Conference on
SOFTWARE TOOLS

April 15-17, 1985 New York, New York

ISBN 0-8186-0628-2
IEEE CATALOG NO. 85CH2188-1
LIBRARY OF CONGRESS NO. 85-80025
IEEE COMPUTER SOCIETY ORDER NUMBER 628

Sponsored by the Center for Advanced Telecommunications Technology of the Polytechnic Institute of New York, with the technical cooperation of the IEEE Computer Society TCSE, the ACM SIGSOFT, and the Software Committee of the National Security Industrial Association

IEEE COMPUTER SOCIETY

THE INSTITUTE OF ELECTRICAL AND ELECTRONICS ENGINEERS, INC.
IEEE

COMPUTER SOCIETY PRESS

COVER DESIGNED BY JACK I. BALLESTERO

Published by IEEE Computer Society Press
1730 Massachusetts Avenue, N.W.
Washington, D.C. 20036-1903

ISBN 0-8186-0628-2 (paper)
ISBN 0-8186-4628-4 (microfiche)
ISBN 0-8186-8628-6 (casebound)
Library of Congress No. 85-80025
IEEE Catalog No. 85CH2188-1
IEEE Computer Society Order No. 628

Order from: IEEE Computer Society
Post Office Box 80452
Worldway Postal Center
Los Angeles, CA 90080

IEEE Service Center
445 Hoes Lane
Piscataway, NJ 08854

THE INSTITUTE OF ELECTRICAL AND ELECTRONICS ENGINEERS, INC.

ii

PREFACE

Martin L. Shooman
Conference General Chairman

Polytechnic Institute of New York

On several occasions in 1983 I held conversations with professionals of various companies in Connecticut and on Long Island about software engineering. At each discussion, we agreed that software tools were of great importance and lamented the fact that there never had BEEN a tools conference in the New York area. Such a conference was deemed important, and a meeting was held in Spring 1984 of an initial planning group; with the encouragement of the IEEE Technical Committee on Software Engineering/ACM SIGSOFT, and the support of the Polytechnic Center for Advanced Tele-communications Technology. Soon thereafter, we received the cooperation of the National Security Industries Association Committee on Software Engineering, and the official cooperation of the IEEE and ACM.

The initial concept was to hold a regional conference in New York City. The initial planning group was expanded to a full conference committee, and a preliminary call for papers was circulated in early June, followed by a regular paper call later in the summer. Early in our planning process, we decided to cover a wide range of software design, development, testing, and management tools, as well as important application areas.

Hotel availability dictated a planning period of about 11 months, somewhat short of the 18 months generally required for a three-day conference. All committee members worked very diligently in their assigned roles, and served on the technical paper committee as well. Only through these dedicated efforts were we able to compensate for the short time period; however, the proceedings could not be distributed at the conference, but would be available a few months later. The proceedings were to be published through the IEEE Computer Society, to assure their wide availability. The conference evolved into an international meeting with participation from throughout the US as well as Austria, Canada, Israel, Japan, The Netherlands, and West Germany.

I would like to thank the members of the organizing committee for their cooperation and hard work in planning this conference. The heart of any technical conference is the program, and the efforts of our Program Co-chairmen, George Estes and Marianne Erdos, and the able assistance of Amy Steinberg are mainly responsible for the review and selection of quality papers. Steven Purdy, our registration chairman, managed the mail and door registration process with tireless effort and efficiency.

Henry Ruston aided by Donald Gormley chaired the local arrangements committee and skillfully handled all negotiations with the conference hotel. John Manning, with the able help of John Luongo, produced these excellent proceedings. Victor Berecz served ably as treasurer for the conference. Check Lao arranged liaison with NSIA and directed all mailings to their members. Bill Turoczy and Paul Janusz publicized our conference to various military groups. Jack Rosenbaum served on the technical program committee and as a session chairman. Ed Miller, Robert Flynn, and John Gaffney were reviewers and also helped with publicity. The committee would like to thank CATT for their sponsorship and Ari Mossman, associate director, who coordinated finances and helped with registration problems. Major thanks go to the Brooklyn CS Secretaries Pearl Brownstein and Linda Louie who helped with correspondence and mailings; and especially to the Farmingdale CS Secretary JoAnn McDonald who served as Conference Secretary, coordinating mailings, correspondence, committee meetings and telephone calls.

The committee's efforts have resulted in a very successful technical conference and a Proceedings volume which will serve as a permanent contribution to the technical literature in the field.

INTRODUCTION

George E. Estes
Program Co-Chairman

AT&T Network Systems

When we set out to assemble the program for this conference, we were faced with a subject which spans an exceedingly wide area. Thus, besides the usual challenges of getting too many papers reviewed, revised, and selected in too little time, we faced the additional task of developing a focus for the diverse viewpoints and perspectives of the accepted papers. We accomplished this by structuring the conference program around two complementary themes:

1. The evolution of software tools, and

2. The user/developer dichotomy.

The evolution of software tools in the last few years has been staggering. From simple programming aids and compilers, we have progressed to sophisticated tools which automate almost all aspects of the software development life cycle. In addition, there are obvious trends toward consolidating discrete tools into comprehensive environments or workstations, as well as many experiments with end user programmability (fourth generation languages, expert systems). Thus we tried to show the progression from Brian Kernighan's opening remarks on the state of software tools today to the closing panel on future developments.

The second theme was the dual role of the software engineer today as both user and developer of software tools. While the job of software developers is to produce tools and systems to automate or facilitate the work of others, we are also a major consumer of tools to automate and control our own work. Thus, we tried to include sessions which took both user and developer perspectives on software tools. Miraculously, we had a fairly even split when we completed the review process.

However, the most important characteristic of the program was the uniform high quality of research and application presented. For this, I must thank the authors and chairmen who prepared and revised their presentations to meet patently impossible deadlines, and the reviewers who contributed so much to the quality of the papers. Finally, I offer a special note of thanks and recognition to my Co-Chairman Marianne Erdos and the program committee secretary Amy Steinberg whose unrelenting efforts were essential to the success of the conference.

CONFERENCE OFFICERS

GENERAL CHAIRMAN

    PROF. MARTIN SHOOMAN
    POLYTECHNIC INSTITUTE OF N.Y.

PROGRAM CO-CHAIRMEN

    GEORGE ESTES
    AT&T NETWORK SYSTEMS

    MARIANNE ERODOS
    HAZELTINE RESEARCH

REGISTRATION CHAIRMAN

    STEVEN PURDY
    AVCO/LYCOMING

TREASURER

    VICTOR BERECZ
    NORDEN SYSTEMS

PROCEEDINGS CHAIRMAN

    JOHN MANNING
    GRUMMAN DATA SYSTEMS

CONFERENCE COMMITTEE

ROBERT FLYNN
POLYTECHNIC INSITUTE OF N.Y.

JOHN GAFFNEY
IBM CORP.

DONALD GORMLEY
GRUMMAN AEROSPACE

PAUL JANUSZ
U.S.A. AMCCOM

CHECK LAO
SPERRY

JOHN LUONGO
GRUMMAN DATA SYSTEMS

EDWARD MILLER, JR.
SOFTWARE RESEARCH ASSOCIATES

JACK ROSENBAUM
EATON AIL DIVISION

HENRY RUSTON
POLYTECHNIC INSTITUTE OF N.Y.

AMY STEINBERG
AT&T NETWORK SYSTEMS

BILL TUROCZY
U.S.A. AMCCOM

LIST OF REVIEWERS

E. BAUDER	J. LUONGO
V. BERECZ	J. MANNING
R. CHARETTE	J. MARCINIAK
E. DORSEY	E. MILLER, JR.
M. ERDOS	C. MOONEY
G. ESTES	S. PREISER
R. FLYNN	S. PURDY
J. GATTNEY	D. REITER
M. HAMILTON	J. ROSENBAUM
H. HECHT	H. RUSTON
P. JANUSZ	M. SHOOMAN
M. KLERER	A. STEINBERG
C. LAO	D. TERCHREOW
J. LAUB	W. TUROCZY
R. LEBLANC	

TABLE OF CONTENTS

Session 1: Software Tools Today
Chairman: George E. Estes, AT&T Network Systems

Session 2: Expert Systems Tools and Applications
Chairman: M.L. Shooman, Polytechnic Institute of New York

Session 3: Program Testing and Configuration Management Tools
Chairman: Gary Cort, Los Alamos National Laboratory

Session 4: Software Design and Development Tools
Chairman: Julie Landstein, IBM

Session 5: Tool Evaluation and Acquisition
Chairman: William Turoczy, U.S. Army AMCCOM

Session 6: Future Tools
Chairman: M.E. Erdos, Hazeltine

Session 1

Software Tools Today

Chairman
George E. Estes
AT&T Network Systems

THE CLASSIC LIFECYCLE

Figure 1 is a generic instantiation of the classic software engineering lifecycle. The output of each phase acts as the input for the following phase. The first activity is to identify a system and its needs that perform some functional requirement. There are no tools currently available to help specifically with this task; however, some tools under development do address support of this effort. These tools typically are called rapid prototyping tools and are used to perform feasibility analysis of required system concepts and designs. This might be something as complex as asynchronous communication between programmed tasks or as simple as the layout of data on a CRT screen. The two basic approaches to the task are to perform a simulation or to do an analytical analysis. Examples of these tools range from systems which automatically generate source code from a formalized requirement specification, such as USE.IT from HOS, Inc., to the many implementations of LISP, an interpreted language.

Other tools supporting this activity help with the analysis of the effort required for implementation. Cost estimating systems provide support through parametric modelling, such as the RCA PRICE system[1], or through analogy with similar efforts in size and complexity, such as the COCOMO system[1]. Project management tools help identify required resources and range in complexity from simple Gantt chart generators to integrated spreadsheet/database systems such as are currently being marketed on personal computers.

REQUIREMENTS SPECIFICATION PHASE

The first software development phase is used to formalize the requirements of the proposed computer program. This phase ideally should only address "what" the system is to accomplish. By restricting the requirements specification in this manner, design decisions will be delayed as far into the development lifecycle as possible. This is important because it allows the system's designers to have the greatest degree of flexibility in making design decisions. The requirements phase may impact the following phases through the introduction of constraints, such as the choice of implementation language. Constraints should only be imposed when there are no options.

Several tools have been implemented to support this phase, including PLS/PSA[15] and REVS[5]. These tools provide a formal system of specification which can be analyzed for consistency and completeness. A specification for a large system can be hundreds of pages long and be assembled from multiple diverse organizations. Many times this will lead to contradictions or omissions in the requirements specification for the system. If inputs are expressed in the formal language of a requirements specification tool, less ambiguity is likely in the interpretation of the descriptions, and the system can be automatically analyzed as well as automatically documented.

DESIGN PHASE

The design phase specifies "how" the requirements are to be accomplished. In the design phase the idea is to specify the "how" with minimal impact on the implementation phase. Through the process of "abstraction", design decisions are identified without detailing the specific implementation choices. The primary tools to support this phase are structurizers and pseudocode. Structurizers are tools which help the user specify the control strategy of the program. Through one of several methods the modules of the system are described as processes, data objects, or interfaces; and a structurizer will document and analyze the design specification. Program description languages (PDL's) are used to implement pseudocode. Pseudocode provides a language which is between the free form, ambiguous English language and the structured, formalized programming language. A PDL tool also will implement, for a specific project, a formal pseudocode syntax which will have the same benefits as the formal requirements language: enhanced understanding among users, automated analysis of decisions (usually of a limited nature), and automated documentation. SDDL is an example of a generic PDL tool[2]. Several Ada™ oriented PDLs have been developed, and there is an IEEE effort to define a standard for an Ada PDL.

CODE PHASE

The implementation phase specifies the "with" decisions of the design phase. Each design decision is implemented "with" the best available constructs and data types and then implemented in the chosen programming language. A multi-way branch may be implemented as a CASE construct or as a series of IF-THEN-ELSE constructs or any of a number of other ways, primarily dependent upon the definition of the language being used, and the available extensions to the language which might be implemented on a particular host computer. The selection of integer instead of floating point as a data type representation may be selected because of limited floating point processing speed. The implementation issues include speed and size of compiled code, use of structure, modularization, collection of common components of control and data, readability, reuseability, portability, and others all of which influence the decisions to varying degrees depending on their relative importance.

Tools to support these types of choices are not generally available except as systems which check for compliance with standardization. Even though most of the tools developed in support of the development of software have been in the implementation phase, they have primarily been built to increase the quantitative productivity of the programmer, not to support his decision processes. These tools are various compilers, language constructs, smart editors, code libraries, optimizers, symbolic debuggers, and many others. The Ada programming support environment is the first real attempt to provide the programmer with a set of implementation tools which will support qualitative as well as quantitative productivity improvements[3]. This is an extensible environment proposed to provide a wide set of tools integrated through a common data library package. An effort named the Joint Services Software Engineering Environment within the DOD is addressing the mix of tools and their method of application that might best support quality programming.

TEST PHASE

The test phase as described here represents the unit test of each code module, the test of module integration, and the system test. These activities are functional tests rather than operational (debugging) and are usually described as verfication and validation. The system must be tested functionally between each step in the development process with no known errors (verification); and also must implement the total system requirements specification of functionality (validation). The tools which support verification arc PDL's which allow traceability of multiple steps through a common tool, and integrated methodologies and tool databases which can be used to support multiple tools with the same data structures. Gypsy is an example of a tool which supports verification[10].

There are multiple tools to help with the validation process, but by nature these tools are tied closely to the implementation language. Examples of these tools, which happen to be in the public domain, are the Fortran Automated Verification System, the Cobol Automated Verification System, and the Fortran '77 Analyzer, all of which support control path and data flow analysis. These tools perform testing coverage to determine if all of the code has been exercised by the test set developed, static analysis to generate statistics about the implementation details such as number of branches and number of variables, and dynamic analysis to evaluate performance characteristics. The tools in combination with historical databases are also used to support regression testing. Other tools exist, but have never been accepted widely, which perform the function of test data generation. The development of test data and code is usually performed in a parallel effort using the same tools as the application code development[11].

MAINTENANCE PHASE

The final phase, maintenance, is a recursion through the previous phases to correct deficiencies. The phase to which the recursion returns is dependent on the nature of the deficiency. An error in the specification of the system requirements will require a total recursion of the lifecycle for some segment of the system. The most important tools for this phase are documentation control systems such as SCCS[14]. These tools include a database in which all development and test documentation, source files, object files and deliverables reside; and a control mechanism which can regenerate any historical version of the database. Without this capability, modifications to the generated system are complex and sometimes impossible. Most major computer manufacturers now offer these systems. Other tools which support maintenance are those that support regression testing and those that support reuseability.

The earlier in the development life cycle a product is generated, the more likely it can be reused. Specifications and designs are more reuseable than code due to their relative generality. The first tool identified to support reuseability is usually the software library. Software libraries are easy to establish, and hard to make useful. The primary reason is that the products put into a library usually have not been designed nor documented for reuse. This reduces the chance that a potential user will have faith in its capabilities. There are no tools which provide a formal method for describing what a software component does or how it should be used. Software libraries are a first step, but currently require the reuse of personnel to make them productive.

THE ARTIFICIAL INTELLIGENCE APPROACH

In the field of artificial intelligence the primary language in use is LISP[4]. LISP is a procedural language (process versus declarative oriented) which has undergone many modifications and generated many dialects (reference Table 1), but has retained the implementation of functions as its primary construct. Other artificial intelligence oriented languages have been used in the research communities; but only PROLOG, a declarative oriented language, has gained wide acceptance. PROLOG will not be discussed since very few systems have actually been built in PROLOG, but it is important from the standpoint of being selected as the base language for the Japanese 5th generation project[7].

TABLE 1   LISP DIALECTS

DIALECTS	VENDOR*
COMMON LISP	SRL
FRANZ LISP	U. C. BERKELEY
INTERLISP-D	XEROX
INTERLISP-VAX	USC
INTERLISP-10	BBN
IQ LISP	INTEGRAL QUALITY
EXPERLISP	EXPERTELLIGENCE
DOMAIN LISP	APOLLO
NISP	SST
LISP 1.6	STANFORD UNIV.
ZETALISP	SYMOBLICS
MACLISP	MIT
NIL	MIT
PSL	UNIV. OF UTAH
T LISP	YALE UNIV.
UCI LISP	U. C. IRVINE

LISP was invented to solve the symbolic manipulation problems that FORTRAN did not seem to be able to handle. The attempt to instill "intelligence" into computers was approached by attempting to model the human thinking processes, which did not appear to work in numerics but

* There are usually multiple vendors of each even though only one is identified.

instead, symbolics[17]. Because LISP was interpreted rather than compiled, there was also a tendency towards interactive versus batch programming.

THE AI LIFECYCLE

The software product lifecycle presented in Figure 2 has been in existence almost as long as the classic lifecycle (1950's)[12]. To develop a system in LISP, the total system needs do not need to be identified prior to addressing design, code and test. If a specific requirement can be identified, then a function is developed to satisfy the "functional validity" of the requirement. This is then followed by a similar effort for the next identifiable requirement until the total system has been implemented as a set of functions. System integration and testing is performed in increments and a final validity check accomplished. Maintenance then becomes a task of modifying an existing function, or in the case of an error of omission in the requirements, simply the generation of another function. Since LISP has been in use primarily in the university research environment, tools to support the symbolic programming lifecycle are not extensive. The decomposition of the requirements does not lend itself to analysis, nor does the incremental design of functions provide for design analysis. In some systems coding is supported through syntax editors which generally are not considered very powerful, but necessary; and testing is supported through run-time symbolic debuggers. Other systems have very powerful editors which perform some semantic checking, as well as provide for foreground editing through interpretation in combination with background processing of compiled code. These more powerful systems also have very friendly interfaces using graphics and specialized built-in support functions, such as the highlighting of active processes displayed in a process invocation tree. Current application oriented tools are emerging with greatly enhanced features to support design, coding and test. However, these are tools which define a new programming lifecycle approach embodying concepts such as object-oriented programming, top-down decomposition, code libraries, and others; with LISP as the underlying language of implementation.

AI ENVIRONMENTS

Numerous computer environments that are

SYMBOLIC PROGRAMMING LIFECYCLE

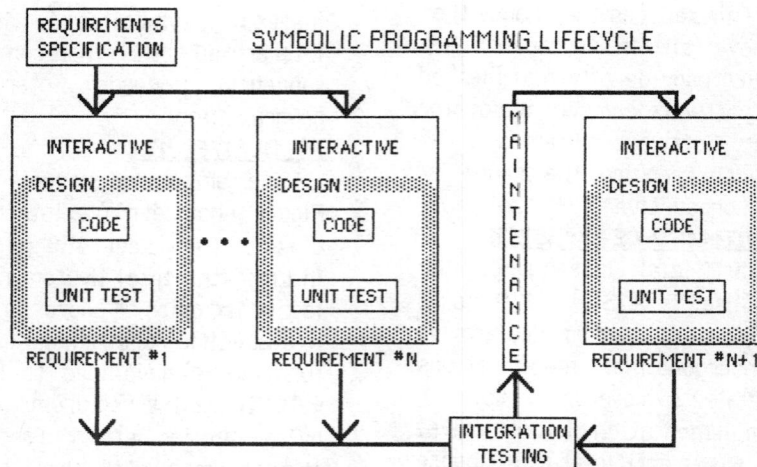

FIGURE 2   THE ARTIFICIAL INTELLIGENCE LIFECYCLE

available to perform artificial intelligence (AI) projects are identified in the AI Environment Support Matrix, Table 2. The primary considerations of a system are hardware, software environment, language, and the capabilities of each. However, the software environment is the critical resource, which when selected, relegates the capabilities of the hardware and languages to less importance.

Table 2, the AI ENVIRONMENT SUPPORT MATRIX, presents a list of development environments cross referenced with their identified capabilities and hosts. The capabilities listed represent a core of those identified in the available literature, mostly from marketing sources. Some capabilities, such as "FRAME BASED REPRESENTATION", may only be partially supported because many of the capabilities listed lack a good definition of consensus. Most systems have some unique capability not identified because it was not necessarily an AI support capability, or it was very unique. Other capabilities might be derived through the particular host on which the system resides, such as a PROLOG interface. With these considerations in mind, the matrix provides a rough cut at identifying which systems would best be useful for a particular task. Some would provide more capability than needed for most tasks, whereas others would not support a sometimes required capability such as "CONFIDENCE FACTORS."

Conspicuous absences in the list of characteristics are the language (or dialect) supported and language of implementation. Most of the development environments support multiple LISP dialects and at least one version of PROLOG, and are implemented in LISP.

There are some key factors not identified in the

TABLE 2 AI ENVIRONMENT SUPPORT MATRIX

```
- - - X X - - - - - - - -   IBM PC
- - X - - - - - X - - - -   TI EXPLORER
- - X - - - - - - X - -     APOLLO
- X - - - - - - - - - -     TEKTRONIX
- - - - - - - - - X -       INTELLIMAC
- - - - - X - - X X - -     XEROX
- - - - - - X X - X - X     SYMBOLICS
- - - - - - X X - - - X     LMI
X - - X - X X X - X - X     VAX
- - X - - - X X X X X X     FOREIGN CODE INTERFACE
X - - - - - - - - - X - X   NON-MONOTONIC REASONING
X - - - - - - - X - - X     PERFORMANCE ANALYSIS
- - X - - X X - - - - X     HELP FACILITY
X - X - X - - - - - - -     SYNONYMS
- - - X X - - X X - - - -   USER FRIENDLY INTERFACE
X - X X - - X X X X X X     RULE BASED PROGRAMMING
X X - - - - X X - - - -     FRAME BASED REPRESENTATION
- - - - - - X X X - X -     LOGIC PROGRAMMING
- X - - - - X X X - -       OBJECT PROGRAMMING
- - X - - - X X X X - X X   PROCEDURAL PROGRAMMING
X - X X - X X - - - - -     EXPLANATION FACILITY
- X X - X X - - X X - X X   DEBUGGING AIDS
X - X X X X - - - - - - X   CERTAINTY FACTORS
- - X - X - X - - - X - X   FOWARD CHAINING
- X - - - - - - - X - X     BACKWARD CHAINING
- X X - - - X X - - - X     INHERITANCE
- - - - - X - X - - X       INTERPRETATION OF CODE
- X - X - - X - - - - X     COMPILATION OF CODE
- - X - - - X X X - X X     EXTENSIBLE SYSTEM
- - X - - - - - - X - - X   STRUCTURE EDITOR
- X - - - X - X X - - X X   GRAPHICS INTERFACE
```

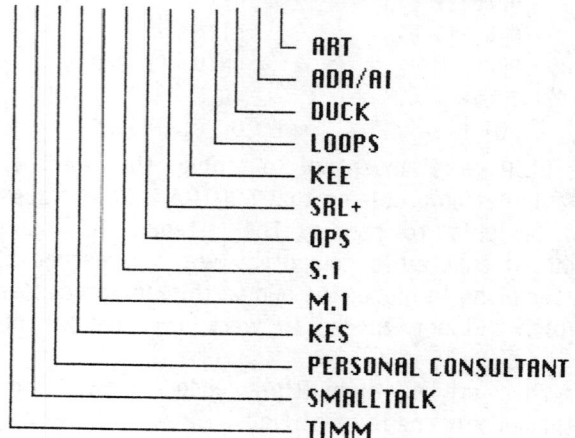

- ART
- ADA/AI
- DUCK
- LOOPS
- KEE
- SRL+
- OPS
- S.1
- M.1
- KES
- PERSONAL CONSULTANT
- SMALLTALK
- TIMM

support matrix: cost per user, training provided, company history, and hardware maintenance support. Training provided with the system is a very important consideration. Most new applications have short schedule expectations which do not include a training period. These systems are very complex with a wide variety of capabilities and varying qualities of documentation. The final, and driving consideration is cost. Specifically the cost per user is important in an application oriented environment where productivity and return on investment are measured. These systems range in cost from $5,000.00 to more than $60,000.00 per user.

EXECUTABLE REQUIREMENTS SPECIFICATIONS

Not everyone wants the flexibility of the previously described programming lifecycles. Ideally once the requirements for the system have been established, the rest of the process could be automated. This would mean that, given that the automation methodology was correct, there would be no errors except for those described in the requirements or caused by operator error. The system would only be modified when there was an identified requirement error or a need for an update in requirements. No documentation, design decisions, programming, or incremental testing need ever occur beyond the requirements specification phase.

Figure 3 represents the tools approach which attempts to implement this executable requirements specification lifecycle. These tools require the use of a formal requirements specification language which can be analyzed for consistency and completeness. Once accepted, the specification is then used to automatically

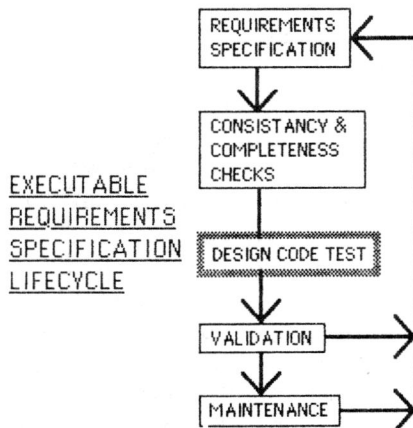

FIGURE 3 EXECUTABLE REQUIREMENTS LIFECYCLE

generate source code in one or more of multiple languages, that can then be compiled and executed, or interpreted.

System performance tuning is limited with this approach, but even when this is necessary it might be accomplished through manual modification of the source code. Even when this is not possible, the execution of the requirements prior to being used in the classic lifecycle would provide insight into requirements errors which would be extremely expensive to correct in later phases. PAISLEY[10] and USE.IT[9] are examples of such systems. Several Knowledged based approaches to this paradigm are being researched including Glitter[8], PSI/CHI[6], and Programmer's Apprentice[6].

A KNOWLEDGED BASED APPROACH

The Development Arts for Real Time Systems (DARTS™) lifecycle is one of several called "knowledge-based" approaches, a subfield of artificial intelligence[13]. DARTS technology is oriented to the archetyping of existing application programs. The intent is to use knowledge of previously developed systems and knowledge of the targeted application to generate a new system.

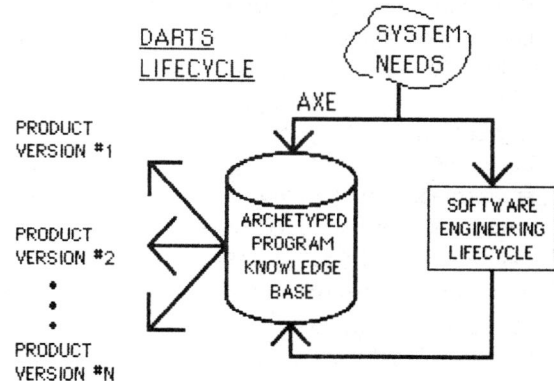

FIGURE 4 A KNOWLEDGE BASED LIFECYCLE

In this and other similar systems, which were alluded to in the symbolic programming discussion, tools exist as primitive functions to be used to build other tools, which eventually bootstrap the desired system. A unique feature of the DARTS lifecycle is the use of previously developed systems, decomposed into semantic units, to baseline the new system. As much code as can be identified as useful by its semantic description will be reused in producing the new system. The AXE™ feature of the DARTS technology is a powerful programming language which is simply a set of tools to help build other tools (possibly as functions) such as graphics interfaces, domain-specific natural language interfaces, or specialized pattern recognition systems. A component of DARTS called the BOLT™ processor encodes and interpretively executes AXE statements. The AXE language was designed by first addressing the tasks which were to be accomplished as listed above, and then selecting the capabilities of various languages which were beneficial. Concepts from Snobol (pattern matching), LISP (list processing), and structured languages such as Ada were included. Additional capabilities to provide for database access and rapid prototyping were incorporated as necessary. The AXE language, being interpreted, is easily extended.

When a system is built, its unique features are incorporated (archetyped) into the DARTS database as new semantic units for future use. Many versions of the same system with small variations can easily be produce with this method, but new instances of a software system can contain only those features that have been previously archetyped or are implemented in AXE. The primary thrust of the knowledge based approach is to give the user a good set of primitive yet flexible tools with which to implement a new system.

SUMMARY

Many of the lifecycles and tools discussed overlap in use and application. Specific implementations of the tools have been evaluated by various universities (MIT, Univ. of Michigan, CMU, ...), agencies (DMA, USAICS, NADC, RADC, NBS, NASA, ...) and businesses (General Dynamics, TRW, Boeing, General Electric, Softech, ...). These results are readily available in the open literature, especially in the proceedings of IEEE and ACM. The DARTS technology is a product of General Dynamics and further information can be obtained by contacting the author.

The classic life cycle has been more formalized and historically been shown to be effective. The methodology of tool support is the primary thrust of research in this life cycle. The AI approach to software development is in a state of flux and is likely to remain so for some time. The emergence of the techniques from the university environment combined with the rapid advances in hardware technology are the main destablizing forces. However the DARPA programs attempting to transfer these technologies into industry practice

may provide for some structure formalism. The requirements for AI/knowledge based systems support is resource intensive. In general, attempting to develop these type systems on other than dedicated processors results in unacceptable performance. The following are the driving criteria: 1) a processor with sufficient resources to support interactive debugging (memory intensive), incremental compilation, and interpretive development (cpu intensive), 2) special tools specifically designed to support AI development, 3) extensibility as new applications required new functionality, 4) flexibility of interfacing to other computers for application support.

The development of executable requirements specification systems has been in research for several years. The lack of research into language theory, and the required mode of interpretation will trend an evolutionary rather than revolutionary development of these executable specification systems. One significant factor which could speed up the evolution is advances in computer processing speed. The potential for use of such systems is extremely high as quality support tools.

The changing scope of computer software development and the use of the associated products will drive the process of finding new paradigms such as the DARTS technology approach[16]. Concepts such as software manufacturing, software brassboarding, software reuseability, automated programming and many others will all lead to new paradigms.

REFERENCES

[1] BOEHM B. - Software Engineering Economics, Prentice-Hall, Inc., (1981)

[2] BOND R. - "Ada as a Program Description Language (PDL): A Project Software Management Perspective", ACM Ada LETTERS IV, 1 (July, August 1984), 67-73.

[3] BOOCH G. - Software Engineering with Ada, Benjamin/Cummings Publishing Company, (1983).

[4] CHARNIAK E., RIESBECK C. and McDERMOTT D. - Artificial Intelligence Programming, Lawrence Erlbaum Associates, (1980).

[5] CHILDS D., WHALEN D. and KEITH L. - "USAICS USAMS Evaluation of SREM/REVS/RSL and PSL/PSA", Proceedings of the Symposium on Application and Assessment of Automated Tools for Software Development, (November 1983), 89-98.

[6] FEIGENBAUM E. and BARR A. - The Handbook of Artificial Intelligence, Volume II, HuerisTech Press, (1982)

[7] McCORDUCK P. and FEIGENBAUM E. - _The Fifth Generation: Artificial Intelligence and Japan's Computer Challenge to the World_, Addison-Wesley, (1983).

[8] FICKAS S. - "Automating Software Development: A Small Example", _Proceedings of the Symposium on Application and Assessment of Automated Tools for Software Development_, (November 1983), 3-9.

[9] HAMILTON M. and ZELDIN S. - "Higher Order Software-A Methodology for Defining Software", _Tutorial: Automated Tools for Software Engineering_, (1979), 72-95.

[10] HUGHES AIRCRAFT - Ground Systems Group, _Reusable Software Implementation Technology Reviews_, (December 1984).

[11] JOINT LOGISTICS COMMANDERS - _DEFENSE SYSTEM SOFTWARE DEVELOPMENT_, MIL-STD-SDS, (5 December 1983).

[12] NILSSON N. - _Principles of Artificial Intelligence_, Tioga Publishing Company, (1980).

[13] RAWLINGS T. et. al. - "The Central Valley Project Computer Systems", _Proceedings of the 2nd International Symposium on Mini and Micro Computers in Control_, (December 1979).

[14] ROCHKIND M. - "The Source Code Control System", _Tutorial: Automated Tools for Software Engineering_, (1979), 233-239.

[15] TEICHROEW D. and HERSHEY K. - "PSL/PSA: A Computer-Aided Technique for Structured Documentation and Analysis of Information Processing Systems", _Tutorial: Automated Tools for Software Engineering_, (1979), 32-39.

[16] WINOGRAD T. - "Beyond Programming Languages", CACM 22, 7 (July 1979), 391-401.

[17] WINSTON P. - _Artificial Intelligence_, 2nd Edition, Addison-Wesley Publishing Company, (February 1984).

THE LOS ALAMOS HYBRID ENVIRONMENT:
AN INTEGRATED DEVELOPMENT/CONFIGURATION MANAGEMENT SYSTEM

G. CORT

Los Alamos National Laboratory
Los Alamos, New Mexico

Details are presented for a hybrid configuration management system that utilizes a commercial configuration management tool (Softool's Change and Configuration Control environment) to monitor and control the development of mission-critical software systems at the Los Alamos Weapons Neutron Research Facility. The hybrid system combines features of the VMS host operating system and elements of the tool environment to integrate a flexible development environment with a very powerful automated configuration management system. System features are presented with particular emphasis on the benefits of the hybrid approach. By employing a special interface data structure, the hybrid environment supports a much higher level of automation (of both development and configuration management activities) than is realizable in either environment individually. It is shown that in the process of providing a rigorous configuration management environment, the system remains virtually transparent to software development personnel and actually enhances the programmer's capabilities.

Introduction

As has been the case for most of the disciplines of software engineering, the evolution of the principles of software configuration management has been driven mainly by the requirements of large-scale software development projects. Although this situation has resulted in very effective and efficient strategies for managing these giant projects, the very different needs of small or intermediate sized projects have been largely ignored. This has served effectively to deny both the immediate and the long term benefits of software engineering in general, and software configuration management in particular, to the majority of software development projects. Far more serious is the dangerous attitude fostered by the large scale approach to these very important disciplines, namely that the techniques of software engineering and configuration management can only be cost-effective when applied on a grand scale.

This paper presents the experiences of a small group responsible for the development of a moderately large real-time data acquisition system. It describes our approach to the utiliza-tion of the Softool Change and Configuration Control environment, a commercially-available configuration management tool (CMT), and the steps taken to develop a very powerful development/configuration management environment incorporating this CMT.

Project Organization

In order to establish the requirements and operational constraints which led to the development of the Los Alamos system, a brief description of our facility and the organization of our project is appropriate. The Los Alamos Weapons Neutron Research Facility (WNR) is a world-class neutron scattering installation devoted to basic research in physics, chemistry, materials science and biology. Operating in conjunction with the 800 MeV linear accelerator at the Los Alamos Meson Physics Facility (LAMPF) the facility supports an expanding, international user community. A major facility upgrade currently being implemented will significantly enhance present capabilities and will transform WNR into one of the world's premiere neutron scattering centers.

This upgrade, however, will render the existing real-time data acquisition system obsolete. Its replacement, which is currently under development by the Computer Section of the WNR Operations Group, will ultimately consist of a network of 8-12 computers of the VAX 11/780 class each hosting the VMS operating system. Each computer will be dedicated to acquiring data from a single spectrometer. To accomplish this task, each computer will execute identical data acquisition software.

The projected size of the software system being developed to meet the data acquisition requirements of the new facility is approximately 250 K executable lines. Reliable operation of this system is essential as software failures can result in total disruption of the operation of the facility. Because of the great expense incurred in producing the neutron beam, and the high demand by users for access to the facility, the economic, political and scientific consequences of a system failure can be quite serious.

Our organization consists of three very senior

CH2188-1/85/0000/0010$01.00 © 1985 IEEE

staff members with full-time responsibility for software design and implementation. In addition, we have available the equivalent of approximately two full-time people to support the development effort. These individuals range in experience from very senior staff members with partial responsibility for software to junior programmers and data analysts.

The project management structure is also quite different from that associated with most large-scale development efforts. The small staff attached to the project does not warrant the multilayered, highly stratified management structure imposed on large development projects. Indeed, a single manager oversees the entire software development effort. Heavy reliance on the experience and judgement of the software staff further reduces management visibility to a minimal level.

The CMT Environment

The CMT chosen for the Los Alamos system, was selected for a combination of features including security, flexibility and automatability. The CMT environment provides virtually unbreachable security for system sources (and documentation), thereby eliminating the possibility of inadvertent or unauthorized modification of any of these key system components. This capability is of particular importance in a highly volatile development environment such as ours: one in which every programmer has access to system management resources and therefore is potentially capable of bypassing all file protections established by the operating system.

The CMT environment also provides a comprehensive, automated version control system, a feature that is essential to the conduct of an effective configuration accounting effort. This feature gives us the capability to define the precise configuration of any software component of the data acquisition system. In addition, it provides for fallback configurations that can be utilized in the event of a serious failure of a primary software component, thus allowing the data acquisition task to continue (though possibly with reduced capability) while the primary component is under repair.

The CMT also features a macro facility that provides the potential for almost unlimited automation of the configuration management environment. This capability is particularly attractive within the context of our project for which the relatively small size of the technical staff demands that the overhead associated with support functions (such as configuration management) be kept to an absolute minimum.

The Need for an Extended Environment

Although the CMT environment is an extremely powerful tool to support configuration management activities, the conventional methodologies for

utilizing such a tool are not adequate to meet the needs of a small software development project such as ours. At the extreme of maximum CMT utilization, the methodology requires that every development and maintenance programmer work entirely within the confines of the CMT data base, using CMT commands and the built-in CMT line editor to accomplish all programming and maintenance activities. At the opposite extreme, programming and maintenance staff do not interact with the CMT data base, but instead conduct their programming activities externally. A manager is then responsible for copying all work from the users' environments into the CMT data base at regular intervals. The deficiencies of these methodologies are discussed below.

The policy of maximum CMT utilization allows management to exercise a high level of visibility throughout the development process, and provides the capability to identify software version changes with an extremely fine time resolution. Unfortunately, this approach also imposes severe overheads on both configuration management and development personnel. The most severe management overhead derives from the necessity for a data base administrator to define and maintain access control information for every CMT user. This problem is further complicated by the extremely volatile development environment that is often associated with small projects: users' access control information may require modification on a daily or even hourly basis. Add in a constraint that requires all maintenance operations to be performed in a modular fashion (programmers are allowed access to only those modules of a software component that actually require modification) and the process of maintaining access control information becomes increasingly error-prone and time intensive. It should be noted that this activity cannot be extensively automated, so there is little hope of reducing these overheads through the use of the CMT macro facility.

Also, the maximum utilization strategy imposes intolerable overheads on the technical staff. The effective relocation of the development environment to within the confines of the CMT data base has the immediate consequence of making standard development tools (compilers, linkers, etc.) as well as locally developed automated software support tools inaccessible to the developer (Fig. 1). As a result, what should be a simple compile-link procedure becomes tedious, time consuming, multi-step operation involving exportation of the appropriate modules from the data base, performance of compilation and link steps in the host operating system environment, and importation of the source modules back into the data base. In addition to the direct deleterious effects upon developer productivity, the imposition of such overheads can foster resentment and can result in serious erosion of morale within the technical staff. To support a modular maintenance effort within this environment becomes even more difficult, requiring a significantly increased level of participation by the data base administrator.

Additional unacceptable overheads are also characteristic of the maximum utilization implementation. Developers are required to become proficient with new software interfaces in order to operate within the CMT data base. In some cases these new interfaces may be perceived as less effective than tools that exist at the operating system level (for instance. programmers resist abandoning the versatile. full-screen and familiar VMS EDT editor for the less powerful. line-oriented CMT editor). Additionally. response times deteriorate rapidly as more users are forced to access the data base simultaneously. Coupled with the extra response time overhead introduced by a policy of archiving incremental changes for most recent versions. these delays can seriously degrade development productivity.

The minimum utilization methodology (Fig. 2) also presents serious problems as a configuration management implementation strategy. Although access control. tool accessibility and response time overheads are largely eliminated by this approach. significant new management overheads are introduced. Foremost among these is the increased effort required to export modules from the CMT

data base for maintenance. especially in a modular maintenance environment. When used in this mode. the CMT environment seems to be reduced to an extremely sophisticated (and expensive) backup utility.

Both methodologies seem to allow the CMT data base to become cluttered with uncertified intermediate software versions. This generally results in rapid increase in data base size and decreased intervals between data base maintenance and backup activities. Almost regardless of the time resolution associated with the the smallest increment of change. the benefits to be gained by saving uncertified versions in the data base are offset by the increased maintenance burden placed on the data base administrator.

In summary. there seems to be a basic incompatibility between environments that promote a strong development effort (the host operating system environment, for example) and those, such as the CMT, that support rigorous, automated configuration management activities. Environments in which developers thrive present severe dif-

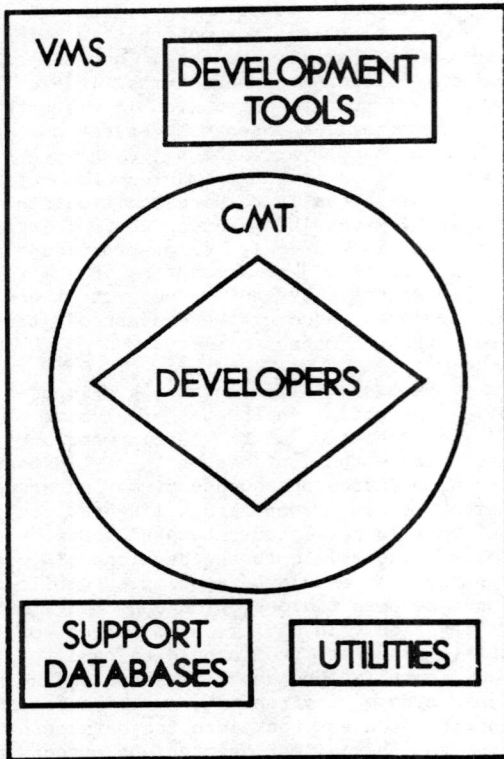

Fig. 1. Impact of the maximum utilization strategy. Development activities are subordinated to the configuration management effort and developers are isolated from tools that exist at the operating system level.

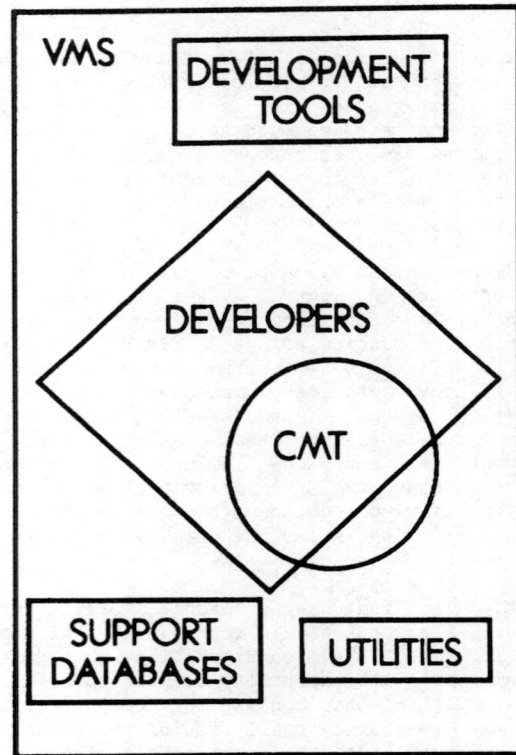

Fig. 2. Impact of the minimum utilization strategy. The configuration management effort is subordinated to development activities. Developers can access tools but configuration management overheads are significantly increased.

ficulties for configuration management personnel. The converse also appears to be true. Conventional approaches to the resolution of these problems generally force one of these groups to work within an inadequate environment in order to preserve the effectiveness of the other group. In worst case situations, each group is forced to endure a compromise solution in which both parties sacrifice significant capabilities and neither is satisfied. The Los Alamos approach, however, defines a new methodology that completely isolates development activities from the configuration management effort, thereby allowing the full power of each environment to be exploited to its fullest. The unique feature of this strategy is the provision of an interface between the two environments that allows for automated interaction between them, and actually melds them into a single, comprehensive hybrid environment for software development and configuration management.

The Hybrid Environment: Specifications

Within the context of our project, the following properties were identified as required features of the hybrid environment and its associated configuration management methodology:

User exclusion from the CMT data base. All development/maintenance activities must be conducted within the host operating system environment. This requirement was specified in order to eliminate the management and developer overheads associated with CMT data base transactions and maintenance. Only the CMT data base administrator is permitted access to the data base.

Only certified software is maintained under configuration control. Only software that has been reviewed and passed by the facility Configuration Control Board (CCB) is accepted into the configuration management environment. Likewise, specific approval of the CCB is required before any software is released from configuration control (by transfer to the development environment). All uncertified software versions (generally intermediate versions of modules undergoing maintenance or development) remain in the development environment. Reliance is placed upon ordinary facility software backup procedures to provide adequate capability for reconstruction of modules in the development environment.

The hybrid environment must impose no additional overheads upon the developer. All configuration management tasks must be the exclusive responsibility of configuration management personnel. In addition, there must be no degradation in system response attributable to the hybrid environment.

The hybrid environment must support the automation of virtually every configuration management task. Because the configuration management staff is responsible for all aspects of the configuration management effort, and because these staff members

generally have significant development responsibilities as well, automated procedures must be available to reduce the effort and increase the reliability of all configuration management transactions.

The Hybrid Environment: Implementation

The hybrid environment (Fig. 3) is comprised of a development environment and a configuration management environment, each of which is strictly isolated from the other. The development environment consists of the VMS operating system utilized in the conventional manner and partitioned into the usual user accounts and directories. All activities that take place within the development environment are the exclusive responsibility of the software developer and are not monitored or influenced in any manner by the configuration management staff.

The configuration management environment consists of a Configuration Data Base (CDB) and automated procedures (VMS command files and CMT macros) to operate on CDB elements. The configuration management staff is responsible for performing all operations on the CDB.

The organization of the CDB reflects our operational requirement that modules be maintained at different levels of configuration control depending on function, utilization and current change processing status. To meet this requirement, the CDB is divided into a Class 1 and a Class 2 partition. The Class 1 partition consists of the CMT data base and is intended to hold modules for which access must be restricted to configuration management personnel only. Certified source code, user's documentation and test results are examples of modules that must be maintained under Class 1 configuration management. Only the CMT data base administrator is authorized to access structures that reside within the Class 1 partition.

The Class 2 partition consists of a hierarchy of protected VMS directories that contain software modules that must be accessed on an on-demand basis by data acquisition system users or development personnel. Included in the list of Class 2 modules are executable images, libraries of object modules and support data bases. All users have read-access to Class 2 modules; only configuration management personnel have modify-access. Obviously, modules that exist in the Class 2 partition are not as secure as those in the Class 1 partition. However, because these modules exist in non-ASCII format, and because any Class 2 module can be simply rebuilt (usually by a compile or link operation) from one or more Class 1 modules, the reduced security is not considered a serious problem.

The CDB structure reduces developer overheads to levels comparable to those that would exist in the absence of any configuration management activities. By extensively automating the CDB (using CMT macros for the Class 1 partition and VMS command files for the Class 2 partition) management overheads can also be drastically reduced. Indeed, the only aspects of the configuration management process that do not lend themselves to automation under the hybrid environment are those of 1) releasing software from the Class 1 partition into the development environment and 2) admitting software (after certification) from the development environment into the CDB. This inability to integrate the constituent environments in an automated fashion was considered a serious deficiency of the hybrid approach in light of the fact that these processes comprise the vast majority of the activities of the configuration management staff.

Integrating the Environments

In order to address this deficiency, we further extended the hybrid environment by defining an interface data structure that enables the complete automation of software transfers between the constituent environments. The structure is called a Program Source File List (SFL) and consists of a text file that describes the structure of a program. Each program that is maintained in the Class 1 partition has a corresponding SFL that resides with the program source code.

An SFL consists of a list of each software module that must be compiled/linked to build the executable image for a particular computer program. The SFL is organized with one module name per line and allows commentary material to be included after any module name. The SFL also contains information that defines the status (unmodified, modified, or new) of each module in the list. A sample source file list is shown below.

Source File List for Program ADD :

```
ADD             ! Main program
VALDATBAS       ! Data base validation routine
SEEKENTRY       ! Entry locate routine
UPDATE          ! New entry addition routine
PMPTUSER        ! General prompting routine
PARSELINE       ! Command decoding routine
```

As shown in Figure 4, the SFL data structure integrates the the CDB and host operating system into a flexible, automated environment. In order to demonstrate the degree to which SFL's support the unification of the hybrid environment through automation of the interface between the constituent environments, we present the following example of a simple maintenance operation. Consider the ADD program for which the SFL is presented above. Consider also that a software

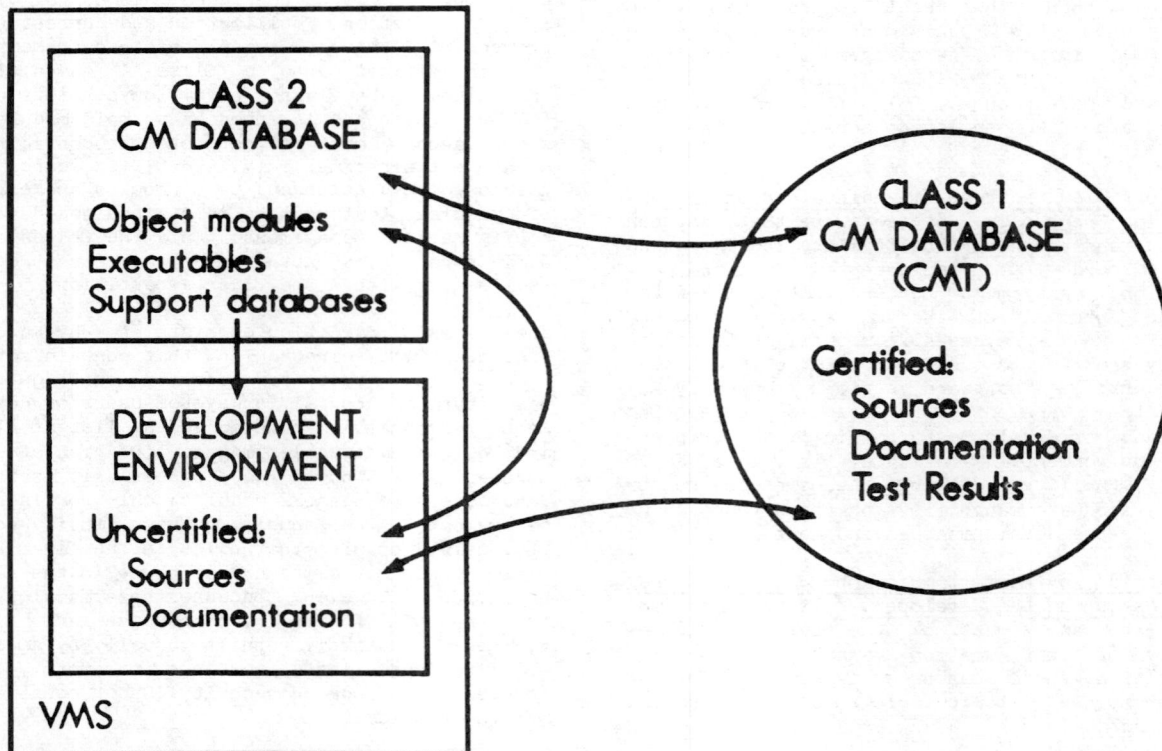

Fig. 3. The hybrid environment. Development and configuration management activities are completely separated. Arrows indicate required interactions between the constituent environments.

fault associated with the execution of ADD has been identified and reported. Analysis indicates that bugs exist in the SEEKENTRY and the PARSELINE subprograms and (in accordance with the modular maintenance policy) a request has been placed with the configuration administrator to release these modules into the development environment (i.e. into the maintenance programmer's local VMS directory). Using manual procedures to accomplish the appropriate transfers from the CMT data base to the maintenance programmer's VMS directory is a tedious and error-prone operation. This is especially true in light of the fact that a transfer operation must be performed on every module of the computer program, regardless of how many modules are to be modified. (This results from the fact that object modules must be generated for all modules that are not subject to modification, and these object modules must be transferred to the Class 2 partition in order to allow the ADD program to be linked prior to testing.)

By utilizing the ADD source file list, however, the entire manual process described above can be replaced by an automated procedure that reduces the overhead imposed upon the CMT data base administrator to trivial levels. The only step performed manually involves editing the SFL to indicate which modules are to be transferred to the maintenance programmer. This is accomplished by editing the appropriate SFL (with the CMT editor to place an asterisk (*) before the name of each module to be transferred. Within the context of this example the edited SFL for the ADD program would appear as follows:

Edited Source File List for Program ADD :

```
  ADD          ! Main program
  VALDATBAS    ! Data base validation routine
* SEEKENTRY    ! Entry locate routine
  UPDATE       ! New entry addition routine
  PMPTUSER     ! General prompting routine
* PARSELINE    ! Command decoding routine
```

A CMT macro is then invoked that parses the edited SFL and transmits the source code for the flagged modules to the appropriate maintenance account, and sends object modules for all other SFL entries to the Class 2 partition from where they can be accessed by the maintenance programmer at link time. In addition, the macro sends a copy of the edited SFL to the maintenance account.

Within the development environment, the SFL can also be utilized to streamline the job of the developer or maintenance programmer. To

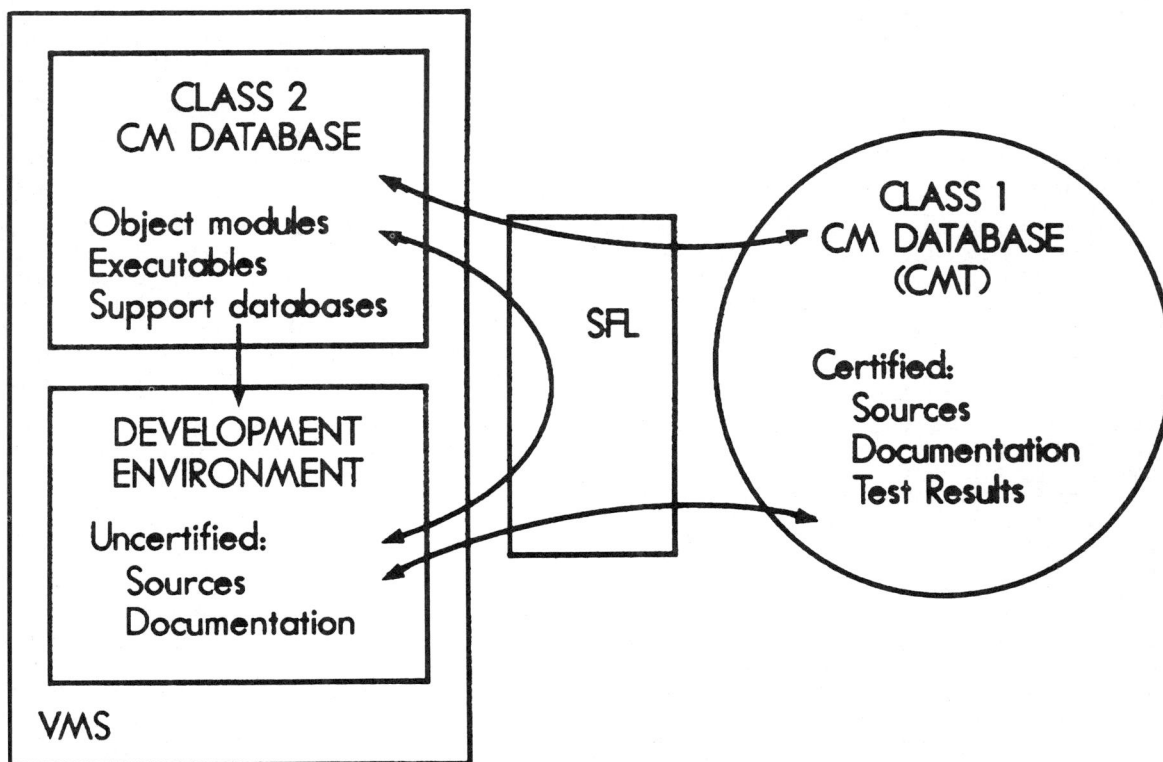

Fig. 4. The integrated hybrid environment. Paths that intersect the SFL token represent transactions that can be automated through the use of SFL data structures.

demonstrate this let us continue our example by assuming that appropriate modifications have been made to SEEKENTRY and PARSELINE. We will also assume that the programmer has decided that, in addition to these modifications, an entirely new module (called VALCOMMND) is also required and has been developed.

The maintenance programmer is now prepared to recompile all of the modified modules and the newly developed module prior to relinking the ADD program. This could be done manually, or even with a command file written and maintained by the programmer. A far simpler approach is to use the information contained in the SFL as input to an automated utility (a VMS command file) that recompiles all modified or newly developed modules. Prior to invoking this utility, the programmer must re-edit the SFL to indicate any newly developed modules associated with the program. This is accomplished by flagging the names of all newly developed modules with two asterisks and adding them to the SFL. For this example the re-edited SFL would appear as follows:

Re-edited Source File List for Program ADD :

```
  ADD          ! Main program
  VALDATBAS    ! Data base validation routine
* SEEKENTRY    ! Entry locate routine
  UPDATE       ! New entry addition routine
  PMPTUSER     ! General prompting routine
* PARSELINE    ! Command decoding routine
**VALCOMMND    ! Command validation routine
```

The utility parses the SFL and compiles any module that is flagged as new (**) or modified (*).

Similar support is provided for the link activity. An automated procedure is supplied that parses the SFL and retrieves each required object module from one of several locations depending on the status (new, modified or unmodified) of the corresponding entry in the SFL. Objects for new and modified modules are linked from the maintenance account; objects for unmodified modules are linked from the Class 2 partition.

In addition to reducing the overheads imposed upon the maintenance/development programmer, utilization of these standard compilation and link tools guarantees that the same set of compilation and link options are used in every operation. This promotes a level of software uniformity that would be difficult to obtain with manual procedures.

The final step in the maintenance cycle for program ADD involves readmitting (after certification) the modified and newly developed modules to the Class 1 partition (CMT data base). To accomplish this task a CMT macro can be invoked to import and parse the SFL, and to import all modules that are flagged within the SFL as new or modified. As a final step, the macro deletes all status flags from the SFL. Again, virtually all manual procedures are eliminated from what would otherwise be a very complex task.

In addition to eliminating the tedium and significantly reducing the time involved in processing new and modified modules, use of SFL-based automated procedures and utilities at all levels of the development and configuration management efforts virtually eliminates the possibility of corrupting the Class 1 partition due to an error or oversight on the part of the developer or the configuration management staff. Configuration management efforts that rely upon manual procedures to update a data base of protected software are susceptible to admitting uncertified modules to the data base, or failing to admit all new or modified modules to the data base. In either case, if these errors are not immediately detected and rectified, the integrity of the data base can be seriously compromised. By providing SFL-based tools that are used by both the development/maintenance and the configuration management communities, however, one can guarantee that all modules and the same modules that comprise a (successfully tested) program are readmitted to the data base.

The final aspect of SFL utilization that we will present is the application of SFL's to the automation of software system rebuilds. Within the context of our system, the term system rebuild denotes a process whereby all software subordinate to a particular data structure in the Class 1 partition (CMT data base) is recompiled and relinked, and the appropriate components of the Class 2 data base are updated (with the new executable images, for example). To perform this task manually, even for a very small system, can be an enormously complex and time-intensive undertaking.

By utilizing the information within source file lists, however, this process can be completely automated. A CMT macro is invoked to modify the SFL for each program in the data base, flagging each constituent module for transfer out of the Class 1 partition. This macro then invokes the software release macro (discussed above) to transfer all source modules and the corresponding SFL's to a location in the Class 2 partition. The standard compilation and link utilities can then be executed from a command file to accomplish the recompilation, relink and recataloging of the resulting executable images for all exported software. All sources and objects are then deleted from the Class 2 partition. In this manner the entire system can be rebuilt extremely quickly and reliably.

Conclusions

In this paper the results of our efforts to implement an effective automated configuration management environment to support a small software development project have been presented. It has been demonstrated that the introduction of a hybrid environment that exploits features of a CMT (for configuration management support) and the host operating system (for development support) provides an extremely powerful structure within which both of these complementary activities can be conducted. It has been further demonstrated

that a simple interface data structure (the SFL)
can be defined that allows automation of the interactions that must take place between the
constituents of the hybrid environment. Finally
it has been shown that the performance of this
system (in terms of operational overheads, convenience and user training) significantly exceeds
that of conventional configuration management
environments. Indeed, the capabilities of a
developer operating within the hybrid environment
are actually enhanced, without imposing any significant additional overheads.

The hybrid environment approach to configuration
management was developed specifically to address
the requirements of a small software development
project. These requirements dictated the elimination of intrusions upon the development effort by
configuration management activities. In addition,
the ability to automate all phases of the configuration management effort was deemed the only
practical way to guarantee that all configuration
management activities could be carried out by a
very small staff. It is the opinion of this
author, however, that the hybrid environment approach is also appropriate for use in conjunction
with large-scale software development projects.
Although the level of management visibility supported by the hybrid environment, and the
prohibition against retaining uncertified versions
within the CMT data base may be considered limitations, the tremendous reduction in the overheads
imposed upon both management and technical staffs
could potentially result in even greater productivity gains than are seen on a small project.

It is expected that the minimum impact of the implementation of the hybrid environment upon a
large-scale software development project would be
the re-assignment of a large fraction of the configuration management staff from tedious manual
tasks to (more productive) development-oriented
activities. Certainly, it is true that the
automated procedures that have been described in
this paper constitute a minimum exploitation of an
extremely powerful resource: a subset that enables
the small project to conduct effective configuration management. The enhancements to this system
that might be realized by redirecting the efforts
of staff formerly engaged in manual configuration
management activities to the development and support of new automated capabilities could
revolutionize this very important software engineering discipline.

THE SLIM SOFTWARE COST
AND
SCHEDULE ESTIMATING MODEL

Lawrence H. Putnam and Ralph M. Cline

Quantitative Software Mgmt. Inc.
1057 Waverley Way
McLean, Virginia 22101

ABSTRACT

SLIM is a versatile, interactive software product designed to help managers and analysts estimate the time, effort, and cost to build software systems. Users can tune the model by inputting size, time, and effort data from completed projects. For the project being estimated, descriptive information about system complexity and developer proficiency are input. SLIM then calculates the minimum time and associated cost and effort to build the system. Users can either accept the minimum time or consider longer times at reduced cost. Once a solution has been determined, the model can generate a consistent set of life cycle projections. Staffing and cashflow plans, risk assessments, and reliability predictions are examples of these outputs. Through better planning and control, SLIM enables managers to stay within budget, on schedule, and meet reliability goals.

SOFTWARE LIFE CYCLE

The life cycle (Figure 1) for large software systems used in government and in the private sector typically begins with a study phase to assess whether the development is technically and economically feasible. During the functional design phase which follows, the software requirements are written and a preliminary design is prepared. Next, up to two to three years for development will be required for detailed design, coding, testing, validation and documentation of the system. The operation phase, covering an average of six to ten years, completes the life cycle. During this phase, maintenance is performed to correct hidden design and coding errors that periodically surface and, as the system matures, modifications and enhancements are made to update and increase the capability of the system.

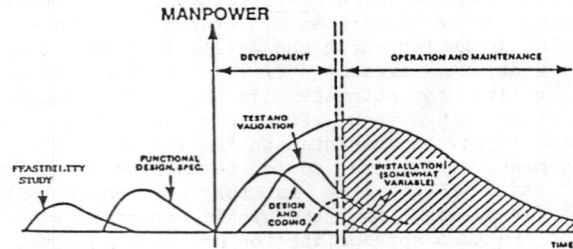

FIGURE 1 SOFTWARE LIFE CYCLE

The development and operational phases characteristically have moderately steep initial manpower buildup rates that level off near the peak and then gradually decline. It has been empirically determined by others that a form of the Rayleigh distribution, shown below, closely fits this type of staffing profile:

$$y = 2Kate^{-at^2}$$

where
y = manpower utilized at time t
K = cumulative manpower utilized for development and operation
a = shape parameter
t = elapsed time from start of development phase

NEED FOR BETTER ESTIMATING METHODS

With few exceptions, personnel involved in planning budgets and schedules over the life cycle of new software systems have consistently underestimated what the various costs will be and how long each milestones will take. This is because planners tend to base their budget and schedule estimates on factors other than those related to the actual effort required to do the job. For example, the date when the hardware is to be delivered to the customer becomes the planned software completion date, and a cost per line of code multiplied by the expected size of the system becomes the dollars budgeted for

18

the project. Little or no regard is given to the inherent difficulty of the effort. As a result, midway through the development, milestones will have been missed and the budgeted funds will be nearly depleted. Once again, management will be forced to accept a schedule slippage and a cost overrun because they do not have an effective means for making reasonably accurate predictions.

A survey conducted by the General Accounting Office quantified the frequency with which software developers exceeded their early estimates for cost and schedule (Table 1). Over 50% of those surveyed reported that cost overruns were either very common or fairly common; whereas, over 60% reported very common or fairly common overruns for schedule.

TABLE 1 GAO SURVEY RESULTS

"Software development has dollar overrun."		
	Respondents	
Response	Number	Percentage
Very common	24	21.2
Fairly common	33	29.2
Not very common	29	25.7
Very rare	11	9.7
Never occurs	7	6.2
Don't know	9	8.0
Total	113	100.0

"Software development has calendar overrun."		
	Respondents	
Response	Number	Percentage
Very common	34	30.1
Fairly common	36	31.9
Not very common	29	25.7
Very rare	9	8.0
Never occurs	2	1.8
Don't know	3	2.7
Total	113	a/ 100.0

a/Does not add due to rounding

SLIM - A COST-SCHEDULE ESTIMATING MODEL

The Software Life Cycle Management Model (SLIM), based on the Rayleigh equation, is a versatile, interactive software product that is designed to help software managers, financial managers and analysts estimate the time, effort and cost required to build medium and large size software systems. It allows users, with relatively little effort, to tailor their estimates to meet all realistic constraints imposed on the development. Staffing and cashflow plans, risk assessments and reliability predictions are examples of model outputs that are available to answer management's questions. Specific questions which the model can answer are as follows:

How long will the development take and what is the duration of the life cycle?

How much will the effort cost and what is the cashflow?

What are the trade-offs between time and cost?

What are the manpower requirements with time?

How can the constraints imposed by management and the customer best be accomodated?

What are the risks associated with the planned development?

What is the expected mean time to failure of the system upon completion of development and for the rest of its life cycle?

INITIAL INPUTS - TUNNING THE MODEL

The algorithms used in SLIM allow the user to input descriptive information about the development environment, the software system being developed, and the developer's capability to do the job. Table 2 is an example of the inputs for an inventory management system (business application) that will (a) be coded on-line in an interactive mode, 95% in COBOL and 5% in ASSEMBLY language, (b) be developed on a dedicated computer that is aided by a data base management system (25% coded in DBMS language) and report writer (20% of output formats prepared using the writer), (c) contain 5% realtime code, (d) utilize 50% of the target computer's memory, and (e) have interfaces that are moderately difficult and logic and algorithms that will be 85% newly designed. The table also shows that the developer intends to use three of the listed modern programming practices to a high degree and the fourth to an average degree. About 90% of the personnel assigned to the development will be available immediately and will have average overall skills and and experience building like systems. They also have extensive experience using the development computer and language. The management team assigned to the project is know to have had experience directing two projects that were similar in difficulty to the inventory management system.

Two additional inputs, defined by index numbers, also are shown in the table. One, the Manpower Buildup Index, imposes a one sided constraint that determines the maximum effective staffing build up rate. The maximum rate will vary according to how much of the effort must be accomplishd in a sequential manner versus in a parallel manner. For example, an entirely new system designed and coded from scratch and having many interfaces will have to be built sequentially; whereas a system that already has been operational, and hence has all of its algorithms and functions in place, can be converted from one language or machine to another by building the pieces concurrently or in parallel. In this case, people can be added to the project at a much more rapid rate than for the new system that must be built sequentially.

TABLE 2 PROJECT INPUT

TITLE: INVENTORY MANAGEMENT   PROJECT START: 0185

COST ELEMENTS
    LABOR RATE: 110000   MONETARY UNIT: $
    STD DEV (LABOR RATE):   11000   INFLATION RATE: 6.5%

ENVIRONMENT
    ONLINE DEVELOPMENT: 100%   COMPUTER AVAILABILITY: 100%
    PRIMARY LANGUAGE: COBOL   SECONDARY LANGUAGE: ASSEMBLY
    ASSEMBLY: 5%   HOL: 95%
    4TH GENERATION: 0%   DBMS: 25%
    REPORT WRITER: 20%   SCREEN WRITER: 0%

SYSTEM CONSTRAINTS
    TYPE: BUSINESS APPLICATION   REAL TIME CODE: 5%
    MEMORY: 50%   INTERFACES: MODERATE
    NEW DESIGN: 85%   MANPOWER AVAILABILITY: 90%

MODERN PROGRAMMING PRACTICES
    STRUCTURED PROGRAMMING: HIGH   DESIGN/CODE WALKTHROUGHS: HIGH
    TOP-DOWN DESIGN: HIGH   PROGRAM LIBRARIAN: LOW

EXPERIENCE
    OVERALL: AVERAGE   SIZE AND APPLICATION: AVERAGE
    LANGUAGE: EXTENSIVE   DEVELOPMENT COMPUTER: EXTENSIVE
    MANAGEMENT: TWO

PRODUCTIVITY INDEX: 13   MANPOWER BUILDUP INDEX: 2

SIZE:

FUNCTION	SMALLEST	MOST LIKELY	LARGEST	EXPECTED	STD DEV
ON HAND	3500	6000	9500	6167	1000
ON ORDER	5000	9000	14000	9167	1500
BACK ORDER	4500	7500	13000	7917	1417
BEING SHIPPED	6500	10000	15000	10250	1417
BEING PROCESSED	3500	7200	11500	7300	1333
TOTAL				40800	3007

The Manpower Buildup Index of 2 that is shown for the inventory management system in Table 2 represents a relatively slow staffing rate for the project. The system being built is made up of interdependent subsystems with moderately complex interfaces thereby requiring the build to be mainly sequential. However, since the index is a one sided constraint, users will still be able to examine other viable options that build up more slowly, have a lower peak staffing and take a little longer to complete. A manpower Buildup Index of 1 corresponds to the most gradual staffing rate; a 6 corresponds to the steepest.

The other index, the Productivity Index calibrates or tunes the model to the expected level of efficiency of the developer and to the complexity of the system being developed. A developer who employs modern programming practices and utilizes state of the art equipment will have a higher Productivity Index than one who does not. Also the same developer will have a higher Productivity Index when building a straight forward banking system vis a vis a more complex real time weapons control system. The index of 13 shown in Table 2 for the example inventory management system represents an average productivity for building management information systems. The range of Productivity Index values for industry as a whole for all types of systems extends from 1 (the lowest) to 25 (the highest).

SLIM calculated the productivity index that was given in Table 2 based on the user inputting historical size, time and effort data from software systems recently completed by the developer. Table 3 shows the inputs to SLIM for the completed systems and the Productivity Index and Manpower Buildup Index that were calculated for each. Since 2 systems calibrated at 13 and one at 12, a Productivity Index of 13 was used to calibrate SLIM in the example. Also management has agreed to give the project first priority on all company resources, a decision that will allow the development team to perform at the higher level of demonstrated proficiency. Furthermore, since there is a high degree of similarity between the system being developed and the completed systems (e.g. all are management information systems), we can expect the calculated index number to be a very good representation of the developer's productivity.

TABLE 3 CALIBRATION DATA

CALIBRATE INPUT SUMMARY

SYSTEM NAME	SIZE (SS)	TIME (MOS)	EFFORT (MM)	APPLICATION TYPE	OPERATIONAL DATE
SYSTM INVENTORY	217360	28.0	624	BUSINESS	0683
FINANCE	19000	10.0	15	BUSINESS	0983
ADMINISTRATION	95000	20.0	325	BUSINESS	1183

MANAGEMENT METRICS

SYSTEM NAME	PRODUCTIVITY INDEX	MANPOWER BUILDUP INDEX	PRODUCTIVITY (SS/MM)	AVG MANPOWER (MM/MO)	AVG CODE PRODUCTION RATE (SS/MO)
SYSTM INVENTORY	13	2	348	22	7763
FINANCE	13	2	1267	2	1900
ADMINISTRATION	12	2	292	16	4750

In the absence of historical data for similar systems, the productivity index could have been approximated by SLIM from an industry average that will be adjusted by the model based on the previously discussed descriptive information about the system being developed and the developers capability to do the job. Because this method is based on an industry average, the preferred method for determining the productivity is to input historical data for similar systems recently completed by the developer.

One final input is the expected size (number of developed, delivered, executable lines of code) of the system. Recognizing that there are uncertainties in these size estimates, SLIM utilizes a range estimating approach. The size inputs consist of estimates of the smallest, most likely, and largest possible number of lines of code that could be developed for the final product. The estimates should be broad enough to encompass a 99% high-low range. Depending on the stage of development, the size estimates should be for the whole system, for each major subsystem or for each module. Shown at the bottom of Table 2 are the smallest, most likely and largest size estimates for the 5 major subsystems of the inventory management system.

MINIMUM TIME SOLUTION

Based on the initial input values, SLIM automatically gives the minimum feasible time schedule and associated cost and effort to complete development of the system. This output is based on a Monte Carlo simulation that produces a solution in terms of expected values and standard deviations (statistical measures of uncertainty). Because of the uncertainty in system size, a sensitivity analysis is provided to show how the expected values for time, effort and cost change as the expected value for size varies by one to three standard deviations. In addition, the consistency of the solution is checked by comparing the calculated values for effort, duration, staffing and productivity with their corresponding means from the SLIM data base. The check identifies those values that are greater than, less than, or within the normal range of the data base (the normal range includes systems that are within one standard deviation of the mean of the data base).

Table 4 shows the minimum time solution for the inventory management system. The shortest schedule for the development is 13.2 months based on 78.4 manmonths of effort at a cost of

$725,000. The expected system size is given as 40,800 statements with an uncertainty (one standard deviation) of plus or minus 3,007 statements. According to the size sensitivity profile, if the statements increased by one standard deviation to 43,807, the expected development time would be increased to 13.5 months and the expected cost increased to $810,000. Likewise, the analysis shows that there would be a corresponding decrease in the expected time and cost if the size of the system were one standard deviation smaller. A check of the model outputs for consistency shows that the solution is within the normal range of values for similar size systems.

TABLE 4 MINIMUM TIME SOLUTION

MANAGEMENT METRIC	EXPECTED VALUE (50% PROBABILITY)	STD DEV
SYSTEM SIZE (STATEMENTS)	40800	3007
MINIMUM DEVELOPMENT TIME (MONTHS)	13.2	0.5
DEVELOPMENT EFFORT (MANMONTHS)	78.4	10.6
DEVELOPMENT COST (x 1000 $)		
(UNINFLATED)	725	131
(INFLATED 6.5%)	751	136
PEAK MANPOWER (PEOPLE)	8	1

SENSITIVITY PROFILE FOR MINIMUM TIME SOLUTION

	SOURCE STMTS	MONTHS	MANMONTHS	UNINFLATED COST (X 1000)
-3 STD DEV	31779.	11.8	49.	452.
-1 STD DEV	37793.	12.7	68.	628.
EXPECTED	40800.	13.2	78.	725.
+1 STD DEV	43807.	13.5	88.	810.
+3 STD DEV	49821.	14.3	109.	996.

QSM DATABASE CONSISTENCY CHECK

MANAGEMENT METRIC	VALUE	ASSESSMENT
TIME (MONTHS)	13.2	IN NORMAL RANGE
EFFORT (MANMONTHS)	78	IN NORMAL RANGE
AVERAGE STAFFING (PEOPLE)	6	IN NORMAL RANGE
PRODUCTIVITY (LINES/MM)	520	IN NORMAL RANGE

ALTERNATIVE SOLUTIONS – TRADING OFF TIME AND COSTS

The user either may accept the minimum time solution or may consider longer times and thereby reduce the cost of development. One way to arrive at a longer schedule is to let SLIM determine the new time based on a specified acceptable risk for not overruning the schedule. In the example illustrated by Table 5, management specified that it wants to have at least a 90% probability that the development will not exceed 16 months. Output from the model shows that by planning to complete the development in 15.2 months, the assurance required by management will be satisfied. Furthermore, by increasing the schedule from the minimum time to 15.2 months (a change of two months), the cost can be reduced by over $300,000 --- a very significant savings. In software development productivity increases as the size of the project team decreases (less intercommunication) and as a result, projects cost less even though they may take longer.

TABLE 5 DESIGN TO RISK

WITH A 90% ASSURANCE OF NOT EXCEEDING 16.00 MONTHS, YOUR EXPECTED SOLUTION IS:

CURRENT SOLUTION

MANAGEMENT METRIC	EXPECTED VALUE (50% PROBABILITY)	STD DEV
TIME (MONTHS)	15.21	0.61
EFFORT (MANMONTHS)	43	6
COST (X 1000)	397	72
PEAK MANPOWER (PEOPLE)	4	1

QSM DATABASE CONSISTENCY CHECK

MANAGEMENT METRIC	VALUE	ASSESSMENT
TIME (MONTHS)	15.2	IN NORMAL RANGE
EFFORT (MANMONTHS)	43	IN NORMAL RANGE
AVERAGE STAFFING (PEOPLE)	3	IN NORMAL RANGE
PRODUCTIVITY (LINES/MM)	941	IN NORMAL RANGE

Reliability of the system could be a factor in determining how much time should be allowed for the main build. Table 6 shows the time, effort, cost, staffing and expected errors if the system is designed to have 0.15 months mean time to failure when it reaches full operational capability. The new development time of 13.9 months is greater than the minimum time solution but less than the 90% assurance solution. Consequently, the cost of this solution ($563,000) is between the costs calculated for the previous two. Also, because the time for this solution (13.9 months) is less than the time for the 90% assurance solution (15.2 months), the assurance of completing the development in 16 months will now be greater than 90%.

Additional management constraints are considered in the solution presented in Table 7. The maximum cost of the development was limited to $700,000, the time to 16.0 months, and the peak staffing to 3 people minimum and 7 people maximum. The model automatically imposes one additional constraint, the development time must be greater than the 13.2 months previously calculated for the minimum development time.

TABLE 6 DESIGN TO RELIABILITY

WITH A MEAN TIME TO FAILURE OF 0.15 MONTHS, YOUR EXPECTED SOLUTION IS:

CURRENT SOLUTION

MANAGEMENT METRIC	EXPECTED VALUE (50% PROBABILITY)	STD DEV
TIME (MONTHS)	13.94	0.56
EFFORT (MANMONTHS)	61	8
COST (X 1000)	563	102
PEAK MANPOWER (PEOPLE)	6	1
MTTF (MOS)	0.15	0.02
EXPECTED ERRORS	311	42
EXPECTED ERRORS/1000 SS	7.63	-
EXPECTED ERRORS/1000 SS (FROM SIT TO TD)	1.34	-
ERRORS REMAINING AT 13.9 MOS	16	-

QSM DATABASE CONSISTENCY CHECK

MANAGEMENT METRIC	VALUE	ASSESSMENT
TIME (MONTHS)	13.9	IN NORMAL RANGE
EFFORT (MANMONTHS)	61	IN NORMAL RANGE
AVERAGE STAFFING (PEOPLE)	4	IN NORMAL RANGE
PRODUCTIVITY (LINES/MM)	665	IN NORMAL RANGE

TABLE 7 LINEAR PROGRAM

MANAGEMENT CONSTRAINTS

DEVELOPMENT TIME (MONTHS)	16.00
DEVELOPMENT COST (X 1000 $)	700
MINIMUM PEAK MANPOWER (PEOPLE)	3.0
MAXIMUM PEAK MANPOWER (PEOPLE)	7.0

RESOURCE CONSTRAINED SOLUTIONS

	MINIMUM TIME	MINIMUM COST
TIME (MONTHS)	13.6	16.0
EFFORT (MM)	69	35
COST (X 1000)	628	324
PEAK MANPOWER (PEOPLE)	7.0	3.1

GOVERNING CONSTRAINT	MAXIMUM PEAK MANPOWER	MAXIMUM TIME

A linear program algorithm in the model uses the constraints to determine a region of feasible solutions. As shown by Figure 2, the region lies along line Ss (system size) and is bounded by the intersection of Ss with Time (maximum time) and with Max MP (maximum peak staffing). Asterisks locate the two intersections on the graph and identify the bounds of the feasible region. The solutions at the bounds give the minimum feasible cost and minimum feasible time within the constraints of the problem. Other lines shown are Min MP (minimum peak staffing), MBI (maximum buildup rate) and Cost (maximum cost). These lines intersect line Ss outside the feasible region in this example and thus are not the values that constrain the solution.

The table and graph both show that the range of feasible solutions extends from 13.6 to 16.0 months. Because of the constraint at 13.6 months, we can no longer consider schedules as short the minimum time of 13.2 months.

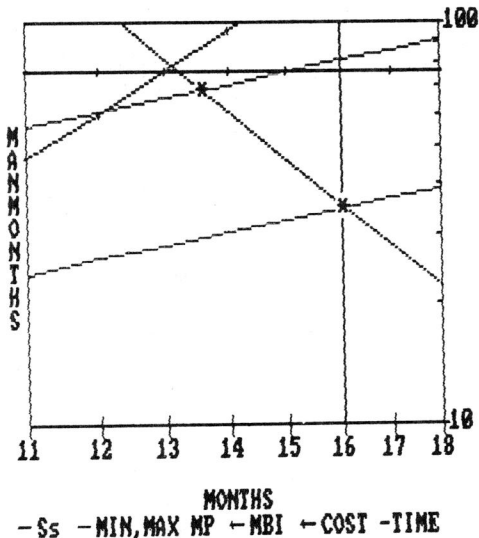

FIGURE 2 LINEAR PROGRAM GRAPH

It is often possible to incorporate assurance and reliability constraints directly in the Linear Program solution. Instead of entering the development time as 16 months, we can enter 15.21 months (the time that assures a 90% probability of completing the build in 16 months) and instead of entering the cost as $700,000, we can enter $563,000 (the cost of building a system with a 0.15 month MTTF).

Table 8 and Figure 3 give the new linear program solution. The feasible region has been reduced from 2.4 months (between 13.6 and 16.0 months) to 1.3 months (between 13.9 and 15.2 months), but the region now satisfies all of the constraints imposed on the problem. That is, all solutions within the smaller feasible region will give at least a 90% assurance of completing the development within 16 months and also will result in at least 0.15 months MTTF. Cost and peak staffing constraints also will be satisfied.

A preferred solution can be selected from the range of feasible solutions. Table 9 gives an example of a solution that maximizes the joint probability of not exceeding 16 months and $700,000. By planning to complete the build in 14.58

months at a cost of $471,000 and 51 manmonths of effort, the developer is virtually assured of not overruning the constraining cost and schedule (99% assurance). Figure 4 depicts the solution graphically based on 500 iterations of a Monte Carlo simulation. Essentially every simulation (dots on the graph) resulted in a development time less than 16 months and $700,000. Since this solution (14.58 months) is also within the previously determined smaller feasible region (13.9 to 15.2 months), it will satisfy all of the management constraints. Also, from the consistency check, we see that the effort, time, manpower, and productivity calculated for the solution are within the normal range for the SLIM data base.

TABLE 8 ALTERNATIVE LINEAR PROGRAM

MANAGEMENT CONSTRAINTS

DEVELOPMENT TIME (MONTHS)	15.21
DEVELOPMENT COST (X 1000 $)	563
MINIMUM PEAK MANPOWER (PEOPLE)	3.0
MAXIMUM PEAK MANPOWER (PEOPLE)	7.0

RESOURCE CONSTRAINED SOLUTIONS

	MINIMUM TIME	MINIMUM COST
TIME (MONTHS)	13.9	15.2
EFFORT (MM)	61	43
COST (X 1000)	563	397
PEAK MANPOWER (PEOPLE)	6.1	3.9

GOVERNING CONSTRAINT	MAXIMUM COST	MAXIMUM TIME

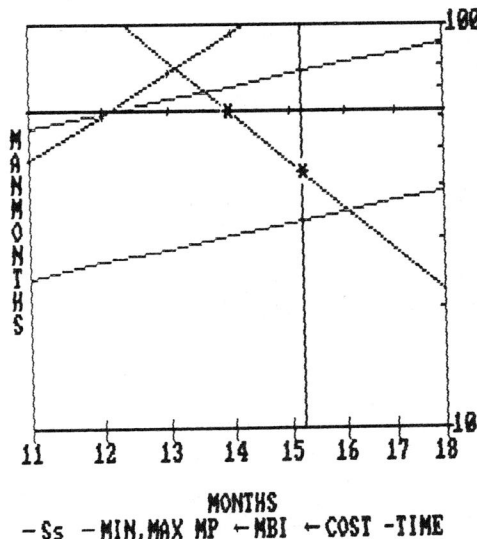

FIGURE 3 ALTERNATIVE LINEAR PROGRAM GRAPH

TABLE 9 BEST BID

WITH A 16.00 MONTH SCHEDULE AND A $ 700000 COST, YOUR EXPECTED SOLUTION IS:

CURRENT SOLUTION

MANAGEMENT METRIC	EXPECTED VALUE (50% PROBABILITY)	STD DEV
TIME (MONTHS)	14.58	0.59
EFFORT (MANMONTHS)	51	7
COST (X 1000)	471	85
PEAK MANPOWER (PEOPLE)	5	1

PROBABILITY OF NOT EXCEEDING COST & SCHEDULE: 0.99

QSM DATABASE CONSISTENCY CHECK

MANAGEMENT METRIC	VALUE	ASSESSMENT
TIME (MONTHS)	14.6	IN NORMAL RANGE
EFFORT (MANMONTHS)	51	IN NORMAL RANGE
AVERAGE STAFFING (PEOPLE)	4	IN NORMAL RANGE
PRODUCTIVITY (LINES/MM)	794	IN NORMAL RANGE

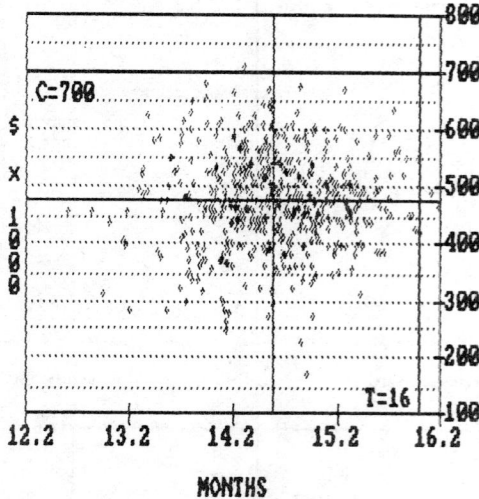

FIGURE 4 BEST BID GRAPH

IMPLEMENTING THE SOLUTION – MANAGEMENT ORIENTED PROJECTIONS

Once it has been determined that a solution is optimum or at least in agreement with the constraints, the model can be used to generate a consistent set of development and life cycle projections. The projections can be used at the start of the project, for example, to schedule major milestones, estimate the cashflow, and plan the work breakout by principal tasks (e.g., design, coding, testing). As the development progresses, estimates of the initial SLIM inputs will become better known and new estimates should be used to update the initial projections. This will provide management with a more accurate means for monitoring the development and detecting emerging problems early enough to do something about them.

The user should keep in mind that the outputs to SLIM are not single values but rather are expected values and standard deviations. As the accuracy of the inputs increases the standard deviations decrease and the expected values converge to their true values.

Table 10 gives a starting month for each of the major milestones. This projection can be used to plan and control the software development. Missing a major milestone is a strong indication that the development is headed for trouble and redirection by management may be required.

TABLE 10 MAJOR MILESTONES

MILESTONES

#	EVENT	MONTHS FROM START OF DETAILED LOGIC DESIGN	EARLIEST CALENDAR MONTH
0	FEASIBILITY STUDY REVIEW	-4.9 *	AUG 84 *
1	PRELIMINARY DESIGN REVIEW	0.0	JAN 85
2	CRITICAL DESIGN REVIEW	6.3	JUL 85
3	FIRST CODE COMPLETE	8.4	SEP 85
4	SYSTEM INTEGRATION TEST	10.3	NOV 85
5	USER ORIENTED SYSTEM TEST	11.7	DEC 85
6	INITIAL OPER. CAPABILITY	13.6	FEB 86
7	FULL OPER. CAPABILITY (95% RELIABILITY LEVEL)	14.6	MAR 86
8	(99% RELIABILITY LEVEL)	18.1	JUL 86
9	(99.9% RELIABILITY LEVEL)	22.2	NOV 86

* TIME WILL HAVE TO BE ADJUSTED IF FUNCTIONAL DESIGN AND MAIN SOFTWARE BUILD OVERLAP OR HAVE A GAP BETWEEN THEM.

A breakdown of time, effort, and cost for the front end phases (feasibility study and functional design) and by work category for the development phase is given in Table 11. These outputs let managers better plan the allocation of their resources by giving them projections of effort and schedule by skill category.

Figures 5 and 6 show the probability that the development time and cost respectively will not exceed the various values shown on the graphs. The expected time (50% level) to reach full operational capability is shown as less than 15 months and the expected cost (also 50% level) is shown as less than $500,000. Notice that these values are consistent with the solution that we selected (development time equal to 14.58 months at a cost of $471,000). Also shown on the graphs are probabilities other than at the 50% level and milestones other than Full Operational Capability (FOC). The probabilities range from 1% to 99%; the milestones in addition to FOC are Critical Design Review (CDR), First Code Complete (FCC), System Integration Test (SIT), User Oriented System Test (UOST), and Initiel Operational Capability (IOC). The standard deviation lines on the graph facilitate determining the probabilities of overruns and underruns.

TABLE 11 EFFORT BETWEEN MILESTONES

THE TABLE BELOW SHOWS THE PROJECTED TIME (MONTHS), EFFORT (MANMONTHS), PERCENT OF TOTAL DEVELOPMENT AND COST REQUIRED FOR EACH ACTIVITY PHASE DURING DEVELOPMENT. THESE VALUES ARE BASED ON A DEVELOPMENT TIME OF 14.6 MONTHS AND A TOTAL DEVELOPMENT EFFORT OF 51.4 MANMONTHS. THE FOLLOWING COSTS ARE INFLATED BY 6.5%.

BREAKDOWN BY PRINCIPAL ACTIVITY

PRINCIPAL ACTIVITY	TIME (MONTHS)	EFFORT (MM)	UNINFLATED (COST X 1000)	INFLATED (COST X 1000)	% OF TOTAL
FEASIBILITY STUDY	3.6	10.9	100	101	14.72
FUNCTIONAL DESIGN	4.9	11.9	109	113	16.07
LOGIC DESIGN	6.3	13.0	119	126	17.45
CODING	2.1	9.0	83	90	12.17
INTEGRATION	1.9	8.9	82	90	12.04
PRELIMINARY VERIFICATION	1.4	6.6	61	67	8.90
FINAL VERIFICATION	1.9	9.1	84	93	12.29
QUALIFICATION	1.0	4.7	43	49	6.35
TOTAL	23.1	74.2	681	730	100.00

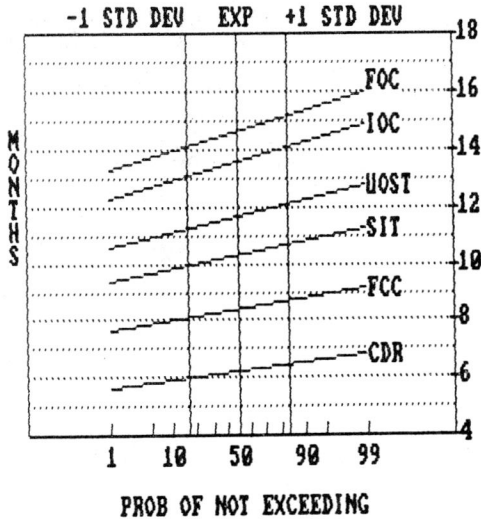

FIGURE 5 RISK ANALYSIS (TIME)

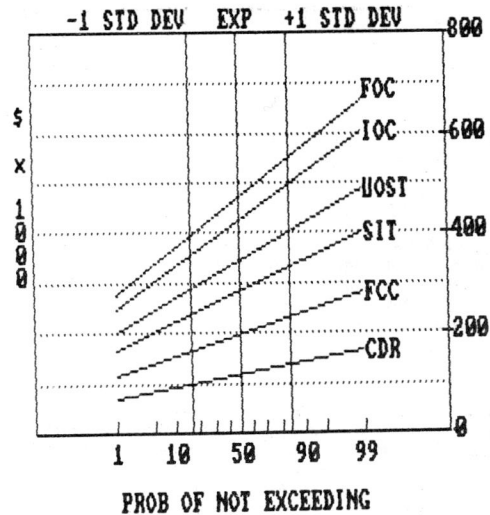

FIGURE 6 RISK ANALYSIS (COST)

Code production rates, like some other SLIM outputs, can be presented in several different forms -- table, histogram or simulation plot. Figure 7 shows the expected rate for the inventory management system as a simulation. Two simulations are plotted for each month and are shown on the graph as small crosses. A best fit Rayleigh curve is drawn through the simulation points and gives the expected code production rate as a function of time. The spread of crosses shows the uncertainty associated with the rate. The number of lines of valid code that eventually will be delivered to the system user are shown. They do not include code that is written but subsequently rejected. Thus, the code actually written during any period should exceed that shown by the graph.

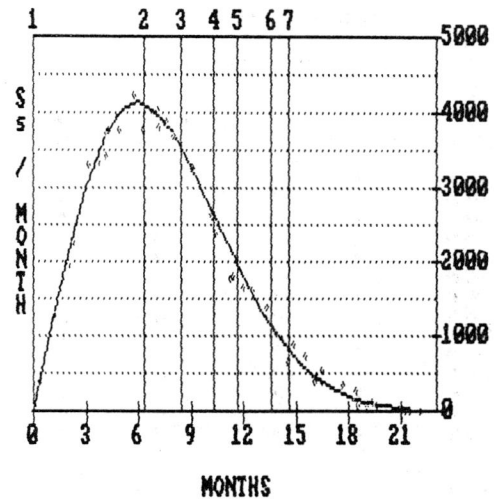

FIGURE 7 CODE PRODUCTION

The expected reliability of the system is shown in Table 12. The table projects a mean time to failure upon completion of the development of almost 4 days (0.18 months). After 6 months of operation the expected rate will be reduced to one failure in 2.5 months.

TABLE 12 RELIABILITY

THE TABLE BELOW SHOWS THE EXPECTED ERROR RATE, MEAN TIME TO FAIL-URE (MONTHS), AND EXPECTED CUMULATIVE ERRORS FOR DEVELOPMENT THROUGH THE .999 RELIABILITY LEVEL. THESE VALUES ARE BASED ON A DEVELOPMENT TIME OF 14.6 MONTHS AND A TOTAL DEVELOPMENT EFFORT OF 51.4 MANMONTHS.

EXPECTED ERRORS

MONTH	MEAN ERROR RATE	ERROR RATE RANGE	EXPECTED CUM ERRORS FIXED	RANGE CUM ERRORS FIXED	MTTF (MONTHS)
JAN 85	3.7	2.5 - 4.9	4	3 - 4	-
FEB 85	10.7	7.3 - 14.1	14	11 - 18	-
MAR 85	16.8	11.7 - 22.0	31	24 - 38	-
APR 85	21.7	15.3 - 28.0	53	41 - 64	-
MAY 85	24.9	17.8 - 31.9	78	60 - 95	-
JUN 85	26.4	19.2 - 33.7	104	81 - 127	-
JUL 85	26.4	19.4 - 33.3	130	101 - 159	-
AUG 85	25.0	18.5 - 31.4	155	120 - 190	-
SEP 85	22.6	16.9 - 28.2	178	138 - 217	-
OCT 85	19.6	14.8 - 24.3	197	153 - 241	0.051
NOV 85	16.3	12.4 - 20.1	213	166 - 261	0.061
DEC 85	13.1	10.1 - 16.1	227	176 - 277	0.076
JAN 86	10.1	7.8 - 12.4	237	184 - 290	0.099
FEB 86	7.6	5.9 - 9.3	244	190 - 299	0.132
MAR 86	5.5	4.3 - 6.7	250	194 - 306	0.182
------- FOC -------					
APR 86	3.8	3.0 - 4.7	254	197 - 310	0.261
MAY 86	2.6	2.1 - 3.1	256	199 - 313	0.385
JUN 86	1.7	1.3 - 2.1	258	200 - 316	0.586
JUL 86	1.1	0.9 - 1.3	259	201 - 317	0.922
AUG 86	0.7	0.5 - 0.8	260	202 - 318	1.496
SEP 86	0.4	0.3 - 0.5	260	202 - 318	2.502
OCT 86	0.2	0.2 - 0.3	260	202 - 319	4.318

Other examples of SLIM output are given in the following table and figure. Table 13 gives a monthly staffing plan for the development phase. Figure 8 gives a cashflow plan for the entire life cycle.

TABLE 13 MANLOADING

STAFFING PLAN

MONTH	PEOPLE/MONTH	STD DEV	CUMULATIVE MANMONTHS	CUM STD DEV
JAN 85	0	0.1	0	0
FEB 85	1	0.2	1	0
MAR 85	2	0.3	3	0
APR 85	2	0.4	6	1
MAY 85	3	0.5	8	1
JUN 85	3	0.6	12	2
JUL 85	4	0.6	16	2
AUG 85	4	0.7	20	3
SEP 85	5	0.7	25	3
OCT 85	5	0.7	29	4
NOV 85	5	0.7	34	5
DEC 85	5	0.7	39	5
JAN 86	5	0.7	44	6
FEB 86	5	0.6	49	7
MAR 86	5	0.6	53	7
------- FOC -------				
APR 86	2	0.3	55	8

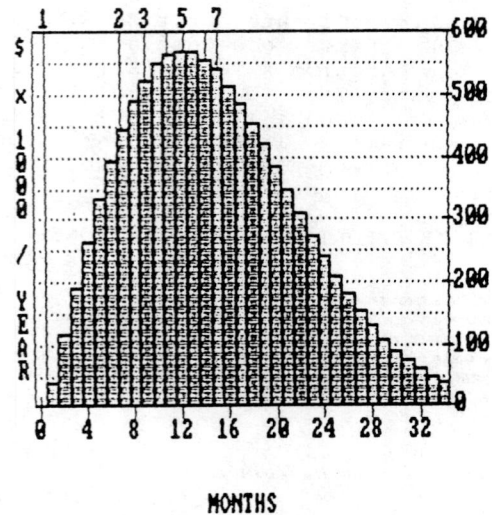

FIGURE 8 LIFE CYCLE (CASHFLOW)

SUMMARY

SLIM is an interactive model that can be tuned to a particular requirement. It then allows the user to tailor the model outputs of time, effort and cost to meet realistic constraints that have been imposed on the development. With relatively little difficulty, a favorable solution can be determined and the model then used to provide schedule, cost, manpower, risk and reliability projections based on the solution. Projections that are made before development starts can be a basis for planning the development; subsequent projections, updated as the development progresses, can be used to monitor the effort and identify emerging problems. Through better planning and control, SLIM gives managers an effective way to stay within budget and schedule and meet reliability goals.

Session 2

Expert Systems Tools and Applications

Chairman
M.L. Shooman
Polytechnic Institute of New York

OBIE-1: A KNOWLEDGE-BASED SOFTWARE TOOL FOR SIMULATION

Jeffrey P. Rosenking   Roy S. Freedman

Software Systems Laboratory
Hazeltine Corporation,   Greenlawn, N.Y.   11740
(516) 261-7000

ABSTRACT

OBIE-1, an object-based intelligent editor that is currently under development by Hazeltine Corporation, is a knowledge-based software tool for developing interactive simulations. OBIE-1 helps a programmer develop interactive simulations more productively. The programmer is not required to keep track of graphic names, variable names, or a particular programming language syntax that expresses the behavior of the simulated object. OBIE-1 automatically develops these programming representations internally, and exploits the common-sense knowledge that the programmer "knows" about most interactive devices.

Introduction

Instrument panel simulations are used in many military training applications to train personnel how to operate certain pieces of equipment. The equipment may consist of several related devices. The operator of the equipment is required to possess a certain level of expertise about the equipment in order to operate it correctly. To construct an interactive simulation of the equipment, the expertise of the operator must be put into a form which can be recognized by a computer, i.e., in some programming language. The relationships which exist between the several devices that make up the equipment must be specified, so that the simulation can operate as if it were the actual hardware. An example of an instrument panel for which a simulation may be constructed may be seen in Figure 1.

The creation of an interactive simulation for a given piece of equipment requires the effort of at least two individuals: an equipment operator and a programmer. The equipment operator must be able to convey all the information needed about how the equipment operates to the programmer, who will then construct a program to simulate the exact operation of the equipment. The only case where both of these individuals would not be needed is where one individual was an expert operator and an expert programmer or was willing to develop an expertise in the area in which he was lacking knowledge. Therefore, a minimum of two people are most often needed to develop interactive panel simulations using the tedious and laborious methods which are currently in use.

The Software Systems Laboratory at Hazeltine Corporation has developed a tool called OBIE-1 (an Object Based Intelligent Editor), which allows interactive panel simulations to be created in an easier and more productive way than is currently available. OBIE-1 allows an individual, such as an equipment operator - who has developed expertise on the operations of a specific piece of equipment - to author a simulation without the need of a programmer. This tool is being designed to assist with the development of Hazeltine TICCIT computer based training systems (see Reference [3] and [4]). One important component of TICCIT involves the creation of interactive panel simulations. OBIE-1 may be used to generate a large number of interactive simulations, which may consist of many different devices (switches, indicators, meters).

OBIE-1 will alleviate the author's concern with the programming step of the simulation creation process. There is still programming involved in this process, but OBIE-1 performs the programming, at a level which is unseen by the simulation author. The "common sense knowledge" of the author is exploited by this tool and is used to assist in creating a simulation. Therefore, the author is not required to have knowledge of a formal programming language.

Knowledge Representations

The critical component in the design of OBIE-1 is in knowledge representation. We have chosen a two-fold approach to knowledge representation:

(a)   to define an abstract object to represent all the knowledge associated with a particular device; and

(b)   to utilize a basic model to represent the relationships which exist between abstract objects.

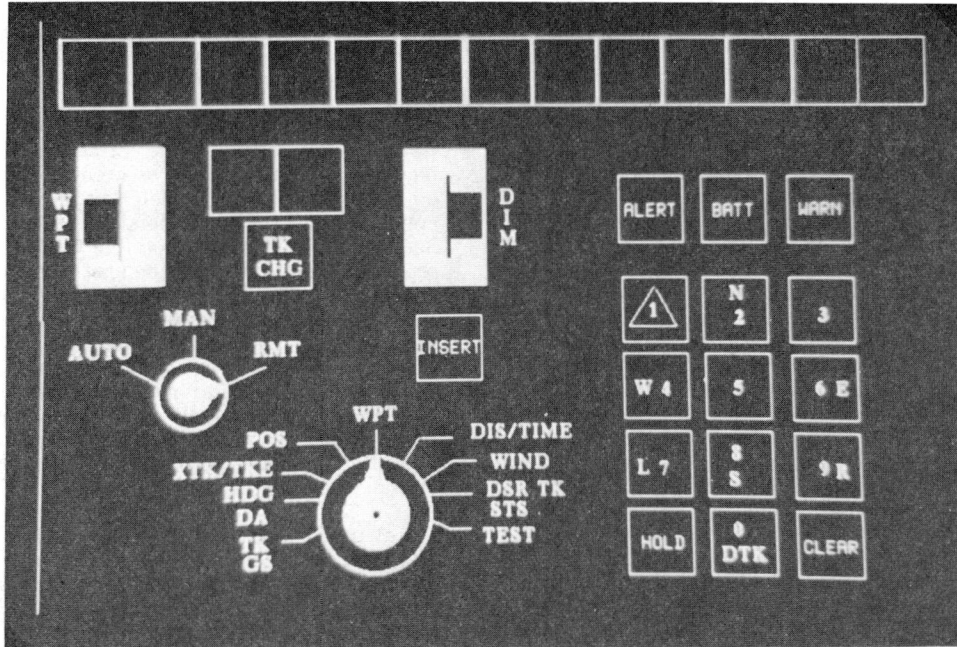

Figure 1. The LTN-72 Inertial Navigation System

OBIE-1, which was developed using knowledge base technology, facilitates the creation and manipulation of interacting abstract objects. This is why we describe OBIE-1 as "object-based". Each device on some piece of equipment is represented as an abstract object in a simulation. An abstract object consists of a name, an associated definition and a knowledge base. The definition is defined in terms of the graphics, states and state values which are associated with the object. The knowledge base of an object contains all the relationships that exist between other objects in a simulation and itself. Relationships between objects are defined by the author and are then transformed and represented in the individual object knowledge bases by OBIE-1.

Constructing the graphics for abstract objects is a simple task. The area of difficulty in the simulation creation process, using current methods, is in modeling the knowledge associated with an abstract object and forming the relationships that exist between the several objects. Each one of the relationships must be tediously programmed, to create an interactive simulation using current techniques. OBIE-1 provides an alternative, easier approach.

Each object contains knowledge about itself and knowledge about how it interacts with other objects in the simulation. To allow objects to interact with each other, OBIE-1 provides a means for objects to pass "messages" to each other. The content of these messages promote some action to be taken by the objects (such as the changing of the state of a device). We use message passage techniques which

were modeled after those used by Clinger (see Reference [1]).

We have defined a basic model to provide a structure to represent the form of a relationship which exists between two or more abstract objects. This model represents the knowledge that an author has about how an object interacts with other objects. In our model, a simple interaction is a "cognitive connection". A cognitive connection is an author defined rule of the form: IF x THEN y, where substituted for x and y are one or more abstract objects and their states. An example might be:

> if MSU-SWITCH is in the ALIGN state and READY-NAV-LIGHT is in the OFF state
> then ALERT-INDICATOR is in the ON state and INSERT-LIGHT is in the BRIGHT state.

According to the rule, the objects substituted for x are affecting the objects substituted for y. When the x-objects are in their defined states then the y-objects must be in their defined states.

OBIE 1: AN OBJECT-BASED INTELLIGENT EDITOR

OBIE-1 is composed of four distinct tools: the Graphics Interface Editor, the Cognitive Connection Editor, the Panel Sequencing Editor and the Student Mode Verifier. Each of these tools is responsible for performing individual functions.

The Graphics Interface Editor constructs the abstract objects that make up an interactive simulation. This tool combines the graphical representations of an object with all the state information associated with that object, to form the object definition. The state information is dynamically defined by the author, during the construction of the object, and represents the author's "knowledge" about an object. The knowledge is acquired by OBIE-1 during an interactive process using specially designed queries and menus. The output of the Graphics Interface Editor is the addition of a new abstract object to the OBIE-1 library of objects, from which any object may be created and manipulated at any time.

The graphics associated with an object are generated by a graphics editor. OBIE-1 is not a graphics editor, but utilizes the output of a graphics editor. In developing OBIE-1 we developed our own graphics editor, called DaVINCI (see Reference [2]), to create the graphics that we would need to construct panel simulations.

The Graphics Interface Editor classifies objects into three categories: discrete, analog and sequential. The reasons for this classification of objects was for the benefit of the author. When using OBIE-1 the author may better identify different types of objects and understand how they interact together. A discrete type object is an object whose states have a finite number of values. An example of a discrete object is the switch or one of the indicator lights which may be seen in Figure 2. An analog object contains states which may contain an infinite number of values over a specified range. An example of this type of object is a clock, a meter or a thermometer. A sequential object is an object which has certain state values which are dependent on other state values. An example of a sequential object is a display (see Figure 1), since the current value of a display is always dependent on the previous value of the display.

The Cognitive Connection Editor allows the simulation author to create relationships or "connections" between abstract objects using a common sense (rule-based) model. The input of the Cognitive Connection Editor is the output of the Graphics Interface Editor: the abstract objects. The output of the Cognitive Connection Editor is the programmed object relationships defined by the simulation author and generated by OBIE-1.

To create a connection between objects one must identify the affector objects - those that affect state changes in other objects - and the affectee objects - those that are affected by such state changes. Once the affectors and affectees are chosen, with the use of several menus and a mouse, the author has the ability to "make", "remove" or "quit" an existing connection. Making a connection results in the creation of a rule which specifies that when the affector objects are in some specified state the affectee objects should be in some other specified state. If the author chooses to "remove" a connection, if it was determined that the rule was no longer needed, he may also do that. The author can also abort the connection process by selecting the "quit" choice from the connection menu. The model used to create the connections between objects embodies the common sense notion associated with the assertion, "This is what happens to these objects when I perform this particular action." Affectors and affectees make up a cognitive connection and cognitive connections make up a simulation.

The Graphics Interface Editor and the Cognitive Connection Editor help an author specify the declarative semantics associated with abstract objects; these editors help an author specify the behavior of objects independent of time. The Panel Sequencing Editor is responsible for incorporating the procedural semantics of the abstract objects into the simulation. This editor helps an author plan a sequence of display panels for a training session. If one considers the results of the Cognitive Connection Editor to consist of a "scene", then the results of the Panel Sequencing Editor can be considered to be a "script" which links all the scenes together. The Panel Sequencing Editor allows the author to teach operating procedures for normal and abnormal modes of simulated device behaviors.

The Student Mode Verifier allows the author to see how the interactive simulation appears to the student, i.e., without auxilliary menus and queries which appear during authoring mode. This tool helps the author evaluate the simulation, so that any necessary modifications can be made.

Using OBIE-1

Several components of OBIE-1 execute on a Symbolics 3600 Lisp Machine. OBIE-1 is designed to accommodate some of the problems and mistakes that new users - either new computer users or new OBIE-1 users - might have when using OBIE-1. One example is the inclusion of an abort or "quit" choice in some of the menus. This allows authors who have made a mistake in choosing some menu choice to abort from a choice without any serious ramifications. Another example of how OBIE-1 helps the author is by allowing most author interaction with OBIE-1 involve the use of menus and a mouse (light pen for later TICCIT implementation), which is used to make the menu selections. A keyboard is also used to enter responses to queries, such as "What is the name of this object?". OBIE-1 provides a description of the menu selections available and also notifies the author when improper selections have been made, such as affector choices without any corresponding affectee choices. An example of a menu is the system command menu, which enables the author to "Create a Thing", add a previously created object into the temporary OBIE-1 library of objects, "Destroy a Thing", delete an object from OBIE 1's list of created objects, "Connect Things", use the Cognitive Connection Editor, or "Simulate", use the Student Mode Verifier (see Figure 2).

When a simulation author wants to create an abstract object he/she uses the Graphics Interface Editor. This tool utilizes simple queries to acquire knowledge from the author. The author responds to the queries via the computer keyboard. The following is an example of using the Graphics Interface Editor to create the abstract object WARNING-INDICATOR, which is part of the LTN-72 Inertial Navigation

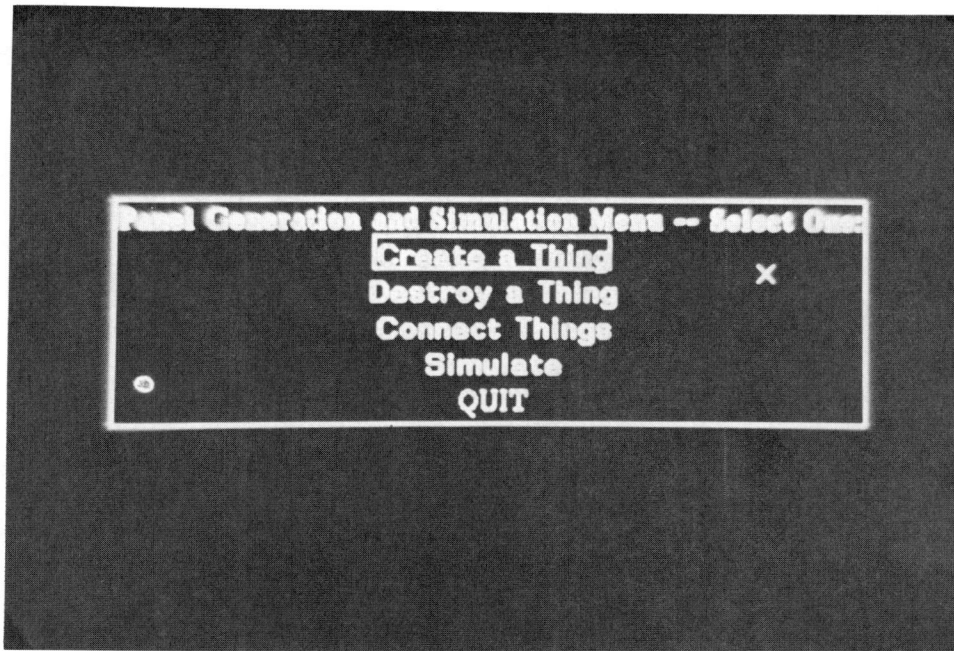

Figure 2. OBIE-1 System Command Menu

System (see Figure 1). The first step is to create all the graphics that are to be associated with the abstract object. This is done with the use of a graphics editor, such as DaVINCI. For the WARNING-INDICATOR, a minimum of two graphics must be created; one graphic to represent the object in the "ON" state and one to represent the object in the "OFF" state. An abstract object may contain several graphics, which represent different states of the object. Once the graphics have been created the author chooses the Graphics Interface Editor option from a provided menu, to initiate the abstract object creation process. After the Graphics Interface Editor has verified that all the graphics have been created it then asks the author for the name which will be assigned to the abstract object.

Once the object name is verified the state knowledge about an object is acquired from the author. First, the Graphics Interface Editor generates a query which asks the author for a state name for the abstract object. Then this tool generates a query which asks for one or more values of this state. After each state value is input, an associated graphic is chosen, from the screen, to represent the abstract object with the specified state value. For example, for the WARNING-INDICATOR, the author inputs "ON-or-OFF", when prompted for a state name. The author assigns the first value of this state to be "ON", by responding to the query, "What is the value of ON-or-OFF?". Once the state value is acquired

from the author the Graphics Interface Editor generates a query which asks the author to choose the graphic on the screen which represents the abstract object, when it has the specified state value. Graphics are chosen from the screen using the mouse. Therefore, in our example, the WARNING-INDICATOR graphic that resembles a "bright" indicator, is chosen to represent the "ON-or-OFF" state with the value of "ON" for the WARNING-INDICATOR abstract object.

Similarly, the WARNING-INDICATOR graphic that resembles a "non-lighted" indicator is chosen to represent the "ON-or-OFF" state with the value of "OFF", for the WARNING-INDICATOR abstract object. Once all the states and state values are acquired from the author, and after the graphics are associated with the state values OBIE-1 generates a query which asks the author to identify the type of abstract object: discrete, analog or sequential. After the choice is made other specific queries are presented to the author in order to acquire additional knowledge which is needed to construct the specified type of object. After OBIE-1 acquires all the knowledge necessary to construct the type of object which the author specified, during the process of using the Graphics Interface Editor, it will signal the author with a message indicating that a new abstract object has been added to the library of objects.

For an example of a cognitive connection consisting of three objects, one affector object, MSU-SWITCH

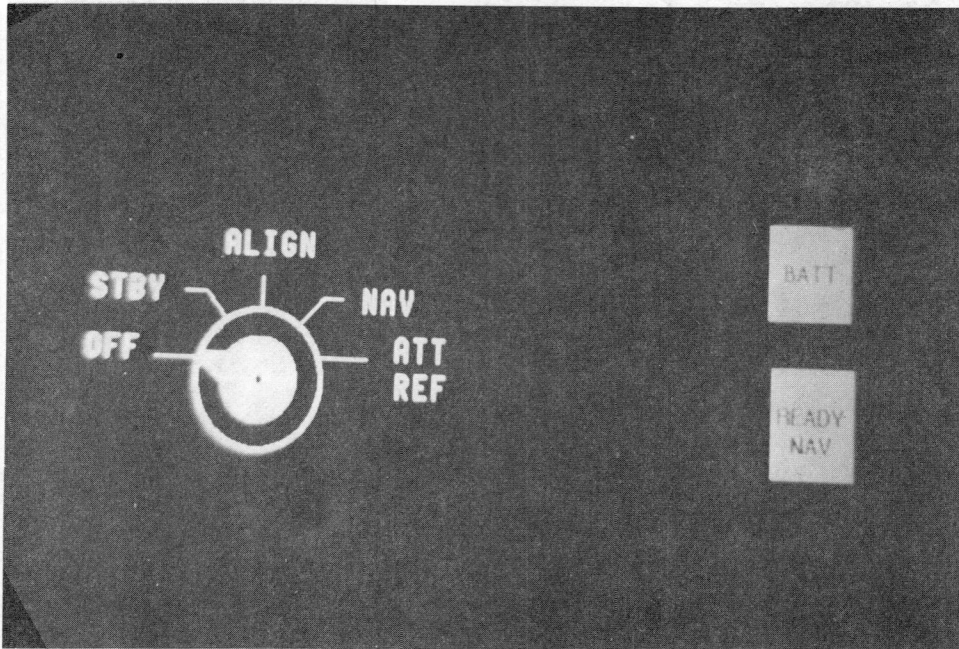

Figure 3. MSU-Switch (OFF), BATT-Light (ON),
READY-NAV-Light (ON)

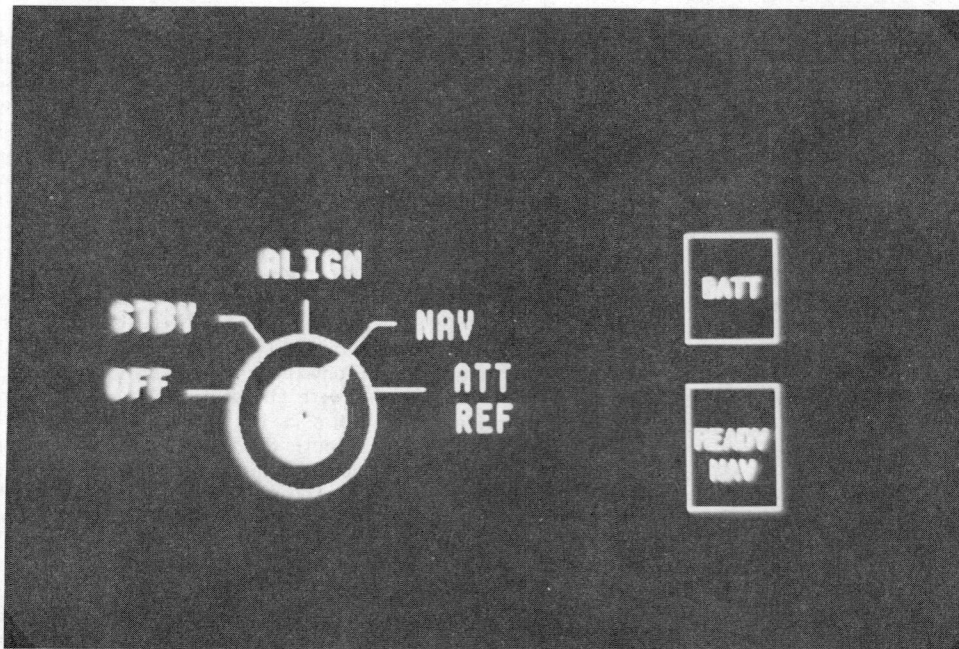

Figure 4. MSU-Switch (NAV), BATT-Light (OFF),
READY-NAV-Light (OFF)

and two affectee objects, READY-NAV-LIGHT and BATT-LIGHT, see Figures 3 and 4. In Figure 3 the connection was made that when MSU-SWITCH is in the OFF state READY-NAV-LIGHT and BATT-LIGHT would be in the ON state. When we change MSU-SWITCH to the NAV state we see that another connection was made which states that when the MSU-SWITCH is in the NAV state the READY-NAV-LIGHT and the BATT-LIGHT should be in the OFF state. To illustrate the simplicity involved in using OBIE-1 we will show how we created the connections represented in Figures 3 and 4. The first step to take is to select "Create A Thing" choice from the OBIE-1 main menu (see Figure 2), so that the author can add the objects which will be connected from the library of objects to the OBIE-1 panel simulation display.

Once the objects are selected each of their states must be assigned the appropriate values for the connection, by modifying each object menu, as is done for the MSU-SWITCH in Figure 5. To connect the objects we must now choose the "Connect Things" choice from the main menu (see Figure 2). This causes a menu to appear on the terminal screen which allows the author to choose which object or objects are to be the affector objects. If the user has made a mistake by choosing the "Connect Things" choice from the menu he need only move the mouse into and then out of the menu and OBIE-1 will abort

the connection process. This is just one way which OBIE-1 anticipates, and allows for, an author making a mistake.

Otherwise, if the author did not make a mistake, he will pick the affector(s) using the mouse (see Figure 6). When the affector(s) are chosen the author will then choose the affectee object(s) from the affectee menu (see Figure 7). After both the affector(s) and affectee(s) are chosen the author has the option to make or remove the connection, or if for some reason the author wants to abort the connection process, he may choose the quit choice (see Figure 8). This connection would take approximately two minutes for an inexperienced OBIE-1 user to initiate and less than one minute for an experienced one. This reduces the amount of time necessary to create interactive simulations by several orders of magnitude.

An example of some "common sense" which is incorporated into OBIE-1 may be shown when an object (which is one of several affectee objects connected in a rule) has been deleted. When the affector object(s) are changed to the appropriate state(s) the affectee object(s) change to their appropriate state(s) and the rule will still hold, even though one of the affectee objects that was a part of the rule is removed it will instantiate any part of it that exists.

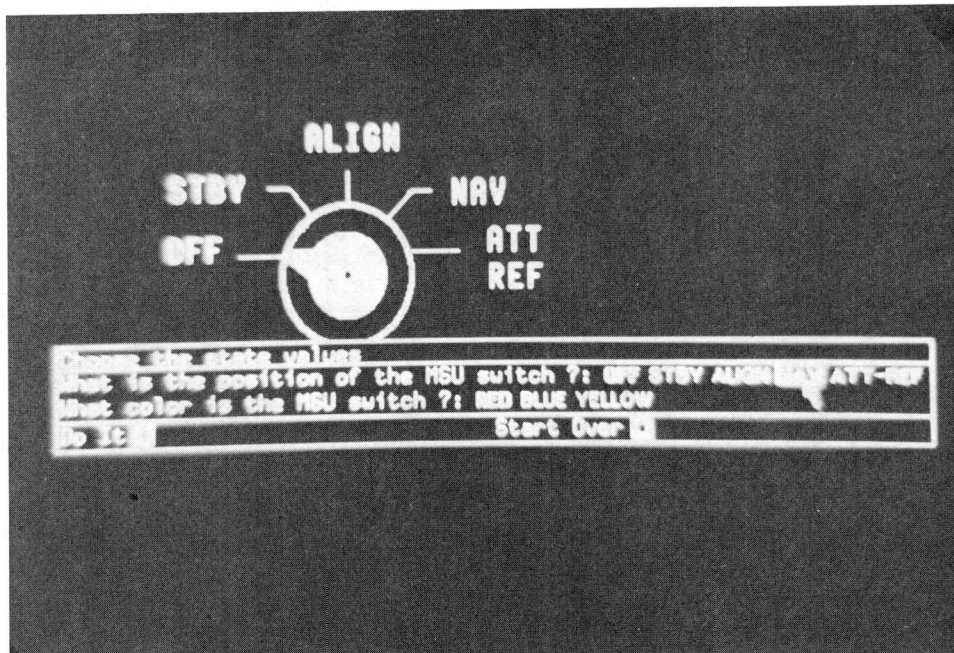

Figure 5. MSU-Switch With Associated Object Menu

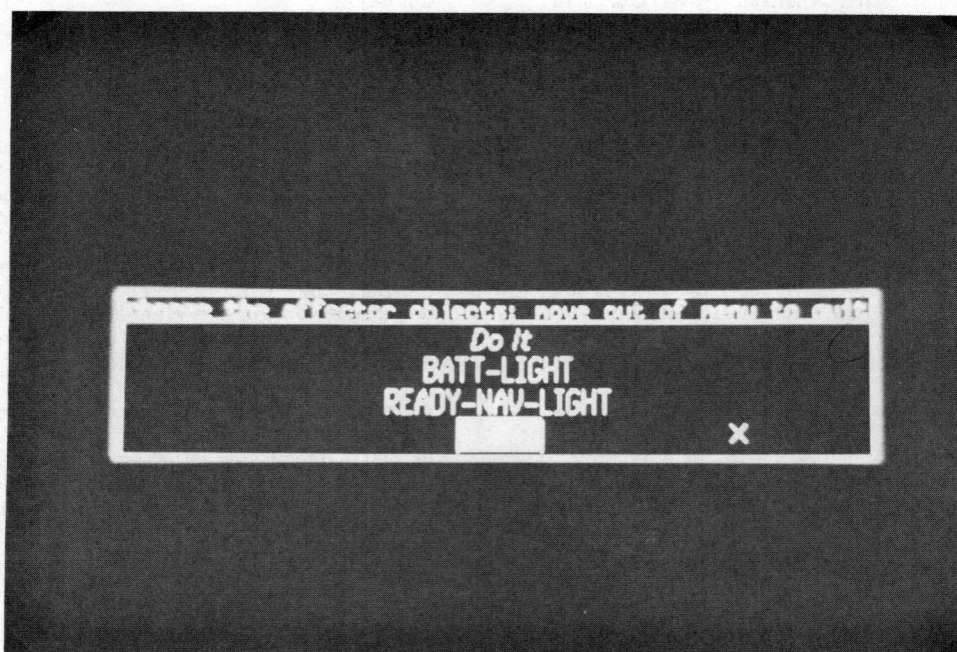

Figure 6. Making a Cognitive Connection:
Choosing the Affectors

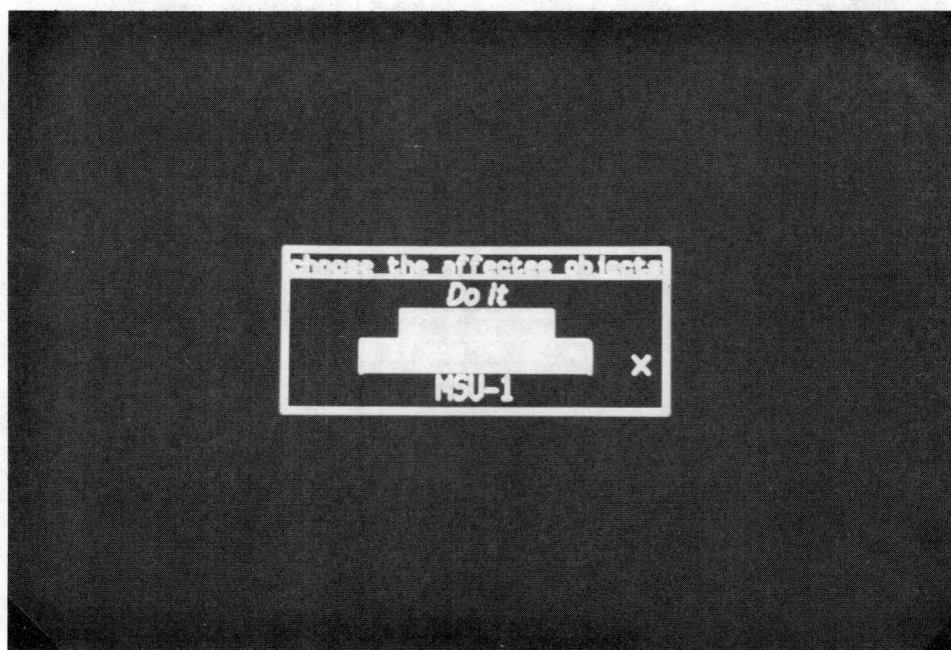

Figure 7. Making a Cognitive Connection:
Choosing the Affectees

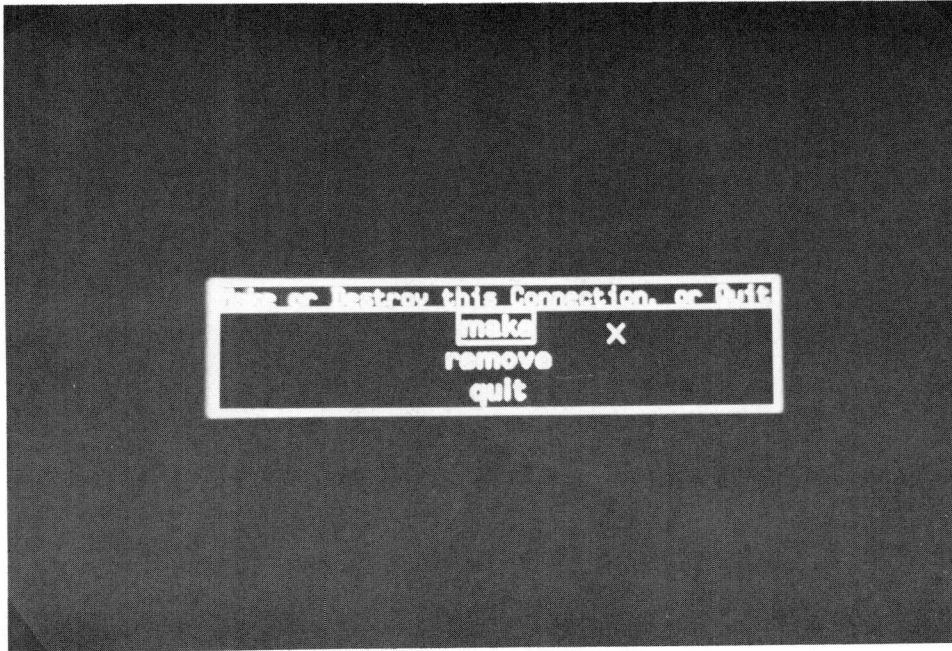

Figure 8. Making a Cognitive Connection:
Choosing the Connection Choice

SUMMARY

OBIE-1 allows interactive graphical simulations to be constructed by individuals without rigid programming language constructs. Therefore an individual need not know a programming or authoring language to construct an interactive simulation but need only use "common-sense" knowledge which OBIE-1 transforms into programmed code. The use of this tool eliminates the need for the intermediate programmer, who had to translate the knowledge of the author via a long and tedious process, and decreases the length of time to produce an interactive simulation. Therefore, OBIE-1 is efficient as well as cost effective and will surely increase productivity.

Although in its prototype development stage presently, OBIE-1 is already operational and shows potential for major benefits for the simulation author. OBIE-1 is currently being designed to develop interactive panel simulations for training and future applications are being investigated to utilize OBIE-1 for other types of simulations.

ACKNOWLEDGEMENTS

We would like to thank the following people who helped develop OBIE-1: Rob P. Frail and William F. Griese, members of the Hazeltine Research Labs, and Lois Wilson and Steve Fine, members of the Hazeltine Training System Center.

REFERENCES

(1) Clinger, W., Foundations of Actor Semantics, (MIT Technical Report AI-TR-633), May, 1981.

(2) Frail, R. P., Freedman, R.S., "DAVinci: An Extendible Knowledge-Based Software Tool for Graphics". (These proceedings)

(3) Wilson, L. S., "Presenting TICCIT. State-of-the-Art Computer-Based Instruction", Training Technology Journal, Vol. 1, No. 2, 1984.

(4) Freedman, R. S., "Knowledge-Based Courseware Authoring", Training Technology Journal, Vol. 1, No. 4, 1984, pp. 4.

LANST
A Local-Area Network Simulation Tool

Rui-Yuan Dong
Jane W. S. Liu

Department of Computer Science, University of Illinois at Urbana-Champaign
1304 West Springfield Avenue
Urbana, Illinois 61801

Abstract

LANST is a software tool which may be used to construct simulators of different types of local-area networks. LANST provides an environment which supports the reuse of software modules. More specifically, LANST has the following features: 1) It allows the user to specify interactively the target local-area network. 2) It selects and instantiates the appropriate modules from its library to construct the simulator. 3) It allows the user to add new modules to its library. This paper describes the architecture of LANST.

1. Introduction

Recently, several studies have been carried out in order to find means to reduce the cost of software development. These studies exam how and where man power has been spent in typical software development projects. One of the results conclude that only 15 percent of the code written in 1983 is unique and novel[1], the rest appears to be common and generic. This fact has motivated many research works in software reusability. One of the software reusable techniques proposed is the parameterized programming[2]. This technique is used in the design and development of LANST, a software tool for construction of local-area network simulators.

The concept of *local-area network (LAN)* was originated in 1970s. Now, LANs are widely used to connect computers, workstations, terminals and peripheral devices in distributed systems. To date, many different types of LANs based on different technologies, different structures and different protocols have been developed. The diversity of LANs makes it difficult for a user to select a specific type of LAN to suit his needs. A number of performance evaluation studies[3,4,5] have been carried out to determine the relative merits of different LANs. These studies deal with one or more specific types of LANs. For this reason, they provide only limited help to the user in the task of selecting a LAN which can best meet his requirements.

The goal of LANST is to provide a software tool useful in the simulation of different types of LANs. More specifically, LANST provides an environment which supports the construction of LAN simulators using the reusable software modules. In particular, LANST applies the technique of the parameterized programming[2] to a specific application, the construction of LAN simulators. LANST constructs the LAN simulator by using the *parameterized modules* contained in the library. These modules can be instantiated to construct simulators of different LANs. A user of LANST specifies his target LAN system to be simulated through the user-interface of LANST. From the user specification, LANST selects and instantiates the appropriate modules to construct a simulator of the target LAN system. In addition, LANST also provides facilities for a user to add new modules to the library and to make them available for later use. The architecture of LANST may be easily extended to support the development of LAN software systems.

The basic assumptions on the target LANs to be simulated using LANST are summarized in Section 2. The terminology used in our discussion is also defined in this section. Section 3 discusses the structure of LANST. The last section summarizes our current and future work. There are two appendices at the end of this paper. Appendix A is an example illustrating the interaction between the user and the USER-INTERFACE of LANST. Appendix B discusses the parametrized modules in the library of LANST.

2. Assumptions and Terminology

A LAN is "a communication network that provides interconnection of a variety of data communicating devices within a small area"[6]. The geographic scope of a LAN usually covers several miles to tens of miles. In most cases, a LAN is owned and operated by a single organization. The functions supported by a LAN correspond to the functions of the physical layer, the data link layer and the network layer of the Open System Interconnection (OSI) reference model by International Standard Organization (ISO)[7]. Because of the special characteristics of LANs, not all functions of these three layers are required. For example, routing is one of the functions of the network layer. However, in a LAN, when the stations are connected together by a common broadcast medium, routing is not necessary.

Since 1980, the Institute for Electrical and Electronic Engineers (IEEE) has developed a series of standards for LANs, collectively known as the IEEE Project 802[6,8,9,10,11]. IEEE Project 802 divides the functions of a LAN into three layers: the *logical link control (LLC)* layer, the *medium access control (MAC)* layer and the *physical* layer. The correspondence of the layers in IEEE Project 802 and the layers in ISO OSI reference model is as shown in Figure 1.

The LLC layer is the interface of the LAN with the hosts. It provides media-independent data link functions to the *service access points (SAPs)* by using the services of the underlying MAC layer. The functions of the LLC protocol handler include exchanging control packets, organizing data flow, generating acknowledgements and responses, performing error control and error recovery, and so on. In the current draft of IEEE Standard 802.2[8], two kinds of LLC layer services are defined: *unacknowledged connectionless service* and *connection oriented service*. The MAC layer protocol handler controls the access of the common medium. IEEE Project 802 defines three different MAC protocols: *carrier-sense multiple access with collision detection (CSMA/CD)* [9], *token bus* [10], and *token ring* [11]. IEEE Project 802 also includes standards of the physical layer. However, the only few physical layer characteristics which affect the performance of a LAN are transmission delays, signaling rate and error rate. Therefore, details on the physical layer protocols are not modeled in LANST. The relevant physical layer characteristics are modeled in the form of actual parameters of the appropriate modules.

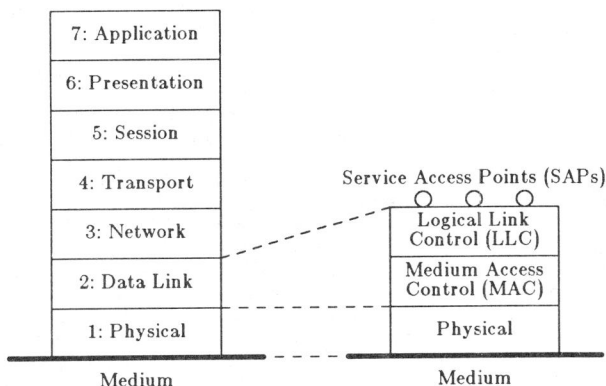

Figure 1: The Correspondence Between the ISO OSI Model and the IEEE 802 Model

The general form of a distributed computer system supported by a LAN is depicted in Figure 2. The target system of the simulator generated by LANST is the part enclosed in the dashed box. It is assumed that the target LAN is a packet switching or message switching network supported over a common broadcast medium. More specifically, its structure is compatible with the layering concept of IEEE Project 802. The LAN interacts with its environment through the station-to-host interfaces shown schematically as arrows across the boundary of the dashed box. Each station on the LAN provides one or more SAPs to the hosts served by it. There are buffer spaces in each station for temporarily storage of packets to and from the hosts. The buffer space is assumed to be divided into buffers, each buffer can hold a packet of the maximum size. The functions of disassembling files into packets and assembling packets into files are performed by the transport layer protocol handler[12] residing on the hosts. The traffic accrosses the station-to-host interfaces is the input parameter of the LAN simulator. It is in the form of packet streams. Since packets can have variable lengths, this assumption leads to no loss of generality. Besides the traffic accrosses the station-to-host interfaces, other details on system configuration outside the dashed box are not considered.

The reusable modules of LANST are stored in the LANST library. Again, these modules are called *parametrized modules* in the terminology of the parameterized programming[2]. For simplicity, the term *module* is used hereafter to refer to a *parameterized module* or a *reusable module*. A module is an encapsulated program unit implemented to carry out a natural function and has well defined global properties and interfaces. It is parameterized so that it can be used in different ways. A parameter can be a value that is a part of the specification of an algorithm implemented by the module. A parameter of a module may also be another module which interfaces with it. To *instantiate* a module is to use the function implemented by the module in a specific environment with a specific set of actual parameters.

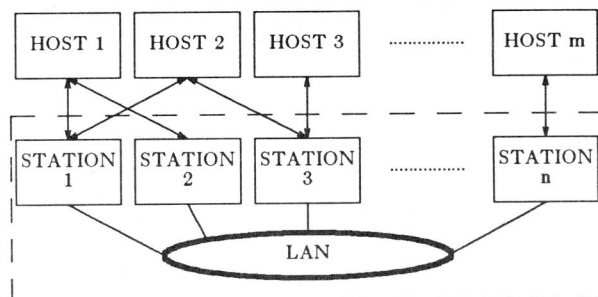

Figure 2: The General Form of a Distributed System Supported by a Local-Area Network

3. The Structure of LANST

A primary design objective of LANST is that it can be used to construct simulators of different types of LANs. When the target LAN uses standard protocols, LANST constructs the simulator with the modules already exist in the library. When a protocol used in the target LAN is not modeled by any existing module, LANST assists the user with the task of writing a new module needed to model the protocol, enforces the documentation of the new module and adds the new module into the library. Once a module is added to the library, it can be used later on as any other modules in the library. As shown in Figure 3, the input to LANST is the user specification of the LAN system, the output is the source program of the LAN simulator.

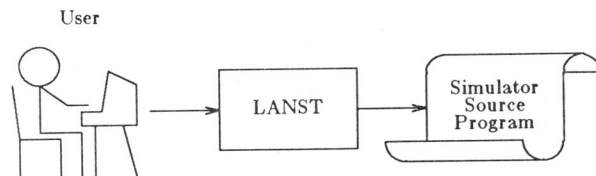

Figure 3: Input and Output of LANST

As depicted in Figure 4, LANST consists of five components: the USER-INTERFACE, the SIMULATOR-CONSTRUCTOR, the LIBRARY-MANAGER, the MODULE-LIBRARY and the MANUAL-LIBRARY. To build a simulator of a LAN, the user specifies the configuration of the LAN via the USER-INTERFACE. The USER-INTERFACE assists the user in the task of completing the specifications of the LAN. The USER-INTERFACE displays appropriate manuals selected from the MANUAL-LIBRARY and sets flags and variables according to the user responses. These flags and variables are used by the SIMULATOR-CONSTRUCTOR to select and instantiate modules from the MODULE-LIBRARY. When a user wants to write new modules and to add them to the MODULE-LIBRARY, the LIBRARY-MANAGER is called to assist the user. When the MODULE-LIBRARY is updated, the LIBRARY-MANAGER also updates MANUAL-LIBRARY correspondingly.

MODULE-LIBRARY

The MODULE-LIBRARY contains all the modules which can be used to construct simulators of different LANs. There are five classes of modules in the MODULE-LIBRARY: 1) the LLC class, 2) the MAC class, 3) the MISC class, 4) the MNG class and 5) the IO class.

Modules in the LLC class may be used to simulate different LLC layer protocols. To construct a LAN simulator, one of the LLC class modules must be instantiated. The formal parameters of a LLC class module include the sending station, the receiving station and a module in the MAC class to simulate the underlying MAC protocol. The parameters may also include modules in the MISC class used to model flow control algorithms, error recovery procedures and other functions.

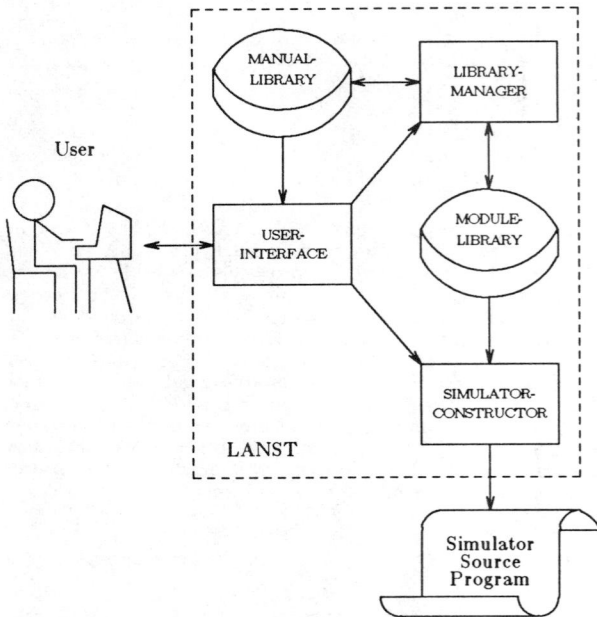

Figure 4: The Structure of LANST

Modules in the MAC class are used to simulate different MAC layer protocols. In a LAN, when a LLC layer protocol handler is ready to transmit a packet, a MAC layer protocol handler is called to access the medium and to supervise the transmission. Hence, one MAC class module must be instantiated to simulate the MAC layer protocol used in the target LAN. A formal parameter of a MAC class module is a LLC class module which models the LLC protocol. Formal parameters may also include numerical values which specify the MAC protocol. Modules in the MISC class which model retransmission scheme, error control scheme, and physical layer characteristics may also be parameters of the MAC class module.

Both the LLC protocol and the MAC protocol in the target LAN may support miscellaneous optional functions such as flow control, retransmission control, error recovery, and so on. These miscellaneous functions are modeled by the modules in the MISC class. Also contained in the MISC class are modules which model the relevant physical layer characteristics such as transmission error rate, transmission delay, and so on. Appropriate MISC class modules may be instantiated and used as actual parameters in the instantiation of the LLC class modules and the MAC class modules.

The resource management of a station connected to the LAN includes the management of the SAPs and the buffers. The SAP management is straight forward. When a station is

selected either as a sender or as a receiver, transmission to and from the station can proceed only if there is a SAP available. Buffer management schemes categorize buffers into classes, allocate and return buffers of different classes with different priorities. The modules in the MNG class are used to model SAP management schemes and buffer management schemes. By instantiating modules in the MNG class with the appropriate actual parameters, the resource management schemes used in a station can be modeled.

The simulator generated by LANST, after being compiled, can run in two modes: the trace-driven mode and the distribution-driven mode. The input parameter of the simulation is the load traffic accrossing the station-to-host interfaces between all the stations on the LAN and the hosts served by them. This load traffic is specified by a load-script. If the simulation is run in the trace-driven mode, as in Figure 5, the user must provide the trace in the form of a load-script. If the simulation is run in the distribution-driven mode, as in Figure 6, a load-generator module must be instantiated and included in the simulator. After compilation, the load-generator will generate the load-script according to the user specified distributions. The load-generator module is contained in the IO class. Also contained in the IO class are modules to accumulate, calculate and report simulation results. When instantiated appropriately, these modules are used to collect the statistical data during the simulation and to derive the simulation results.

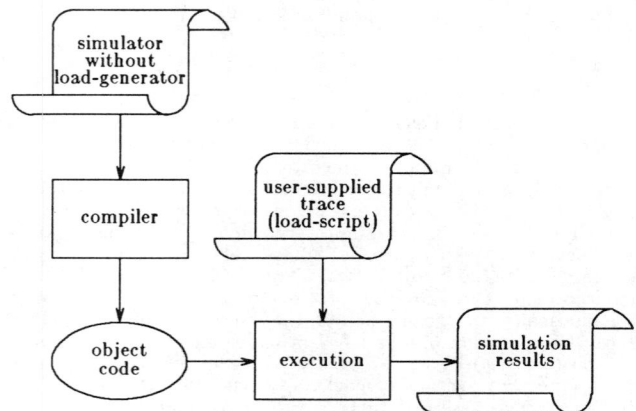

Figure 5: Simulation in the Trace-Driven Mode

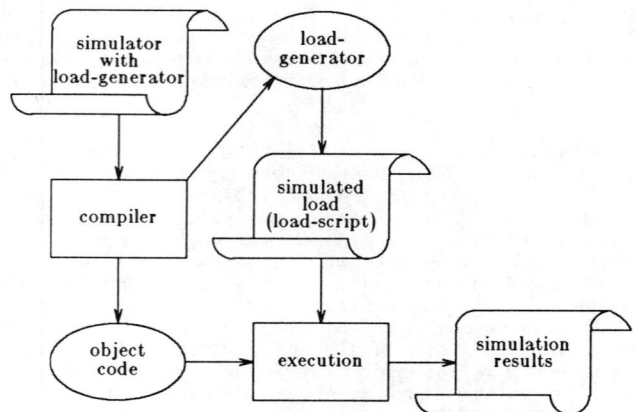

Figure 6: Simulation in the Distribution-Driven Mode

In summary, the MODULE-LIBRARY serves as a knowledge base in LANST. Whether LANST can be used to construct a simulator of a specific LAN depends on whether appropriate modules exist in the MODULE-LIBRARY. The MODULE-LIBRARY is designed to allow new modules to be added incrementally. Appendix B of this paper describes the global properties and the interfaces of the modules in different classes in the MODULE-LIBRARY.

MANUAL-LIBRARY

During an interactive session, the USER-INTERFACE communicates with the user by displaying various manuals to the terminal. These manuals are stored in the MANUAL-LIBRARY. More specifically, there are two types of manuals, general manuals and specific manuals. General manuals give general information and guide the user in specifying general characteristics of the target LAN system. These manuals are displayed to the terminal in every user session. Specific manuals are related to specific modules. The documentation of every module in the MODULE-LIBRARY is contained in the corresponding specific manual. The manual describes the function or algorithm implemented by the module and the interface of the module with its environment. This manual also guides the user in entering actual parameters and instantiating the module. These specific manuals are stored in the MANUAL-LIBRARY in a similar manner as the modules are stored in the MODULE-LIBRARY. When user wants the description of a module or when the module is selected to be instantiated, the corresponding specific manual is selected by the USER-INTERFACE and displayed on the terminal. The MANUAL-LIBRARY is also designed to allow addition of new manuals when new modules are added to the MODULE-LIBRARY.

USER-INTERFACE

In order to use LANST to construct a simulator for a LAN, the user must provide to LANST the specifications of the target LAN system. The input and output parameters of the simulation should also be specified. The user specification is done via the USER-INTERFACE, which communicates with the user interactively. The USER-INTERFACE selects the appropriate manuals from the MANUAL-LIBRARY, displays them on the terminal, and reads the user responses. When the user wants to construct a simulator using only the existing modules, the USER-INTERFACE sets up internal flags and variables according to the user specification. Then, the SIMULATOR-CONSTRUCTOR is called to produce the source program of the simulator. When no existing module can be used to simulate the protocol used in a LAN, a new module must first be written by the user. In this case, the USER-INTERFACE calls LIBRARY-MANAGER to assist the user in writing the new module and adding it to the library.

The specification of the target LAN system consists of: 1) the specification of the protocols used in the LLC layer and the MAC layer and 2) the specification of all the stations connected to LAN. An example of an interactive session between the user and the USER-INTERFACE to specify a target LAN system is given in Appendix A.

To specify the LLC layer protocol, the user selects a LLC class module and provides the appropriate actual parameters. MISC class modules may be instantiated to model functions supported in the LLC layer. The MAC layer protocol is specified in a similar way, by selecting a MAC class module and instantiating with the appropriate parameters. Again, MISC class modules may also be instantiated to supplement the MAC class modules. The packet length of a LAN must also be specified. The user can specify the packet length in two ways. Fixed packet length is specified explicitly. Variable packet length is specified by the packet length distribution.

The stations connected to LAN are specified by the configuration of each station and the topology of the network connecting them. The configuration of a station is specified in terms of the maximum number of SAPs supported, the total number of buffers, the SAP management scheme and the buffer management scheme used in the station. The topology of the network is specified by the transmission delays between stations.

During the interactive session with the USER-INTERFACE, the user is required to specify the input and output parameters of the simulation. As mentioned earlier, the simulation may be carried out in either the trace-driven mode or the distribution-driven mode. In the trace-driven mode, the input of the simulation is the trace provided by the user, as shown in Figure 5. In the distribution-driven mode, the load-generator module in IO class must be instantiated to generate the simulated load as the input to the simulation, as shown in Figure 6. To instantiate the load-generator module, the user must provide the distribution functions of the file lengths and the file inter-arrival times of all the files to be transferred from all stations. The output parameter of the simulation is specified in terms of the statistical data to be collected. Among all the statistical data and results that LANST will be able to generate, the user may select a subset to meet his needs. The corresponding modules in the IO class are instantiated accordingly.

Termination condition of the simulation must also be specified by the user. In case of a trace-driven simulation, the end of the trace is a default termination condition. In case of a distribution-driven simulation, the termination condition may be specified by a preset value of simulated time. Other termination conditions, such as after a certain number of files been transferred, after a certain number of medium access failures, and so on, can also be specified.

SIMULATOR-CONSTRUCTOR

Figure 7 shows a typical structure of a target LAN system. The arrows in this figure represent the traffic flows. The structure of the simulator generated by LANST follows closely the structure of the target LAN system. Therefore, Figure 7 also shows the structure of the simulator, with arrows represent the interfaces between modules of the different classes.

The construction of the simulator is carried out by the SIMULATOR-CONSTRUCTOR. To construct a simulator, a LLC class module, a MAC class module and optional MISC class modules are instantiated to model the protocols of the LAN. In addition, MNG class modules may be instantiated to model the resource management schemes used in all stations. Based on the internal flags and variables set up by the USER-INTERFACE, the SIMULATOR-CONSTRUCTOR selects the appropriate modules and instantiates them with the appropriate parameters. The interfaces between the selected modules are defined upon instantiation.

Since the reusing of modules is done in the source program level, the selection of the modules means the inclusion of the selected modules in the source program of the simulator. To instantiate a module, the appropriate names and variables in the module are initialized. The output of the SIMULATOR-CONSTRUCTOR is the source program of the simulator. The SIMULATOR-CONSTRUCTOR ensures the syntactic correctness of the source program generated.

LIBRARY-MANAGER

The task of LIBRARY-MANAGER is to assist the user in adding new modules to the LANST library. In order to create a new module, the user must have basic knowledge about the programming language in which the module is written. The LIBRARY-MANAGER provides the user with a template containing information on the internal structure of the module, the required global properties of the module, the dependency of the module on other modules, and so on. The LIBRARY-MANAGER also informs the user about the global environment of his new module. In other words, by providing information hiding, the LIBRARY-MANAGER isolates the user from the implementation details as much as possible. With the help of the LIBRARY-MANAGER, the user can create a new module and integrate it into LANST without the complete knowledge about other parts of LANST.

Another function of the LIBRARY-MANAGER is to enforce the documentation of the new module. When a new module is created, the user is required to supply the documentation together with the syntacticly correct module to the LIBRARY-MANAGER. The LIBRARY-MANAGER updates the library by adding the module to the MODULE-LIBRARY and adding the documentation to the MANUAL-LIBRARY in the form of manuals.

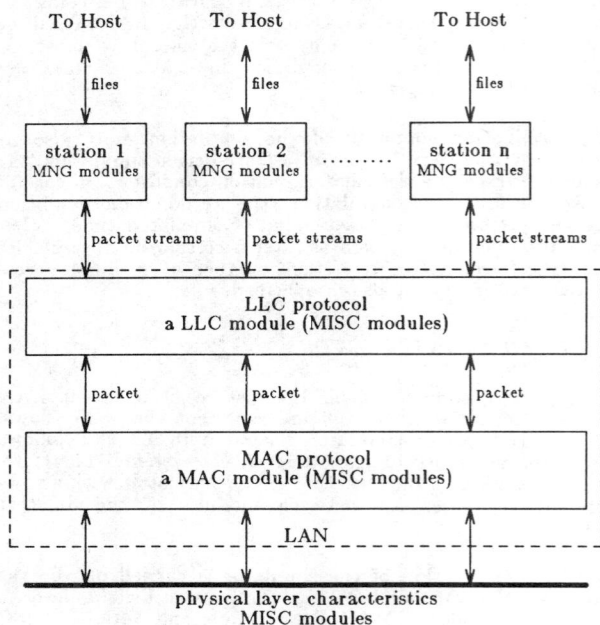

Figure 7: The Structure of the Target LAN System and the Structure of the Simulator

4. Summary

LANST is implemented on a 4.2 bsd UNIX system in the Department of Computer Science at University of Illinois. The programming language in which all the modules are written is a general purpose simulation language called SIMSCRIPT II.5[13]. Since our UNIX system does not have a SIMSCRIPT compiler, the source program of the simulator generated by LANST must be compiled and run on another system with a SIMSCRIPT compiler. In the development of LANST, we use the CYBER 175 system in University of Illinois to compile and run the SIMSCRIPT simulator.

With the basic modules in the library, LANST can be used to generate simulator of LANs with two different types of LLC protocols and two different types of MAC protocols.

Modules for modeling several miscellaneous functions and physical layer characteristics are also available. Moreover, LANST also provides support to model resource management schemes used in the stations.

LANST is designed to accommodate the rapid development of new LANs and new LAN protocols. Effort has been made to allow the users to extend the capability of LANST by creating new modules and adding them to the library of LANST. With this facility, we will build more modules, especially modules in the LLC class and the MAC class to enable LANST to generate simulators of a wider variety of LANs in the future.

Acknowledgement

This work is partially supported by the U. S. Army CONRADCOM, Fort Monmouth, New Jersey 07703, under Contract No. US Army DAAB07-84-K526.

References

[1] T. C. Jones, "Reusability in Programming: A Survey of the State of the Art," *IEEE Transactions on Software Engineering*, vol. SE-10, No. 5, pp. 488-493, September 1984.

[2] J. A. Goguen, "Parameterized Programming," *IEEE Transactions on Software Engineering*, vol. SE-10, No. 5, pp. 528-542, September 1984.

[3] F. A. Tobagi and V. B. Hunt, "Performance Analysis of Carrier Sense Multiple Access with Collision Detection," *Computer Networks*, vol. 4, pp. 245-259, 1980.

[4] A. K. Agrawala, J. R. Agre and K. D. Gordon, "The Slotted Ring vs the Token-controlled Ring: A Comparative Evaluation," *Proceeding COMSAC 1978 Chicago, IL: IEEE*, pp. 674-679, 1978.

[5] W. Bux, "Local Area Subnetworks: A Performance Comparison," *IEEE Transactions on Communications*, vol. COM-29, No. 10, October 1981.

[6] W. Stallings, *Local Networks — An Introduction*, New York, NY: Macmillan Publishing Company, 1984.

[7] H. Zimmermann, "OSI Reference Model — The ISO Model of architecture for Open Systems Interconnection," *IEEE Transaction on Communications*, vol. COM-28, pp. 425-432, April 1980.

[8] Institute for Electrical and Electronic Engineers, *IEEE Project 802, Local Area Network Standards, Draft Standard P802.2 Logical Link Control, Draft D*, November 1982.

[9] Institute for Electrical and Electronic Engineers, *IEEE Project 802, Local Area Network Standards, Draft IEEE Standard 802.3 CSMA/CD Access Method and Physical Layer Specifications, Revision D*, December 1982.

[10] Institute for Electrical and Electronic Engineers, *IEEE Project 802, Local Area Network Standards, Draft IEEE Standard 802.4 Token-Passing Bus Access Method and Physical Layer Specifications, Draft D*, December 1982.

[11] Institute for Electrical and Electronic Engineers, *IEEE Project 802, Local Area Network Standards, Draft IEEE Standard 802.5 Token-Passing Ring Access Method and Physical Layer Specifications, Draft D*, December 1982.

[12] A. S. Tanenbaum, *Computer Networks*, Englewood Cliffs, NJ: Prentice-Hall, 1981.

[13] CACI Inc.-Federal, *SIMSCRIPT II.5 Programming Language*, Los Angeles, CA: CACI Inc.-Federal, 1983.

Appendix A

As an illustrative example, the following is an interactive session between the user and the USER-INTERFACE of LANST. In this session, the user specifies a target LAN system as shown in Figure A-1. The USER-INTERFACE is manual driven. During an interactive session, manuals are actually displayed one by one on the terminal. Here, just for the purpose of readability, all the manuals and user responses are listed continuously. The words in Roman letters are the manuals and prompts of the USER-INTERFACE and the words in bold-face are the user responses.

WELCOME!
This is the USER-INTERFACE of LANST. Please read the manuals carefully before selecting a specific manual entry. Please enter you manual selection or other response after the prompt ">". You may ask for help on manual entry n by typing "?n". You may abort the USER-INTERFACE session by typing <esc>.
Please note: <esc> is the escape key, <sp> is the space bar, <cr> is the carriage return key.
Ready? Please type <sp> to continue:
> **<sp>**

Please select one of the following task:
    1 — Specify the target LAN
    2 — Construct the simulator
    3 — Add new module
    ?n — Help on manual entry n (n = 1, 2, 3)
    <cr> — Return
    <esc> — Abort
> **1**

Please select the following manual entry:
    1 — Display the available modules
    2 — Specify the LAN protocols
    3 — Specify the stations
    4 — Display the target LAN specified so far
    5 — I/O and termination specification
    ?n — Help on manual entry n (n = 1, 2, 3, 4, 5)
    <cr> — Return
    <esc> — Abort
> **1**

Available LLC class modules:
    Dummy LLC
    Unacknowledged Connectionless
    Connection Oriented
Please type <sp> to continue, or <cr> to return:
> **<sp>**

Available MAC class modules:
    Dummy MAC
    CSMA/CD
    Token Ring
Please type <sp> to continue, or <cr> to return:
> **<cr>**

Please select the following manual entry:
    1 — Display the available modules
    2 — Specify the LAN protocols
    3 — Specify the stations
    4 — Display the target LAN specified so far
    5 — I/O and termination specification
    ?n — Help on manual entry n (n = 1, 2, 3, 4, 5)

    <cr> — Return
    <esc> — Abort
> **2**

Please specify the logical link control (LLC) protocol used in the LAN by choosing one of the following:
    0 — Dummy LLC
    1 — Unacknowledged Connectionless
    2 — Connection Oriented
    ?n — Help on manual entry n (n = 0, 1, 2)
    <cr> — Return
    <esc> — Abort
> **?2**

Connection Oriented Service — According to this protocol, a connection is established between a SAP in the sending station and a SAP in the receiving station prior to the transmission of any data packet. Three-way handshake is used to establish and close any connection. Reliable, sequenced delivery of data packets is provided over each connection. Several flow control schemes may be used to regulate traffics between sending and receiving SAPs.
Please type <cr> to return:
> **<cr>**

Please specify the logical link control (LLC) protocol used in the LAN by choosing one of the following:
    0 — Dummy LLC
    1 — Unacknowledged Connectionless
    2 — Connection Oriented
    ?n — Help on manual entry n (n = 0, 1, 2)
    <cr> — Return
    <esc> — Abort
> **2**

LLC protocol: Connection Oriented
Do you want to model a flow control algorithm?
Please answer by choosing one of the following:
    0 — No flow control
    1 — Sliding Window
    2 — Pacing
    ?n — Help on manual entry n (n = 0, 1, 2)
    <cr> — Return
    <esc> — Abort
> **0**

Please specify the medium access control (MAC) protocol by choosing one of the following:
    0 — Dummy MAC
    1 — CSMA/CD
    2 — Token Ring
    ?n — Help on manual entry n (n = 0, 1, 2)
    <cr> — Return
    <esc> — Abort
> **1**

MAC protocol: CSMA/CD
Please select one of the following:
    1 — Non-persistent
    2 — P-persistent
    3 — 1-persistent
    ?n — Help on manual entry n (n = 1, 2, 3)
    <cr> — Return
    <esc> — Abort
> **2**
Please enter the value for P ($0 < P < 1$):
> **0.8**
Please specify the backoff algorithm by choosing one of the following:
    1 — Constant backoff
    2 — Binary exponential backoff
    ?n — Help on manual entry n (n = 1, 2)
    <cr> — Return
    <esc> — Abort
> **2**
Please specify the end-to-end delay in bit-time:
> **30.0**
Please specify the maximum number of collisions allowed before give up:
> **16**

Please specify the probability Pr of the physical layer transmission error ($0 \leq Pr \leq 1$):
> **0**

Please specify the packet size by choosing one of the following:
    1 — Fixed size packet
    2 — Uniformly distributed packet size
    3 — Normally distributed packet size
    4 — Exponentially distributed packet size
    ?n — Help on manual entry n (n = 1, 2, 3, 4)
    <cr> — Return
    <esc> — Abort
> **3**
Please enter the mean and the standard deviation of the normally distributed packet size (in number of bytes), separated by a space:
> **1024 20**

You have finished the specification of the LAN protocols. Please type <cr> to return:
> **<cr>**

Please select the following manual entry:
    1 — Display the available modules
    2 — Specify the LAN protocols
    3 — Specify the stations
    4 — Display the target LAN specified so far
    5 — I/O and termination specification
    ?n — Help on manual entry n (n = 1, 2, 3, 4, 5)
    <cr> — Return
    <esc> — Abort
> **3**

Please specify the number of stations connected to the LAN by entering an integer:
> **4**

Please specify the characteristics of Station 1:
Is this station the same as another station?
Please enter 0 if not or N if this station is the same as station N (station N must already been defined):
> **0**
Number of SAPs supported:
> **2**
Total number of buffers:
> **15**
Please specify the buffer management scheme:
    1 — 4-classes buffer management scheme
    2 — I/O-reserved buffer management scheme
    3 — SAP-reserved buffer management scheme
    ?n — Help on manual entry n (n = 1, 2, 3)
    <cr> — Return
    <esc> — Abort
> **1**
Number of common buffers:
> **15**

Please specify the characteristics of Station 2:
Is this station the same as another station?
Please enter 0 if not or N if this station is the same as station N (station N must already been defined):
> **0**
Number of SAPs supported:
> **3**
Total number of buffers:
> **13**
Please specify the buffer management scheme:
    1 — 4-classes buffer management scheme
    2 — I/O-reserved buffer management scheme
    3 — SAP-reserved buffer management scheme
    ?n — Help on manual entry n (n = 1, 2, 3)
    <cr> — Return
    <esc> — Abort
> **3**
Number of SAP1 buffers:
> **6**
Number of SAP2 buffers:
> **3**
Number of SAP3 buffers:
> **4**

Please specify the characteristics of Station 3:
Is this station the same as another station?
Please enter 0 if not or N if this station is the same as station N (station N must already been defined):
> **0**
Number of SAPs supported:
> **2**
Total number of buffers:
> **21**
Please specify the buffer management scheme:
    1 — 4-classes buffer management scheme
    2 — I/O-reserved buffer management scheme
    3 — SAP-reserved buffer management scheme
    ?n — Help on manual entry n (n = 1, 2, 3)
    <cr> — Return
    <esc> — Abort
> **1**
Number of common buffers:
> **5**
Number of common input buffers:
> **9**
Number of common output buffers:
> **7**

Please specify the characteristics of Station 4:
Is this station the same as another station?
Please enter 0 if not or N if this station is the same as station N (station N must already been defined):
> **1**

Please specify the delays between stations by choosing the following:
    1 — Default
    2 — Linear delays
    3 — Non-linear delays
    ?n — Help on manual entry n (n = 1, 2, 3)
    <cr> — Return
    <esc> — Abort
> **?2**

The delays between every adjacent pair of stations must be specified. The delays between non-adjacent stations are assumed to be linear. That is, for all stations, if station y is between station x and station z, then the delay between x and z is equal to the delay between x and y plus the delay between y and z, plus the possible internal delay of y. The sum of the delays between all adjacent pairs of stations should be less than or equal to the total delay.
Please type <cr> to return:
> **<cr>**

Please specify the delays between stations by choosing the following:
    1 — Default
    2 — Linear delays
    3 — Non-linear delays
    ?n — Help on manual entry n (n = 1, 2, 3)
    <cr> — Return
    <esc> — Abort
> **2**

The delays are shown in the following matrix. The off-diagonal element in row R and column C ($R \neq C$) represents the delay from station R to station C. The diagonal elment in row R represents the internal delay in station R.

    0 10 20 30
  10   0 10 20
  20 10   0 10
  30 20 10   0

To change the element in row R and column C of the above matrix to value d, enter three numbers R, C and d. All numbers are separated by spaces.
Only the delays between the adjacent stations can be modified.
After finish all the changes, please type <cr> to return:
> **1 2 5**
> **2 1 5**
> **2 3 15**
> **3 2 15**
> **<cr>**

You have finished the specification of stations.
Please type <cr> to return:
> **<cr>**

Please select the following manual entry:
  1 — Display the available modules
  2 — Specify the LAN protocols
  3 — Specify the stations
  4 — Display the target LAN specified so far
  5 — I/O and termination specification
  ?n — Help on manual entry n (n = 1, 2, 3, 4, 5)
  <cr> — Return
  <esc> — Abort
> **4**

LLC Protocol —
Connection Oriented: no flow control
MAC protocol —
CSMA/CD: 0.8-persistent, binary exponential backoff,
end-to-end delay=30.0, maximum collision=16
Physical layer —
error free
Packet Length —
normally distributed: mean=1024, standard
deviation=20
4 stations —
Station 1: 2 SAPs, 15 buffers, 4-classes buffer
management scheme, 15 common buffers
Station 2: 3 SAPs, 13 buffers, SAP-reserved buffer
management scheme, 6 SAP1 buffers, 3 SAP2 buffers, 4
SAP3 buffers
Station 3: 2 SAPs, 21 buffers, 4-classes buffer
management scheme, 5 common buffers, 9 common input
buffers, 7 common output buffers
Station 4: Same as station 1
Delay between stations —
    0   5 20 30
    5   0 15 25
  20 15   0 10
  30 25 10   0
Please type <cr> to return:
> **<cr>**

Please select the following manual entry:
  1 — Display the available modules
  2 — Specify the LAN protocols
  3 — Specify the stations
  4 — Display the target LAN specified so far
  5 — I/O and termination specification
  ?n — Help on manual entry n (n = 1, 2, 3, 4, 5)
  <cr> — Return
  <esc> — Abort
> **5**

Please select the input mode of the simulation:
  1 — Trace-driven
  2 — Distribution-driven
  ?n — Help on manual entry n (n = 1, 2)
  <cr> — Return
  <esc> — Abort
> **1**

Please specify the output of the simulation by a list of
numbers correspond to the desired statistical data,
separated by spaces:
  1 — Maximum delay
  2 — Average delay
  3 — Throughput
  4 — Utilization
  5 — Retransmission count
  6 — Transmission failure count
  ?n — Help on manual entry n (n=1,2,3,4,5,6)
  <cr> — Return
  <esc> — Abort
> **1 2 4**

You have finished the specification of input output
parameters and termination condition.
Please type <cr> to return:
> **<cr>**

Please select the following manual entry:
  1 — Display the available modules
  2 — Specify the LAN protocols
  3 — Specify the stations
  4 — Display the target LAN specified so far
  5 — I/O and termination specification
  ?n — Help on manual entry n (n = 1, 2, 3, 4, 5)
  <cr> — Return
  <esc> — Abort
> **<cr>**

Please select one of the following task:
  1 — Specify the target LAN
  2 — Construct the simulator
  3 — Add new module
  ?n — Help on manual entry n (n = 1, 2, 3)
  <cr> — Return
  <esc> — Abort
> **2**

The SIMSCRIPT program of the simulator is in the file
"simulator".
Please type <cr> to return:
> **<cr>**

Please select one of the following task:
  1 — Specify the target LAN
  2 — Construct the simulator
  3 — Add new module
  ?n — Help on manual entry n (n = 1, 2, 3)
  <cr> — Return
  <esc> — Abort
> **<cr>**

THANK YOU!

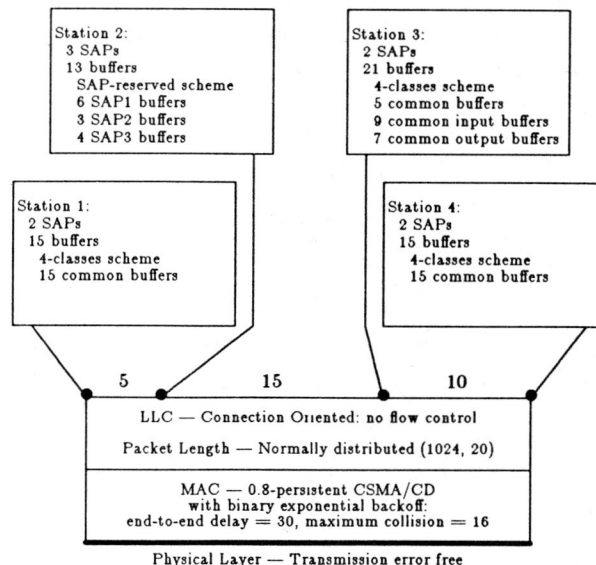

Figure A-1: The Target LAN Specified

Appendix B

By categorizing the modules into classes with each class having common global properties and similar interfaces, software reuse is facilitated in LANST. In this appendix, the global properties and the interfaces of the modules in different classes are discussed.

The LLC Class

The modules in the LLC class implement the LLC layer protocols. All the modules in this class contain three concurrent processes: the basic process, the sending process and the receiving process. The execution of the LLC module starts with the activation of the basic process. The basic process activates the sending process and the receiving process. The LLC module interacts with the MAC module in the similar way as the LLC protocol calls the MAC protocol to access the medium. The MAC module is activated by the sending process of the LLC module. The receiving process of the LLC module is resumed by the MAC module. The interface between the LLC module and the MAC module and the internal relation between processes of the LLC module is depicted in Figure B-1. The LLC module may call the modules in MISC class to model miscellaneous functions.

In the basic MODULE-LIBRARY, the LLC class contains three modules. The first two modules implement two LLC protocols defined in IEEE Standard 802.2: the *Unacknowledged Connectionless Service* and the *Connection Oriented Service*. The third module is a dummy LLC protocol. It can be used in observing the performance of a MAC protocol without the interference of the LLC protocol.

The MAC Class

The modules in the MAC class implement MAC layer protocols. A MAC module is a single process. The MAC module interacts with the LLC module through the interface shown in Figure B-1. It is activated by the sending process of the LLC module. It resumes the receiving process of the LLC module. Like the LLC module, the MAC module can call the modules in the MISC class for modeling functions to supplement the MAC protocol. In addition, MISC modules can also be called to model the physical layer characteristics.

Basically, three MAC modules are provided in LANST. Two of them may be used to model two MAC protocols defined by IEEE Standards 802.3 and 802.5, respectively. These two MAC protocols are known as the *CSMA/CD* and the *Token Ring*. The third module is a dummy MAC protocol which waits for a fixed period of time.

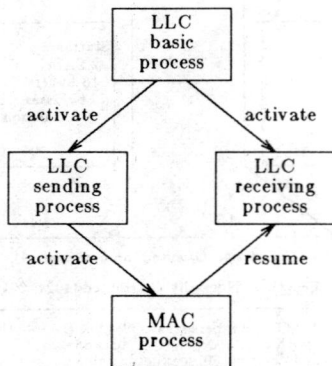

Figure B-1: The Interface Between the LLC Module and the MAC Module and the Internal Relation of the LLC Processes

The MISC Class

The MISC class contains modules to model various functions used in the LLC layer and the MAC layer. It also contains modules to model physical layer characteristics. All the modules in the MISC class are in the form of functions. These functions may have global variables associated with them. In general, the MISC modules is called by either the LLC module or the MAC module to perform well defined functions.

Currently, the MISC class contains modules for modeling sliding window flow control, pacing flow control, binary exponential backoff, and transmission error in physical medium.

The MNG Class

This class contains modules to model the resource management schemes used in the stations. These modules are implemented as boolean functions which return yes or no depending upon the availability of the resources. These functions have global variables associated with them to keep records of availability.

Currently available in the MNG class are one module of SAP management scheme and three modules of buffer management schemes. The SAP management scheme simply keeps the record of the number of the free SAPs. The first buffer management scheme is the "4-classes scheme". It partitions the buffers into four classes and allocating and deallocating the buffers in different classes with different priority. The four buffer classes are: 1) buffers which can be used only by a specific SAP for either incoming packets or outgoing packets, but not for both; 2) buffers which can be used by a specific SAP for both incoming packets and outgoing packets; 3) buffers which can be used by all SAPs for either incoming packets or outgoing packets, but not for both; 4) buffers which can be used by all SAPs for both incoming packets and outgoing packets. The other two buffer management schemes are the "I/O-reserved scheme" and the "SAP-reserved scheme". The "I/O-reserved scheme" categorizes buffers into two classes, one class is reserved only for incoming packets, the other only for outgoing packets. The "SAP-reserved scheme" categorizes buffers into classes which are reserved for specific SAPs.

The IO Class

An important module in the IO class is the load-generator. When instantiated with the specified distributions of the file lengths and the file inter-arrival times, the load-generator generates the load-script containing the description of all the file transfers between stations. The description of a file transfer has 6 fields:

1. Arrival time to the sending station
2. Sending station identification
3. Incoming rate to the sending station
4. Receiving station identification
5. Outgoing rate from the receiving station
6. File length in terms of the number of packets

The load-script is arranged in the increasing order of the arrival times of file transfers.

Currently, the modules available in the IO class may be used to generate the following simulation result:

1. Maximum delay time
2. Average delay time
3. LAN throughput
4. LAN utilization
5. Retransmission count
6. Failure count

BES/SSD : Expert Systems Providing Diagnostic Support
For Large Scale Software Systems

Robert I-Fang Chou, Wang-Chuan Tsai, and Steve Radtke

Operating System and Language Division
Bell Communications Research
Piscataway, N.J. 08854

ABSTRACT

In this paper, development of the Bellcore Expert Systems for System Software Diagnosis (BES/SSD) is discussed. BES/SSD is a series of online consultation expert systems primarily for system fault diagnosis. A prototype expert system for UNIX* (1100) support has been implemented. Other knowledge bases are under development for supporting other system software components of a very large software project.

By writing the tool called B-EXPERT (Bellcore Expert) in the C programming language, it has been possible to achieve portability as well as efficiency and maintainability. The Rutgers EXPERT [1] system developed by Weiss and Kulikowski was selected as the basis for the tool design.

However, B-EXPERT is extended with an enhanced control strategy design, a utility for interpreting the expertise embedded in the knowledge base and an interface to the underlying UNIX system. In order to provide the knowledge base builder a clear guideline in designing their application domains, problem solving methods and modeling mechanisms were developed.

I. Introduction

Support for large scale software systems has always been a costly task. System malfunctions can be attributed to any combination of causes such as user mishaps, procedural/operational errors, incorrect configurations, scarce system resources, incompatible environments and component failure avalanches. These problem situations constitute the majority of requests for system support. Expert systems techniques have readily been applied to solve problems in this category. For instance, DART [2] is a consultation system to advise IBM field service personnel on the diagnosis of faults occurring in computer installation. CRIB [3] is a computer engineer's diagnosis aid in detecting faults in computer components. YES/MVS [4] is a continuous real time expert system for reducing a computer operator's workload.

---

* UNIX is a trademark of AT&T Bell Laboratories.

To solve some system problems requires an experienced domain expert. Because years of experience are needed to build up necessary expertise, it can be very difficult to maintain the system when these experts become unavailable or expensive. The BES/SSD Consultation Systems were developed to alleviate this difficulty by providing on-line diagnosis support.

A tool, namely B-EXPERT, is written entirely in the C programming language to achieve highly desirable features such as simplicity, portability, high efficiency, and maintainability. Rutgers EXPERT [1] developed by Weiss and Kulikowski was selected as the basis of the tool design. However, various modifications, simplifications, and enhancements to EXPERT have been made in order to accommodate different models which simulate the problem solving methods of human experts. The modified tool is named B-EXPERT to distinguish it from the original Rutgers EXPERT system.

The B-EXPERT tool can run on many UNIX and UNIX-compatible systems. The most important advantages of using this non-LISP-based approach are that there is no LISP portability problem, and it provides great flexibility in implementing a real-time system interface.

In this paper, we briefly discuss problem domain design approaches which can be used with our tool in addition to the EXPERT approach. The knowledge acquisition process is described to reflect the differences from the conventional extremes. Also introduced are particular features of B-EXPERT including an enhanced control strategy design, a utility for interpreting the expertise embedded in the knowledge base, and an interface to the underlying UNIX system.

II. The Problem Domains and the Use of Expert Systems

The aims for Bellcore Expert Systems for System Software Diagnosis (BES/SSD) are

1. to provide on-line support to reduce service requests for human experts,
2. to support and train new field support staffs and system administrators, and
3. to preserve the expertise.

The possible problem domains we have are UNIX (1100) system support, applications support, communication networks, and various Sperry system software components. Each of these has its own procedures for generation and installation as well as run time administration and recovery methods.

The support requests/service calls can be made by various users and system administrators. A significant percentage of these help requests are predictable problems (based on past interactions between the field support people and users) and can be answered by an expert system.

Following are the typical causes of system faults.

C1. User made operational/procedural mishaps.
C2. User violated or misunderstood system specification.
C3. Resource unavailable.
C4. Inadequate/incompatible environment.
C5. Subcomponent malfunctions - software bugs.
C6. Other system failure - software failure avalanche.

The expected services/advice from an expert system could be as follows:

S1. Identify appropriate documents.
S2. Display the correct operations/procedures with brief explanations.
S3. Indicate the incompatible configuration.
S4. Identify the failed components.
S5. Give directions for recovery procedures.
S6. Give detailed interpretations of the error codes and error messages.
S7. Give a list of the interrelated expert systems to consult next if needed.

A prototype expert system for UNIX (1100) system support has been implemented under B-EXPERT. The UNIX (1100) system is a virtual operating system implementation under the OS-1100 executive on Sperry Series 1100 mainframes. Many UNIX (1100) system problems are created by administrators still learning their jobs (usually 6 to 12 months), while other problems are shortcomings of the existing implementation. In either case when system errors are trapped, a generic warning message is issued. Interpreting such messages, and appropriately recovering from the error, requires that the SAs (system administrators) use concepts from SPERRY Series 1100 architecture and from UNIX internals. Error messages and ongoing actions to change system configurations or components (if any) must be identified, then the appropriate recovery actions should be taken. In some instances the manuals do not supply the information in ways that allow it to be quickly found and interpreted. For example, the SA is unable to locate the information, because it is not cross-indexed by error condition. This system is intended to provide an interactive tool to be used in conjunction with standard manuals and assistance from field support personnel.

III. *The Knowledge Engineering and Problem Solving Models*

In many applications, eliciting problem-solving knowledge from domain experts has been the main obstacle in building expert systems; usually it is difficult for the domain experts to adapt their problem-solving knowledge to suit the knowledge representation approaches of a particular expert system tool.

Even though our domain experts, all highly trained computer scientists, would not have trouble learning the basic principles of expert systems, substantial time and effort may still be required for them to develop a high degree of proficiency in the use of the tool. According to the EXPERT user guide [5], domain experts start with the conclusions and then decide upon the questions or findings which can reach these conclusions. However, the problem-solving steps suggested may not be presented in such a way that domain experts feel comfortable. It would certainly be more flexible and natural if domain experts are allowed to choose a model which is better tailored to their individual preferences.

To overcome these apparent deficiencies and to accelerate the knowledge engineering process, the domain is designed in two phases. Phase one includes model selection and knowledge formalization. Based upon his/her preference and implementation considerations, a domain expert has the freedom to choose one among several proposed models. Once the model is selected, the domain expert follows the model to draw inference graphs and to formalize knowledge. Phase two converts the results of phase one into the style as required by the tool. For each model selected in phase one, there is a corresponding conversion mechanism.

With these two distinct phases, our domain experts can choose, as close as possible, the models that most readily describe their problem-solving knowledge and, as a result, they may even perform the coding and debugging process themselves. The interview process between the knowledge engineer and the domain expert is thus bypassed. The current models supported for representing problem domains are the decision tree model, the top-down model, and the original liberal model suggested in EXPERT. Following, we discuss the first two approaches.

III.1 *Decision Tree Approach*

The inference graph associated with a decision tree may look like Figure 1.

The nodes Q1-Q7 are possible questions; they can be numerical, single choice, multiple choice, or yes/no questions. Q2, Q3 and Q4 are grouped as one questionnaire QN1. The branches c_1-c_{11} are conditions under which the next move can be selected. Multiple conditions can be set after one question is asked. The node CLi denotes one of the possible conclusions during a consultation session. The node Ti denotes the corresponding treatment with respect to CLi.

The following is a sample B-EXPERT run for a case of a UNIX (1100) system installation problem; the system is based on the decision tree approach. The UNIX (1100) diagnosis prototype contains approximately 200 inference rules (FF, FH and HH rules) and 100 questions.

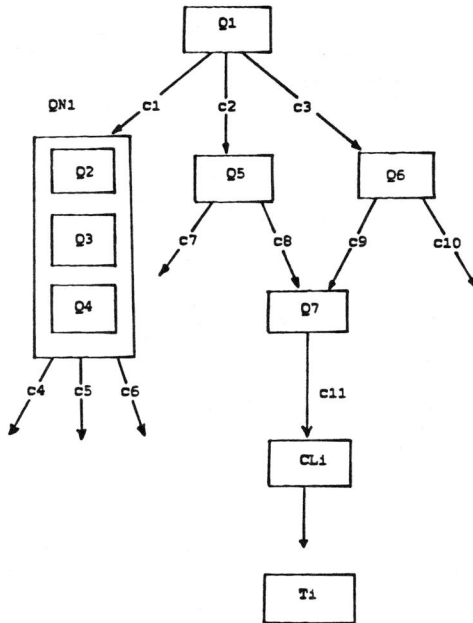

Figure 1. A Decision Tree

--- EXPERT CONSULTATION SESSION ---

Type ? for a summary of valid responses to any question asked by the program.

CASE TYPE:
  (1) Case Entry (2) Visit Entry (3) Case Review (4) Case Deletion
  (5) Demo Entry (6) Batch Entry (7) Edu Entry   (8) Program Exit
Enter Case Selection: 1

Enter Name or ID Number: u1100s

Press 'Y' to Enter Initial Findings, or 'N' to Begin Questioning:N

1. Answer Yes or No:
   Is this the inital installation of the UNIX(1100) system
   *yes

2. What problem are you having?
   1) can't read release tape
   2) problems cataloguing files for UNIX system
   3) problems booting the starter system read from tape
   4) problems logging in to unix
   5) problems in the generators
   6) down runstream failed to take down starter system
   7) install runstream failed
   Choose one:
   *3

3. Where did boot fail?
   1) common bank reload failed
   2) bad ER ATIME$
   3) no common bank defined in EXEC gen
   4) no configured common banks in EXEC gen
   Choose one:
   *1

4. Did the reload get iopr or eabt failure?
   1) reload got iopr
   2) reload got eabt
   Choose one:
   *2

5. What was the rentr adr from reload abort?
   1) rentr adr 1032
   2) rentr adr 1036
   3) rentr adr 1044
   4) rentr adr 1405
   5) rentr adr 1154
   6) rentr adr 1157
   7) rentr adr 1421
   8) rentr adr 1432
   9) rentr adr 1207
   10) rentr adr 1221
   11) rentr adr 1225
   12) rentr adr 1267
   Choose one:
   *2

End of Findings (Press Return for Summary Report):

SUMMARY

Name: u1100s
Case: 1 Visit: 1 Date: 03/26/85

Is this the inital installation of the UNIX(1100) system
    Answer: YES

What problem are you having?
    problems booting the starter system read from tape

Where did boot fail?
    common bank reload failed

Did the reload get iopr or eabt failure?
    reload got eabt

What was the rentr adr from reload abort?
    rentr adr 1036

End of Summary (Press Return for an Analysis Report):

INTERPRETIVE ANALYSIS

Diagnostic Status:

1.00 problem occured during new system installation
1.00 @use failed

Treatment Recommendations:

1.00 check for existing file with @use name and re-name it

Command Mode: Fix x, Why, Dx, Sum, New, Hypo, Quit, or ? for Help
-> quit

End of Consultation

III.2 *Top-Down Approach*

A backward chaining scheme is widely adopted in problem diagnosis expert systems. The deduction works backward from the root (the general goal) of the inference graph toward the leaves (evidence provided by the users during the consultation). The inference sequence implemented in B-EXPERT strictly follows the exhaustive depth first search which makes the system behavior of this type of model very easy for a model builder to predict. The search tree is implicitly defined in the rules. To make this notion clear, an example is given in Figure 2 (the treatment part is not shown).

A boxed node denotes an abstract concept in the problem space. The higher in the graph, the more general the concept it designates; the lower, the more specific (the mnemonic name of a node is shown in the upper-left corner). The double circled nodes denote the findings (observables).

An "askable" node denotes that the system will first ask a user a question directly associated with the meaning of that node when it is visited. By answering such a question, the user can provide information which allows the subtree to be pruned. In figure 2, an end user may be confident, even before answering any question, that S1 is not possibly the source of the problem but he/she has no idea about S2 and S3. By providing the truth values False, True, True to the questions fs1, fs2 and fs3 respectively, he/she can then avoid the unnecessary search of deducing S1. A "nonaskable" node usually denotes some internal deduction step or concept for which it is impossible for a user to discern.

Figure 3 is an example of the inference graph for an application domain being developed. The problem

domain addressed in this example is Session Control, a system software component which directs terminal messages to the appropriate application program and also enforces security. The diagnostic process adopted by the designer in this domain is a top-down approach.

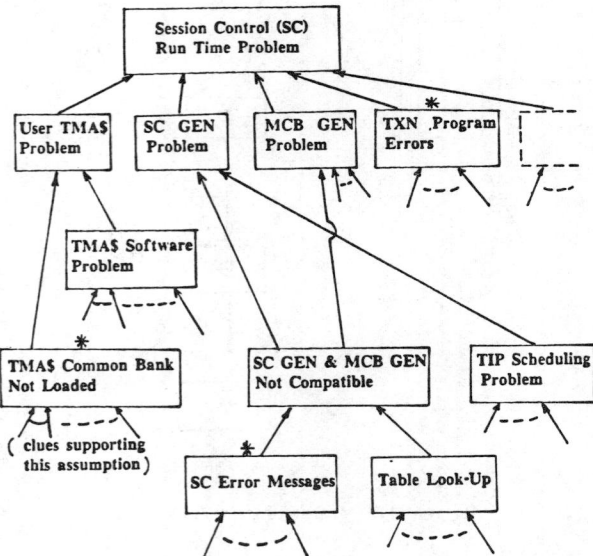

* The marked nodes denote the askable nodes

Figure 3. An Incomplete Inference Graph for Session Control Diagnosis

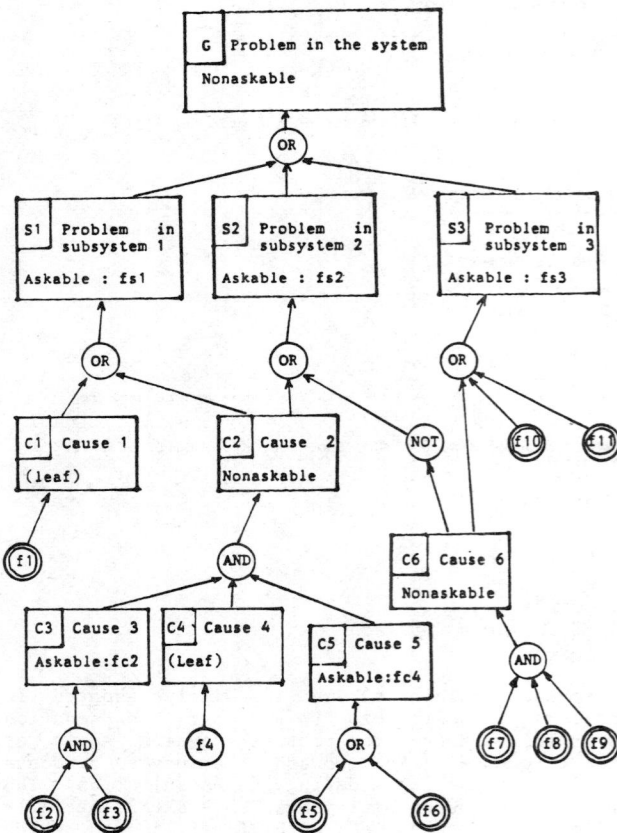

Figure 2. Top-Down Approach

IV. Tool Implementation and Features

For our consultation type of application, we first considered the EMYCIN [6] and EXPERT tools. Eventually, we decided to develop our own tool based on the EXPERT framework mostly because of our concern over the tool's simplicity, availability, efficiency, portability, and maintainability of our particular application environment. Moreover, a non-LISP-based tool can relieve our domain experts the overhead of learning the LISP language.

The B-EXPERT tool has been implemented completely in the C language on the UNIX (1100) system. Since the tool is highly portable, it can run on many other UNIX and UNIX-compatible systems. The tool consists of two phases, namely compilation and consultation. The compilation phase reads the domain file and translates it into a knowledge base. The consultation phase contains the inference engine which controls the questioning sequence in reaching conclusion, and the user interface which interprets users' consultation requests.

The B-EXPERT tool retains approximately 90% of the primary functionality of the original Rutgers EXPERT tool, which was implemented in FORTRAN. In addition, B-EXPERT contains an enhanced control strategy, an interface to the underlying UNIX system, and a subsystem for transferring expertise (see Section V).

Our tool is still undergoing development to include the remaining 10% of the capabilities of the Rutgers EXPERT, such as case analysis, case conversion, and some other minor consultation commands. The next phase of development also includes the design of an intelligent knowledge acquisition editor. As the application domain file increases in size, an intelligent editor will alleviate the overhead and complexity involved in maintaining domain knowledge.

IV.1 *Control Strategy*

The enhanced control strategy of B-EXPERT is capable of supporting domain models employing either the data-driven or goal-driven scheme (The Rutgers EXPERT system tool does not have the goal-driven control capability. The problem of processing simultaneous goals cannot be easily handled within the EXPERT control structure [7]). But, since B-EXPERT has included goal-driven control strategy, domain experts can easily implement their applications by following any one of the problem-solving models discussed in the last section.

In order to provide goal-driven control, an extra HH-rule section is included in our tool to allow domain experts to specify backward chaining inference in their models. The new HH-rule section is as shown in Figure 4. The rules in this section reflect the inference graph as shown in Figure 2. Internally, no inference tree is constructed to implement the backward chaining. Instead, an alternative approach simulating depth-first search is used to control the question asking sequence.

```
*HH Rule

{****    Backward chaining HH rule section    ****}

{* The following three rules deduce goal G. *}
F(FS1,T) & H(S1,0.5:1.0) -> H(G,1.0)
F(FS2,T) & H(S2,0.5:1.0) -> H(G,1.0)
F(FS3,T) & H(S3,0.5:1.0) -> H(G,1.0)

{* The following rule deduces S1. *}
[1:H(C1,0.5:1.0),H(C2,0.5:1.0)] -> H(S1,0.8)

            :

{****       Treatments       ****}

*IF
        F(TRUE,T)
*THEN
            :
        H(S1,0.4:1.0) -> H(T1,1.0)
        H(S2,0.5:1.0) -> H(T2,1.0)
            :
*END
```

Figure 4. Backward Chaining HH-rule Section

IV.2 *UNIX System Interface*

B-EXPERT has been extended with an interface to the underlying UNIX system. In particular, it is possible for knowledge bases to invoke UNIX commands to obtain knowledge, and to effect "treatments". With these extensions, B-EXPERT can now support applications in real-time diagnosis and treatment, and performance interpretation and tuning.

To implement the new rule-controlled system interface, a "standout" finding has been added to the tool for calling the external program and passing data. Different from "askable" findings, a "standout" finding issues a UNIX shell command or executes a user program. This design is necessary when information cannot be obtained through the interactive questioning of the consultation phase, or would inconvenience the user to have to find the information.

The treatment section has also been modified to allow a system interface declaration. An invocation of a shell command or a user program can be associated with a treatment hypothesis. If a program-call treatment is concluded, the corresponding program call will be issued during the generation of the interpretation report.

Several other facilities have been studied to provide more flexible system interface capabilities in B-EXPERT. For example, accessing an external file is necessary when the expert system is used to interpret data stored in that file.

V. *Expertise Transfer and Knowledge Base Maintenance*

Transferring problem solving expertise and providing explanation have become important demands on expert systems. It has been confirmed by researchers that the knowledge base can be used for purposes other than problem-solving.

By using B-EXPERT, a domain expert constructs a knowledge base from his/her years of experience. This valuable expertise is codified into B-EXPERT rules. In order to disseminate this problem solving expertise, as well as to facilitate both the knowledge debugging process of building a knowledge base and the task of maintaining a knowledge base, software which is capable of translating the expertise embedded in a knowledge base into English is needed. The EDU (Education Subsystem) and other explanation utilities in B-EXPERT were developed for these purposes.

In EDU, both the meaning of an individual rule in a model and the relationships among rules are described in English. For a forward chained model, there are three available report sections:

1. The Knowledge Base Text File section,
2. The Interpretation Of Individual Rule section, and
3. The Cross Reference section.

For a backward chained model, there is an additional section, the Problem Solving Strategy section, which explains the implicitly defined inference graph in an explicit manner (in depth first order).

A model builder or a knowledge-base maintainer can optionally specify which report sections he/she needs. Also, he/she can specify (redirect) the output device (or file) of the report sections.

If the model is chained backward and the output device selected is a terminal, the user has two alternatives to interactively 'trace' the problem solving expertise (i.e. the inference graph). The system can explain the graph exhaustively or selectively. By 'selectively' we mean the user can walk along the inference graph step by step. This capability is useful when only a small portion of the graph is interesting to the user.

Besides EDU, there are several interactive commands for a user to obtain explanation of the system behavior. At any point of time during a consultation session, a user can ask the system:

1. to explain why the current question is asked,
2. to display all the currently concluded hypotheses and how they were deduced,
3. to report the current state of each rule, and
4. to summarize the answers to questions which have been asked.

Employing the utilities just discussed, a learner is able to gain the problem solving expertise in an efficient way and a knowledge base maintainer can comprehend the structure of a knowledge base in a very short period.

VI. *Conclusion*

The BES/SSD Expert System is a series of System Software Diagnosis expert systems being developed at Bell Communication Research. A prototype for UNIX (1100) system installation problem diagnosis has been implemented and is currently being used by the user community.

The tool was developed using the C language in eight months, while the UNIX (1100) application domain prototype took one month. The UNIX (1100) diagnosis prototype follows the decision tree approach and the result, up to the present, satisfies our original design goal.

The most significant features of the BES/SSD system are the portability of the tool, the system interface for knowledge bases to invoke UNIX commands or user programs, the rich utilities for transferring expertise and providing explanation, the flexibility of the model selection, and the systematic and clear guidelines for knowledge modeling. The domain experts have the freedom to choose the most suitable model so that their ideas and skills can be most effectively transformed into the B-EXPERT representation.

There are several other potential application domains being considered at Bellcore for the same tool. In the near future, we expect to upgrade our current tool and to have the intelligent knowledge acquisition editor available to decrease the overhead of implementing knowledge bases.

VII. *Acknowledgements*

The authors wish to thank Brian Minnihan for his helpful discussions and suggestions on the subject of the paper. Thanks also due to Joe Carfagno and Gene Cracovia for their support.

VIII. *References*

1. Weiss, S., and A. Kulikowski, "EXPERT: a system for developing consultation models," Proceedings of the sixth IJCAI, Tokyo, Japan, 1979, pp. 942-947.

2. Bennett, J. S. and C. R. Hollander, "DART: An Expert System for Computer Fault Diagnosis," Proceedings of the seventh IJCAI, Vancouver, Canada, 1981, pp. 843-845.

3. Hartley, R. T., "CRIB: Computer Fault-finding Through Knowledge Engineering," Computer Magazine, March 1984, pp. 76-83.

4. Griesmer, J. H., et al., "YES/MVS: A Continuous Real Time Expert System," Proc. AAAI, Austin, Texas, 1984.

5. Weiss, S., et al., "A Guide to the Use of the EXPERT Consultation System," Dept. of Computer Science, Rutgers Univ., CBM-TR-94, Nov. 1983.

6. Van Melle, W., et al., "The EMYCIN Manual," Dept. of Computer Science, Stanford Univ., STAN-CS-81-885, Oct. 1981.

7. Frederick Hayes-Roth, Donald A. Waterman, Douglas B. Lenat, "Building Expert Systems," Addison Wesley, 1983.

8. Weiss, S., and A. Kulikouski, "A Pratical Guide to Design Expert Systems," Rowman & Allanheld, N.J., 1984.

9. Boose, J. H., "Personal Construct Theory and the Transfer of Human Expertise," Proc. AAAI, Austin, Texas, 1984.

SOFTWARE PRODUCTIVITY AND CONTROL ENVIRONMENT - SPACE II

Paul Sonnenblick, Louis M. Picinich
EXPERTWARE, Inc.
2685 Marine Way, Suite 1209
Mountain View, CA. 94043-1125
(415) 965-8921

and   John J. Marciniak
Marciniak and Associates
1600 South Eads Street
Arlington, VA. 22202
(703) 920-9116

ABSTRACT

SPACE II is being developed to satisfy the requirement for a life cycle program management tool which spans the development and maintenance phases of systems. The tool provides full documentation and configuration management support, supports high level and detailed design by incorporating design methodologies of Yourdan, Constantine, and Jackson, and supports Ada PDL. The tool is compatible with recent direction in the DoD to create a common software engineering environment based on the Ada Programming Support Environment, and the provisions of the draft Joint Logistics Commander's Software Development Standard. It has been designed as an integrated engineering management system that assists in the practice and enforcement of a life cycle management methodology.

INTRODUCTION

Software acqustion has been a major problem for the Department of Defense for at least the past decade. In the early 70's the emergence of software as an integral part of avionics systems signalled a new era in systems, completing the introduction of software across the spectrum of DoD systems.

The attention that software received was not due to its ability to introduce flexibility and capability into weapons, but due to the many problems it seemed to cause in weapon systems development. Software appeared to be on the critical path of every development schedule, and accounted for more acquisition problems than all of the other possible causes combined. Major weapon systems were delayed because the "software" did not work, causing multimillion dollar overruns. In some cases entire systems had to be scrapped as schedules got so out of hand that the integrity of the budget for the system was indefensible before Congress. This "schedule" problem was only the tip of the iceberg.

DoD was also concerned with the high cost of software. Accompanying this problem was an inability to deal with estimation of software costs up front, therefore, an inability to adequately project weapon system costs. The escalating costs of software resulted in increased management awareness and led to numerous studies to analyze the problem. In the late 70's and early 80's a cohesive management direction emerged in DoD with first the DoD-1(Ada) program, and subsequently, the STARS program. These major DoD programs were intended to deal with the productivity of the software development process and the quality of the delivered product.

The DoD-1 program introduced a modern High Order Language, named Ada. Ada was more significant for setting the pace for a concentration on the support environments necessary to build applications or systems software. The concept of the Ada Programming Support Environment (APSE) was innovated. This environment created interest across industry and academias quest for a disciplined software engineering process - the accumulation of tools and methodologies to deal with the creation of weapon systems software in an orderly and engineered process.

The Software for Adaptable Reliable Systems (STARS) program, initiated in 1983, tackled the software engineering process and specifically, the issues of software programmer productivity and software quality. This broad front program is just beginning. Its products, new tools, practices, and methodologies will be transitioned into use through a common software engineering environment, namely the APSE.

The Need for Effective Communication on Software Projects

Tool development during the eighties has focused on automating the discrete tools that assist the process of software development. Each of these tools have, in fact, served a useful function and improved the productivity of the software engineer and the quality of his product. The industry has not, however, seen the improvement in project productivity and quality that was expected. This shortfall is due to the fact that the development of large, complex software systems is a complicated and abstract process requiring a coherent management methodology to tie together all the engineering processes that are required for a software project.

Such management methodologies have been proposed by Yourdon[1], DeMarco[2], Boehm[3], Evans[4], and others. While the various approaches may differ, they all agree that the methodology must be based on a life-cycle model that encourages good software engineering practices. In particular, requirements must be clearly specified and allocated, and design of process and data must be based on modern practices and must be clearly documented.

In addition, the project should be structured to ensure that requirements and design errors are caught and corrected during the phase in which they occur, not the coding or testing phases. The main roadblock to successfully executing this management methodology is the data produced during each phase of the development effort. Figure 1 shows a typical software development life cycle together with the data products that are produced during each phase. Each of the data products noted are produced either as formal documents (that may go unread), or as design notes on scraps of paper, or as information retained in the creator's head. It is problematical, however, if the data products are fulfilling their primary function of communicating ideas/information. The solution to this problem is to automate the data management and communication tasks.

This paper describes a system, SPACE II, that provides this automation in an integrated engineering management system that assists in the practice and enforcement of a life cycle management methodology. It will be noted that SPACE II is compatible with Ada and may be used as the front end of an APSE (Ada Programming Support Environment) to complement the compiler, debuggers, etc. that comprise the minimal APSE (MAPSE).

THE SOFTWARE PRODUCTIVITY AND CONTROL ENVIRONMENT (SPACE II)

SPACE II is an interactive, multi-user development environment that was created to satisfy the need for a life cycle management tool which spans the development and maintenance phases of software systems and aids both management and development personnel. SPACE II supports all of the life cycle phases; from planning to maintenance, and serves management by providing support to development personnel. SPACE II provides principal support to the requirements and design portions of the development process.

User Support

SPACE II is intended for use on medium to large scale software development projects utilizing from 4 to 50 or more developers. Space II provides support to the following major areas: Management, Design Documentation, and Development.

Management Support

SPACE II supports the assignment of tasks to personnel, provides automatic task statusing, enforces review/approval checkpoints, and performs the configuration management function by automating the program support library function, the component identification function, revision numbering, release packaging, and trouble/error report processing.

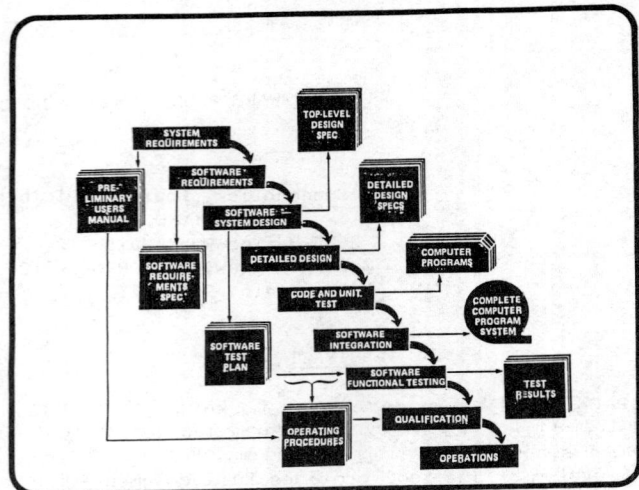

Figure 1.

A number of additional management aids are being added to the management support feature already provided in the tool. Perhaps the area which is most interesting is the full scheduling tracking capability. Another function of the tool is to provide a cost estimating capability. By defining work packages in accordance with work breakdown structures and cost accounting codes, a fully automated capability to generate work flow and total cost projections is provided. Additional aids could be added to check the validity of these projections based upon current analysis techniques.

Design Documentation

SPACE II captures the design as it is entered by system users and stores it in its data base. Design information is entered once and only once, thus minimizing the opportunity for error. SPACE II automatically generates the requested design documentation according to predefined user-specified formats by accessing its data base.

Software Development

SPACE II provides significant automation support to the portions of the software development life cycle possessing the largest potential for productivity improvement; requirements and design. The system automates the vital but tedious tasks of requirements specification/allocation/traceability, supports the development of the data dictionary during the design phase (and checks to ensure typing and usage legalities), prompts for decomposition to the lowest required level, assists the detailed design process through the use of a high-level pseudocode, and automates the consistency checking portions of requirements and design walkthroughs.

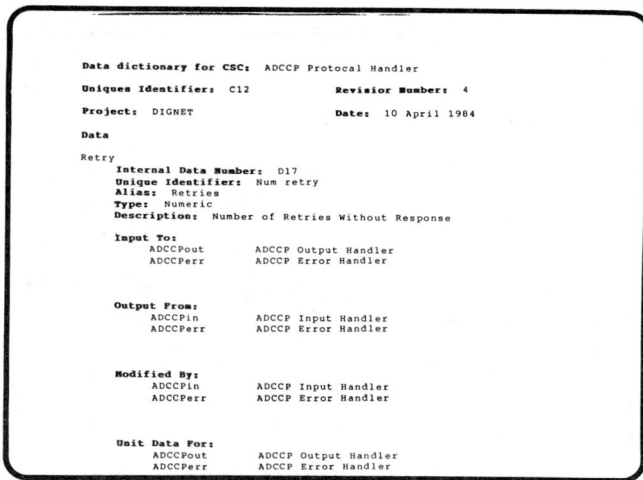

```
Data dictionary for CSC:  ADCCP Protocol Handler

Uniques Identifier:  C12          Revision Number:  4

Project:  DIGNET              Date:  10 April 1984

Data

Retry
      Internal Data Number:  D17
      Unique Identifier:  Num retry
      Alias:  Retries
      Type:  Numeric
      Description:  Number of Retries Without Response

      Input To:
           ADCCPout       ADCCP Output Handler
           ADCCPerr       ADCCP Error Handler


      Output From:
           ADCCPin        ADCCP Input Handler
           ADCCPerr       ADCCP Error Handler


      Modified By:
           ADCCPin        ADCCP Input Handler
           ADCCPerr       ADCCP Error Handler


      Unit Data For:
           ADCCPout       ADCCP Output Handler
           ADCCPerr       ADCCP Error Handler
```

Figure 2.

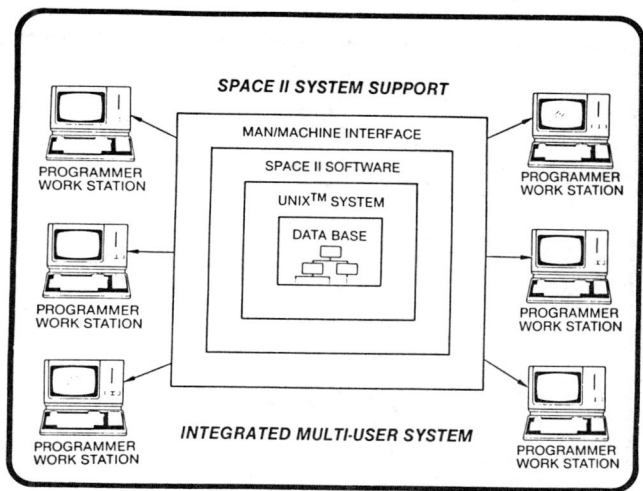

Figure 3.

SPACE II is being extended in the requirements analysis area by adding automated capabilities for consistency and redundancy checking. This enhanced requirements process will be accomplished by extending the current features and by integrating exisiting requirements tool into SPACE II.

SPACE II will graphically support number of design practices such as Yourdon's Structured Design and/or Data Flows. Figure 2 is a Data Dictionary Report.

In future releases, SPACE II will also compare the source code generated by the programmer with the corresponding detailed design. It will then flag inconsistancies in naming and logic, thus performing a significant portion of the code walk-through.

Test plans, specifications, and procedures can be generated using SPACE II. The traceability of requirements and data usage to software processes will be a significant aid in the development of cost-effective and efficient test procedures.

During maintenance, the automatic configuration management capabilities of SPACE II ensure product control despite multiple releases. In addition, the traceability provided by SPACE II permits development personnel to ascertain, prior to implementation, the effect that a change in one area of the software will have in other parts of the system.

General Features

As mentioned above, the system is interactive and multi-user. It is written in C and runs on UNIX Version 7, System 3, or System 5. Depending upon the computer used and its storage capability, up to 50 or more users may be accommodated. SPACE II utilizes color graphic terminals together with full screen editing and a multi-window display capability to ensure a viable user interface.

Figure 3 illustrates the multiuser configuration of SPACE II. SPACE II operates by considering all the information pertinent to a project as a set of related data objects that are connected to one another through a variety of relationships. SPACE II maintains traceability of these relationships, updates them in real-time and flags changes and discrepancies to affected users.

The software developer is not required to learn a formal specification language; plain text is used for requirements and process/data descriptions, while an Ada-like PDL is used for detailed logic design. In addition, the software developer is required to master only three basic working screens (and associated actions). These screens are

1.   A description screen used to create and describe both process or data, (See Figure 4).

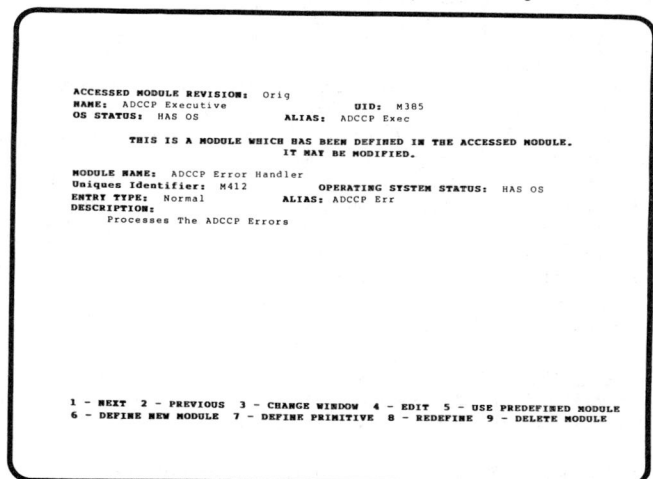

```
ACCESSED MODULE REVISION:  Orig
NAME:  ADCCP Executive           UID:  M385
OS STATUS:  HAS OS       ALIAS:  ADCCP Exec

      THIS IS A MODULE WHICH HAS BEEN DEFINED IN THE ACCESSED MODULE.
                        IT MAY BE MODIFIED.

MODULE NAME:  ADCCP Error Handler
Uniques Identifier:  M412            OPERATING SYSTEM STATUS:  HAS OS
ENTRY TYPE:  Normal        ALIAS:  ADCCP Err
DESCRIPTION:
      Processes The ADCCP Errors




1 - NEXT  2 - PREVIOUS  3 - CHANGE WINDOW  4 - EDIT  5 - USE PREDEFINED MODULE
6 - DEFINE NEW MODULE  7 - DEFINE PRIMITIVE  8 - REDEFINE  9 - DELETE MODULE
```

Figure 4.

```
                    APPROVED CSC LIST


  APPROVED CSC:
  NUMBER    UNIQUE IDENTIFIER    NAME                        REVISION
  1         C12                  ADCCP Protocal Handler      4
  2         C 4                  ASYNC Handler               1
  3         C17                  BI-SYNC Protocol Handler    2
  4         C 1                  Channel Controls            8
  5         C14                  Utilities                   Orig
  6         C 7                  TCP                         Orig



                    1 - CONTROL CSC   2 - PRINT LIST
```

Figure 5.

```
  ACCESSED MODULE REVISION:  Orig
  NAME:  ADCCP Timer
  OS STATUS: HAS OS              ALIAS:  Timer

  REQUIREMENT FROM SPEC TITLED:  ADCCP Requirement Specification
  A   NUMBER UNIQUE IDENTIFIER          TITLE
  *   412     R112              Inter-Message Timeout
  *   413     R118              Intra-Message Timeout
  *   414     R 92              4le Timer



  1 - NEXT SCREEN          2 - PREVIOUS SCREEN      3 - CHANGE WINDOW
  4 - DEFINE DERIVED REQ   5 - DELETE DERIVED REQ   6 - MODIFY DERIVED REQ
  7 - ALLOCATE REQ         8 - DEALLOCATE REQ
  TO MODULE OR PREIMITVE:
  A   NUMBER UNIQUE IDENTIFIER          NAME
  *   1001    M 85              ADCCP Executive
  *   1002    M 87              ADCCP Timex
  *   1003    M217              ADCCP Input Handler
  *   1004    M218              ADCCP Output Handler
  *   1005    M386              ADCCP Error Handler


  9 - MODULE  10 - PRIMITIVE  11 - DELETE  12 - MODIFY  13 - USE PDEF-MOD
  14 - VIEW PDEF-MOD
```

Figure 6.

2. An allocate screen used to allocate requirements and data, (See Figure 5).
3. A list screen which hierarchically lists
   related entities, (See Figure 6).

An overview of the system's key features are given
below.

Methodology - As mentioned above, the tool directly supports DoD software development methodo-
gies, specifically MIL STD SDS, and its accompanying Document Standards (Data Item Descriptions). The decomposition methodology starts with
a software Computer Software Configuration Item
(CSCI), progresses to a Computer Software Component (CSC) and finally ends with the lowest level
of the hierarchy, the Unit. The documentation
function addresses DoD documentation standards and
the tool directly supports configuration management practices specified in Mil Std 483.

Standards - One of the strong points of the tool
is its capability to support development standards. The Project Manager establishes standards
that are used throughout the life of the project.
Standards that may be defined by the Manager include: the development language to be used, defining names used to describe the various design and
coding units, (e.g. Computer Software Component,
Unit, Module, etc.), setting limits (e.g. number
of lines of PDL per unit), and establishing points
at which various components are brought under
configuration control. The tool also provides a
set of default standards.

Enrollment - This feature controls who may have
access to the system for the various functions to
be performed. Initially, the Project Manager is
enrolled and from then on controls who is enrolled onto the system, and for what function. The
Project Manager enrolls other system users by task

and function assignment to include the right to
work on, review, or control the specific components of the system. A user is then assigned
certain privileges according to his role in project development. This feature provides an excellent way for the manager to exercise overall control over the project.

Schedule - While the tool, at this time, does not
provide for automatic scheduling mechanisms, scheduling is supported by the generation of activities reflecting the work to be accomplished and
automatically marking them as completed. All of
the tasks of development are in the system, and
control over their generation and review is determined by the Project Manager through the User
Activity feature. As activities are completed,
their status is entered into the system. The
status of the activities for a particular task is
affected by at least two people: the person having
responsibility for task completion and the person
having review responsibility. Thus, the Project
Manager can audit system status through his terminal. As the project proceeds, the manager can
compare actual with projected accomplishment to
assess the status of the development project.

Archive - The SPACE II tool places controlled
files which are no longer used in any revision of
the product in a file directory under the control
of a system administrator. This administrator has
the overall responsibility for archiving the data
or deleting it, depending on the procedures installed by the Project Manager.

Move/Copy - The move and copy commands are an
important and labor saving feature of the system.
The move command allows the user to move a component from one part of the system to another. All
ties with the original part of the system are
broken and ties to the new link are established.

The copy command allows the user to duplicate a component to use in another part of the system. The tool automatically performs all necessary reallocations of requirements and data in support of these functions.

Common Package - A function is provided to mark a CSC as a Common Package. This allows the linking of that CSC's subordinate units to other units under the same operating system in the CSCI detailed design.

Help - A help function is provided to the user. This function, which is activated by a dedicated function key, provides a help screen for each individual screen of the system.

USE OF SPACE II IN AN ADA PROGRAMMING SUPPORT ENVIRONMENT

The major emphasis of current APSE tool development is concentrated on the backend of the development life cycle: coding, debugging, testing, system generation etc. SPACE II compliments these tools by providing support to the specification and design processes, as well as providing automatic configuration management, automatic design specification generation and support to management in the form of scheduling, resource allocation, and status monitoring.

General Interfaces

SPACE II runs on the UNIX Operating System. The system is being initially implemented on the Perkin Elmer 3205, 3210 and DEC VAX 11/780. Since the system has been coded in the "C" programming language using the standard "C" subset, problems associated with transportability have been minimized. SPACE II provides primary support to the data management aspects of design, to configuration management, and to project visibility and control. As such, it is independent of any specific design methodology, however, supports five principal methodologies:

- Top-Down Structured Design - e.g. Constantine
- Data Structure Design - e.g. Jackson
- Modular Decomposition Criterion - e.g. Parnas
- Object Oriented Design - e.g. Liskov
- Structured Code - e.g. Djikstra

SPACE II supports the above methodologies by enforcing decomposition and allocation procedures; maintaing hierarchical requirements and design traceability; and providing for structured pseudo-code process discriptions.

The developer uses other development tools for compilation, debug, and integration testing. Configuration management is automatically performed on all requirements, data, software design, and source code, as well as other associated documentation.

APSE Interfaces

Ada is a very powerful, expressive language that supports the principles of good software engineering. The following are some of the key capabilities provided by Ada:

- Structured Constructs
- Strong Typing
- Relative and Absolute Precision Specification
- Information Hiding and Data Abstraction
- Concurrent Processing
- Exception Handling
- Generic Definition

Any programming support tool must compliment and enhance these capabilities, giving the software developer access to the full range of Ada's power and versatility. The following describe how SPACE II supports the development of software that will be based on Ada.

Structured Constructs - SPACE II provides a high level pseudo-code that is used to specify detailed logic design. The constructs provided by SPACE II fully support the Ada constructs on the design level and provide a natural transition to code generation.

Strong Typing - SPACE II starts with a basic set of types and permits the definition of new types to be built based on the basic set. The formation of Arrays and Records is supported and overloading is permitted.

Relative And Absolute Precision Specification - SPACE II supports the specification of both floating point (relative) and fixed point (absolute) values.

Information Hiding and Data Abstraction - SPACE II allows a designer to consider a software entity as a "black box". That is, the designer sees the inputs, outputs, and function of the entity and uses that information in performing his design task. Only personnel directly given access to that entity can modify its internals.

Concurrent Processing - SPACE II supports the Ada ability to implement tasks with concurrent processing using the rendezvous technique. During design, another program may be invoked by use of a "Service Request" which requests the Operating System to activate the other program. This is identical to the rendezvous function in Ada.

Exception Handling - While the initial release of the tool will not fully support exception handling, an additional construct, Exception, will be added in a subsequent release to permit the forthright specification of exception handling during design.

Generic Definition - Through the Copy Command function, a predefined generic function can be moved into another part of the structure. The types for the pertinent data are then specified.

In addition, the Predefined Command function provides the capability to reuse specifications and high level design as well as complete systems.

TRENDS

The use of tools and software development environments will be the dominant theme in software engineering practice during the next decade. The employment of tools is not new; it has been the leadership of the Department of Defense in software engineering environments and the availability of inexpensive personal computers, fostering the introduction of software work stations, that have brought new initiative and innovation into the tools area. The software engineering environment, as previously stated, has created the focus for integrating all tools into a common environment, while the availability of inexpensive personal computers has motivated the concentration of development on automating specific procedures and practices to create individual automated tools. The general trend will be to flesh out the definition of the common software engineering environment with tools and methodologies while software work stations become more sophisticated. Sometime in the future these efforts will truly coincide, as it will be possible to host a full environment on a small personal "work station". At the moment, the DoD environment seems destined for a medium to large scale computers while the work station is presently being targeted for small to medium machines.

It is clear that the driving force in environments is the assimilation of all the assets of development into an integrated whole. The use of discrete tools, while still valuable, will diminish as they give way to tools that are integrated into an environment. We believe this means that tools must support a standard way of doing business; essentially the practice of software engineering as a generic methodology. That is, a common set of procedures and practices that define the practice of software engineering. In this way tools will have meaning to a large set of engineering practice.

SPACE II has been designed from the onset to support accepted software engineering practice instead of defining its own peculiar practice. While it provides a reasonable set of management and development aids, it can be embellished with additional features to enlarge its capability.

As an example SPACE II, can be extended in the software testing area with additional path testers. When a path tester is included additional capabilities can also be added. Another example of an enhancement would be a requirements matrix tool that could be used to automatically drive test documentation.

In all, there are numerous additions that can be incorporated into the tool to increase its value to the user whether he/she is a manager, developer, or support specialist.

SUMMARY

The approach that has been taken in developing SPACE II is to provide a tool that supports the entire life cycle and both the development and project management functions. The developers believe that the tool will fill a void in current tool availability. The tool has been designed to take into consideration current development practices and direction with respect to software engineering and management methodologies. SPACE II is neither a perfect nor exhaustive tool; it does, however, contain the basis for providing a full development and project manager's workbench through normal enhancements after its initial development period. The current development schedule calls for availability in mid 1986. The tool will be introduced through several Beta sites, and then offered to the general marketplace. As the DoD common software engineering environment evolves, the tool will be modified to retain compatibility with that environment.

BIBLIOGRAPHY

1. Structured Design, E. Yourdon and L. Constantine, Prentice-Hall, 1979.

2. Controlling Software Projects, T. DeMarco, Yourdon Press, 1982.

3. Software Engineering Economics, B. Boehm, Prentice-Hall, 1981.

4. Principles of Productive Software Management, M. Evans, P. Piazza, J. Dolkas, John Wiley & Sons, 1983.

ARTIFICIAL INTELLIGENCE AT THE FEDERAL RESERVE: AN EXPERT SYSTEM FOR MONETARY CONTROL

Robert T. Chang
Polytechnic Institute of New York

501 West 123rd Street
New York, New York 10027

Home: (212) 222-7773
Office: (212) 558-7373

Abstract

This paper describes a backward-chaining production rule system in which the concepts of monetary theory are used to formulate monetary policy.

Such an expert system would be an indispensible tool for a country which wants to control its money supply in order to maximize real economic growth.

An example of this expert system was written in PROLOG under the PDP-11 UNIX operating system. Its output is shown in the appendix of this paper.

Overview

Milton Friedman, the 1976 Nobel Prize Winner in Economics, recently said that the Federal Reserve Board, a group of seven men and women who regulate our nation's money supply, should be replaced by a computer which will have our money supply grow at a steady rate of two percent each year. In saying this, he was quite serious; rather than have these people respond to the jawboning of the President or of the members of Congress, he would much prefer a system free of political pressures which would allow the supply of money in our economy to grow at a slow but steady rate. In addition, the seven members of the Board are not necessarily the most qualified experts who could be chosen to undertake the responsibility of deciding monetary policy. Many of the most qualified economists would prefer to work in the more lucrative world of Wall Street and private industry.

One of the most important functions of the Federal Reserve Board and its subordinate Federal Reserve Banks is to control the money supply. The Board consists of seven Governors who must monitor, interpret, predict, and at times, change the money supply of the United States. The objective is to exercise money and credit policies which are designed for high production and price stability in the economy. Because control of the money supply is not a trivial matter, Congress has authorized the experts at the Federal Reserve to control the money supply. This paper will discuss how artificial intelligence can be used to control the money supply, or, at least, help the Fed control it.

Motivation

The use of expert systems in the control of the money supply is an ideal application because it involves several of the categories of knowledge engineering applications: interpretation, prediction, diagnosis, monitoring, repair, and control. Because the Governors of the Federal Reserve Board are appointed and are independent of the federal government, it is supposedly a non-political entity; this makes expert systems even more ideal for this type of application.

The wide swings in the levels of the money supply in recent years are an indication that the Federal Reserve Board is indecisive about monetary policy; it often cannot justify its actions. As a result, its credibility has been diminished. What is needed is an expert system which uses the knowledge of the leading economists, and either seeks a consensus or represents their different opinions. In any case, it must justify and explain its actions.

This paper will present a plan for an expert

system which will incorporate a number of ideas from existing expert systems used for other applications, and can be used to solve the problems of monetary control. I shall call this expert system MONETARIST, named after one who believes that monetary policy is the primary determinant of the level of economic activity. Note that the use of this type of expert system is not restricted to the United States. In fact, every country can make use of such a system because every country has a responsibility and an interest in regulating its own money supply in order to have an economy with reasonable price stability and one which lives up to its full production potentials.

Overview of Monetary Theory

Every day, the Fed Takes actions which increase, decrease, or stabilize the community's stock of money. One who is unfamiliar with monetary policy may wonder how and why this is done. First, the definition of the money supply must be given. A narrow definition of the money supply is the sum of paper currency, coin, and demand deposits (also known as checking accounts). A broader definition of the money supply would add on savings deposits. We do not include commodities such as gold or silver in our definition of the money supply in the United States because people usually do not pay for goods and services using these commodities. Also, the Fed has no control over the supply of gold and silver; such control is in the hands of silver- and gold-producing firms and countries such as South Africa.

Suppose high unemployment exists, factories are shut down, home-building is off, we're in a recession. The Fed's responsibility is to increase the money supply in order to achieve full employment and full production without inflation. It works as follows. A decreasing function known as liquidity preference describes interest rates as a function of the money supply. It is decreasing because when the supply of money increases, people have an easier time borrowing money, making interest rates decline. The function is also asymptotic, causing interest rates to change rapidly when the money supply is small. Also, changes in the money supply when it is large will not affect interest rates very much.

Another decreasing function known as the marginal efficiency of investment describes the level of investment as a function of interest rates. When interest rates drop, the attractiveness of borrowing money for investment rises; therefore, investment rises. This function is also asymptotic; therefore, investment expenditures will change rapidly when interest rates are low. They will not change much when interest rates are high.

Investment is one component of the gross national product. Therefore, an increase in investment will increase the gross national product, but it will increase it by a multiplied amount! Why is this so? It is because the gross national product is expressed in terms of dollars per year, but for each dollar spent on investment, the one who received that dollar will probably spend some percentage of it pretty soon within a year. The next person who receives that dollar will also probably spend part of it again within the same year, and so on and so on. The number of times a dollar is spent within a year is defined as the velocity of money.

What we see now is a composite function which relates the money supply to the gross national product. When the money supply rises, the gross national product will also rise. We have the following equation:

$$M \times V = GNP$$

where:

    M   = money supply (dollars)
    V   = velocity of money (times per year)
    GNP = gross national product (dollars per year)

From historical experience, velocity is relatively constant. Therefore, one may wonder why the Fed would ever decrease the money supply. It does so because of the following equation.

$$GNP = P \times Q$$

where:

    P = prices of goods (dollars per unit)
    Q = quantities of goods (units per year)

This gross national product is nominal. But economists want to maximize real gross national product, i.e. the gross national product assuming that prices did not change. When the economy is already at full employment and the money supply were to increase, then prices will rise. Why? At full employment, the economy can not produce any more goods (Q can not rise); therefore, an increase in M will increase P. So the Fed will contract the money supply to reduce inflation.

Tools of Monetary Policy

There are three basic tools of monetary policy: open-market operations, discount rate policy, and changing reserve requirements. These tools are used in different situations and for different purposes, with open-market operations being used most frequently, and changing reserve requirements being used least frequently.

Through open-market operations, the Fed buys or sells government securities. Such buying and selling is done every day, and how much is done is kept highly confidential. The names of the buyers and sellers themselves are also confidential. When the Fed wants to contract the money supply, it will sell government securities to the open market. Buyers write a check to the Fed, which will then debit the buyers' balances in their checking accounts; by definition, the money supply has been reduced. Conversely, in order to increase the money supply, the Fed will buy government securities; as a result, the sellers' bank accounts will get more money. This tool in monetary policy is the least drastic and provides for a steady change in the money supply.

When the Fed loans money to private banks at its discount window, it charges an interest rate known as the discount rate. The Fed can tighten up on the money supply by raising the discount rate, or loosen it by lowering the discount rate. Generally this action is used to reinforce the tool of open-market operations described earlier. Banks generally will not borrow from the Fed if they don't have to. But if the Fed tightens up the money supply by other means, bankers will be tempted to borrow from the Fed unless the discount rate has been raised.

The most infrequently used, but most drastic, monetary policy tool is to change the reserve requirement. The reserve requirement is the percentage of a bank's deposits which must be kept idle as reserves, i.e. it may not be loaned out to borrowers. By lowering the reserve requirement, the money supply is increased because banks can "create" more money by loaning it out. In other words, it sets up a checking account from which the borrower may withdraw the money. When the reserve requirement is increased, banks must call in their loans in order to satisfy the requirement. Borrowers will have to use up their checking accounts in order to pay back the loans. All of this must happen in a very short period of time. This is why the changing of reserve requirements is the most drastic tool of monetary policy.

Operational Environment and Principal Features of the Expert System

Presently, the Fed uses its computers to collect deposits data from financial institutions on a daily basis, and can compute the money supply accurately. Economists at the Fed look at this data, along with price indexes and business activity data in order to determine which monetary policy actions should be taken. Our expert system, MONETARIST, shall be designed to replace these economists, or at least, to interact with them in formulating the appropriate monetary policy actions.

MONETARIST will interpret the data it sees. For example, it will try to identify the cause of a change in the money supply. Since it knows the level of deposits and loans from every financial institution in the nation, it should be able to detect and identify the source(s) of the change.

MONETARIST will monitor money supply data to ensure that banks are maintaining correct reserve requirements, that there is no unusually excessive borrowing at the discount window by any particular bank, that there is no unusual change in interest rates since interest rates are closely related to the supply of money.

MONETARIST will attempt to predict levels of inflation and business activity given the historical data and different tools of monetary policy. It will explain and justify its reasoning for different scenarios.

MONETARIST will suggest various courses of action to take in order to correct outcomes which have not met expectations (e.g. too fast or too slow growth in the money supply).

Transfer of Expertise

One must realize that an expert system such as MONETARIST must deal with a problem which is not completely understood. Therefore, we may have a feature in our system which will formulate theories of its own and present them to the expert or to the user. The nature of this domain is very much similar to that of medicine. This is one reason why the transfer of expertise is especially important in such a system.

Not all experts, especially economists, agree on everything. Many fundamental things in economics, however, are accepted by most economists, such as liquidity preference, the marginal efficiency of investment, and the multiplier theory, all of which have been discussed earlier in this paper. MONETARIST should be able to recognize the points at which economists differ.

Ideally, MONETARIST will be able to interact with the expert in order to acquire and use new knowledge. In this process, MONETARIST may point out some phenomenon which contradicts rules given to it earlier. For example, the rule of liquidity preference may be contradicted by the fact that market interest rates rose shortly after the Fed announced that the money supply had sharply gone up. Clearly the phenomenon is counterintuitive because interest rates should drop if the availability of money is greater, and MONETARIST will point this out to the expert. The expert is aware that the market was fearing that the Fed would tighten up the money supply as a result of the announcement of the rise in the money supply. So the expert might add a rule indicating that changes in interest rates which occur shortly after Fed announcements are to be regarded as temporary aberrations.

Knowledge Representation

Many of these so-called "exception" cases occur in monetary policy; therefore, it is imperative to allow the user to be able to make changes or add onto the knowledge base easily. Even if economists were to present all of their knowledge to the system, new "exception" cases always pop up. One of the best ways to facilitate such incremental changes to a knowledge base is to represent the knowledge in the form of production rules. From the descriptions of monetary theory and monetary policy, we can devise some sample production rules (in English):

- If the money supply is increased AND velocity of money is held constant, then the nominal gross national product will increase. (tautology)

- If the Fed sells government securities, then the money supply will drop. (definition of money supply)

- If the money supply drops, then interest rates will increase. (liquidity preference)

- If interest rates increase, then investment will decrease. (marginal efficiency of investment)

- If investment decreases by x, then the gross national product will decrease by a multiplied level of x. (multiplier theory)

- If the economy is at the full-employment level AND the money supply is increased, then increased inflation will occur. (quantity theory of money)

- If excessive borrowing occurs at the discount window, then the discount rate does not reflect market interest rates. (theory of supply and demand)

It can be seen that these production rules facilitate a backward-chaining control structure which can help the system explain and justify its reasoning. This type of control structure and others will be discussed later in this paper. Before we discuss the production rule system in MONETARIST further, let us examine other possible representations of knowledge for a monetary policy application.

One possible knowledge representation method to be considered for this system could be the semantic network. In a semantic network, we have nodes representing various objects, and links representing the relationships between the nodes. This can be useful in representing the relationships between the money supply, interest rates, inflation, and the level of economic activity. But it appears to be very difficult to represent the so-called "exception" cases described earlier. In other words, semantic networks can easily relate the attributes of an object, but how does it represent its non-attributes (i.e. that which it's not)? In addition, it is questionable whether semantic networks can represent intangible things such as time lags among these relationships. Therefore, it probably is an infeasible method.

Logic is one popular method of representing knowledge in expert systems. Through the use of the predicate calculus and the propositional calculus, one can express certain things in a natural, but precise, manner. Unfortunately, for an expert system which must rely on inexact reasoning, heuristics, and uncertainty factors, logic does not seem to be a feasible method.

Many of the rules in monetary policy are not hard and fast rules. One must remember that economists almost always add the following caveat to their rules: ceteris paribus, i.e. all other relevant things, factors, or elements remain unaltered. For example, they would say, "all other things being equal, an increase in the money supply will lower interest rates." Only for a tautology would they not add this warning. For example, they would say, "the supply of money multiplied by the velocity of money equals the prices of goods and services multiplied by the quantities of goods and services; this arithmetic product also equals the gross national product."

Control Structure

The production rule system in MONETARIST should not and can not be a pure production rule system because of the uncertain nature of the application. In formulating monetary policy, there is never complete certainty that something will work, but there do exist probabilities, or as described in the expert system MYCIN, certainty factors. Unlike MYCIN, our expert system should implement standard statistical methods in the certainty factors because economists always use such methods in

their analyses. By incorporating findings from econometric studies, we would add a measure of objectivity to our expert system.

The control structure will be very similar to that of MYCIN. It will use a backward-chaining mechanism when examining the production rules, but it would also use the certainty factors to confirm various states along the way. This control structure also facilitates the system's ability to explain and justify its reasoning. MONETARIST will simply show the path it followed and display it to the user. There may be alternative paths which the user may want to see (since economists often differ on these matters). The expert who disagrees with the path which MONETARIST chose may wish to add to or change the knowledge base. The certainty factors probably should not be changeable by the user into subjective probabilities since they are meant to be obtained from standard objective statistical methods.

Let us examine an example of the backward-chaining control strategy which MONETARIST would use in order to diagnose and interpret an unfavorable economic situation. This is a very much simplified example which is intended only to illustrate the control strategy of this expert system. Suppose there was a resurgence of inflation, and economists wanted to find out from MONETARIST the cause for it:

Some rules might make use of the following tautology:

$$P \times Q = GNP$$

Note that GNP represents nominal gross national product, P represents prices, and Q represents quantity produced (which is the same as real gross national product). The following rules can come from this:

(a) If (nominal) gross national product increases AND quantity produced fails to increase, then inflation will occur.

(b) If (nominal) gross national product decreases AND quantity produced remains the same, then prices will drop.

We also have the following definition as a production rule:

(c) If investment spending increases, then (nominal) gross national product will increase.

Suppose we take rule (a) since its consequent is our goal: "inflation will occur." We look for another rule whose consequent is the antecedent of (a): "(nominal) gross national product increases AND quantity produced (or real gross national product) fails to increase."

We can see that the consequent of rule (c) satisifies one part of the antecedent of rule (a): "(nominal gross national product increases." We look for a rule whose consequent is the same as the antecedent of rule (c): "investment spending increases." We note the following rule which follows from the marginal efficiency of investment:

(d) If interest rates fall, then investment spending increases.

Since the consequent of rule (d) matches the antecedent of rule (c), we then look for a rule whose consequent is the same as the antecedent of rule (d): "interest rates fall." We note the following rule which follows from the theory of liquidity preference:

(e) If the money supply is increased, then interest rates will fall.

We now look for a rule whose consequent is the same as the antecedent of rule (e): "the money supply increases." Suppose there is no such rule; MONETARIST will then find out if the money supply actually did increase. If the expert system knows (from its monitoring activities) or it found out by asking the user that the money supply actually did increase, it will then proceed to look for a rule whose consequent is the same as the other part of the antecedent of rule (a): "quantity produced fails to increase." As explained earlier, this statement is equivalent to saying that the real gross national product fails to increase. We note the following rule which is a definition:

(f) If the economy is at full

employment, then the real gross national product will fail to increase.

MONETARIST will now look for a rule whose consequent is the same as part of the antecedent of rule (f): "the economy is at full employment." Suppose that no such rule exists; then it will try to find out if the economy really is at full employment. By examining its knowledge base of national income statistics or by asking the user, suppose it did determine that the economy is at full employment. MONETARIST will now be able to diagnose and interpret the cause of the inflation, and will be able to explain to the user its findings:

"Since there was a dramatic increase in the money supply, interest rates in the credit markets took a dive. The low interest rates encouraged business to substantially increase their level of investment which subsequently increased business activity. This increase in business activity made the nominal gross national product increase, but since the economy was already at full employment, real gross national product was not able to increase at all. An upward pressure on prices occurred, which resulted in renewed inflation."

As one can see, the backward-chaining control strategy provides a straightforward mechanism for explanation and justification of the expert system's reasoning. This diagnosis of an economic problem would be only one of MONETARIST'S many activities. Ideally, we could also provide it with prediction and repair capabilities.

Conclusion

It is clear that an expert system can facilitate control of the money supply by using many of the same methods as those used in existing expert systems for other applications. However, it is unfortunate that experts in this field disagree on a number of things, and it is unclear how MONETARIST should handle the differing points of view. Nevertheless, such a system should be able to justify its actions and perhaps return credibility to the Federal Reserve. As we have seen, a backward-chaining control strategy is an ideal method for this type of application which would make the expert system an indispensible tool for those who want to control a nation's money supply.

References

[1] Barr, A., and Feigenbaum, E.A., 1981. The Handbook of Artificial Intelligence, Volume I, William Kaufman, Inc.

[2] Barr, A., and Feigenbaum, E.A., 1981. The Handbook of Artificial Intelligence, Volume II, William Kaufman, Inc.

[3] Hayes-Roth, F., Waterman, D.A., and Lenat, D.B., 1983. Building Expert Systems, Addison-Wesley Publishing Company, Inc.

[4] Nilsson, N.J., 1980. Principles of Artificial Intelligence, Tioga Publishing Company.

[5] Winston, P.H., 1977, Artificial Intelligence, Addison-Wesley Publishing Company, Inc.

APPENDIX:
Sample PROLOG Runs on the PDP-11 UNIX System

The following sample PROLOG runs of the expert system illustrate different economic situations: an inflationary economy, an inflationary economy despite tight monetary policy, and a depressed economy despite loose monetary policy.

Generally, the goals of monetary policy are to increase the real GNP and decrease the inflation rate. Certain goals, such as reducing the interest rate, are of particular interest to politicians.

The expert system receives questions concerning these goals and will advise the user of the appropriate monetary policy measures which should be taken. Note that the user's comments are indicated as follows:

/* This is a comment */

The accompanying comments should help to explain the thinking process of the user as he interacts with the expert system.

Computer output and user input can be distinguished via the different fonts as follows:

Computer output has this font.

User input has this font.

SAMPLE RUN FOR AN INFLATIONARY ECONOMY

```
$ cat inflat.pro
current_policy(open_market,moderate).
current_policy(discount_rate,moderate).
current_policy(reserve_requirements,moderate).
current_level(gnp,high).
current_level(investment,high).
current_level(interest_rates,moderate).
current_level(money_supply,low).
$ prolog
PROLOG Version NU7.1
?- consult('inflat.pro').  /* Load conditions */
yes
?- consult('fed.pro').    /* Load expert system */
yes
?- inflation_rate(decrease,X).
                    /* How can I decrease inflation? */
** (top) PROVED :
    inflation_rate(decrease,policy(_54,tighten)) ?
yes
?-  /* O.K. I can decrease inflation by */
    /* tightening monetary policy      */
inflation_rate(decrease,X),
    /* Can I decrease inflation, and */
real_gnp(increase,X).
    /* increase real GNP at the same time? */
no
?- real_gnp(increase,X).
    /* What about just increase real GNP? */
no
?- inflation_rate(decrease,X),
    /* Can I decrease inflation, and */
real_gnp(stable,X).
    /* at least keep real GNP stable? */
** (top) PROVED :
    inflation_rate(decrease,policy(_72,tighten)),
    real_gnp(stable,policy(_72,tighten)) ?
yes
?- real_gnp(decrease,X).
    /* But can real GNP go down? */
no
?-
```

SAMPLE RUN FOR AN INFLATIONARY ECONOMY DESPITE TIGHT MONETARY POLICY

```
$ cat tight.pro
current_policy(open_market,tight).
current_policy(discount_rate,tight).
current_policy(reserve_requirements,tight).
current_level(gnp,high).
current_level(investment,high).
current_level(interest_rates,high).
current_level(money_supply,low).
$ prolog
PROLOG Version NU7.1
?- consult('tight.pro').   /* Load conditions */
yes
?- consult('fed.pro').     /* Load expert system */
yes
?- inflation_rate(decrease,X).
       /* How can I decrease the inflation rate? */
** (top) PROVED :
    inflation_rate(decrease,
          policy(reserve_requirements,tighten)) ;
    inflation_rate(decrease,
          policy(reserve_requirements,no_change))
?-   /* O.K.  I should either tighten or not change */
     /* the already tight reserve requirements    */
inflation_rate(decrease,X),
     /* Can I decrease the inflation rate, and */
real_gnp(increase,X).
     /* increase the real GNP at the same time? */
no
?- real_gnp(increase,X).
     /* Can I just increase the real GNP? */
no
?- inflation_rate(decrease,X),
     /* Can I decrease the inflation rate, and */
interest_rates(decrease,X).
     /* lower interest rates at the same time? */
** (top) PROVED: inflation_rate(decrease,policy(
               reserve_requirements,no_change)),
               interest_rates(decrease,policy(
               reserve_requirements,no_change))
?- inflation_rate(decrease,X),
     /* Can I decrease the inflation rate, and */
interest_rates(stable,X).
     /* just keep interest rates stable? */
** (top) PROVED: inflation_rate(decrease,policy(
               reserve_requirements,tighten)),
               interest_rates(decrease,policy(
               reserve_requirements,tighten))
?-   /* I should tighten reserve requirements. */
```

SAMPLE RUN FOR A DEPRESSED ECONOMY DESPITE LOOSE MONETARY POLICY

```
$ cat loose.pro
current_policy(open_market,loose).
current_policy(discount_rate,loose).
current_policy(reserve_requirements,loose).
current_level(gnp,low).
current_level(investment,low).
current_level(interest_rates,low).
current_level(money_supply,high).
$ prolog
PROLOG Version NU7.1
?- consult('loose.pro').   /* Load conditions */
yes
?- consult('fed.pro').     /* Load expert system */
yes
?- real_gnp(increase,X).
       /* How can I increase the real GNP? */
** (top) PROVED: real_gnp(increase,policy(
          discount_rate,loosen)) ;
** (top) PROVED: real_gnp(increase,policy(
          discount_rate,no_change)) ;
** (top) PROVED: real_gnp(increase,policy(
          reserve_requirements,loosen)) ;
** (top) PROVED: real_gnp(increase,policy(
          reserve_requirements,no_change)) ;
?-   /* O.K. I can do it by not tightening the */
     /* already loose discount rate and        */
     /* reserve requirements.                  */
real_gnp(increase,X),
     /* Can I increase the real GNP, and */
inflation_rate(decrease,X).
     /* lower the inflation rate at the same time? */
no
?- real_gnp(increase,X),
     /* Can I increase the real GNP, and */
inflation_rate(stable,X).
     /* at least keep the inflation rate stable? */
** (top) PROVED:
    real_gnp(increase,
          policy(discount_rate,loosen)),
    inflation_rate(stable,
          policy(discount_rate,loosen))
?-   /* Great!  I can simply loosen (lower) the */
     /* discount rate in order to increase the  */
     /* real GNP and keep the inflation rate    */
     /* stable at the same time.                */
```

64

DA VINCI: AN EXTENDIBLE KNOWLEDGE-BASED
SOFTWARE TOOL FOR GRAPHICS

R. P. Frail
R. S. Freedman

Software Systems Laboratory
Hazeltine Corporation
Greenlawn, NY 11740
516 261-7000

ABSTRACT

In our paper, we describe a general-purpose paint system, called Da Vinci, that was developed in the Hazeltine Corporation Software Systems Laboratory. Da Vinci evolved from an immediate need for a paint system that could be used in a powerful interactive Lisp programming environment. From the user's view, Da Vinci "knows" about brushes, paint textures, and shapes. In this perspective, Da Vinci is similar to other paint systems (e.g., Mac Paint) or graphics editors. From the implementor's view, however, Da Vinci is a good example of a software tool that was rapidly prototyped using knowledge-based technology. Da Vinci is easily extendible because of the knowledge-based representation of its graphics knowledge in terms of frames and message-passing objects.

THE PROBLEM

Computer-generated graphics show up in a large range of applications because of the increasing sophistication of today's graphics production systems[1]. This sophistication allows the relatively rapid creation of graphics that are either impossible or too time consuming to produce using conventional graphic arts. Another advantage that computer-generated graphics have over conventionally generated graphics is that they can be stored on-line.

Applications of computer-generated graphics include video animations, graphics for computer-based training lessons, mathematical function plotting, business graphs, 35-millimeter slide reproduction for audio-visual presentations, and hard-copy reproduction for the printed medium.

The problem for graphics tool implementors is to provide the user--especially the casual user--a means of easily generating these application graphics. Part of the problem is to overcome the computer's (somewhat deserved) reputation for being intimidating or difficult to use. If a powerful graphics tool is to attract a large following, its operation and capabilities must be relatively easy to understand.

Additional design requirements of our particular graphics tool were that it be developed very rapidly and be easily extendible, without compromising its user operability.

DA VINCI: AN EXTENDIBLE GRAPHICS TOOL

Da Vinci is a general-purpose graphics editing tool recently developed in the Hazeltine Corporation Software Systems Laboratory. It allows its users to create and modify black-and-white graphics in a powerful, interactive, Lisp programming environment.

We developed Da Vinci because we needed to create graphics quickly. The graphics were to be used to test a graphics-based generator of instrument panel simulations. Da Vinci was prototyped in three weeks. Its initial command set included many commands common to other paint systems: commands to draw freehand with a variety of "brushes," commands to create geometrical shapes, and commands to store graphics on disk. Da Vinci's command set has grown beyond the initial one in response to new functional requirements.

Da Vinci satisfied the need to easily and rapidly create graphics largely through its human-machine interface. In general, contemporary human-machine communication is based on the concept of a virtual window; the machine provides a figurative window through which the user can view and relate to some aspects of the machine's environment. Multiple-window interfaces allow a relatively higher degree of productivity because of the great ease with which users can shift between and relate to different views of the computing environment.

Window-oriented operations are often mechanized by a device called a mouse.

A mouse is an electronic pointing aid; moving the mouse across a flat surface causes a pointer on the CRT to move correspondingly. The human clicks a button on the mouse to get the machine's attention. By pointing and clicking, the human uses the mouse to focus the machine's attention on a specific view of the computing environment or on some information within a view. This eliminates much keyboard entry and speeds up the human-machine interaction. Window and mouse complement each other nicely; the machine talks to the human via windows, the human talks to the machine via mouse.

The window-and-mouse-based interface represents one of the more significant steps in bringing the human-machine communication level closer to the level of the human. Indeed, much work in knowledge-based systems can be thought of as an attempt to narrow the human-machine communication gap.

Da Vinci provides effective human-machine communication based on the window-and-mouse interface. Da Vinci appears to the user as a "window frame" filling the entire CRT screen. This window frame is divided into three horizontal "window panes" (see figure 1). Each pane defines an interface for specific kinds of information (e.g., textual, graphical, input, output). We were naturally led to this window-pane concept when we realized that Da Vinci's communication knowledge could be factored into conceptually independent categories based on functional requirements (e.g., graphical input, textual

output). Inter-pane communication is provided through a shared input-output (I/O) buffer, thus forming an integrated wholistic interface. The division of the frame by the functional requirements of the interfaces means that at any given moment, the user can easily associate his focus of attention with the particular method of communication that is required-- the user knows how to talk to the machine based on where she/he is within the frame.

The upper (and largest) pane is called the canvas pane. It is both an input and output interface for graphical information. It is the area on which graphics are either drawn freehand with the mouse, or displayed and manipulated as the result of the execution of a command.

The middle pane in the Da Vinci window frame contains a command menu that constitutes an input interface for text. Most of the comments of the Da Vinci vocabulary are listed in mouse-selectable form. Following each command, a character is listed in parenthesis that indicates how to actuate that particular command via the keyboard.

The lower Da Vinci pane is called the query pane. This is an input and output interface for text. Here, supplementary command information is solicited from the user (e.g., file names, angles of rotation, scale factors, text strings). Da Vinci also displays status messages here. The query pane can also be used as an entry point for interaction with the rest of the programming environment.

Figure 1. How Da Vinci Appears to the User

66

Da Vinci's current command set can be roughly divided into two areas: those dealing with the creation and modification of graphics, and those dealing with the input and output of graphics.

Commands to create basic variable-sized geometric shapes (e.g., circles, squares) are invoked by a simple mouse button click. These same geometric shapes can be created by selecting a "brush" function with which to paint freehand on the CRT screen. Another mouse button click allows menu selection of the brush parameters (size, shape, bit-map logic). Mouse button clicks are also used to create a large variety of shade patterns.

There are a variety of commands that perform some action to graphics already displayed on the canvas. For example, the transform command employs an optimized, output-driven transformation algorithm that can rotate a graphic about any point on the canvas and simultaneously scale it in either one or two dimensions. Copy and Move commands control the placement of a graphic on the canvas. There are also line-drawing and rectangle-drawing commands. A text command allows the placement of text in a variety of selectable fonts.

The Da Vinci input/output functions allow users to retrieve previously constructed graphics and store their creations either within the existing environment or on disk. Da Vinci also provides a number of "auxiliary canvases" to hold temporary and intermediate graphic constructions. These canvases are separate from the canvas pane itself but, at any given time, there is always one auxiliary canvas associated with the canvas pane. This is called the "current canvas." Commands are provided to change the current canvas and transfer the contents of the canvas pane to the current canvas, and vice versa. The canvases are convenient as graphical breadboards--component constructions can be stored on auxiliary canvases, then combined to form more complicated pictures.

It takes less than an hour for someone with no computer programming background to learn the use of all Da Vinci commands.

SAMPLE GRAPHIC CONSTRUCTION SESSION

In the paragraphs below, we demonstrate typical steps in the construction of a graphic representing an analog voltage meter. This construction illustrates uses for many of the Da Vinci commands.

Figure 2 depicts two concentric circles, the inner one filled. These were created by the Circle command. These will form part of the outline of the meter face.

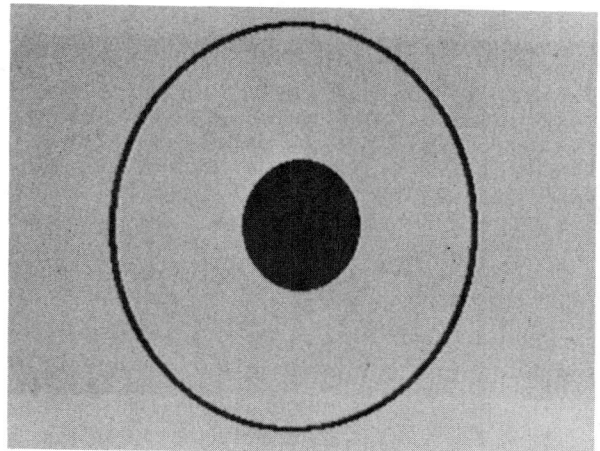

Figure 2. Concentric Circles

Figure 3 shows three line segments, constructed on a different portion of the canvas pane. The middle segment, created by the Rectangle command, was copied twice using the Copy command. The left and right segments were then formed by rotating these copies by 315 and 45 degrees, respectively, using the Transform command. These outer line segments will form two of the boundaries of the meter face.

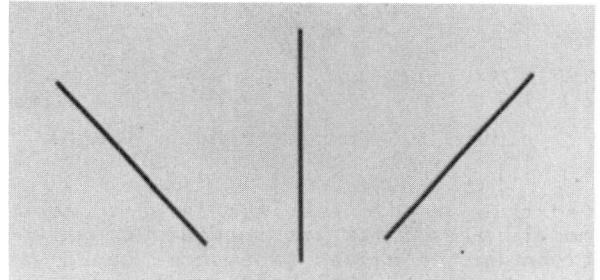

Figure 3. Boundary Segments

Figure 4 shows a blank meter face built from the previous constructions. The Copy command was used to place the boundary segments of figure 3 at the desired locations within the concentric circles of figure 2. The Erase command was then used to remove the unwanted circle portions.

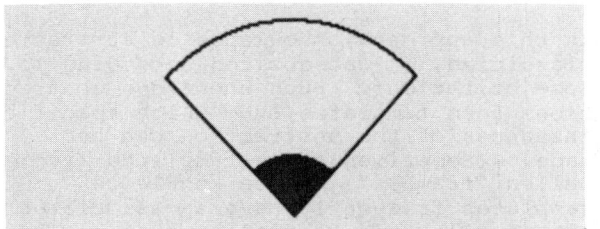

Figure 4. Blank Meter Face

Next, we place a scale (from 0 to 100) on the meter face. The numbers 0, 50, and 100 are placed on yet another part of the canvas, in the desired font, using the Text command. The numbers 0 and 100 are rotated by 315 and 45 degrees, respectively, as were the line segments. The numbers are depicted in figure 5.

84L0611

Figure 5. Numbers for Meter Face

We then copy the numbers, one at a time, to their proper positions and add a pointer, resulting in the completed meter shown in figure 6. Satisfied with our work, we use the Write command to copy this graphic to the disk.

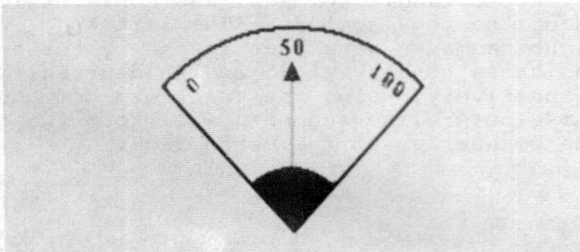

84L0603

Figure 6. Completed Meter Graphic

Had this graphic been too large to accommodate all of its intermediate constructions on the canvas pane, some could have been stored on the auxiliary canvases. The meter face graphic takes a novice Da Vinci user about 15 minutes to construct.

DA VINCI ARCHITECTURE

Da Vinci is constructed in a modular fashion to facilitate easy extension of its command repertoire. Da Vinci's modularity is achieved by a knowledge-based programming approach that emphasizes the application of several knowledge representation techniques.

In this approach, knowledge is abstracted, classified, or categorized according to some criterion[2]. Such knowledge abstractions form templates from which specific instances of the abstraction can be made. (Sometimes these templates are called "frames.") These knowledge templates frequently have an associated set of allowable operations that may be performed on specific instances.

One example of this knowledge abstraction is the classification of numbers into real, complex, and integer; each with its own set of instances, and each with its own set of allowable operations.

Sometimes the set of allowable operations includes an operation that allows instances to communicate with each other by sending and receiving messages. In this case, this knowledge representation scheme is frequently called "object-oriented" and the specific instances are called "objects."

The knowledge-based programming representations of frames and objects provide a highly modular way of representing knowledge in Da Vinci because knowledge can be encapsulated to a high degree. Changes in the content of the knowledge do not propagate unexpectedly throughout the system.

Our knowledge-based programming representations also accommodate the integration of other component representations to form hybrids. Knowledge bases built on hybrid representations also limit the unexpected propagation of changes. For example, an object can be an abstraction represented with rules, frames, and even other objects. Changes are relatively easier to manage because of the more clearly defined interfaces naturally resulting from the employment of different knowledge representations.

In Da Vinci, the canvas is represented as an object that understands messages (operations) about drawing and graphics. These messages are the Da Vinci commands; each command corresponds to one message.

The overall system architecture of Da Vinci consists of just two main components--pictured in figure 7--the message dispatcher, and the canvas. The message dispatcher receives user input, one character at a time, via either the keyboard or command menu. The message dispatcher then sends the message associated with that character to the canvas. The user is warned when there is no message corresponding to the character he has entered.

However, knowledge of how to execute commands is not represented in the canvas. This knowledge is distributed in the messages, rather than centralized in a single knowledge base. The factoring of graphical knowledge into messages is based on command function. For each command, there is a corresponding message. The message for a particular command acquires from the user any necessary supplementary information and performs the desired function

USER INPUT

CHARACTERS

MESSAGE DISPATCHER

MESSAGES

CANVAS

8504013

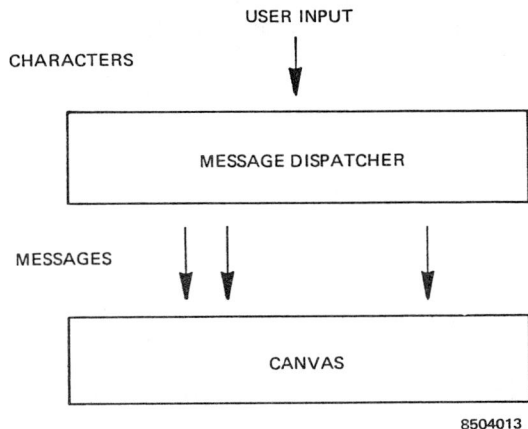

Figure 7. Da Vinci's Data Flow--
A Message-Passing Architecture

(painting, transformation, input-output, etc). The message is the means by which the user communicates his ideas to the canvas. In short, the message is the medium.

Because all command knowledge is encapsulated within individual independent messages, new commands are easily installed and tested (it takes about 5 minutes to install a new command in Da Vinci). This enabled very rapid prototyping of Da Vinci during the first few weeks of its evolution.

A SAMPLE EXTENSION: A HIGH-LEVEL I/O FACILITY

We recently installed a High-Level I/O Facility (HLIOF) in Da Vinci, listed on the command menu as "Edit Object (O)." One application of the HLIOF is in device simulation[3], where large numbers of graphics (corresponding to different states of a device) must be conveniently referenced.

The HLIOF provides the user with a high-level, interactive way of making an association between the graphics of a simulated device and the different state values of the device. As a simple example, if the user wishes to simulate a two-position toggle switch, he uses Da Vinci to create two graphics: one of the switch in its on position, and one of the switch in its off position. He then invokes the HLIOF to provide names with which to reference the graphics. The HLIOF encapsulates this device knowledge and solicits a name for the device. It then infers a file name from the device name and stores the "device" on disk. The author provides what is minimally required; he need not concern himself with the details of file naming or knowledge

representation. This "device" is the output of the HLIFO. It is actually a frame-based representation of the knowledge needed to create any number of instances of a particular device.

SUMMARY

We have described a paint system for the production of two-dimensional graphics for a variety of applications. From the user's point of view, the functionality of Da Vinci is not much different from paint systems that are commercially available for use on personal computers. Those systems usually have a mouse-driven user interface.

From the implementor's point of view, however, Da Vinci is easily extendible because of the knowledge-based representation of its graphics knowledge in terms of frames and message-passing objects. The resulting modularity allows the addition of new commands with a minimal amount of programming effort.

Commands under current development include a canvas magnifier. This command would create a "magnifying glass" with which to magnify a selected portion of the canvas to a selectable degree. The mouse would control the screen placement of the magnified portion of the pixel level and would also control editing the contents of that portion.

Also under development is a command to provide continuously varying shading within an enclosed area. User-supplied parameters would include a starting shade density and a finishing shade density.

Da Vinci represents a successful application of knowledge-based, object-oriented programming techniques, developed under a rapid prototyping regime. It provides implementors with an easy way to maintain and add to their system. This facility has been achieved without sacrificing ease of user operability.

ACKNOWLEDGEMENTS

We would like to thank various persons from the Software Systems Laboratory for their support: W. Wagner for suggesting the transformation algorithm used in Da Vinci, W. F. Griese for his encouragement, and J. P. Rosenking for his helpful critiques.

REFERENCES

[1] C. C. Cortes, "The Vital Statistics on Major Paint Systems," Computer Pictures, Volume 2, Number 4 July/ August 1984.

[2] R. S. Freedman, "The Common Sense of
     Object Oriented Languages," Computer
     Design, February 1983.

[3] J. P. Rosenking and R. S. Freedman,
     "OBIE-1: A Knowledge-Based Tool for
     Simulation," (These Proceedings).

Session 3

Program Testing and Configuration Management Tools

Chairman
Gary Cort
Los Alamos National Laboratory

ASSET : A SYSTEM TO SELECT AND EVALUATE TESTS

Phyllis G. Frankl, Stewart N. Weiss and Elaine J. Weyuker

Department of Computer Science, Courant Institute of Mathematical Sciences
New York University

Abstract

This paper describes ASSET, a tool which uses information about a program's data flow to aid in selecting test data for the program and to evaluate test data adequacy. ASSET is based on the family of data flow test selection and test data adequacy criteria developed by Rapps and Weyuker. ASSET accepts as input a program written in a subset of Pascal, a set of test data, and one of the data flow adequacy criteria and indicates to what extent the criterion has been satisfied by the test data.

1. Introduction

The selection of test data and evaluation of its adequacy are among software engineering's most important problems today. We have designed and implemented a tool, called ASSET, which uses data flow information to aid in the selection and evaluation of test data for programs written in a small subset of Pascal. It can also be used to aid in debugging and to detect data flow anomalies. We intend to use this tool as a prototype for one which performs these functions on programs written in Pascal.

The goal of testing is to detect errors. The program is run on a subset of its input domain, and the output is compared to the expected result. We will assume the availability of an "oracle" which can determine whether or not a given input-output pair is correct. If the test data set has been carefully selected, then its failure to expose errors should increase one's confidence that the program behaves according to its specification. Since nothing short of exhaustive testing, which is usually infeasible, can guarantee that the program is correct, research in testing aims at finding methods of producing test sets which are small enough to be useful in practice, yet which are likely to expose existing errors.

There are two aspects to this problem: the selection of test data and the evaluation of test data adequacy. A *test data selection method* is a procedure for choosing elements to include in the test set. An *adequacy criterion* is a rule used to determine whether "enough" testing has been done.

Several sources of information are available for use in test data selection and in adequacy determinations, the most important being the program text and the specification. Those methods which are based on the program text are called *program-based* and those based on the specification are called *specification-based*. Program-based methods have the advantage of being more amenable to automation.

A number of program-based test data selection methods and adequacy criteria have been proposed and tools to implement them have been built. These include statement testing, branch testing, and path testing [2,3,4,6,13]. All of these are based on control flow. They are based on the idea that one cannot have much confidence that the program is correct if some statement, branch, etc. has not been executed by any test data.

Rapps and Weyuker [9,10] have proposed a family of test data selection and adequacy criteria which are based on data flow analysis. Similar criteria were proposed in [5] and [7]. The intuition motivating these criteria is that one cannot have much confidence that the program is correct if the result of some variable definition has never been used during testing. These criteria are program-based and have been shown to be more powerful than branch testing.

ASSET determines whether a given test set adequately tests a given program with respect to the test data adequacy criteria defined in [9,10]. In section two we summarize this theory. Section three describes the design and implementation of ASSET. Section four presents a number of applications. An example is given in section five.

2. Data Flow Testing

A family of test data selection criteria, each based on the program's data flow characteristics, was defined in [9] and [10] for a very simple universal programming language consisting of assignment statements, conditional and unconditional transfer statements, and input and output statements. This language has the same structure and semantics as the subset of Pascal accepted by ASSET (see figure 1.) We now present a summary of the terminology used.

A program can be uniquely decomposed into a set of disjoint *blocks* of ordered statements having the property that whenever the first statement of the block is executed, the other statements are executed in the given order. Furthermore, the first statement of the block is the only statement which may be executed directly after the execution of a statement in another block. Intuitively, a block is a chunk of code which is always executed as a unit. The program is represented by a *program graph* in which the nodes correspond to the blocks of the program, and edges indicate possible flow of control between blocks. The node corresponding to the block containing

```
<program>        ::= <program heading>;
                     <label declaration part>;
                     <variable declaration part>;
                     begin <stmt>{;<stmt>} end.

<stmt>           ::= [<label>:]<simple stmt>

<simple stmt>    ::= <assignment stmt>
                   | <conditional transfer stmt>
                   | <unconditional transfer stmt>
                   | <input stmt>
                   | <output stmt>

<assignment stmt>
                 ::= <identifier> := <expression>

<conditional tranfer stmt>
                 ::= if <expression> then goto <label>

<unconditional transfer stmt>
                 ::= goto <label>

<input stmt>     ::= read [(<identlist>)]
                   | readln [(<identlist>)]

<output stmt>    ::= write [(<exprlist>)]
                   | writeln [(<exprlist>)]

<identlist>      ::= <identifier> [,<identlist>]

<exprlist>       ::= <expression> [,<exprlist>]

where
    <program heading>, <label declaration part>,
    <variable declaration part>, <label>,
    <identifier>, and <expression>
are defined as in Pascal.
```

Figure 1

the first statement in the program is the *entry node* and any node having no successors is an *exit node*.

The test data selection criteria are based on the ways in which values are associated with variables, and how these associations can affect the execution of the program. This analysis focuses on the occurrences of variables within the program.

Data flow analysis was originally used for compiler optimization, and generally classifies each variable occurrence as being either a definition or a use [1, 11]. We distinguish between two substantially different types of uses. The first type directly affects the computation being performed or allows one to see the result of some earlier definition. We call such a use a computation use or a *c-use*. Of course, a c-use may indirectly affect the flow of control through the program.

In contrast, the second type of use directly affects the flow of control through the program, and thereby may indirectly affect the computations performed. We call such a use a predicate use or *p-use*. Occurrences of variables in the language's statements are thus classified as follows:

1) The assignment statement "y := <expression>" where the variables $x_1, \ldots, x_n$ occur in the expression on the right-hand side contains c-uses of $x_1, \ldots, x_n$ followed by a definition of y.

2) The input statement " read $(x_1, \ldots, x_n)$" contains definitions of $x_1, \ldots, x_n$

3) The output statement " write $(x_1, \ldots, x_n)$" contains c-uses of $x_1, \ldots, x_n$

4) The conditional transfer statement "if <expression> then goto <label>", where the variables $x_1, \ldots, x_n$ occur in the expression, contains p-uses of $x_1, \ldots, x_n$

We say that a node of a program graph contains a c-use or a definition of a variable if there is a statement in the corresponding block containing, respectively, a c-use or a definition of that variable.

Since we are interested in tracing the flow of data *between* nodes, any definition which is used *only* within the node in which that definition occurs is of little importance to us. We thus make the following distinction: a c-use of a variable x is a *global c-use* provided there is no definition of x preceding the c-use within the block in which it occurs. That is, the value of x must have been assigned in some block other than the one in which it is being used. Otherwise it is a *local c-use*. Global c-uses are often called locally exposed uses in the data flow analysis literature [1].

A conditional transfer statement can only occur as the last statement of a block. It has two executional successors, which are always in two different blocks. Since the values of the variables occurring in the predicate portion of the conditional transfer statement directly determine which of these two blocks is to be executed next, we associate p-uses with edges rather than with the node in which the predicate portion occurs. If the final statement of the block corresponding to node i is " if <expression> then goto <label>", where the variables $x_1, \ldots, x_n$ occur in the expression, and the two successors of node i are nodes j and k, then we will say that edges (i,j) and (i,k) contain p-uses of $x_1, \ldots, x_n$. Note that since p-uses are associated with edges, no distinction need be made between local and global p-uses.

Let x be a variable occurring in a program. A path $(i,n_1,\ldots,n_m,j)$, m≥0, containing no definitions of x in nodes $n_1,\ldots,n_m$ is called a *definition clear path with respect to (wrt)* x from node i to node j and from node i to edge (n_m,j). A definition of a variable x in node i is a *non-local definition* if it is the last definition of x occurring in the block associated with node i. It is a *global definition* if it is a non-local definition and there is a definition clear path wrt x from i to either a node containing a global c-use of x or an edge containing a p-use of x. Thus, a global definition assigns a value to a variable which can be used outside the node in which the definition occurs. A definition which is non-local but not global can never be used; if the program contains any such definitions, it should be examined for possible error.

We now define several sets which will be needed below (see figure 2.) The *def-use* graph is obtained from the program graph by associating a set with each edge and two sets with each node. *p-use(i,j)* is the set of variables for which edge (i,j) contains a p-use. *def(i)* is the set of variables for which node i contains a non-local definition. *c-use(i)* is the set of variables for which node i contains a global c-use. Let i be a node and let x ∈ def(i).

```
V         = {variables}
N         = {nodes}
E         = {edges}
def(i)    = {x ∈ V | x has a non-local
                     definition in block i}

c-use(i)  = {x ∈ V | x has a global c-use in block i}

p-use(i,j) = {x ∈ V | x has a p-use in edge (i,j) }

dcu(x,i)  = {j ∈ N | x ∈ c-use(j) and there
                     is a def-clear path from i to j}

dpu(x,i)  = {(j,k) ∈ E | x ∈ p-use(j,k) and there is
                     a def-clear path from i to (j,k) }
```

Figure 2

Then $dcu(x,i)$ is the set of all nodes j such that x has a global c-use in node j, and for which there is a definition clear path wrt x from i to j; $dpu(x,i)$ is the set of all edges (j,k) such that (j,k) contains a p-use of x, and for which there is a definition clear path wrt x from i to j.

We now informally introduce the family of path selection criteria which are formally defined in [9] and [10]. Let G be a program graph, and P be a set of paths from the unique entry node of G to the unique exit node of G. We say that P is *executed* if every path contained in P is traversed during the course of executing the program on a set of test data. Then:

- P satisfies the **all-nodes** criterion if every node of G is included in some path of P.

- P satisfies the **all-edges** criterion if every edge of G is included in some path of P.

- P satisfies the **all-definitions** criterion if for every node i of G and every x which has a global definition in i, P includes a definition clear path wrt x from i to some element of dcu(x,i) or dpu(x,i). That is, every global definition must be used.

- P satisfies the **all-p-uses** criterion if for every node i and every x which has a global definition in i, P includes definition clear paths wrt x from i to each element of dpu(x,i). That is, P includes a path from every global definition to each of its potential p-uses.

- P satisfies the **all-c-uses/some-p-uses** criterion if for every node i and every x which has a global definition in i, P includes some definition clear path wrt x from i to every node in dcu(x,i); if dcu(x,i) is empty, then P must include a definition clear path wrt x from i to some edge contained in dpu(x,i). This criterion requires that every global c-use of a variable x globally defined in node i must be included in some path of P. If there is no such c-use, then some p-use of the definition of x in i must be included.

- P satisfies the **all-p-uses/some-c-uses** criterion if for every node i and every x which has a global definition in i, P includes some definition clear path wrt x from i to every edge in dpu(x,i); if dpu(x,i) is empty, then P must include a definition clear path wrt x from i to some node contained in dcu(x,i). That is, every p-use of each variable x globally defined in node i must be included in some path of P. If there is no such p-use, then some global c-use of the definition of x in i must

be included.

- P satisfies the **all-uses** criterion if for every node i and every x which has a global definition in i, P includes definition clear paths wrt x from i to each element of dcu(x,i) and to each element of dpu(x,i). Thus, P must include a path from every global definition to each of its uses.

- A *simple path* is one in which all nodes, except possibly the first and last, are distinct. A *loop-free path* is one in which all nodes, are distinct. A path $(n_1,...,n_j,n_k)$ is a *du-path* with respect to a variable x if n_1 has a global definition of x and either

    i) n_k has a c-use of x and $(n_1,...,n_j,n_k)$ is a def-clear simple path with respect to x

    or

    ii) (n_j,n_k) has a p-use of x and $(n_1,...,n_j)$ is a def-clear loop-free path with respect to x.

  P satisfies the **all-du-paths** criterion if for every node i and every x which has a global definition in i, P includes every du-path wrt x. Thus, if there are multiple du-paths from a global definition to a given use, they must all be included in paths of P.

- A *complete path* is a path $(n_1,...,n_m)$ such that n_1 is the entry node and n_m is an exit node. P satisfies the **all-paths** criterion if P includes every complete path of G. Note that programs which are represented by graphs containing loops may contain infinitely many complete paths.

We call the criteria all-definitions, all-p-uses, all-c-uses/some-p-uses, all-p-uses/some-c-uses, all-uses, and all-du-paths *data flow criteria*.

We say that criterion c_1 *includes* criterion c_2 if for every program graph G, any set of paths from the entry node of G to the exit node of G that satisfies c_1, also satisfies c_2. We say that c_1 *strictly includes* c_2, denoted $c_1 => c_2$ provided that c_1 includes c_2, and for some G there is a set of paths of G that satisfies c_2 but not c_1. The following is proved in [9]:

Theorem:

The family of criteria is partially ordered by strict inclusion as shown in figure 3. Furthermore, criterion c_i strictly includes criterion c_j, if and only if it is explicitly shown to be so in figure 3 or follows from the transitivity of the relationship.

3. Design and Implementation of ASSET

ASSET takes as input a program called the subject program, written in the subset of Pascal described above, one of the data flow adequacy criteria, and a set of test data. It is assumed that the program is syntactically correct and that

i)   If L is the target of some goto then there is exactly one labeled statement with label L.

ii) All transfers are effective, i.e. a statement **goto** L cannot immediately physically precede the statement labeled L.

iii) There are no syntactically endless loops, i.e. on every path $(n_1,...,n_k,n_1)$ there is some block containing a conditional transfer to a block which is not on the path.

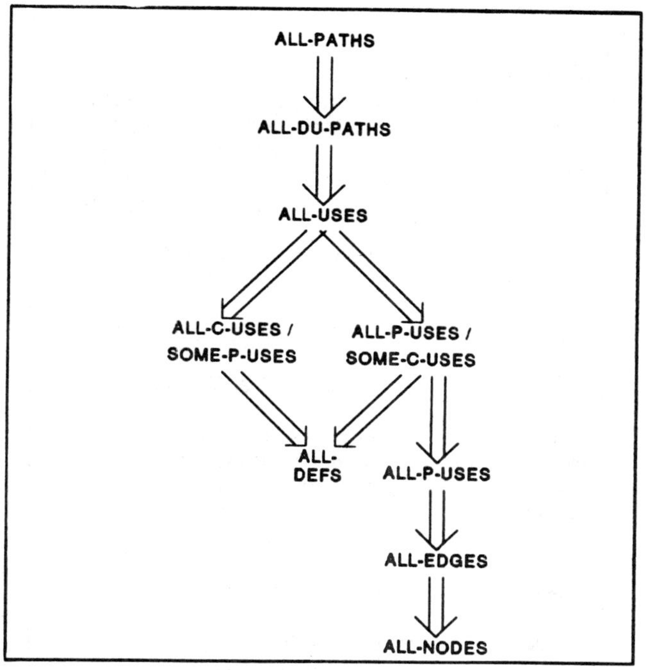

Figure 3.

iv) There is no syntactically unreachable code, i.e. there are paths from the start node to every node in the flow graph.

ASSET checks that these conditions are met and flags any violations.

ASSET's first step is the production of the subject program's def-use graph (see figure 4). On the first pass through the subject program, a table of label occurrences in labeled statements and their uses in transfer statements is constructed. On the second pass, statements are classified as labeled or unlabeled, and as conditional transfer, unconditional transfer, or other, and this information, along with the label table, is used to divide the program into blocks and to produce the flow graph, which is represented as an array of adjacency lists.

Variables are inserted into a symbol table called the def-use-table. Variable occurrences are classified as c-use, p-use, or definition (see section 2) according to whether they appear on the right hand side of an assignment statement or in a write statement, in a conditional transfer statement, or on the left-hand side of an assignment statement or in a read statement. In each block the global c-uses and non-local definitions are distinguished from the local ones according to position within the block. The global c-uses, p-uses, and non-local definitions (which we will refer to as c-uses, p-uses, and definitions) are recorded in the def-use-table. The flow graph along with the def-use-table constitute the def-use graph.

The flowgraph provides the information needed to insert probes in the subject program. A statement of the form **writeln** (traversed,<block number>) is inserted into each block. The modified subject program is then compiled by a Pascal compiler and executed on each element of the test set. A record of each test is written,

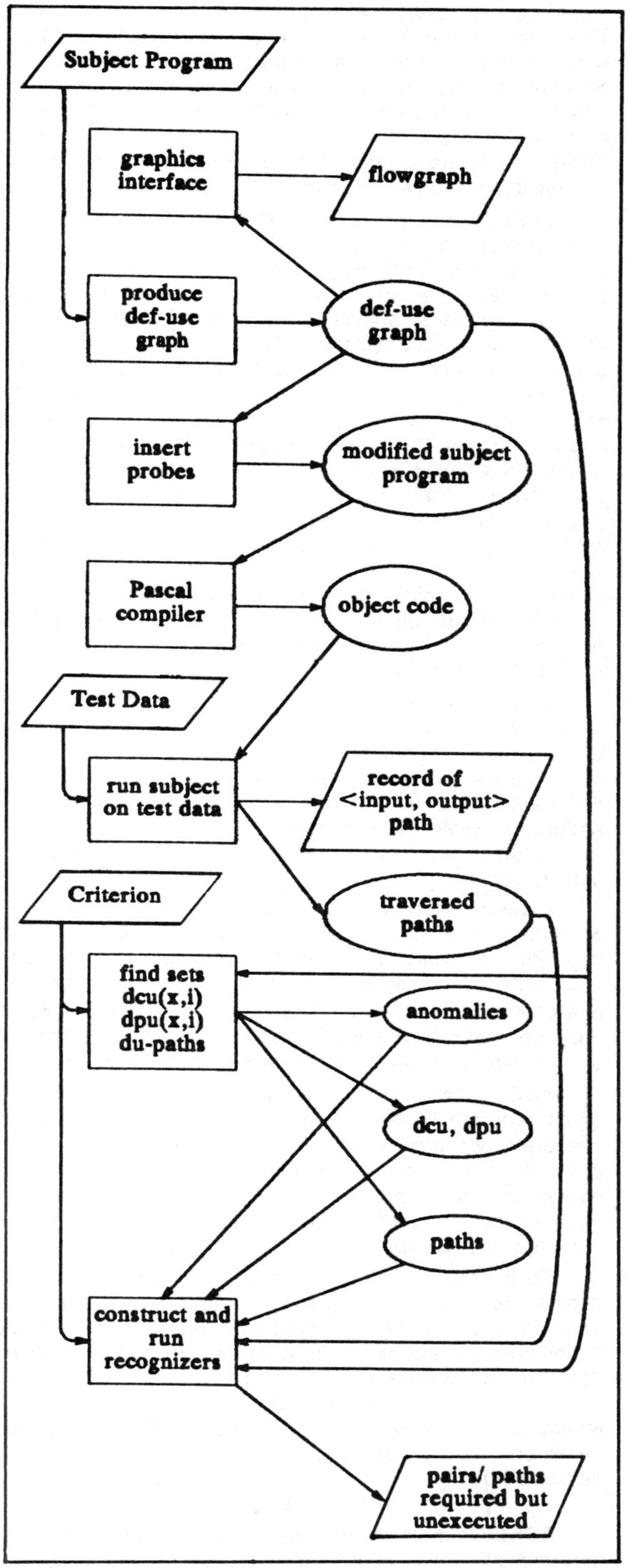

Figure 4. ASSET

75

including the input, the output, and the path traversed. These results can be examined by the person testing the program to determine whether the test was successful, i.e. whether the program met its specification on each test datum. The paths executed by the various test data are recorded in the file "traversed", separated by markers. These will be used later to determine whether or not the test fulfilled the given adequacy criterion.

ASSET uses the def-use graph to determine which pairs or paths are required by the given criterion. For the criteria all-definitions, all-p-uses, all-c-uses/some-p-uses, all-p-uses/some-c-uses and all-uses, this entails constructing the sets dcu(x,i) and dpu(x,i), defined above. These sets are constructed by performing a series of depth-first searches, one for each non-local definition of a variable. To construct dcu(x,i) and dpu(x,i) a depth-first search is performed beginning at node i. Each time a node j is visited, the def-use-table is checked to determine whether x ∈ c-use(j), x ∈ p-use(j), or x ∈ def(j). If x ∈ c-use(j) [respectively, p-use(j)] then j is added to dcu(x,i) [respectively, dpu(x,i)]. If x ∈ def(j) then the search backtracks; otherwise it continues. In effect, the search visits every node which is syntactically reachable from i by some definition-clear path. After each search, the sets dcu(x,i) and dpu(x,i) are recorded in a file. These sets will be used later to determine whether the paths executed by the test data include the required def-use pairs.

This series of searches takes time $O(N^2V)$ in the worst case, where N = number of blocks and V = number of variables, since at most NV depth-first searches are performed, each taking time O(N) because the graphs involved are sparse. In fact, since only those nodes reachable along a definition-clear path from node i are visited on a search starting at i, the worst case will not usually occur.

If the criterion is all-du-paths, then for each definition of variable x in node i, ASSET explores the graph in a depth-first manner, recording in a file every du-path from i to a node containing a c-use or an edge containing a p-use of x. Since there are $\Omega(2^N)$ du-paths, each of which must be explicitly visited, this portion of the algorithm has an exponential lower bound on worst-case behavior.

ASSET next determines which, if any, of the pairs or paths required by the given adequacy criterion were not executed by the given test data. This is done by treating paths as strings on the alphabet A = {node numbers}, expressing the required conditions in terms of regular expressions on A, and running the paths traversed by the test data through appropriate acceptors.

To handle the criteria all-definitions, all-p-uses, all-c-uses/some-p-uses, all-p-uses/some-c-uses, all-uses, observe that the set of complete paths which include definition-clear subpaths from node i to node j can be described by the regular expression
$$A^*i(A - D)^*jA^*$$
where D = { nodes k | x ∈ def(k) }. Those including definition-clear subpaths from i to edge (j,k) can be described by
$$A^*i(A - D)^*jkA^*$$
ASSET simulates the parallel execution of a family of deterministic finite automata, one dfa for each def-use pair, as indicated by the algorithm in figure 5. After

```
type
automaton = record
          variable: hashrange; {index of defined
                            variable in def-use-table}
          def,      {node in which def occurs}
          use  : node number;
                    {node in which use occurs}
          state: (q1,q2,qf);
          accepted: boolean;  {initially false}
          end;

var
c-use,
p-use : array [1.. max # uses] of automaton;

{This algorithm simulates the execution of
the automata which recognize def-c-use
associations. The algorithm for def-p-use
associations is similar. }

initialize;
repeat   {process next node in input string}
     read(node);
     for i:= 1 to max # uses do
       {update state of ith automaton }
          with c-use[i] do
          case state of
          q1: if node = def then
                    state := q2;
          q2: if node = use then
                    begin
                    state := qf;
                    accepted := true
                    end
               else
                    if (variable ∈ def (node)) and
                    (node <> def) then state := q1;
          qf: {null};
          end {case}
until end-of-path;
```

Figure 5.

running these automata on all of the paths traversed by test data, ASSET determines which of the criteria all-definitions, all-p-uses, all-c-uses/some-p-uses, all-p-uses/some-c-uses and all-uses have been fulfilled by examining the arrays p-use and c-use.

In order to determine which, if any, of the paths required by the all-du-paths criterion have not been exercised by the test data, ASSET uses the fact that a traversed path, p, exercises the du-path q if and only if p is of the form A*qA*. ASSET uses a pattern matching algorithm to determine which of the required du-paths appear as subpaths of some traversed path.

4. Uses of ASSET

ASSET has many uses, both practical and experimental. It can be used to evaluate test data, to aid in the selection of test data, to enhance program reliability through data-flow anomaly detection, to aid in program debugging, to augment program documentation, and to gather information on the cost and effectiveness of data flow testing.

Given a subject program, a test set, and one of the data flow test data adequacy criteria, ASSET determines whether the test set is adequate with respect to the criterion. In addition, it produces a list of those pairs of nodes (or in the case of the all-du-paths criterion, paths), if any, which are required by the criterion, but not exercised by the test data. The person testing the program can then use this list to guide the selection of additional test data. Of course, running ASSET with the empty test set as input, provides guidance for the initial selection of test data.

While constructing the def-use graph and the lists of pairs or paths required, ASSET looks for data flow anomalies which may indicate the presence of errors. In [8], Osterweil and Fosdick point out that along any complete path the following "rule" is expected to be obeyed: "A definition must be followed by a reference, before another definition or undefinition." They call a violation of this rule a type 2 data flow anomaly. Such a data flow anomaly is not necessarily an error, but often indicates the presence of an error, such as a misspelled variable name.

ASSET detects such data flow anomalies under certain circumstances. Any type 2 anomaly occuring within a single block is detected while the def-use graph is being constructed. During the construction of the sets $dcu(x,i)$ and $dpu(x,i)$, all occurrences of a definition which is never used in another block and some (but not necessarily all) occurrences of two definitions of the same variable without an intervening use are detected. The nature and location of any anomalies detected are reported to the user, who should then examine the relevent portions of the program for possible error.

ASSET also serves as a debugging aid. If the program outputs the wrong value for variable x on test case t, the programmer can use information about the path executed by t and the def-use associations for x to help focus the search for the bug. ASSET can be modified so that it can serve as an interactive debugging aid. This can be done by modifying the probes which are inserted into the subject program so that in addition to recording the node number on the file "traversed", they would serve as optional stops at which the values of any variables having non-local definitions or uses in the block could be reported to the user.

ASSET produces several useful documents pertaining to the subject program. Graphical output of the flow graph makes it easier to read and understand the program. The file containing the inputs, outputs, and paths traversed by the test data provides a well organized record of the testing session. This can be useful if a modified version of the program is to be tested or if the test data is to be subjected to another adequacy criterion. ASSET can easily be modified so as to include other information, such as performance statistics in this file.

5. An Example

We now present an example of ASSET's operation. Figure 6 shows the listing and flow-graph produced by ASSET for the sample program, which computes $x^y + 1$

for integers x and y. The remainder of this section consists of an annotated record of an ASSET session, which has been slightly edited to preserve space.

ASSET **begins** by analyzing the program in file "EXAMPLE", constructing its def-use graph and inserting probes. We **select a criterion** and ASSET **finds** the required def-use **associations**, then **checks** which pairs still need to be exercised in order to satisfy the criterion. At this point the test set is empty; the results will aid in the initial selection of test data.

```
>>>:begin EXAMPLE

>>>:select-criterion
          SELECT A CRITERION

A.  All-defs
B.  All-c-uses
C.  All-p-uses
D.  All-c-uses/some p-uses
E.  All-p-uses/some c-uses
F.  All-uses
G.  All-du-paths

Enter letter representing the selected
criterion
>>>:A
Criterion is All-defs

>>>:find-associations

>>>:check

ALL-DEFS:

Still must exercise at least one of
the following def-clear paths:
with respect to      from      to
      x                1         7
AND
Still must exercise at least one of
the following def-clear paths:
with respect to      from      to
      y                1         2
      y                1         3
      y                1       ( 1,  3)
      y                1       ( 1,  2)
      y                1       ( 6,  9)
      y                1       ( 6,  8)
AND
Still must exercise at least one of
the following def-clear paths:
with respect to      from      to
   power               2         7
   power               2       ( 5,  7)
   power               2       ( 5,  6)
AND
Still must exercise at least one of
the following def-clear paths:
with respect to      from      to
   power               3         7
   power               3       ( 5,  7)
   power               3       ( 5,  6)
AND
Still must exercise at least one of
the following def-clear paths:
with respect to      from      to
      z                4         7
      z                4         8
      z                4         9
AND
```

Still must exercise at least one of
the following def-clear paths:

with respect to	from	to
z	7	7
z	7	8
z	7	9

AND
Still must exercise at least one of
the following def-clear paths:

with respect to	from	to
power	7	7
power	7	(5, 7)
power	7	(5, 6)

AND
Still must exercise at least one of
the following def-clear paths:

with respect to	from	to
z	9	8

We now try to find test data which will satisfy the all-defs criterion. Inspecting the above results, along with the flow graph, we see that in order to include both blocks 2 and 3 in traversed paths, we need some test data with $y \geq 0$ and some with $y \leq 0$. Furthermore, to include a path from 7 to 7 we must traverse the loop at least twice, so we require some data with $|y| \geq 2$. We compile the modified subject program, run some tests, and check the results.

```
>>>:compile

>>>:runtest

Executing modified subject program ...

Enter x and y
2    3
answer =  9.000
More test data? (Y/N)
>>>:y

Executing modified subject program ...

Enter x and y
2   -3
answer =  1.125
More test data? (Y/N)
>>>:n

>>>:check

>>>:view results
ALL-DEFS:
CRITERION SATISFIED
```

Having found a test set which is adequate for the all-defs criterion, we check whether this same set is adequate for all-uses. The results follow.

```
ALL-USES
Still need to exercise all of the
following of def-clear paths:
```

with respect to	from	to
z	4	8
z	4	9
power	2	(5, 6)
power	3	(5, 6)

Four required def-use pairs remain. Inspecting the flow graph, we see that any *def-clear* path with respect to z from 4 to 8 must include the path (4,5,6,8). This

```
program example (input,output);
          label 100,200,300,400,500;
          var x,y,power :integer;
          z,answer : real;

          begin

Blk Stmt     Statement

1   s1       writeln('Enter x and y');
1   s2       readln( x , y );
1   s3       if y < 0 then goto 100;
3   s4       power := y;
3   s5       goto 200;
2   s6   100: power := - y;
4   s7   200: z := 1;
5   s8   300: if power = 0 then goto 400;
7   s9       z := z * x;
7   s10      power := power - 1;
7   s11      goto 300;
6   s12  400: if y >= 0 then goto 500;
9   s13      z := 1 / z;
8   s14  500: answer := z + 1;
8   s15      writeln('answer = ',
                       answer:6:3);

8   s16      end.
```

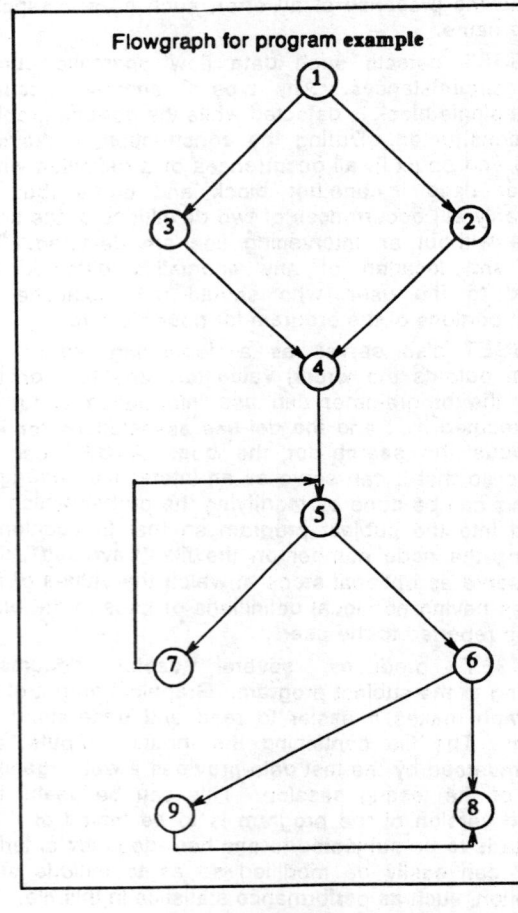

Flowgraph for program example

Figure 6.

means that power must initially be 0, so y must be 0. We add a test case with y = 0 and check whether all-uses is satisfied.

```
>>>:runtest

Executing modified subject program ...
Enter x and y
1    0
answer =  2.000
More test data? (Y/N)
>>>:n

>>>:check

ALL-USES
Still need to exercise all of the
following of def-clear paths:

with respect to      from      to
      z               4         9
      power           2       ( 5, 6)
```

We now look for test data which will exercise the two remaining pairs. Refering to the flow graph, we see that the only def-clear path with respect to z from 4 to 9 is (4,5,6,9). But any data which executes this path must have y = 0, to insure that the loop is never traversed and y < 0, to insure that edge (6,9) is traversed, so the required path is not executable. Similarly, there is no executable def-clear path with respect to power from node 2 to edge (5,6).

We see that for this program no test set can satisfy all-uses. However, we have found a set which "almost" satisfies the criterion, in the sense that it exercises every required def-use pair which can be exercised by any test data. This example also shows that although the question of whether or not a given path is executable is formally undecidable, in practice it is often quite easy for a person looking at the program to determine the answer.

6. Conclusions and Future Work

We have described the design and implementation of a tool based on the theory developed in [9,10]. ASSET uses data flow information to aid in the selection and evaluation of test data for programs written in a small subset of Pascal. It also enhances program reliability by performing data flow anomaly detection, by aiding in debugging and by providing useful documentation. The utility of ASSET is limited by the fact that subject programs must be written in an extremely simple language which permits only simple variables and elementary control flow mechanisms (sequential flow, conditional and unconditional transfers.)

We plan to use ASSET to do empirical studies of the cost and effectiveness of the data flow criteria. Weyuker [12] has shown that for a program with n variables, m assignment statements, i input statements, and t conditional transfer statements, the all-nodes and all edges criteria require at most $t+1$ test cases; all-definitions requires at most $m+i \times n$ test cases; The all-p-uses, all-c-uses/some-p-uses, all-p-uses/some c-uses, and all uses criteria require at most $\frac{t^2+4t+3}{4}$ test cases.

All-du-paths requires at most 2^t test cases. In each case there exist programs requiring that number of test cases. However the types of programs which require these upper bounds are peculiar. We plan to use ASSET to obtain empirical results indicating the number of test cases required by "real" programs. The effectiveness of the various criteria can be investigated by using ASSET on programs with known errors and attempting to categorize which errors each criterion is likely to detect.

We also plan to extend the theory developed in [9,10,12] to cover a more sophisticated programming language, including such features as arrays, dynamic allocation, aliasing, procedure and function calls, and recursion. The tool described in this paper can then be used as a prototype for a tool which aids in selection and evaluation of test data for programs written in such a language. We expect that the upgraded tool will prove to be an effective, reasonable-cost aid to significantly enhancing software reliability.

7. References

[1] M. S. Hecht, *Flow Analysis of Computer Programs*, North Holland, 1977.

[2] W.E. Howden, "Reliability of the Path Analysis Testing Strategy", *IEEE Trans. Software Eng.*, Vol. SE-2, No.3, 1976, pp. 208-215.

[3] W.E. Howden, "A Survey of Dynamic Analysis Methods" in *Tutorial: Software Testing and Validation Techniques*, eds. E. Miller and W.E. Howden, IEEE Computer Society, 1978.

[4] J.C. Huang, " An Approach to Program Testing," *ACM Computing Surveys*, 7(3), Sept. 1975, pp. 113-128.

[5] J. W. Laski and B. Korel, "A Data Flow Oriented Program Testing Strategy," *IEEE Trans. Software Eng.*, Vol. SE-9, No.3, May 1983, pp. 347-354.

[6] E. F. Miller, Jr. M. R. Paige, J. P. Benson, and W. R. Wisehart, "Structural Techniques of Program Validation," *Dig. Compcon*, Spring 1974, pp.161-164.

[7] S. Ntafos, "On Required Element Testing," *IEEE Trans. Software Eng.*, Vol. SE-10, No.6, Nov. 1984, pp. 795-803.

[8] L.J. Osterweil and L. D. Fosdick, "DAVE- A Validation Error Detection and Documentation System for Fortran Programs," *Software- Practice and Experience*, Oct-Dec 1976, pp. 473-486.

[9] S. Rapps, E.J. Weyuker, "Data Flow Analysis Techniques for Test Data Selection," Department of Computer Science Technical Report # 023, Courant Institute of Mathematical Sciences, New York University, New York, Dec. 1981.

[10] S. Rapps and E. J. Weyuker, "Data Flow Analysis Techniques for Program Test Data Selection," *Proceedings Sixth Int'l Conference on Software Eng.*, Tokyo, Japan, Sept. 1982, pp. 272-278.

[11] M. Schaeffer, *A Mathematical Theory of Global Program Optimization*, Prentice-Hall, Englewood Cliffs, N. J., 1973.

[12] E.J. Weyuker, "The Complexity of Data Flow Criteria for Test Data Selection," *Information Processing Letters*, Vol. 19, No.2, August 1984, pp.103-109.

[13] M. R. Woodward, D. Hedley, and M. A. Hennell, "Experience with Path Analysis and Testing of Programs," *IEEE Trans. Software Eng.*, Vol. SE-6, May 1980, pp. 278-286.

COMPLEXITY ANALYSIS AND AUTOMATED VERIFICATION

John R. Hlotke

A T & T Technologies
28 W615 Ferry Road
P. O. Box 450
Warrenville, Illinois 60555

The most important consideration in a software development effort is the production of software that functions as defined by the user requirements, is easily maintained and demonstrates a high degree of reliability. A large number of analytical tools and procedures exist to assist in that endeavor; however, most concentrate on only one aspect of the problem.

The purpose of this paper is to present a methodology developed at the Warrenville facility of AT&T, combining the McCabe complexity metric, a tool designed to view the logical structure of a program in graphical form with the XPEDITER® test tool® , an interactive test tool developed by Application Development Systems, Inc., (ADS). An increase in the test coverage of a module and the corresponding decrease in redundancy between test cases has been realized. The verification of test output has been automated, reducing manual verification effort, with an increase in module reliability and adherence to user requirements.

Test repeatability or regression testing is supported, reducing the costs and efforts of modifications while insuring module integrity and reliability. Application of the procedure during the design and specification stages can aid in the packaging of system functions resulting in modules that will permit standardized testing procedures to be employed.

★ XPEDITER® is a registered trademark of Application Development Systems, Inc.

Costs accrued during the life of a software system can be split across the development process and system maintenance. Studies focusing on the software development phase have shown that 40-60 percent of the total cost incurred during the phase is attributable to testing and quality assurance activities (walk-thrus, code inspections, etc.) (1) System maintenance can be divided into two; (2) subdivisions, system enhancements (processing refinements, functional add-ons, etc.) and the correction of program bugs that were missed in the initial testing effort. Both maintenance subdivisions will follow similar development steps; specification, analysis, design, testing, etc. and can be considered as a development process in their own right. Combining development and maintenance costs, it becomes apparent that a large chunk of the costs accrued during the life of a software system are attributable to quality assurance-related activities. With present cost trends for software development on the increase, the dollar amount for these activities will continue to increase. (2) It is in this area that significant cost savings can be realized.

One of the easiest approaches to reduce costs, and most unsatisfactory from a systems development standpoint, is to shortcut the quality assurance process. This normally occurs during the formal testing phase which is undertaken relatively late in the development process, when time and budgeting constraints are most likely to affect the process. (3) Shortcutting on testing is often not met with a great deal of resistance. Testing "output," in terms of enhancements to the program, tend to be intrinsic and not as readily observable to someone not directly involved in the process, especially to upper-level management who are removed from the development process. Most programmers dislike testing, since for a test to be considered successful, a program must be in error. Discovering bugs during testing often does not carry the same reward level as that for a programmer who writes a difficult piece of code, even if it contains bugs (the irony is that the tester sometimes receives the "blame" for finding the bug and lessening the "work of art").

The various phases of a project have well-defined physical outputs, analysis specifications, program specifications, etc. Procedures are defined where inputs to the process are taken and physically transformed. The testing phase lacks this. A syntax-free program goes in and a syntax-free program (hopefully) comes out. No noticeable physical transformation takes place during the phase (although, if done properly, the quality and reliability increases). With progress typically being measured on a project in terms of program completions, testing can appear to be holding up progress. The end result is to shortchange the testing process and hurry testing along to meet completion dates.

Adding to the problem are some of the structured methodologies that are in use for system development. The design and analysis processes, as discussed above, characteristically contain well-defined quality assurance procedures (walk-thrus, inspections, etc.) to increase the probability of errors being uncovered. Yet during the testing phase quality assurance procedures are fuzzy or lacking entirely. Determination of test cases is usually dependent on a programmer's intuition and not a careful examination of the program or program specification. Testing strategy is developed on a modular basis and "test plans" are developed accordingly. At the completion of testing hard copies of the test plans, results and data may be retained for future reference, but the physical input data may be deleted. A great deal of redundant effort results as the information must be recreated for each subsequent test execution of the program. A tester confronted with this will often create input to test only the changes made to a program, not fully testing the impact of the modification across the entire program. The handling of testing is ironic. Testing should be considered a crucial phase of the development process, representing the first opportunity to check the physical implementation of the logical design.

Increased system life cycle costs result from the above process. Bugs missed during the early quality assurance activities can conceivably go undetected until well after system implementation. (4) Data processing studies have shown that the later a bug is found in the life cycle of a system, the more complex the solution tends to be (i.e. programs requiring changes, notification of those changes to responsible people, etc.) and consequently the more expensive to fix. (5) Statistics kept on error rates indicate that even on programming done well (following a methodology with well-defined quality assurance and testing procedures) it is not out of the ordinary to encounter error rates of 1 per every 100 statements of code. (6) Skimping on testing during the development process can only increase that ratio. To reduce costs over the life cycle of a system, standardized, well-defined testing procedures must be employed.

To develop a testing methodology, a separate Quality Assurance group was established at the Warrenville facility. The methodology they were to develop had to meet three (3) management criteria:

★ Increase test coverage of a module;

★ A standardized procedure to follow when creating test plans and test cases such that verification of test results is improved and modifications required for regression testing are kept to a minimum;

★ With a large number of programs that could require testing during a development effort, the procedure had to allow for rapid generation of test scripts without a sacrifice in test reliability.

The first step was to examine the development procedures, based on AT&T's Total Systems Development (TSD) methodology, currently being used. Reviews of the documents produced during the process were held at required intervals and verified against the original user requirement specification. Checklists of points to cover were prepared, and responsibility for correction was assigned. Points of contention were to be resolved prior to the next review of the document. Development could not proceed to the next phase until all open items had been resolved and agreement that the document represented the user request was reached. The testing phase lacked the same set of controls. Program walk-thrus were required but often emphasized a comparison of the program source to coding standards and not a comparison of program logic to program specification (not finding the forest for looking at all the trees?). Test case generation was the responsibility of each programmer and his project leader (each programmer tested his own code). The program source code was usually the main testing document although some programmers used the program specification for that purpose. There was a tendency in tests based on the source code, for the test cases to expect exactly what the source code indicated, i.e. if the program indicated 1 + 1 = 3, the test cases would accept that as valid output. Test coverage of a program also varied across programmer/tester, leaving parts of a program well-tested and other parts barely touched. One programmer was insistent that his code could be tested sufficiently using, at the most, three (3) test cases.

The Quality Assurance group decided the primary emphasis of testing would be a verification of the program functions against the user specifications. Since the prior steps in the TSD methodology produced logically accurate representations of the user requirements, the program specifications document was to be used as the primary test resource.

The final methodology adopted combined the McCabe Complexity metric with XPEDITER®, an interactive test tool of Application Development Systems, Inc. Test cases were generated by applying the McCabe metric to each program. The metric involved creating a "bubble chart" based on the outcomes of the decisions made within a program, depicting the number of linearly independent paths data could take through a program. (7) Once the bubble chart was drawn, a complexity factor was calculated using an equation developed by McCabe, based on the number of outcomes versus the number of decision (8). This number could then be used for three (3) purposes:

★ To rate a program's complexity. The higher the number the more complex and the more difficult a program should be to test;

★ To indicate the minimum number of test cases that needed to be developed to test a program.

★ To allow better planning for the test effort based upon the indicated complexities of individual programs.

The complexity factor indicates the number of linearly independent paths data could follow through a program. Once a base set of test paths has been established, any test case generated must be some combination of the base set. The generation of paths is done from the bubble chart. Following McCabe's guidelines, a functional path through the chart is selected. When choosing the initial path it is beneficial to pick a path that encompasses the greatest number of decisions on the bubble chart. From this initial or "baseline" path, all other paths are derived. To derive the next path the outcome of the first decision on the baseline should be flipped, i.e. if the first outcome defined A equal B the second would assume A not equal B, while keeping as many of the subsequent decisions on the path equal to their "baseline" outcome. For the next path the outcome of the second decision on the "baseline" would be flipped. This process continues until all decisions in the bubble chart have been flipped. Each

path is then equated to a test case and data picked to exercise those conditions. The test cases derived from the metric were also added to, using a "boundary values" construct, i.e., when dealing with logic that involved testing for ranges of values, test cases had to be generated, if not explicitly defined in the paths, to test just above and below the ranges being tested for in the program.

It should be noted that the McCabe methodology does not view the outcomes of decisions as only a true and false branch. Instead it considers the number of ways a decision can be true or false. For example, if the statement

A EQUAL B and C EQUAL D

were examined, three conditions would have to be considered:

★ A equal B and C equal D

★ A not equal B and C equal D

★ A equal B and C not equal D

Resulting in two false conditions and one true.

Adopting McCabe's complexity metric met the requirements for Quality Assurance testing. The bubble chart would be generated by applying the metric to the program specification document. This removed the need for having the source code available early in the test phase and removed the option of using the source code in test creation. The test paths derived from applying McCabe's complexity metric illustrate how data flows logically through a program. The paths for a given program, taken as a group, will cover all portions of a program; basing test cases on those paths will increase overall test coverage within a program. By using the McCabe complexity chart (bubble chart) and procedures for identifying test paths the process of test case identification achieved a degree of independence from the tester. By following McCabe's methodology similar test plans would be derived regardless of which tester created the plan. To simplify regression testing documentation was retained from the initial test creation. Program modifications could be highlighted and appropriate changes made to reflect the new processing logic. The existing test cases can then be compared against the revised test documentation and modified. The test creation process does not have to be repeated and the effects of the modifications across the entire program can be tested by re-executing the original test.

McCabe's complexity metric simplified the logical testing process; however, the physical process of data creation and output validation were not addressed. Output validation was viewed very critically. If a program runs to "successful" completion (i.e. does not abnormally terminate) it is only through examination of the output that errors can be uncovered. A problem encountered with visual verification involves the "law of diminishing returns." When beginning the verification process, output tends to be scrutinized very carefully. Checking normally proceeds on a field-by-field basis. As the process continues, as with any tedious task, the verifier begins to increase speed, glancing at records, no longer checking field by field. This is especially true if the early test cases uncovered no errors. The end result is that there is an increased probability of errors going through undetected. Creating test cases to thoroughly test a program is a waste of effort if the output is not carefully verified.

Test data creation presented still another problem. Several options were considered for test file creation:

★ Using copies of production files.

★ Creating new files based on test cases identified in the programs.

★ Using a subset of production files and modifying it.

The use of production files was discounted for several reasons. Using the full set of production files could result in excessive test run times and large volumes of output leading to operational and verification problems. The test cases needed may not all be present on the files. With a large physical volume of data it would be quite cumbersome for a tester to search through a file, verify that the conditions needed were present and then verify the results. The test files were to be a controlled environment containing selected conditions not the "uncontrolled" environment of production.

The last two options were given careful consideration. Creating test files based on test cases identified was recommended in several testing methodologies. The required test conditions are represented, the volume of the output is kept to a manageable level and execution time is reduced significantly. The tester has increased control over the contents of the files. However, creating the entire file from scratch was recognized as a time-consuming process. Testers would need to assemble not only records containing error conditions but also a large number of "valid" records. The final option seemed to offer the compromise. Subsetting production files allowed the tester to take advantage of conditions that exist on those files. File size is bounded, output volume is reduced and test run times will be down from a straight production file choice. With the decreased file size it is easier for a tester to check for missing conditions, the volume of records to examine does not exist. Test conditions not present can be added to the file, either through modification of existing records or addition of new records.

Identification of test data and conditions is simplified by using the paths derived from the McCabe bubble chart. Each path identified from the McCabe bubble chart defines a set of conditions that identifies a unique piece of data. If the conditions defined by a particular path are not present on the data base, a tester would be required to add them. For example, if a test case required an item on an inventory file to have only five component parts and the test file did not contain any parts that met this criteria, the tester would create a part (by modifying an existing record or adding new records to the test file) containing only five components. Prior to test file modification an examination of record usage in other tests was required to preserve testing integrity. If modification of existing records was not possible, new records would be added to the file.

The ability to quickly change data on the files was still a problem. The tester still had to assemble his modifications and submit them for an update run. If a tester felt it was necessary to check conditions different from those specified in the test cases, turnaround time for the file update could become a factor. Also the problem of conflicting conditions between programs needed to be addressed. A test condition required for one program may cause an abnormal termination condition in another.

A number of interactive test tools and test data generators were examined to resolve the test data modification and creation problems discussed above. The XPEDITER® interactive test tool of Application Development Systems, Inc., has the capabilities to assist in those areas. A tester can take control at any executable point within a program, assign the values necessary to create a given condition to the aproriate data items and then resume program execution at the breakpoint or at any other executable point within a program. The tester has the flexibility to modify data and the execution sequence of a program to temporarily create condtions that are not present on the test files. At the completion of testing an update of the test files can be submitted to permanently add the conditions.

The big advantage of the XPEDITER® test tool came in the verification of test output. The least exciting phase of testing is verification, yet it is one of the most important since it is by an examination of expected and actual results that program errors will be uncovered. The attention of a tester decreases over time as the volume of output requiring verification increases, raising the probability that errors will be missed. (9) Ideally verification of test output should occur at the time of output. If a problem exists the conditions that led to it are still present and can aid in debugging. Automatic verification would remove the drudgery from output verification and would require tester intervention only when a discrepancy between expected and actual results occur.

The XPEDITER® test tool contains two (2) command groups that enhanced its ability in this area:

★ The ability to define data fields both internal and external to a program and reference them logically;

★ Commands to logically test conditions that were dependent on program execution (i.e. which physical iteration of a particular statement or paragraph the program was executing).

When a test run was being assembled the tester would examine the test cases noting the outputs defined for each input condition. Breakpoints would be established at the proper locations in the programs to capture data prior to program modification (at invocation of called routines, after a read of a file or databases, etc.) and stored in externally defined fields. This would involve both fields that were to be modified and those that would remain unchanged. Similarly breapoints would be established and the data content of the output would be verified using the logical compare commands of the XPEDITER® test tool, against the externally stored data or a literal constant. For example, the input transaction for a file update program would be stored at program access in an externally defined XPEDITER® test tool data area. For the records to be updated off the file, the data will be similarly stored. When the actual update was performed (i.e., the record replaced in the file) the XPEDITER® test tool compare commands would be executed to verify the data being replaced. For modified fields the compares would be done between the external data in the XPEDITER® test tool and the fields in the actual record being replaced. If a compare should fail, indicating an unexpected result, the tester would be prompted and given an opportunity to investigate further. At completion of a test run the tester would scan the XPEDITER® test tool output, which shows the order in which the breakpoints were invoked, to verify that all breakoints were executed as expected.

To reduce the number of XPEDITER® tool command streams required to test a program, each stream covered several test cases. A problem encountered was that while most outputs were always formatted in the same manner (i.e., the data always came from the same sending field), formatting could be dependent on logical decisions made within a program. The ability of the XPEDITER® test tool to test for which physical execute of a breakpoint the program was executing proved invaluable.

Each input case defines a particular path through a program. A tester has control over the sequence in which the inputs are processed. It can be determined, based on the prior inputs in a run, when a particular input would invoke a particular breakpoint (its 5th invocation, 6th). By logically testing for this, any processing differences between input conditions can be accounted for and the XPEDITER® test tool command stream can verify output data content. Similarly the command stream can logically check for input conditions that the program was not designed to handle yet are on the test files for other programs. When encountered, the command stream can bypass processing for that record.

Another feature of the XPEDITER® test tool that reduced testing time was the capability of creating the XPEDITER® test tool command stream prior to test execution. The command stream could be entered, saved on disk and included in processing when required. Two advantages were realized:

★ Data entry at test execution was reduced.

★ Similarities between command streams could be capitalized on.

Testers were relieved from the tedious job of re-entering large command streams every time a program required testing. Each subsequent execute used the same command stream, barring required modifications, lending continuity to the external manipulations done to a program. Tester entry error was reduced. As command streams increased in length, the probability of a tester entering the wrong program position for a break increased. Saving the command stream allowed the errors to be caught and corrected without having to re-enter an entire command sequence.

Many of the command streams generated for a program shared common processing similarities. The same breakpoints would be established and the same data fields would be verified. After creation of the initial script for a program, a tester could copy the "model" and modify it for the conditions being analyzed. The net result was a reduction in test script creation time.

Regression testing was also simplified by storing the command streams. Scripts did not need to be re-created for subsequent program modifications but only altered to reflect the modifications. Using the same set of input and verification procedures lent a degree of continuity to the testing phase that had been lacking. The impulse to "only test the changes" was sidestepped to some extent since the majority of the test set-up work is completed. The tester modified the scripts to reflect the program changes but the entire test would be re-run.

A test plan was created to coordinate the running of each test. The format of the plan was dependent on whether the program was batch or online. A batch test plan would identify the datasets and data bases required, the XPEDITER® test tool command streams and the sequence in which they would be invoked, the files to be dumped at test completion and any special instructions required to test the program (i.e., run specific programs to set up conditions, etc.). Online test plans contained the same information in a slightly different format. An online test plan contained the screen entries to be made by the tester. The entries would define the input to be made on each screen and detailed the output to be expected (i.e., screen or transactions output, etc.). Interspersed within the screen entries were references to specific XPEDITER® test tool command streams and the test cases that were being tested.

At the completion of testing a test documentation binder was assembled. The folder contained a copy of the program specification, McCabe complexity chart, test case list, dumps of the XPEDITER® test tool command streams, test plan sheets, dumps of output files, for batch programs copies of the input data sets and a cross-reference between the test case list and the input transactions. This documentation formed the basis for regression testing.

The testing procedures as defined were first applied to the testing of an in-house manufacturing control system. An online/batch system supporting MRP II (Materials Resource Planning, it consists of procedures that help to better manage inventory levels and production scheduling within a factory). With the exception of several very complex programs (complexities greater than 60), most programs were charted and test data prepared in substantially less time than had been the case before. Since implementation of the system in the Spring of 1983, a substantially decreased number of program bugs have been found in production. Regression testing for systems enhancements can easily be handled without requiring extra staffing.

An analysis of the error rates versus the complexities of the tested programs was undertaken to attempt to establish guidelines for upper limits of desirable program complexity. By limiting complexity, programs would be designed with testing and maintenance in mind. The process of testing would not be viewed as an impossible task by the tester. Benefits of limiting module complexity can be found in three (3) areas:

★ Testing

★ Maintenance

★ Development

Since the complexity factor is based on the number of outcomes of a decision versus program size or number of decisions, the higher the complexity the greater the possibility of having introduced extremely complicated decision structures into a module. In a module with a high complexity factor it was not uncommon to have logical paths that spanned 30 to 40 different logical conditions. When defining test data for these conditions it was difficult, if not impossible, to find inputs that satisfied all the conditions. Items had to be added to the databases causing delays in turnaround or special instructions had to be included in the test scripts detailing to the tester how specific conditions were to be created. When dealing with modules in either a new development or regression test mode, a high complexity factor is usually indicative of nested or compound decisions. These constructs have traditionally been hard to code, modify and debug. The possibility of programmer error is increased along with the effort involved in initial coding. During design, by applying the complexity calculation, modules found too high in complexity can be redesigned without loss of coding time or be flagged as requiring special attention.

An interesting outcome when applying this to the above-mentioned

system was that as the program complexities increased, the number of errors uncovered expressed as an average number of errors per path decreased. The more complex a program was the fewer errors were uncovered during testing. Two reasons were initially advanced for this seeming contradiction. The first, which was supported by most literature on testing psychology, involved the largeness of the programs. The tester did not view testing as being an accomplishable goal and a much more lackadasical attitude was undertaken during testing. (10) An examination of the test documentation resulting for these programs showed no great deviation in procedure than programs with lower complexity. The other reason, which appears to be backed up by the track record of the system, was that design and development recognized these programs as having a high internal complexity and as such greater detail was paid to these programs overall. It will take continued study on future projects before any definitive conclusions can be adequately characterized. Low essential complexity within the design constraints of the system should still be the goal. In our experience this will still provide the best opportunity for simplified maintenance and test generation.

APPENDIX A
A Test Example

Program A will accept five input transactions A1, A2, A3, A4 and A5. Any other transaction should be rejected as an error and the next transaction read. Transaction A1 will invoke program B, transaction A2 will invoke program C, transaction A3 will invoke program D, transaction A3 will invoke program E and transaction A5 will invoke program F. The McCabe complexity chart follows:

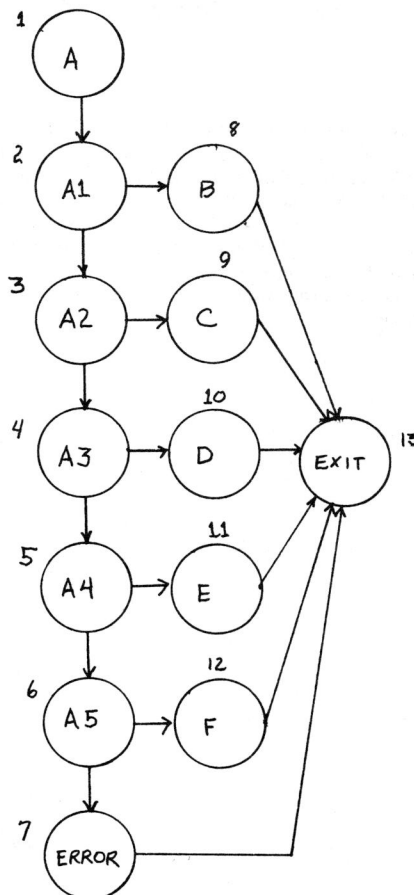

The complexity factor calculated would be

17 lines - 13 bubbles + 2 = 6

The test paths that can be derived from the bubble chart, picking the longest path first (in this case it happens to be an error path) are:

1) 1 2 3 4 5 6 7 13

Invalid transaction code

Flipping the first decision in the above path:

2) 1 2 8 13	--- A1 transaction

Repeating for the remainder of the chart gives:

3) 1 2 3 9 13	--- A2 transaction
4) 1 2 3 4 10 13	--- A3 transaction
5) 1 2 3 4 5 11 13	--- A4 transaction
6) 1 2 3 4 5 6 12 13	--- A5 transaction

All decisions have been flipped through their range of outcomes. The test cases used for the program would correspond to the paths defined above.

Assuming the following is a portion of the COBOL code for the example:

```
100 READ INPUT-FILE
150     AT END GO TO EXIT-RTN
200 IF INPUT-CODE EQUAL "A1"
250     CALL "PRGM-B" USING INPUT-REC
300 ELSE IF INPUT-CODE EQUAL "A2"
350         CALL "PRGM-C" USING INPUT-REC
```

The XPEDITER test tool command stream breaks would be established at line 200 to store a copy of the input transaction in an external XPEDITER test tool data area. The break must come after the read since the XPEDITER test tool breaks prior to execution of the line the command references. Breaks would also be established at lines 250 and 350 and a verification made that the record in the external hold area is of the type that should cause that call to be executed. If an invalid response is returned, a message would be displayed and control would be returned to the tester.

FOOTNOTES

(1) Davis, C.G., "Testing Large Real-Time Software Systems," Software Testing; Vol 2: Invited Papers, Infotech Intl Limited, 1979.

(2) Capron, H.L. and Williams, Brian K., Computers and Data Processing, Benjamin/Cummings Publishing Company, Inc., 1982.

(3) Davis, C.G., op cit.

(4) Bezier, Boris, Software Testing Techniques, Van Nostrand Reinhold Company, 1983.

(5) DeMarco, Tom, Structured Analysis and System Specification, Prentice Hall, 1978.

(6) Bezier, Boris, op cit.

(7) McCabe, Thomas, "A Complexity Measure," IEEE Transactions On Software Engineers, Vol SE-2, Number 4, Dec. 1976.

(8) McCabe, Thomas J., op cit.

(9) Weinberg, Gerald, The Psychology of Computer Programming, Van Nostrand Reinhold Company, 1971.

(10) Ibid.

REFERENCES

Beizer, Boris, Software Testing Techniques, Van Nostrand Reinhold Company, 1983.

Capron, H.L. and Williams, Brian K., Computers and Data Processing, Benjamin/Cummings Publishing Inc., 1982.

Chow, T.S., "Software Quality Assurance For Large Scale Systems," Software Testing, Volume 2: Invited Papers, Infotech International Limited, 1979.

Clarke, L.A., "Automatic Test Data Selection," Software Testing, Volume 2: Invited Papers, Infotech International Limited, 1979.

Davis, C.G., "Testing Large Real-Time Software Systems," Software Testing, Volume 2: Invited Papers, Infotech International Limited, 1979.

DeMarco, Tom, Structured Analysis and System Specification, Prentice Hall, 1978.

McCabe Thomas J., "A Complexity Measure," IEEE Transactions On Software Engineers, Volume SE-2, Number 4, December 1976, pgs. 308-320.

McCabe, Thomas J., "A Testing Methodology Using The McCabe Complexity Metric," NBS Special Publication, Contract NB82NAAK5518, 1982.

Myers, Gleford, The Art of Software Testing, John Wiley and Sons, 1979.

Weinberg, Gerald, The Psychology of Computer Programming, Van Nostrand Reinhold Company, 1971.

CONTROL FLOW ASPECTS
OF
GENERATING RUNTIME FACILITIES
FOR
LANGUAGE - BASED PROGRAMMING ENVIRONMENTS

K.A. MUGHAL

Visiting Fellow, Cornell University,
Dept. of Computer Science, 405 Upson Hall,Ithaca, NY 14853.

ABSTRACT

We present preliminary results in the study of problems concerned with generation of runtime facilities for language-based programming environments. Our aim is to provide *one uniform operational model* based on attribute grammars that allows runtime semantics to be incorporated with the syntax and static semantics of the language. We will demonstrate the feasibility of specifying such facilities along with the syntax and static semantics of language constructs found in block-structured languages. The specification is written in SSL (Synthesizer Specification Language) and forms the input to the Cornell Synthesizer Generator.

INTRODUCTION

We are concerned with the generation of execution/debugging facilities for language-based editors (LBEs) from formal language specifications. The description is based on the formalism of attribute grammars (AG)[13,14] and forms the input to the Synthesizer Generator[24]. [24] also presents an overview of the facilities found in the Synthesizer Generator for specifying LBEs. [22] is a discussion of *static semantic analyses* in LBEs. This paper describes the incorporation of *runtime or execution semantics* in such editors, with emphasis on the control flow aspects. We will use the term *runtime facilities* to mean both execution and debugging facilities.

"Hand-crafted" LBEs that provide runtime facilities have usually done so using ad hoc techniques for incremental compilation[3,6,15,30]. Other interactive programming environment (IPE) generators based on AGs, but supporting only syntax and context-sensitive analyses, include POE[5] and TRIAD[18]. The PECAN editors[19,20] provide runtime facilities and are created from formal specifications, but the hybrid approach, based on *semantic actions* and AGs, is closer to the Gandalf approach[8] rather than our approach based primarily on attribute grammars.

The AG-based specifications for compiler generators like GAG[12] and HLP[26] distinguish themselves from AG-specifications for IPEs as they generate "batch-oriented" systems that can afford to discard attribute values once these values are no longer required in the compilation process. However, in an interactive environment, all attribute values have to be maintained simultaneously. Control flow aspects described in [27] are based on the denotational semantics model pertaining to compiler generation rather than the operational model described in this paper for interactive LBEs.

Another AG-based semantics model for LBE specifications is described in [21]. In contrast to our model, it however uses semantic functions with side effects to mutate the internal values of generated code blocks. Handling of recursive procedure calls, parameter transmission and non-local gotos in the semantics model are not discussed in [21]. [21] makes the case for automatically generating AG-based specifications from *continuation* semantics.

Specifications for the Synthesizer Generator are written in SSL (Synthesizer Specification Language)[24,25]. The power of such specifications lies in the property that repropagation of semantic information after program modification is implicit in a pure AG formalism. The concept of explicit undoing or rollback is not necessary, and thus does not form part of the specification.

One major issue for LBEs providing execution facilities is that of incremental compilation. The techniques used are distinguished by the granularity of recompilation performed in response to changes to the program. The Cornell Program Synthesizer[30] analyzes just the *phrases* of the program when a change invalidates the generated code. In DICE[6], the granularity level is the statement, with as much of the old code being reused as possible. PECAN[20] tries to limit the amount of undoing necessary to what it calls a *compilation unit* which may be a statement or a procedure, depending on the context, to make the program consistent. Magpie[28], on the other hand, employs a background processor that operates on a procedural granularity. However, the attribute evaluation mechanism in language-based editors generated by the Synthesizer Generator, is an *optimal-time incremental attribute updating strategy* with respect to the number of attributes that need reevaluation[23]. Consequently, the granularity is dependent on the attributes that change values. Our aim is to make use of this powerful mechanism for incremental code generation as well.

As a first step towards generating such facilities for language-based environments, we have written a specification that augments an SSL specification of syntax and static semantics of Pascal[29] to produce a LBE that incorporates program execution and debugging in addition to allowing syntax and static semantics analyses. Initial emphasis of our work has been on flow of control: execution of simple and structured statements, allowing recursion and various parameter transmission modes available in that language. The code generated by the attribute evaluation mechanism is interpreted at execution time.

The aim is to make the task of designing LBEs easier by providing the necessary "hooks" for including runtime facilities in the generated environment. The system designer need only specify the code generation together with the syntax and static semantics of the language. The runtime facilities are automatically generated for the LBE. In order to facilitate the specification of the code generation, the system designer is provided with a runtime specification interface which includes the entry point of the code of the root of the abstract syntax tree and the specification of the abstract code instructions recognized by the interpreter.

ATTRIBUTE GRAMMARS

An attribute grammar (AG) is a context-free grammar augmented by attributes attached to the symbols of the grammar. A set of *semantic equations* is associated with each production p in the grammar. Each semantic equation defines an attribute as the value of a *semantic function* applied to other attributes in the production. The attributes of a symbol X can be classified into two disjoint sets: *synthesized* and *inherited*.

If an attribute b is an argument of the semantic function for attribute a then we have a *dependency* from attribute b to attribute a. The directed *dependency graph*, representing dependencies among the attributes, would have a directed arc from the graph node denoting attribute b to the graph node denoting attribute a.

A important constraint imposed on AGs accepted by the Synthesizer Generator is that there be no *circular* dependencies among the attributes.

In SSL, we define an attribute of a nonterminal by specifying the name of the nonterminal, the type of the attribute, and the class (synthesized or inherited) of the attribute. For example,

statement { synthesized CODE entry; };

associates a synthesized CODE-valued attribute **entry** with the nonterminal **statement**. We reference the value of an attribute using the '.' notation: **statement.entry**. Attribute **entry** of the i-th. occurrence of nonterminal **statement** in a given production is denoted by **statement\$1.entry**.

In SSL, we can also define what are called *local attributes* of a *production*. These attributes cannot be referenced directly from outside the production they are defined in. They allow computation of attribute values that are specific to the production.

In the generated editor, the program is represented as an attributed tree. Program modifications affect the values of the attributes at the nodes in the attributed tree. Incremental attribute analysis updates these attributes values throughout the attributed tree in response to modifications. Only a subset of attributes need reevaluation. However the size of this subset is not known at the start of the updating process. Its size is computed as a result of the incremental analysis itself. The Synthesizer Generator uses algorithms that require steps proportional to the size of the subset of the affected attributes. These algorithms are "optimal" in the sense that the minimum amount of work required to update the attributed tree after modification is proportional to the size of the above mentioned subset.

[24], [25] and [23] are the authoritative references on SSL, the Synthesizer Generator and optimal-time incremental attribute updating algorithms employed by the Synthesizer Generator.

UNIFORM OPERATIONAL SEMANTIC MODEL

We would like to define a mapping of the abstract syntax tree to an executable form which not only allows efficient execution but also facilitates the implementation of debugging techniques such as control-flow tracing, single-stepping and value-monitoring. A number of other desirable debugging facilities are found in the Cornell Program Synthesizer[30], Magpie[4] and PECAN[19].

CODE GENERATION SCHEME

Since we want to make use of the incremental attribute evaluation mechanism for code generation, we can define an attribute that represents the code for a node in the abstract syntax tree. The code for the program is thus fragmented and attached to various nodes of the abstract syntax tree as attribute values.

One could *synthesize* the code for the *root* of the abstract syntax tree from the code fragments. This approach is used in [16] for the generation of a Pascal p-code compiler. However, in an incremental attribute evaluation scheme , any change to a code fragment would mean propagation of this change to the root of the tree. Our code generation scheme limits this change propagation.

Another approach would be to coalesce this code just prior to executing it. For debugging purposes this would entail extra book-keeping in mapping the code *back* to its respective node in the abstract syntax tree.

We have chosen to execute the fragmented code directly. In order to do this, the interpreter must know the entry point to a code block and the entry to the next code block to execute on completing the execution of the current one. The approach is described below in more detail in terms of code generation for statements found in a block-structured language. The scheme described here limits the change propagation necessary due to changes in the value of the code block to its production. Our scheme also avoids any circular dependencies among the code attributes that might otherwise appear in the attribute grammar defining the language.

For a *statement* node, we define a *synthesized* attribute **entry** that indicates the entry point corresponding to the code block of that statement and whose value is then available to the statement's parent and siblings in the abstract syntax tree. In addition we define an *inherited* attribute **completion** whose value the statement node inherits from its parent or siblings and can incorporate in its own code. The value of **completion** is effectively the entry point of the next code block to be executed after the current statement is completed. A *completion* is a concrete operational representation of a *continuation* in the denotational semantics model[9]. These two attributes thread the fragmented code together while allowing the individual code blocks to remain attached to the nodes of the abstract syntax tree as attribute values.

The diagram in Figure 1 shows the *flow of control* in the linked code structure for the **while** statement. We note that this structure is cyclic. The code blocks are mutually dependent: change in the value of one requires incremental reevaluation of the value of the others. The grammar is thus circular. The Synthesizer Generator requires a noncircular attribute grammar as its input. We can overcome this problem by introducing a level of indirection in referencing the code via the **entry** attribute. We also define code as a *local* attribute of the *production*, rather than that of the *statement* nonterminal. This allows us to specify code for only those productions that need to have such code. Code as an attribute of a *nonterminal* would require specifying its value even for cases where the nonterminal did not require the specification of code. The location of the code is fixed when the production is applied. The *value* of **entry** attribute is this location. This strategy effectively breaks the circularity as the value of the **entry** attribute is no longer dependent on the *contents* of the code block. During execution, a special operation performs the indirection required to access the code block, given the entry point or link to its location.

Figure 2 depicts this strategy for the **while** statement. As mentioned above, this approach has the advantage that any changes in the value of the code block are not propagated outside of the production for the **while** statement since the location of the code block does not change once the production is applied. It also facilitates the tracing of control flow in the abstract syntax tree, requiring only a simple mapping from the attribute (in this case, the code block) to its production subtree in the abstract syntax tree.

CODE SPECIFICATION FOR STATEMENTS

In this section we consider examples of code specification for *simple* and *structured* statements. Although the discussion will be specific to Pascal, it can be extended to other block-structured languages.

The code blocks mentioned in the previous section could be any of the representations discussed in the literature: machine language (eg. 68000 code), virtual stack-machine code (eg. p-code) or even executable metalanguage (eg. lambda-expressions). In our model, the instruction set that the interpreter recognizes is defined by the same sort of *productions* using SSL as the rest of the

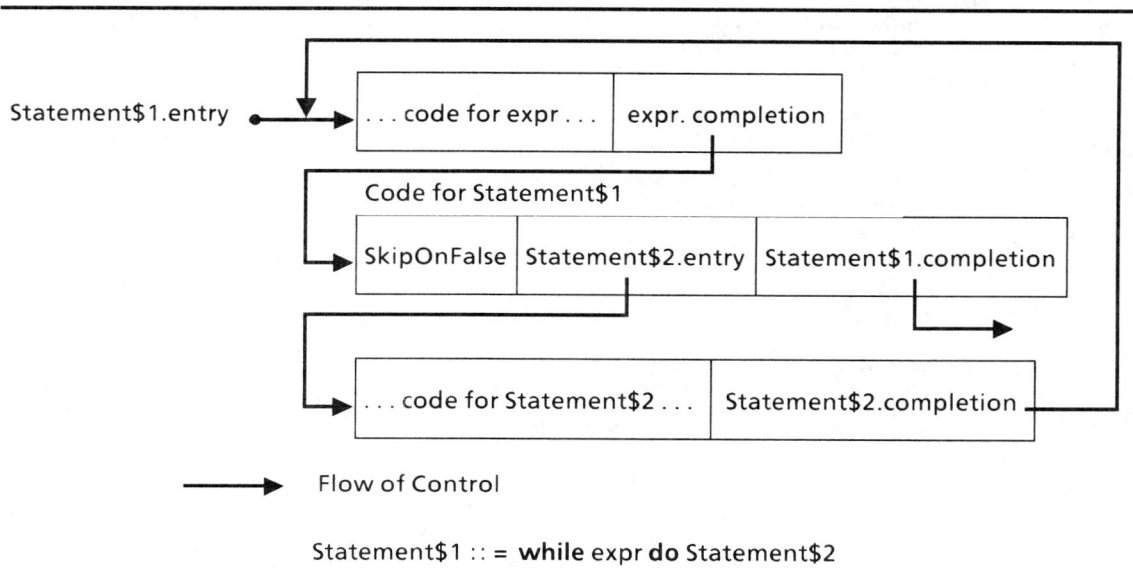

Flow of Control →

Statement$1 :: = **while** expr **do** Statement$2

Figure 1: Circularity in the Control Flow Graph for the While Statment.

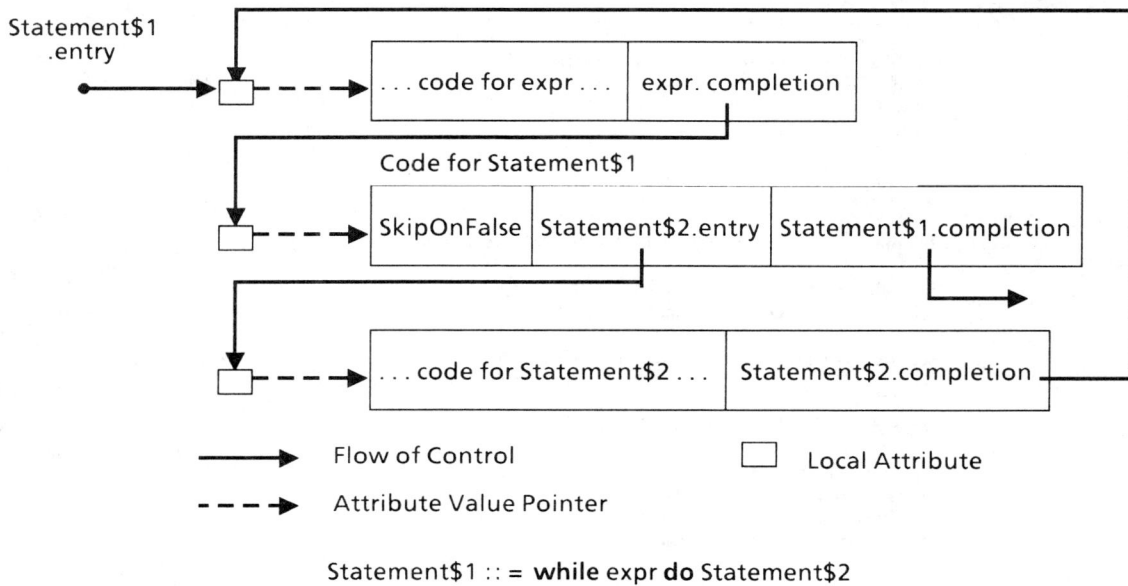

Flow of Control →   ☐ Local Attribute

- - → Attribute Value Pointer

Statement$1 :: = **while** expr **do** Statement$2

Figure 2: Code Generation for the While Statement

```
statement, expr {
    synthesized PTR entry;
    inherited PTR completion;
    };

statement: Assign( variable expr ) {
    local CODE code;

    code = AssignCode(variable, statement$1.completion);
    statement$1.entry = expr.entry;
    expr.completion = &code;
    }

| While( expr statement ) {
    local CODE code;

    code = SkipOnFalseCode(statement$2.entry, statement$1.completion);
    statement$1.entry = expr.entry;
    expr.completion = &code;
    statement$2.completion = statement$1.entry;
    }
;
```

Table 1: Code Specification for Assignment and the While Statement

language. It is a new attribute "type", called CODE. (For a discussion of the unification of types in the Synthesizer Generator, see [24]).

The runtime semantics of the appropriate productions in the language is expressed in terms of CODE. Table 1 shows excerpts from the SSL-specification of the **assignment** and the **while** statement respectively, showing the specification of their code blocks. PTR and STR are the builtin pointer and string types in SSL, respectively. &X creates a pointer or a link to X.

Some productions may require more than one code block to define their runtime semantics. The **for** statement is shown in Table 2 with four code blocks or instructions which specify its runtime semantics. Figure 3 shows the control flow graph for the **for** statement.

```
statement: Forto( identifier expr expr statement ) {
    local CODE initcode1;
    local CODE initcode2;
    local CODE testcode;
    local CODE incrcode;

    local STR tempid;

    tempid = GenSymb(&(statement$1)); /* generate a unique identifier */

    initcode1 = AssignCode(identifier, expr$2.entry);
    initcode2 = AssignCode(tempid, &testcode);

    testcode = GreaterRelCode(identifier, tempid,
                              statement$1.completion, statement$2.entry );

    incrcode = IncrCode(identifier, &testcode);

    statement$1.entry = expr$1.entry;
    expr$1.completion = &initcode1;
    expr$2.completion = &initcode2;
    statement$2.completion = &incrcode;
    }
;
```

Table 2: Code Specification for the For Statement

Statement$1.entry

```
●──→□ · · · [ . . . code for expr$1 . . . | expr$1.completion ]

initcode1 □ · · · → [ Assignment to control variable | expr$2.entry ]

          □ · · · → [ . . . code for expr$2 . . . | expr$2.completion ]

initcode2 □ · · · → [ Assignment to temporary variable | &testcode ]

testcode  □ · · · → [ IfGreater | . . . | Statement$1.completion | Statement$2.entry ]

          □ · · · → [ . . . code for Statement$2 . . . | Statement$2.completion ]

incrcode  □ · · · → [ Increment control variable | &testcode ]
```

───────→ Flow of Control   □ Local Attribute

· · · · ·▶ Attribute Value Pointer

Statement$1 ::= for identifier := expr$1 to expr$2 do Statement$2

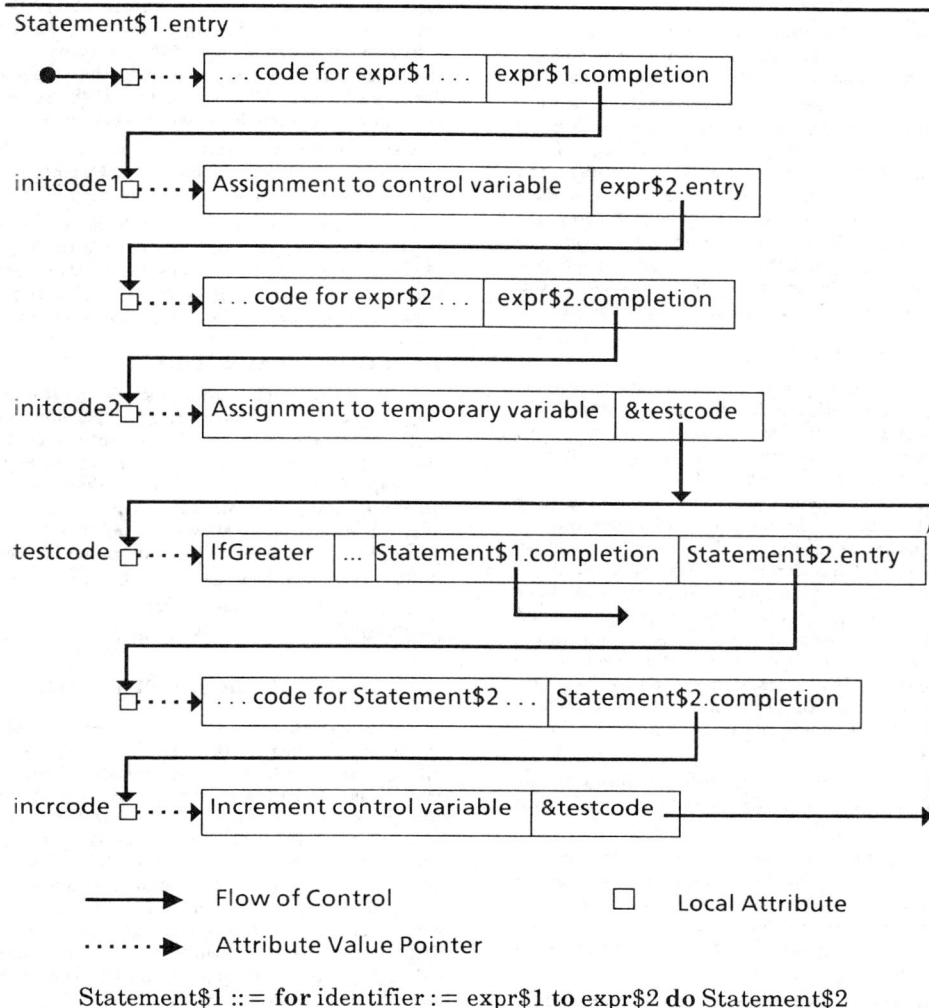

Figure 3: Control Flow Graph for the For Statement

The paradigm for execution is that the program is always executable. If unexpanded nonterminals or errors due to context constraint violations are encountered along the path of execution then the execution is aborted on encountering the first such anomaly and the appropriate place indicated in the abstract syntax tree. This requires specifying the HaltCode as an alternative in each context where such anomalies can occur. Reporting of *runtime* errors is done in a similar manner: execution is aborted and the relevant node in the abstract tree highlighted.

The next section presents a summary of some of the implementation features of the runtime semantics. Implementation of procedure calls and GOTOs is also postponed til the next section since their runtime interpretation requires an understanding of the underlying store management scheme.

IMPLEMENTATION OF RUNTIME SEMANTICS

At runtime, the interpreter fetches the value of the **entry** attribute of the root of the abstract syntax tree and executes the linked code structure described above. The interpreter is a tail-recursive procedure that has the *current instruction pointer*, the *control stack*, the *expression-evaluation stack* and the *store* as parameters.

STORE

Primarily because of the functional nature of the SSL (Synthesizer Specification Language), it was decided to implement the store in an applicative fashion. In fact the store is an AVL tree[1] where the key is an identifier name and the value is a *value stack* (i.e. the usual runtime activation stack is distributed over the identifier names), thus implementing *shallow binding*. Basic operations like value lookup/update for an identifier and insertion/deletion of identifier-value pairs in the store, all have approximately the same constant cost: $O(\log n)$, n being the number of identifiers in the store. However in case of *indirect* references (see below) into the store, the cost is slightly higher due to the cost of accessing a value down in the *value stack*; this additional cost being proportional to the height of the value stack.

RECURSIVE PROCEDURE CALLS

Implementation of recursive procedure calls is conventional in its approach. Procedure invocation is handled in two stages. On the *call side*, the actual parameters are evaluated and are to be found on the expression-evaluation stack. The return address is pushed onto the control stack. On the *entry side*, the formal parameters are matched to the actual parameter values and their bindings pushed into the store. The temporary variables and the local declarations, together with the label definitions, are also pushed into store and control transferred to the entry point of the procedure code. All the necessary information required is available as operands for the code blocks generated for procedure call and entry. The code of the procedure declaration always ends with the ReturnCode block whose operands indicate the information that is to be popped from the store. It also transfers control to the return address that was pushed into the control stack at procedure invocation. In the case of a function, its value is pushed onto the expression-evaluation stack.

Call-by-value parameter passing is straight forward: the expression is evaluated and its value bound to the formal parameter.

Call-by-reference parameters are implemented by an *indirection* consisting of the name of the actual parameter and the height of its value stack at the time of the call. Chains of indirection (i.e. reference parameters passed as reference parameters) are avoided by copying the indirection rather than making a new indirection.

Procedure parameters require a more elaborate scheme which essentially involves creating a *closure* for the procedure at the time when it is passed as a parameter. The closure consists of the entry point of the code for the actual procedure and *indirections for all the non-local variables referenced* in the procedure. It captures the "environment" at the time the procedure is bound to the formal procedure name. When this procedure parameter is invoked, the indirections in the closure are distributed over the respective non-local variables in the store. Thus the procedure is always executed in the correct environment existing at the time it was passed as a parameter. The indirections of the non-local variables are popped on return from the procedure. We distinguish between an ordinary *procedure declaration* call and a formal *procedure parameter* call. The later requires handling of a closure.

HANDLING OF GOTOS

Implementation of *local* gotos is straightforward. A label is bound to the value of the **entry** attribute of the statement it prefixes. To perform a local goto, control is transferred to this value and no changes are necessary in the store.

Non-local gotos are handled in the *activation-frame stack* model by popping the activation frames until the "right" frame becomes visible. In our store, the frames are distributed over the value-stacks of the variables. We have to "unwind" the store to what it was when the procedure, (the label is declared in), was activated. (In ISO Pascal, a label can only prefix a statement in the block of the procedure in which it is declared.) Unwinding the store should give us a store that contains the *same number of entries* as the store existing at the time when the procedure was activated. Also the *heights* of the corresponding value-stacks in the two stores must be the same; only the values in the stacks have possibly changed. This means that if the store at the time of the procedure activation is saved, it can easily be updated from the new store at the time when a nonlocal goto is done. Control would be transferred to the relevant statement and from this point onwards the updated store would be used in the execution.

The scheme outlined for nonlocal gotos requires that for each label pushed into the store, we include in its binding the value of the store just prior to handling the labels on procedure activation. Although the store is a shared-data structure (like all attribute values in the system), a nonlocal goto is an expensive operation.

DEBUGGING FACILITIES

Facilities implemented include control-flow tracing, single-stepping and value-monitoring. The implementation of these facilities is influenced by the semantic model. Code blocks are treated as single instructions by the interpreter; single-stepping is in terms of the execution of a code block. A code block is a local attribute; mapping from the attribute to its production in the abstract syntax tree allows control-flow tracing. The store is passed as a parameter to the interpreter and can thus be queried during execution. Other facilities like reversible execution[3,30], COME command[2] and execution resumption after program modification[3,30] are possible in the future and are being considered.

CONCLUSION & FUTURE RESEARCH

An operational semantics model that allows generation of execution/ debugging facilities in LBEs has been described. It allows runtime semantics to be specified along with the syntax and static semantics of a language. It limits the incremental change propagation due to changes in the value of a code block to the production in which the code block is defined. The model avoids the excessive copying of attribute values (for code generation); a criticism often voiced about AG-based systems. The control-flow graph built and maintained by the attribute evaluation mechanism can be used for providing different *views* of the program as in the PECAN editors. It facilitates the implementation of certain debugging features desirable in a LBE: control-flow tracing, single-stepping and value-monitoring.

The approach has been used to implement the salient aspects of control flow in the execution of statements in Pascal. At the moment, only values of the *simple* type are allowed during runtime. Work in progress will lift this restriction. New debugging facilities alluded to in the previous section will also be investigated for implementation.

We believe that the approach can be generalized to generate LBEs with runtime facilities for other block-structured languages.

ACKNOWLEDGEMENTS

The driving force behind this work has been Tim Teitelbaum. His encouragement and participation permeate all aspects of this work. I am also very thankful to Alan Zaring, Tom Reps and T.K. Srikanth for many helpful suggestions and ideas.

I thank Tim Teitelbaum, Tom Reps, Kari Raiha and Alan Zaring for reading this paper and suggesting improvements.

REFERENCES

[1] G.M. Adelson-Velskii and E.M. Landis, "An algorithm for the organisation of information," Doklady Akademia Nauk SSSR, pp. 263-266, 146, 1962. English translation in Soviet Math. Dokl., pp. 1259-1263, 3, 1962.

[2] C.N. Alberga, A.L. Brown, G.B. Leeman Jr., M. Mikelsons, M.N. Wegman, "A Program Development Tool," IBM J. Res. Develop., pp. 60-73, Vol. 28, No. 1, January 1984.

[3] J.E. Archer Jr., *The Design and Implementation of a Cooperative Program Development Environment.* PhD dissertation, Department of Computer Science, Cornell University, Ithaca, NY.,1981.

[4] N. M. Delisle, D. E. Menicosy, M. D. Schwartz, "Viewing a Programming Environment as a Single Tool," In Proceedings of the ACM SIGSOFT/SIGPLAN Software Engineering Symposium on Practical Software Development Environments, Pittsburgh, Penn., 1984. (Joint issue: SIGPLAN Notices (ACM), 19, 5 (May 1984) & Software Engineering (ACM) 9, 3 (May 1984), pp. 49-56).

[5] C.N. Fischer, A. Pal, D.L. Stock, G.F. Johnson, J. Mauney, "The POE Language-based Editor Project," In Proceedings of the ACM SIGSOFT/SIGPLAN Software Engineering Symposium on Practical Software Development Environments, Pittsburgh, Penn., 1984. (Joint issue: SIGPLAN Notices (ACM), 19, 5 (May 1984) & Software Engineering (ACM) 9, 3 (May 1984), pp. 21-29).

[6] P. Fritzson, "Preliminary Experience from the DICE system: a Distributed Incremental Compiling Environment," In Proceedings of the ACM SIGSOFT/SIGPLAN Software Engineering Symposium on Practical Software Development Environments, Pittsburgh, Penn., 1984. (Joint issue: SIGPLAN Notices (ACM), 19, 5 (May 1984) & Software Engineering (ACM) 9, 3 (May 1984), pp. 113-123).

[7] D.B. Garlan, P.L. Miller, "GNOME: An Introductory Programming Environment Based on a Family of Structure Editors," In Proceedings of the ACM SIGSOFT/SIGPLAN Software Engineering Symposium on Practical Software Development Environments, Pittsburgh, Penn., 1984. (Joint issue: SIGPLAN Notices (ACM), 19, 5 (May 1984) & Software Engineering (ACM) 9, 3 (May 1984), pp. 65-72).

[8] A. N. Habermann, R. Ellison, R. Medina-Mora, P. Feiler, D.S. Notkin, G.E. Kaiser, D.B. Garlan, S. Popvich, *The Second Compendium of Gandalf Documentation.* Dept. of Computer Science, Carnegie-Mellon University, 1982.

[9] M.C. Henson, R. Turner, "Completion Semantics and Interpreter Generation," In Conference Record of the 9th. ACM Symposium on Principles of Programming Languages, Albuquerque, N.M., pp. 242-254, January 25-27, 1982.

[10] G.F. Johnson, *An approach to incremental semantics.* Ph.D. dissertation, Dept. of Computer Science, Univ. of Wisconsin, Madison, Wisc., 1983.

[11] G.F. Johnson, C.N. Fischer, "Non-syntactic attribute flow in language based editors," In Conference Record of the 9th. ACM Symposium on Principles of Programming Languages, Albuquerque, N.M., pp. 185-195, January 25-27, 1982.

[12] U. Kastens, B. Hutt, E. Zimmermann, *Lecture Notes in Computer Science,* Vol. 141: *GAG: A Practical Compiler Generator.* Springer-Verlag, New York, 1982.

[13] D.E. Knuth, "Semantics of context-free languages," Mathematical Systems Theory, pp. 127-145, 2, 2 (June 1968).

[14] D.E. Knuth, "Semantics of context-free languages: correction," Mathematical Systems Theory, pp. 95-96, 5, 1 (March 1971).

[15] R. Medina-Mora, P.H. Feiler, "An Incremental Programming Environment," IEEE Transactions on Software Engineering, pp. 472-482, Vol. SE-7, No. 5, (Sept. 1981).

[16] D. Milos, U. Pleban, G. Loegel, "Direct Implementation of Compiler Specifications or The Pascal P-Code Compiler Revisited," In Conference Record of the 11th. ACM Symposium on Principles of Programming Languages, Salt Lake City, Utah, pp. 196-207, January 15-18, 1984.

[17] L. Paulsen, *A compiler generator for semantic grammars.* Ph.D. dissertation, Dept. of Computer Science, Stanford University, Calif., 1981.

[18] J. Ramanathan, D. Soni, The model for program development and analysis used in TRIAD. Tech.Rep. TRIAD-TR1-80, Dept. of Computer and Information Science, State Univ., Columbus, Ohio, May 1980.

[19] S. P. Reiss, "Graphical Program Development with the PECAN Program Development Systems," In Proceedings of the ACM SIGSOFT/SIGPLAN Software Engineering Symposium on Practical Software Development Environments, Pittsburgh, Penn., 1984. (Joint issue: SIGPLAN Notices (ACM), 19, 5 (May 1984) & Software Engineering (ACM) 9, 3 (May 1984), pp. 30-41).

[20] S. P. Reiss, "An Approach to Incremental Compilation," In Proceedings of the SIGPLAN '84 SYMPOSIUM ON COMPILER CONSTRUCTION, Montreal, Canada, 1984. (SIGPLAN Notices (ACM), pp. 144-156, 19, 6, (June 1984)).

[21] J.H. Reppy, C.M.R. Kintala, Generating Execution Facilities for Integrated Programming Environments. Technical Memorandum, AT&T Bell Laboratories, Murry Hill, 1984.

[22] T. Reps, "Static-semantic analysis in language-based editors," In Digest of Papers of the IEEE Spring CompCon 83, San Francisco, Calif., pp. 411-414, Mar. 1983.

[23] T. Reps. *Generating Language-Based Environments.* M.I.T. Press, Cambridge, Mass., 1984.

[24] T. Reps and T. Teitelbaum, "The Synthesizer Generator," In Proceedings of the ACM SIGSOFT/SIGPLAN Software Engineering Symposium on Practical Software Development Environments, Pittsburgh, Penn., 1984. (Joint issue: SIGPLAN Notices (ACM), 19, 5 (May 1984) & Software Engineering (ACM), pp. 42-48, 9, 3 (May 1984)).

[25] T. Reps and T. Teitelbaum, The Synthesizer Generator Reference Manual. Tech.Rep. 84-619, Dept. of Computer Science, Cornell University, Ithaca, N.Y., July 1984.

[26] K.-J. Raiha, "Attribute Grammar Design Using the Compiler Writing System HLP," *Methods and Tools for Compiler Construction,* B. Lorho (ed.), Cambridge University Press, 1984.

[27] R. Sethi, "Control Flow Aspects of Semantic Directed Compiling," ACM TOPLAS, pp. 554-595, 5, 4 (October 1983).

[28] M. D. Schwartz, N. M. Delisle, V. S. Begwani, "Incremental Compilation in Magpie," In Proceedings of the SIGPLAN '84 SYMPOSIUM ON COMPILER CONSTRUCTION, Montreal, Canada, 1984. (SIGPLAN Notices (ACM), pp. 122-131, 19, 6, (June 1984)).

[29] T. Teitelbaum, SSL-specification of Pascal. (private communication).

[30] T. Teitelbaum and T. Reps, "The Cornell Program Synthesizer: a syntax-directed programming environment," Communications of ACM , pp. 563-573, 24, 9 (September, 1981).

[31] W. Teitelman, Interlisp Reference Manual. Xerox Palo Alto Research Center, 1978.

AUTOMATED CONFIGURATION MANAGEMENT ON A DOD SATELLITE GROUND SYSTEM

SANDRA ZUCKER   KATHLEEN B. CHRISTIAN

GENERAL ELECTRIC SPACE SYSTEMS DIVISION

ABSTRACT

An Automated Configuration Management System (CMS) was developed at General Electric and is in use on a DOD satellite ground system maintenance contract. CMS improves and enhances the manual techniques for project tracking and change control and allows for reliable management of large projects. Because CMS works with any file, it can perform Configuration Management on all items in a configuration. The CMS Bookkeeping and Status Accounting forms are displayed on a terminal and the user is guided into filling them out correctly. New configuration items or changes can be entered into the system only after approval has been supplied by the proper authority. Since a common project data base is built by CMS, visibility of current system status is available to those who are permitted project access. Standard report forms as well as user defined report forms are used when viewing the current or historic system information. CMS not only controls the configuration, but also the paperwork, change approval cycle, and the quality of the product.

INTRODUCTION

When a DOD Satellite Ground System went into the maintenance phase, and multiple versions of the Ground System software were required, it was decided to use an automated Configuration Management System (CMS). Although the Ground System software was developed for the MODCOMP computer and the CMS program ran on the VAX, it was expected that enough benefits would be derived from the control of source code files and configuration management paperwork to warrent the acquisition and the use of the VAX tool.

A prime concern of the software maintenance phase was the control of software modifications made as a result of customer requested enhancements, upgrade of Vendor hardware and software, and software rework for the correction of problems found at the sites. This was a very difficult configuration management chore since each of the ground system sites contained different hardware and software configurations. Each site had about 1000 source modules and over 300,000 lines of code. The controlled master copies of all the ground software versions as well as associated documentation and manuals had to be stored and maintained. The automated Configuration Management System was needed to facilitate and control the process of analyzing and approving problem reports and enhancement requests, integration of multiple modifications into a block change, validation of new versions of software, and tracking associated documentation. We believe CMS is the only software program that integrates code control and forms control for configuration management. It merges the "paperwork" with the control so that changes cannot be made without the proper approvals. By combining the two into a data base, we are able to generate unique status reports on this information.

AUTOMATED CONFIGURATION MANAGEMENT SYSTEM (CMS)

CMS was developed at GE under a research project in 1982. The objective was to automate the manual procedures used for change control, configuration item control and identification, and status accumulation and reporting for software projects. The result was a program that can perform the major functions for identifying, controlling and tracking of any configuration item. A paperless system where forms are filled out at a terminal where users are aided by system prompts and help responses to questions, simplifies CM procedures.

Because large projects require a high degree of coordination, a single master data base accessible to all project personnel via a computer terminal is a necessity. CMS has a master data base which is protected and cannot change unless the proper approval has been entered. The status data base is available to enhance project visibility, aid in coordination of activities, accumulate historical data and improve product quality.

USER FRIENDLY

Because CMS must handle many different types of users, its man/machine interface is very user friendly. It is menu driven with a HELP feature available at any prompt, and where the prompt responses are almost always obvious. Each response is assigned a priority level so that only those users having passwords which allow for this priority may execute the response. All CMS transactions may be saved on a file during a session for future retrieval and printing.

STATUS ACCOUNTING

The bookkeeping and the related forms required by Configuration Management have been standardized and computerized for CMS. Discrepancy Reports, Change Proposals and Work Orders are entered into the system on a form displayed at a terminal. The CMS system performs error checking, fills in known data (e.g., form identification number and date), provides a help facility for explaining the needed data fields, and rejects records containing detached errors indicating the field in error. New configuration items or changes to items already under control are accepted into the system only after the paperwork for them is completed, they have been properly approved, and they follow project standards.

CONTROL AND TRACKING

The control and tracking of the configuration items of a project are accomplished in CMS with three controlled areas of storage; Development, Test and Release. Each area contains a tree defined by the project manager which reflects the project structure. The tree is used to locate, control, and logically link the configuration items of a project.

The nodes are collections of items (directories). These items may be files of source code in any language, executable code, object modules, command files, data base files, documentation files, test procedures and/or hardware descriptions. Figure 1 shows the tree built for the ground system software. At each level a single node is taken and further defined into its next level of structure.

A configuration item is placed by its implementer into a node of the development tree. After being used locally by the developers, the item must be released for formal testing requiring it to be placed under configuration control. Items can be placed from the Development areas into the Test area only after all the "paperwork" has been completed and approved, and QA standards have been met. Similarly, when configuration items have been tested and are ready for customer release, approval must be entered to enable these items to be moved to the Release area for use by the customer and in the field. Figure 2 shows the movement of configuration items through the system using an archive function which is also used for off-line storage of configuration items.

CMS CONFIGURATION MANAGEMENT (CM) PROCEDURES

The CM procedures start when the required paperwork describing a problem, change proposal or new function is entered into the CMS system. Discrepancy Reports (DR) define errors to the current configuration and are normally filled out by a tester or operator. Change Proposals (CP) are requests to change current controlled items in the system and are often filled out by the customer or an operator. Work Orders (WO) are requests to start new work, and are initiated by the system engineers or the project manager. Standard forms are used at the terminal in order to enforce the format and structure of fields, check errors, ensure mandatory fields are filled in and to provide help to the person filling in the forms. Figure 3 indicates the process of entering these records into CMS and Figure 4 is an example DR entry form that is displayed on the terminal.

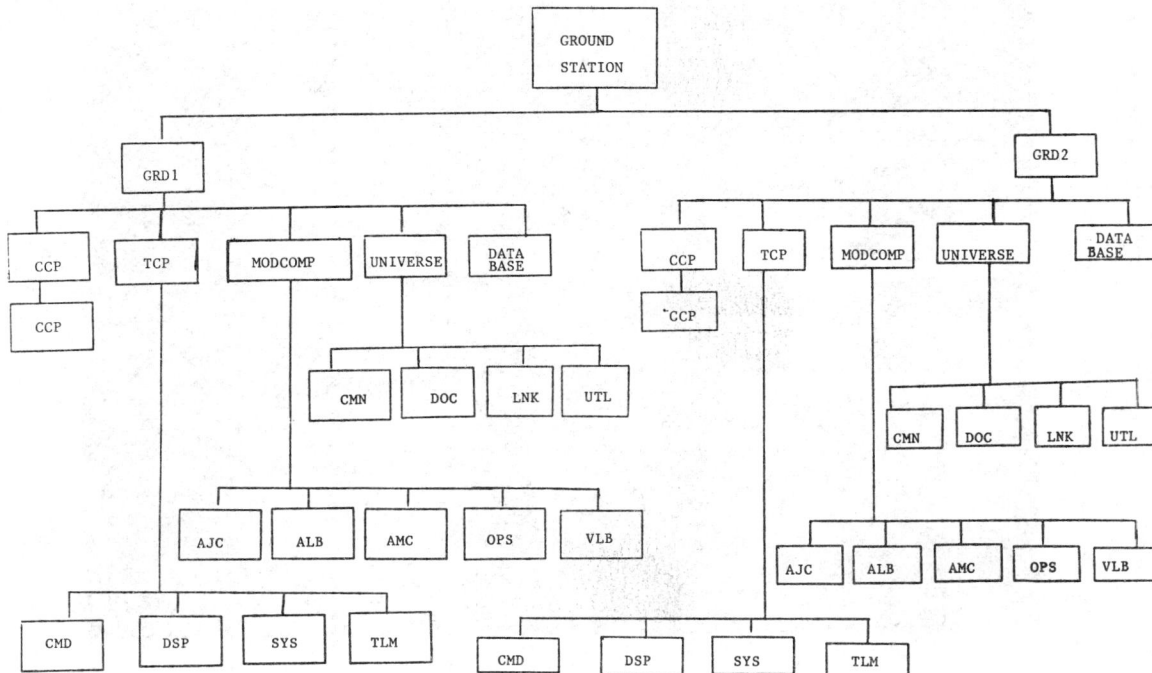

GROUND SYSTEM CMS TREE
FIGURE 1

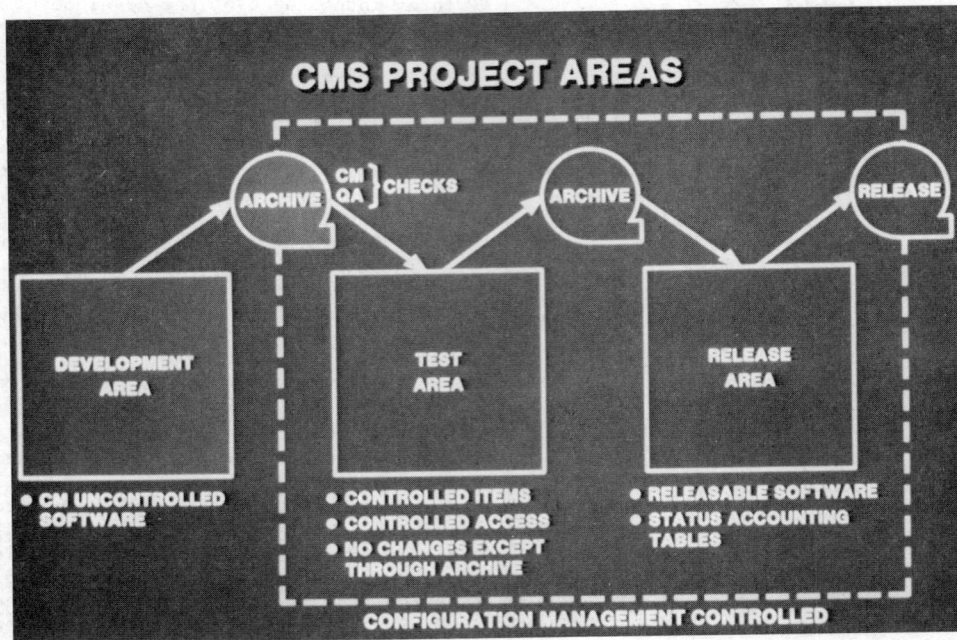

CMS PROJECT AREAS
FIGURE 2

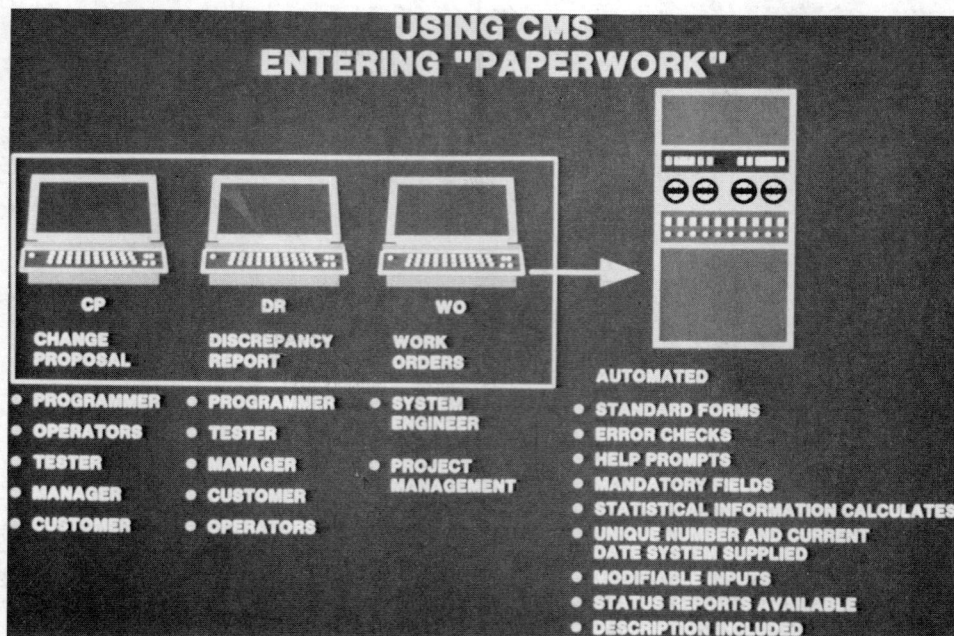

ENTERING THE CONFIGURATION MANAGEMENT SYSTEM
FIGURE 3

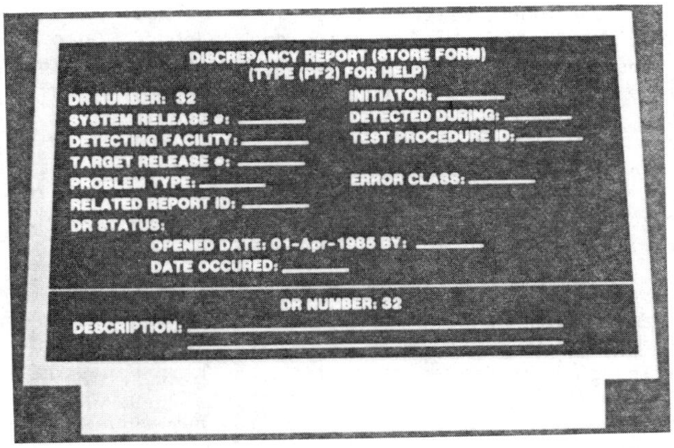

DR STORE FORM
FIGURE 4

Added data is included on the DR form as it progresses through the CMS process. On a regular basis the CM paperwork is received to determine which items will be approved and which will be rejected. A technical investigator is assigned to a report to determine the extent of work required. The technical investigator must perform the analysis to determine the extent of work/cost/schedule and the method required to implement the approved change or new work. He must prepare Change Notices (CN) for each different type of change required (e.g., software, hardware, test procedure, data base, documentation). CN defines how to implement a change or new function. The CN form at the terminal is used by the technical investigator to create one or more CNs for each initiating document (DR, CP or WO).

CNs are reviewed to determine whether they should or should not be implemented. Rejected CNs are closed by the CM manager. Approved CNs are locked so they can no longer be modified by anyone except the person who gives the approval.

An approved CN is the work assignment for the responsible person designated in the CN. In order to work on implementing a change to a file, a Get with Lock operation is performed to retrieve the file from the test or release area. The Get with Lock function will put a copy of the most current version of the requested file into the user's directory and lock the file in the controlled area. Subsequently, anyone who wants to update this file must wait until the borrower returns the new version to the test area or until the file is unlocked. Reports are available which display the name of the locked file, the date and time it was locked, and the person who locked it. However, no one but the borrower may resubmit a new version of this file while the file remains locked.

When the implementer is ready to release the file to be placed under CM control (Test Area), he must prepare a Transmittal Notice (TN), one for each node which will receive one or more new files. Each changed file is noted on a TN which must be approved

by the CM manager. CMS uses the approved TNs for actually moving a file under control.

The CM manager performs a restore function of all new files that have been approved for movement on the TNs, and that pass the standards check and the lock check, are placed in the test area by the system. All items moved into the test area are assigned unique version numbers, and are compared against the last version to produce a set of hard copy differences.

The CM Manager may request reports indicating which CNs have been satisfied. These CNs are then closed and a report is generated which determines which of the DRs, WOs, and CPs may be closed because all CNs they initiated have been closed. The CM Manager then closes these documents.

Once files are under configuration control, the CM Manager can perform builds and releases as requested by the different users. A build request when executed will perform compiles and links, creating a final image for execution. The identification of the entire environment during the build will be saved, including source version numbers and the compiler, linker and operating system versions.

SATELLITE GROUND SYSTEM MAINTENANCE CM

The satellite ground system source files are kept under control with CMS. Source code is edited, updated and controlled on the VAX and then released and translated to MODCOMP format for compilation and object code control on the MODCOMP. Master copies of the documentation are kept in a hard copy library with a characteristic file stored under CMS control to record the change process for the documentation.

A controlled release tape is constructed by CMS, run through the MODVAX utility (changes VAX to MODCOMP format and vice versa), and placed on a tape. The new source files on this release tape are compiled on the MODCOMP producing corresponding controlled object files. Linking these new object files with existing unchanged object files under control, an executable file for the MODCOMP is produced. The Software Engineering personnel on the ground system project use the CMS forms displayed at the terminal to enter Discrepancy Reports (DR), Work Orders (WO), and Change Proposals (CP) as needed. When the corresponding Change Notice (CN) and Transmittal Notice (TN) forms are approved the new configuration items (e.g. source code, test procedures, document descriptions) are placed under control. A release of the source code files is created in MODCOMP compatible form for transfer to the MODCOMP computer for subsequent compilation to produce controlled object files. The object files are then linked to produce controlled executable files. These files are then placed under CM control for subsequent release to the field. The application programmers use the VAX for editing changes to the controlled source code. Once the source code changes are complete, the file is translated into a MODCOMP compatible form and transferred into the programmers own MODCOMP source area. After compilation of the new source code, the resultant object files are

95

linked with the controlled object files on the MODCOMP to form an executable file for debugging the changes. Once the changes have been validated, the source files on the VAX 11/780 are placed under CM control.

SPECIAL CHARACTERISTICS OF CMS

CMS is unique in that it combines the complex forms of configuration management and the control of the CM forms and management approvals into a single integrated system. These features enable the building of a data base useful to the entire project.

There are several differences between an automated and a manual configuration control system. Manual paper forms were often "misplaced" on people's desks during the times they were transferred for approval. With the automated CMS, anyone with access to the VAX can find the status of any paperwork or forms on the system. Closed forms that were several months or even years old were diffecult to locate in a manual system but currently are located within a couple of minutes in CMS.

People interested in the status of a form, (e.g. whether a DR was approved, or the TN was satisfied) can have this information at their fingertips. There is no need to find the Software Configuration Manager to find out the status of the project. Everyone saves time in this way.

The Automated Configuration Management System allows for the generation of reports from the information contained on the different forms. We can selectively report different information (e.g. all DR problems greater than 75 for all DRs written between January 1, 1984 and January 1, 1985). As long as the information is contained on a form, a report can be generated. This reporting allows the users of CMS to generate trending reports. For example, how many DRs were written against software, hardware, documentation, data base, or test procedures? How many of the software DRs were caused by coding errors for formatting errors? These reports can be used currently by the managers to follow the work being done now or in the future for cost proposals.

The manual CM method allows two different people to submit updates simultaneously to the same file. These concurrent updates are usually not discovered until after CM is in the process of performing software builds. At this point CM must stop the build and locate the project leader to determine if both updates should be in the build, or just one. CMS does not allow two different people to update the same file. Files are locked via CMS until they are built. CMS will even notify the second programmer as to who has locked the file and when it was locked.

With CMS one has easy access to the controlled software on the VAX without being able to make changes to it. Using the manual system, the programmers must read from tape to get the latest controlled software. CMS gives high visibility of the system status to the programmers, managers, and CM.

The manual sign-off of forms has lead in the past to many delays for different reasons. Some forms were misplaced, and sometimes it could take days for someone to return a form they were approving. If CM was waiting for that particular form to do a build, this would pose multiple problems. With the automated CMS System, paperwork does not get misplaced, the paperwork is approved at a meeting, and since all necessary lead analysts attend, any questions could be answered at the meeting.

CMS provides a help facility for filling in forms displayed at a terminal. If the user is unsure of what is expected in a particular field, help can be received by pushing the help key. On a manual form, the writer would have to locate the original procedures distributed to them when they first started on the project.

Although the Digital Equipment Corporation (DEC) has created a Code Management System (DEC/CMS), it does not reflect the features of true configuration management. There are not forms. DEC/CMS only controls software where CMS controls any files. The DEC program lacks security. It leaves control open to both intentional and unintentional damage. There are also no files kept for statistics.

REPORTS

Personnel coordination and high visibility of project status occurs when using CMS because it constructs a common data base. Anyone can retrieve the information, if he has access to the computer and the project. Users may create their own reports or use already prepared report formats which are part of CMS. The user can define the domain of records, for which these reports are run, the particular items to be reported, and the sorting parameters of the data.

The figures on the following pages represent a sample of the multitude of reports CMS generates. Figure 5 and Figure 6 are summary reports. Figure 7 and Figure 8 contain information about specific DRs.

CONCLUSIONS

Many benefits were accrued by the entire project by going from a manual to an automated CM system. CMS has been used for over one year, and it has been found to be labor saving to CM, Quality Assurance, testers, programmers, and Project Management. The paperwork associated with deliverable software is more accurate and the customer seems more likely to accept it coming off a machine. People tend to believe more in the accuracy of information that is automatically generated on the computer.

The more CMS is used on a job, the more the configuration management organization becomes dependent upon it to perform the drudge work as well as security checks. When a computer refuses to accept undocumented or unapproved changes, the users cannot be angry at the CM manager. Information and status reports are easy to create allowing the CM

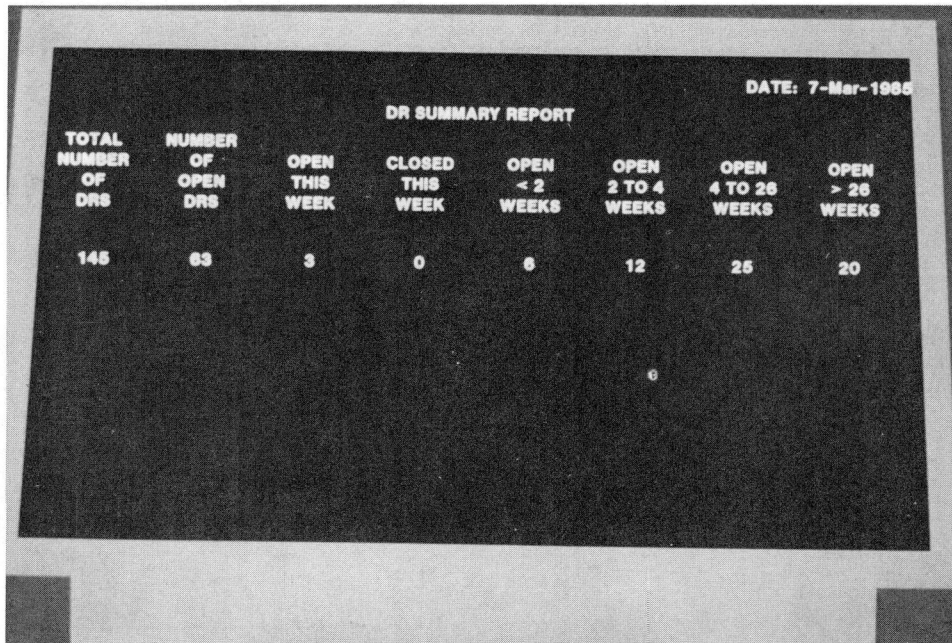

FIGURE 5

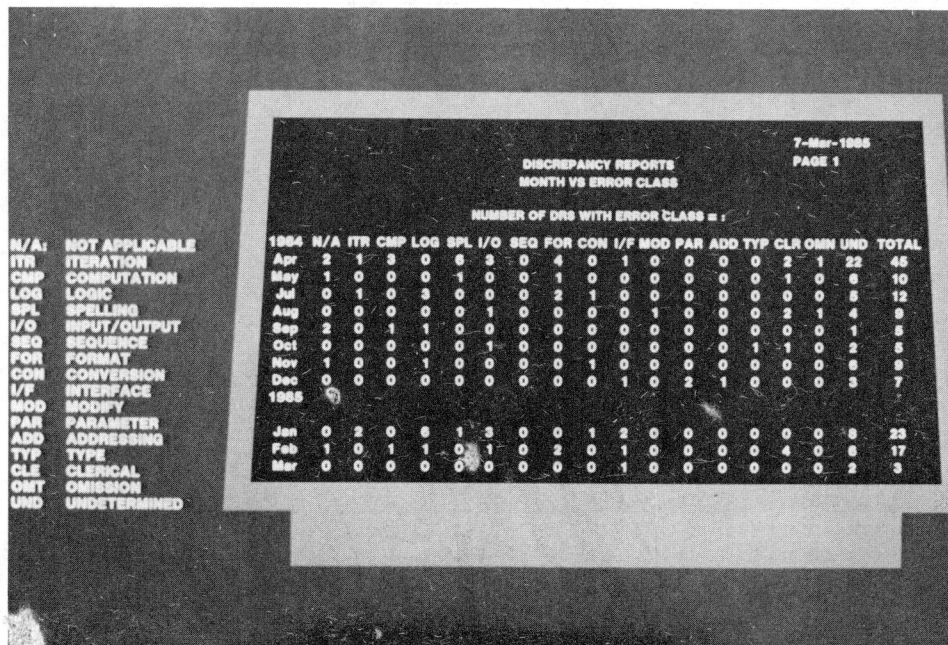

FIGURE 6

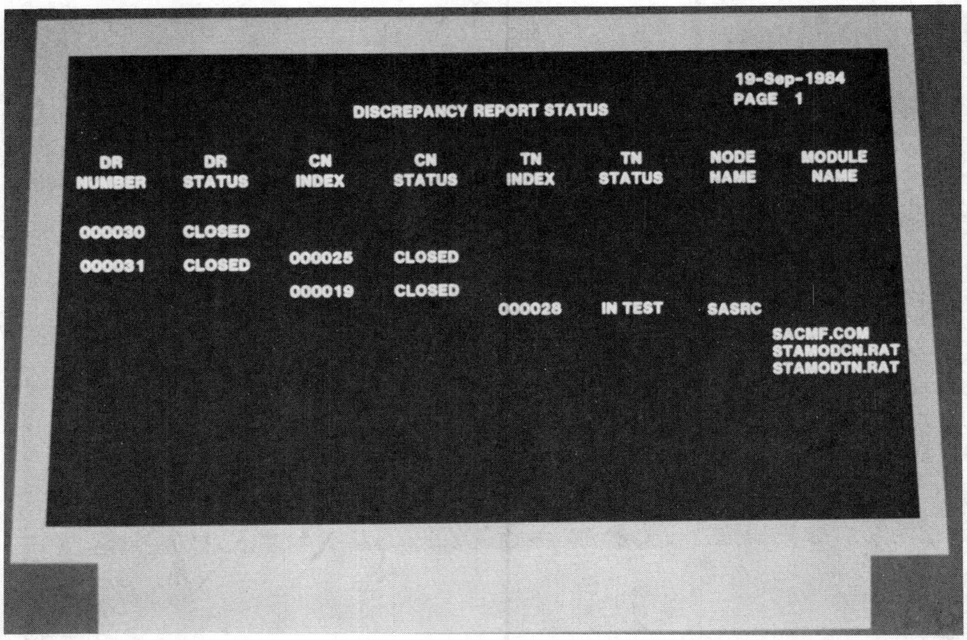

DISCREPANCY REPORT STATUS

19-Sep-1984
PAGE 1

DR NUMBER	DR STATUS	CN INDEX	CN STATUS	TN INDEX	TN STATUS	NODE NAME	MODULE NAME
000030	CLOSED						
000031	CLOSED	000025	CLOSED				
		000019	CLOSED				
				000028	IN TEST	SASRC	

SACMF.COM
STAMODCN.RAT
STAMODTN.RAT

FIGURE 7

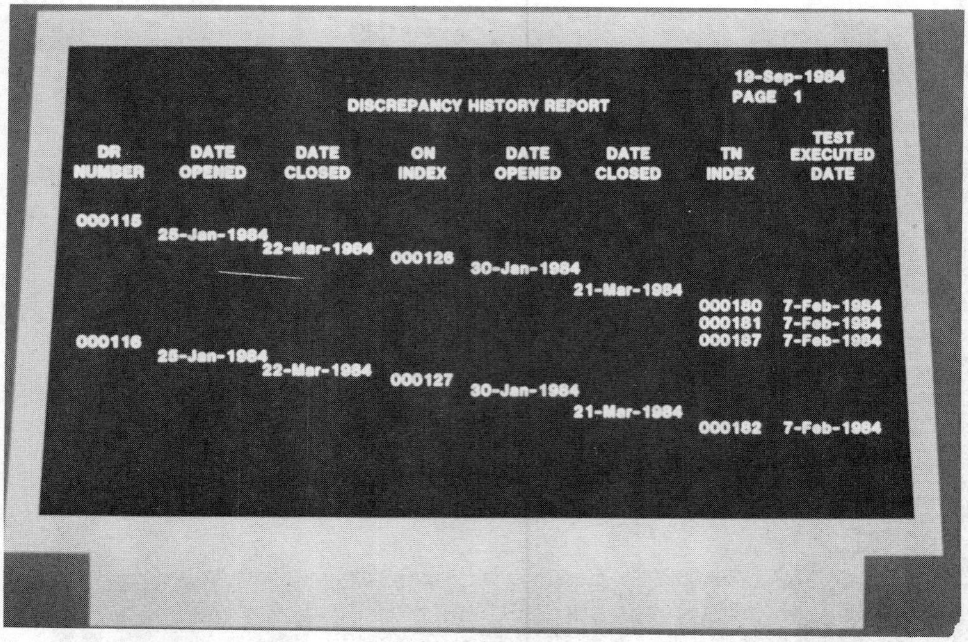

DISCREPANCY HISTORY REPORT

19-Sep-1984
PAGE 1

DR NUMBER	DATE OPENED	DATE CLOSED	ON INDEX	DATE OPENED	DATE CLOSED	TN INDEX	TEST EXECUTED DATE
000115	25-Jan-1984	22-Mar-1984	000126	30-Jan-1984	21-Mar-1984		
						000180	7-Feb-1984
						000181	7-Feb-1984
						000187	7-Feb-1984
000116	25-Jan-1984	22-Mar-1984	000127	30-Jan-1984	21-Mar-1984		
						000182	7-Feb-1984

FIGURE 8

98

complete knowledge about the entire software system.

The security felt because no change in the software can be made to a baseline without the approval and knowledge of the system is comforting. Best of all, no DRs or CNs can get lost on someone's desk for several weeks. Access to forms as well as their status is always available to CM as well as project management.

Prior to CMS reports that made up deliverable software releases used to take up to a week to prepare. Now these reports are processed in minutes.

Management and Software Quality Assurance have access to the complete status of the system at all times. A great savings in verbal communication occurs because the time previously required for programmers and CM to explain their status (especially in crisis mode) is obsolete. Programmers can find out the status of software builds themselves without requiring the attention of the Configuration Manager.

In general CMS makes a very complex system manageable and the data base developed by CMS is available to all so that everyone is aware of the total traceability of problems.

REFERENCES

Sandra Zucker, Automating Configuration Management Process, Software Proceedings, IEEE Computer Society, July 25-28, 1983, pp 164-172

Sandra Zucker, Configuration Management System, Proceedings of the Third General Electric Software Conference, April 21-23, 1982

Military Standard MIL-STD-480, Configuration Management Practices for Systems, Equipment, Munitions and Computer Programs, December 31, 1970

General Electric Quality Assurance Procedures and Software Configuration Management Procedures, October 1980 - January 1982

Digital Equipment Corporation, User's Introduction to DEC/CMS, Order No. AA-L371A-TE, May 1982

AUTOMATED CONFIGURATION MANAGEMENT

Alex Lobba

Softool Corporation

Abstract

The purpose of Configuration Management (CM) is
to identify all the interrelated components of
a body of information and to control its
evolution throughout the various phases of its
life cycle.

The need for CM is ubiquitous. Among its
important applications are: software development and maintenance, document control,
problem tracking, change control, and many
more.

At present, CM is addressed mostly through
manual means which are inadequate and cannot
cope with the problem. Automatic CM is an
absolute necessity. The purpose of this
paper is to discuss the automation of CM and
to illustrate the utilization of an automated
tool currently in wide use.

The Situation Today

The last few years have witnessed a tremendous
increase in the amount of information that is
handled by computers, and in the quantity of
software being developed. The problem of
keeping track of all this information has grown
as well. With the aid of computers, information
is manipulated at a rate that produces different
versions and revisions faster than they can be
documented manually.

Configuration Management (herein referred to as
CM) is the discipline that addresses this
problem. The purpose of CM is to identify all
the interrelated components of a body of information and to control and document its evolution
throughout the various phases of its life cycle.

The need for effective CM is felt in a wide
range of environments and applies to different
types of information. From the software
developer entangled in the complexity of requirement documents evolving into design
documents and then actual code, to those responsible for maintaining all the different
versions of the final software product, to the
engineering firm trying to keep track of the
changes in their computer generated drawings,
to the government agency maintaining documents
and their amendments, to the government contractor who needs to comply with defined standards ... the list goes on and on.

The Conventional Approach

A manual approach to the problem is unmanageable
because it cannot keep up with the speed at which
changes take place. Moreover, as the volume of
information that needs to be managed increases,
the manual approach breaks down. To obtain
up-to-date documentation of the status of information requires that the process of making modifications be interrupted; this is clearly unacceptable. Furthermore, manual or semiautomated
procedures provide little or no control over who
can make changes and where, and over the integrity
of information.

The Need

An automated approach to CM is essential in
implementing the following major aspects of
functionality effectively[1]:

* IDENTIFICATION of all the components of a body
  of information

* STATUS ACCOUNTING reports to document what
  changed, when, and who made the changes

* AUDITING the history of components to verify
  their integrity and compliance with the
  original specifications

* CONTROL over what changes should be made and
  incorporated, and over who can access what
  information.

An automated CM tool should also provide the
ability to identify and document changes as they
occur, without interfering with the process;
thus allowing verification, in real time, that
the right changes were made in the right places.
It should restrict access to information to
selected personnel, and should eliminate the
redundant storage of information that is shared
by multiple versions or baselines.

In summary, what is required is a tool in which
the various aspects and functions of CM are integrated in one consistent environment.

Softool's Change and Configuration Control
(CCC™)

The following is a discussion of Softool's Change and Configuration Control Environment (CCC). A software development environment is used as an example to explain CCC's capabilities.

Identification - Structure of Information in CCC

The first function of CM is to be able to identify all the components of a product.

Information in CCC is organized as a hierarchy of data structures, with the DATA BASE at the highest level.

The data base is composed of SYSTEMS. To relate the diagram in Figure 1 (next column) to a typical situation, System 1 might be a manufacturing control system, System 2 might be a simulation program, and System 3 might be an accounts payable or payroll system, and so on.

Each of these systems is composed of one or more CONFIGURATIONS (baselines or versions) of the parent system. For example, Configuration 1 of the manufacturing control system, might consist of production routines, whereas Configuration 2 might be a development version, and Configuration 3 might be an enhanced version of the exact same system being developed to run on machine B rather than machine A.

Each configuration is in turn composed of MODULE data structures. Modules may represent the different routines or programs that make up a specific configuration of a given system, with corresponding TEXT structures to hold each module's source code, object code, and accompanying documentation.

In another situation, it might make more sense to store all the source routines for a given version in text structures under Module 1 and all the accompanying objects for each routine under Module 2.

In any event, a key feature of CCC is the flexibility it provides in both the representation of, and subsequent access to stored information.

Please note that any level in the CCC hierarchy may have text associated with it, providing a convenient mechanism for associating documentation, job control language procedures, macro procedures, test cases, or any other pertinent pieces of information, with an entire level or structure, from the system data structure on down.

Status Accounting and Auditing - Changes

With the internal structure in mind, we will examine how CCC keeps track of and permits users to manipulate changes made to stored information.

Figure 1

Structure of Information in CCC

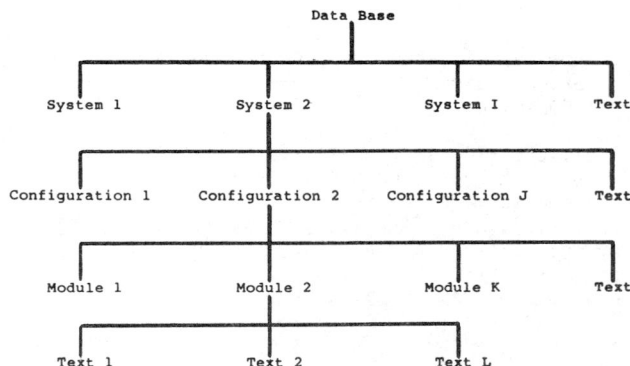

CCC also provides status accounting reports that support the activity of auditing the history of components to verify their integrity.

When a change is made, CCC gives the user an opportunity to enter a change name and a description of the change he or she made, providing a key by which a change, or group of related changes, may be readily accessed and displayed.

For example, a programmer modifying three separate routines to resolve software trouble report (STR) number 65 might name all three changes "STR65". The project manager could then examine, with a single command, all the changes made in order to address STR65.

CCC automatically records who makes a change and when the change is made.

In addition, CCC only keeps track of the actual changes made to a given text structure. This means, for example, that if a programmer changes three lines of a one hundred line program or routine, CCC only saves the three lines that have changed, not a whole new version of the entire 100 lines of information.

This tracking capability of CCC enables a user to maintain a complete audit trail history of all changes made to any structure within the CCC hierarchy. Also, it provides the ability to reconstruct a component as it was at any point in time. In addition to being able to display the actual lines that have been changed in any text component, one is able to generate a number of useful reports based on any one of several change attributes. For example, the following are typical user requests:

. What changes were made by programmer SMITH

. What changes were made to text structure SOURCE1, and by whom

. What changes were made to components of SYSTEMA, After September 27, 1982, at 3:00 PM

. Show me a list of all changes made that have a name of STR65

. Show me the latest version of ROUTINE1, or the version being used on January 23, 1982, at 1:00 AM, etc.

Thus, CCC allows programmers and managers to keep track of all changes, recreate or examine any change made (based on a number of relational criteria), and effectively minimize disk storage by only storing actual changes made to a component structure, rather than storing a whole new copy of the revised structure.

Figure 2 (below) contains a sample change report in which one can see a succinct summary of all the changes made to the component structures of module "SOURCE" in configuration "DEVELOPMENT" of system "SYSTEM1". For each structure, one can see all the versions (e.g., ";1", ";2", etc.), when the changes were made and who made them. Each version is identified by a change name (e.g., STR65).

Figure 2

Configuration Status Accounting Report

```
-  CHANGE REPORT
-
-  STRUCTURE LEVEL:   SYSTEM1.DEVELOPMENT.SOURCE/MOD
-
-  STRUCTURE            DATE;TIME           USER      NAME
-
   DM003/SRC;1          05/02/84;13:20:01   SANDY     STR65
   DM007/SRC;1          05/03/84;15:50:12   SANDY     STR65
   DM007/SRC;2          06/06/84;08:51:20   SANDY     STR18
   DM007/SRC;3          06/09/84;09:04:16   BRUCE     STR76
   DM011/SRC;1          05/03/84;10:34:22   SANDY     STR65
   DM012/SRC;1          05/18/84;09:06:28   BRUCE     STR73
   DM013/SRC;1          05/19/84;12:27:24   BRUCE     STR73
   DM015/SRC;1          04/17/84;11:52:24   SANDY     STR45
```

                    version number

               structure type, in this case SRC stands for source

        structure name

Figure 3

Detailed Change Report

```
-  CHANGE REPORT
-
-  STRUCTURE LEVEL:   SYSTEM1.DEVELOPMENT.SOURCE/MOD
-
-  STRUCTURE            DATE;TIME           USER      NAME
-
   DM007/SRC;3          06/09/84;09:04:16   BRUCE     STR76
-
-  DESCRIPTION
-
   This change was made to accommodate a special graphics device
   (Graphile Mode 13) attached to our compilers.  It was approved
   in Management Request No. M3-42.  It is documented in detail
   in our Internal Memo No. C3-42.
-
-  ACTUAL CHANGES
#1    DELETE 1 LINE BEGINNING WITH LINE 18 :

          ARRAY = 300

#2    INSERT 1 LINE :

18:1      ARRAY = 2500

      AFTER LINE 18:0
```

In Figure 3, an example of a more detailed change report is shown. Here a user asked for a listing of the description and actual changes made in version 3 of text structure DM007/SRC.

Trouble Reports

CCC also provides the ability to keep track of documents such as software trouble reports and engineering change proposals. The first report in Figure 4, contains a listing of the current status of all STR's. In the second report, one can see the complete history of STR number 51. Also, one can selectively ask for a summary description of each change of status, and list the actual contents of each STR document.

Figure 4

```
-  CHANGE REPORT
-
-  STRUCTURE LEVEL:   SYSTEM1.DEVELOPMENT.STR/MOD
-
-  STRUCTURE            DATE;TIME           USER      STATUS
-
   14/STR;3             04/06/84;09:36:19   BRUCE     FIXED
   77/STR;2             05/03/84;16:14:21   BRUCE     ASSIGNED
   39/STR;2             04/11/84;10:08:28   BRUCE     ASSIGNED
   51/STR;4             05/23/84;14:42:09   BRUCE     CLOSED
-
-  CHANGE REPORT
-
-  STRUCTURE LEVEL:   SYSTEM1.DEVELOPMENT.STR/MOD
-
-  STRUCTURE            DATE;TIME           USER      STATUS
-
   51/STR;1             04/25/84;11:08:49   BRUCE     REPORTED
   51/STR;2             04/30/84;09:39:06   BRUCE     ASSIGNED
   51/STR;3             05/15/84;16:00:32   BRUCE     FIXED
   51/STR;4             05/23/84;14:42:09   BRUCE     CLOSED
```

Control - Configurations (Baselines)

CCC offers true configuration control:

All components of a given software release or baseline can be organized and managed as a single entity that preserves the relationship between components. Then, all distinct but related releases can be handled as separate units with CCC doing the busy work of managing the changes that define the separate versions.

In addition, CCC provides the capability to operate on configurations as a whole. For example, one can combine the changes made in two separate configurations into a single configuration. CCC will flag any conflicts encountered when combining the two configurations.

Finally, CCC maintains a complete history of exactly what has been changed in moving from the original configuration of a given product to its latest version. The ability to document the changes from baseline to baseline gives full auditing and traceability, thus allowing the user to verify that each component is evolving in a logical and consistent progression from the previous stages.

For the purpose of describing how CCC maintains different versions of components, we have coined the terms "virtual" configurations. What this means to a CCC user is that whenever he or she uses the latest version of a piece of information, it appears as though that person has a complete, up-to-date copy of the information in question. In fact, the user really has only a virtual copy of the baseline configuration.

For example, the production version of a software product contains 20 routines. Configuration 1 of the same product also contains these 20 routines, but 5 of them have been modified to make the system functional under a different host computer. Physically, CCC only stores the changes to those 5 routines under Configuration 1, eliminating the redundancy inherent in duplicating the whole product.

All of this is transparent to the user of CCC.

Access Control and Protection

CCC provides powerful access control features to define who can do what and where (Figure 5 below).

Figure 5

Access Control

. USER-ID AND PASSWORD CONTROL

. THREE TYPES OF USERS:

    Data Base Administrator
    Manager
    User

. ACCESS CONTROL BASED ON:

    Structure
    User
    Class of User

. ENCRYPTION

To ensure that no unauthorized users log into CCC, there is log in user-ID and password control. User-ID and passwords may only be established by a user with data base administrator privileges, and must be correctly entered to gain admittance to CCC upon initial log in.

Furthermore, CCC users are divided into three categories with different degrees of privileges:

. Data Base Administrators

. Managers

. Users

In addition to controlling the access of users to CCC as a whole, CCC provides the capability to limit user access to a specific structure, on a per user, or class of user, basis. Thus, all users of class UPDATER, for example, might only be permitted to log into a development configuration, effectively locking out the corresponding production version from any accidental modification.

Users requiring tighter controls can also request that information be encrypted.

Traits

To determine how data is internally stored, and how difficult it is to access that data, CCC allows the assignment of structure traits.

These traits determine:

. whether a unit of information will be shared among derived configurations (i.e., virtual copy), or its storage will be duplicated (i.e., physical copy)

. whether CCC maintains a complete audit trail of all changes, or only the most recent version of a component

. the degree of compression by which information is stored

. the degree of encryption by which information is encoded.

Conclusion

Keeping track of evolving information is a critical issue with which the current manual methods cannot cope. The automation of configuration management is essential. Softool's CCC provides the high level of automation that is needed in a comprehensive change and configuration control environment.

[1] "Software Configuration Management", An Investment in Product Integrity, by Edward H. Bersoff, Vilas D. Henderson, Stanley G. Siegel

Session 4

Software Design and Development Tools

Chairman
Julie Landstein
IBM

AVOID DISASTER: THE USE OF AN INTEGRATED TOOL FOR MANAGING THROUGHPUT AND RESPONSE TIME REQUIREMENTS IN EMBEDDED REAL-TIME SOFTWARE SYSTEMS

David L. Hall, John J. Gibbons, and David A. Woodle

HRB-Singer, Inc.
P. O. Box 60
State College, PA 16804
(814) 238-4311

The development of large-scale, real-time software systems is plagued by throughput problems typically discovered during system integration. At that phase of system development, measured contention response times often reveal that the software does not meet system throughput constraints. Redesign and tuning result in schedule and cost overruns. This paper describes a strategy for avoiding these problems by a threefold approach: (1) well-defined system response time and throughput requirements identified early in system development and allocated to software units via resource budgets; (2) an Integrated Software Design Tool (ISDT) providing requirements traceability, consolidated design data base, and software performance analysis capability; and (3) management of the software resource budgets via frequent performance predictions and monitoring of unit budgets during software design, coding and unit test. This approach is uniquely keyed to using software design and metrics data available from the ISDT data base thereby ensuring consistent timing and functional design verification. As a result, the development risks of real-time software systems are reduced by early identification of potential response time problems. The techniques and tools for implementing this strategy are described in this paper.

INTRODUCTION

The development of software for large-scale systems has matured to the point that the methodology is well-defined. A progression of project phases including requirements analysis, preliminary design, detailed design, code and unit test, software integration and test (I&T) and system I&T provide for an orderly top down creation of a software system. As illustrated in Figure 1, each project phase is concluded by formal reviews with associated documentation and baselined design or products. In the DoD community, formal documentation exists which prescribes the standards for products, contents of documentation, and appropriate levels of detail of design at each project phase (e.g., (1)). Many software industries have developed their own software standards and procedures which parallel and augment the DoD standards (reference (2)).

The development of real-time systems, particularly in an embedded environment, poses throughput problems which are only marginally addressed by standard methodologies. Typically, real-time systems exhibit throughput problems during I&T

which may include; failure to meet response time requirements in a contention environment, excessive use of one or more computer resources (e.g., CPU, disk, bus or device I/O, etc.), and nonrobust system behavior in which small changes in system loading result in large changes in response times. These problems are usually first detected during software or system integration since this is the first project phase at which response times can be measured on a transaction basis vice a software unit level. (A transaction is defined here as a sequence or thread of software functions initiated by an external stimulus and resulting in an external response). Although detected during integration, these problems have roots in the very early phases of design. At the integration and test phases, the options for resolving the throughput issue are severely limited and, even when effective, may result in schedule and cost overruns.

This paper describes a strategy for minimizing or avoiding throughput problems by an integrated process including:

1) precise definition of system response time and throughput requirements early in the design phase with definition of resource budgets allocated to software units;

2) the use of an Integrated Software Design Tool (ISDT) for requirements traceability, management of a consolidated design data base, and software performance analysis tools based on analytical queuing models; and

3) management of software resource budgets allocated to individual software units during software design, code, unit test, and integration and test.

This strategy augments classical software development methodology to meet the needs of real-time system development.

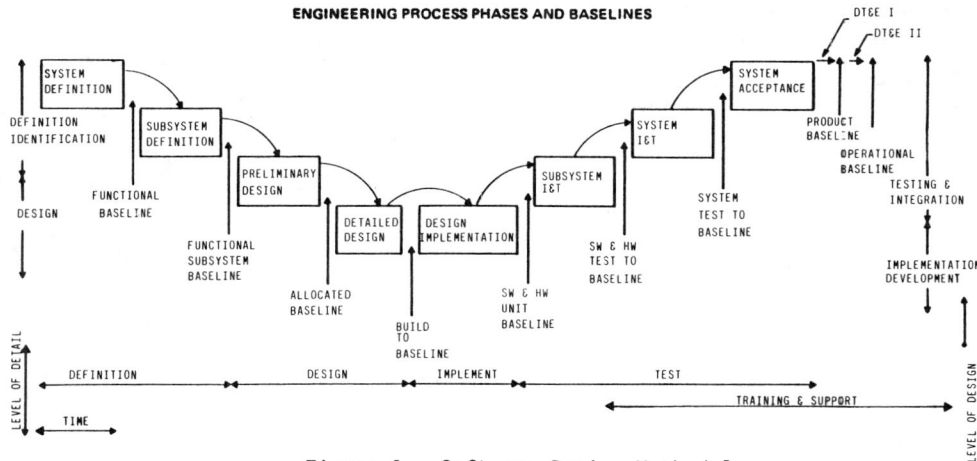

Figure 1: Software Design Methodology

PERFORMANCE PROBLEMS IN REAL-TIME SYSTEMS

Embedded real-time software systems are subject to constraints on available computer resources and yet must meet throughput requirements while multiple software units are simultaneously contending for those resources. Complex computer architectures may be used with multiple processors linked via a local area network (LAN) to peripherals such as data storage and output devices. Real-time aspects of such systems may involve real-time control of hardware (e.g., receivers, data collection devices) or highspeed synchronous external interfaces. The design of systems of this type require decisions concerning; choice of basic architecture, selection of specific computer equipment, partitioning of software functions among devices, software architecture (software environment, use of operating system functions, data record management services, etc.), detailed software unit design (data flow, control, design of computer program components and routines) and finally detailed issues such as sizes of data buffers, specification of system generation parameters and overlay or paging considerations. Although modern sophisticated commercial software such as operating systems and data base management software tend to ease the burdern of system design by providing for built-in resource management, they also tend to obscure resource overhead and to make designers complacent about resource utilization.

The performance problems of real-time systems have beginnings even in the procurement stage. Considerable work is required to specify the response time requirement for individual transactions in a system (e.g., the response time for display of a histogram shall not exceed 2 seconds measured from the depression of the execute key on the user's keyboard to the display of the final character on the display screen). In typical systems developed at HRB-Singer, between 30 and 60 transactions may be defined. Even more difficult is the specification of the contention environment, or system workload, at which the response times must be met. This entails specifying the average and peak frequency of instantiation of each transaction. The performance requirements and workload for a real-time system need to be developed. Part of the difficulty in such specification is that in the procurement stage, only a subset of transactions necessary for a system are known. Further design is required to identify all the system transactions. Thus, part of the system requirements analysis and design process is the identification of transactions and specification of associated response requirements.

During subsequent design phases (preliminary and detailed design), software designers tend to focus on hierarchical breakdown of functions (e.g., identification of subsystems, computer program components (CPCs), and units) and flow of data control between and within units. Tools for this design, such as Program Design Language (PDL) (reference (3)) aid the identification of units, establishment of interfaces, and logical flow within units. These tools, however, do not support performance analysis. Indeed, although numerous commercial software tools are available to support detailed design, code and unit test of software, few tools are available to support the early requirements analysis and preliminary design phase. This is illustrated in Figure 2.

The early requirements analysis and preliminary design are key to successful development of real-time systems. Not only are errors in design more difficult to detect and correct the later the development phase at which they are discovered, but, in addition, the available options to resolve the problems become more limited in later phases. This is especially true for performance issues. If performance problems are identified during integration and test, the available options to resolve the problems are very limited and relatively ineffective. Figure 3 illustrates the availability of design and implementation decisions which affect system performance as a function of development phase. The solutions become progressively limited and relatively ineffective with each succeeding phase. Clearly, for example, the selection of a fundamental system architecture has a greater effect then selection of data buffer sizes.

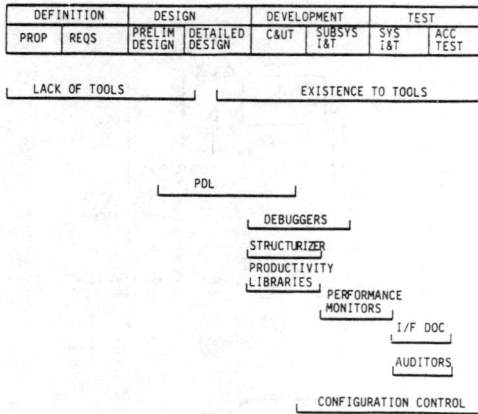

Figure 2: Current Status of Software Tools Over the System Development Life Cycle

DEVELOPMENT PHASE	PERFORMANCE SOLUTIONS
Requirements Analysis	o Definition of Response Requirements o Definition of System Workload o Identification of System Constraints
Preliminary Design	o Architecture Selection o Selection of Computer Hardware o Partitioning of Functions Among H/W and S/W o Partitioning of Functions Among Subsystems o Allocation of Performance Budgets to Subsystems
Detailed Design	o Partitioning of Functions Among CPCs o Selection of Algorithms o Design of Detailed S/W Architecture
Code & Unit Test	o Allocation of Budgets to Routines o Use of Assembly Language vs. HOL o Detailed Code/Logic Structure o Selection of Buffer Sizes, etc. o Partitioning of Data Among Routines
Integration and Test	o System Generation (SYSGEN) Parameters o Tuning of Buffer Sizes, etc.

Figure 3: Available Solutions for Performance Problems vs. Development Phase

If the available solutions are ineffective in resolving performance problems at the phase at which the problems are discovered, then considerable rework may be required to effect the solution from an earlier phase.

AN INTEGRATED SOFTWARE DESIGN TOOL (ISDT)

In order to address these issues at HRB-Singer, a systematic effort has developed management techniques to augment classic software system project management, and developed an Integrated Software Design Tool (ISDT).

The ISDT is a tool aimed primarily at the early phases of project design, but applicable throughout the software development life cycle. This tool is described in detail in references (4) and (5). The tool executes on a VAX 11/780 computer using a VT-241 color alphanumeric terminal for man-machine interface. A commercial relational data base management system (ORACLE) is used to perform data management. Figure 4 illustrates the basic ISDT architecture, and Figure 5 summarizes the required hardware and software environment.

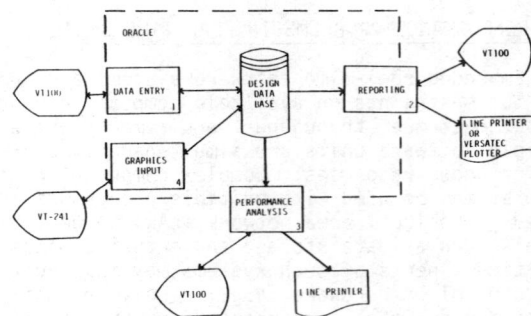

Figure 4: Architecture of the Integrated Software Design Tool (ISDT)

ENVIRONMENT	REQUIREMENT
Hardware	
o computer	DEC VAX 11/7XX
o memory	2 Mbytes
o data storage	RA 81 disk drive
o line printer	any
o alphanumeric terminal	VT-100 compatible
o color graphics terminal	VT-241 (optional)
o graphics plotter	VERSATEC plotter or equivalent
Software	
o operating system	DEC VAX/VMS v 3.5
o DBMS	ORACLE DBMS v 4.0.12
o compiler	FORTRAN - 77+
o graphics software	DI-3000 Graphics Interface package

Figure 5: Hardware and Software Environment Required for the ISDT

The ISDT provides four basic functions; (1) a relational data model to support system design, (2) data entry via both alphanumeric and graphic input, (3) output reports which describe the system design, and (4) several performance analysis algorithms to analyze computer system performance in both a contention and non-contention environment. Each of these functions is summarized below.

The heart of the ISDT is a centralized relational data model to support system design. The model consists of twenty-one two-dimensional views of data which are created to design a system. These data include requirements, software and hardware functions, transactions, computer equipment, scenarios, interface control documentation (ICDs), system elements (e.g., system, subsystem components, CPCs, units, etc.), and connections among the data. The creation and evolution of these data constitutes an evolving system design. The data model was selected to represent the views typically envisioned by system designers.

Data entry is accomplished in two modes, either alphanumeric data entry on the alphanumeric keypad (using function keys) on the VT-100, or graphics data entry using the VT-241 color graphics device. The data is accessible via a SEQUEL query language and predefined queues. Figures 6 and 7 illustrate displays associated with alphanumeric and graphic data input, respectively. The graphics data entry is particularly applicable for defining data flow and connections between functions (transactions) and defining the residency of software functions on computer equipment and required computer resources. The graphic interface also provides for automatic translation between the graphic input and the underlying tabular data model. Another feature reorganizes messy displays to provide visually pleasing displays.

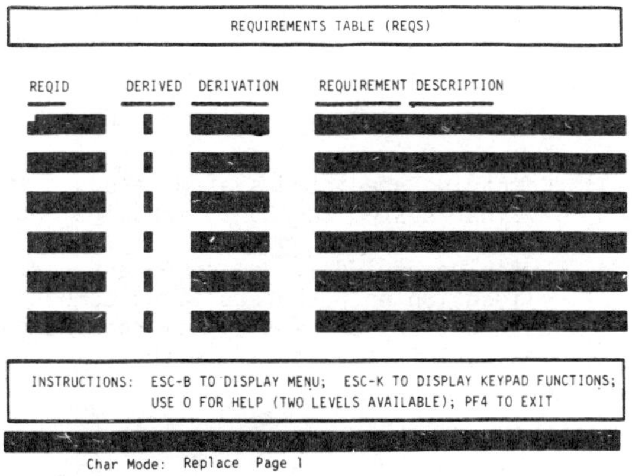

Figure 6: Requirements Data Entry Screen

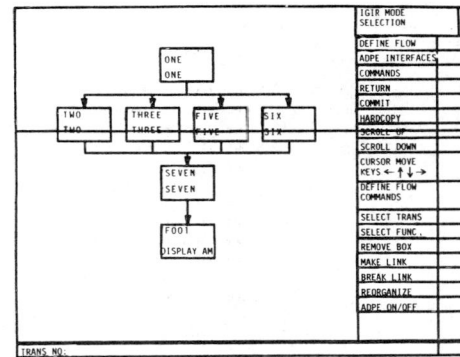

Figure 7: Graphics Display

Forty-one data output reports are provided to document the emerging system design. These reports include all of the two dimensional data relations and a number of indirect relations. Examples of output reports include software hierarchy diagrams, compliance matrixes (e.g., requirements mapped to software units, and requirements to test cases), ICDs, and graphical output of transactions. These reports are used directly in software documentation and for formal design reviews such as preliminary design reviews (PDRs) and critical design reviews (CDRs). The output reports allow system designers to have current hard copy of the system design data.

The final function provided by the ISDT is a set of computer performance models. The performance models are based on analytical queuing models including; (1) an open network of queues (references (6) and (7)), (2) several models for Ethernet local area networks, (3) models for priority queuing of transactions within a scenario, and (4) the linearizer model which uses a closed network of queues as an approximation (reference (8)). These models provide a complete capability to analyze response times for transactions and the contention for resources in complex computer architectures.

Several output reports are available from the computer performance models. A transaction time-line report (Figure 8) graphically shows the sequence of software functions required to complete a specified transaction and the elapsed time required for each function. The time for each function is computed based on the required resource utilization (viz. CPU time, number of I/Os, etc.). Total duration of the transaction is normalized to 100 so that the relative effect of each software function can be easily compared. The transaction time-line report can be output for either a contention environment, in which multiple transactions are competing for computer resources, or in a non-contention environment with only a single transaction.

Another type of performance report summarizes the average percent utilization of each computer resource. A sample report is shown in Figure 9. This report shows designers which resources have high utilization rates and must be carefully managed. A related output record can be obtained for

```
                                              TIMELINE
FUNC. DESCRIPTION          0   10  20  30  40  50  60  70  80  90  100   (TIMES FACTOR = 0.8353598E-01)

1401  T14.GET COMPOSE FILE REQU 0   .   .   .   .   .   .   .   .   .   .   FUNC DUR:.3000000E-02 SECS ( 0.036%)
1402  T14.SEND REQUEST TO VAX  >>   .   .   .   .   .   .   .   .   .   .   FUNC DUR:.9908000E-01 SECS ( 1.186%)
1403  T14.OPEN/CREATE COMPOSE F .>>  .   .   .   .   .   .   .   .   .   .   FUNC DUR:.1680556 SECS ( 2.012%)
1404  T14.SEND FULL TEXT BUFFER .>==========>  .   .   .   .   .   .   .   FUNC DUR:1.894012 SECS ( 22.673%)
1405  T14.RECEIVE TEXT BUFFER   .   .>=======>  .   .   .   .   .   .   .   FUNC DUR:1.200000 SECS ( 14.065%)
1406  T14.ENTER MODS/NEW TEXT   .   .   .  >==>  .   .   .   .   .   .   .   FUNC DUR:.4000001 SECS ( 4.788%)
1407  T14.SEND VAX MODS/NEW TEX .   .   .   .>================>.   .   .   FUNC DUR:2.701800 SECS ( 32.343%)
1408  T14.RECEIVE MODS/NEW TEXT .   .   .   .   .   .   .   .>>  .   .   .   FUNC DUR:.2222223 SECS ( 2.660%)
1409  T14.UPDATE COMPOSE FILE   .   .   .   .   .   .   .   .   >  .   .   FUNC DUR:.5483627E-03 SECS ( 0.007%)
1410  T14.CLOSE COMPOSE FILE    .   .   .   .   .   .   .   .>=========>.   FUNC DUR:1.456000 SECS ( 17.430%)
1411  T14.SEND PC STATUS        .   .   .   .   .   .   .   .   .   >.   FUNC DUR:.9908009E-01 SECS ( 1.186%)
9004  TXX.DECODE STATUS FROM VA .   .   .   .   .   .   .   .   .   .>X  FUNC DUR:.1098003 SECS ( 1.314%)

SYMBOL-EXPLANATION
>---> DURATION OF A NORMAL FUNCTION
0---> DURATION OF A FUNCTION WITH NO PREDECESSORS
>--X  DURATION OF A FUNCTION WITH NO SUCCESSORS
*     ZERO-LENGTH FUNCTION


                                 TRANSACTION          14 --> MAINTAIN COMPOSE
TOTAL DURATION (NON-CONTENTION) FOR TRANSACTION       14 -->   8.354   SECONDS
```

Figure 8: Transaction Time-Line

```
                              LOAD PER TRANSACTION FOR THE VAX

TRANS    TRANS                                        UTIL/TRANS HISTOGRAM
NUMBER   DESCRIPTION              UTIL/TRANS  0     .25     .50     .75       1.00

  1      INDEX SEARCH CMF            0.05
  2      INDEX SEARCH PRIVATE        0.09
  3      TEXT SEARCH CMF           689.52    |=================================
  4      TEXT SEARCH CMF (HIT)      53.98    |==
  5      TEXT SEARCH COMPOSE         2.17    |
  6      TEXT SEARCH PRIVATE       306.63    |=============
  7      INDEX SEARCH STRUCTURE      0.03    |
  8      NON-INDEX SRCH STRUCT.(M    3.30    |
  9      TEXT SRCH STRUCT.(HIT)     34.96    |==
 10      UPDATE PRIV.(HIT/HOLD)      0.00    |
 11      UPDATE PRIV.(SINGLE TRAN    0.00    |
 12      UPDATE CMF (SINGLE TRANS    0.00    |
 13      CREATE NEW PRIV.(HIT/HOL    0.02    |
 14      MAINTAIN COMPOSE            0.86    |
 15      STRUCT. MAINT.(MASS UPDA    0.00    |
 16      STRUCT. MAINT.(ONLINE UP    0.00    |
 17      STRUCT. MAINT.(BATCH UPD    0.00    |
 18      MAIL BROWSE                54.82    |==
 19      CMF (HIT) BROWSE            0.04    |
 20      PRIV.(HIT) BROWSE           0.01    |
 21      STRUCTURE (HIT) BROWSE      1.59    |
 22      USER -> USER MESSAGE        0.00    |
 23      PRINT REPORT                0.00    |
 24      CREATE ARCHIVE              0.01    |
 25      RELOAD FROM ARCHIVE         0.00    |
 26      CMF INPUT                   9.03    |
                                 ----------------------------
```

Figure 9: Computer Resource Utilization

each computer resource, showing the extent to which each transaction uses the specified resource. This allows designers to quickly determine key trans-actions which use significant amounts of resources.

PERFORMANCE ANALYSIS AND RESOURCE MANAGEMENT

The ISDT can be used for consolidating design data and performance analysis throughout the design and implementation of a real-time software system. Special management attention must also be directed towards the definition and control of computer resources. During each project development phase, performance analysis activities include:

(1) Estimating the computer resource re-quired by individual system components (e.g., subsystems, computer program components, software units, as appropriate).

(2) Inputting the component level resource estimates into the ISDT data base.

(3) Using the ISDT to predict system perfor-mance (e.g., contention response times for transactions).

(4) Comparing predicted system response times against system throughput requirements.

(5) Redesign of individual components or re-allocation or resources among components as necessary to meet system requirements. The options available are those listed in Figure 3.

(6) When performance predictions indicate that the current design meets system re-quirements, the allocated resources are specified as resource budgets for soft-ware engineers to meet.

As the system design progresses, the allocation of resources to system components is refined from sub-systems to computer program components, software units, and ultimately to individual subroutines. During implementation, estimates of resource re-quirements can be replaced with actual measurements of resources using software monitoring tools. The accuracy of the performance predictions successively improves and the allocation of resources among com-ponents becomes finer and finer.

The resource budgets must be monitored to en-sure compliance for each system component during design and implementation. To ensure adherence to these goals, the resource budgets are reported on a monthly basis. As part of the software unit development process, the source budgets are included in the unit development folders (UDFs). During design walkthroughs, code ready reviews, etc., the budgets are monitored. In addition, the resource budgets are included as part of unit level tests. Strict adherence to budgets at a unit level will guarantee that the system meets overall through-put requirements at the completion of system integration. Although this strategy appears elementary, it is frequently forgotten during the pressured efforts to develop software to meet functional requirements.

EXPERIENCE AT HRB-SINGER, INC.

The ISDT and associated management techniques have evolved at HRB-Singer, Inc. over the past few years. Recent use of the ISDT on seven projects is summarized in Figure 10 which lists project identifier, total size of the software to be developed (viz. number of lines of code of higher order language), the development schedule, the approximate number of requirements, current project status and comments on the primary use of the ISDT.

Preliminary use of both the ISDT and management attention to computer resource budgets have been encouraging. Training in the resource analysis techniques has been initiated for software engineers. In general, a higher awareness of real-time problems has been created. Further experience, however, needs to be gathered to determine if a measurable increase in software productivity results from the use of the ISDT and associated management methodology.

REFERENCES

[1] NSA/CSS Software Product Standards Manual, NSAM 81-3, National Security Agency.

[2] Software Standards and Conventions Document, HRB-Singer, Inc., 1982.

[3] Program Design Language Reference Guide, Technical Manual produced by Caine, Farber, and Gordon, Inc., 750 East Green Street, Pasadena. CA, 91101, February 1977.

[4] D. L. Hall, J. J. Gibbons, and D. A. Woodle, "An Integrated Software Tool Set", presented at the 1984 AFCEA Symposium, Naval Surface Weapons Center, September 1984.

[5] P. Hastings and B. Fike, "An Integrated Software Design Tool Built on ORACLE", presented at the Third International ORACLE User's Group Conference, San Francisco, August 1984.

[6] D. Finkel, D. L. Hall, and J. Beneke, "Computer Performance Evaluation: The Use of Time Line Queuing Method Throughout a Project Life Cycle," Modeling and Simulation, 13 (1982) pp.729-734.

[7] T. Elchak, D. Finkel, and D. L. Hall, "Planning for Performance: Computer Performance Evaluation in the Early Stages of Project Development", The Modeling and Proceedings of Simulation Conference, Pittsburgh, PA, April 1983.

[8] K. M. Chany and D. Neuse, "Linearizer: A Heuristic Algorithm for Queuing Network Models of Computing Systems", Comm. of the ACM, Vol. 25, 1982.

PROJECT	LOC	SCHEDULE	REQS	STATUS	USAGE/COMMENTS
1	80000	30 MONTHS	300	∼CDR	o PERFORMANCE ANALYSIS
2	9000	24 MONTHS	30	∼PDR	o REQUIREMENTS MAPPING o TRANSACTION DEF'N
3	10000	12 MONTH DESN 15 MONTH DEV	100	∼CDR	o REQUIREMENTS MAPPING
4	STUDY	6 MONTH DEFN 24 MONTH DEV	209		o REQUIREMENTS MAPPING o PROPOSAL ONLY
5	22000	24 MONTHS	300	∼PDR	o REQUIREMENTS MAPPING o PERFORMANCE ANALYSIS o JUST STARTING
6	40000	36 MONTHS	700	PROP	o REQUIREMENTS MAPPING o PERFORMANCE ANALYSIS o JUST STARTING
7	85000	36 MONTHS	200	PRE-SRR	o REQUIREMENTS ANALYSIS o JUST STARTING o PORT TO IBM/PC

Figure 10: ISDT Usage During 1984

AN ENVIRONMENT FOR WORKSTATIONS*

Steven P. Reiss, Joseph N. Pato, Marc H. Brown

Department of Computer Science, Brown University, Providence, RI 02912

ABSTRACT

In this paper, we describe an environment for powerful graphics-based personal workstations. The environment consists of a collection of sophisticated packages for window management, graphical and textual output, menu-based input, program control, and communications. This "toolset" simplifies developing interactive graphics applications that are both consistent in the interface that they present to users and portable to a large number of workstations.

1. Introduction

Not too long ago, only a small select group of computer scientists had access to the expensive and scarce hardware required for building interactive graphics applications. Now, powerful workstations with pointing devices and high-resolution bitmapped displays (e.g., Apollo, Sun) are readily available, and graphics applications are fast becoming quite common. Although the effective development of such applications requires sophisticated software support, there is no good understanding nor standard as to what this support entails. All too often the available software is primitive and difficult to use. Inevitably, the software varies from one machine to another.

To address these problems we have developed an integrated "toolset" of software packages for workstations that is collectively called the Brown Workstation Environment. This toolset provides mechanisms that make graphical output as simple to produce as textual output has traditionally been. It provides graphical input mechanisms that make a pointing device coupled with menus, icons, and "picking" as simple to use as textual input has traditionally been. It provides window management facilities that allow applications to run in a multi-window environment without dealing with the complexities of window-management. In addition, the toolset is designed to be easily ported, thus ensuring that applications based on it can run on a variety of workstations.

The Brown Workstation Environment is currently running on Apollo and Sun workstations, and has been in "production use" within the Computer Science Department at Brown for teaching, research, and student programming projects since the Fall of the 1982. We have used feedback from the users of the environment to continually upgrade and augment the facilities it provides.

In this paper we present a description of the Brown Workstation Environment. The next section provides some of the motivation and design goals of the environment and briefly compares it to other environments. Section 3 contains an overview of the design of the environment, followed by a summary of each toolset component in Section 4. Section 5 offers some concluding remarks.

2. Background

Throughout the design and development of the environment, we have stressed machine-independence, extensibility, ergonomics and integration.

Machine-independence is important because there will be a variety of workstations available and the cost of redeveloping an application for each one is too high. While some of the interfaces for these workstations are relatively standard (such as the Unix** operating system), the interfaces involving graphical input and output almost always differ from one workstation to another both in terms of the available software and the hardware support. We believe that such differences will become even greater in the future as workstations evolve to fit a wide variety of needs, from the entry-level machine for students and secretaries, to the advanced-level machine for researchers and software developers. Our environment is flexible and forward-looking so that applications written today will run efficiently with little or no modifications on new machines with different hardware and software capabilities.

Extensibility is a key part of a research or academic environment. The toolset structure of our environment allows tools to be easily added, modified or replaced. Our initial set of tools has stressed extensibility in and

* This research was supported in part by National Science Foundation grants MCS-8200670 and MCS-8121806, by the ONR and DARPA under Contract N00014-83-K-0146 and ARPA Order No. 4786, and by a grant from Digital Equipment Corporation. Partial equipment support was provided by NSF Grant SER80-04974 and by Apollo Computer, Inc. Partial support for the third author was also provided by the Exxon Education Foundation and by the IBM Graduate Student Fellowship Program.

** Unix is a trademark of Bell Laboratories.

of itself, by providing general purpose, program-definable features such as a message mechanism for windows or the ability to use different window manipulation methods.

Ergonomics are essential to a viable graphical interface. Our environment provides the tools necessary to support highly-interactive and user-friendly window-based systems in a consistent manner. It provides a window manager that can be tailored by both the particular application and the user; a common tool for menu-based input that offers consistency between and within applications; a standard "help" mechanism for all applications; utilities that encourage an "undo" feature to be built into an application; and the facilities needed for a user-controlled multi-window output interface for each application. The extensible nature of the tools has encouraged experimentation with different approaches to user-interfaces before actually settling on a default interaction technique.

Integration makes an environment out of a set of tools. This is seen in the application's ability to use a combination of tools and in consistency among the toolset. The environment is designed with a layered approach, with tools at the outer layers making use of tools at the inner layers. As a result, all input and output go though a common interface. At the same time, applications are free to make use of tools at each level of the environment. The set of tools provides consistency to the programmer through common naming and calling conventions. It provides consistency to the user through a common interface.

Our environment is different from most current computer science environments such as the Unix user environment because of its emphasis on graphics for both input and output and its basis in networked personal workstations. In developing this environment, we have drawn on the display and user interface components of programming environments developed at research centers and in commercial offerings. Many workstation environments have been heavily influenced by the pioneering work of the Xerox Palo Alto Research Center beginning in the early 70's. The Xerox environments of Smalltalk,[1] Interlisp,[2] Mesa,[3] and CEDAR[4] provide excellent examples of what can be done in language-specific environments. Unfortunately, these environments have never been made readily available to the academic community (nor the commercial market-place), nor do they exist on non-Xerox hardware. Recently, several products have been developed that are based on this work at Xerox. The Xerox Star office environment is a commercial product with an integrated environment for a single application domain; however, it does not yet provide for programming support or portability to other machines. The Apple Lisa/Macintosh, Microsoft's Windows package, Apollo's display manager and graphics primitives package, and Sun Windows provide simple but efficient general-purpose environment.

These environments provide support for a small class of menus, a single type of window, and a single method for manipulating windows. They assume and support a particular style of user interface rather than allowing different user interfaces for different users and providing for experimentation.

3. Design Overview

The Brown Workstation Environment is a layered structure that attempts to take advantage of the hardware and software provided by the manufacturer in a machine-independent manner.

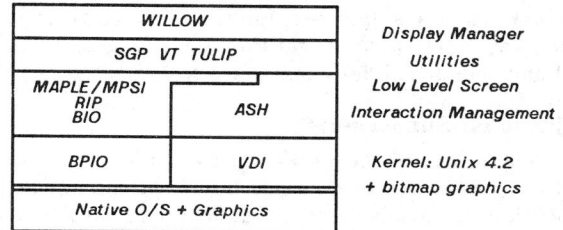

Figure 1. Single Process Model

Machine Assumptions

The environment assumes that workstations will support a basic set of graphics primitives including raster operations on both a high-resolution display and on non-displayed bitmaps. The workstations may or may not provide hardware or firmware support for high-performance graphics. For graphical input, we assume the workstation provides a pointing device such as a mouse with switches for selection.

The environment also assumes that the workstations will provide Unix or a Unix-like operating system. Building on top of Unix has many advantages. It is supported by most of the commercial workstations. It is a general-purpose operating system that is not restricted to a particular language or application. It provides a large set of utility programs for applications and users. It is easily extensible. Moreover, it is fast becoming the de facto standard operating system, especially in academia. From the user's perspective, our environment is built on top of Unix and the various packages become extensions of the operating system.

The Machine-Dependent Layer

While we make assumptions as to the essential functionality of workstations, we expect that they will not all provide the same or a similar interface to this functionality. Indeed, experience has shown that the interfaces differ significantly. To isolate applications as well as the components of the toolset from the differences between workstations, the innermost layer of the environment consists of virtual device interfaces for input and output. These map a standard set of graphics calls to the interface that is provided. The complete environment, including applications, can be ported to a new machine by simply rewriting the virtual device interfaces. If the graphics support on the workstation is adequate, this can be done in about a week.

The Basic Tools

Our basic system-support facilities are layered on top of the virtual device interfaces. A screen handler provides the abstraction of a bitmap or window to the user program. It allows arbitrary graphics to be done in these windows and it allows the visibility of the various windows to be manipulated. Input is handled through a menu-based system that uses the screen handler for output and the virtual device interface for input.

Additional Functionality

The power of the workstation environment derives not only from the basic tools, but from the advanced tools that are available to the applications programmer and the user. Several packages have been designed to provide additional functionality to a single window: there are a number of traditional graphics packages that provide various types of modelling worlds; text packages provide intelligent editing of text that can contain multiple, different-sized and proportionally spaced fonts; a user-level window manager allows applications to provide a multi-window environment within an arbitrary window; and communications facilities allow multiple processes to run in the graphics environment. These will be described in detail in the next section.

4. The Toolset Components

In this section we consider specific tools that provide the functionality outlined in the preceding overview. For each tool we attempt to describe its basic philosophy, its place in the environment, and the functionality it provides.

Virtual Device Interface

Basic Output: The output virtual device interface, VDI, provides a device-independent method for accessing graphical primitives, based on the emerging ANSI-standard virtual device metafile.[5] It supports a single screen bitmap and an arbitrary number of off-screen bitmaps. The single screen bitmap corresponds to the environment visible to the user as the system is being run. The VDI allows it to be the complete display, or a window in the underlying environment (thereby allowing our entire environment to coexist with an externally supplied window manager).

The VDI provides all the necessary graphics operations to be performed on the screen or on any of the off-screen bitmaps. This includes points, lines, ellipses and polygons; text operations that display a given string in a given font at a given position; and bitmap operations such as bit-blt, reading and writing of pixels into a user array, and disk storage and retrieval.

The VDI provides each bitmap with its own set of attributes. These describe the current color, line styles, the pattern to use for filled polygons, the raster-op for the bit-blt and drawing primitives, and the clipping-rectangle. Each bitmap also has its own integer coordinate system defined by the VDI. The off-screen (i.e., non-displayed) bitmaps are widely used in our applications for storing the image of a partially or totally obscured window for later refresh, for saving the contents of the screen underneath a pop-up menu, and for computing graphics images that can later be quickly displayed on the screen using a bit-blt. Finally, the VDI provides full support for multiple-plane color bitmaps.

Basic Input Package: The low-level component of the input interface, BPIO, takes input from the keyboard and mouse (or other pointing device), serializes it into a sequence of "events", and transforms it into a machine-independent format. The single stream allows clients to access the user's actions in the order they occur. This is necessary when the client wants to allow the user to use the pointing device to move around the screen while also using the keyboard to enter text in different places. Each event in the stream denotes the action causing the event, the position of the pointing device when the event occurred, and the time of the event. Events include characters typed on the keyboard, function keys, mouse buttons, and movement of the mouse.

Basic Support Environment

Screen Management: The task of the screen management package ASH is to provide an output abstraction to the client program that is both easy to use and that can make effective use of the underlying hardware. Since the environment is designed for raster graphics on workstations, we have chosen the "window" as the abstraction. A window is a virtual bitmap into which a program can perform a full range of raster graphics operations. Each window can be displayed on the screen in full or in part, with those windows currently displayed being allowed to overlap. ASH allows the client program to use windows without worrying about the complexities that arise when these displays are partially or fully obscured.

It is important to note that ASH is a *screen handler* that only provides the abstraction of windows to client programs. It is not a *window manager* that supplies an interface to the user for managing such windows. (The latter task is handled by a separate component.) Several existing systems on workstations provide functionality similar to ASH. These include CANVAS[6] in the CMU SPICE environment for PERQs, VIEWERS in the Xerox CEDAR system, PADS in the

Apollo Aegis environment, and Sun Windows for Sun workstations. Most of these perform some of the tasks of the window manager as well. One important design feature of our environment is the distinction between these two tasks. The abstraction of windows is useful to the program in ways independent of the user interface for manipulating them. Many of our applications exploit the fact that ASH supports internal windows in the same way as it supports the main window assigned to a program. These applications create hierarchies of windows, assigning the independent subwindows to different components of the program. The distinction between the tasks is also important because it allows different window managers to coexist on the same system, just as different shells can be used in Unix. ASH, like all of our toolset components, is an "open" package. That is, it is used by both other toolset components and also by applications.

In addition to window-oriented output, ASH provides general facilities for input support. "Sensitive areas" are regions within a window that can be used for input selection. ASH determines which sensitive area the cursor is over and will optionally highlight the regions as the cursor moves over them. This facility is used for buttons in menus by other components of the toolset.

There are many instances where parts of the environment or the user program will need to communicate with the module in charge of a given window. To facilitate such communication, ASH supports a window-based message facility. Each window can have one or more message processing routines registered with it. Each routine can reject the message so that the next message routine for the designated window is called, or it can accept the message and return a status code to the message sender.

The message facility is used as the primary means whereby the environment communicates with itself and with the applications. The messages allow a client of ASH to keep track of the state of its window and to adjust its processing accordingly.

Machine-Independent Input: Applications usually do not call the primitive BPIO directly; rather, they use a machine-independent package BIO to gain selective access to the event stream. BIO allows the clients to associate a set of input characteristics with each ASH window. In addition to the events generated by BPIO, there are also events at this level for entering and exiting an input window, and notification that the mouse has stopped moving. The input characteristics associated with a window are the cursor style for tracking, the events to accept or ignore, and keyboard and function key mappings (a key can be used to generate any valid type of input event, to invoke a function directly, or to simulate mouse activity). BIO tracks and performs primitive input processing as the user causes

the event rather than when the application actually reads the event.

Typically BIO is actually accessed by RIP, a region oriented input package, rather than a client application. This package makes use of BIO and ASH to provide a building block for Menu packages.

Menu-Based Input and Program Control: MPSI and its predecessor MAPLE are front-ends modeled after work done by the SIGGRAPH committee on graphical input interaction techniques[7] and elsewhere.[8] They are designed to allow programs to do sophisticated graphical input as easily as possible and to provide a standard input interface for all applications. General facilities for menu and locator based input allow programs to easily define a finite-state program control based on menus.

Both systems provide "pop-up" and "sticky" menus, as well as general mechanisms for character and pointer-based input. Pop-up menus appear at the current position of the cursor when needed and disappear after a button on the menu has been selected. Sticky menus are displayed on the screen in a fixed location at all times. Whenever the cursor is moved over a selectable menu button, the button is highlighted. Buttons within these menus may be either textual or iconic, and the menus themselves can be displayed in a variety of formats. A different menu can be associated with any keyboard character or, more commonly, with a switch on the pointing device.

Higher-Level Utility Packages

Graphics Packages: Several packages have been developed to provide additional graphics functionality within an ASH window. The primary package is SGP, a high-level machine- and device-independent 2D graphics subroutine package, modeled after the ACM/SIGGRAPH CORE.[9] SGP has been in use at Brown and elsewhere since the mid-70's, and is supported on a wide variety of computer systems for a variety of devices, including both raster and vector displays. The implementation of SGP that the workstation environment provides has been extended to support raster graphics primitives and some GKS[10] facilities.

Two other graphics packages have been developed, primarily for introductory computer science courses. A floating point package provides a double-buffering capability for simple animation. This allows the user to create the next display off-line while showing the complete current display. Another is a simple graphics package developed for doing graphical output from Pascal programs. It uses a fixed integer coordinate system, provides primitive segmentation, a wide range of drawing operations, and input correlation.

Text Packages: ASH provides a primitive text facility that allows a string to be output in any font at any position of the display. There are many applications for which this interface is too primitive. In order to facilitate such applications, the toolset contains packages that allow an ASH window to be used as a fancy terminal.

A simple text output interface is provided by the TULIP terminal utility package. TULIP provides a stream interface to an arbitrary size window that acts as an intelligent terminal. It provides a variety of escape sequences for use within the window including inserting and deleting characters and lines and absolute cursor positioning. It provides correlation between screen coordinates and line/column addressing. TULIP differs from a normal terminal in its variable sizing and its support for multiple fonts including proportionally spaced fonts. Fonts can be intermixed on the display, with TULIP taking care of character alignment and variable line sizes. TULIP also provides both rectangular boxes and line-oriented boxes for highlighting portions of text. These boxes may be displayed either in outline form or in reverse video. Finally, TULIP allows the program to query about the contents of the screen and to correlate a position in the window to a particular line and character.

The VT package enhances TULIP by providing a semi-infinite quarter-plane of text. This allows applications to let the user scroll over all his past output. Additional text facilities in the form of a generic text editor are currently being worked on. This editor has features of both structure editors and pure text editors.

A Multiprocess Environment

COMM is a message-based communications package that provides the Brown Workstation Environment with interprocess communication and remote procedure call capabilities. While these features can be used by any program, they have been specifically developed to allow multiple processes to share the screen and the associated input devices.

The communications package is split into two parts. The first provides a bi-directional message protocol between processes in a machine-independent manner. The second is a pre-processor that generates client and server components of a remote procedure call facility automatically from a C source file.

A graphics server provides clients with two services, input and output. Input is provided by having BIO send events over the message mechanism. Output is provided by a special version of the VDI, called VCS, that makes use of the remote procedure call facility.

User Window Management

The Brown Workstation Environment provides window management facility that is independent of processes. It can be used within a single process so that an application can have the user organize the screen the way he wants and change this organization dynamically. Or it can be used as a base level window manager providing multiple processes in multiple windows. Since the same package, WILLOW, is used in both instances, a consistent interface is provided.

WILLOW is a general purpose window manager that provides both a user and program controlled interface to multiple window displays. It also offers a window-oriented button interface that is consistent with MAPLE or MPSI.

Rather than enforcing a single window manipulation philosophy, WILLOW provides several methods for manipulating windows and allows either the user or the application to choose which is to be used. Two basic methods and some variations are provided in the initial implementation. One of these allows overlapping windows and has the user specify the coordinates of each window he wants to create by rubber-banding a box over the display. The other uses a tiled method similar to that used in the Xerox Cedar system with two columns of windows for which WILLOW does constraint satisfaction to correctly size new windows. In addition, WILLOW allows new methods to be added. This can be done with a simple modular addition to WILLOW or dynamically by the application program.

5. Conclusion

In summary, we have developed a portable interactive graphics environment for Unix based graphics workstations. This environment has made it easy for application programmers to create sophisticated systems that exploit the hardware facilities in a relatively painless manner. The environment has been used to improve the productivity of students and researchers alike. It is a step toward changing the way one interacts with computers.

6. Acknowledgements

Many people, too numerous to cite individually, have helped in the design and the implementation of the environment prototypes. Those of particular note include Rob Rubin who has used the environment for several projects and aided in its design, John Bazik who worked on a drawing package and the VDI for both the Apollo and Sun, and Stefan Tucker who worked on RIP and MPSI.

References

1. Adele Goldberg and Dave Robson, *Smalltalk-80: The language and its implementation*, Addison-Wesley (1983).
2. Warren Teitelman, *Interlisp Reference Manual*, XEROX (1974).

3. James G. Mitchell, William Maybury, and Richard Sweet, "Mesa language manual," *Xerox CSL-79-3*, (April 1979).

4. R. Beach, "Experience with the Cedar programming environment for computer graphics research," *Proceedings of Graphics Interface 84*, (June, 1984).

5. ANSI, "Draft Proposed American National Standard for the Virtual Device Metafile," ANSI X3H3 83-15 R1 (August 1983).

6. J. Eugene Ball, "Canvas -- the Spice graphics package," Carnegie-Mellon Computer Science Department (1981).

7. James J. Thomas, chairman, "Graphical Input Interaction Technique (GIIT) Workshop Summary," ACM/SIGGRAPH (June 1982).

8. Andrew J. Schulert, George T. Rogers, and James A. Hamilton, "ADM: A dialog manager," *Proceedings of the CHI '85 Conference*, ((to appear) April 1985).

9. GSPC, "Status report of the Graphics Standards Committee," *Computer Graphics* **13**(3)(August 1979).

10. ANSI, "Draft Proposed American National Standard Graphics Kernel System," *Computer Graphics*, (February 1984).

Documentation for all software packages described in this paper are available from the Computer Science Department at Brown University.

SCHEMACODE,

A SOFTWARE TOOL TO DESIGN OR TO RETROFIT PROGRAMS

PIERRE N. ROBILLARD
JEAN-LOUIS HOULE

Department of Electrical Engineering
Ecole Polytechnique of Montreal
P.O. Box 6079, Station A
Montreal, Quebec, H3C 3A7
Canada

Abstract

Schemacode is a software tool that provides a systematic approach to program design and implementation. The objective of the tool is to increase the readability of programs as well as the reliability of the documentation. This is achieved by using schemas to represent the program constructs. This methodology is called schematic pseudocode (Schemacode). The step-wise refinement approach is automated in such a way that it provides most of the documentation. Source code is automatically generated from the 9hematic pseudocode.

The steps require to build a program are presented. The self implementation of Schemacode is stressed, and the details of retrofitting an unstructured program are revealed. The salient features of the tool are presented.

Introduction

The SCHEMACODE software-tool allows the user to develop programs interactively by means of a top-down modular approach, and assists the user in writing quality, well-structured, well documented, and easily maintained programs [1].

It solves the problem of poor readability and unreliable documentation by providing a systematic approach to program design and documentation supported by an automatic code

generation [2]. A distinction must be made between "structured programming and "structured coding": a program is structured if it represents the structure of a problem; a code is structured if the coding constructs used are easy to control. SCHEMACODE provides assistance in both these areas, i.e. design and coding.

It is involved in design in that it enables the programmer to build an abstract schematic version of his program using the successive refinement technique. It is a coding aid in the sense that it contains code generators.

The modular approach consists of subdividing a general function into a number of independent subfunctions. This method enables the programmer to concentrate on one specific part of the program or subprogram, thereby making the logic of the program easily understandable. When each subfunction has been identified, it is refined gradually, still with the modular approach, until the formal code can be defined.

A refinement is defined as the specification of an abstraction. Editing a program is accomplished by means of a series of abstractions. SCHEMACODE forces the user to document each refinement and automatically integrates this information into the program, thereby providing a communicable product.

The next step is to define the control steps within a refinement. Sequential, conditional, and repetitive constructs are represented on the screen in a mnemonic schematic form: hence the expressions schematic pseudocode (SPC).

Once the program has been developed in schematic pseudocode, a code generator, an integral part of SCHEMACODE, translates the SPC into the target language (FORTRAN, PASCAL, C, or any some other programming language).

Thee source language, in which the program is described, is actually a mixture of two differents languages:

- the target language, which is the one used by the programmer to introduce assignments, calls to external procedures, declarations and Boolean expressions:

- the schematic pseudocode, which makes possible a schematic representation of constructs.

We describe in the following how the user can built his program.

Refinements

In the first phase, the SCHEMACODE user specifies the major steps involved in solving his problem. SCHEMACODE automatically creates a refinement for each step specified. Each step is called an operational comment. The use of this comment is described in the next section.

A program is a set of refinements. The mechanism for developing refinements makes it possible to design an algorithm in top-down form. When an operational comment is written, SCHEMACODE creates a new numbered refinement. Its number is the one assigned by the editor, and its name is automatically the text of the comment.

The first refinement is created at the same time as the file that will contain the program, and the number assigned to it is zero. As a result, a refinement may only be created once, within another refinement. There is thus only one reference to each refinement in a program.

Sequential constructs

Figure 1 gives an example of sequential structures together with each of the commands needed to create them.

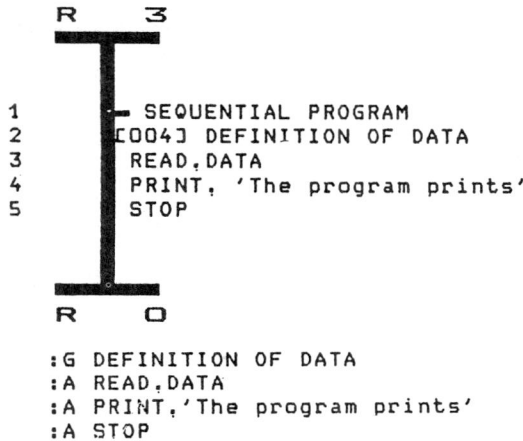

```
R  3

1       — SEQUENTIAL PROGRAM
2       [004] DEFINITION OF DATA
3       READ,DATA
4       PRINT, 'The program prints'
5       STOP

R  0

:G DEFINITION OF DATA
:A READ,DATA
:A PRINT,'The program prints'
:A STOP
```

Figure 1

Example of Sequential Structure

There are three kinds of sequence: narrative comments, operational comments and target language instructions.

The purpose of the narrative comment is to provide immediate information that is complete in itself: it is by no means the expression of an abstraction. The narrative comment is a free text. The most typical comments are those that identify the module (name, date) or justify specific steps. These comments will be part of the source program during the coding phase.

The operational comment is used to define an abstraction. It summarizes a set operations that are to be executed later. The operational comment is a free text containing no more that 72 characters. An operational comment automatically generates a refinement.

The target language instruction is an instruction in the target language, i.e. an assignment, a call to an external procedure or a declaration.

A narrative comment is preceded by a dash. An operational comment is preceded by a number. An instruction in the target language is written as is.

Conditional constructs

Figure 2 provides an example of the commands used to create a conditional structure. Note that only the operational comment is used as a sequential structure, even though any of the other structures may also be used.

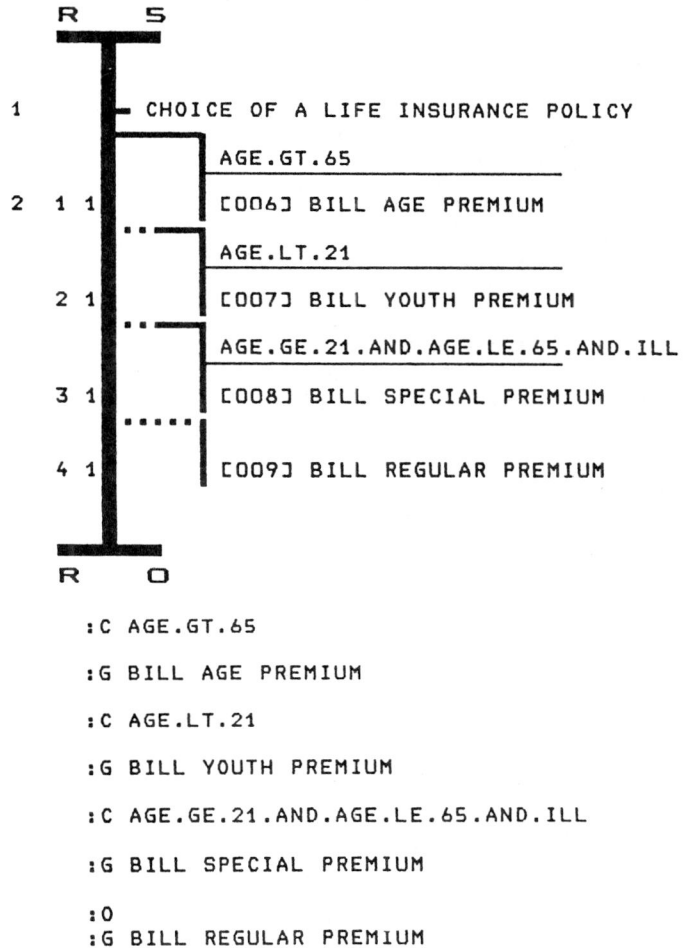

```
R  5

1       — CHOICE OF A LIFE INSURANCE POLICY
            AGE.GT.65
2  1  1     [006] BILL AGE PREMIUM
            AGE.LT.21
2  1        [007] BILL YOUTH PREMIUM
            AGE.GE.21.AND.AGE.LE.65.AND.ILL
3  1        [008] BILL SPECIAL PREMIUM
4  1        [009] BILL REGULAR PREMIUM

R  0

:C AGE.GT.65
:G BILL AGE PREMIUM
:C AGE.LT.21
:G BILL YOUTH PREMIUM
:C AGE.GE.21.AND.AGE.LE.65.AND.ILL
:G BILL SPECIAL PREMIUM
:0
:G BILL REGULAR PREMIUM
```

Figure 2

Example of Conditional Structure

These constructs are composed of an execution condition for each case and the exclusion of all previous conditions (ELSE). The body of each case is obviously composed of the sequential constructs described above. When a case is checked, only that case is executed and any others are ignored. If none of the cases have been checked, the ELSE case is executed. It is not necessary for all cases to exist at the same time. In fact, several combinations are allowed.

Boolean expressions are underlined and connected to the preceding flowpath with a horizontal line. The sequential constructs to be executed when the condition is true are aligned with another vertical line indented from the previous one. The numbering and the line drawing are done automatically by the SCHEMACODE editor.

Repetitive constructs

Figure 3 provides an example of the use of the commands to create a repetitive construct.

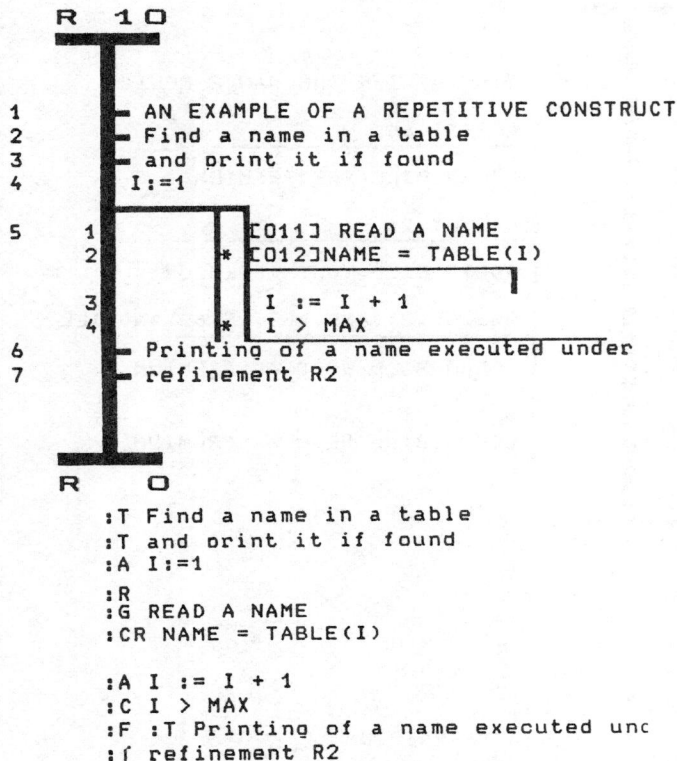

```
R 10
       ├─ AN EXAMPLE OF A REPETITIVE CONSTRUCT
1      ├─ Find a name in a table
2      ├─ and print it if found
3      ├─ I:=1
4
5    1     [011] READ A NAME
     2   * [012]NAME = TABLE(I)

     3     I := I + 1
     4   * I > MAX
6      ├─ Printing of a name executed under
7      ├─ refinement R2


R  0

  :T Find a name in a table
  :T and print it if found
  :A I:=1
  :R
  :G READ A NAME
  :CR NAME = TABLE(I)

  :A I := I + 1
  :C I > MAX
  :F :T Printing of a name executed unc
  :f refinement R2
```

Figure 3

Example of Repetitive Structure

Schematic pseudocode allows a representation of more general structures than is offered by programming languages. For example, a loop may have as many exit conditions as are needed, and these may be placed anywhere in the body of the loop.

The body of the repetitive construct is identified by two parallel vertical lines. These lines are idented from the previous operation and are connected to it by a horizontal line. The point where the horizontal line meets the vertical is the entry and exit point of the repetitive construct. Within the body of the repetitive construct there must be at least one exit condition. This is an underlined Boolean condition and is identified by an asterisk, which is located between the parallel lines. The numbering and the line drawing are done automatically by the SCHEMACODE editor.

Interaction level

The user can interact with the SCHEMACODE tool at three different levels, that are called mode. These levels are perfectly hierarchical, i.e. it is not possible to access one level without going through the preceding one, and it is impossible to leave a level without going to the preceding or following level.

The utility mode provides all the file management mechanisms. It makes using SCHEMACODE independent of the operating system supporting it. The monitor mode makes it possible to access the refinements within a subroutine and obtain the various code generator. The editor mode enables the programmer to edit the structures within a given refinement.

When the programmer has specified all the refinements, SCHEMACODE integrates them into the appropriate control statements generated from the pictorial representation to produce an executable program. The schematic form remains, however, so that the software is documented. Figure 4 illustrates sample program written in schematic pseudocode.

Classification of Schemacode

Reifer [3] proposes a taxonomy with three categories. Within each group of "software development tools", for example, each aid or tool is classified according to its inputs, functions and outputs.

This taxonomy classifies Schemacode in the following way. Its input is a very high level language (schematic pseudocode). Its functions are processing, editing, formatting and re-structuring code generation. And its output takes two forms: a pictorial form, which lets the user read his program in schematic pseudocode, and a source code form, which is a computer program.

One method of classifying design tools is the following [4,5]. Certain tools aid in expressing specifications and we can call these "pre-design tools". Schemacode operates on this level by allowing the programmer to sidestep the complexities of the program by using successive refinements. Because the structural outline of the program is defined from the very beginning, the programmer is not walking blindfolded.

There are also design tools to automate a programming methodology by guiding programmers and preventing them from deviating from it. Schemacode operates on this level by supporting the schematic pseudocode.

Continuing with this classification method, there are the coding tools, which produce the source code from the design phase. Schemacode operates with the following code generators: FORTRAN, PASCAL, C, or any other programming language.

```
PAGE   :              ACMF77  -  0
SCHEMACODE   VERSION  VMS  10.0
CODE      FICHIER   DATE DE        DATE DE DERNIERE :   HEURE
USAGER              CREATION   UTILISATION  CODIFICATION  D'IMPRESSION
BEAUCAGE  ACMF77    1NOV84    12MAR85     10JAN85       09:35:00
```

```
         R   O

0  1        ACMF77   - Ecole Polytechnique de Montreal - Schemacode ver.VMS 10.0
   2        SCANNING A FILE AND COUNTING ALL THE NAMES
   3        THAT BEGIN WITH THE SAME CHARACTER
   4        001 INITIALISATION
1  1
   2        INTEGER*4 TOTAL/0/,GROUP/0/
   3        LOGICAL*1 END
   4        CHARACTER*1 LAG/' '/,TAG,RECORD*80
   5        EQUIVALENCE(TAG,RECORD)
0  5        002 GROUP START
2  1
   2   1        READ(5,*,END) RECORD
       2    *   END
       3        004 PROCESS A RECORD
4  1
                    TAG.EQ.LAG
   2  1 1           GROUP=GROUP+1
                    ......
   2  1          005 GROUP ENDING
5  1
                        GROUP.NE.0
   2  1 1               TYPE *,' THE NUMBER OF NAMES BEGINNING WITH ',
      2                 ... LAG,' IS ',GROUP
      3                 TOTAL=TOTAL+GROUP
4  2  2 2       LAG=TAG
      3         GROUP=1
0  6        003 FINAL ENDING
3  1
   2        TYPE *,' THE NUMBER OF NAMES BEGINNING WITH ',TAG,' IS ',GROUP
   3        TOTAL=TOTAL+GROUP
   4        TYPE *,' THE TOTAL NUMBER OF NAMES IS ',TOTAL

         R   O
```

Figure 4

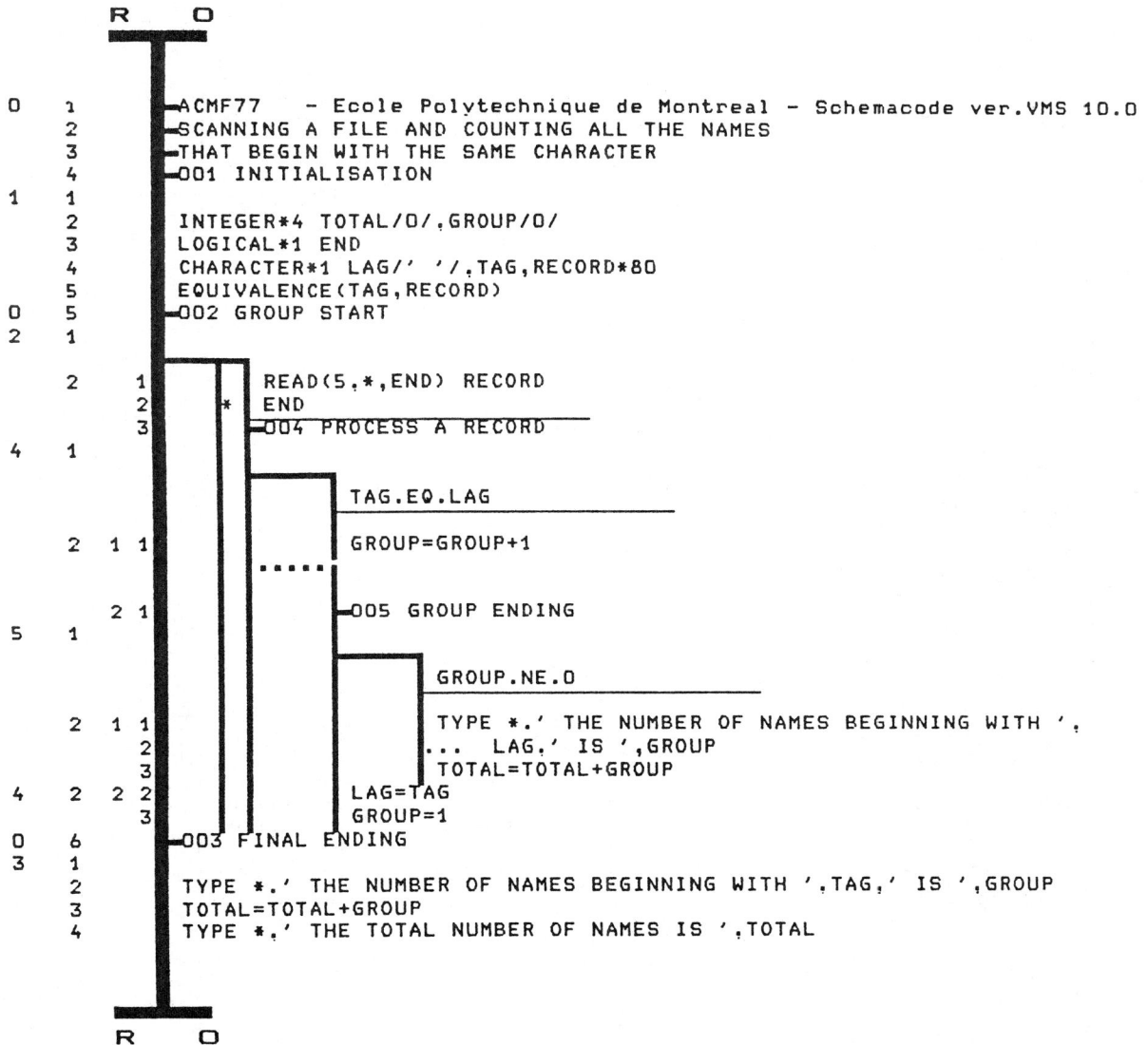

Example of Program in Schematic Pseudocode

Figure 5 shows the modular architecture of Schemacode.

Case studies

Schemacode has been entirely designed in schematic pseudocode and the running version VMS 10.0 has been automatically coded by the

prototype version 3.0 [6]. The tool is available on the IBM 4341 machine under MUSIC (McGill University System for Interactive Computing) and on the VAX machine under VMS or UNIX.

121

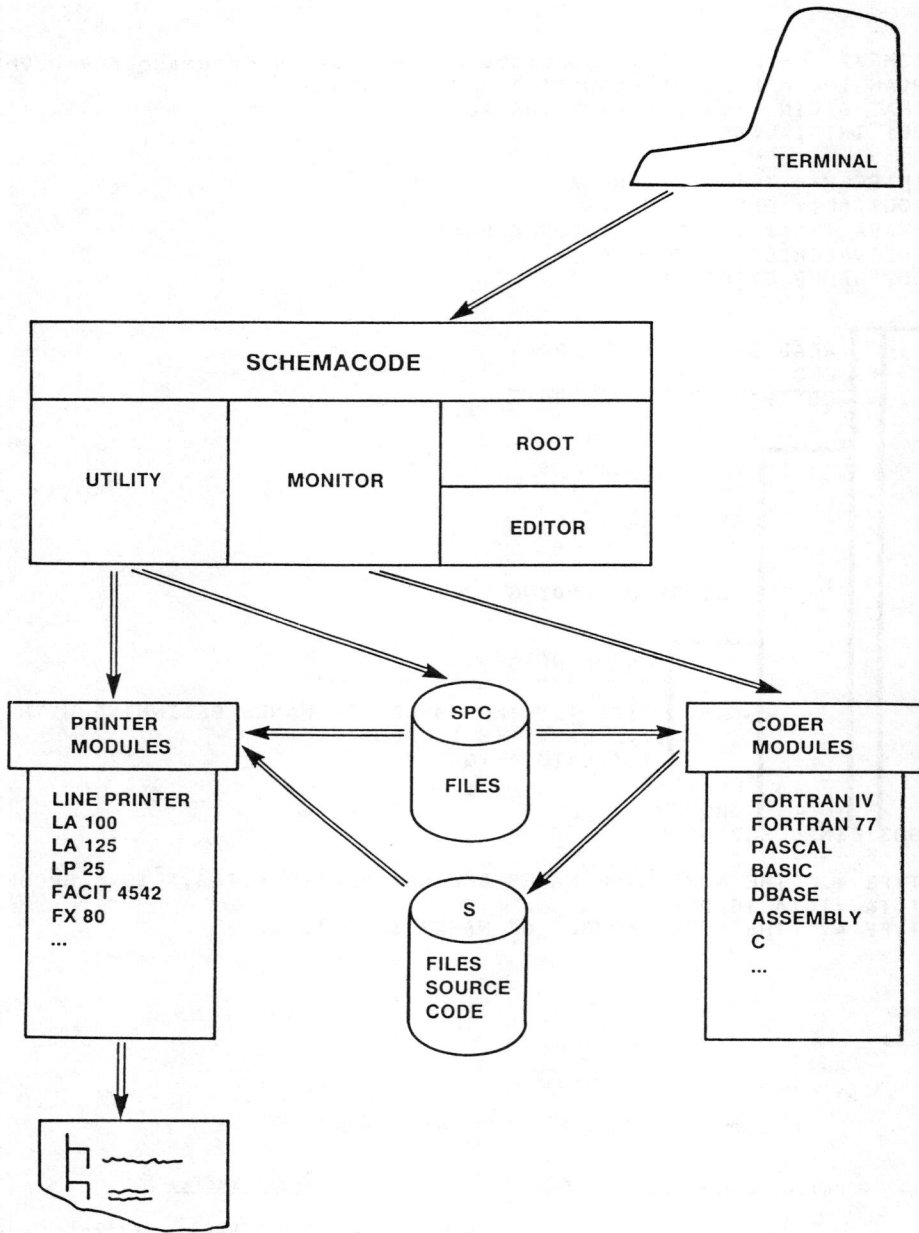

Figure 5

Architecture of SCHEMACODE

122

Schemacode is used for research [7] at the Ecole Polytechnique, Laval University, the University of Quebec in Montreal, and the Telecommunications Department of the INRS. To date, close to a million lines of code have been generated in various languages. The tool was also used for retrofitting a non-structured FORTRAN IV program. The retrofit was done on a program developed as part of a Ph.D. research project.

Since the software was developed in a research environment, the code produced was functional but poorly structured. It became obvious that the software obtained had a potential commercial value and would need to be supported and easily maintainable. Two solutions were available; we had to either completely rewrite the program or to retrofit it using Schemacode. The second alternative was chosen because of the program's size and because of the usefulness of having a unified coding style that could be automatically retained in the future. All the sequential constructs and the already well formed structures were automatically regenerated. Human intervention was required only when the modules were too long or the code too tangled.

The restructuring and documentation of the source program was done by a team of two programmers not familiar with the original program. They spent 150 hours to entirely retrofit the 12,000 lines of code of the non-structured program. The rate of 80 lines per hour was made possible with Schemacode. The use of this tool to maintain the program will keep it well structured and documented. As can ben seen, Schemacode automatically translates the high level schematic structure into a programming language. The retrofitted program has been automatically recoded in FORTRAN, which has been translated from non structured FORTRAN ANSI 66 to structured FORTRAN ANSI 77.

Concluding remarks

The new version of the program is well structured and documented. The salient features are the following:

- All unreachable statements are detected and removed.

- All constructs are documented.

- The program is entirely structured.

- Any modifications may be done with Schemacode, doing so the program will remain structured and documented, and further retrofitting will not be required.

- High level documentation is readily available in schematic form, an up-graded alternative to a flowchart.

- Documentation in any form, source code or schematic pseudocode are always up-to-date since the link between the two is automatically done.

The schematic pseudocode and the tool have been used for four years within our research group, resulting in a great improvement in the quality of our programs. Although it is hard to define program quality, we base our statement on the fact that since we have been using the tool for all program developments, all programs are continually in use. Programs are now understandable by people other than the designer, and large scale projects are passed along successfully to different groups of programmers.

In summary, the salient features of the schematic pseudocode and its computer automation are the following:

- It is easy to learn and understand, even by a non professional.

- Is is a systematic, uniform and rigorous way of designing programs.

- It is a representation of the structure of a program which is language independant; this representation is seen by most as the skeleton of the program.

- It is an embedded top-down and step-wise refinement approach.

- It is an automatic integration of the documentation.

- As far as structures are concerned, Schemacode provides reliable and error-free code generation.

- It is an efficient alternative to flowcharts.

References

[1] Robillard, P.N., Plamondon, R., Planning for software tool implementation: experience with SCHEMACODE. National Computer Conference, Houston, June 1982.

[2] Robillard, P.N., Plamondon, R., An Interactive tool for descriptive, operational and structural documentation. COMCON '81, 23rd IEEE Computer Society International Conference, Sept. 1981, pp. 291-295.

[3] Reifer, Reifer consultants software tools directory. 2733 Pacific Coast Highway, suite 203, Torrance Ca. 90505.

[4] Schindler, M., Todays software tools point to tomorrow's tool systems, Electronic design, July 23, 1981.

[5] Miller, E., Tutorial: automated tools for software engineering, IEEE catalog EHO 150.3. COMPSAC 1979.

[6] Robillard, P.N., Plamondon, R., Interactive Schematic Pseudocode for Program Development, Documentation and Structured Coding. 5th Int. Conf. on Soft. Eng., Proceedings of Tool Fair NBS Special Publication, March 1981, pp. 164-169.

[7] Davidson, J., Houle, J.L., On the Design of Hierarchical Process Control Computer Systems. IFAC, Distributed Computer Control Systems, Tallinn, USSR, 1982, pp. 83-92.

SOFTWARE DEVELOPMENT FACILITIES FOR EMBEDDED COMPUTER SYSTEMS

David A. Feinberg, C.D.P.

Energy Control Systems Division
The Boeing Company
P. O. Box 24346, M/S 1E-56
Seattle, Washington 98124

ABSTRACT:

This paper discusses technology available to enhance development of software for embedded computer systems. Special emphasis is placed on non-Department of Defense products; where costs and functionality are more intimately related. Characteristics and side-effects emphasized by the civilian cost vs. performance relationship as applied to embedded software development and production execution are described. Generic requirements for any embedded software development facility are then outlined.

Three software development facility strategies available for civilian projects are defined. The first strategy, "embedded computer upgrade," uses one or more expanded versions of the same processor delivered with the product. The second strategy, "separate support computer," uses an independent computer equipped with extensive embedded processor software generation utilities. The third strategy, "linked separate and embedded computers," employs an interconnected independent and embedded computer architecture requiring only minimal new software generation utilities. An exposition of each strategy is presented. Discussions outlining requirements applicability plus advantages and disadvantages of each are included.

A case history describing an implementation of the third type of embedded software development facility concludes the paper. Based on this case history, a set of generic rules for selection of an embedded software development facility is proposed.

1.0 INTRODUCTION

Over twenty-five years ago, the United States Department of Defense (DoD) commenced the development of the first in a long series of projects which utilized a digital computer as an integral, but not total, component of a complex weapons system. The Semi-Automatic Ground Environment (SAGE) system and its successor DoD projects utilized a computer for navigation and guidance computations, but the radar sensors, communications facilities, and interceptor airframes were equally important portions of the total air defense package.

In the decades since SAGE, DoD and its vendors have become expert in techniques for development of embedded computer systems. With the advent of minicomputers, microcomputers, and most recently, super microcomputers, the civilian sector has recently commenced numerous projects which can also be characterized as embedded computer systems. Examples of such projects include Computer Aided Design (CAD) systems, Computer Aided Manufacturing (CAM) tools, transportation and power distribution control systems, and even video games.

The long-standing techniques preferred for implementation of embedded DoD software are not necessarily appropriate for highly cost-conscious civilian sector embedded systems. Subsequent sections of this article define the characteristics of non-DoD embedded computer systems, itemize generic development facility requirements, outline several strategies for developing embedded computer system software, illustrate a case history of one civilian sector Embedded Software Development Facility (ESDF), and hypothesize a set of rules for ESDF selection.

2.0 KEY EMBEDDED COMPUTER SYSTEM CHARACTERISTICS

The essential characteristic of an embedded computer system is that the computer and its programming are invisible within the shell of the overall product. For example, the typical player of a video game is totally unaware of the presence (or absence) of a computer within his or her game box. In fact, the player doesn't even care whether there is a computer or not. For the most part, the primary concerns of a purchaser of a civilian embedded system are: (1) How much does it cost?, and (2) How much does it do?

These two concerns define a key civilian (and to some extent, DoD) embedded computer system characteristic: minimum necessary functionality. The system's required computational performance must be obtained at the lowest possible production costs. This applies to both hardware and software. Two side-effects occur as a consequence.

The first, common to all of an embedded product's hardware, is the issue of component replication. Computer hardware has weight, requires power and cooling, and consequently costs money for every copy constructed. Keeping a civilian product price-competitive demands that the costs and numbers of these components be kept as low as possible. Software, on the other hand, is usually considered a one-time development charge that costs nothing to replicate. This situation routinely causes complex computing tasks to be relegated to software in lieu of adding additional, special purpose, "assist" hardware. The conventional wisdom is that this will minimize a product's unit cost; however, this only works if the software development cost is low and/or can be amortized over a large quantity of sales.

The second side-effect is stabilization of a common hardware environment. In order to minimize costs and maintain consistent configuration, the same minimum computer hardware embedded in a product's production package is often utilized in the development laboratory. For software personnel, this means that many of the facilities normally available with today's large minicomputers and mainframe systems (e.g., virtual memory management, full-screen editors, symbolic debuggers, timing instrumentors) are absent or severely limited. This is particularly acute for those capabilities used only during development of a product's software, and not its post-delivery execution.

It is these two side-effects which cause the most difficulty in the development of software for embedded computer systems; particularly in a highly cost-driven civilian product.

3.0 DEVELOPMENT FACILITY REQUIREMENTS

Figure 1 summarizes the primary requirements for a software development facility. While these requirements can be applied to facilities for developing traditional as well as embedded software products, the key characteristics and needs of embedded computer software frequently lead to special interpretations and/or emphasis.

3.1 Accessibility

Useful access to a software development facility should be available during all normal and extended employee work shifts. In the case of DoD work, this can approach seventeen to eighteen (out of twenty-one) shifts per week. As a consequence, it is routinely possible to segregate work on product components and/or phases into distinct, non-interfering time periods.

For civilian projects, generally only five to six shifts per week are worked. Thus the ability to segregate work by time period is more severely restricted and the risks of interference from one subtask to another are increased.

3.2 Capacity

A software development facility must provide sufficient capacity to "turn around" work within acceptable time periods. This is no different than the processing standards for any production data processing shop; which is what a software development facility is. A development facility should also have the capacity to store (preferably, online) all relevant software information (e.g., design documents, source code, test programs, users manuals) used during the full course of a product's development and maintenance.

3.3 Stability

Personnel must be able to depend on a reliable, constant (or at worst, slowly evolving) hardware and software development environment. Also included as part of stability is the need for a controlled hardware and software "test bed." Embedded computer products traditionally have critical performance goals; both in terms of program size and execution speeds. Any variations or impacts to software development activities should not impact product testing for compliance with critical goals.

3.4 Capability

The tools provided by a software development facility should contain all of the features necessary to support a product's development. Wherever possible, the latest technologies consistent with other requirements (e.g., stability) should be used.

For embedded computer software, these tools have traditionally included text editors, compilers, link-editors, and "master tape" generators/loaders. Realistically, in today's environment, the traditional list can be routinely expanded to

---

DEVELOPMENT FACILITY REQUIREMENTS

ACCESSIBILITY	Available whenever needed for all product development tasks.
CAPACITY	Good processing turn-around plus sufficient online product development data storage.
STABILITY	Consistent working environment for all product development tasks.
CAPABILITY	Powerful tools for all product development tasks.
REUSABILITY	Applicability to broadest possible spectrum of organization's products.
IMPLEMENTABILITY	Facility's implementation cost and schedule support overall product development cycle and pricing.

Figure 1

include design tools (e.g., Program Design Languages), automated documentation packages, configuration control systems (e.g., UNIX* Source Code Control System), program generation processors (e.g., UNIX Make), problem reporting systems, and project management software (e.g., PERT).

Additionally, it is highly desirable that data from one tool be available to other tools to allow for cross-correlation of information (e.g., noting problem report closures resulting from source code module or design document changes).

3.5 Reusability

Software development facility tools should be usable on the broadest possible spectrum of an organization's products. For civilian embedded computer projects, this quite often means that tools must be able to support variations in deliverable hardware configurations as well as evolutions in product operating systems and utilities.

3.6 Implementability

The cost and schedule needed to implement a software development facility is crucial. Lead times and expenses must be consistent with and supportive of the delivery dates and pricing of the product being developed.

4.0 DEVELOPMENT FACILITY STRATEGIES

In addition to the always present option to "do nothing," three primary strategies are available for the development of embedded computer software: (1) upgrade an embedded computer's hardware configuration to support the required software development tools, (2) utilize a different (more powerful) stand-alone computer equipped with tools for directly generating embedded computer software, and (3) utilize a different (more powerful) computer with a downlink to one or more embedded computers.

4.1 Embedded Computer Upgrade

The first strategy, that of upgrading the development laboratory embedded computer hardware, is currently the most common civilian sector option. It's applicability to the development facility requirements discussed in Section 3.0 is summarized in Figure 2.

In general, this strategy has the advantage of not introducing a new equipment type into the development environment. In the case of a small software development effort, this is a most acceptable approach. For anything beyond a small software effort, however, this option has several drawbacks. First and foremost, use of this strategy too easily causes loss of distinction between an embedded computer configured for development and one configured for production.

Thus a piece of software which executes properly on the development computer may inadvertently take advantage of a capability which is not available on the deliverable computer and fail during final testing or after delivery.

The second drawback is that, for all but the smallest of projects, only one upgraded system is not enough. Multiple copies of a development environment are expensive; particularly in terms of the human labor required to schedule computer usage as well as coordinate and exchange interrelated data from different individuals or groups which use the separate systems.

The third and final drawback of using an upgraded embedded computer as a software development facility results from the general unavailability of sufficiently powerful tools that can significantly impact the development process. While many of the computers currently selected for embedded products have reasonably functional development tools, very few of them contain the high-powered, sophisticated

---

REQUIREMENTS APPLICABILITY OF THE
EMBEDDED COMPUTER UPGRADE STRATEGY

ACCESSIBILITY	Possible when sufficient numbers of computers are available (e.g., for twenty person five shift per week development effort, three computers would be required if each one can support eight users).
CAPACITY	Possible when sufficient numbers of computers and storage devices are configured.
STABILITY	Difficult to achieve; particularly when more than one computer is used. Testing environments tend to become confused and/or interfere with environments used for other tasks/phases.
CAPABILITY	Full range and/or power of tools generally not available (e.g., program design languages).
REUSABILITY	Usually restricted to embedded machine's architecture and operating system (e.g., difficult to migrate from Z80 to 8086 to 68000 processors and their various operating systems.)
IMPLEMENTABILITY	Easy to achieve so long as multiple, differing computer configurations are minimized.

Figure 2

---

* UNIX is a trademark of Bell Laboratories

capabilities of well established minicomputer and mainframe systems. (For example, consider the text editors available on a typical microprocessor compared with Digital Equipment Corporation's EDT or International Business Machine's SPF-EDIT and XEDIT.) The alternative, to develop in-house tools, while potentially effective, is not usually supportable in a cost-conscious environment: in-house tool development and maintenance is overhead that can only be recovered by increasing the price of each copy of the final product.

4.2 Separate Support Computer

The second strategy, utilizing a different, more powerful computer equipped with tools for directly generating embedded computer software is currently the one most frequently utilized by DoD projects. Its development facility requirements applicability is illustrated in Figure 3.

This strategy easily solves most of the drawbacks of the first strategy, but has three serious drawbacks of its own: (1) large initial costs, (2) long implementation schedules, and (3) restricted adaptability to ther rapidly evolving embedded computer hardware and operating system architectures currently underway in the civilian sector.

Development and maintenance of specialized tools for directly generating embedded computer software (e.g., cross compilers, cross assemblers, linkage editors, master disk/tape builders, instruction-level simulators) is expensive. In addition, the schedule lead times necessary to specify, design, develop and test such cross-software tools can be extensive (e.g., the initial Ada* Integrated Environment was estimated to require thirty months to develop for one development/embedded computer pair). Historically DoD has had no option but to pay these charges; the alternatives in terms of national defense have been considered sufficiently more expensive. To mitigate these charges, DoD has for many years taken steps to standardize development computers, embedded computers and the software which operates between them.

Unfortunately, while DoD has "clout" to enforce such standardization, the civilian sector has not and probably will not be able to standardize on a minimal set of development and embedded computers and their associated cross-software.

4.3 Linked Separate and Embedded Computers

Use of a separate more powerful computer with one or more downlinks to embedded machines is the third possible strategy. Essentially, the embedded computer is used as an execution and test "back end." Figure 4 summarizes the applicability of this strategy to the requirements discussed in Section 3.0.

Using this approach, a variety of effective, commercially available, development tools can be fully and economically utilized. No cross-software is used. Only the compiler, link-editor and testing tools usually delivered with the embedded hardware need actually execute on the deliverable computer. All other tools are those already provided as standard vendor or third-party facilities with the more powerful "host."

This final strategy is in many ways a compromise: it does not completely satisfy the drawbacks associated with the earlier two strategies, yet it is reasonably cost-effective and quite powerful. For example, configuration differences between the delivered embedded computer and the ones used for development will exist; yet they can be isolated to the downlink interface with relatively little effort. Similarly, the cost and schedule of implementing downlink hardware and software is significant, yet it is enormously less than that associated with construction and maintenance of a full complement of direct generation cross-software.

In fact, one of the key reasons for even considering the third strategy is the current off-the-shelf availability of downlink facilities in the guise of local area networks. These networks allow functional and performance segregation of software development tools. Those

---

REQUIREMENTS APPLICABILITY OF THE
SEPARATE SUPPORT COMPUTER STRATEGY

ACCESSIBILITY	Excellent (e.g., usually a commercial mainframe or minicomputer is used for development).
CAPACITY	Excellent (e.g., usually a commercial mainframe or minicomputer is used for development).
STABILITY	Excellent (e.g., usually a commercial mainframe or minicomputer is used for development).
CAPABILITY	Limited only by availability of cross-software for particular development / embedded computer pair.
REUSABILITY	Usually restricted by cross-software for particular development / embedded computer pair.
IMPLEMENTABILITY	Time consuming and expensive (e.g., Ada* Integrated Environment is estimated to require thirty calendar months).

Figure 3

---

* Ada is a trademark of the U. S. Dept. of Defense

tools which do not require embedded computer access are used only on the more powerful development (host) computer. Tools which best operate on the embedded computer are retained there. Integration of the segregated tools and computers is then accomplished by using the network for programmer/analyst terminal connections to all computers as well as for file transfers between them.

A typical software modification cycle illustrates this strategy. When a new capability for an embedded computer program is identified, it is documented and entered in the Software Change Request file on the host computer (i.e., no embedded computer access is required). The programmer/analyst assigned to implement the request then continues to use only the host computer to update the program design information and subsequently the program source code. Once a new version of the program source code is ready for compilation, it is entered into the Configuration Control File on the host computer and then downloaded to the embedded computer for compilation and link-editing. Resulting listings are then uploaded back to the host computer for online review and/or printing. Once the programmer/analyst is satisfied that the new version of the program is ready for testing, she logically disconnects her terminal from the host and reconnects, using only the network, to the embedded computer and issues the necessary execution and testing commands. Alternatively, the programmer/analyst could connect to the embedded computer via a host/network conduit without disconnecting and reconnecting: all the host need do is download commands in much the same manner as source programs are downloaded for compilation.

5.0 CASE HISTORY

The Energy Control Systems Division of The Boeing Company produces powerful Energy Management Systems (EMS) for the electrical power distribution industry. An EMS qualifies as an embedded computer system as described in Section 2.0: for the general user, the computer and its programming are invisible within the shell of the overall product. Additional attributes of an EMS are: (1) computers selected primarily for execution speed and durability, (2) large initial software development (greater than five hundred thousand lines of program source code plus program specification, design, maintenance, and usage documentation aggregating several thousand pages), and (3) significant customer software maintenance capability available concurrent with delivered system production execution.

The software maintenance tools delivered with an EMS are of special note in this situation. Unlike the DoD case where only the most primitive capabilities are generally available, the tools embedded in an EMS allow a significant range of customer-implemented modifications and customizations to be made. This allows each EMS system to be upgraded and adapted to a changing environment without mandating automatic Energy

Control Systems' involvement.

Because of the potency of the EMS software tool set, Energy Control Systems began its product development effort using the Embedded Computer Upgrade strategy described in Section 4.1. Up to six processors at one time were scheduled functionally (e.g., operating system/utilities, data base, data acquisition/control, displays, models) for use as development environments. Though this approach worked well while each function was in its early stages, it began to fail once testing began in earnest. By the time integration of the separate EMS functions began, it was clear that the use of the Embedded Computer Upgrade strategy was failing.

In the EMS case, the reasons for this were twofold. First, when functional testing began, the ten to fifteen individuals working on each computer began to interfere with each other. One person running a test would all too frequently cause a system failure which would in turn destroy any development (e.g., editing) work simultaneously in progress. Secondly, as functional integration progressed, it became exceedingly difficult to reflect one functional group's changes to all the other computers in a timely, effective and controlled manner.

To support its EMS product development, Energy Control Systems was faced with the need to adopt a

---

REQUIREMENTS APPLICABILITY OF THE LINKED SEPARATE AND EMBEDDED COMPUTER STRATEGY

ACCESSIBILITY   Excellent (e.g., usually a commercial mainframe or minicomputer is used for development).

CAPACITY   Excellent (e.g., usually a commercial mainframe or minicomputer is used for development).

STABILITY   Excellent (e.g., usually a commercial mainframe or minicomputer is used for development).

CAPABILITY   Excellent (e.g., usually a commercial mainframe or minicomputer is used for development).

REUSABILITY   Restricted by local area network downlink facilities.

IMPLEMENTABILITY   Moderately time consuming and expensive (e.g., Energy Control Systems ESDF required ten weeks for first capability, eight months for full linkage).

Figure 4

different development strategy. Because the equipment and programming languages selected for use in an EMS do not match any of the counterparts used by DoD embedded computer systems, use of the Separate Support Computer strategy would have been prohibitively expensive; Energy Control Systems could not afford either the time or the resources necessary to develop a full complement of cross-software. As a result the Linked Separate and Embedded Computer strategy was selected.

Using this strategy, Energy Control Systems implemented a full-scale Embedded Software Development Facility (ESDF). In addition to superbly satisfying the particular EMS development facility requirements, this strategy also provides numerous advantages to Energy Control Systems for multiple EMS preparation without detracting from the self-sustaining features of distinct EMS's once they are installed at a customer's site. For example, (1) program source code and associated documentation are maintained in a sophisticated host computer configuration management system which identifies text which is common to all customers or unique to just some, (2) embedded computers are configured to their deliverable/production configuration without the need to establish an initial development-only environment, (3) the continual expense of cabling development-only programmer/analyst terminals from one computer to another is eliminated, and (4) development efficiency and cost effectiveness is enhanced by segregating program source code and document preparation from the integration and test environment.

Implementation of the ESDF with both its more powerful computer and downlink network was accomplished without impacting ongoing EMS development. The computer and the network were installed in parallel except in the final stages where interfaces were established. The ESDF configuration finally constructed is shown in Figure 5. With the exception of the downlink file transfer software (represented in the figure by wide lines), all of the capabilities of the ESDF were available from the vendors at the time of initial receipt. As a result, the elapsed time to install and make the initial ESDF operational was just over ten weeks. This period covered all hardware and software installation as well as a thirty day component burn-in and integration test period prior to shifting into a "production" mode of operation.

Development of the downlink file transfer software required eight months. The vast majority of this time was spent in specifying, designing, programming and testing of the embedded computer interface to the network. (The host computer network interface was very close to an off-the-shelf item and was working within three months.) The relatively long time for this portion of the work resulted from two causes: (1) general lack of an embedded computer hardware/software interface to the local area network selected (or to almost any general purpose network for that matter), and (2) the strong desire to integrate the network interface with the deliverable computer in such a manner that when an Energy Control Systems' product is shipped, the ESDF "umbilical" can be

BOEING ENERGY CONTROL SYSTEMS
EMBEDDED SOFTWARE DEVELOPMENT FACILITY

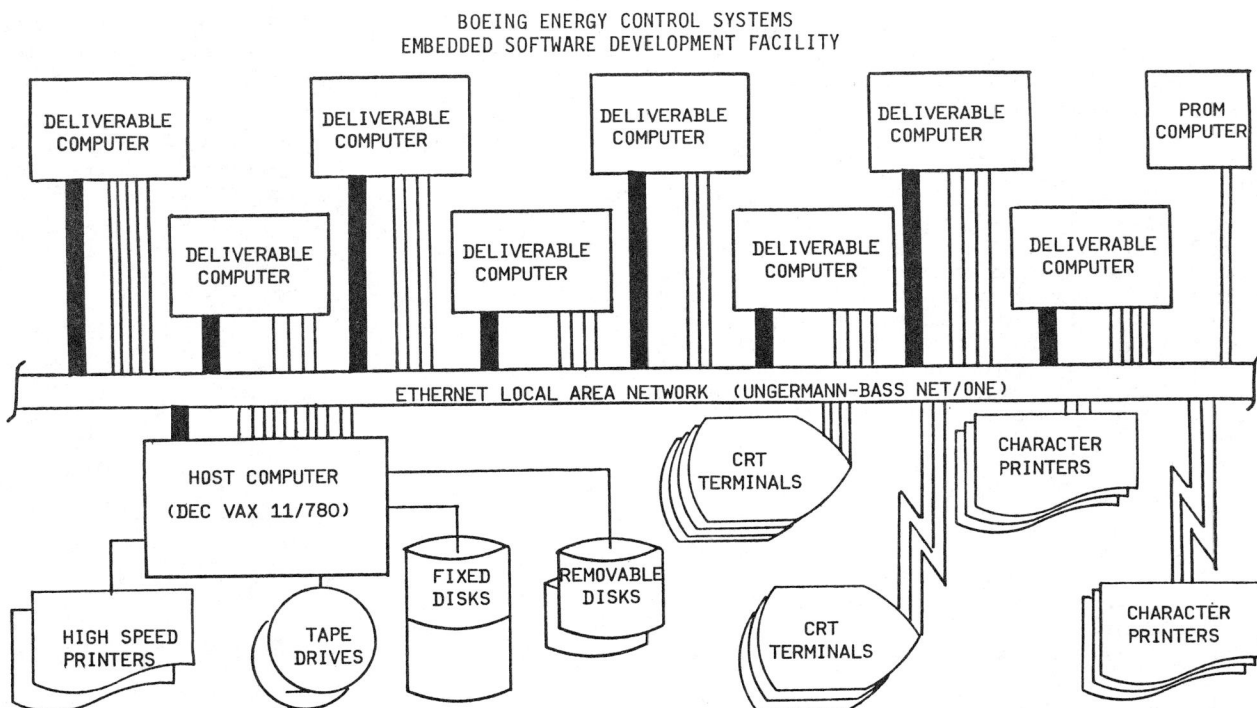

Figure 5

severed quickly, neatly and with no ill effects to the product itself.

6.0 CONCLUSION

The ESDF implemented by Energy Control Systems has markedly enhanced The Boeing Company's ability to develop large complex software systems for embedded computer products. Unlike the DoD technique of using cross-software with its associated long lead times and high "up-front" costs, the use of a host software development computer connected with the embedded computers via a local area network has proven to be both easy to implement and cost effective. Analysis of the costs of the ESDF versus labor and schedule savings indicates that improved productivity has recovered the basic ESDF investment in approximately one year. Additionally, several procedural and human factors problems have been either mitigated or resolved; thus promising even better software development efficiencies for the future.

As an extrapolation of Energy Control Systems' efforts, it appears that a generic set of rules for selecting embedded computer software development facilities can be hypothesized:

(1) If a project is small and development can be supported on a "controllable" number (i.e., 1) of computers, the Embedded Computer Upgrade strategy is feasible.

(2) If a project is not small, but uses equipment and programming languages which match DoD equipment and languages, use of the Separate Support Computer strategy is economically possible.

(3) If a project is not small and does not use DoD equivalent equipment and programming languages, the Linked Separate and Embedded Computers strategy is an effective software development technique.

It is not yet clear if the ESDF implemented by Energy Control Systems represents a universal solution for other non-DoD embedded computer projects. Obviously, differing host and embedded computer hardware coupled with evolving software development languages and tools present a wide set of conditions which must be accounted for in each specific case. Yet, the success of the ESDF strategy demonstrates that it can be used as at least one model for future attempts to establish environments which are conducive to the efficient, cost-effective production of embedded computer software.

REFERENCES:

1. Clark, D. D., Pogran, K. T., Reed, D. P., "An Introduction to Local Area Networks," Proceedings, IEEE (November, 1978), pp. 1497-1517.

2. Davies, D. W., Barber, D. L., "Communications Networks for Computers," Wiley, New York, 1973.

3. Everett, R. R., Zraket, C. A., Bennington, H. D., "SAGE: A Data Processing System for Air Defense," Proceedings, Eastern Joint Computer Conference (1957), pp. 148-155.

4. Fraser, A. G., "A Virtual Channel Network," Datamation 21 (February, 1975), pp. 51-56.

5. Karplus, W. J. (ed.), "On-Line Computing: Time-Shared Man-Computer Systems," McGraw-Hill, New York, 1967.

6. Metcalfe, R. M., Boggs, D. R., "Ethernet: Distributed Packet Switching for Local Computer Networks," Communications, ACM 19 (July, 1976), pp. 395-404.

7. Tannenbaum, A. S., "Computer Networks," Prentice Hall, Englewood Cliffs, N. J., 1981.

8. Thurber, K. J., Freeman, H. A., "Tutorial: Local Computer Networks," second edition, IEEE Computer Society Press, 1981.

9. Thurber, K. J., Trent, B. A., "Local Networks: What's Available?," Data Management 20, (April, 1982), pp. 20-22.

10. White, D., "Ada Integrated Environment," JOVIAL Language Control Facility Newsletter 14 (June, 1982), p. 5.

11. ------, Computing Surveys 11, (December, 1979).

12. ------, "EDT Editor Manual," Digital Equipment Corporation document AA-J726A-TC, Maynard, Mass., 1980.

13. ------, "Virtual Machine/System Product: System Product Editor User's Guide," International Business Machines document SC24-5220-0, White Plains, New York, 1980.

14. ------, "Virtual Machine/System Product: System Product Editor," International Business Machines document SC24-5221-0, White Plains, New York, 1980.

CAS
A TOOL FOR THE INTERACTIVE PROGRAM DESIGN

ARNO SCHULZ

University of Linz/Austria
Computer Science Department

ABSTRACT

The design of software development tools, also
called software engineering environments, is yet
an unexplored discipline. We therefore started
three years ago on a project under the name of CAS.
These three letters form the abbreviation of "Computer aided software design". In this presentation
I would like to give a report on the goals and the
present status of this project. The first part is
dedicated to the theoretical background of interactive program design such as the design of a man-
machine-interface realized by a graphical language.
In the second more practically oriented part the
fundamental structure of CAS-systems is investigated. Two implementations will be described.

1. Introduction

In order to put this study into the framework of
software engineering I will start with a short
description of its history.

- 1968: Dijkstra suggests "structured programming"

- 1968 - 1971, first software-engineering-phase:
  Discussion of the advantages and disadvantages of programming without GOTO-state-
  ments. Introduction of the stepwise refinement process. The name "software-
  engineering" originates from NATO conference Garmisch. The programming world
  accepts the principles of structured
  programming.

- 1972 - 1975, second software-engineering-phase:
  Structured design methods are proposed on
  the basis of structured programming (e.g.
  HIPO, Jackson, Constantine, Warnier, SADT).

- 1978, start of the third software-engineering-
  phase: It has been recognized, that the
  use of design methods without any support
  facilities is troublesome. Therefore software tools have been created (first generation: batch tools).

- 1982, start of the fourth software-engineering-
  phase: Interactive program design by
  CAS tools.

The interaction between software-engineering principles, methods and tools can be expressed by a
triangle:

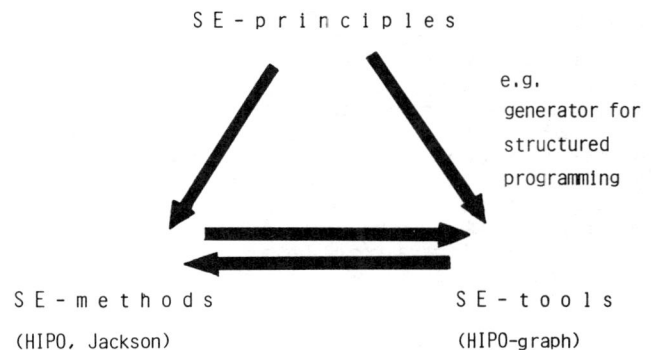

Principles are to be realized by methods, for instance the Jackson design method. In order to make
methods applicable, tools have been introduced.
This scheme represents the approach of the last
decade. Of course it is possible to pass this triangle in the opposite direction. In this way software-engineering principles are directly implemented in tools. As an example for this procedure I
refer to a generator, which produces well structured programs. In this manner the correct use of
methods is enforced. We try to follow this philosophy.

2. The fundamentals of CAS-systems

The name CAS associates the idea of transferring
the approved CAD/CAM methods to software design
tasks. A software system should be designed on a
screen without paper and pencil. Just as in CAD/
CAM system we need graphic means for this purpose.
A major objective of our research-work therefore,
is to find an adequate graphic design-language.

CAS systems consist of three components:

- problems
- methods and tools
- human beings, who solve problems in
  a CAS system by using methods and
  tools.

131

This situation is a very old one. In prehistoric times of mankind, the first human beings had to solve the problem of killing a bear with the tool 'stone'. For the solution of this problem an appropriate method was necessary, otherwise the human beings were killed. This example shows that each tool has two interfaces, the first between user and tool, the second between tool and problem. The tool has to solve this problem by use of adequate methods or principles.

Consequently we started our CAS project investigating the question how to arrange the interface between software designer and software tool. We are of the opinion that precisely this interface has been neglected for a long time. For this reason we asked psychologists what their science could contribute to design the interface between software designer and software tool. Professor Kraft, a German psychologist, states that the best way of understanding the programming problem is to write a program, due to the fact that it is impossible to foresee the level of required details in advance. Thus a feedback mechanism exists in writing a program, understanding the problem in detail and improving the written program. In other words: program design is an iterative activity, working alternately top down and bottom up. Software design tools have to support this trial-and-error philosophy. In order to achieve this objective modern software tools have the following fundamental structure:

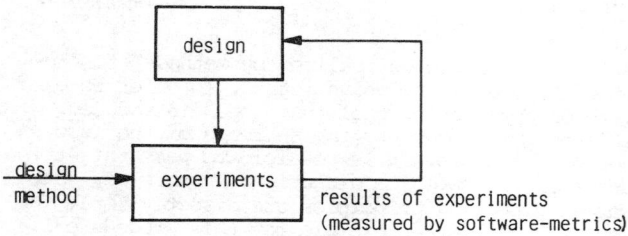

In transferring the trial-and-error philosophy to the structuring process of the software lifecycle a sequence of feedback loops arises:

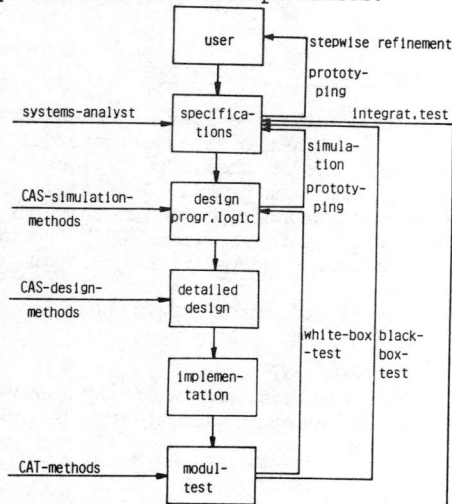

The first loop represents the specification phase in the software lifecycle. Psychology states that no specification can ever be totally complete. A specification is always an abstraction of a real situation. For this reason the user together with a system-analyst tries to write down specifications in a trial-and-error manner. To test these specifications a tool is needed which is capable of dealing with imperfection. Prototyping is a tool of this kind.

The second loop supports the global design of the program logic checked by simulation. In the third loop the local design of each program function is achieved together with the design of the input-output data flow. An interactive design-tool has to support the verification as well as the testing of the individual system components. We have developed a tool of this kind, allowing path testing in an interactive manner (CAT: Computer aided testing).

When designing the interface between software tool and user, an important question has become dedicated to design language. Should it be a kind of pseudocode or graphical tool, which plays an important part in CAD/CAM systems? This is a question for human factors research. I would like to sketch some results. I am sure that you are acquainted with the sentence: "One picture is worth more than 1 000 words". As an engineer I believe in this sentence. Many CAD/CAM systems demonstrate the advantage of graphical means in the daily work of designers. But is it founded on psychological experiments? In a series of investigations Kammann displayed the advantage of flowcharts versus written information containing telephone dialing instructions for a complex network [Kammann 75]. Two groups of subjects participated in his investigations, namely employees of Bell Laboratories and housewives. Kammann measured the mean time to comprehend a problem and the error rate in solving this problem. The results are:

Mean time (sec) per problem (n=30):

Subjects	DIR	F1	F2
Housewives	72.0	59.4	51.0
Employees	34.8	33.6	30.6

DIR: Instruction by directory (text)
F1, F2: two types of flowcharts

Percent error for present experiment and a similar earlier experiment:

Subjects	DIR	F1	F2
present experiment (n=30)			
Housewives	60.7	41.4	728.1
Employees	20.8	6.5	6.0
previous experiment (n=20)			
Housewives	59.7	29.1	
Employees	21.6	5.9	

Professor Shneiderman explained that the results of Kammann's investigations were not applicable to computer programming [Shneiderman 77]. He started his own experiments to investigate the utility of detailed flowcharts in programming. His intention was to ascertain under which conditions flowcharts are helpful. At the end of his experiments he had a more sceptical opinion of the ability of flowcharts under modern programming conditions. Three years later Brooks demonstrated the methodical weakness of Shneiderman's studies [Brooks 80]. For this reason up to now the claim to design a user-friendly interface between software designer and software tool is more a slogan than a method based on facts. In this situation we have decided to create a graphical design language using tree structures which represent the functions of a software system. The first question of our investigations referred to the set of statements which are needed in a graphical design tool. We found 14 basic statements grouped into three classes.

1. Generation of the tree structure:

    1.1 Generation of a root node
    1.2 Generation of a father-son-relation
    1.3 Generation of a brother-brother-relation
    1.4 Insertion of the control flow (sequence, iteration, selection)
    1.5 Definition of a data element (name, type)
    1.6 Connection of data elements and nodes (input-flow, output-flow)
    1.7 Insertion of text to a node

2. Output:

    2.1 Output of a tree or a subtree
    2.2 Output of data and control flow

3. Processing:

    3.1 Store of a tree or a subtree
    3.2 Delete of a tree or a subtree
    3.3 Copy of a subtree
    3.4 Treesplitting
    3.5 Generation of a new abstraction level.

The first three statements (1.1 - 1.3) are necessary in order to design a tree top down. The interaction of the software designer with the CAS-system is shown in the next picture.

1.1 Generation of a root node:

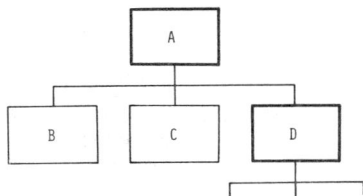

1.2 Generation of a father-son-relation:

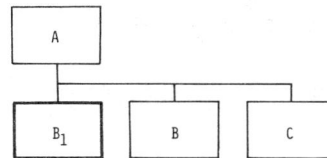

1.3 Generation of a brother-brother-relation:

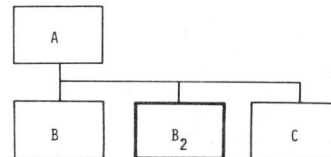

In the case of creating a tree the first step is the generation of a root node. This task shows the node "A". With the command "FATHER" and the parameter "A", this node becomes a root node. In general, when using the same command every node that already exists can be declared as root node of a subtree. Example "D" demonstrates the use of this general function.

For the designing of a tree the second step is the use of the father-son-relation. The command "SON" generates a new node under that node which is active at present. If a node already possesses a son, the same command will generate a node left from the first son. Example B_1 shows this generalized function.

As third relationship the brother-brother-connection is required. Therefore the command "BROTHER" generates a new node right from the marked node, for instance B_2 right from B.

These three commands are sufficient to design the architecture of software systems. Of course, in practice more comfort and therefore also more commands are needed. We call this first design phase "rough design". It is comparable with the first design phase in the HIPO technique which creates a tree showing the major functions to be performed by the software system. Computer science calls the result of this first design phase a tree, showing the "Consist of Relationship".

The next phase in our design system inserts the control flow (statement 1.4) together with the data flow (statements 1.5 and 1.6) and decomposites the tree in depth. The control flow consists of the three basic control structures of structured programming, namely:

    - sequence,

    - iteration and

    - selection.

In our system, sequence is expressed by an arrow, iteration by the capital letter "I" and selection by the capital letter "S". The iteration- and selection conditions are summarized in a table shown by the next picture.

1.4 Insertion of control flow:

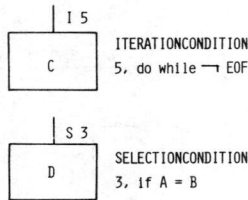

```
        | I 5
  ┌──────────┐
  │    C     │        ITERATIONCONDITION
  └──────────┘        5, do while ¬ EOF

        | S 3
  ┌──────────┐
  │    D     │        SELECTIONCONDITION
  └──────────┘        3, if A = B
```

For better understanding I am going to demonstrate these basic functions of a CAS-system by means of a simple example. It is the classical sequential file processing problem. A transaction file contains records which update an old masterfile, thus generating a new masterfile. This task is a typical matching problem. Therefore from a functional point of view the following functions can be founded:

- The updating of matched records.
- For a missing master record a new master record has to be created in the output file.
- For a missing transaction record the old master record has to be written into the new masterfile without any change.
- Finally a protocol of all these processes will be printed.

The next picture demonstrates the design of the first and the second abstraction level of this system using the three basic statements:

- generation of a root node
- generation of a father-son-relationship
- generation of a brother-brother-relationship

1. design of the 1. and 2. abstraction level

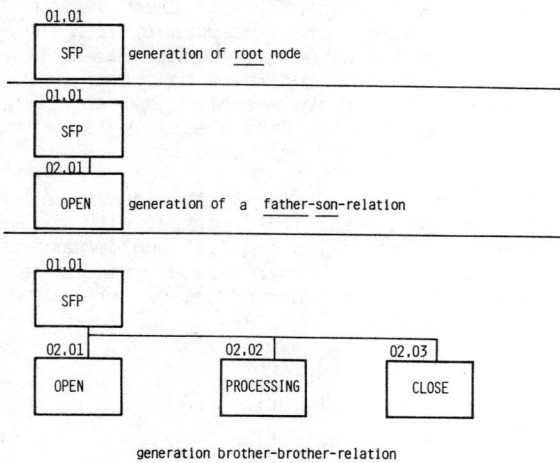

```
01.01
┌──────┐
│ SFP  │   generation of root node
└──────┘
─────────────────────────────────────
01.01
┌──────┐
│ SFP  │
└──────┘
02.01
┌──────┐
│ OPEN │   generation of a father-son-relation
└──────┘
─────────────────────────────────────
01.01
┌──────┐
│ SFP  │
└──────┘
02.01        02.02        02.03
┌──────┐   ┌──────────┐  ┌──────┐
│ OPEN │   │PROCESSING│  │CLOSE │
└──────┘   └──────────┘  └──────┘

   generation brother-brother-relation
```

The CAS-system automatically numbers the nodes top-down and left to right.

The following picture shows the design of the third abstraction level together with the insertion of the control flow. In this case the third abstraction level consists of the functions updating, missing transaction record and missing master record.

2. design of the 3. abstraction level and design of the control flow

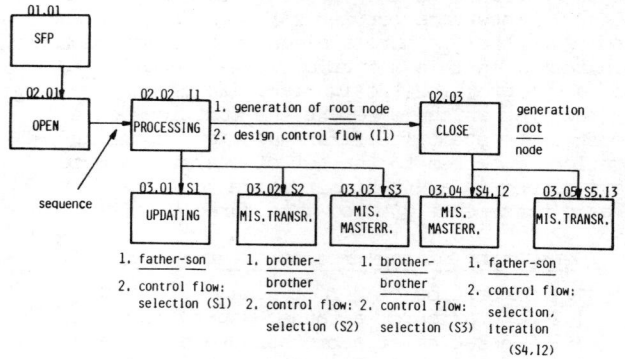

```
01.01
┌──────┐
│ SFP  │
└──────┘
02.01                02.02  I1                              02.03
┌──────┐   sequence  ┌──────────┐  1. generation of root node  ┌──────┐   generation
│ OPEN │ ──────────▶ │PROCESSING│  2. design control flow (I1)  │CLOSE │   root node
└──────┘             └──────────┘                              └──────┘

   03.01 │S1   03.02 │S2   03.03 │S3   03.04 │S4,I2   03.05 │S5,I3
  ┌────────┐ ┌──────────┐ ┌────────┐ ┌────────┐    ┌──────────┐
  │UPDATING│ │MIS.TRANSR│ │  MIS.  │ │  MIS.  │    │MIS.TRANSR│
  └────────┘ └──────────┘ │MASTERR.│ │MASTERR.│    └──────────┘
                          └────────┘ └────────┘

  1. father-son  1. brother-   1. brother-   1. father-son
                    brother        brother
  2. control flow: 2. control flow: 2. control flow: 2. control flow:
    selection (S1)   selection (S2)  selection (S3)   selection,
                                                      iteration
                                                      (S4,I2)
```

In the next step the control flow has to be designed. The control flow transfers the "Consist of Relationship" to the "Call up Relationship". For this purpose the three control structures sequence, iteration and selection are used, for instance the three functions OPEN, PROCESSING and CLOSE form a sequence. The three functions UPDATING, missing transaction record (MIS. TRANSR.) and missing master record (MIS. MASTERR.) constitute a selection because either the updating function or one of the both unmatched functions will be called up. The processing function (PROCESSING) forms an iteration controlled by the end-of-file signals of both input files. If one end-of-file condition arises the control flow goes to the close function. At the end of the design phase the data flow has to be inserted. For this purpose data elements are to be defined by the basic statement 1.5. With the statement 1.6 data elements will be connected with nodes. The result is a matrix showing the input and output data flow for each node.

NODE NUMBER	INPUT-DATA FLOW	SENT BY	OUTPUT-DATA FLOW	RECEIVED FROM
01.01	MASTERFILE OLD	FILE	MASTERFILE NEW	FILE
	TRANSACTIONS	FILE	LIST	PRINT
02.01	MASTERRECORD	01.01	MASTERRECORD	02.02
	TRANSACTIONRECORD	01.01	TRANSACTIONRECORD	02.02
			EOF TRANSACTION	02.02
			EOF MASTER	02.02
02.02	MASTERRECORD	02.01	MASTERRECORD	02.03
				03.01
				03.02
	TRANSACTIONRECORD	02.01	TRANSACTIONRECORD	02.03
				03.01
				03.03

The results of the design process can be printed or given out by a screen (statement 2.1 and 2.2). The next picture shows an example for a print output.

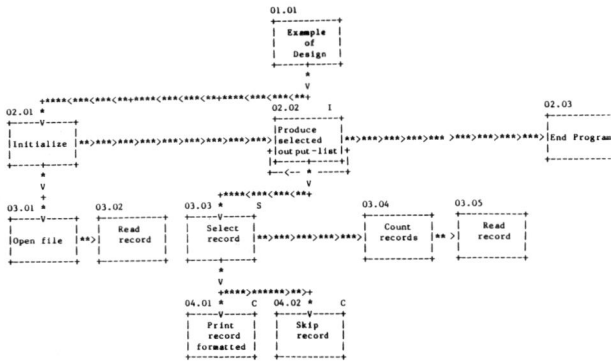

The third group of statements, the processing statements (3.1 - 3.5), is responsible for deleting or copying a tree or a subtree. One important function besides this is treesplitting. In practice it must be possible to use subtrees at various points of a software system in the sense of subprograms.

3.4 T r e e s p l i t t i n g :

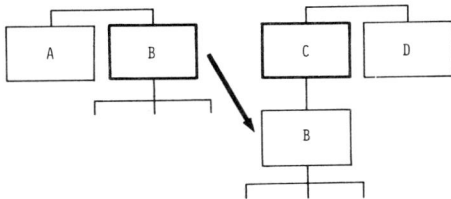

3.5 Generation of a new a b s t r a c t i o n l e v e l :

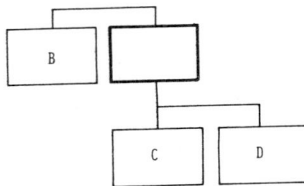

The first part of our CAS project was dedicated to the designing of a graphical design language as I have already pointed out. Naturally its command-set is larger than 14 statements. At present it consists of 57 commands. Many of them are responsible for organizational functions, managing screen and editing tasks.

This language supports the whole software-life-cycle. In the definition phase it helps by documentation of the specifications. Within the project it is planned to make use of the entity-relationship-model for verification of the specifications.

The program logic is tested by simulation in a dialogue between the software-designer and the CAS-system. For this purpose specific commands permit to show a path through the program on the screen, stop the execution of the program logic at predefinded positions and show the value of selected variables. They can be changed by the software-designer. Test coverage metrics are calculated automatically.

3. The structure of CAS-systems

As mentioned before CAS-systems are related to CAD-systems. Therefore it is useful to investigate the question as to whether CAD-systems can be used for CAS purposes. CAD-systems fulfil three tasks:

1. the shape design: input of geometrical data by screens, two and three dimensional processing

2. the functional design: black box design of functional units and connection to a system

3. the numerical design: calculation of physical elements (e.g. gears).

Center of a CAD-system is the shape design. Therefore the computerized drawing board is a main component of a CAD working station. In a CAS-system the functional design and not the shape design is the main objective. As already mentioned in the first part of this presentation the shape of a program tree, for instance the shape and the size of a node, is given by the design language and not by the designer.

CAD is referred to geometrical design, but CAS is functional design of the program structure represented by a program-tree. Therefore the goals of CAS-systems can be summarized as follows:

1. functional design:
   - method-independent design: design based on software engineering principles (structured programming, stepwise refinement, information hiding)
   - method-dependent design: e.g. Jackson-method (structured clashes, program inversion, backtracking)

2. dialogue user - CAS-system:
   screen facilities (interactive design-language)

3. documentation of the inputs and outputs of every software lifecycle (graphics and text)

4. project planning and project controlling:
   selected information for the project management

5. <u>On-line-training</u>: e.g. by a typical example.

It is useful to distinguish between method-independent and method-dependent design. Method-independent design is based on the software-engineering principles such as structured programming or information hiding. If necessary, the method-independent design stage is followed by method-dependent design like the application of the Jackson method. It provides special design features like program inversion or backtracking.

As mentioned in the first part of my report, the dialogue interface between user and CAS-system has to be designed in a very careful way. As the use of paper and pencil is forbidden, documentation of every activity and of every result is very important. Managers at all levels have discovered their "need to know" about all phases of a software project, a special kind of documentation has to be created for this purpose.

Training of programming people in modern software design philosophy and design methods is a big problem in practice due to lack of time. On-line-training can help in this situation. It means that a typical example of a software problem is built in the CAS-system. Programming people can use this example for training but also as a help function.

An important question in designing a CAS-system is concerned with decentralization or centralization of the design tools. Pros and cons can be summarized as follows:

1. <u>decentralized computers</u>:

   - microcomputers
   - PC's

   <u>advantages</u>:

   - optimal adaption to CAS-requirements
   - transportable tools (e.g. by cars).

   <u>disadvantages</u>:

   They need the central system to store the design-data and gain access to the design-database.

2. <u>centralized computers</u>:

   <u>advantages</u>:

   - high performance
   - software design on the production computer
   - easily portable.

   <u>disadvantages</u>:

   The workload of the computer influences the design process (production has higher priority).

Centralized software development is of the disadvantage that interactive software development on the same main frame supporting daily production is troublesome. Production work always has a higher priority than development activities. In order to increase productivity by reducing lost time, the decentralized use of microcomputers and PC's is recommended. Naturally this kind of software development also has some disadvantages because it needs the central system for storing the design data in a data base. On the other hand centralized software design and programming has the advantage that it can be done on the same computer for which programs are made.

Functional structure of CAS-systems

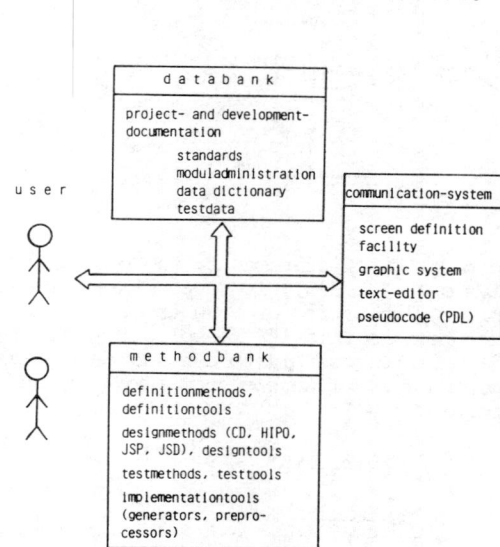

Now I will report on our considerations of the structure of CAS-systems. The activities of the software design process can be summarized in three subsystems:

   - a databank
   - a method- and toolbank and
   - a communication-system.

The databank manages any kind of documentation such as modules, its input- and output data stored in a data dictionary, specifications, test data. In this manner the databank acts as interface between the phases of the software-lifecycle. The communication-system supports the dialogue between software-designer and software-tool by use of a graphic design language as mentioned before. A large part of software development is text processing like writing, modifying or reading specifications, memoranda, test protocols, programcode etc. Therefore an efficient text-editor is necessary.

The methodbank contains methods and tools for every phase of the software-lifecycle. Of course they should be integrated as far as possible by including standardized interfaces between the several phases in order to be able to hang up tools of different manufacturers.

A project control system rules these three subsystems and is responsible for the management of the whole CAS-system and its components.

We have carried out two implementations of CAS-systems in our institute. For the first version we used the MAESTRO software engineering environment which has been installed in our institute since 1979. The hardware is manufactured by Philips, the software by Softlab in Munich. The next picture is a graphical representation of the system concept showing the work distribution between the decentralized software design workstations and the host computer.

STRUCTURE
of
CAS-system
(1. version)
Institute of Informatics
University Linz

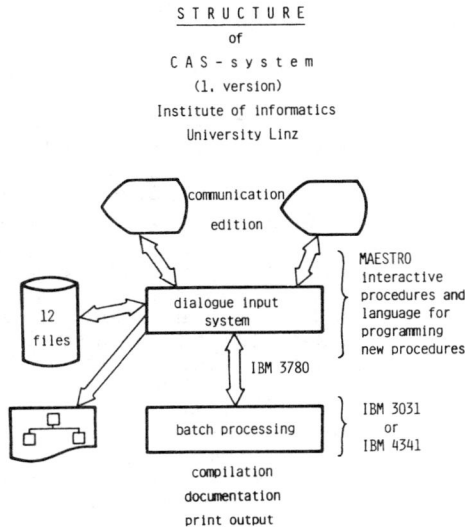

Some features of MAESTRO are very attractive. A procedure language permits the creation of new features. In this manner our graphical design language has been implemented. Furthermore the "multi-camera" principle also called "television principle" allows users to switch tasks, reference documents, copies from existing work and also to send messages, whilst retaining complete control over their position in the overall job. This feature simulates up to 12 logical screens on one physical screen. In batch processing compilation of long term documentation and printing are done.

In order to compare decentralized software design with the centralized one a second version of a CAS-system has been implemented on our host computer. The software contains 13 000 loc written in PL/1 plus some lines assembler needed for interfaces to TSO and library management. It requires a partition (region) of 256 KB memory. In order to get a feedback of non university environment, three installations have been made outside of our own university at present.

2. Version CAS System LITOR

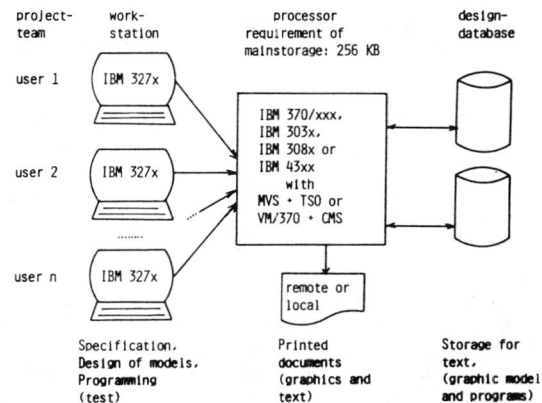

4. Conclusion

Our investigations yield that the requirements of a CAS-system can be summarized in eight criteria:

1. Automatic documentation (specifications, design, code, test data)

2. Support of the software design (high-low level design, design of data structure) by a design language using graphical means

3. On-line updating of documentation

4. Verification of the program logic by simulation

5. Generation of a program frame

6. Support of the coding process

7. Support of the program tuning

8. Support of various software design methods by tools.

5. References

[Brooks 80] R. E. Brooks, Studying Programmer Behaviour Experimentally: The Problems of Proper Methodology. Communications of the ACM, April 1980, Volume 23, Number 4, 207-213

[Kammann 75] R. Kammann, The Comprehensibility of Printed Instructions and the Flowchart Alternative. Human Factors, 1975 17(2), 183-191

[Shneiderman 77] B. Shneiderman, R. Mayer, D. McKay, P. Heller, Experimental Investigations of the Utility of Detailed Flowcharts in Programming. Communications of the ACM, June 1977, Volume 20, Number 6, 373-381

GRIP : A FORMAL FRAMEWORK FOR DEVELOPING A SUPPORT ENVIRONMENT FOR GRAPHICAL INTERACTIVE PROGRAMMING.

David A. Workman
Farahangiz Arefi and Mahesh Dodani

University of Central Florida.
Dept. of Computer Science
Orlando, FL. 32816

ABSTRACT

This paper proposes a methodology for designing and implementing tools to support interactive, graphical programming. Our approach combines the formalism of attributed, graphical context-free grammars with the object-oriented philosophy of implementation. The concepts are illustrated by examining their application to the development of an interactive, syntax-directed editor for D-Charts. Using our methodology the syntax tree describing a D-Chart becomes an instantiation of the objects and methods comprising the editor itself; conceptually, nodes in the tree become related tasks of the user process, cooperating to carry out the editor functions.

1. Introduction

GRIP (GRaphical Interactive Programming) is a support environment for graphical programming under development in the Computer Science Department at the University of Central Florida. The goals of this effort are: 1) to provide an integrated interactive system for developing and maintaining software, 2) to exploit graphics as much as possible in representing program information during each phase of the software life span, and 3) to apply state-of-the-art techniques and methodologies in the design and implementation of this system. With regard to the use of graphics in representing the various "views" of software, we recognize no single paradigm is suitable. Thus a programming environment such as GRIP should support a variety of graphical paradigms and ideally provide tools enabling the user to define a personalized graphical interface for the display and manipulation of program entities. It is necessary, therefore, to develop formalisms suitable for specifying and implementing graphical languages for programming.

This paper proposes a class of 2-dimensional attributed context-free grammars as a formal vehicle not only for specifying graphical programming languages, but also for implementing the tools used to edit and view programs expressed in such languages. The implementation methodology we are developing is based on the object-oriented philosophy of Smalltalk [8]. It treats the syntax tree defining a program in some graphical language as an instantiation of the objects and the methods forming a particular editing or viewing tool for that program. We illustrate our approach by describing a few of the object classes and methods required to implement a syntax-directed editor for D-Charts.

The paper is organized as follows. Sections 2 and 3 survey some of the literature on languages used for the specification of interactive interfaces to motivate the need for techniques more suitable to graphical programming. Section 4 develops the formalism of 2-D attributed grammars we propose to meet this need. Section 5 presents the application of our implementation methodology based on graphical grammars to the design and implementation of a D-Chart editor. The paper concludes with section 6 where we review major issues and concepts and point out some of the theoretical avenues that might be pursued.

2. Interface design and Specification Languages

The dialogue between the user of an interactive system and the system itself can be viewed as a string in a language, $(LI.LO)*$, where LI denotes some language of user inputs and LO denotes the language of system responses to those inputs. Under this interpretation we may think of the system as a translator or compiler which decodes a user input, $x \in LI$, to "learn" the semantics of the user's request and responds in some fashion producing an encoded output, $y \in LO$.

This view of man-machine interaction naturally suggests a syntax-directed design of the user interface (if not the system as a whole) where semantic actions are tied to syntactic elements through some type of formal specification language such as BNF grammars or state-

138

transition diagrams. Many researchers have taken this approach. Reisner [24,25], Bleser and Foley [4] used BNF grammars as a specification language primarily to study the human factors aspects of an interface design, in contrast to its actual implementation. Others [9,17,18,27,19] have used BNF-style specifications more as a language for design leading directly to implementation. Jacobs [11,13] surveys much of the literature on interface specification techniques and in [12] describes a specification language based on state-transition diagrams(STDs). Other applications of STDs in the design and specification of interactive interfaces can be found in [20,28,32]. Pilote [22,23] describes an interesting interface specification styled after the methods of denotational semantics [26,29].

A shortcoming of many proposed interface specification languages lies in their use of string oriented formalisms to deal with or describe inherently graphical concepts. This conceptual mismatch is typically resolved by adding to the input language, LI, primitives and operations that encumber the user with the mechanical aspects of graphical display. This results in diminished concentration on the conceptual aspects of the task. For example, when displaying a 2D object, such as a circle, the user is usually required through some input sequence to specify the exact location and size of the object. In contrast it would be better if the interface and dialogue were structured so that the location and size of the next object to be created is implicit from context. Putting this point another way, incorporating into the user interface more knowledge about the problem domain can lead to a more structured and intelligent dialogue, thereby reducing the distractions that interfere with the essentials of problem solving. Our thesis, therefore, is that user interfaces must incorporate more of the inherent structure of the problem domain. This requires more powerful specification languages and techniques.

3. Graphics in Programming

One area where software engineering and computer science have merged is in the development of programming environments, in particular, graphical programming environments. In [1,2,3] numerous examples are given of such systems demonstrating the vigorous activity in this emerging discipline. The proliferation of systems such as these clearly establishes a direction for future research, namely, the development of fully graphical programming languages together with

the formal specification techniques and implementation tools necessary to deal with them. In the next sections we introduce a class of 2-dimensional BNF grammars and show how they can be used not only as a formal specification language for describing the syntax and semantics of graphical languages, but also as a framework for their implementation.

4. Attributed Graphical Grammars

Two principles undergird our approach to graphical language specification and implementation. The first is the building of graphic forms through recursive substitution of syntactic templates. This notion is incorporated in the Cornell Program Synthesizer [30] which is a syntax-directed editor for PL/I. For example, the recursive description of D-Charts [33,10], a graphical language for describing structured control flow, can be expressed using a 2-dimensional BNF notation such as that shown in Figure 1. By starting with rule 1 and replacing the bracketed variables ("<Body>" , "<Loop>" , "<Cases>" , "<Case>" , "<Default>") on the left side of rules with the structure(s) on the right an arbitrary D-Chart can be produced.

While recursive substitution is conceptually powerful, its implementation as the controlling mechanism of a syntax-directed D-Chart editor leaves a number of geometric and screen allocation problems to be solved. These are in addition to the usual problems of semantic analysis associated with any language implementation. The second principle addresses the syntactic display problems by associating with each graphic primitive (terminals and variables) a rectangular region that represents the minimum area necessary to display the primitive. Thus each rule of syntax specifies how the rectangular region associated with the syntax variable on the left side can be computed in terms of the rectangular areas associated with symbols on the right. When a new syntax rule is applied the dimensions of all rectangular regions enclosing the replaced variable must expand according to geometric relationships specified by their defining rules.

To illustrate this second principle consider an "editing session" with a D-Chart editor where the variable "D-Chart" appears in the upper left corner of the CRT screen as shown in Figure 2a. The icon of the unexpanded "DChart" could be just the text "D-CHART" highlighted in a particular color to indicate the next point of expansion. The minimum width

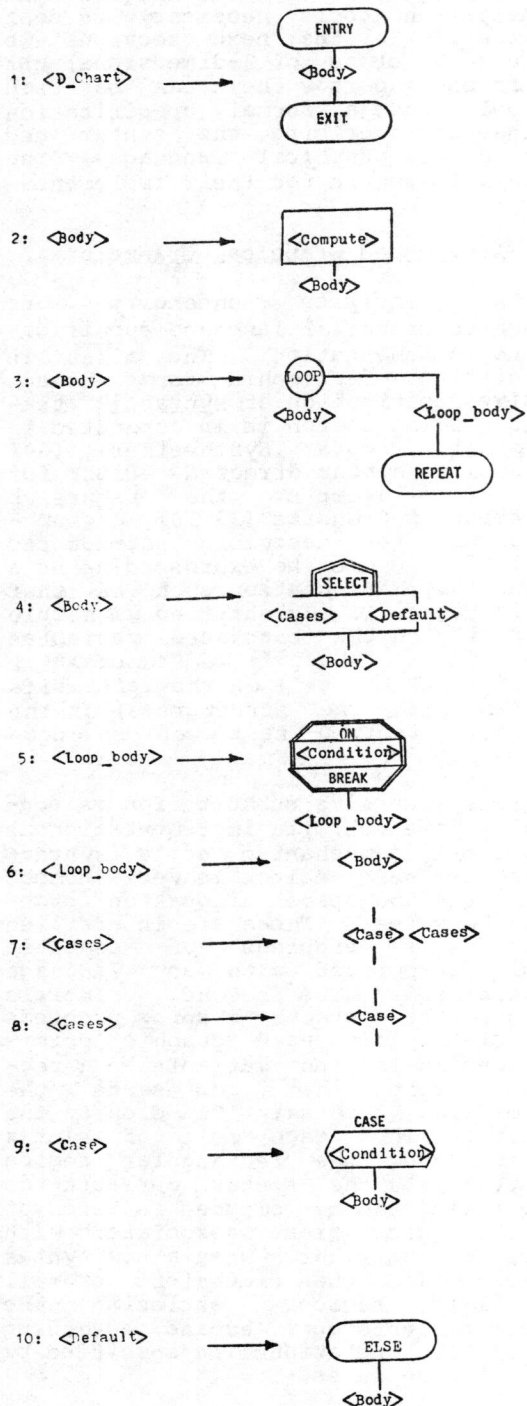

Figure 1. A Sample D_Chart Grammar

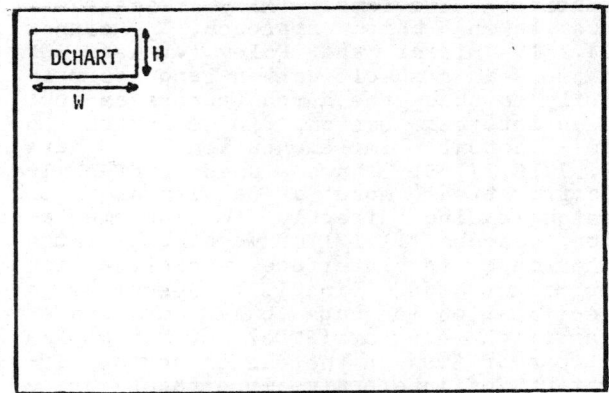

(a) Before DCHART Expansion

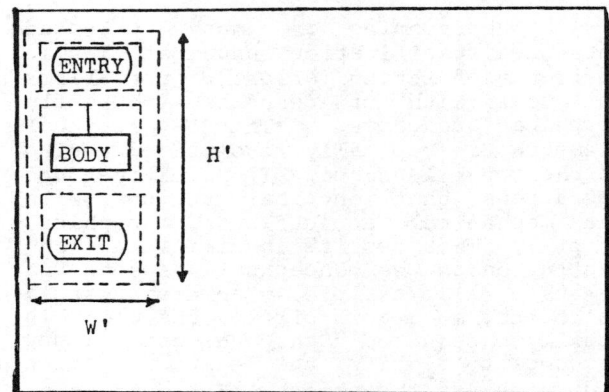

(b) After DCHART Expansion

Figure 2. Geometry of Node Expansion

(W) and height (H) of the <D-Chart> icon is easily computed from known charac-teristics of the display device. When <D-Chart> is expanded by applying rule 1 the geometry changes as shown in Figure 2b.

The outside dimensions of the smal-lest rectangle enclosing the expanded <D-Chart> is given by the simple equa-tions:

$$W' = \max\{ \text{Width}(ENTRY), \text{Width}(<Body>), \text{Width}(EXIT)\};$$
$$H' = \text{Height}(ENTRY) + \text{Height}(<Body>) + \text{Height}(EXIT).$$

These equations follow directly from the vertical stacking of the symbols ENTRY, <Body> and EXIT comprising the rightpart of rule 1 of the D-Chart grammar given in Figure 1. Implicit in these relation-ships is a third parameter, we shall call "E" for "Entry point", which denotes the position of the "control flow path" through the symbol. The vertical connector lines associated with various grammar symbols are syntactic encodings of this semantic property of control flow and are positioned a distance E from the left edge of the symbol's rectangular region. Normally E = 1/2 W, but for loop structures, which are asymmetric, this relationship does not hold.

To formalize the geometric properties of the display we associate with each graphic symbol a set of display attributes. The subset of these display attributes used to control geometry will be called geometric attributes. For D-Charts three such attributes are required:
  (1) Symbol Width (W),
  (2) Symbol Height (H),
  (3) Entry point (E), where E = (Ex,Ey) denotes a reference point in relative coordinates with (0,0) defined to be the upper left corner of the symbol's rectangular region; Ey=0 for all D-Chart symbols.
Using the terminology of attributed grammars [14,15] the geometric attributes for the display of <D-Chart> in rule 1 of the grammar were synthesized from the geometric attributes of symbols in the right part. Unfortunately, there are instances where not all geometric attributes can be synthesized. For example, the conditional structure given by rules 4,7,8,9 and 10 of Figure 1 represent a situation where inherited attributes must be used to describe the geometry. The reason for this relates to the requirement that the vertical dimension of <Cases> in rules 4 and 7 must be the same (+ or - some fixed constant) as the vertical dimension of <Default> in rule 4 or <Case> in rule 7. Since the minimum rectangle enclosing <Cases> in rule 4 will in general have a different (and independent) vertical height relative to <Default> it is necessary to "force" agreement by the use of inherited attributes. Specifically, this problem was solved by defining distinct height attributes Ha and Hm. Hm denotes the minimum vertical dimension of the enclosing rectangle and is always synthesized. Ha denotes the actual vertical dimension and in rule 4 must be an inherited attribute of both <Cases> and <Default>. Thus we can write:

$$\text{Ha (<Cases>)} = \text{Ha (<Default>)} + c$$
$$= \text{max } \{\text{Hm (<Cases>)},$$
$$\text{Hm (<Default>)} + c\},$$

where "c" is a constant allowing for fixed length connectors.

A comment about implementation of these concepts is appropriate at this point although issues concerning implementation will be addressed at greater length in the next section. In order to manage the display and update the geometry according to the principles described above it is necessary (and desirable) to maintain a syntax tree in memory corresponding to the current state of the D-Chart display. Symbols on the frontier of this tree produce visible images (terminals and syntax variables alike) while interior nodes (denoting expanded variables) serve to record the display and other attributes of the entire subtree they represent. In this framework the root node denotes the start symbol (<D-Chart>) of the grammar and contains the Wa, Ha and Ea attributes for the entire display. For frontier symbols a display attribute (c) will indicate the "color" of the node and will have a unique value for the syntax variable next to be expanded. The syntax tree defined in this way superimposes on the vertical display area a hierarchical organization of nested invisible windows permitting efficient management of display space and other display properties. A similar kind of organization is suggested in [27] and [16].

4.1 Semantic Attributes

Semantics for D-Charts reduces to a description of control flow; that is, a complete specification of the relation, "B follows A", where A and B can be any symbols of the grammar. For the most part, this relationship is made explicit through the syntax via connector lines joining one symbol to its possible successor(s). The exceptions to this rule occur with the BREAK and CASE symbols introduced by rules 5 and 9, respectively. We associate with both symbols a logical expression defined by the variable, <Condition>. The value of this expression gates control flow along alternate paths as illustrated in Figures 3a and 3b.

The control flow relation is specified formally by associating semantic attributes with each symbol of the grammar. These semantic attributes take the form of "links" (pointers) connecting related nodes on the frontier of the syntax tree describing some D-Chart. In general, three distinct link types are required to express D-Chart semantics. They are:
  L1 : primary link; (A,B) is a directed link of type, L1, iff B is an immediate successor of A at the same nesting level;

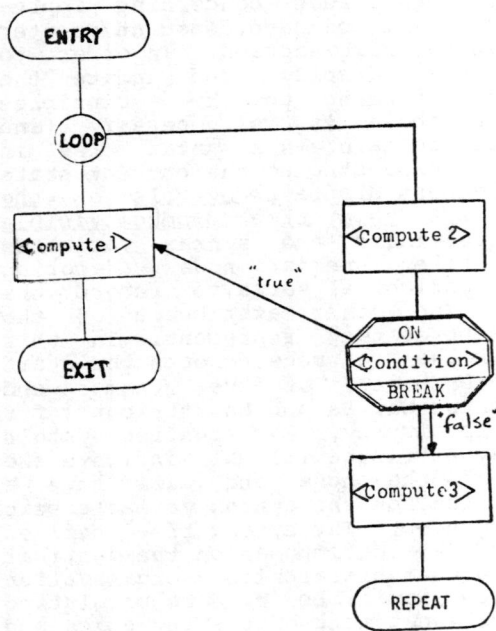

Figure 3a. Semantics of the BREAK Symbol.

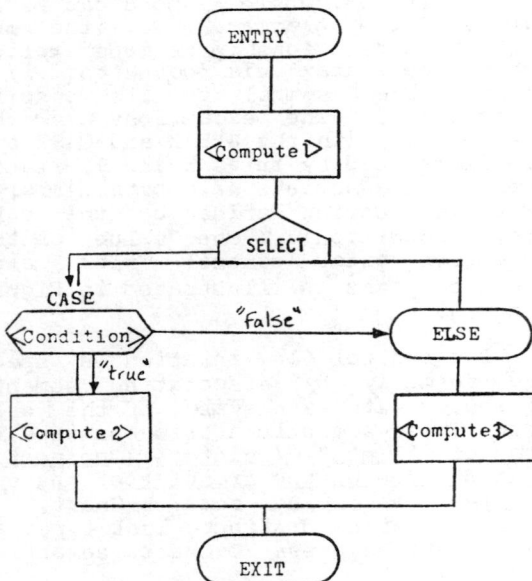

Figure 3b. Semantics of the CASE Symbol.

L2 : <u>secondary link</u>; (A,B) is a directed link of type, L2, iff B is an immediate successor of A and the nesting levels of A and B differ by one.

L3 : <u>expression link</u>; used to associate a semantic expression with some symbol, A; e.g. CASE and BREAK.

As was the case for geometric attributes, semantic attributes may be synthesized or inherited. If we let labeled "boxes" denote grammar symbols, then the following convention can be used to describe the synthesized and inherited link attributes : the link, L, in the diagram below is denoted by the synthesized attribute , y, of B and inherited attribute, x, of A.

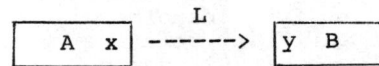

Applying this convention to the symbols in the rightpart of some production yields a "graph" where nodes represent grammar symbols and directed arcs represent semantic links. Links in the rightpart having no source node denote synthesized attributes of the leftpart, while links with no destination denote inherited attributes of the leftpart. These conventions are illustrated in Figures 4a and 4b for grammar rules 3 and 5 which define loop structures in D-Charts.

The attributes defined in Figure 4 are summarized in the table of Figure 5.

The propagation of semantic attributes when a node is expanded in the syntax tree requires two passes: first, a top-down pass during tree expansion is required to distribute independent inherited links; finally, a bottom-up pass is necessary to compute synthesized links and remaining inherited links. The result of expanding <Body> using rule 3 and <Loop-body> with rule 5 is illustrated in Figure 6. When <Loop-body1> is expanded its "c" link is inherited by BREAK and <Loop-body2>, while its "b" link is inherited only by <Loop-body2>. On the returning bottom-up pass the address of BREAK (denoted by its "a" link) becomes the synthesized attribute of <Loop-body1> used to define inherited attribute "c" of LOOP. The principles outlined above are sufficient to completely specify and implement the semantics of D-Charts.

142

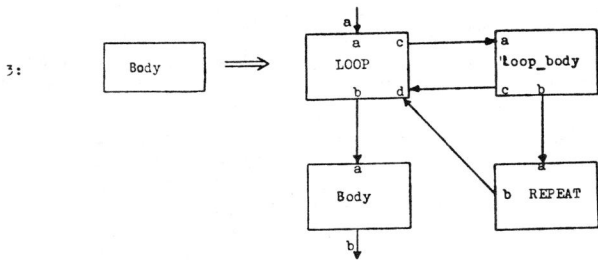

Figure 4a. Semantic links of a Loop Structure.

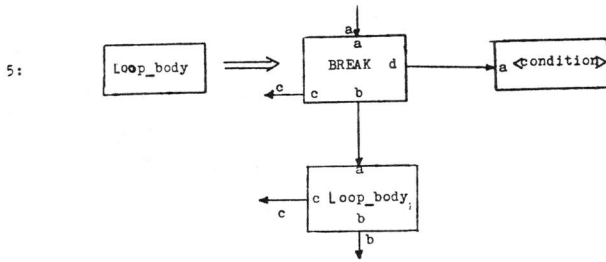

Figure 6. Syntax tree with Semantic links.

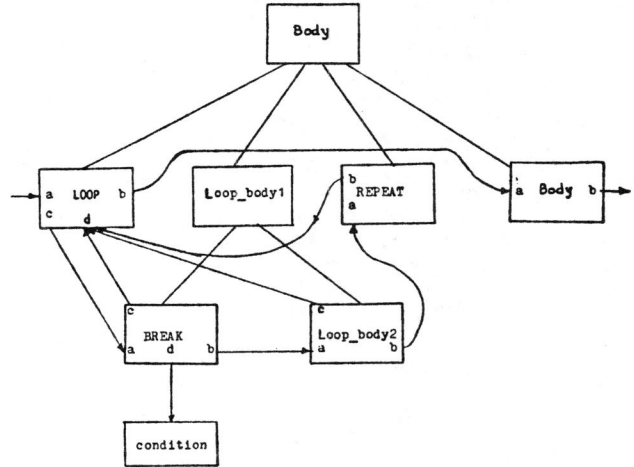

Figure 4b. Semantic links of a BREAK Symbol.

4.2 A Formal Definition

The discussion to this point has introduced the attributed graphical grammar as a vehicle for formal specification of graphical languages. Most of the principles involved have been illustrated by example and have not been set down in formal terms. Here we present a formal definition of attributed graphical grammars.

DEFINITION (Attributed Graphical Grammar): An attributed graphical grammar (AGG) is a 6-tuple,
$$G = (V, T, P, S, Ad, As)$$
where

V: set of syntax variable,
T: set of terminal symbols,
$S \in V$: denotes the start symbol,
Ad: denotes a set of display attributes
As: denotes a set of semantic attributes
P: a finite set of attributed productions satisfying
  (a) For X ---> w in P, X is a member of V and w is a subset of (V+T)* (V "union" T), perhaps the empty subset;
  (b) For each a in Ad+As, D(a) shall denote the set of possible values of attribute, a;
  (c) For each X in V+T, ATR(X) is a subset of Ad+As denoting the attribute set defined for X. ATR(X) is a partitioned into disjoint subsets, SYN(X) and INH(X) denoting, respectively, the synthesized and inherited attributes of X.

symbol	attribute	link type	Inh/Syn
Body	a	L1	Syn.
	b	L1	Inh.
LOOP	a	L1	Syn.
	b	L1	Inh.
	c	L2	Inh.
	d	L2	Syn.
REPEAT	a	L1	Syn.
	b	L2	Inh.
Loop_body	a	L1	Syn.
	b	L1	Inh.
	c	L2	Inh.
BREAK	a	L1	Syn.
	b	L1	Inh.
	c	L2	Inh.
	d	L3	Inh.

Figure 5. Synthesized and Inherited Semantic Attributes of LOCP Structure.

143

Furthermore, SYN(X) * Ad ("*" denotes set intersection) contains the geometric attributes : width(X), height(X) and entry(X) defining the minimum rectangular region necessary to enclose the display image of X.

(d) Let Y(i,0) ---> Y(i,1) Y(i,2) ... Y(i,ni) denote the ith production where ni >=0. For each i,j and a such that 0<=j<= ni, and "a" is in ATR(Y(i,j)) there is an attribute function
f_a(i,j) : D(b1) x D(b2) x ... x D(br) ---> D(a), where

   (i) if j=0, a ∈ SYN(Y(i,0)) and for each k, 1<=k<=r, bk is a member of SYN(Y(i,m)) for some m, 1<=m<=ni;

   (ii) if j>0, a ∈ INH(Y(i,j)) and for each k, 1<=k<=r, bk is a member of INH(Y(i,m)), 0<=m<j, or SYN(Y(i,m)), 0<=m<=ni.

(e) For each X in V+T and a in SYN(X), there is a value, default(a), in D(a) that applies when X appears at the frontier of some syntax tree. Furthermore, for the start symbol, S, default(a) is defined for each a in INH(S).

5. Implementation Methodology

The central concepts forming the foundation and framework of an object-oriented implementation methodology based on attributed graphical grammars are the following:

[a] Interaction with the user is conducted through a set of viewports distributed among some collection of display devices. The collection of possible display images associated with a given viewport will be called the viewport language and is assumed to be specified in terms of an appropriate attributed graphical grammar.

[b] The syntax tree representing a given viewport image defines the relationships among the object-oriented tasks controlling interaction with the user through that viewport and managing the viewing resources allocated to that viewport.

[c] Each node of the viewport syntax tree denotes an object-oriented task together with its local environment and is responsible for managing the subtasks below it in the tree.

[d] At any time while a viewport is engaged in interaction with the user there is a unique task, called the viewport's active task, in control of viewport activities.

The application of these principles in the design of interactive programming tools yields an implementation where the syntax tree representing a particular program "view" in some viewport language becomes an instantiation of the object-oriented tasks comprising the tool itself. The rest of this section attempts to make these ideas more concrete by considering the design of a syntax-directed D-Chart editor. The discussion is organized in two parts, first, a brief overview of the user interface characteristics, and second, a description of the internal system architecture in terms of the most important object-tasks and the methods and messages by which they communicate.

5.1 System Interface Characteristics

Interaction with the GRIP programming environment, of which the D-Chart editor is a part, is assumed to be conducted via a simple interface consisting of a graphics CRT, a pick device, such as a mouse, and a keyboard. The CRT display is organized as shown in Figure 7.

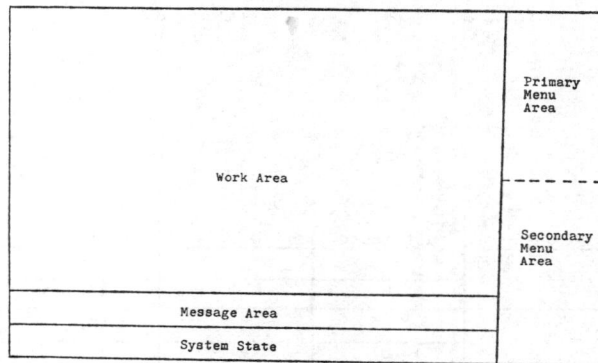

Figure 7. Screen Layout for User Interface.

The workarea serves as the primary output port of the D-Chart editor and is used to display the current image of a control diagram expressed as a D-Chart. Symbols involved in an insertion or deletion operation can be selected from the current workarea display. The menu area is partitioned into two parts, the primary menu and the secondary menu. The primary menu displays menu items, typically in the form of icons, representing operands or options applicable to the current editor function. The secondary menu normally presents the functions the editor can perform in any given system state. Menu selection is made either via the pick device or by depressing an appropriate function key. The message area is provided for system prompts, error messages and text input by the user in response to simple system requests. Icons denoting prominent tasks along the path in the system hierarchy of tasks supporting the current editor function are displayed in the port labeled "system state". This display is manipulated as a LIFO list and serves as a navigational aid permitting the user to know at all times his/her location in the system; it also functions as a menu when the user wishes to "force" a transition to some previous state.

Most of the discussion in the next section deals with three functions every syntax-directed editor should support: adding symbols, deleting symbols and inserting symbols. The user interaction scenario for each of these is described briefly below.

Symbol Addition: The generation of a D-Chart occurs by expanding a syntax variable with an appropriate production of the graphical grammar. In the expansion state the workarea contains an image of the partial D-Chart with at least one syntax variable visible and exactly one highlighted to indicate the next point of expansion. The highlighted variable on the D-Chart display is called the active node and represents the image of the object-task in control of activity within the workarea. The primary menu area in the expansion state always contains a list of icons that uniquely identify and correspond 1-to-1 with the possible productions available for expanding the active node. When the user selects a choice from this menu the syntax tree is expanded at the active node, the display is regenerated, the menu is updated, and a new variable becomes active by default. This cycle is repeated until the state is changed as a result of picking a different function from the secondary menu. One such function could be to designate a different variable on the diagram as the active node.

Symbol Deletion: Symbol deletion is performed by picking the delete function from the secondary menu followed by picking a symbol or region to be deleted on the workarea display. If the user picks a symbol that cannot be deleted according to the rules of syntax, then an error message is generated and the operation is aborted. The user must then try again. Syntax variables can be deleted from the diagram by applying an erasing rule in the grammar. Internally the syntax tree must be pruned appropriately to accommodate the change.

Symbol Insertion: Symbol insertion is performed by selecting the appropriate item from the secondary menu and then picking the insertion point (some terminal symbol) on the workarea display. Again, if syntax does not permit the insertion to take place at the designated point an error message is issued and the pick must be repeated. If insertion is valid, then the primary menu is updated to present a list of symbols that can be inserted. This list is determined by some syntax variable on the interior of the tree that must be expanded with a different production than was used originally. This "grafting" operation must be accomplished without polluting the structure of the tree as defined by the grammar.

5.2 System Architecture

The architecture of the GRIP environment in general, and the D-Chart editor in particular, is founded on the general principles and concepts exemplified by the Smalltalk environment [8]. Consistent with the Smalltalk framework we envision the GRIP environment as being a multiprocessing system where the editor executes under the user process and independent system processes exist to manage the various system resources such as, memory, input/output devices, etc. For our purposes the following system processes are of particular relevance.

Screen Manager: The Screen Manager will be a system process whose function is to manage output directed to the graphics CRT, the primary system output device. The CRT will be treated like a virtual memory whose space is allocated in logical segments called viewports. Viewports can, of course, overlap and from the user's perspective represent logical display devices that respond to messages for displaying graphic objects of any type. Each viewport has an associated world coordinate system and parameters that describe the location of the viewport in that world system. Viewports clip objects that lies outside the visible frame defined by the viewport's location. Viewports respond to messages that change their position in their world system. Messages to a viewport suspend the user process until the message has been processed.

Input Manager: This process monitors user activity with the mouse and keyboard. Keystrokes and button pushes on the mouse generate interrupts that can be sensed by a "Wait" message to the Input Manager. The Input Manager responds with an interrupt-id and input-data that depend on the interrupting device.

Cursor Management: Independent processes are associated with a text cursor and a graphics cursor. The graphics cursor display is coupled with the mouse locator; movement of the mouse locator generates an interrupt which results in a display message to the graphics cursor. The user can send messages to these processes to change their location on the screen either in absolute device coordinates or relative to some viewport.

The remainder of this section describes the object classes and key methods comprising a typical editor that might execute under the user application process. While our discussion centers on the details specific to a D-Chart editor, the concepts and principles generally apply to other program editors and tools.

5.2.1 GRIP Object Classes. The user-process under control of the D-Chart editor is composed of the methods defined by a number of object classes. The most important of these classes and their relationships are depicted in Figure 8.

The class VIEWPORTS and its subclasses, WORKAREA, MENU, MESSG, and STATE contain the methods and the objects necessary to manage the various viewports described in the previous section. In effect, VIEWPORTS represents the software interface between various tools in the system and the Screen Manager process discussed earlier. Subclasses WORKAREA, MENU, MESSG and STATE are necessary because each must support distinct functional capabilities. Messages recognized by all viewports, such as moving the viewport in world coordinates, are supported by the superclass VIEWPORTS.

The class TOOLS and its subclasses define the environmental framework in which all software tools function and communicate. A detailed description of this hierarchy and its capabilities are still under investigation and lie outside the scope of this paper. Of relevance here is the class DCHARTEDITOR which defines the messages and methods directly supporting the creation and editing of program modules in the D-Chart language.

The class GRAMMARS defines and manages the data structures required for specifying attributed graphical grammars to the GRIP environment. In fact, included in the class, TOOLS, is a grammar editor and a grammar compiler the user can exercise to develop new graphical languages for integration into the system. Each such grammar drives a syntax-directed editor (within TOOLS) similar in behavior to the D-Chart editor we are presenting here as the paradigm.

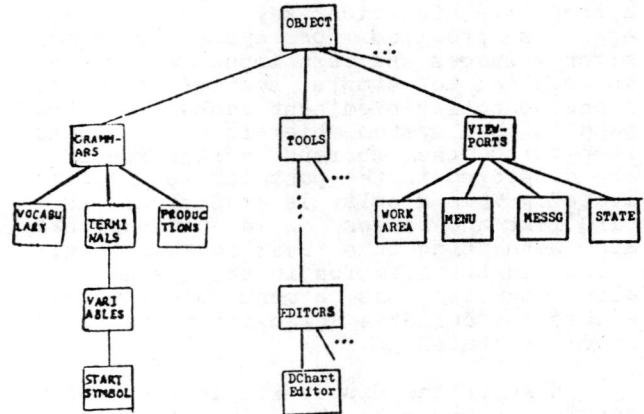

Figure 8. Object Class Hierarchy in GRIP.

One instance of GRAMMAR creates different instances of VOCABULARY and PRODUCTIONS. These structures contain the obvious syntactic information, but, in addition, include all semantic information necessary to drive an editor. For example, an instance of VOCABULARY contains the Vocabulary Table which includes for each grammar symbol the following information:

Symbol Name - unique identifier associated with each terminal and syntax variable;

Symbol Type - indicates whether a symbol denotes a terminal or syntax variable;

Attribute Symbol Table - contains the names, types and descriptions of all synthesized and inherited attributes (syntactic and semantic) associated with the symbol;

Display Routine - this is not the DISPLAY method (which is defined for the class GRAMMARS), it is a block of display instructions which when interpreted by the DISPLAY method of GRAMMARS produces the graphic image of the associated symbol in a predefined viewport.

An instance of PRODUCTIONS contains the Production Table illustrated in Figure 9. It contains an entry for each syntax variable in the grammar's Vocabulary Table. Associated with each variable is a Rightpart Set. Each element of the Rightpart Set denotes the righthand side of some production with the same leftpart variable and consists of the following components.

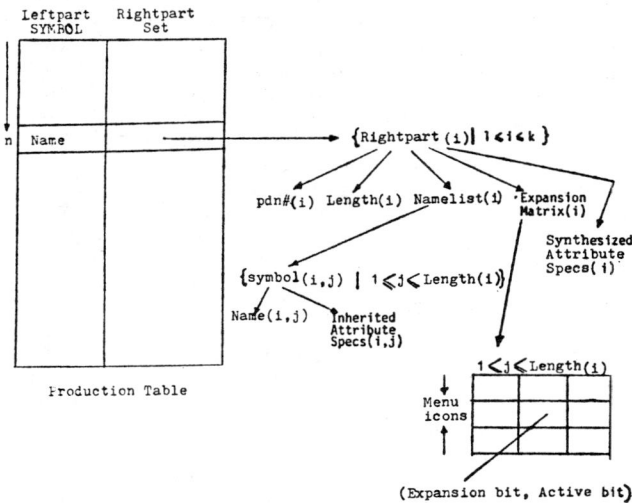

Figure 9. Grammar Production Table.

Pdn# - unique production identifier; used as a key in some messages to retrieve information from the production table;

Length - number of symbols in the rightpart;

Namelist - an ordered list of elements corresponding to the symbols in the rightpart; this list is empty if Length = 0. Each Namelist element consists of a symbol identifier and a set of specifications for the inherited attributes associated with the rightpart symbol. These attribute specifications are interpreted by methods in classes TERMINALS and VARIABLES during edit operations that alter the syntax tree according to the specifications defined by a particular production.

Expansion Matrix - this table is used whenever the leftpart variable is expanded by the corresponding rightpart; it indicates which variables in the rightpart (if any) must be further expanded to produce the terminal symbol selected by the user from the primary menu. The principle applied here is that the expansion of any syntax variable by one of its rightparts is uniquely determined by some terminal symbol, either present in the rightpart or present in the frontier of the subtree produced by a unique sequence of productions. The expansion bits correspond 1-1 with symbols in the rightpart, a "1" indicates which variables must be further expanded for the given menu selection (a terminal). The set of terminals appearing as row labels accumulated across all rightparts defines the set of menu items to be displayed whenever the leftpart variable is selected for an expansion (or inser-

tion) operation.

Synthesized Attribute Specification - each rightpart defines a set of specifications for the synthesized attributes (semantic and geometric) associated with the leftpart variables. These specifications are interpreted by methods exercised during expansion and insertion operations.

The object classes TERMINAL, VARIABLES and STARTSYMBOL define the data structures and the methods used to build and maintain the syntax tree denoting some D-Chart. Instances of these types respond to messages such as: DISPLAY, INSERT, DELETE, and EXPAND. Among the instance variables defined are those specifying: the parent node, the neighboring nodes, viewport description, geometric attributes (including width, height and entry point), semantic attributes, display attributes such as pickability and visibility, and symbol name.

5.2.2. DCHARTEDITOR Methods. In this section we describe in detail the structure of the methods, Starteditor , which controls the user-editor dialogue, and Expand, which drives the expansion of the active syntax variable. Before presenting these two methods we note that each valid editor function will be implemented as a method in the class, DCHARTEDITOR. For example, HELP, EXIT, LOAD, SAVE, CREATE, EXPAND, DELETE, INSERT, REFINE, ABSTRACT, etc., are a few of the possible functions the editor might support. Following our discussion of Starteditor and Expand we comment briefly on methods "Insert" and "Delete" which expose issues of a theoretical nature.

5.2.2.1 Starteditor. Starteditor is executed in response to the "Starteditor" message sent to a newly created instance of the class, DCHARTEDITOR, by some supervisory method of the executing user-process. The algorithm for this method is presented below.

Step1. (setup).

The D-Chart grammar is loaded into the GRIP environment from a system file. New instances of WORKAREA, MENU, MESSG and STATE are created and allocated viewports of a particular size and location on the CRT. Each viewport is sent messages to initialize its display: MENU is sent an initial list of function items to display in the secondary menu; MESSG is sent an initial "instruction" message; and STATE is sent an icon for the initial editor state. The text cursor is turned off and the graphics cursor is positioned in MENU.

Step2. (main body)

(a) Set class variable (global to editor methods), Done, to "false".
(b) While Not Done, do
    { (1) Send a "Wait" message to the Input Manager to suspend the editor task until an interrupt occurs from either the keyboard or mouse. The return message will contain a device id and interrupt data.
      (2) Select on device id:
        if <u>Mouse</u>
            { ask MENU to "Identifypick: coordinates" and let Pickid hold MENU's response. Then if Pickid "Isnil", then send error message to MESSG.}
        if <u>keyboard</u>
            { ask MENU to "Identifykey: keystroke" and let Pickid be its response. Then if Pickid "Isnil", send error message to MESSG.}
      (3) While Pickid "Notnil" do { send self (the editor) the message 'Pickid' (the function defined by Pickid) and update Pickid with its response; each editor function-method returns the identity of the next function to perform, or it returns Nil.}
    } end (b)

Step3. (exit)

When an editor EXIT is selected by the user, Done will be set to "true" and the above loop will terminate. The editor returns to its calling task.

    5.2.2.2 Expand. To recap, in an earlier section we described the object class GRAMMAR and its subclasses as a framework providing the necessary data types for implementing attributed graphical grammars. We also described the class DCHARTEDITOR and its controlling method, Starteditor. To show how these classes interact to effect the editor functions we describe the method Expand of class DCHARTEDITOR. This method will illustrate: 1) how instances of TERMINALS and NONTERMINALS are created and linked to form the syntax tree of a D-Chart, 2) how attributes are propagated during tree construction; and 3) how a newly created or updated structure is displayed.

    At the outset we assume a partial D-Chart exists with some syntax variable designated as the active node. The object structure representing the active node will be accessible via a class variable, Activenode, in DCHARTEDITOR. The MENU port will be configured to display in the primary area a list of icons denoting terminal symbols that can be legally introduced by expanding the active variable; the secondary menu will contain a list of function identifiers that can legally be selected in the expand state. The algorithm for Expand is given below.

<u>Expand</u> (of DCHARTEDITOR)

Step1. Send messages to MENU, STATE and MESSG reflecting the change in editor function. Initialize Nextfunction to Nil.

Step2. While Nextfunction "Isnil" do{
    (a) Send "Wait" to Input Manager to suspend editor until an interrupt occurs from Mouse.
    (b) Request MENU to "Identifypick: coordinates" and let Pickid be its response.
    (c) If Pickid "Isafunction" { set Nextfunction to Pickid.} else {
        1: Send "Expandfor: Pickid" to Activenode and set local variable, Newactive, to the response.

        2: The syntax tree below Activenode has been fully expanded at this point and its synthesized geometric and semantic attributes recomputed accordingly. Now the synthesis of attributes must be continued to the ancestors of Activenode. Synthesis terminates when either the root node (start symbol) is reached, or when the attribute values stabilize. The node on the path from Activenode to the root of the syntax tree at which the geometric attributes stabilize determines the smallest window (in the world system) that must be redisplayed. The above computation is initiated by sending Activenode the message, "Propagateattributes". The response will be a node pointer identifying the node at which redisplay must begin (this could be the

148

root); call this node, Displaynode.

3: Displaynode is sent the message, "Erasewindow", to clear its window for redisplay. Then it is sent the message, "Display". The Display method uses the node's name to lookup the node's display procedure in the Vocabulary Table of the instance of VOCABULARY. This procedure is interpreted to produce the visible image of nodes on the frontier of the syntax tree. For interior nodes, the production used to expand the node is used to locate and interpret the inherited geometric attribute specifications of each child before the "Display" message is sent to them.

4: When "Display" completes, control returns to this step and the expansion process is complete. Activenode is then updated with Newactive, the next active variable on the frontier.

5: Production Table is sent the message, "Getmenu-listfor: Activenode", to compute the list of menu items defining the possible ways to expand the new Activenode. Let this list be denoted, Menulist.

6: Finally, MENU is sent the message, "Displayprimary: Menulist".
} end-else.
} end (Step 2)

Step3. return Nextfunction.

   5.2.2.3 Other Editor Methods. Space limitations prevent us from presenting here other editor methods in the same detail as "Expand". However, the methods "Insert" and "Delete" bring to light implementation problems raising theoretical issues in our approach.

Insert: The method for inserting terminal symbols in a D-Chart is a variation of the algorithm for expanding a syntax

variable. The primary difference is that some interior node must be re-expanded using another, possibly different, production than the one used when it was on the frontier. Figure 10 illustrates a typical syntax tree before and after a request has been made to insert Terminal-a before Terminal-b. The difficulty with the transformation suggested by Figure 10 is that it need not be unique. The grammar obviously dictates the number of possible ways the insertion

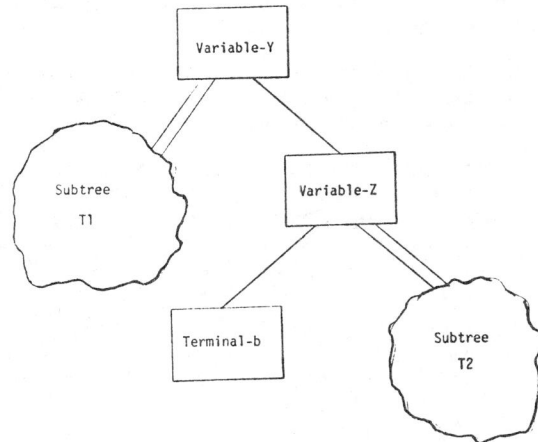

Figure 10a. Syntax Tree Before Insertion at "b".

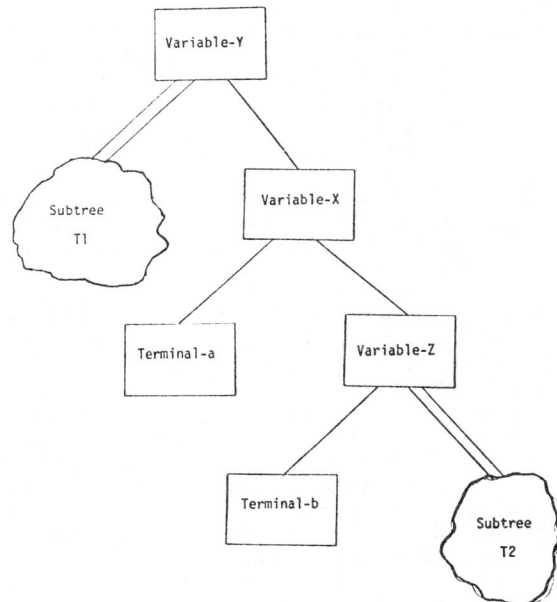

Figure 10b. Syntax Tree After Insertion at "b".

could be made. To mitigate this problem we constrain productions introducing _insertion_ _terminals_, a, to be of the form: X --> a X, for some _insertion variable_, X. With reference to Figure 10 this implies Variable-Z and Variable-X denote instances of the same symbol. Furthermore, the grammar must be _locally unambiguous with respect to insertion_; that is, given some _insertion locator_, b, there must exist a unique syntax variable, X, on the path from b to the start symbol that introduces the set of possible insertion terminals appearing adjacent to b on the frontier.

Assuming the above constraints on the grammar, insertion is accomplished with the following steps:

Step1. The pick coordinates are used to identify the insertion locator, b, by a top-down tree traversal beginning at the start symbol. The locator, b, is passed up the tree along the same path until it is recognized by the unique insertion variable, X. The identity of the insertion variable is then passed on and returned by the start symbol.

Step2. The set of insertion terminals defined by X in step 1 is displayed in the primary area of MENU. The user makes a selection which uniquely determines the production to use in expanding X.

Step3. Variable X is sent an "Insertfor: a" message which behaves just as "Expandfor: a" except that X and its associated subtree becomes its own child along with the insertion terminal, a.

Step4. Attribute propagation and redisplay is performed in the same manner as described for the Expand function.

Delete: Deletion is essentially the inverse of insertion. By convention, only insertion terminals can be deleted. The deletion method follows essentially the same sequence of steps defined for insertion. Step 1 locates the symbol to be deleted, say a, and the variable, X, that introduced it. Step 2, menu display, is unnecessary. Step 3 executes the deletion by overwriting X with its child of the same name. Step 4 updates geometric and semantic attributes and re-generates the display.

5.2.3 TERMINAL and VARIABLE Methods. In this section we present the "Expandfor" method of class VARIABLES. This method reveals many of the implementation principles necessary for the development of other methods. Expandfor is a paradigm for another reason, it makes reference to numerous other key methods that must be defined for the class TERMINALS and VARIABLES and provides a stage where the interplay between these methods can be observed.

Step1. Activenode requests the rightpart of its production determined by Menuitem. The "Fetchrightpart" message returns the rightpart structure described in Figure 9. Activenode saves this structure in local variable, _Rightpart_. Save "Pdn#" of Rightpart in an instance variable of Activenode.

Step2. Set Namelist to the "Namelist" of Rightpart. Then send "Addchildrenwith: Namelist" to the self (Active node). This method looks up the name of each rightpart symbol in the Vocabulary Table to determine its type. Based on type an instance of TERMINALS or VARIABLES is created and added to the list of children of the Activenode. "Nextneighbor" and "Previousneighbor" links each child in the list to its predecessor and successor, respectively.

Step3. Set Expansionmat to the row of "Expansion Matrix" determined by Menuitem.
Let Newactive be a local variable used to hold the object pointer to the next node to become active as a result of expansion of Activenode, and set it to Nil.
For each _Child_ in the Rightpart list of Activenode, do {
    (a) Set _Symbol_ to the entry from Namelist corresponding to Child and set _Matentry_ to the entry of Expansionmat corresponding to Symbol.
    (b) Send Child the "Inheritattributes" message using the "Inheritspecs" of Symbol. Inheritattributes interprets Inheritspecs and as a side effect defines the inherited semantic attributes for Child. Inherited geometric attributes are computed by the "Display" method described in step 2.c.3 of the editor's method "Expand".
    (c) If Matentry "Expansionbit" equals 1,
    {send Child the "Expandfor: Menuitem" message returning an object pointer, say P. If P is

not Nil, then save it in Newactive.}
else
{send Child the message "Frontierattributes" to compute its synthesized attributes as a frontier node. If Matentry "Activebit" equals 1, set Newactive to Child.}
} end-For.

Step4. At this point the attributes of all children of the expanded node have been computed and the syntax tree fully expanded below. To complete the definition of the expanded node it must compute its synthesized attributes. This is done by sending the message "Synthesizedattributesof: Rightpart", to itself. The Synthesizedattributesof method interprets the attribute specifications stored in Rightpart to compute both geometric and semantic attributes. Let Newsynset be a local variable holding the resulting set of synthesized attributes.

Step5. Before returning to the calling method the expanded node (originally Activenode) records its old synthesized attributes in an instance variable, Oldsynset, and then updates their values from Newsynset computed in step 4. Oldsynset is required by the "Propagateattributes" method introduced in step 2.c.2 of the editor's Expand method.

Step6. Return Newactive to calling method. This transfers control to step 3.b of the Expandfor method of the parent node except when returning from Activenode, in this case control returns to step 2.c.1 of the editor's "Expand" method.

6. Conclusions

In this paper we have presented the key concepts and principles undergirding the development of GRIP, an interactive environment for graphical programming. The three major principles forming the basis of our approach to designing this system are the following:

[1] Interaction with the user is conducted through a collection of display viewports. The collection of possible images associated with a given viewport defines a viewport language.

[2] The syntax and semantics of a viewport language is described formally using an attributed graphical context-free grammar.

[3] A program tool which communicates with the user through one or more viewport languages is implemented as a collection of Smalltalk style object classes and methods in such a way that the syntax tree defining a particular viewport image is an instantiation of the objects defining the tool. The operation of the tool is realized through inputs by the user which invoke incremental transformations on the syntax tree; that is, the tool modifies its syntactic and semantic structure to reflect a given user input - this results in a new display image.

These concepts were illustrated by considering as an example the design and implementation of a syntax-directed D-Chart editor. The actual implementation of such an editor based on our methodology is well under way at the University of Central Florida. Other graphical editors and tools are being designed and when integrated within the GRIP environment will provide a fully graphical interface for program development.

In addition to presenting a methodology for developing a syntax-driven graphical interface, we have identified a number of problems requiring further investigation and more formal treatment.

[1] Our implementation of syntax-directed editors is "interpretive" in nature. Display methods and attribute computations were carried out by interpreting some formal specification recorded in the Vocabulary and Production tables. The development of a suitable semantic specification language for implementing the intended scope and capabilities of the GRIP environment is a subject of future research.

[2] In developing a grammar for editing D-Charts, it was necessary to restrict the form of productions and the method of parsing to accommodate editing operations such as insertions and deletions. Defining a formal class of graphical grammars supporting a given set of editing operations may have theoretical as well as practical merit.

[3] Attributed graphical context-free grammars were found to be sufficient to implement a syntax-directed D-Chart editor. As we investigate and implement other graphical languages, such as Data Flow Diagrams, Petri Nets, etc., this model may prove to be inadequate. More work is needed

in this direction.

[4] The principles and methodology presented here have their most obvious application to program editing and viewing tools. Can they be extended to apply to the design and development of all software comprising a programming environment? If so, there would need to exist some "super grammar" or collection of grammars that would define not only the user interface to the entire system, but also the internal interfaces among various system components.

REFERENCES

[1] -----, in Software Engineering Environments, Proceedings of the symposium held in Lahnstein, Germany, June 80, ed. Horst Hunke, North-Holland, 1981.

[2] -----, "The Proceedings of the ACM SIGSOFT/SIGPLAN Software Engineering Symposium on Practical Software Development Environments," Software Engineering Notes, vol. 19, #5, May 1984.

[3] Barstow, D.R., Shrobe, H.E., and Sandewall, E., Interactive Programming Environments, McGraw-Hill, 1984.

[4] Bleser, T. and Foley, J.D., "Toward Specifying and Evaluating the Human Factors of User-Computer Interfaces," Proceedings of the Conference on Human Factors in Computing Systems, NBC, Gaithersburg, Md., 1982.

[5] Carlson, E., Rhyne, J., and Weller, D., "Software Structure for Display Management Systems," IEEE Transactions on Software Engineerig, vol. SE-9, #4, pp. 385-394., 1983.

[6] Feder, J., "Plex Languages," Inf. Sci., vol. 3, pp. 225-241, 1971.

[7] Fu, K.S., Syntactic Pattern Recognition and Applications, Prentice-Hall, Englewood Cliffs, N.J., 1982.

[8] Goldberg, A. and Robson, D., Smalltalk-80 - The Language and Its Implementation, Addison-Wesley, Reading, Mass, 1983.

[9] Hanau, P.R. and Lenorovitz, D.R., "Prototyping and Simulation Tools for User/Computer Dialogue Design," Proc. ACM SIGGRAPH 80, pp. 271-278, 1980.

[10] Hwang, C.J., "Structured D-Charts: A Diagramatic Methodology in Structured Programming," AFIPS Conference Proceedings, vol. 51, pp. 735-748, Jun. 1982.

[11] Jacobs, R.J.K., Survey of Specification Techniques for User Interfaces, Naval Research Laboratory Tech. Memo. 7590-303:RJ:rj, Aug. 1981.

[12] Jacobs, R.J.K., "Using Formal Specifications in the Design of a Human-Computer Interface," Proceedings of the Conference on Human Factors in Computing Systems, NBC, Gaithersburg, Md., 1982.

[13] Jacobs, R.J.K., Examples of Specifications of User Interfaces, Naval Research Laboratory Tech. Memo. 7590-008:RJ:rj, Jan 1983.

[14] Knuth, D.E., "Semantics of Context-Free Languages," Math. Systems Theory, vol. 2, #2, pp. 127-146., 1965.

[15] Lewis, P.M.II, Rozenkrantz, D.J., and Stearns, R.E., "Attributed Translations," J. Comput. Sys. Sci., vol. 9, #3, pp. 279-307, 1974.

[16] Lipkie, D.E., "STAR Graphics : An Object-Oriented Implementation," Computer Graphics, vol. 16, #3, pp. 115-124, 1983.

[17] Moran, T.P., "The Command Language Grammar: A Representation for the User Interface of Interactive Computer Systems," Int. J. Man-Machine Studies, vol. 15, pp. 5-50., 1981.

[18] Schneiderman, B., "Multi-Party Grammars and Related Features for Defining Interactive Systems," IEEE Transactions on Systems, Man, and Cybernetics, vol. SMC-12, #2, pp. 148-154., 1982.

[19] Olsen, D.R. and Dempsey, E.P., Syntax-directed Graphical Interaction, 18, #6, pp. 112-117., 1983.

[20] Parnas, D.L., "On the Use of Transition Diagrams in the Design of a user Interface for an Interactive Computer System," Proc. 24th National ACM Coference, vol. 15, pp. 379-385, 1969.

[21] Pflatz, J.L. and Rosenfeld, A., "Web Grammars," Proc. First Int. Joint Conf. Artif. Intell., pp. 609-619, Washington D.C., 1969.

[22] Pilote, M., A Framework for the Design of Linguistic User Interfaces, Ph.D. Dissertation, Dept. of Computer Science, Univ. of Toronto., 1983.

[23] Pilote, M., "A Programming Language Framework for Designing User Interfaces," Proceedings of the 83 Symposium on Programming Language Issues in Software Systems, SIGPLAN Notices, vol. 18, #6, pp. 118-133., 1983.

[24] Reisner, P., "Further developements toward using formal grammars as a design tool," Proceedings of the Conference on Human Factors in Computing Systems, NBC, Gaithersburg, Md., 1982.

[25] Reisner, P., "Formal Grammar and Human Factors Design of an Interactive Graphics System," IEEE Transactions on Software Engineering, vol. SE-7, #2, pp. 229-240, Mar. 1981.

[26] Scott, D.S., "Logic and Programming Languages," CACM, vol. 20, #9, pp. 634-641., 1977.

[27] Shaw, M.et.al., "Descarte : A Programming Language Approach to Interactive Display Interface," Proceedings of the 83 Symposium on Programming Language Issues in Software Systems, SIGPLAN Notices, vol. 18, #6, pp. 100-111., Jun. 1983.

[28] Singer, A., Formal Methods and Human Factors in the Design of Interactive Languages, Ph.D. Dissertation, Dept. of Computer and Information Science, U. of Mass., 1979.

[29] Stoy, J.E., Denotational Semantics: The Scott Strachey Approach to Programming Language Theory, MIT Press, Cambridge, Mass., 1977.

[30] Teitelbaum, T. and Reps, T., "The Cornell Program Synthesizer : A Syntax-directed Programming Environment," CACM, vol. 24, #9, pp. 563-573, 1981.

[31] Tennent, R.D., Principles of Programming Languages, Prentice-Hall, Englewood Cliffs, N.J., 1981.

[32] Wasserman, A.I., "USE: A Methodology for the Design and Development of Interactive Information Systems," in Formal Models and Practical Tools for Information System Design, ed. H.J. Schneider, pp. 311-350., North-Holland, 1983.

[33] Workman, D.A., "GRASP : A Software Development System Using D-Charts," Software Pract. and Exper., vol. 13, #1, pp. 17-32, 1983.

A SOFTWARE DEVELOPMENT ENVIRONMENT CALLED STEP

A. Frederick Rosene

GTE Communication Systems Division
77 "A" Street
Needham Heights, Massachusetts 02194

STEP is an automated software development environment which helps produce more reliable software. It consists of a methodology employed throughout the software development cycle and an integrated system of computer programs which automate, control, support and enforce the methodology. The STEP environment is composed of three parts, a database, a core system and a set of tools. At the heart of the system is an architectural framework which incorporates principles essential to the design of quality software. STEP was first released for use in 1978 and has improved the quality of software generated at GTE while reducing the life cycle cost. In particular projects developed on STEP have turned out to be easy to test, to have low maintenance cost; STEP has made it possible to reuse design and code.

The STEP System

Introduction

In 1976 GTE's Communication Systems Division began creating a software development environment called "Phoenix". A few years later, the project obtained corporate support and the name was changed to "STEP" (Structured Techniques for Engineering Projects). Today CSD policy calls for the STEP system to be used in all major software development programs in the division. STEP is continually being improved and expanded in response to user feedback and software engineering progress. This paper describes STEP from the user's perspective and from a design perspective. We will also review our experience in using STEP for over six years.

Section 2 gives an overview of STEP. Section 3 describes the architectural framework on which the STEP environment is based. Section 4 describes the structure of the database, the core system and the tools of the STEP system. Finally, Section 5 describes some reactions to and experience in using STEP.

Overview

STEP is an automated software development environment[1] which helps produce reliable software, both a life-cycle methodology and an integrated system of computer programs which automate, control, support and enforce the methodology. It meets most of the requirements of an Ada environment as described in the STONEMAN document[2].

The STEP methodology is a set of design steps that results in a controlled, structured approach to software system development. Figure 1 shows the phases into which the system life-cycle is divided.

A measurable result, called a milestone, marks the end of each phase. At each milestone someone in authority must certify that the project is ready to advance to the next phase. The key features of the methodology are:

- a standardized software architecture for projects
- enforcement of standards throughout the development
- documentation that is concurrent with development
- top-down structured programming for all development
- periodic reviews for early detection and correction of errors.

The STEP system combines human procedures with software tools, a database and an interactive computer in order to structure:

- software engineering
- software quality assurance
- configuration control
- project management.

STEP is founded on the theory that a large software project is a group effort and thus information must be accessible to everyone. Progress is recognized only when it is reflected in the project's database, and reviews and audits are performed only on database contents.

Software Architecture

The heart of the system is an architectural framework[3,4] which is designed on time-sharing principles. That is, the program is partitioned into subprograms, each of which has a control interface with an executive which schedules its use.

The architectural template, shown in Figure 2, is a generalization of the classical time-sharing approach, which allows tradeoffs between efficiency and isolation for specific applications. It can expand to include the most complicated real-time system or compress to meet simpler requirements. Mapping a project to this architecture is

154

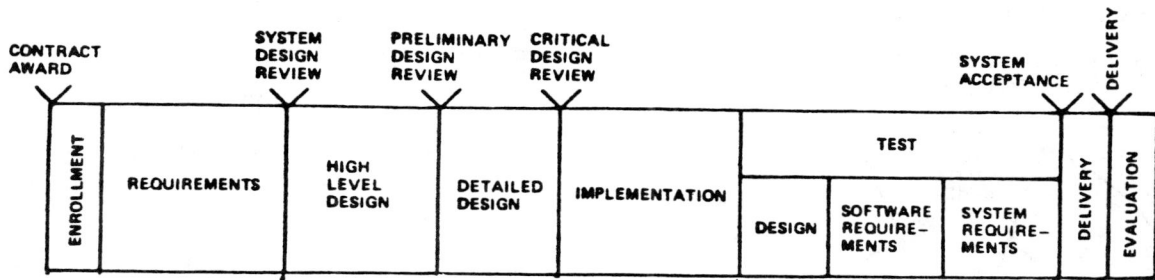

Figure 1

Software Development Phases

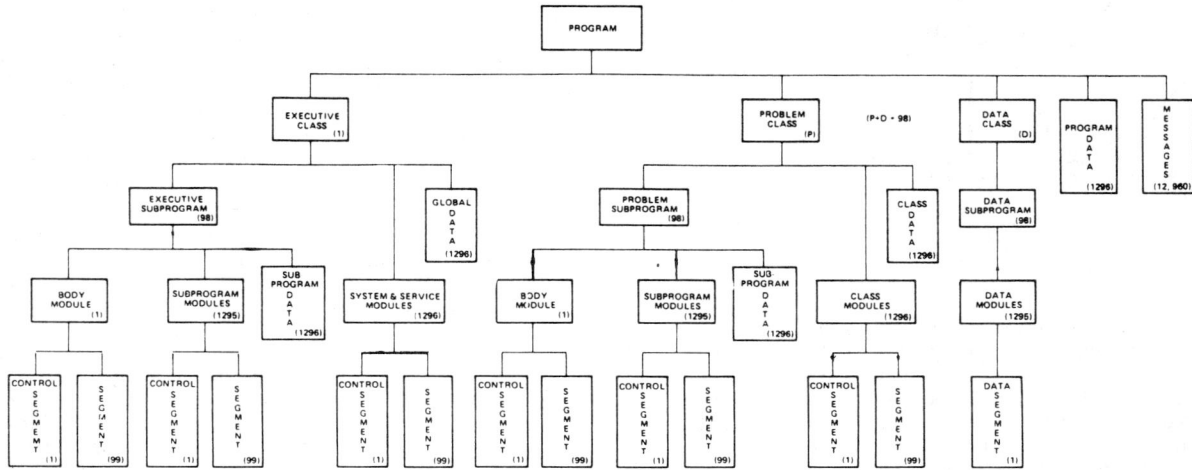

Figure 2

STEP Architecture

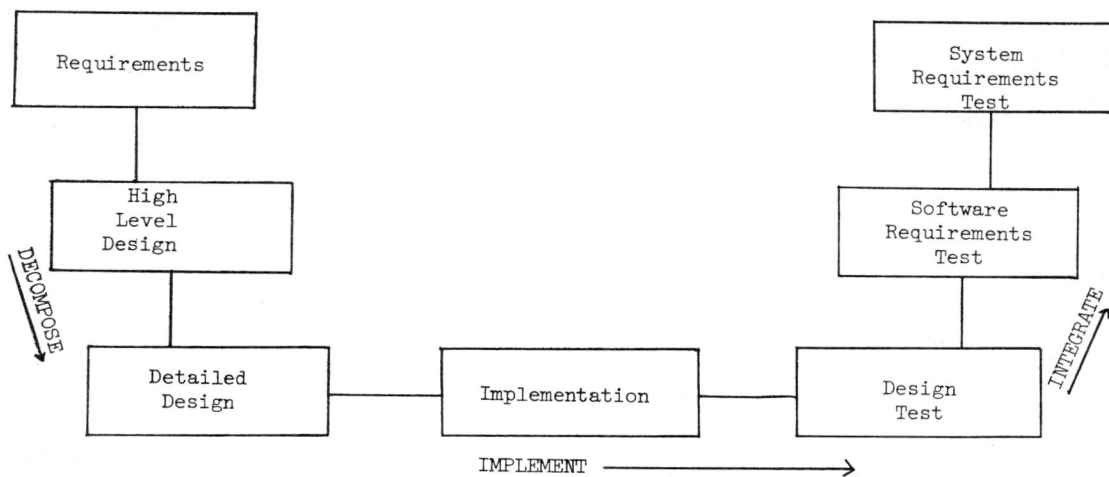

Figure 3

Development Levels of STEP Phases

a major part of high level design.

Figure 3 shows the STEP phases divided into three levels of development.

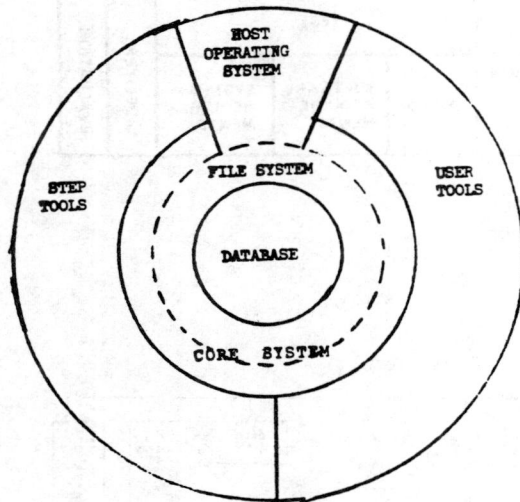

HOST OPERATING SYSTEM

STEP TOOLS

FILE SYSTEM

USER TOOLS

DATABASE

CORE SYSTEM

Figure 4

STEP Environment

As the project moves to lower levels, the program is divided into smaller and smaller pieces, until at the lowest level, implementation occurs (i.e., coding in Pascal, Ada, Chill,...). Integration takes place when the project reaches the testing phases, proceeding from design test to software test to systems level.

Because STEP understands the hierarchical relationship between architecture elements and establishes a common architecture for all GTE software, it has the following benefits:

- Increases probability that each project is on a solid footing.
- Configuration and project management controls may be applied, as a function of architecture.
- The exact state of any architectural subdivision may be documented.
- Personnel may be moved from project to project, even location to location, with little loss of productivity.
- A new architecture is not reinvented for each new project.
- The architecture is enforced during implementation.
- Testable, maintainable, and hence reliable software.

The accumulation of metrics is a byproduct of combining a standard architecture and database. Information that assists in predicting program testability and maintainability before the detailed design is begun[4], and information that can be used to improve the development process on future projects, is easily kept in the database. Furthermore, it is possible to produce performance

data down to the level of each user. The only cost is efficiency: The more data collected, the more processing required per user action.

Structure

Figure 4 shows the three principal features of the STEP system:

- the database
- the core system
- the tools - both STEP and user-supplied

Database

Each project has its own database, which is the central storage for all information associated with that project thoughout its life cycle. A named collection of information in the database is known as a component; for example, a module or a subsection of a document. Each component stored in a project database is related to the the architectural framework and the methodology. A module's relationship determines what can call it, what it may call, and what data it may reference. A document component is related to the methodology in two ways: The point in the life cycle when it can be created, and the point at which it must be completed. Also, users may instruct the system to maintain additional relationships among components. For example, an association may be maintained between requirement document components and software architecture components.

The database for a project is a tree structure of nodes in which each node can store all components needed during the life cycle of a project. In fact, small and medium-sized projects normally require only one node. Multiple node structures are used for several reasons:

Efficiency - if a node gets too large, data retrievals take too long.
Security - access is assigned by node as well as by function.
Support - database backups and audits get cumbersome if a node exceeds the capacity of one disk drive.
Resources - large projects require more computing resources than one computer can provide. Nodes or subnets of nodes may be on different computers.

Each node is divided into five volumes:

Volume 1 contains skeleton files used to initialize files in the other volumes, and instruction files that can be displayed at the user's option. Files in Volume 1 may be modified by authorized users but may not be deleted or created.

Volume 2 contains user aid files. These files are used to predefine commands and parameters to be run either on line or in batch. They also are used to store the rules by which components are selected and processed. They are also used to construct compound commands.

Volume 3 contains all documentation associated with the software lifecycle other than test and software design documentation. This includes requirements, hardware description, user manuals, maintenance manuals, etc.

Volume 4 contains all test documentation including test plans, test procedures and test results.

Volume 5 contains high level design and detailed design documentation and source code.

The contents of Volumes 2, 3, and 5 are not controlled by the user through the use of DEFINE, DATA, DELETE and EDIT commands. Components of volume 4 track the structure created in Volume 5. The files with each component vary with volume, and within Volume 5 with function and source languages used.

Core System

The Core system consists of:

- STEP commands
- Development standards
- File system
- Configuration management

STEP commands. The STEP commands provide a variety of capabilities associated with a project's database. After logging into the host operating system, a user runs STEP by entering the word "STEP" and a node ID. Now STEP commands and normal operating system commands may be executed. STEP commands, which in turn affect the node database, allow the user to create, modify, display, document and delete information. Questions regarding who has done what and where are easily resolved by up-to-date reports based on information in the project's database. Table 1 summarizes the commands available.

Table 1

STEP Commands

Commands which create components

DEFINE - creates all components in Volumes 2 to 5 except high level data
DATA - creates high level data components (in Volume 5)

Commands which insert information

EDIT - modifies contents of any file of any component
ALTER - global edit or replacement across any or all components
ALLOCATE - inserts data that associates components
CERTIFY - marks external progress, e.g., a successful review

Commands which generate data

ANALYZE - checks syntax, enforces standards and generates reference data

COMPILE - selects components for a release, builds source for a release, exports source ready to compile and/or object for source already compiled.

Development Levels of STEP Phases

STATUS - estimates, stores current status and reports on status
TRACK - creates and maintains an audit trail of changes
PHASE - controls when phases of project are started
GLOSSARY - maintains a naming glossary of all mnemonics used in source code

Commands which view the state of components

BROWSE - selectively views and searches files
TYPE - displays any file of any component
PRINT - prints any file of any component
INFORMATION - displays state data for any component

Commands which create documents

DOCUMENT - selects, combines and processes STEP components
PROLOG - generates a high level - detailed design document
REPORT - provides information on the state of a node.

Commands which provide file handling capabilities

IMPORT - transfers a file from host operating system to STEP
EXPORT - transfers a file from STEP to host operating system
DOWNLOAD - transfers files from STEP to a workstation
UPLOAD - transfers files from a workstation to STEP
APPEND - appends STEP files
CHANGE - changes names of STEP files
DELETE - deletes STEP files

Commands which aid users

EXECUTE - allows STEP to run without user input
SUBMIT - allows STEP to run in batch
CALL - allows users to interface tools with STEP
SET - allows user to set personal defaults

Commands which monitor and control a project

NAMING All names used in source code are made up of fixed length mnemonics whose definitions are maintained in a naming glossary. Code will not be prompted to the level necessary for compiling unless all mnemonics of all its names are defined in the glossary.

ARCHITECTURE All procedure calls and data usage must agree with the architecture specified in the high level design. Code that violates the architecture will not be promoted to the compile level.

CODING The user may define format and design language content standards that are enforced by the system. This is done both by activating built-in checks made on source and design language documentation, and by tailoring of source code processors which analyze code.

DOCUMENTATION Use of documentation processors, such as flowcharters, result in documents that follow a specific standard. User-defined processors are also linked in using the CALL command to further tailor documentation formats. Skeletons are used to preset component formats such that the user essentially fills in the blanks.

A variety of control options are incorporated in the core system to enable a manager to tailor the system to project needs. In particular, command and subcommand rights may be tailored to each user or type of user, standard enforcement parameters may be tailored for each node, and password protection may be applied to any component of any volume.

File System. The STEP File System serves as a machine-independent foundation for the STEP command system. This greatly reduces the need for special programming for computer systems with different operating system architectures.

This portable file system uses the host computer services available in most mainframe operating systems. Each version has been optimized to perform efficiently on its host. Usually, the limiting factors are the efficiency of the host Pascal compiler, the capabilities of the host's asynchronous, direct-access disk systems, and the operating system's interprocess communication.

The STEP File System is implemented on a host computer through a direct-access data file. Disk blocks are accessed asynchronously using a low-level, host computer method which does not see any block structure. The file system operates using disk blocks of equal length organized into structure, data, and internal pointer categories. The structure blocks represent directory structure and file storage information. The data blocks store file data, and the internal pointer blocks relate combinations of various block types. Individual formats may exist within a category, according to use; unused blocks generally have no type. The types of blocks are defined below.

Block Type 0: An internal pointer block. It contains a sequential list of integer block numbers. These pointer lists chain unused blocks together.

Block Type 1: A structure. It represents a directory and contains the appropriate series of directory entries. A subdirectory is viewed as a file in the parent directory with the reserved extension "DIRECT".

Block Type 2: Another type of structure block. This block type is used to link the pieces of large directories of large files.

Block Type 3: A data block.

Configuration Management. The configuration management system provides: (1) interlocks to ensure information in use by one person is not changed or deleted by another, (2) reports which summarize the conditions and associations of all components, (3) records of all changes made to all controlled components, (4) a framework for all user actions. This framework provides users with complete information about any components associated with a user's action. Each component defined to STEP has one or more revisions. Whenever a component name is specified in a command, the following actions occur:

1. The system displays the revision for the named component and its associated control levels. A "?" input calls up the date of the revision, the name of the user who created it, and the reason it was created.

2. The user selects a revision.

3. The system checks to make sure the selected revision is at a level consistent with the command to be executed. For example, if an EDIT command is given and the revision selected is at a level that cannot be edited, the EDIT will not be allowed. However, the user has the option of creating a copy of the requested revision with a new revision number.

The revision selection logic may be prespecified so that commands with multiple selections such as DOCUMENT and COMPILE may be run in batch or on line without user inputs. The important thing is that users always know the framework within which they are working.

A variety of reports are associated with configuration management:

CONTROL LEVEL REPORT - summarizes the levels of each component.

RELEASE SUMMARY REPORT - summarizes releases that have been created.

RELEASE CONTENTS REPORT - identifies the revision of each component of a release.

USAGE REPORT - identifies the releases containing component revisions.

TROUBLE AND CHANGE REPORTS - provide an audit trail of changes.

Tools

A variety of tools are used with STEP. They fall into two categories: tools that check user input and tools that transform user input. Checking tools include syntax analyzers for each language. Transforming tools include formatters, flowcharters, datamappers, design language proces- and text processors.

The STEP command being executed runs the tools. Users do not need to know the details of running a tool. STEP provides the necessary interface. STEP also allows users to integrate their own tools, either called directly from STEP commands or indirectly through its CALL command facility.

Use Experience

The STEP environment was first used on a project in 1978[5], It has subsequently been used on a variety of real-time and non-real-time applications totalling more than 500,000 source lines and is used to maintain itself and extend its capabilities. These projects include telephone switching systems, air traffic control simulators, and communications control systems. Its first use was mandated by top management and supported by appointing one of the developers as software task manager. Initial use met with numerous complaints because the methodology demanded a lot of work and significant effort in the design phases. Yet the benefits from this extra effort are not apparent until the testing phases. However, by the time the project was completed most users were sold on the advantages of STEP and looked forward to using it on other projects. As could be expected with any large complex system, experience in using it was essential to maximizing the benefits. Our experience showed that users got more out of STEP the second time they used it.

Experience to date has shown:

1. Testing goes much faster than expected.
2. The resulting programs are reliable and maintainable.
3. Projects are coming closer to budgets and schedules and have even met them.
4. Documentation is extensive, sometimes too extensive.
5. Documentation is consistent with code.

The following discussion deals with a variety of topics relating to the use of STEP.

Human Interface

1. Consistency is extremely important.
2. Upper and lower case is much easier to read than all upper case.
3. Users resent "smart" responses.

   Because STEP continually tells users when they have done something wrong, we thought humorous comments might eliminate user re-

sentment. Instead users felt they were not being treated as professionals. In fact, one user was reduced to tears after being called a "dummy" by the system.

4. Extensive on-line help is more important than documentation.

   We made the mistake of providing on-line help only at the command level. The resolution is to provide an expert mode for experienced users.

User Documentation

1. The three most important things in documenting a system are examples, examples and examples.
2. Two types of documents are needed: one that explains the theory, i.e., what's done and why, and a reference manual.

Efficiency (Workstations)

A mainframe environment will always be overloaded.

If you provide more computing resources, you get more users. The only solution is to provide smart workstations which can be added as users are added. Still, every effort should be taken to make the mainframe as efficient as possible. We removed some functions because efficiency was more important than having those particular functions.

Performance

1. Users are afraid of performance measurement.

   The ability to collect data on individual performance and to compare user's work was designed into STEP but never implemented because of user resistance. It was difficult enough just getting people to try a new system.

2. Young users became efficient quickly and tended to get more out of the system than programmers who had been around for a few years. In fact, it turned out that novice programmers became contributers more quickly.

3. Users need to feel they are part of the action.

   It is important to find ways to make users feel they can contribute to the evolution of the system. It is also a good idea to publicize success using STEP to give credit to the people using it.

Portability

1. It was possible to make an environment that was transportable among computers as different as IBM and DEC-20 and still have the same user interface.
2. It would have been a lot easier not to.

Conclusions

1. The architectural framework was essential to the design of STEP. It made many things possible that otherwise would have been impractical.

2. The decision to make configuration management part of the backbone of the system instead of a separate tool worked out well. It allowed users to always be aware of the context in which they were working and ensured that all actions on all data were within the prescribed boundaries.

3. The design techniques resulted in code that stood the test of many changes and extensions.

4. Separating the actual compiling and testing from the rest of the system worked well. That is, when the source code was exported, it was syntactically and architecturally correct and in the proper format for compiling. The test results were inserted into STEP by the CERTIFY command. This provided a flexible interface with language-dependent environments (i.e., compilers, debuggers) and target systems.

5. Given the advances in microprocessors and user interface techniques over the last few years, it is questionable whether a mainframe system is still appropriate. A distributed microprocessor based system with smart workstations, file and compute servers seems a better way to go today.

6. The most important part of an environment is user documentation. It was the most underestimated item in the development.

REFERENCES

1. A. F. Rosene, "Phoenix Software Development System Overview." Presented at 15th Design Automation Conference, June 1978.

2. STONEMAN, "Requirements for the Programming Environment for the Common High Order Language," DOD, February 1980.

3. J. Roder, "Phoenix Architecture." Presented at 15th Design Automation Conference, 1978 June. Published in ACM SIGDA Newsletter, Vol. 8, No. 2, Summer 1978.

4. A. F. Rosene, J. E. Connolly, K. M. Bracy, "Software Maintainability What It Means and How to Achieve It." IEEE Transactions on Reliability, Vol. R-30, No. 3, August 1981.

5. E. Erickson, and J. Roder, "A Generic Approach to Software Validation", Phoenix Conference on Computers and Communications," May 1982.

Session 5

Tool Evaluation and Acquisition

Chairman
William Turoczy
U.S. Army AMCCOM

UNIX USG V.2 and BSD 4.s
Comparative Study

Sinan Neftci
Associate Professor CCNY

1. ABSTRACT Operating System Interface (system Calls) and User interface aspects of the two common versions of the UNIX systems are compared for the type of tools and utilities they provide.

2. Introduction

The objective of this report is to give the reader a concise but complete comparison between the two major versions of UNIX namely the AT&T V.2 and 4.2BSD (sometimes referred to as Berkeley UNIX).

The document is organized into sections and subsections that parallels the traditional format of the UNIX documentation.

In the following two sections a brief historical sketch of UNIX developments and an overview of the functional nature of the two major UNIX evolutions are given.

3. A Historical Perspective

The origins of the UNIX Operating System goes back to the work of Ken Thompson and Dennis Ritchie both members of research staff at Bell Telephone Laboratories.

The two earlier versions V6 (1975) and V7 (1978) were widely deployed at Academic and Research circles. But it is a later AT&T release called System III (at about 1982, which is also the first AT&T UNIX standard) that forms the origins of most of todays commercial UNIX offerings and its look-alikes.

Late in 1983 AT&T released the System V which has now been followed by two subsequent versions V.1 and V.2 the later one is the most current version of UNIX available from AT&T at the time of writing of this report.

At about 1975 on a totally separate track a group of researchers at University of California at Berkeley initiated a series of UNIX enhancements. Their enhanced releases are 1.0, 2.0, 3.0 and 4.0 at 1977, 78, 79, and 80 respectively (sometimes the release number is followed by BSD for Berkeley Software Distribution).

As the result of the R&D efforts funded by DARPA (Defense Advanced Research Projects Agency) two more BSD releases 4.1 (1981) and 4.2 (1983 and most current at this point) have followed.

The subject of this report is the comparison of these two most recent releases from both groups.

4. An Overview of System Differences

The major Berkeley enhancements to the UNIX are the Paging and Virtual Memory, LISP and PASCAL compiler, the "vi" editor, job control, a new shell, longer variable names, Network Support, a faster file system and inter process communications.

A commercial version of 4.2 on SUN Workstation has the additional support for networked diskless workstation, windowing and bit mapped graphics.

CH2188-1/85/0000/0162$01.00 © 1985 IEEE

Within the Bell System UNIX took its place as the main Time-Shared System available to the employees for the purpose of document preparation, electronic mail and Software Development. This resulted in many localized enhancements and additions to the basic system. Among these are numerous communication interfaces, and document processing packages. May be it is because of this dispersed nature of developments that AT&T UNIX V.2 still lacks a general and clean Network support structure. However more recent developments from AT&T are distinctive for their seriousness completeness and functionality. A sample of these are;

SCCS: Source Code Change Control system is a utility with a large set of commands for creation and maintenance of source code implementation increments called "deltas".

b16: A collection of Cross Compiler, Libraries, Debug and Emulation utilities intended for 16 bit microprocessors but implemented for 8086.

sar: A system activity reporter for helping the UNIX administrators mostly with system tuning and scheduling.

It is difficult to make a functional classification of various flavors from a flexible system such as UNIX. With this word of caution we would like to observe that AT&T UNIX paralleling its major environments has evolved in the direction of centrally administered time-sharing system for target and/or cross software developments, and daily office chores.

The Berkeley version however with its support for a generic [1] IPC and Network Support and some academically favored languages like PASCAL and LISP found itself closer to general purpose graphics workstation market.

5. System Calls

---

independence from the protocols and Network specifics along with the IPC and Network interface similarities

In the following an itemized list of system calls are presented for both versions and the discrepancies are commented on.

5.1. 4.2 BSD Calls not present in 5.2

The first table in this section summarizes the System calls in 4.2 BSD that are either absent or somewhat different from their V.2 counterparts. All system calls that are grouped under Table 1. will be discussed in more detail in a later section. Briefly their purpose is the management of a network port while making it look like an object similar to the usual file descriptor from the application process point of view.

Both systems include software signal utilities next to the older type of UNIX signal utilities. The V.2 software signal utility (named ssignal) is put under section 3 of the user manual along with library routines. Despite their similarity 4.2 software signals offers more control and flexibility to the users with the signal stack and software signal utilities. The "Kill" system call of V.2 can accomplish the same effects of the "killp" system call in 4.2 but it is not implemented as separate command. The signal related calls in 4.2BSD with no direct counterparts in V.2 are listed in Table 2.

In the following table we summarize the 4.2 System Calls of general utility and administrative nature that are not present in V.2. Among the calls in this table we would like to point that "mman" call which enables the user to map a page of memory to a device is an especially interesting one. However the mman implementation is not complete in the sense that it works with some character oriented devices only. In some cases it may be possible to obtain the same functionality using the older **kmem** and **mem** drivers found on both systems.

A new entity called "group access lists" is defined that will permit the access across group boundaries without changing the actual group id. The BSD concept of a symbolic link which basically looks like a path name translation table is also new one to the UNIX environment. **Vfork** (which is an efficient way of forking) is a useful improvement that may be difficult to implement with the current memory management support of V.2.

5.2. V.2 System Calls not present in 4.2 BSD

The most important group of system calls incorporated to the V.2 are the ones related to Inter-Process Communication, Shared Memory and Semaphore support. These are summarized in Table 4.

The V.2 IPC utilities although powerful and somewhat complete for most applications lack some desirable features. As an example we can observe the rendez-vous mechanism that is utilized within V.2 to enable two cooperating process to communicate. In such a mechanism the message queues (or similar objects) are identified with keys which has the possibility of colliding (same key for intended to be different queues) therefore there is always the possibility of interference if the keys are not selected with care. But the new utilities relieves the user from the restrictive requirement of "common ancestor" (i.e forked from same parent process) for communicating processes which had to use "pipes".

There are also a set of shared memory utilities that are specific to the PDP-11 machines. These utilities are listed in Table 4 & 5.

Table 6 lists the system calls that have either different names or some variations in 4.2 system.

In 4.2, some V.2 System Calls are placed with library routines in section 3. Most of these calls have newer variants implemented in 4.2. These system calls are displayed in table 7.

As a final note on system calls we should note that as a variant of the exec function common to both systems the **Execve** in 4.2 has the capability of taking an interpreter input file and calling the interpreter defined in the file itself. **Fcntl** in 4.2 allows owner information to be obtained about a descriptor. **Open** in 4.2 has an option to create if the file does not exist. **Stat** for file status gathering has an **estat** variation in 4.2 for obtaining status information on symbolic links which are not present in V.2 The command names **utime** in V.2 and **utimes** in 4.2 are synonyms

doing file access and modification time set in V.2 and 4.2 respectively.

6. Comparison of Library Calls

The library organization in 4.2 has the same structure but a finer subgrouping named as general, compatibility, math, network, standard I/O and miscellaneous library routines. Some of the now more or less redundant system calls of V.2 are moved to the compatibility Library section. Network library subsection of 4.2 is a totally new section that will be dealt with more detail in a later section.

6.1. 4.2 Library Routines

The most substantial addition to the 4.2 library is the Networking support routines. These routines performs mostly a directory assistance type of support to the communicating application processes.

We should also note that some of these calls are somewhat specific to the currently implemented "domains" in 4.2 BSD.

Among the more general type of new library routines in 4.2 the memory allocation on the user stack, a new directory file handler and a generic queue handler are noteworthy. There is also a group of 4.2 library additions that are more general in nature. Table 9 shows the general 4.2 library implementations which are not present in V.2. In this table the **bcmp** library for bit and byte string operations can be observed to have a parallel in **memory** utility of V.2 (memcmp(3), memcpy(3), memset(3)) with the exceptions of "find set bit" operation of 4.2 that is not present in V.2 and memset operation of V.2 which will set the region of the memory to any desired character where the corresponding 4.2 command will simply zero out the region.

6.2. V.2 Library Routines

There are two major groups of library additions to the System V.2 besides some scattered general routines. One group is the extensive set of utilities added for the handling of the archived object files. Such utilities are designed to work in a uniform manner with either an archived object file or with an individual object file. There is no need to make a long list for all archived object handling utilities but they consist of all library calls that begins with ld and they perform functions like open, close, read, write and seek etc.. The other significant library addition to V.2 is the extensive X.25 support. These library routines are illustrated in the table 10 .

We must also note without listing that the FORTRAN support libraries are more extensive in the V.2 UNIX environment including a FORTRAN version of "signal" and "system" calls. Other more general library additions are listed in the following table. We must note that some of the library routines has equivalent counterparts in 4.2 (like bcmp and memory, ftime and ctime, directory operation and ftw etc). Please compare Table 9 and 11 for general Library Differences.

7. Commands and Intrinsics

A complete list of all differences in the user commands (section (1) of standard UNIX documentation) would be a prohibitively long one for this document. We have counted a total 95 commands in 4.2 that are not present in V.2 and about 200 V.2 commands not present 4.2. The following sections offers a sampled comparison of the User Commands in both systems.

7.1. BSD 4.2 Commands not present in V.2

The Communication functions implemented in 4.2 result in a few user level applications commands that are provided in separate listing below.

These applications are totally built on the new Network Support utilities listed in previous sections on System Calls and Libraries. Among the other more diverse commands the following list summarize the

important ones in 4.2 with no immediate counterpart in V.2.

7.2. V.2 Commands not present in 4.2

The User Commands sections of V.2 is much more crowded then its counter part in 4.2. Most of these commands are related to text processing and many variants of communication interfaces. None of the new document processing and network interface related utilities are in 4.2.

There is also an extensive support in V.2 for Bell developed processors like Mac4 and Mac8. Table 14 lists some of the basic V.2 commands that are absent from 4.2.

8. Communication Support and Related Enhancements

In 4.2 Network interface utilities are same or at least has the same user interface as Inter Process Communication Utilities. The differences between the two and the difference between different Networks are parametrized into the function calls. One of the main advantage of this architecture is the possibility of starting a development as a multi process single processor environment then at a later phase distribute the applications over a network. Such an approach may save debugging and development time.

Besides the application level generality described above the 4.2 Network Architecture is also structured with generalities at lower levels. None of the hardware and protocol specifics of a network that is being supported is hard wired to the system implementation. Instead the specifics are hidden in the corresponding driver structure and as usual in UNIX the drivers are supplied with a standard interface to the kernel. This flexibility is accomplished with a protocol switch (just like the block or character device switches) implemented within the kernel. In that respect the Network interface in 4.2 is similar to the block device interfaces which hides the specifics of a disk drive from the file system or other higher levels. The 4.2 Network Interface Architecture does not provide protocol functions like flow or error control by its own but rather it adopts the constructs of the Network that is being interfaced and builds its services on top of them. This is unlike for example of UUCP which has its own set of protocols for such functions. The 4.2 implementation of the Network Support relies heavily on implementations within the kernel. If the same functionality were implemented as user level process (with no or minimal kernel change) it would be very difficult to maintain the same level of performance because of the data moves and context switching. The performance of a network interface is also related to other factors like file system and memory management. It is very likely that the limiting factor for the performance of a file transfer protocol will be the transfer process to/from the disk. A file system with 50k per second bandwidth will be the bottle neck in any file transfer protocol.

System V is still lacking a memory management feature that will reduce the swapping for large processes and would permit processes requiring more than the size of main memory to run. One difficulty in adding such an enhancement to the System V would be the backward compatibility (which AT&T is committed to) without a sacrifice in performance. This may also require some File System enhancements. In General the traditional UNIX File System relies on the sorted and interleaved free block list for reducing seek time but the free list will change in time leaving a more or less random free list which will result in a new file creation with inefficiently distributed blocks. Also the physical record size in V.2 and earlier AT&T UNIX systems is 512 bytes. Therefore a large file would necessitate too many seek operations to penalize the performance of the transfer operation. In 4.2 the block size is increased to 4K and the device drivers for disks are modified to make more use of the data for disk geometry. As a result it is being reported that file handling in 4.2 has accomplished a major improvement of performance.

Signal Related System Calls	
killp	send signal to a process group
sigblock	prevent signal from delivery
sigpause	release and wait for signals blocked
sigsetmask	set current signal mask for blocking
sigstack	to define a stack for signal processing
sigvec	software signal utility

General 4.2 Library Routines	
alloca	memory allocator
cfree	memory allocator
bcmp	bit and byte string operations
bcopy	bit and byte string operations
bzero	bit and byte string operations
scandir	scan a directory
asctime	convert date and time ascii
closedir	directory operations
opendir	directory operations
readdir	directory operations
telldir	directory operations
seekdir	directory operations
rewinddir	directory operations
closedir	directory operations
isinif	test for indeterminate floating point values
isnan	test for indeterminate floating point values
insque	insert element to the queue
remque	remove element from queue
openlog	initialize logfile
syslog	control system logfile
closelog	close logfile
frexp	split into mantissa end exponent
ftime	get date and time
initgroups	Initialize group access lists
psignal	system signal message

Table 9

4.2 BSD Commands not Present in 5.2	
csh	C shell
dbx	An improved and repaired version of SDB
ctags	To create a tags file for use with ex (or vi)
indxbib	make inverted index to a bibliography
looklib	find reference in bib.
roffbib	print record in bib. file
startbib	set bibliographic data
lastcomm	show last commands executed in reverse order
mt	a magnetic tape manipulation program
pc	pascal compiler(also a set of pascal support etc commands)

Table 13

Communication Related System Calls	
accept	accept a connection on a socket
bin	bind a name with a socket
connect	initiate a connection on a socket
gethostid	get unique identifier of current host
gethostname	get name of current host
sethostname	set name of current host
getpeername	get name of the session peer name
getsockname	get socket name
getsockopt	get socket options
setsockopt	set socket options
socket	create a communication endpoint
socketpair	create a pair of communication endpoints
listen	wait for or service a connection request
shutdown	call take-down on a socket
recv	receive a message from a connected socket
recvfrom	receive message from a socket regardless of connectedness
recvmsg	same as recvfrom with calling variation
send	opposite of recv
sendto	opposite of recvfrom
sendmsg	opposite of recvmsg
select	synchronous I/O multiplexing
readv	scattered (de-multiplexed) input of data
writev	inverse of readv

Table 1

General Utility and Administrative 4.2 Syscalls	
mmap(unmmap)	map(unmap) pages of memory
quota	manipulate disk quotas
reboot	reboot system or halt processor
rename	change the name of file
rmdir	remove a directory entry (unlink in V.2)
set(get)groups	set (get) group access list
swapon	add a swap device for interleaved paging/swapping
symlink	make a symbolic link to a file
readlink	read value of symbolic link
syscall	indirect system call
truncate	(and ftruncate) truncates a file to specified length
utimes	set file times
vadvise	to give advice to the paging system
vfork	memory efficient fork
vhangup	to give clean terminal at next login
wait3	wait with options to non-block
dup2	give a desired new descriptor value
flock	advisory lock handling to a file
fsysnc	update on a single file return when done
gettimer	return current value of timer
settimer	set timer value
getpagesize	get system page size
getpriority	get program scheduling priority
setpriority	set program scheduling priority
getrlimit	(setrlimit) control system resources utilization
getrusage	get info about resource utilization of current proc.
gettimeofday	get date and time
settimeofday	set date and time

Table 3

4.2 Network Distributed Commands	
rcp	remote file copy
rlogin	remote login
rsh	remote shell
ruptime	show host status of local machines
rwho	a remote who

Table 12

Interprocess Communication Related Syscalls	
msgctl	inter process message queue control
msget	get a message queue identifier
msgop	message operations
msgsnd	put a message to a queue
msgrcv	opposite of msgsnd
semctl	semaphore control
semget	get a semaphor identifier
semop	semaphore operations
shmctl	shared memory control
shmget	get a shared memory segment
shmop	shared memory operations

Table 4

PDP-11 Shared Memory Syscalls	
getmaus	shared memory operations for PDP-11
freemaus	close the maus descriptor
enabmaus	attach a maus file descriptor
dismaus	free maus file
switmaus	attach a maus file descriptor

Table 5

General Utility System Calls	
plock	prevent swapping of data or text segment of caller
sys3b	3B specific system calls
timer	get process and child process times
uname	get name of current UNIX system(gethostname in 4.2)
ustat	get file system statistics

Table 6

V.2 System Calls Moved to Library Section in 4.2	
alarm	send SIGALRM to caller when time elapsed
stime	set time
ulimit	get and set user limits
umount	unmount file systems
nice	change scheduling priority of a process
pause	suspend calling process until a signal
exit	exit with cleanup
signal	specify signal actions
exec	exec calls with l,v,le,lp,vp extensions are replaced by execv
time	get time

Table 7

V.2 Library Calls for X.25 Support	
X25alnk	attach a device to a logical link id
X25ilnk	initialize the link
X25clnk	change from primary to backup device
X25hlnk	halt link
X25dlnk	detach link
X25ipvc	install private circuit
X25rpvc	remove a private circuit

Table 10

4.2 Network Library Routines	
endhostent	get network host entry
endnetent	get network entry
endprotoent	get protocol entry
endservent	get service entry
gethostbyaddr	get network host entry
getbyname	get network host entry
gethostent	get network host entry
getnetbyaddr	get network entry
getnetbyname	get network entry
getnetent	get network entry
getprotobyname	get protocol entry
getprotobynumber	get protocol entry
getprotent	get protocol entry
getservbyname	get service entry
getservbynumber	get service entry
getservent	get service entry
htol	convert between host and network byte order
htos	convert between host and network byte order
inet_adr	Internet address manipulation
inet_lnaof	Internet address manipulation
inet_makeaddr	Internet address manipulation
inet_netof	Internet address manipulation
inet_network	Internet address manipulation
inet_ntoa	Internet address manipulation
nhtol	convert between host and network byte order
nhtos	convert between host and network byte order
rcmd	for returning a stream to a remote command
sethostent	get network host entry
setnet	get network host entry
setprotoent	get network host entry
setservent	get service entry

Table 8

General V.2 Library Routines	
a64l	Long integer to ASCII base 64 conversion
eatab	ASCII to EBCIDIC conversion
aetab	EBCIDIC to ASCII conversion
bsearch	binary search a table
cpyfile	format and copy file
ctermid	generate the path of control terminal
ctime	a set of time and date string conversion utilities
cuserid	Get login name of current process owner
drand	double random
ftw	walk a file tree
getpwent	get fields of a passwd entry
getutmp	get a utmp file entry
hsearch	manage hash search tables
lsearch	Linear search and update
matherr	mathematical error handling functions
memory	memory efficient copy, compare, and set functions
sar	direct read from kernel utility for users
sputl	long integer access utilities
stdipc	standard interprocess comm package
tsearch	management of binary trees

Table 11

V.2 Commands not Present in 4.2 BSD	
shl	shell layer manager
send	(gath) IBM RJE interface
usl	uniform job submittal language
kasb	DEC KMC-11 assembler
ipcs	report IPC facility status
ipcrm	remove a message queue semaphore or shmem id
makeky	make a unique key for ipc use
ctrace	C program tracing tool
b16..	Basic 16 support tools
sar	system activity report
usors	collect UNIX response time

Table 14

ACCOUNTING TOOLS FOR UNIX™ SYSTEMS

Edward Levinson, Ph.D.

Bell Communications Research, Inc.
Piscataway, New Jersey 08854

This paper describes a method, and its implementation, that identifies machine resource usage by transaction instead of individual UNIX* process. A transaction is a shell file containing a collection of application and UNIX commands that performs an application function. The method is readily extended to provide information about the environment in which the transaction is executed. The method does not require changes to the operating system.

Special programs that run at the start and end of each transaction are required to identify transaction resource usage. These programs plus a set of tools that manipulate the UNIX accounting log and convert it to *ascii* are described in this paper. The paper begins with an analysis of existing UNIX accounting tools and then describes the method and its associated tools. In addition the paper includes a skeletal transaction, a manual page for the Accounting Tools, and a sample report.

1. INTRODUCTION

A UNIX operating system usually provides several tools that tell you what resources a process uses, *prof(1)* and *times(1)* for example. While useful when developing individual processes, they are limited when dealing with functional units or transactions that combine shell commands, pipelines, and user written programs into a single unit. These units will be called *transactions*.

For a transaction, you cannot use a system-wide average of each individual process' resource usage, available from *sa(8)*†, because one process, *nroff(1)* for example, may be used in several contexts with different usage patterns. Consequently, the individual process executed in each transaction invocation must be identified and accounted.

---

* UNIX is a trademark of AT&T Bell Laboratories.

† All references to commands in the UNIX User's Manual have the form *cmd*(section), where section is the manual section that contains the command. Section 8 commands are sometimes in a separate System Administrator's Guide.

The data for each process is accumulated by the UNIX kernel and, when accounting is enabled by *accton(8)*, written into a log file. Each record contains the following data:

— the command name,
— cpu execution time while in user mode,
— cpu execution time while in system mode,
— elapsed (wall clock) time,
— process start time,
— user ID,
— group ID,
— memory usage,
— disk block reads and writes, and
— terminal issuing the command.

This file is difficult to use because the UNIX kernel produces a record for each command, not each transaction. In addition each record is written whenever its corresponding process completes, thus the log file interleaves the records of all users in a single sequential file.

The Accounting Tools overcome these problems. They scan the log file, separate the data by user, and group together the commands that make up complete transaction.

A set of UNIX shells and programs, the Accounting Tools aggregate resource usage by transaction; the data can then be used to project a machine's usage and capacity. The tools extract data by transaction on cpu and disk usage and produce resource usage reports. The report contains information about complete transactions that is not available from the standard UNIX accounting reports.

In our application we also want to identify the mode in which the transaction runs: input, immediate, or deferred. In the input mode our programs prompt the user for the data needed to run the application and queue the application software to be run later. In immediate mode, the application is not queued but is run as soon as the input data is available. When a queued application is run it is in deferred mode. The mode is an example of information about a transaction that is important to recorded for later analysis.

2. HOW IT WORKS

The LEIS accounting software works by placing special markers in the UNIX accounting log. The markers are specially named commands, _ac_a and _ac_z, which are invoked at the beginning and end, respectively, of a transaction. In the log file they identify the beginning and end of the transaction. Each log record also contains the user and group IDs plus the name (inode number) of the terminal issuing the command. These data items enable all the records for a single transaction to be grouped together. This data and the markers are used by the Accounting Tools to collect and delimit the records generated by the transactions.

To identify a transaction's mode, two techniques are used. Both are based on finding a specific command between a transaction's start and end markers. In one case there is a command (process) that is unambiguously associated with one mode; in our application a command named "q" always appears in input mode transactions ("q" is the command that queues a transaction for later execution once its input is obtained). In the other case, the end marker command, _ac_z, generates a special marker. It examines a variables in the UNIX shell environment; if it has a specific value then the end marker invokes another command, _ac_run, via the *fork(2)* and *exec(2)* system calls. This second command identifies the mode and in our application is used for the deferred mode. By default, immediate mode is assumed for any transaction not otherwise classified.

Because the accounting records are written at process termination, the record for the transaction process, i.e. the user invoked process, follows the end marker. This detail is handled by the Accounting Tools.

3. A TRANSACTION OUTLINE

The following skeletal shell is a guide to creating transactions that can take advantage of the Accounting Tools. The skeleton also shows how the execution modes are used. This shell is normally executed twice; first by the user, in *Input* mode, to enter the report request and once, in *Defer*red mode, under the "q" command's control. Both passes can be combined in *Immed*iate mode.

```
#! /bin/sh
# begin marker
_ac_a
# when things go wrong
trap "_ac_z" 1 2 15

# gather input
case ${QMODE-Input}in
Input |Immed)
        . . .
esac

# run reports
case $QMODE in
Input) # run this shell later
        QMODE=Defer q $0
        ;;
Immed |Defer)
        # now it's later or
        # immediate execution
        . . .
        ;;
esac

# end marker (normal termination)
_ac_z
```

The first line identifies the command that will process this file and insures that the file name appears in the accounting record; otherwise the record would contain the name of the shell program, *sh*. The first and last statements cause the start and end markers to appear in the accounting log. The *trap* command insures that the end marker is created even if an interrupt occurs.

The two *case* statements control the transaction's operation using the shell environment variable QMODE, to the identify the different modes. The first one sets the default mode (*Input*) and controls gathering the transactions input. The second *case* statement controls the transaction's output generation. If the transaction is running in the input mode the mode is changed to *Defer* and the queuer, *q*, is invoked to execute the transaction (shell variable *$0*) in the background; otherwise the output is generated *Immed*iately.

In operation the transaction starts execution and the start marker is generated. For input mode, *QMODE=Input*, the transaction enters the input gathering phase and then is queued for later execution with *QMODE=Defer*. When executed with *QMODE=Defer*, the transaction skips the input phase and starts the output generation phase. (Note: data is transferred between phases through files and shell variables). In *Immed*iate mode both phases are executed.

4. THE ACCOUNTING TOOLBOX

The software is organized as a group of tools that can be used to manipulate the UNIX accounting log. The log is not a printable *ascii* file; instead it consists fixed length records with binary data, some of which are encoded.

The first set of tools described below take the log, or similar files, as input and produce output in the same format [*cf. acct(4)*]. The next set are tools, not described here, that generate the reports; the final set, tools that can be used with an individual transaction.

The accounting tools start by extracting from the UNIX log the commands that are used in a transaction's execution. The command **acx** performs this function; it takes the UNIX log as its input and, using the start and end markers, produces a file, in the same format as the UNIX log, of the extracted records. The **acseg** command can split a log file, it copies the *i* through *j*th input record to the output (*i* and *j* are command line parameters). **Acprt** converts the records to printable (*ascii*) format. Once in this format the data can be manipulated using standard UNIX software (*awk, sed, sort, etc.*).

Three commands are executed as part of a transaction: **_ac_a** and **_ac_z**, that mark the beginning and end of each program, and **_ac_run** that indicates the deferred execution mode.

Using these tools reports can easily be generated that show resource usage by transaction. Attachment I shows a sample report we use in our system. The data is grouped by mode and a count of executions for each transaction plus the average resource usage is given.

Portability

The accounting tools are implemented on a BSD 4.1 variant and use the declaration in *acct.h(4)* to interpret the accounting records. In porting to other systems, care must be taken to account for differences in

- the structure that defines the layout of the log record and its fields,
- the time interval represented by a clock tick,
- the file system locations of header files needed in the C code.

The Accounting Tools have been running for five months and have recently been ported to a 4.2BSD system. We are in the process of porting them to AT&T's UNIX System V and DEC's ULTRIX*.

5. ACKNOWLEDGEMENT

The contributions of Jim Weythman, who first suggested the use of the accounting file markers and whose discussions of the UNIX kernel were invaluable, and Shelly Becker, who carefully reviewed and critiqued early drafts of this paper, are gratefully acknowledged.

---

* DEC and ULTRIX are trademarks of Digital Equipment Corporation, Inc.

APPENDIX I - Sample Statistics Report

Oct 16 00:00 1984 statistics for Mon Oct 15 Page 1

cmd	cnt	cpu sec	elapsed sec	memory ave k	io blks
*** grp: lead ***					
immediate mode:					
acr	5	4.9	126.6	46.6	69.2
assign	9	1.9	9.9	22.4	15.2
ca	2	2.4	18.0	26.7	46.5
count	6	4.0	8.8	106.9	52.3
lead	11	1.6	6.8	21.6	15.5
ta.update	3	21.1	478.7	157.0	295.7
table	2	1.6	8.5	22.1	13.0
term	1	3.3	38.0	26.2	33.0
valid	2	1.4	5.0	21.2	13.0
input mode:					
acr	5	3.8	30.0	26.5	60.0
ca	2	3.3	18.0	27.8	47.0
ca.fil	2	4.2	9.5	22.8	80.5
cnt.bndr	1	5.0	21.0	24.1	77.0
cnt.brdg	1	4.5	23.0	23.6	83.0
cnt.fil	4	7.1	20.3	25.1	108.3
cnt.term	5	5.3	22.6	23.6	95.2
cnt.termfi	1	4.6	15.0	23.8	86.0
sterm	3	11.8	107.3	125.0	156.3
term.fil	4	3.9	21.0	22.7	81.3
wc.ca	3	4.9	19.0	23.1	86.0
wc.ta	1	3.5	14.0	24.5	52.0
deferred mode:					
acr	5	30.8	56.4	250.9	540.8
ca	2	609.9	1008.0	232.8	5862.5
ca.fil	2	41.2	62.5	237.2	473.0
cnt.bndr	1	27.8	83.0	148.7	496.0
cnt.brdg	1	33.8	42.0	162.7	447.0
cnt.fil	4	36.4	61.0	196.1	513.8
cnt.term	5	80.3	125.2	406.3	583.6
cnt.termfi	1	37.0	45.0	185.4	499.0
sterm	3	130.3	511.3	300.4	551.0
term.fil	4	19.2	26.8	101.6	260.3
wc.ca	3	25.3	50.7	155.2	432.0
wc.ta	1	17.4	27.0	66.9	215.0

NAME
_ac_a, _ac_z, acprt, acseg, acsize, acx — accounting data

SYNOPSIS
_ac_a

_ac_z

acprt file

acseg [+start] [—end] file

acsize file

acx file

DESCRIPTION
These commands permit data for specific commands to be extracted from the accounting records. This data will be used to determine patterns of usage and computer resource requirements. They can be used on an individual basis display a program's performance characteristics.

The commands _ac_a and _ac_z serve as markers in the accounting data file and delimit the beginning and end of the commands that will be extracted by *acx*.

Acprt formats and prints the accounting records in *file* on *stdout*; accounting files contain binary, and encoded, data.

Acseg copies accounting records from *file to stdout*. Records are copied beginning at *pos1* and ending just before *pos2*.

Acsize determines the number of accounting records in *file*.

Acx will write on *stdout* all commands in *file* that were executed between instances of _ac_a and _ac_z; _ac_a and _ac_z and the accounting record of the parent process are included in the output.

EXAMPLES
Shell files should be set up as shown below to have their use and statistics extracted.

```
#!  /bin/sh
_ac_a
. . . your commands and programs . . .
_ac_z
```

SEE ALSO
time(1), acct(5), /etc/accton(8), /etc/sa(8).

Embedded Computer System Requirements Workshop

Stephanie M. White, Grumman Aerospace Corporation, Workshop Chair
Jonah Z. Lavi, Israel Aircraft Industries

Developing embedded computer systems requires extensive requirements analysis, support methodologies, and software tools. A Naval Research Laboratory workshop provided the forum for identifying specific recommendations and areas where standards could be developed.

The complexity of modern embedded computer systems such as those that are integral parts of spacecraft systems, advanced military weapon systems, command and control systems, robots, industrial control systems, and medical systems is increasing steadily. The cost associated with imprecisely specifying embedded computer system requirements has led engineers to the realization that the process of developing such requirements is not thoroughly understood. A workshop sponsored by Grumman Aerospace Corporation and the Naval Research Laboratory was held at NRL in Washington, DC, November 27-29, 1984, to address problems associated with the requirements specification process.

Workshop participants included representatives from private companies, universities, and military agencies, who work extensively in the area of system and software requirements analysis and in the development of methodologies and tools. There was general agreement among them that there are specific problems crucial to embedded computer system requirements analysis and documentation, which are usually not addressed in current methods and standards. This report summarizes the problems and describes recommendations for improvement to system and software standards and to computerized tools supporting the requirements process.

Crucial problems

Embedded computer systems—computer systems that are an integral part of a physical system—have to react quickly and correctly to very complex sequences of unpredictable external events. The system response varies according to the order of these events. Consequently, the accurate description and analysis of the desired system reaction to sequences of external stimuli is a very important step in the specification of embedded systems. Insufficient analysis of external phenomena will lead to the development of systems that do not meet the basic expectations of users and developers.

Most embedded computer systems have not only a complex external interface but also a complex internal structure. The software can be functionally allocated (apportioned by function) among many computerized subsystems and implemented on many diverse computers. Then the behavior of each subsystem is affected by events external to the entire system and by the behavior of the other subsystems.

Specifications are a continuing problem. As changes are made in the system operating rules, the problem of specifying complete, consistent, and correct embedded computer system requirements grows. These changes, which can occur during or after system development, are caused by better understanding of the processes controlled by the system, the need for improved performance, such as fault detection and recovery, changes in the behavior of the external environment, and technical advances that result in changes in the physical system configuration. Any such changes require the re-analysis of the system behavior and may require the re-programming of the software.

Unfortunately, most of the current systems and software engineering practices and standards do not adequately address these specification issues. In addition, the methodologies and tools developed for analysis and documentation of information processing systems are not adequate for embedded computer systems, since they do not allow for the description of complex dynamic phenomena or for analysis of the distributed nature of modern embedded systems. A number of methodologies and tools have been proposed for the analysis of embedded systems.[1-7] They are still evolving, however, because systems and software engineers do not yet completely understand the embedded computer system requirements analysis process, and the complex dynamic behavior of embedded computer systems is difficult to capture in a simple understandable representation. Consequently, development time for many of these systems extends beyond expectations. Furthermore many are not tested properly, nor do they meet customer requirements or expectations.

Workshop overview

The following were the major workshop obectives:

(1) To determine what knowledge about an embedded computer system is needed to define software requirements and what should be the relationships between system and software requirements;

(2) To determine if there exists an acceptable methodology to acquire and document this knowl-

edge, especially for new systems without historical or empirical information on their behavior;

(3) To identify those issues inadequately addressed in current system requirements analysis methods, standards, and specifications; and

(4) To determine the characteristics of tools necessary to support embedded computer system requirements analysis and specification.

The workshop included presentations and discussions on the embedded computer system requirements process, methods, models, and tools. All presentations were followed by extensive discussions of the basic issues. Several participants spoke about developing and/or integrating methodologies to support the embedded com-

---

Methodologies and tools developed for information processing systems are not adequate for embedded computer systems.

---

puter system requirements process.

The ISDOS System Encyclopedia Manager[8,9] was shown to support methodology prototyping. With it, a project can define its own requirements language and specify the format and contents of needed reports.

After a comparison of models, attendees agreed that some form of state machine representation was helpful. However, since the number of states of a finite state machine that models an embedded computer system is too large at the discrete level, workshop participants agreed that structuring/partitioning based on the system environment is necessary.

The differences between the various systems and software requirements approaches were illustrated by specifications of the requirements for a software controller for a home heating system. Five basic specifications were presented: the TRW specification, based on Systems Requirements Engineering Methodology (SYSREM),[1] an

extension of Software Requirements Engineering Methodology (SREM); the NRL specification based on the NRL Methodology developed for the Software Cost Reduction (A-7 Aircraft) Program[4,10]; and three other specifications based on synergisms of various known approaches.[4,10] Grumman's approach,[11] is a modification of the NRL Methodology; SofTech's approach, a combination of the NRL Methodology; Structured Analysis Design Technique (SADT) and Systems Analysis of Integrated Networks of Tasks (SAINT)[12]; and the Israel Aircraft Industries' methodology, which was presented in detail at the workshop.

Basic findings—consensus

There were three categories of agreement: recommendations for standards and tool development, recommendations concerning an embedded computer system model, and recommendations concerning methodologies and the need for tool support. Issues about which there was agreement are very important, since they are the issues not currently addressed in most embedded computer systems and software requirements analysis methodologies and standards.

Recommendations for standards and tool development. The model that embodies functional hierarchy and dataflow is insufficient for embedded computer systems analysis and specification, since these systems are heavily time- and event-dependent. Workshop participants agreed that requirements for embedded computer systems must include the dynamic view that specifies the changes in system state caused by external events. They modeled this view either as a structured finite state machine or as mechanisms similiar to a set of cooperating finite state machines in which externally visible events replace machine inputs.

The boundaries of the system must be explicitly defined, and the environment of the system must be modeled and analyzed as part of the system requirements development process. The model should include the time-dependent, deterministic and nondeterministic, parallel and serial nature of the inputs.

Nonfunctional requirements such as performance, fault detection and recovery, safety, security, availablility, reliability, and ease of change are major concerns in today's complex embedded computer systems. They must be addressed during the generation of system and software requirements. In fact, fault detection and recovery must be considered at all levels of system and software requirements and design; their impact must be considered after each iteration of functional allocation, as fault-detection and recovery techniques vary with the functional allocation and influence performance.

The systems requirements process is not usually complete when software design begins. In fact, it is normal for algorithms to be refined throughout development, resulting in refinement of the software requirements. It is important, however, that requirements not be left to be determined (TBD). Where exact performance specifications are lacking, the available information should be provided and so tagged so that systems and software analysts can evaluate the impact rather than assume incorrect information.

The systems and software requirements documents should serve as reference tools. They should be accurate, understandable, traceable, precise, consistent, sufficient, testable, and easy to change. They should specify any required constraints on the implementation, but otherwise be implementation-independent. They should include acceptable system responses to undesired events, should record any changes to the system that are expected to occur in the future and should address reuseability. They should acknowledge any assumptions made and carry references to analysis that supports decisions. Documentation on assumptions and decisions is necessary for evaluation of future changes and for conducting system testing. Finally, the requirements document

format should support completeness checking. [13-15]

The embedded computer system model. Workshop participants agreed that it would be desirable to develop an abstract model of embedded computer system(s) that both systems and software engineers could understand. This model would facilitate better system and software requirements analysis and tool support. Models would stimulate questions about the behavior of the system and help in the analysis process. Specific engineering metrics, based on the model, should be developed to allow better description and analysis of system behavior and performance. Examples of current models are the SREM and the NRL models.

It's normal for systems requirements algorithms to be refined throughout development, so software requirements are also refined.

The model should include all properties necessary to describe embedded computer systems. Properties not included in the model will probably be omitted in the analysis and the resulting specification.

The model should be consistent across system life cycle phases (systems and software requirements, systems and software design) to facilitate analysis of change and testing. The model should be described in a language of objects, relationships, and attributes. Such a language contributes to the discussion of the nature of information about embedded computer systems that should be captured in a database, and it stimulates further discussion for model enhancement.

Methodologies and tool support. It was agreed that methodologies that assist in the system and software requirements analysis and specification process must be used. An acceptable methodology must consist of an orderly series of steps to assure that all

aspects of the requirements have been considered. The use of metrics within the methodology is necessary for the analysis of conformance and quality. Methodologies cannot be understood intuitively, only through use.

It is difficult to develop adequate requirements documentation and perform consistency analysis for modern embedded computer systems manually because of these systems' multi-state dimensionality, their dynamic and distributed nature, and their continuous evolution. Automated tools are helpful for the retrieval of information, representation of multiple viewpoints, cross-checking, and simulation of system and software requirements.

Areas of disagreement

Participants were not in agreement on the best embedded computer system model. Several were suggested; all models used some level of state machine representation, but the exact form of representation was in dispute.

A second issue of disagreement was whether a requirements model should show the transformation steps from input to output. Some participants believe that this information belongs in the requirements model, while others want to see it only in the design model.

The allocation of functions to subsystems was another issue at variance. Participants working with extremely large systems believe that definition of subsystems is necessary as a first step in their requirements definition process. Others prefer to specify all the functional requirements first, if possible, and allocate functions to subsystems only after all the requirements have been considered.

Future workshop issues

Future workshops are planned to discuss evolving embedded computer system models and standards for requirements specifications. Issues which should be addressed include

- A checklist of items to be considered during the embedded computer system requirements process;

- The different views synthesized during the requirements process, such as the man-machine interface view, the survivability view, the maintenance view;
- Methods for modeling the environment of the system;
- Rules for system decomposition; is it equivalent to state machine partitioning/structuring?
- Methods for specifying commonality and reuseability;
- Methods for bounding system performance requirements;
- Determination of required system and software metrics;
- Methods for requirements allocation to subsystems/processors; and
- The structure and contents of system and software requirements documents. □

Acknowledgments

We would like to thank all workshop participants for the valuable information they provided. Participants included Mack Alford, TRW; Kathryn Heninger Britton; consultant to NRL; Louis Chmura, NRL; Paul Clements, NRL; Alan Davis, BTG; Richard Edelmann, Grumman Aerospace Corporation; Stuart Faulk, NRL; Sandi Fryer, Naval Weapons Center; Eran Kessler, Israel Aircraft Industries; Bruce Labaw, NRL; H.O. Lubbes, Naval Electronics Systems Command; David E. McConnell, Naval Surface Weapons Center; John Mullen, IBM; Donald Reifer, RCI; Hasan Sayani, ASTEC; John Stockenberg, SofTech, Daniel Teichroew, ISDOS; Donald Utter, AT&T Bell Laboratories; David Weiss, NRL; and Stanley Wilson, NRL. Special thanks to Stanley Wilson and David Weiss for the support they gave to the workshop, to all the NRL participants, Mack Alford and Daniel Teichroew for their careful review of this paper, and to Donna Thibodeau of Grumman, without whom this paper would not have been completed in time for publication.

References

1. M. Alford, "SREM at the Age of Eight," *Computer,* Vol. 18, No. 4, Apr. 1984, pp. 36-46.

2. H. Barina, W. Cobey, J. Rosenbaum, and S. White, "Automated Software Design," *Proc. Compsac,* Nov. 1979, pp. 384-391.

3. M. Hamilton and S. Zeldin, "The Relationship between Design and Verification," *J. Systems and Software,* Vol. 1, North Holland, 1979, pp. 29-56.

4. K. Heninger, "Specifying Software Requirements for Complex Systems: New Techniques and their Application," *IEEE Trans. on Software Engineering,* Vol. SE-6, Jan. 1980, pp. 2-13.

5. "Structured Analysis for Real-Time Systems," Yourdon, Inc., New York, 1984.

6. P. Zave, "An Operational Approach to Requirements for Embedded Systems," *IEEE Trans. on Software Engineering,* Vol. SE-8, No. 5, May 1982, pp. 250-269.

7. J. Z. Lavi, "A Systems Engineering Approach to Software Engineering," *Proc. Software Process Workshop,* Egham, UK, Feb. 1984, pp. 49-57.

8. D. Teichroew et al., "Application of the Entity-Relationship Approach to Information Processing Systems Modeling," in P. Chen, ed., *Entity-Relationship Approach to Systems Analysis and Design,* North Holland, 1980, pp. 15-34.

9. D. Teichroew, "The Development of Software Support Environments," *Proc. Canadian Information Processing Society,* 1982 National Conference, pp. 200-210.

10. K. Heninger et al., "Software Requirements for the A-7E Aircraft," *NRL Memorandum Report 3876,* NRL, Washington, DC, 1978.

11. S. White and S. Meyers, "Software Requirements Methodology and Tool Study for A-6E Technology Transfer," *Technical Report SRSR-A6-83-001,* Grumman, Bethpage, NY, 1983.

12. R. N. Charette and R. H. Wallace, "A Methodology for Addressing System Operability Issues," to be published in *Proc. IEEE 1985 Nat'l Aerospace and Electronics Conference,* May 1985.

13. S. D. Hester, D. L. Parnas, and D. F. Utter, "Using Documentation as a Software Design Medium," *Bell System Technical J.,* Vol. 60, No. 8, Oct. 1981, pp. 1941-1977.

14. D. L. Parnas, "Software Engineering Principles," *INFOR,* Vol. 22, No. 4, Nov. 1984.

15. D. F. Utter, "Properties of the System Design Through Documentation (SDTD) Methodology," *Proc. First Int'l Conf. Computers and Applications,* June 1984, pp. 809-814.

Stephanie White is a group head at Grumman Aerospace, where she is responsible for software requirements analysis and for ensuring application of software requirements engineering techniques. Her research interests include requirements specification theory and application. Prior to 1979, she taught mathematics and computer science at C.W. Post College. A Woodrow Wilson fellow, she received an M. S. in mathematics from New York University in 1962. In 1980, she received an M. S. in computer sceince from Polytechnic Institute of New York, where she is a Ph.D. candidate and adjunct lecturer. She is a member of ACM, the IEEE Computer Society, and Phi Beta Kappa.

Jonah Z. Lavi has been corporate R&D manager for the Israel Aircraft Industries since 1978. His current research interests are in embedded computer systems engineering and software engineering, particularly in systems and software requirements analysis.

He received a BSc in electrical engineering from the Technion-Israel Institute of Technology in 1955, an MS in electrical engineering from Northwestern University in 1957 and a PhD in systems engineering from Case-Western Reserve in 1965.

For questions about this article, contact White at Grumman Aerospace Corp. MS B38-35, Bethpage, NY 11714.

EXPERT SYSTEM SOFTWARE FOR TELECOMMUNICATIONS APPLICATIONS

Evelyn Roman
Assistant Professor Computer Science

Polytechnic Institute of New York
333 Jay Street, Brooklyn, New York 11201

ABSTRACT

In this paper we discuss the merits of various features of Expert System software tools we have considered in designing Expert Systems for Telecommunications at the Center for Advanced Telecommunications Technology. These Expert Systems help the user to configure, interface and troubleshoot a network with components obtained from different vendors. Because of the wide variety of new products and the complexity of their compatibility requirements and system interactions, the easily modifiable heuristic rule-based features of Expert System software tools were needed. The match capabilities of Carnegie Mellon's OPS5 tool were useful for the database search techniques required in our first multivendor system. The use of cooperative knowledge sources, as in HEARSAY III, or probability propagation, as in the PROSPECTOR or EXPERT tools, were appropriate features for a more complete Expert System. The University of Maryland's YAPS tool was investigated because of a possible analogical task planning ability.

INTRODUCTION

During the past year, in our work for the Center for Advanced Telecommunications Technology, we have been investigating various Expert System software tools, and have been using them to build or design sample Expert Systems dealing with the problems of network configuration, interfacing, and fault diagnosis in a multivendor environment. From[1] we see "As systems become more complex, it is increasingly less likely that a single vendor offers all the devices and services required and even less likely that each of the vendor's offerings is the best available of its type. The trend towards multivendor systems has been accelerated by international standards efforts on open system architecture." A network configuration system is used to determine the type and model of system elements to achieve prescribed system objectives while guaranteeing compatibility. Interfacing instructions can then be given, and the fault diagnosis program can be used by maintenance personnel or users to troubleshoot the resulting network.

In a typical Expert System there is a clear separation between a Knowledge Base of facts and problem-solving rules, and a Control mechanism which decides when to apply each rule. This is in contrast to conventional computer programs where it has been more difficult to incorporate easily modifiable heuristic rules. Recently, the structures of several domain-specific Expert Systems have been abstracted into Expert System software tools. These tools have made the task of developing an Expert System simpler than, for example, writing it completely in the LISP programming language. The particular software tools chosen to implement our telecommunications Expert Systems depended on the type of knowledge incorporated therein. We will concentrate on three types of knowledge: information which is certain, uncertain information, and analogical information.

We used Carnegie Mellon's OPS5[2] tool when the knowledge in our system was given with complete certainty to be true, false or unknown. For example, in our program the user will specify with complete certainty whether a printer prints letters correctly, doubly, or not at all, and the system will give an appropriate response. The facts are stated in terms of object-attribute-value expressions, as in our statement (make v ^printer-response (accept)), where the printer-response attribute of the "object" v is given a value typed in by the user (i.e. accepted).

Often, because of the seemingly random nature of our particular knowledge domain or because of a lack of complete information, we must deal with uncertain knowledge. We will now discuss four different methods of handling such uncertainty. Carnegie Mellon's Hearsay III[3] tool handles uncertainty by allowing for the incremental construction of competing solutions. It supports the codification of diverse sources of knowledge, incorporating domain-dependent consistency constraints which are applied to the competing solutions. Bayesian systems such as Prospector/KAS[4] assume that the apriori probabilities of antecedents (evidence) and consequents (hypotheses) of production rules are known.

This research supported by the New York Foundation for Science and Technology as part of its Centers for Advanced Technology Program.

When the probability of the antecedent is updated by the user, the probability of the consequent is updated by the system by multiplying by a factor which is interpolated between the number 1 (paired with the apriori probability of the antecedent) and a given likelihood ratio factor (paired with the certain knowledge of the antecedent). In a Bayesian system, all the possible outcomes must be disjoint, which will not necessarily be the case in a fault diagnosis system in which two faults may occur simultaneously. An alternative approach would be to use a tool incorporating, with each assertion, a certainty factor defined as the difference between a measure of belief (MB) and a measure of disbelief (MD) of the assertion, i.e. CF=MB-MD. For more than one observation, we then repeatedly use the formula

$$MB(h,o_1 \ \& \ o_2)=$$

$$MB(h,o_1) + MB(h,o_2)*(\text{Maximum possible increase in the belief of hypothesis } h \text{ after observation } o_1)$$

and a similar formula for MD. Finally, fuzzy Expert System software tools enable one to incorporate uncertainty in the language itself, by defining fuzzy terms using probability distributions. For example, one might say that $100 is "low cost", for a particular problem, with a probability of 90% whereas $500 is "low cost" with a probability of 15%.

Whether the knowledge is certain or uncertain, we have been interested in the problem of incorporating analogical problem solving knowledge in our systems. We have conjectured that the object-oriented programming features incorporated in some recently developed software tools can be used for this purpose. In the FLAVORS's object-oriented programming style, rather than having objects (data) passed to procedures, programs send messages to objects specifying the name of an operation (method) to be performed. New objects and operations (abstract types, flavors) may be created by mixing several component flavors. Hence, as in[5], both a ship and a meteor may contain a moving object component. The operations performed on an object may be inherited from the "general" method of one of its components or this component method may be preceded by some operations ("before demons") or succeeded by some operation ("after demons") to provide a method for the basic type containing the component. We will discuss later on the possibility of using the FLAVORS abstraction hierarchy to incorporate analogical problem solving information.

OPS5

For our prototype system, we started in the restricted domain of matching peripherals such as printers, modems, process and control devices, and local area networks to personal computers.

We used Carnegie Mellon's OPS5[2] software tool, in which objects are declared to have various attributes and those attributes are given particular values in the production rules. A built-in data-driven deductive mechanism determines which rules' conditions hold and hence which rules' actions are to be performed, resolving conflicts by essentially, choosing that rule whose conditions were put most recently in the database. The match and search capabilities of OPS5 made it convenient to implement our menu-driven consultation system, in which the user specifies what type of configuration, interfacing, or network testing information he needs, and the Expert System responds appropriately. After choosing a particular computer-printer or computer-terminal model combination, the user is given the appropriate RS-232C pin cross connections.* For testing, the user is reminded of various transmission mode, speed, parity, polarity, and flow control compatibility requirements, and is guided through various diagnostic procedures. By choosing desired values for various network component parameters, the user is able to have a particular brand and model from the database recommended by the Expert System, as illustrated in our sample output in figure 1 below.

To see a suggested modem model first type in suggested price -

```
500       - if less than $500
1000      - if between 500 and $1000
1000+     - if greater than $1000
500
Now type in maximum baud rate desired either 300
9600 1200 or 1200+
300
Now type in computer interface type desired-either
direct or RS232C
RS232C
Type in phone interface type desired-direct or
acoustic
direct
A-recommended-modem-is Bizcomp1022 with-maxi-
mum-baudrate 300 and- computer-interface-type
RS232C and-phone-interface-type direct and-
the-following-additional-features 110-300bps-Bell
103-autodial-autorepeat-autoanswer-fullduplex-self-
test-onboardmicro-$249
```

Figure 1. Sample OPS5 output and user response.

Figure 2 below gives an excerpt of the OPS5 code which produced the output in figure 1. In production rule 01 (i.e. "p 01", in figure 2) we have - if the value "a" to a previously answered question is modem (i.e. the user wants to choose a modem), she should type in suggested pricerange (modem2 ^price), maximum baud rate (modem3 ^baud), computer interface type desired (modem4 ^cint), and phone interface type desired (modem5

_____

*An interesting discovery we made was that only 4 different types of cross connections were necessary for the majority of RS-232C configurations - we later learned[6] that 6 different color-coded connectors to handle over 85% of the asynchronous RS-232C world were being manufactured to capitalize upon this fact.

^pint). In production rule 02 (i.e. "p 02", figure 2) we have -if the values typed in (renamed <p> <b> <c> <i> for matching purposes) match the values for a modem brand in the database (where a sample database model is Bizcomp1022 with price (less than) $500 and other specifications listed) then print out the brand name and all the specifications.

```
(p o1
    (v ^a modem)
-->
    (write |To see a suggested modem model
    first type in suggested price-
           500        -if less than $500
           1000       -if between 500 and
$1000
           1000+      -if greater than $1000|)
    (make modem2 ^price (accept))
    (write |Now type in maximum baud rate
    desired either 300 9600 1200 or 1200+|)
    (make modem3 ^baud (accept))
    (write |Now type in computer interface type
    desired- either direct or RS232C|)
    (make modem4 ^cint (accept))
    (write |Type in phone interface type desired-
    direct or acoustic|)
    (make modem5 ^pint (accept))
(p 02
    (modem2 ^price <p>)
    (modem3 ^baud <b>)
    (modem4 ^cint <c>)
    (modem5 ^pint <i>)
    (modem ^name <n> ^price <p> ^baud <b>
^cint <c> ^pint <i> ^features <f>)
    (v ^a modem)
-->
    (write A-recommended-modem-is <n> with-
maximum-baudrate <b> and computer-interface-type
<c> and-phone-interface-type <i> and-the-
following additional-features <f>)

    (make modem ^name Bizcomp1022 ^price 500
^baud 300 ^cint RS232C ^pint direct ^features
110-300bps-Bell103-autodial-autorepeat-autanswer-
fullduplex-selftest-onboardmicro-$249)
    (make modem ^name Bizcomp1012 ^price 1000
^baud 1200 ^cint RS232C ^pint direct ^features
autodialrepeatanswer-fullduplex-110-1200bps-Be
11103-212-$649)
```

Figure 2. Sample OPS5 code.

HEARSAY III

DEC's R1 (now XCON) Expert System[4] to complete customer's orders and determine configurations for their VAX computer systems, had also been built using the OPS language family. However, since DEC's program dealt with only one company's products, the size of the search space, optimization requirements, and degrees of uncertainty were not as great as in the multivendor environment we were interested in dealing with. Although, for our sample Expert System, OPS5 was adequate, we felt that for a larger more complete configuration program, it would be more useful to decompose the knowledge base into several separate interacting production rule systems, and also to allow for competing hypotheses.

We found that Carnegie Mellon's Hearsay III[5] software, with its opportunistic scheduling of cooperating knowledge sources, provided this capability.

In HEARSAY III, originally used for speech interpretation, independent cooperating knowledge sources post and respond to various levels of hypotheses arranged hierarchically on common "blackboard" data structures. (One usually defines at least two blackboards, one for domain competence knowledge and one for meta-knowledge affecting performance and dealing with knowledge source scheduling). The implementation of the domain blackboard hierarchy is through the use of the ROLE-OF relation incorporated in the AP3 relational database underlying the HEARSAY software. One defines "choice sets" containing alternatives for certain of the UNITS composing the hierarchy, which can be hypothesized within the framework of a particular blackboard context belonging to a context tree. User-defined acceptance routines determine whether currently considered hypotheses are consistent with results from other blackboard levels, and hence see whether a particular context should be eliminated (poisoned) from the context tree. In a multi-vendor configuration environment we have separate documentation sources dealing with individual component specifications, and interfacing and system interactions. We also have the constraints incorporated in network function (capability), reliability, response time performance, and cost requirements. We found HEARSAY III's knowledge sources structure could capture the documentation source and "grammatical" constraint requirements knowledge, in much the same way that the HEARSAY II Speech Understanding[7] program's knowledge sources had represented "grammatical" information on which signals tend to combine into words, words into sentences, etc., in its signals words sentences hierarchy. The basic hierarchy in our network design application consists of the following blackboard levels:

network (i.e. particular configuration)

network component (modems, printers, etc. - particular types, models, etc.)

component characteristics (modem rates, printer speeds, etc.)

Speech constraints such as "u" always follows "q" get replaced by network constraints such as "high speed printers require parallel interfaces."

The speech understanding problem also used several domain Knowledge Sources which could be used directly in our domain, such as BUBBLE-ACCEPTANCE which marks UNITS to be reaccepted by traveling up the blackboard hierarchy. In addition, some of the scheduling Knowledge Sources in the speech application, such as the scheduling of acceptance routines before the solution-detection Knowledge Sources routine, could be used directly in our system. Most of our scheduling Knowledge Sources, reflecting the order in which subproblems are undertaken and decisions are made, would be tailored to our particular domain and to the particular user who might prefer to do, for example, one type of optimization before another type. As in the application of the Hearsay structure to planning in[8] there are in general several possible solutions in our applications, as opposed to only 1 solution in the original interpretive application to speech understanding. By limiting or expanding the size of choice sets in our application we are able to make the problem small enough for an initial pilot program or large enough to handle as many new brands, features, or standards of network components as is desirable. In general, the conceptual framework underlying the HEARSAY III software was very useful. However, the implementation of the knowledge sources and scheduling routines in Hearsay III must be written in INTERLISP, which can be difficult for anyone not thoroughly versed in this language.

FRANZ-LISP-YAPS-FLAVORS

One of our research interests is to incorporate analogical task planning abilities in a system such as in our network configuration application. If a new task for our network configuration Expert System is analogous (similar) to a configuration task whose plan has already been discovered by the Expert System, we do not want to have to replan from scratch. We have conjectured that object-oriented (FLAVORS) programming techniques can be used for this purpose, and are currently implementing a system along these lines, using the University of Maryland's FRANZ-LISP-YAPS (Yet Another Production System)-FLAVORS software distribution[9]. Winston in[10] has noted that abstraction may be necessary before matching analogous situations, and if we define analogous as "having a property in common with," we immediately come up with an abstraction hierarchy of objects and operations similar to that in the FLAVORS system. We are investigating ways of applying appropriate before and after demons to transform the old configuration into the new.

OTHER TOOLS

A more complete fault diagnosis program incorporating probabalistic reasoning, which OPS5 lacks, could be built with a tool such as SRI's PROSPECTOR[4] or Rutger's EXPERT.[4] We have discovered at least one vendor which is collecting statistics on fault occurence which can be used to estimate the apriori probabilities and likelihood ratios in a Bayesian system such as PROSPECTOR, or the certainty values in a system such as EXPERT. For the configuration system, we may eventually want to incorporate the use of fuzzy terms such as a "low cost" network, where "low cost" is defined by a probability distribution, for

the general configuration policies the designer has in mind. Software tools such as REVEAL[11] are available for this purpose. The user, console, monitor, and system specification knowledge involved in a larger, more complete fault diagnosis program would also require some real-time Expert System software development, such as in[12] where timing mechanisms and concurrency extensions to OPS5 were introduced.

Expert System software tools which can run on microcomputers have obvious commercial advantages. It is possible to implement backward chaining search procedures even in as simple a language as BASIC[13], and we have developed a linked list implementation of some of the OPS5 search and pattern matching abilities in PASCAL. A student and a colleague of ours have developed a version of Rutger's EXPERT software tool in C, in conjuction with their work at Bell Corp.[14]. Languages such as MU-LISP[15] are readily available for microcomputers.

CONCLUSION

In conclusion, we have found there exist several moderately priced Expert System software tools available which can simplify the programming task to varying degrees. One must guard against the danger of tailoring one's application to the particular tool available. We have been aiming for a deep enough understanding of the basic building blocks of these tools, so that in the future we will be able to modify the tool or build a custom made tool when the fit is not right.

References

[1] Van Slyke, Richard, "Documentation Methods for Multi-vendor Systems," Center for Advanced Telecommunications Technology, Feb. 1984.

[2] Forgy, Charles, "OPS5 User's Manual," Dept. of Computer Science, Carnegie Mellon University, 1981.

[3] Fickas, S., "Hearsay III Introductory Manual," University of Oregon, Sept. 1983.

[4] Hayes-Roth, F., D. Waterman, D. Lenat, "Building Expert Systems," Addison-Wesley, 1983.

[5] Weinreb, D., David Moon, "LISP Machine Manual," Symbolics Inc., July 1981.

[6] Data Communications, August 1984, p. 54.

[7] Webber, B., N. Nilsson, "Readings in Artificial Intelligence," Tioga Press, 1981.

[8] Hayes-Roth, Barbara and Fred, Stan Rosenschein, Stephanie Cammarata, "Modeling Planning as an Incremental Opportunistic Process," Rand Corp., Santa Monica, California.

[9] Allen, Elizabeth, and University of Maryland A.I. Group, "YAPS" (TR-1146) and "Franz-Lisp Environment" (TR-1226), 1983.

[10] Winston, P., "Learning and Reasoning by Analogy," Communications of the ACM, Dec. 1980, Vol. 23, No. 12.

[11] Negoita, Constantin, "Expert Systems and Fuzzy Systems," Benjamin/Cummings, Inc., 1985.

[12] "YES/MVS - A Continuous Real Time Expert System," Expert System Group and Installation Management Group, IBM Thomas Watson Research Center, Yorktown Heights.

[13] Byte Magazine, Sept. 1981, p. 264.

[14] Chou, R., Wang Tsai, Steve Radtke, "BES/SSD Expert System Providing Diagnostic Support for Large Scale Software Systems," Bell Communications Research Report.

[15] Mu-LISP-83 Manual, The Soft Warehouse, Honolulu Hawaii, 1983.

Additional Readings

[1] Kirshenbaum, Aaron, "Tools for Planning and Designing Data Communications Networks," Network Analysis Corp., 1984.

[2] Seyer, Martin, "RS-232 Made Easy," Prentice-Hall, Englewood Cliffs, 1984.

DESCRIPTION AND APPLICATION OF A SOFTWARE TESTING METHODOLOGY

John G. Brautigam   Marianne E. Erdos

Hazeltine Corporation
Greenlawn, N. Y.   11740
(516) 261-7000

ABSTRACT

We have developed a unique acceptance test methodology to ensure proper operation of all purchased
software tools. This methodology is based on both
general software testing principles and some specific
principles unique to our approach. Our test methodology comprises five major steps: verification of
correct installation, valid input test, boundary
conditions test, extraordinary input test, and
benchmarking. Problems uncovered are documented
and submitted to the vendor for resolution.

INTRODUCTION

We are coming to use more commercially developed
software in our software systems development. This
has spawned a need for a systematic methodological
approach to assessing the quality of the software that
we buy. We have discovered that many organizations
put commercial software into use after only the most
rudimentary acceptance tests, and sometimes with no
tests at all. Jensen and Tomies[1] describe some
alternative testing methodologies useful in acceptance testing, and present typical error types that
may be used to design tests to discover typical
defects during testing. We have recently developed
and are now applying a software testing methodology
based upon general software testing principles.
Goodenough[2] and DeMillo[3] both present selection
criteria for test data that may be used in conjunction
with our testing methodology.

This paper discusses the form of and application of
our software acceptance test methodology. A
description of our methods of software acceptance
testing is presented. Then, the application of our
methodology to the testing of a commercially
developed software configuration management tool is
discussed.

THE BASES OF OUR METHODOLOGY

A method of acceptance testing used by some organizations is simply to let the users apply the newly
acquired software product and monitor what happens.
If the activities undertaken by the users are
relatively non-critical, or if the project schedule is
flexible, this method may work. However, a formal
methodology for testing is needed, especially where
great reliability is a factor, or where the application
is mission-critical and would be threatened by the use
of commercial software of unknown quality. We
believe that the using software developer should not
be caused to waste time on haphazard "testing" of
development tools while he is engaged in the software development process. Accordingly, we have
developed a five-step methodology that we use to
test any commercial software that we purchase. This
methodology allows us to provide a thorough evaluation of purchased software prior to its release to the
software developers. Our methodology is illustrated
in the flow chart in Figure 1. This process is based in
part on the description of test types contained in
Reference [4].

We note also that we prepare a formal test plan for
each occasion of application of our method. This
ensures thorough, relevant, and effective use of this
testing process because it describes the specific
implementation of our methodology as it applies to
the testing of the specified tool.

OUR FIVE-STEP METHODOLOGY

In the first step in our methodology we install the
software as the vendor prescribes in his installation
manual. We require that this include executing
vendor-provided tests to ensure that the software has
been installed correctly. Successful completion of
these tests is necessary to confirm to us that the
software in ready for the next steps in our methodology - the acceptance test kernel.

184

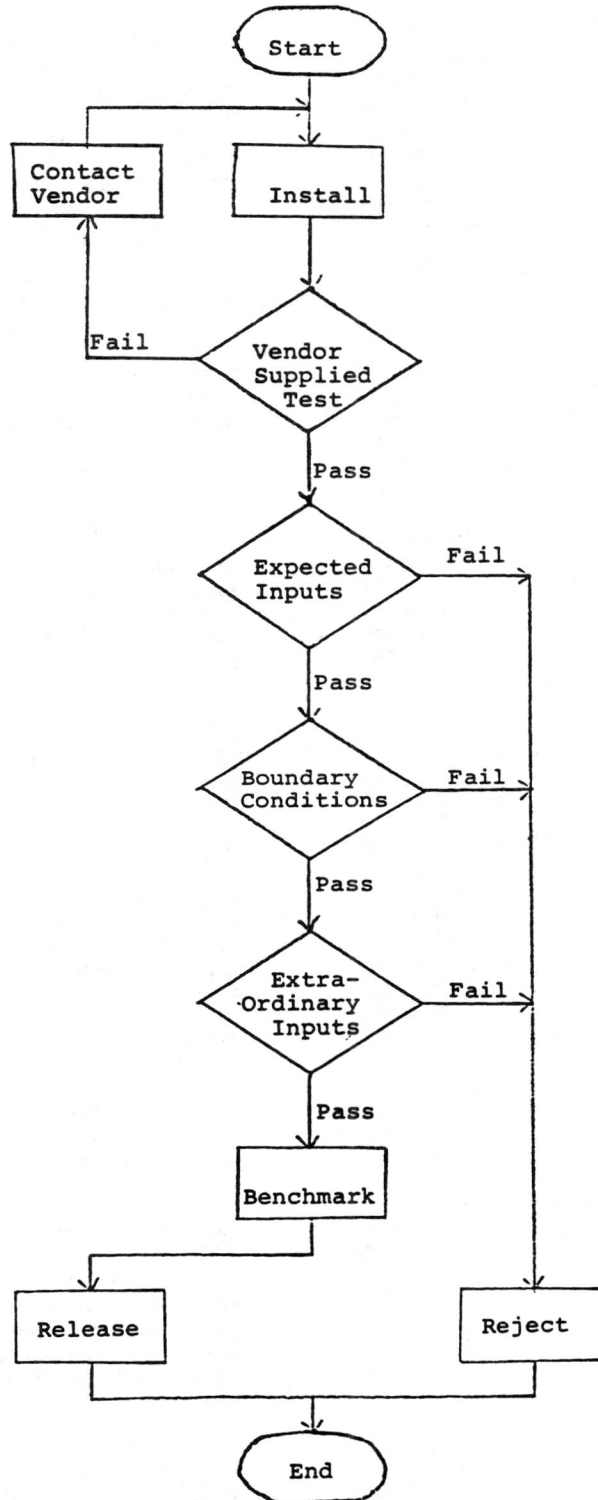

Figure 1. Steps of the Software Testing Methodology

Our Acceptance Test Kernel

The next three steps in our methodology comprise the kernel of our battery of acceptance tests. Three types of tests are used here. These differ based on the type of input applied to the software undergoing testing. These three test types have been devised to ensure a comprehensive test of the new software in an environment that is similar to that in which the software will actually operate in production.

Type One: Testing With Expected Input

The first of our three acceptance test types uses normal, valid (i.e., expected) inputs. Here, each command valid for the software under test is executed using correct input only. The object of this test is to make sure that the software does indeed operate in accord with Vendor's product description and specifications. Since it is not possible to test all combinations of correct input data for a non-trivial software system, we carefully select typical data or data simulating the usual anticipated activities of one or more users. The output from this test (as for all our tests) is examined both manually and by machine for any errors, and for confirmation that the program does indeed perform correct transformations of the input data or correct actions based on the input data. Of course, with valid input data and valid commands, no errors are expected in this test.

Type Two: Testing with Boundary Conditions

In our second type of test, we use input data that should constitute limits to or boundary conditions on the normal or valid input data. The object of this testing step is to assess how the software under test performs under trying conditions. Tests in this category may include, for example, numerical inputs that approach their maximum and minimum allowable values, and may also include inputs that imply or represent demands on host computer resources that tax the performance of the software under test. We use these results to assess how the software will operate in a heavily loaded environment. Output from this test should include predictable errors as well as expected error-free output.

Type Three: Testing With Extraordinary Inputs

In this test, we make an exploration of the software's response to extraordinary and/or pathological inputs. We have decided that this test must consist of at least the following:

1. Input that contains known errors.

2. Input that contains data values outside the normal range.

3. Input that would not be correct or appropriate especially as a function of the state of or operating mode of the software under test.

The expected output from this test step is a collection of error messages and software responses that indicate that the software does in fact recognize the extraordinary or pathological input as being illegal and has reacted to that input as described in the Vendor's documentation (usually, the user's manual or the system manager's guide). This test is important: we decide that if the software accepts as valid or normal input known to be erroneous, and if it operates on that faulty input as if it were valid, a problem exists in the software under test that is serious enough to declare the product unacceptable.

Assessing The Results of Our Kernel Tests

At the conclusion of the kernel acceptance tests, we make a three-step assessment of the tool. We decide to accept or reject the tool based on this assessment.

First, the tool must not produce any errors when tested with valid commands and valid input data. Second, the tool must perform within Vendor's standards for boundary conditions. For example, if the Vendor reports that a linear increase in the tool's response time is to be expected as the number of simultaneous users increases, then if an exponential increase were to be observed, we would judge this to be unacceptable. Finally, the tool must react in a correct manner to extraordinary data. Correctness here may be defined as producing a proper error message for a given invalid input, or as producing an expected or understandable transformation on invalid data.

We combine the results of the kernel tests to reach a balanced conclusion on acceptability by objectively applying assessment steps similar to the typical ones cited above.

Our Last Step: Benchmark Tests

Our final test step comprises a benchmarking or performance evaluation test in which the software is examined for, among other things, memory and disk space requirements, typical execution times, and overt effects on host system load and performance. We consider this last test step to be benign: rarely does a software product fail the benchmark test. Our experience shows it to be an unusual case where the software performance is very far out of step with the information contained in the software product documentation. In short, the information discovered in this last test step should be interesting, but not surprising or damaging.

General Application Statistics

The methodology described above has been applied extensively in our laboratory. The final acceptance testing at our Company of eight different tools has depended on the outcome of tests developed according to our methodology. Of the tools so tested, two have failed.

The number of tests in each of the five test phases has varied from tool-to-tool. The variances are based upon the type of tool under test, our knowledge of the tool and its typical uses, and the applicability of the specific test phase to the tool. For example, in the tests for the Software Configuration Management Tool, described in the following section, the test phase with expected inputs contains 120 individual tests and the test phase with extraordinary inputs contains more than 100 tests. The number of tests for each phase, while larger than is typical, was employed in this instance because of the large number of users expected for this tool.

AN APPLICATION OF OUR TEST METHODOLOGY

Recently, we purchased a Software Configuration Management Tool (SCMT) to help us keep track of code development and to be able to determine exactly at what stage in the software development process any particular user project might be. The test methodology described in the previous section was applied. Our methodology enabled us to perform a quick and comprehensive test. While our testing techniques might seem elaborate, we needed to be sure of the quality of a tool that would subsequently be used extensively and as a matter of routine throughout our Company. In the following section, we describe the details of application of our testing methodology to this important rather substantial tool. The application described takes up our methods at the point where the software product had already been successfully installed according to Vendor's installation procedures.

In the test applications, we introduced iterative incremental changes in the input test sets. Every successful test repetition resulted in a subsequent iteration that employed a larger portion of the total test set. The end result was that the tool was exposed to the entire test in one run. Basically, each test phase was run individually; then a set of test phases was run; finally, the whole test set, one which combined all test phases, was employed in the test .

Testing the SCMT with Normal Input

The first part of our test plan implemented that portion of the test methodology that assessed the behavior of the SCMT in the presence of expected inputs. To do this, we developed a user scenario that would require executing each command of the SCMT in a sequence that was typical of that expected to be employed by users in applying the tool for controlling software development. This scenario was expressed as elements of a VMS command file on our host VAX 785 computer that defined an empty database to be used especially for this test.

In general, the scenario simulated the various manipulations expected of a database administrator, of a project manager, and of two software engineers in their use of SCMT. The operations performed during the test included moving files into and out of the database, allowing access to and denying access to portions of the database, retrieving information about the status of the database, and reviewing transaction behaviour expected of actual users of the database.

Because of its relation to a scenario of normal expected use of the SCMT, errors, or unexpected or unexplainable results produced in this part of the test would have indicated the possibility of very serious problems in the SCMT design or implementation. In our test plan, the SCMT was required to pass all the tests in this portion of the acceptance methodology or we would have summarily rejected this product.

Before selecting the particular SCMT from those commercially available, we developed a set of criteria for an ideal SCMT. We selected our SCMT based on its ability to fulfill more of the criteria than any other SCMT then available. Seven major areas of consideration were the basis for our criteria. These areas were:

1) data integrity in the database
2) access controls over the database
3) database organization
4) operations and commands
5) outputs and reports
6) interfaces to other software
7) applicable standards, military and commercial

Because of the importance of these selection criteria, we developed tests to demonstrate that the SCMT did in fact meet each criterion.

Failure of the SCMT to meet any particular specific criterion would have indicated some inconsistency between the documentation and the software. This could prevent effective use of the tool by software developers, and would have been considered to be a fatal indictment of the quality of the product (or, at least, of its documentation, and therefore, of the Vendor's quality control and market sensitivity).

Testing The SCMT With Data Defining Boundary Conditions

The SCMT passed the first step in our Methodology. Subsequently, we applied the remaining kernel tests previously described. The nature of the SCMT suggested to us that there would be three user-created situations which could define conditions of stress for the product:

1. The existence of multiple software configurations for the same software product under development.

2. The existence of multiple databases reflecting several different unrelated configurations.

3. The presence of multiple concurrent users for each case described.

These areas were also of interest because they lead, at times, to very large demands upon the SCMT, and possibly, on the host computer as well.

Tests To Determine Adequacy to Deal With Multiple Configurations

We developed a specific set of tests to assess the ability of SCMT to deal with operationally defined boundary conditions. The existence of a large number of separate software configurations simultaneously controlled by SCMT is usual and actually is to be expected when SCMT is employed extensively. Accordingly, the multiple configuration test was devised by defining a single database, and by employing a command file script that continually added configurations to the database (in the test case by cloning already existing configurations). SCMT performance under these boundary or limit conditions was monitored during this test, in particular, to determine how the SCMT executed a particular database edit operation on a randomly selected text file within the database, as a function of the number of configurations being controlled. Both the loading of the database on the host computer, and the relative access times to the text file being edited were monitored.

The criteria for passing this section of the acceptance test kernel were: (1) satisfactory accurate SCMT operation without extraordinary demands on host system resources, and (2) SCMT program execution rates in an acceptable range.

We note that this test was not run to benchmark the SCMT's performance when handling multiple configurations: We sought to demonstrate that, under the stress of supporting many configurations within a single database, the SCMT could operate correctly and effectively.

Tests To Determine SCMT Capability To Deal With Multiple Databases

Another set of boundary-condition tests of the SCMT was designed to assess the reaction of this tool when it was required to service multiple databases. (The design of the SCMT required that a separate detached process for each database be defined when run under the VAX/VMS operating system). When SCMT is executed under VAX/VMS, the number of databases that may simultaneously be active on the host VAX is limited by the VMS-imposed limit on the number of simultaneous active processes. This limit protects the SCMT from the deleterious effects of servicing too many databases at one time.

Tests To Determine SCMT Response To Multiple Concurrent Users

The SCMT design is intended to support multiple concurrent users of a single database. This is a very real situation that the SCMT would have to accommodate in actual use. We implemented our methodology kernel so that this situation would be simulated by executing a large number of command files all accessing a previously configured SCMT database simultaneously. In this test, the VMS detached process set up to execute this test queued the requests for access to the database, thus allowing only one access at a time. We needed to answer the important question: what are the consequences of a large number of users trying to access a single SCMT database at the same time? This test, of course, is another example of how we implemented our boundary and/or limit-values philosophy with due regard for the specific characteristics of the software product under test.

Testing The SCMT With Extraordinary and Pathological Inputs

This part of the SCMT acceptance test implemented that part of our methodology which exposes the software under test to extraordinary and/or pathological input. It contained two distinct test components:

1. The error test component;
2. The invalid inputs test component.

The purpose of the error test was to provide such inputs as to force SCMT to reproduce all the error messages described in the documentation for the SCMT. This test tests the robustness of the software product. Careful analysis of the tool's response to the test also served as a springboard from which additional invalid inputs were devised, and against which the outputs from these additional SCMT inputs could be interpreted.

The Error Test Component

Error messages produced by a commercial software product may be assumed to be purposeful system responses that reflect the Vendor's anticipation of user mistakes commonly made when the product is used. The SCMT has more than 100 error messages provided within it. Each of these more than 100 error messages was provoked by executing the tool's operation with a purposefully composed sequence of commands, these sequences being combined into a single command file that attempted to produce all errors publicized for the SCMT. The results we were interested in producing were: messages that were unexpected based upon the inner logic of the commands; or the absence of an error message for a specific sequence of commands that ought to have provoked one; or error messages that could be provoked singly but which could not be provoked when their provoking conditions were combined with other ones so that those error messages were inhibited in some way.

The Invalid Inputs Test Component

Extraordinary, invalid, or pathological inputs to SCMT were synthesized with input data and command parameter values outside known normal ranges, or in the wrong form, or in the wrong sequence, or that were invalid with respect to the current state of the SCMT test database. Our selection of invalid input was also based on the anticipated future actions of SCMT users and project managers. For instance, since a text editor for modifying program text being controlled by the SCMT would be used more often than a "change user password" command, illegal inputs to the text editor were selected more frequently and examined more closely than were illegal inputs to the "change user password" command.

Benchmarking SCMT Operations

The last step in our five-step methodology assesses test-system performance by benchmarking some of the leading features and/or characteristics of the SCMT tool. This test also gathers information about the operational and/or performance maximums and minimums to be experienced using the SCMT. While the benchmark test might appear to be similar to the kernel tests described above, we emphasize that the purpose here is to gather performance information about the SCMT, rather than to produce abnormal conditions, to assess the response to unusual inputs, or to provoke unusual outputs from SCMT. The information required from this benchmark included determination of values for "best" database size, for "best" number of users using a single database, and for "best" concurrent number of SCMT databases. Host system loading effects traceable to running the SCMT were also anticipated observables expected from this test. Finally, information was also sought regarding the robustness of SCMT operation when it is executed under a complex operating system that provides operational features that could lead a naive user astray.

SUMMARY

The amount of time lost by software developers when using untested faulty purchased software; the critical nature of much of the data entrusted to commercial software; and the amount of money spent on acquiring commercially produced software all make acceptance testing of such software imperative. We have developed a method that ensures thorough testing of purchased software. By properly installing the software; by testing tool behaviour in the presence of expected inputs, boundary condition inputs, and extraordinary inputs; and by benchmarking the software, we obtain a composite of performance against which tool quality may be assessed. Our method has instilled much confidence in our installed tools among our user community. By systematically uncovering the tool's defects, we can ensure that our software developers are able to do their work without costly surprises. A comprehensive acceptance test based on methodology such as is described and illustrated in this paper ensures that purchased software performs as advertised.

REFERENCES

(1) Jensen, Randall W, Tomies, Charles C., Software Engineering, Prentice-Hall, Englewood Cliffs, N. J., 1979.

(2) Goodenough, John B., et al., "Toward a Theory of Test Data Selection", The Proceedings of the 1975 International Conference on Reliable Software.

(3) DeMillo, "Hints for Test Data Selection: Help for the Practicing Programmer," IEEE Computer, Vol. 11, No. 4, April 1978.

(4) Shooman Martin L., Software Engineering: Design Reliability and Management, McGraw-Hill, New York, N.Y., 1983.

Modified January 3, 1985

A METHODOLOGY FOR EVALUATING SOFTWARE TOOLS

Stuart Glickman, IEEE Member and
Mark Becker, IEEE Member, ACM Member

Corporate Information Systems
General Electric Company • Building 30EE • 1285 Boston Avenue • Bridgeport, CT 06602

Abstract

Tasks are essential to human activities. Given a task, one must select an appropriate tool. At times this is a simple choice but as problems grow more complex it is often difficult. One way to look at the problem is that the most sophisticated tool is the best tool. There are obvious drawbacks to this approach which actually could negatively affect cost and schedule of a project. This paper steps back from the final decision of which of a tool's characteristics should be chosen to first evaluate the characteristics of a software product for each possible Application Universe. Each product characteristic is then measured against a broad range of management criteria. Finally, the characteristics a tool might offer to the developer is measured for criticality against these management criteria. The product of these three matrices then indicates for each tool characteristic, its critical impact on the application universe one might find oneself in.

Index Terms — Tools, Process Criteria, Product Criteria, Decision Analysis, Application Universe.

Software tools are needed today due to the increasing complexity of software, the increasing importance of software within systems and the need to show that finished products meet specifications. It is commonly known that the demonstration of software correctness is very expensive, whether it be by proof of correctness or by testing. An interesting technique to rationally reduce this cost is explored in [2]. If we could significantly reduce the size of the program to be tested, then our costs would similarly decrease. In their paper they explore the possibility of a smaller program which acts as a kernel program. The kernel program is then extended automatically by source-to-source transformations to become the intended larger program. One method by which economy of scale may be obtained is by having a tool that aids transporting of programs from one machine to another. Their study has gone beyond transportability and precision issues to higher levels of commonality where multiple realizations could be applied.

Due to the increasing cost of software and the large proportion of the software budget devoted to maintenance, there appears to be a need to decrease the overall cost of software projects. One way to attack this problem is by automating some portion of the software lifecycle. In [6], Manley discusses the issue of obtaining the software factory via computer aided software engineering. Computer aided software engineering is the use of microprocessor based software tools for both development and support. The software factory appears to be much more appreciated by Japanese society than ours. Japan seems to be much more comfortable with applying practical tools, whereas we are much more drawn to the latest technological fads.

In [9], the software environment starts to be mapped out and the experimental tools that could fit into niches in this environment start to be examined. Previous efforts in the use of software tools had not reduced cost or improved quality. The catchwords for the new generation of tools is to provide tools which actually aid software engineers in their work. Because of the cost of attaining and using tools, one should select a tool set and use it repeatedly. Previously tools (editors, compilers, linkers), were very narrow in their application or were not noticeably user friendly. The software environment is defined for those tools that would be continuously applicable to the software developer in his or her day to day work. The maintenance software environment would be involved with tools which facilitate the analysis of code, provide for configuration control of the software, and aid in the testing of changed software.

In the large scale production environment, tools should aid in the defining of requirements; creating, controlling and verifying the coding and testing, and finally allowing the altering of code and design requirements. In the management environment, tools should handle resource allocation issues and provide a means to observe the software production and track the progress of the project. Finally, in the quality assurance environment, tools are needed to determine the presence or absence of errors. The software environment is also discussed in [12], where it is indicated that the tool DSEE can handle history management, configuration management, and task management. An interesting feature of this tool is advice management. When a change is made, all modules which call the affected module are alerted, and task management will automatically assign tasks to the responsible module designers.

As can be seen from the above, there are a great many tools that could be applied across the spectrum of possible applications. We will tackle the problem first by looking at the typical set of product characteristics in the context of possible application universes. The product characteristics chosen are indicated in Matrix 1. Language characteristics refer to whether the program source was in assembler to whether it was developed in a very high order language. CPU utilization and I/O utilization refers to the percentage of utilization that the application program would be expected to have. Boundedness refers to whether the program is I/O bound, algorithm bound, or control structure bound and to what degree. Memory utilization (% machine) is similar to the other utilizations consided. Task clock refers to the efficiency issues demanded of a particular application. Change life cycle describes how frequently the program would be expected to require change. Single to multi processors refers to the range of tasks that a software application would be involved with. Degree of interactive processing is involved with the question of the frequency that control is released from one processor to another. Bare machine utilization concerns the question of how much of the hardware is utilized. Finally, design methodology refers to the degree of sophistication of design.

An explanation of some elements of the y-axis is indicated below:

Business Program

This is a business oriented program, often relatively small and ready for use by the author or co-worker's instructed in its use. Documentation is often limited.

Business Program Product

This is a business oriented program that "can be run, tested, repaired, and extended by anybody. It is useable in many operating environments, for many sets of data."[3] It is primarily I/O intensive and the computations that it performs involve simple algorithms.

Business Program System

This is a "collection of interacting programs, coordinated in function and disciplined in format, so that the assemblage constitutes an entire facility for large tasks."[3] The individual tasks are similar to business program products.

Scientific Programs, Program Products, and Program Systems

These are scientific or engineering tasks that are algorithm bound and computationally intensive. They perform relatively little I/O.

Real Time Programs, Program Products, and Program Systems

These are event driven tasks and activities which are bound by strict time constraints. Real Time activities almost always involve asynchronous tasks which must communicate with one another.

We then intuitively correlate the elements of the x and y axis. Though it is a judgement issue, it is probably a much easier task than the final analysis would have had to be.

The scaling is indicated below:

Definitions of Matrix Elements — Matrix 1

The elements within this matrix have a normalized range from 1 to 7. The scale signifies the importance of the independent variable with respect to the dependent variable. The scale is given below:

1 — No impact whatsoever
2 — Very minor impact
3 — Minor impact
4 — Noticeable impact
5 — Significant impact
6 — Very significant impact
7 — Extremely significant impact

				Product Characteristics							
Appli. Universe	Lang. Char.	CPU Util.	I/O Util.	Bound-edness	Mem. Util. % Mach.	Tsk Clk	Chg. Life Cyc.	Single-Multi Procr. (SW/HW)	Deg. of Inter. Procg.	Bare Mach. Util.	Desn. Meth.
Bus. Program	6	2	3	2	1	1	3	4	1	1	3
Sci. Program	6	3	1	2	1	3	3	4	1	2	4
Real Time Prog.	6	4	1	2	1	7	3	4	5	4	4
Bus. Prog. Prod.	7	3	4	4	2	1	3	4	1	2	3
Sci. Prog. Prod.	6	5	2	4	3	4	3	4	1	4	4
R/T Prog. Prod.	6	5	3	4	4	7	3	4	5	7	4
Bus. Prog. Sys.	7	4	5	5	3	2	3	4	4	4	3
Sci. Prog. Sys.	7	6	3	5	4	2	4	4	5	4	4
R/T Prog. Sys.	7	7	4	5	6	7	5	6	5	7	6

Matrix 1: The correlation of Software Product Characteristics to its applicable application universe.

Matrix 2 is developed along a similar theme, but here the question is the critical impact of a software products characteristics versus a set of management criteria.

Maintainability

Perhaps the most pressing problem in software engineering today is maintainability. "Software maintenance is the performance of those activities required to keep a software system operational and responsive after it is accepted and placed into production."[7]

Quality

Software quality [11] is a measure of the degree that a software product meets its stated requirements.

Costs

Software cost is the total cost of developing a software product. Its components include analyst, designer, and programmer time, training costs, machine costs, software tool costs as well as overhead and management.

Schedule

Schedule is a measure not of the absolute time required to complete a given task but rather of the degree to which the schedule is going to be overrun. The authors choose to expect overrun because of the 1st Law of Project Management: "No major project is ever installed on time, within budget or with the same staff that started it."[1]

Productivity

For some authors it is the number of validated lines of code produced on a daily basis by programmers[11] whereas others include the time spent by analysts and designers.

The criteria for Matrix 2 and 3 are indicated below:

Definitions of Matrix Elements — Matrices 2, 3

The elements within these matrices have a range of from 1 to 7. The scale signifies the critical impact of improvement in the independent variable on the dependent variable. If the independent variable increases, there is then a corresponding increase in the dependent variable. One of the easiest cases to consider is that of language — as the language one uses in a project goes from machine language to assembler to an HOL, then the maintainability of the software improves markedly. Another example is that of the significance of the task clock or restraints. As the time restraints become tighter, maintainability suffers as the programmer is forced to "get tricky" or take advantage of seldom used OS or language features. The scale is given below:

1 — Significant negative impact
2 — Moderate negative impact
3 — Minor negative impact
4 — No impact
5 — Minor positive impact
6 — Moderate positive impact
7 — Significant positive impact

Product Characteristics	Process Characteristics				
	Maintainability	Quality	Cost	Schedule	Productivity
Lang. Charac.	5	7	6	5	6
CPU Util.	3	2	2	2	3
I/O Util.	3	2	2	2	3
Boundedness	3	2	2	2	1
Mem. Util. % Mach.	1	1	2	2	1
Task Clock	1	1	3	3	2
Change Life Cycle	1	1	1	1	2
Sing. to Multi.Proc.	2	1	4	2	3
Deg. of Interactive Processes	3	1	1	1	3
Bare Mach. Util.	3	4	2	2	3
Design Methodology	7	6	6	5	5

Matrix 2: Critical impact of each software product characteristic against a set of management criteria.

The final matrix we need to evaluate before we can answer the question of what tool characteristics are appropriate to our particular application is matrix 3. Some of the terms used in the x-axis are explained below.

Code Generation

Code generation in the context of this paper means the capability of producing human and machine readable text suitable for input into one or more compilers or interpreters.

Application Generation

Application generation is the capability to generate a complete application ready for use to include reports, query screens, or update screens, given a user's non-procedural statement of requirements.

Test Generator

Automatic testing or test generation is the capability to create one or more sets of test data based on the user defined requirements (black box testing).

4GL

A fourth generation language is English like and non-procedural. They are often closely tied to a relational data base manager.[4] They have been often praised as the way out of the current "Software Crisis" because they can often allow end users to solve their problems without involving programmers. Also see the works of James Martin.

Design Logic Analysis and Validation

This refers to the capability of a tool to aid the user in analyzing his design and validating it. Tools that have this property can perform a variety of services ranging from proof of correctness to ensuring calling interface compatibility.

Design Decomposition

Tools with design decomposition capability can aid the user in performing hierarchical decomposition of the design—starting at the top and working down to ever finer levels of the design.

Methodology Independent

If a tool exhibits methodology independent characteristics then it does not require the user to alter his existing design methodology. Although this is ostensibly a desirable feature as it reduces the training time needed to use the tool it means that the tool may offer increased flexibility at the expense of ease of use.

Online Documentation

A tool with online documentation offers the user the ability to access a subset of the tool's documentation while the user is using the tool. Several types of online documentation exist. The most useful is a context sensitive help function where the tool is able to supply documentation appropriate to the task at hand. Less useful is context insensitive where the user explicitly asks for documentation on a given subject.

Graphics and Text Capabilities

A tool having graphics and text capabilities will support a high resolution graphics station and will provide the ability to draw and annotate designs.

File Nesting

A tool with file nesting capability will support a generalized "Include" function. Any document or drawing created using the tool can be included in the document or drawing currently being worked on.

Data Flow Diagrams

Support for data flow diagrams is closely tied to graphics support as well as decomposition although it is certainly possible for a tool to have both of these features without providing a mechanism for manipulating data flow diagrams. Ideally, a tool with this capability will provide a simple mechanism for "exploding" diagrams as well as moving rapidly from a level with a great deal of detail to levels higher in the design chain.

Structure Charts

A tool with support for Data Structure charts permits the user to define both input and output data structures, and will presumably support the Jackson or Warnier-Orr methodologies.[11]

Source Editor

A source editor is a screen or line oriented editor. It is primarily used for editing programs rather than documentation.

Syntax Checker

A syntax checker is a program used while editing a program source file. It validates the syntax of program text as it is being entered, rather than during the compilation phase.

High Level Debugger

A tool that supports a High Level Debugger aids the user in debugging compiled code as it permits him to interactively debug using source code and variable names rather than debug his program using the time honored technique of inserting "Write" statements at (in) appropriate points in his program, compiling, linking, and trying all over again.

Tight Integration

A tool exhibiting tight integration is composed of a number of tools that share a similar user interface and common files.

Reuseability

A tool with this property produces output that is reuseable. The best example of this would be a code generator where once the output code was created it could be used by as many people who need it. At the other extreme is a fourth generation language which is usually interpreted.

Central Data Base

A central data base is used to store documents, definitions, programs, drawings, and the like. It is particularly useful on medium and large scale projects, allowing multiple users concurrent access to up-to-date definition of variables, and access to design and program documents and code.

Host Communication

Host Communication refers to the capability of a work station centered tool to communicate drawings, definitions, programs, and the like to a (larger) host.

Networking

Networking is similar to Host Communication with the difference being that the workstations communicate directly with one another rather than via a central host.

Project Management

A tool with a project management capability permits a manager to allocate resources and track schedules. The ideal project management tool would be tightly integrated with the design tools and permit a manager to know that all components of the design have been assigned, that documentation is on schedule, and test plans reflect requirements.

Configuration Control

Configuration Control permits the user to manage the various versions of his programs, files and documentation.

Matrix 4 is the products of the previous matrices and renormalized to be within the range from 1 to 7.

Tool Characteristics for Application Processes	Maintainability	Quality	Cost	Schedule	Productivity
Code Generation	6	6	5	6	7
Applica. Generation	7	7	7	5	7
Test Generation	4	5	3	4	4
4GL	7	7	6	7	7
Design Logic Anal. & Valid.	6	6	4	4	6
Decomposition	6	5	6	4	6
Methodology Indep.	2	2	2	2	1
Online Documen.	4	4	4	4	4
Graphics & Text	5	5	4	4	5
Word Processing	4	4	4	4	4
File Nesting	6	4	4	4	5
Data Flow Analysis	6	4	4	3	5
Structure Charts	6	4	4	3	5
Conventional Source Editor	4	4	4	4	4
Syntax Directed Editor	5	4	4	5	5
High Level Debugger	5	5	5	5	5
Tight Integration of Tools Within Pkg.	4	5	3	3	5
Reuseability of Output	6	6	7	6	7
Central Data Base Used by Tools	5	6	4	4	5
Host Communication Provided by Tool Pkg.	4	5	3	3	4
Networking Environment Avail.	4	4	4	4	4
Project Management Facilities in Tool Set	4	4	7	7	4
Configuration Control	7	5	5	5	4
Support of Multi-Tasking by Generated Application	5	5	4	4	4

Matrix 3 Transposed: The critical impact factor for tools characteristics versus certain management criteria (Process Characteristics). These values being averages over the entire development effort.

Tool Characteristics for Application Processes	Bus. Prog.	Sci. Prog.	R/T Prog.	Bus. Prog. Prod.	Sci. Prog. Prod.	R/T Prog. Prod.	Bus. Prog. Sys.	Sci. Prog. Sys.	R/T Prog. Sys.
Code Generation	4	4	5	4	5	5	5	5	7
Appli. Generation	4	4	5	5	5	6	5	6	7
Test Generation	3	3	3	3	3	4	3	4	5
4GL	4	4	5	5	5	6	5	6	7
Des. Logic Anal. & Valid.	3	3	4	4	4	5	4	5	6
Decomposition	3	4	4	4	4	5	4	5	6
Methodology Indep.	1	2	2	2	2	2	2	2	2
Online Documen.	3	3	3	3	3	4	3	4	5
Graphics & Text	3	3	4	3	4	4	4	4	5
Word Processing	3	3	3	3	3	4	3	4	5
File Nesting	3	3	4	3	4	4	4	4	5
Data Flow Analysis	3	3	4	3	4	4	4	4	5
Structure Charts	3	3	4	3	4	4	4	4	5
Conventional Source Editor	3	3	3	3	3	4	3	4	5
Syntax Directed Editor	3	3	4	3	4	4	4	4	5
High Level Debugger	3	3	4	4	4	5	4	4	6
Tight Integration of Tools Within Pkg.	3	3	3	3	3	4	3	4	5
Reuseability of Output	4	4	5	4	5	6	5	6	7
Central Data Base Used by Tools	3	3	4	3	4	4	4	4	5
Host Comm. Provided by Tool Pkg.	2	3	3	3	3	4	3	3	4
Network Envirn. Avail.	3	3	3	3	3	4	3	4	5
Proj. Mgmt. Facil. in Tool Set	3	3	4	4	4	5	4	5	6
Configuration Control	3	3	4	4	4	5	4	5	6
Support of Multi-Tasking by Generated Appl.	3	3	4	3	3	4	4	4	5

Matrix 4 Transposed: The critical factors for a tools characteristics versus the required application universe.

Definition of Matrix Elements — Matrix 4

The elements of this matrix are the multiplication product of matrices 1, 2, and 3. The range of values has been normalized to fall within 1 and 7. The values indicate the relative utility of choosing a tool with a particular characteristic given a particular class of problems. The value 7 means that a given characteristic is extremely desirable. As one moves from R/T Program Systems toward Business Programs, the complexity of the program, product, or system decreases and therefore the need for the higher index also decreases. Tool characteristics are not mutually independent and the choice of one may obviate the need for another.

Conclusion

Given a tools characteristics which it would inpart to the process of developing software in a particular application universe then one could refer to Matrix 4 to discern how critical that feature was. With this methodology, one could pick a tool set applicable to one's needs.

Reviewing Matrix 4, the following observations can be made. For a Real Time programming system it would be most desirable if a tool had the following characteristics:

Code Generation
Application Generation
Fourth Generation Language
Design Logic Analysis & Validation
Decomposition
High Level Debugger
Reuseability of Output
Program Management Facility in Tool Set
Configuration Control

References

[1] "Laws of Project Management," AGS Management Systems, 1983.

[2] J. Boyle and M. Matz, "Automating Multiple Program Realizations," Proceedings of the Symposium on Computer Software Engineering, Fox, Ed., Brooklyn, NY: Polytechnic Press, 1976.

[3] Frederick P. Brooks, "The Mythical Man-Month, Essays in Software Engineering," Addison Wesley, Jan. 1982.

[4] D.F. Coble, "Fourth Generation Languages will impact productivity — If ...," Data Management, July 1982.

[5] Paul Gillin, "Computer aided software engineering: Automating DP," Computerworld, Aug. 20, 1984.

[6] John H. Manley, "Computer Aided Software Engineering (CASE) Foundation for Software Factories," IEEE Compcon '84 Fall Conference on the Small Computer (R)Evolution Proceedings, IEEE Computer Society, Sept. 1984.

[7] Roger J. Martin and Wilma M. Osborne, "Guidance on Software Maintenance," National Bureau of Standards, 1983.

[8] Edward Miller, "Tutorial: Automated Tools for Software Engineering," IEEE Computer Society, Nov. 1979.

[9] Leon Osterweil, "Software Environment Research: Directions for the Next Five Years," IEEE, Computer, Apr. 1981.

[10] Terrence W. Pratt, "Programming Languages: Design and Implementation," Prentice Hall, 1975.

[11] Roger Pressman, "Software Engineering: A Practitioner's Approach," McGraw-Hill, 1982.

[12] Tom Williams, "Network Environment Manages Software Engineering Projects," Computer Design, Mar. 1984.

Stuart Glickman is a Senior Software Engineer for General Electric's Corporate Information Systems. In this position he is responsible for Software Metrics, Reliability, and Test. He received a B.A. in Physics from Queen's College, CUNY in 1967, and M.B.A in Operations Research from Baruch College in 1967, and an M.S. in Computer Science from Polytechnic Institute of New York in 1984. He is a member of the IEEE Computer Society.

Mark Becker is a Senior Software Engineer for General Electric's Corporate Information Systems. His responsibilities include internal consulting within GE, development of a UNIX based Software Engineering Workstation as well as serving as an instructor in Software Engineering Courses. He received a B.S. from MIT in 1970 and an M.S. in Civil Engineering from MIT in 1972. He is a member of ACM and IEEE and was formerly the Chairman of the Fairfield County, CT IEEE subsection. He is currently Vice Chairman of Outings for the Fairfield County Sierra Club.

Session 6

Future Tools

Chairman
M.E. Erdos
Hazeltine

A LIFE CYCLE ENVIRONMENT FOR INTERACTIVE INFORMATION SYSTEMS

B. I. Blum

The Johns Hopkins University/Applied Physics Laboratory
Laurel, Maryland 20707

ABSTRACT

This paper describes a collection of integrated tools designed to support the life cycle of an interactive information system (IIS), i.e., a "Life Cycle Environment." Such a concept differs from the present efforts relating to "programming environments" in that the objects managed by the environment are applications (i.e., IISs) and not programs. Moreover, the scope of the "life cycle environment" goes from initial requirements documentation through operational support; it is not limited to the "fabrication" (or programming) activities.

The paper begins with a brief overview of the software process and the life cycle. Linkages between methods, tools and environments are considered and a method for IIS development based upon the use of automated tools is described. It then is shown how this method can be supported by an environment with a design database containing all information about an application.

An implementation of this environment is presented. It includes tools for requirements analysis, top level design, semantic data modeling, rapid prototyping, and documentation preparation. It uses program generation to create the object system and has integrated tools to support a relational database, text processing, and system evolution. The environment has been in use for four years; some operational experience is detailed.

1. INTRODUCTION

The Software Engineering Planning Group recently identified the Software Engineering Technology Hierarchy shown in Figure 1. [1] The highest node represents process descriptions, e.g., life

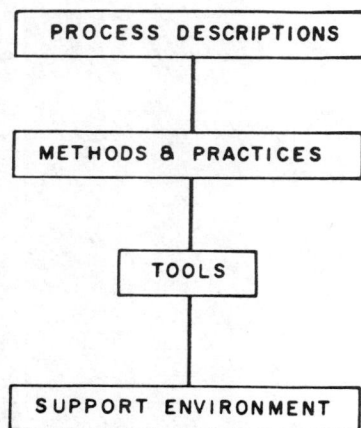

PROCESS DESCRIPTIONS

METHODS & PRACTICES

TOOLS

SUPPORT ENVIRONMENT

Figure 1.   Software Engineering Technology Hierarchy

cycle models. For each model there is a set of methods and practices. Each method defines a set of tools, and each support environment represents an instantation of a set of integrated tools. Upon reflection, the model will be recognized to be a network in that individual environments, tools and methods have more than one parent. Nevertheless, the figure clearly illustrates the linkage between life cycle models and environments.

In this paper we describe an integrated set of tools for the life cycle support of a specific class of application. This implies (a) that the set of tools forms a true software environment and (b) that the environment is structured to support the life cycle model most appropriate for the application class. Thus, the set of tools is not generalized, rather it is tied to a specific method. The purpose of the paper is to describe the objectives and functions of the tools so that (a) they may be understood in the context of their use, and (b) concepts related to them can be transported to other application environments.

The discussion first considers the environment in the context of the application class, its life cycle model and method. Next there is a description of some of the tools in the environment. Finally, there is a brief evaluation of the environment which has been in production use since 1980.

2.   GENERAL CONSIDERATIONS

The application class being considered is the interactive information system (IIS). These systems are characterized by their reliance upon a database, a dependence upon user inputs and actions, the absence of severe real time or computational constraints, and an implementation as an organic (as opposed to embedded) system using off-the-shelf equipment and software tools. The environment, TEDIUM,* has been designed to support all aspects of the life cycle for this specific class of application. The present implementation has been evaluated for a single target language and projects of 30 effort years and smaller. There is reason to believe that alternate target languages or larger projects can be supported. However, there is no evidence that the environment is suited to other application classes. In this sense, TEDIUM is similar to other application specific tool sets, e.g., Toolpack, an environment targeted for mathematical applications using FORTRAN. [2]

2.1   The Life Cycle

Figure 2 presents a very high level view of the software process. Three transformations are identified. The first is from a real world environment into a problem statement. The result is a statement of what is to be implemented, i.e., requirements. Once a problem statement has been provided, it is transformed into an implementation statement. This is typically considered the design process. Finally, the implementation statement is transformed into an operational system. In the case of software, this involves code

---

*   TEDIUM is a trademark of Tedious Enterprises, Inc.

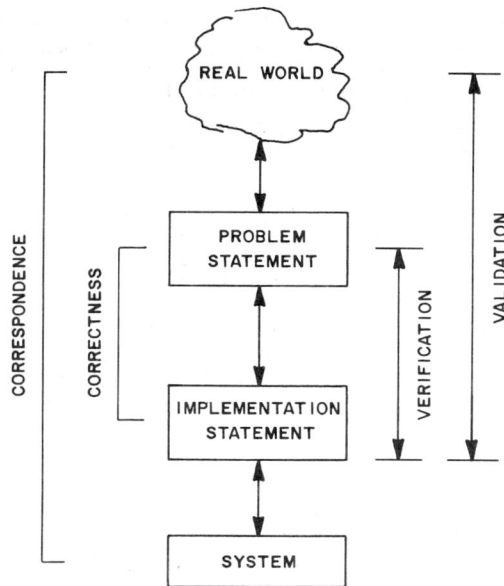

Figure 2. The Software Process

and debug followed by test and integration. The system is then embedded in the real world, thereby modifying the real world and causing another iteration of the process.[3]

In the case of an IIS, the three transformations have the following characteristics:

- **Formulation of the Problem Statement.** This is generally a poorly defined process. The target application is to reside in the real world and alter or enhance some decision making or production process. Thus, it is likely that a product will be developed which will not meet the real world needs (i.e., it will have high application risk).

- **Formulation of the Implementation Statement.** Where the Problem Statement is complete and accurate, this transformation applies rules for system design which are generally accepted. Although there are various methods available, the primary difficulty is in the management of details, the satisfying of constraints, and the trading off among alternatives. When, as is commonly the case, the Problem Statement is not sufficiently explicit, there is also a degree of application risk in this transformation.

- **Creation of the System.** Relative to most other application classes, the transformation of an IIS design into an IIS implementation is a well understood process. Off-the-shelf systems and tools are generally used (e.g., DBMS), and it is seldom that one cannot implement a design successfully. That is, there is low implementation risk.

The life cycle is more commonly displayed as a sequence of activities in a cascading (or waterfall) orientation. Methodologies and tools are then associated with activities in that sequence. Although the previous diagram illustrates the process to be supported, it will be helpful to link the tools to a more conventional view of the life cycle. Using the notation of Freeman and Wasserman,[4] there are the following six processes.

- **Analysis.** This is the preliminary understanding of the problem which results in the definition of the requirements.

- **Functional Specification.** This is a transformation of the requirements (what is to be done) into an external design of how it should be done.

- **Design.** This is a translation of the functional specification into a set of structures which can be implemented as computer programs.

- **Implementation.** This is the translation of the design into executable code. This also implies the testing of the coded units.

- **Validation.** This is the process of assuring that each unit or set of units satisfies its functional requirements. This actually is performed in several steps culminating in an operational acceptance of the entire product.

- **Evolution** (also denoted as Operations and Maintenance). This consists of defect removal and modifications in response to new requirements. (New in the sense that they were not defined in the initial analysis.)

It can be seen that Analysis represents the first transformation, Functional Specification and Design the second transformation and Implementation and Validation the final transformation. Evolution is not shown in Figure 2 because the figure represents a single iteration of the process. It is known that some two-thirds of the life cycle cost is for evolution,[5] and, that it has been characterized as experimentation with the current prototype.[6] Evolution involves all three transformations.

Finally, before concluding this subsection, some comments on Validation are in order. Figure 2 also illustrates some Verification and Validation (V&V) concepts. Verification measures how well a product conforms to its formal requirements. The property of satisfying these criteria is called correctness. Verification (and correctness) have meaning only in the context of a specific set of requirements. Validation, on the other hand, is a subjective projection of the product's utility in the real world. There are no measures, and the most important validation must be performed before products have been implemented. Once the system has been implemented, its ability to meet the needs of the target environment is called correspondence.

The distinction between verification and validation is frequently confused. For example, consider the statistics in Table 1.[7] Where programs had defects which would not allow them to perform as specified, they would be incorrect. However, where the programs did not do what was needed or desired, they would not correspond, i.e., be invalid. In this case, 2% of the software was both correct and corresponded. In general, we know that only 20% of the maintenance costs are for defect removal and some 55% are for enhancement.[5] If we extend these ratios to the data in Table 1, then most of the problems were probably related to invalid products, e.g., solving the wrong problem or implementing an inappropriate (but correct with respect to the contract) design.

Table 1. GAO Report on Software Development Contracting

45% of software contracted for could not be used
29% of software contracted for was never delivered
19% of software contracted for had to be reworked to be used
 3% of software contracted for had to be modified to be used
 2% of software contracted for was usable as delivered

2.2 Method

There are many methods available to implement IISs. They are typically grouped into two categories:[8]

- **Data Flow Oriented** approaches in which processes are identified and linked to each other by the flow of data. Examples are structured analysis as presented by Yourdin, DeMarco or Ross.

- **Data Structure Oriented** approaches in which the structure of the data is first modeled and the system organization then is derived from it. Examples are the methods of Warnier, Jackson or Orr.

Each of the approaches places major emphasis upon a notation which is used to communicate with the users to assure correspondence of the final product. Once the analysis is complete and a model of the system exists, each method suggests ways to perform the second transformation in order to produce an Implementation Statement. This statement is usually in the form of a PDL which can be transferred to code.

The method chosen for TEDIUM makes heavy use of automated tools. Thus many of the concerns associated with manually based methods are eliminated, and the method is free to focus upon the underlying issues. It assumes the existence of the following automated support:

- **Database Management System (DBMS)** functionality. Once a semantic data model of the application domain can be established, it may be readily transformed to a DBMS schema which frees the designer from many of the concerns about data-structures.

- **Program Generation.** Because the IIS implementation process is well understood, much of it can be abstracted in the form of high level specifications which can be transformed to implementable source code. This implies that the specification is produced during the Design activity and that the Implementation activity is eliminated.

- **Housekeeping Free Specification.** It has been shown that over 95% of the code may be used for functions which simply support the underlying purpose of the system. [9] By providing a specification language which minimizes the need for housekeeping, smaller specifications can be produced. These will be easier to understand and will improve productivity.

If these automated tools are available, then the designer should have the ability to rapidly produce models of the target system which can be experimented with by the designer and user. One technique for doing this is called rapid prototyping. [10] A prototype of some portion of the system is implemented quickly, tested in the user's environment (i.e., real world), and then discarded. The knowledge gained from this experimentation is formalized in the requirements document; that is, rapid prototyping is an Analysis activity. The method used by TEDIUM differs from rapid prototyping in that the automated tools generate complete prototypes which are experimented with by the designer and the user. Modifications are made to the specification and a new iteration is generated. Each generated product is complete with respect to the system model, e.g., it performs all error tests on inputs, responds to help queries. The technique is called system sculpture.

Since the method is built upon these automated tools, it has been possible to implement TEDIUM using TEDIUM. One result is that all design activities are viewed as IIS activities. This implies that a reliance upon a design database (DDB) which contains all documentation and implementable objects for each application. This DDB is used to produce prototypes, generate documentation, and support Validation and Evolution.

2.3 Tools and Environments

The term software tool is broadly defined. [11] On the one hand it includes portions of a software development environment which are considered essential, e.g., compilers, link-loaders, and editors. On the other hand, many software tools apply automation in support of traditionally manual operations, e.g., documentation support, static testing, and the tools listed in the previous subsection.

An environment is composed of a collection of tools. However, it is more than just a collection. As Osterweil puts it: [12]

> The essence of a software environment is the synergistic integration of tools in order to provide strong, close support for a software job. This environment must have at least these five characteristics: breadth of scope and applicability, user friendliness, reusability of internal components, tight integration of capabilities, and use of a central information repository. A support system must possess these characteristics if it is to merit the name "environment."

How TEDIUM exhibits these characteristics follows; examples of specific tools will be presented in Section 3.

2.3.1 Breadth of Scope and Applicability

TEDIUM is designed to support the full life cycle of an IIS. Generated programs may run on target machines where TEDIUM is not resident; nevertheless, all maintenance of these applications assumes the use of TEDIUM. The orientation of the tools is toward development and documentation scenarios. Because of the target application class, there are few management or dynamic testing tools. Nevertheless, within the scope of the class and size of intended products, there are no design/maintenance functions which are not primarily or completely supported by TEDIUM.

2.3.2 User Friendliness

Osterweil defines this as the ability of the environment to provide strong, unobtrusive, comfortable support. All designer interactions are managed by TEDIUM. There is a consistent style, help messages are provided, and validation of inputs minimizes inadvertent errors. The system has been used by 100 persons at half a dozen installations. Some users have had no previous programming or design experience; some users had no instruction beyond that provided by the user manuals. For persons whose backgrounds were limited to traditional compiled languages, TEDIUM is easy to learn and use. For persons accustomed to unencumbered use of interpretive environments, TEDIUM is a well chosen name. Finally, for persons responsible for the evolution of an application, TEDIUM is appreciated.

There are deficiencies in documentation and error handling. Nevertheless, the user consensus seems to suggest that it is friendly and — even more important — a natural interface for describing the properties of the application to be implemented.

2.3.3 Reusability of Internal Components

Reusability is a topic of major interest to the Software Engineering community. [13] TEDIUM addresses reusability at three levels:

- Reusability of design materials within the application. Because all materials are maintained in the DDB, the method encourages reuse. For example, user manuals are produced from design text and help messages. Maintenance documentation is generated directly from attributes of the implementable objects in the DDB. Naturally, since the DDB is integrated, there is no redundancy of definition.

- Reusability of design materials across applications. There are a variety of tools to copy objects from one

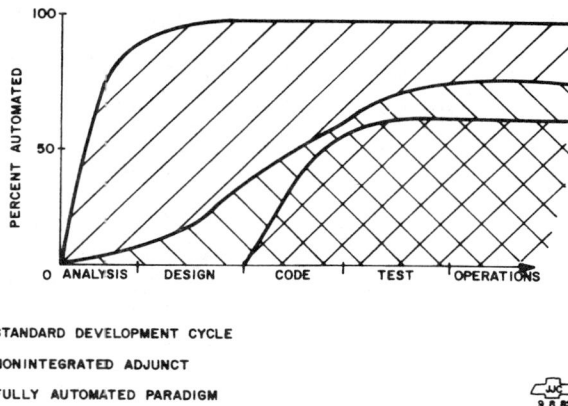

Figure 3. Three Development Paradigms

application set to another. In each case, tests are made to verify that consistency is persevered and that all objects have similar definitions in both applications. More comprehensive tools for sharing definitions are in the planning stage.

- Application independent reusability. Implementation knowledge has been structured in the form of generic programs and a high level specification language. Each formalizes IIS knowledge as "white box" and "black box" structures for reuse. Such knowledge may be modified at the TEDIUM system level to accommodate local requirements.

2.3.4 Tight Integration of Facilities

As previously noted, the user cannot access any of the TEDIUM tools without using TEDIUM. TEDIUM generated applications, on the other hand, may be used without TEDIUM. Figure 3 illustrates three paradigms for development. In the standard paradigm, only the required machine sensible products are maintained in the computer. This is a relic of the era in which computer resources were scarce and their use had to be optimized. The second paradigm introduces tools as an adjunct. TEDIUM is an instance of the fully automated paradigm. The question of tight integration is appropriate only for the tool enhanced paradigm.

2.3.5 User of a Central Information Repository

The concept of a design database (DDB) for each application is fundamental to TEDIUM. The DDB is implemented using a relational data model which provides access to both text and coded objects with fine granularity.

3. SOME TEDIUM TOOLS

This section describes some TEDIUM tools. More complete descriptions of TEDIUM's implementation,[14] tool use,[15] documentation data model,[16] and design concepts[17] have been published elsewhere. In what follows we first describe the process to be supported and the philosophy of the tool's design; then we illustrate how the tool is used.

3.1 Formalization of the Problem Statement

The method used by TEDIUM views the requirements as a text document structured in an outline form, i.e., a hierarchy. Tools are required to enter and maintain both the outline structure and the text contents. The application design is also structured as text documents in outline form. In this case, two documents are required: one for processes which describes the interactions and

functions of the application, and one for data groups which describes the generic organization of the database and any external interfaces. The requirements, processes and data groups are each structured as hierarchies; their nodes are also nodes in a network which links requirements to processes, processes to data groups, data groups to requirements, etc. TEDIUM must supply tools to manage both the hierarchy and network links for editing, listing and auditing purposes.

In addition to the above structures, links are required between design objects and implementation objects, i.e., between processes and programs and between data groups and the table schema. Note that all of this design information is based upon the designer's view of the application; it is subjective and must be manually entered and maintained. TEDIUM requires that this information be entered as part of the final documentation. It provides a "road map" for evolution and a source of text for system documentation. Yet, TEDIUM is permissive in allowing the designer to supply only outline headings (or even bypass entry) until the design decisions are firm. It is the responsibility of management to determine how much documentation is required and when it must be available. The philosophy of documentation is to describe only higher level concepts which are not subject to major change and to confine more detailed documentation to the implemented objects.

Figure 4 illustrates a partial listing of a requirement. Note that the tense and style are appropriate for a user manual. In this case, an initial statement of what the application is to do is now part of the user's documentation. Figure 5 displays an outline of the processes and the programs associated with each process. Only the most important programs are listed; as will be shown below, TEDIUM provides tools to create call trees and show cross-

```
STACK   TEDIUM STACKER

   TEDIUM STACKER

   TEDIUM requires a stacker to queue jobs for both generation and
listing. In the case of program generation, all jobs to be generated are
entered into a queue. If the TEDIUM system is operating in a small
computer which does not support multitasking, then the stacker is started
as a single job. The stacker will read the queue containing jobs to be
generated, generate each, and remove the job from the queue. On the other
hand, where TEDIUM operates in a multijob environment, a stacker job will
be started in the background and it will initiate generation without
interrupting the user processing stream.

   The stacker is also used to produce listings. When in the single user
mode, all requests for outputs must be queued; once a queue has been
formed, the stacker may be started to call the queued jobs which are to be
listed. Since this presupposes a single user environment, the stacker must
allow the user to assign a unit for output. The stacker will then open the
device, run the jobs in the queue directing their output to the device,
and -- when the queue is empty -- close the device.

   When the stacker is to produce output in a multiuser mode, there are
several options. The stacker may be initiated as a background job as soon
as a job is entered into the queue. Alternately, a separate action may be
required to initiate the stacker. The former mode is useful for shorter
jobs; the latter mode is ideal for managing overnight jobs which tend to
use many system resources. Once the queue is empty, the stacker may
terminate; alternately, it may be desirable to keep the stacker active in
a loop waiting for another job to be entered into the queue. Finally, the
stacker may delete jobs from the queue when they are finished or retain
them for later production auditing. Independent of the options chosen, the
stacker must integrate any output with other output produced by the
system. This is done by having the stacker call an open spool routine
before starting and a close spool routine when the queue has been
processed.

   Because there are so many stacker options, the stacker system has
been set up to allow for multiple queues -- each with its unique behavior
parameters. Two queues are provided with the system

      A  Standard printing output queue
      T  TEDIUM generation queue.

These queues have the following characteristics:

                        A    T
      Print output      Y    N
      Auto-start*       Y    Y
      Auto-flush        N    Y

      * Multiuser versions only

   Additional queues may be defined by the local user. Examples are N
for a night time stacker queue, P for a nonprinting processing queue for
small jobs to be acted on quickly, etc. The staker menu (STK) allows the
definition of new queues. The STK and CSTK commands have a QU option which
allows the designer to select the queue for the job to be entered.
```

Figure 4. Partial Listing of a Requirement

```
P      PROCESS STACKER
P.1      ENTER JOBS INTO STACKER QUEUE
         YSTST      SET UP STACKER REQUEST
P.2      PROCESS JOBS IN THE STACKER QUEUE
P.2.1      START STACKER PROCESSING
         STKBG      BEGIN STACKER
P.2.2      PROCESS JOBS IN STACKER QUEUE
         YSTBG      BEGIN STACKER PROCESSING
         YSTBG1     READ IN STK PARMS
         YSTBG2     PROCESSING FOR A SINGLE JOB
P.2.3      STACKER PROCESSING SUPPORT/UTILITY
         YSTERR     STACKER ERROR TRAP
         YSTOPN     OPEN SPOOLER
         YSTCLS     SPOOLER CLOSE ROUTINE
P.3      MANAGE STACKER QUEUES
         SMSTK      STACKER MENU
         STKFL      FLUSH THE STACKER QUEUE
         STKLQ      LIST STACKER QUEUE
         STKLQ1     LIST THE STACKER QUEUE DETAIL
         STKMJ      MODIFY A JOB IN THE STACKER
         STKMP      MODIFY STATUS/PRIORITY
         STKSJ      SET STACKER JOB
         STKSJP     PROCESS STACKER PARAMETERS
P.4      DEFINE/MODIFY STACKER QUEUE PARAMETERS
         STKEQU     DEFINE A STACK QUEUE
P.5      STACKER STANDALONE MANAGEMENT
         MICROS
         TEDIUS     TEDIUM STACKER MENU (S/A)
         SMSTK1     STACKER MENU, SCROLL
```

Figure 5.   Process Outline with Links to Programs

references. Options also exist to include listings of the process text, program text, program-data cross references, etc.

3.2   The Implementation Statement — The Data Model

TEDIUM uses a relational data model and enriches it by providing tools which establish semantic properties. Relations may be organized into structures (hierarchies); relationships between relations may be explicitly defined. Entities may be defined such that a relation will act as a dictionary for an entity. Hierarchical contexts may be defined for entities, e.g., the program "PROG" in the application "TEST". The data dictionary supports enumerated data types and multiple validation criteria. There is a data type called text which uses a text processor for input and output. Elements of type text can be used in any relation as nonkey terms and are integrated into all interactive processing.

TEDIUM provides tools to define and maintain the data model. Every object in the DDB has an identifier, a short name, a text description, and then object-specific details. The text and details are used in help messages as appropriate. Each data element in the data dictionary has validation criteria associated with it. All user interactions automatically test to verify that these criteria are satisfied. Within a specific relation, a data element may be assigned a role; this implies processing which may augment the initial definition.

All defined objects may be listed in a variety of formats, e.g. lists of relations, structures, or data dictionaries. Figure 6 illustrates a portion of a relation definition in the full text format. The text at the element level was designed to be used as an on-line help message in support of data input.

3.3   The Implementation Statement —
Generic Specifications

Certain frequently used processes have been implemented as

```
XSTKA     STACK TASK ABORT MESSAGE          ^XSTK          BIB   07/19/83
                                                           BIB   07/19/83

      This table contains any abort message if a task does not finish normally.

   INDEX TERMS :
YSTQU     STACKER QUEUE                      CHARACTER (1)

             This is the stacker queue identifier.

YSTP      PRIORITY                                      CHARACTER (1)
          0      RESERVED FOR PROGRAM GENERATION
          1      HIGHEST PRIORITY
          2      HIGH PRIORITY
          3      ABOVE DEFAULT PRIORITY
          4      DEFAULT PRIORITY
          5      BELOW DEFAULT PRIORITY

             This is the priority of the job in the stacker queue. It goes
          from 1 to 5 with 4 as the default. A priority of 0 is reserved for
          program generation.

YSTN      TASK SEQUENCE NUMBER               INTEGER (5)

             This is a sequence number for the jobs in the queue.

IKEY      INDEX KEY                          VARIABLE LENGTH (6)
          *** THE INDEX VALUE IN THIS TABLE IS COMPUTED AS "X" ***

   DATA TERMS :
YSTAMS    ABORT MESSAGE                      VARIABLE LENGTH (256)
          ROLE IN TABLE IS MANDATORY

             This message contains information about the status when an
          abort was recorded.
```

Figure 6.   Partial Listing of a Relation, Documentation Format

generic programs. These generic programs require certain nonprocedural statements. Each generic program also has been designed to allow modification by use of procedural statements. The modification cannot communicate outside the function it is designed to augment or replace. Moreover, the processing of the generic program is hidden from the designer and — except for the alterable defaults — is kept secret.

By way of example, assume that a relation R has been defined. The specification of a program to add, edit, delete, or list entries in the relation can be fully specified as

P is an ENTRY program for R

(The actual specification is supplied in a prompting sequence because the program P requires a title and some descriptive text.) The nature of the generated program will be a function of the contents of the relation R. If R contains text data types, then the text processor will be called in at the appropriate time. If R has secondary (related) relations, then these must be updated as well.

Entry programs can be modified in a variety of ways. For example, after all data have been entered and before an update to the database is made, the following prompt is printed

(A)CCEPT   (R)ETRY   (I)GNORE

(A null return will be accepted as the first response, i.e., accept what has been entered.) The user may replace this block with a "no operation" command. In this case, the prompt and associated code will not be generated and processing will resume as if the null option had been selected. Alternately, the designer may enter additional validation code and resume generation with the printing of the prompt.

All generic specifications are prompted for and listed in ways that seem natural to the user. Figure 7 illustrates a portion of a generic MENU program listing.

3.4   The Implementation Statement — Common Specifications

Programs may also be written in the TEDIUM language. Such programs are called common specifications. These statements in the TEDIUM command language tend to be housekeeping free. For example, the statement

```
                 TEDIUM LISTING FOR APPLICATION TEDIUM
      03/22/85
                        SPECIFICATION DESCRIPTION
SPECIFICATION SMSTK                STACKER MENU                      (M)

              BIB  08/05/83         BIB  01/16/85


     This menu is used to manage the TEDIUM stacker.


FRAME STRING 1: TEDIUM STACKER FUNCTIONS

THE FOLLOWING MENU CONTROL IS USED

LINE           TEXT                      COMMAND      PROGRAM

  5    MANAGE STACKER PROCESSING         M,queue
 10    LIST STACKER QUEUE                L,queue      STKLQ
 20    MODIFY JOB                        J,queue      STKMJ
 25
 30    ENTER JOB TO STACKER              E,queue      STKSJ
 35
 40    DEFINE QUEUE                      DQ           STKEQU

THE FOLLOWING PROCESS IS DONE WHEN THE COMMAND M IS ENTERED

          :----------------------------------------------------------:
  5       : I      YSTQU/CMD/MAND                                    :
 10       : G      YSTPRF/XSTKN                                      :
 15       : WR     !,"STACKER QUEUE ",YSTQU," IS ",@WT(YSTPRF)       :
 20   PR  : PR     (Q)UIT    (S)TART    (T)ERMINATE    (F)LUSH       :
          : (R)ESET STATUS                                           :
 22       : ON CONDITION that YC="Q"                                 :
          : N                       ---------------------------------:$QUIT
 23       : ON CONDITION that (YC="S")&(YSTPRF'="I")                 :
          : W      [STACKER CANNOT BE STARTED. RESET STATUS]         :
          :                         ---------------------------------:PR
 25       : ON CONDITION that YC="S"                                 :
          : C      STKBG            ---------------------------------:$QUIT
 30       : ON CONDITION that YC="F"                                 :
          : C      STKFL            ---------------------------------:$QUIT
          :                                      ON ABNORMAL RETURN  :PR
 35       : ON CONDITION that YC="T"                                 :
          : A      YSTPRF="T"       ---------------------------------:PUT
 45       : PR     (A)CTIVE    (I)NACTIVE    (T)ERMINATE AFTER       :
          : JOB//YSTPRF                                              :
 50   PUT : P      YSTPRF/XSTKN                                      :
          :----------------------------------------------------------:

INTERNAL HELP MESSAGES
GENERAL HELP STATEMENT

     This menu provides access to the functions used to manage the TEDIUM
stacker. All functions are associated with a specific stacker queue.
```

This lists the specification for the menu used to control the TEDIUM background job stacker (see Figure 4). There is some preliminary administrative information and descriptive text. Next the menu is defined as sets of tuples <text, command, program>. In this case, for example, entry of the command L will result in a call to the program STKLQ.

The TEDIUM command language is used to create a block to be executed when the Manage Stacker Processing command (M) is entered. Since the stacker manages several independent stack queues, Line 5 begins by prompting for the mandatory input of the desired queue (YSTQU); the CMD option bypasses the prompt if the queue identifier already has been supplied with the command (M, queue). The I command also tests to assure that a valid value has been entered for YSTQU.

The next two lines get the processing status (YSFPRF) from a relation (XSTKN) and then print out the queue and enumerated value for the status (@WT(YSTPRF)). The next line generates a prompt which will set the variable YC to one of the strings in parentheses. (An invalid input will not be accepted.) The following lines are conditional calls and/or returns ($QUIT on the left). Line 45 is reached if the Reset status (R) was selected. It prompts for the new status value and puts the updated value (YSTPRF) in the relation (XSTKN).

Following this block, the help messages are listed. Figure 8 illustrates how the same data are formatted for use in a users' manual.

Figure 7. Partial Listing of a Generic Program Specification

PRompt   (A)CCEPT   (R)ETRY   (I)GNORE

will print the prompt, accept an input and test it for validity. A question mark will result in a help response. (Help messages may be added after program generation.) A null entry will be set to the first valid response, in this case "A". No invalid response will allow passage to the next line, and a special escape character input will cause an "abnormal" return.

A description of the language is beyond the scope of this paper. The following tools are available when processing common specifications in the TEDIUM language:

- Syntax validation at time of entry.

- Automatic conversion to and maintenance in a standard pretty print format.

- Immediate access to a query function which displays program names, relation contents, element definitions, etc.

- Immediate access to utilities for global search and replacement, copying of other programs, etc.

3.5 System Implementation and Test

TEDIUM uses a program generator. The main advantage of generation is the efficiency of the resultant program. Unlike many generators, TEDIUM generates complete programs which are treated as object code; all design and maintenance is done at the TEDIUM level. This implies that TEDIUM should be able to generate code in a variety of target languages.

The TEDIUM generator performs many of the testing functions associated with a static analyzer. With each generation, cross references to tables and programs are updated. All TEDIUM programs tend to be small. The length is about 15 lines, and few cannot fit on one or two CRT screens. Consequently, the emphasis is on specification comprehension and not debugging. Thus, it would be reasonable to say that the TEDIUM tools are deficient in the testing area and rely heavily upon the power of the host environment.

3.6 Document Generation

As previously noted, the DDB is viewed as a resource for documentation preparation. One tool — the user manual preparation system — allows the designer to structure a manual from fragments of documentation, documentation functions and other manuals, e.g., requirements text, help messages, the data dictionary. Figure 8 illustrates a portion of a user manual which describes the use of a menu. It is built from the menu specification and its help messages. (See Figure 7.)

3.7 Application Evolution

Since all information about the application is maintained in the DDB, there is a rich resource to support evolution. Data are organized at two levels:

- **Subjective.** This includes text, cross reference links, etc. It provides top level descriptions and provides a road map to the application. It must be maintained by the designer and should be at a reasonably high level of description.

- **Objective.** This includes all implemented objects. Since TEDIUM uses program generation, the specifications represent the operational system and there is no variation between the detailed design and the final product.

Tools are provided to peruse the subjective data, identify links to objective data and list (or display) specifications, etc. For example, the display shown in Figure 5 could — on option — be

```
STACKER MENU                          MENU DESCRIPTION
:-------------------------------------------------------------------:
:                                                                   :
:     FUNCTION                    ENTER                             :
:                                                                   :
:  MANAGE STACKER PROCESSING      M,queue                           :
:  LIST STACKER QUEUE             L,queue                           :
:  MODIFY JOB                     J,queue                           :
:                                                                   :
:  ENTER JOB TO STACKER           E,queue                           :
:                                                                   :
:  DEFINE QUEUE                   DQ                                :
:                                                                   :
:  ENTER:                                                           :
:-------------------------------------------------------------------:


:---------MENU DESCRIPTION -----------------------------------------:
:                                                                   :
:      This menu provides access to the functions used to manage the :
:  TEDIUM stacker. All functions are associated with a specific     :
:  stacker queue.                                                   :
:-------------------------------------------------------------------:


:---------COMMAND DESCRIPTIONS-------------------------------------:.
:                                                                   :
:  COMMAND M,queue                                                  :
:                                                                   :
:      This command allows the user to perform the following        :
:  functions:                                                       :
:                                                                   :
:      Start the stacker. This will either transfer control to the  :
:      stacker in a single user system or start up a stacker job as a:
:      separate task.                                               :
:      Terminate the stacker. This will set a flag to have the      :
:      stacker terminate as soon as the current stacker task is     :
:      complete. It is used only in multiuser situations.          :
:      Flush the stacker. This will delete any entries in the stacker:
:      queue which are complete. If the stacker is empty, it will    :
:      also reset the job number.                                   :
:      Reset the status. This can be used to alter the status of a   :
:      stacker in the event of recovery from a failure.             :
:  Modifications to a stacker queue may be done with the LIST command.:
:                                                                   :
:  COMMAND L,queue                                                  :
:                                                                   :
:      This command allows the user to list the contents of any     :
:  stacker queue. The listing may be done in the page mode in which  :
:  each entry is listed in a single line. There is also a step mode in:
:-------------------------------------------------------------------:
```

Figure 8. Partial Listing of Menu Description

printed with the specifications of all referenced programs appended. The cross references are always current; they may be accessed directly (Figure 9) or used to produce a call tree (Figure 10). Both displays are available on-line or off-line; printed displays on option, also can be produced with specification listings.

4. EVALUATION

TEDIUM has been in production use since 1980. Four major clinical information systems at the Johns Hopkins Medical Institutions have been implemented with TEDIUM. Each is in daily operational use. The largest of these is generaly accepted as the most comprehensive clinical information system used by a cancer center.[19] It operates on two PDP-11/70s, supports 60 clinical terminals, is composed of over 5,000 programs and uses a database defined by 1,000 relations. TEDIUM installations exist in four states, the District of Columbia and Australia. As previously noted, approximately 100 people have been trained in its use. Virtually all of TEDIUM has been written in TEDIUM.

```
STKBG     BEGIN STACKER

          CALLS          YSTBG

          CALLED FROM     SMSTK

          READS TABLES    XSTKN     XSTKQ

          WRITES TABLES   XSTKQS
```

Figure 9. Cross Listing for a Program

```
        STKBG    BEGIN STACKER                        ^UTMOD9
          YSTBG    BEGIN STACKER PROCESSING           ^UTMODG
            YSTBG2   PROCESSING FOR A SINGLE JOB      ^UTMODQ
              YSTBG1   READ IN STK PARMS              ^UTMODH
              YSTCLS   SPOOLER CLOSE ROUTINE          ^UTMODN
                ^%SC                                  ^UTM
                ^YSYTH                                ^UTM
              YSTOPN   OPEN SPOOLER                   ^UTMODM
                ^%SO                                  ^UTM
                ^YSYTH                                ^UTM
          ^YSYIN                                      ^UTM
        STKEQU   DEFINE A STACK QUEUE                 ^UTMODA
        STKFL    FLUSH THE STACKER QUEUE              ^UTMODB
        STKLQ    LIST STACKER QUEUE                   ^UTMODC
          STKLQ1   LIST THE STACKER QUEUE DETAIL      ^UTMODD
          STKMP    MODIFY STATUS/PRIORITY             ^UTMODE
        STKMJ    MODIFY A JOB IN THE STACKER          ^UTMOEJ
          STKMP    MODIFY STATUS/PRIORITY             ^UTMODE
          STKSJP   PROCESS STACKER PARAMETERS         ^UTMOEI
        STKSJ    SET STACKER JOB                      ^UTMOEH
          STKSJP   PROCESS STACKER PARAMETERS         ^UTMOEI
          YSPGM    SET PROGRAM ID                     ^UTM09X
```

Figure 10. Program Call Tree

Table 2. Overview of TEDIUM Generated Applications

Application	Operational Since	Tables	Number of Elements	Programs
TEDIUM	8/80	119	225	414
SOCIAL WORK	3/81	22	88	87
CORE RECORD	3/81	136	295	751
OCIS	6/81	1045	2398	5023
ANESTHESIOLOGY	1/82	192	356	1043

Table 2 lists some descriptive data about the products developed using TEDIUM. There have been several evaluations of productivity. In one evaluation, all programs completed in the first year of use (10 effort years of activity) were analyzed and the number of lines of specification and generated code were computed. The same analysis was then performed for two smaller applications. These data are presented in Table 3. Subsequent tests showed that the ratio of TEDIUM to generated MUMPS code was

Table 3. Some Productivity Measures

Activity	Effort	Lines Per Man-Day TEDIUM	Lines Per Man-Day Generated[1]
Start-up[2]	10 man-years	13.8	101
Anesthesiology[3]	10 man-days	35.3	247
Symposium[4]	10 man-days	45.5	402

1. Generated lines are based upon 30 characters per line of MUMPS code.

2. All programmer activity from the time TEDIUM was first available to the end of 1981. Includes training of new hires, etc.

3. Prototype of an Operating Room Scheduling system. First use of TEDIUM by the analyst.

4. A symposium program management system developed by the author and a novice.

consistent with these data and that the number of lines of TEDIUM specifications per day were roughly the same as what one would expect for lines of code in any other language.

The next evaluation attempted to compare TEDIUM with MUMPS and COBOL using benchmarks and published results. The conclusion was that TEDIUM was four times more compact than MUMPS and twenty times more compact than COBOL.[20] Since productivity is a function lines of code, these numbers also represent productivity multipliers for the implementation (detailed design and code) activities.

A third evaluation involved the development of a moderate sized application for which productivity data were available. Boehm's two student exercises in implementing the Intermediate COCOMO model were used.[9,21] The author received the project requirements (for the second study) and implemented all of the first semester* and most of the second semester requirements. A total of 28 hours was required for all analysis, implementation, test and documentation tasks. Table 4 compares the author's data with Boehm's two exercises. The differences are attributable to the differences in developers (single, experienced designer vs. student teams) and the environment.

Of more interest than the time or lines data is the number of times each program had to be generated. This is presented in Table 5. Note that seven programs had to be generated only once. This means that the designer's understanding of the problem could be expressed properly the first time. In this case no programs were generated more than six times. The average number of generations per program was 2.5; this figure ± .5 is typical for most experienced designers on well understood problems (excluding evolution). An analysis of the generations of the 5,000 OCIS programs over a three and a half year period showed a median of 11 generations per program.[22]

Table 4. Implementations of Intermediate COCOMO

	Lines	Hours
1978 Study (Large Scale S.E.)		
Pascal Team	2137	611
Fortran Team	1977	771
1982 Study (Specifying vs. Prototyping)		
Specifying Teams	3391	584
Prototyping Teams	2064	325
1984 TEDIUM Benchmark	432	28

Table 5. Program Generations by Type

Number of Generations

	1	2	3	4	5	6
Common	3	5	5	2		2
Generic	4	2			1	2
Total	7	7	5	2	1	4

26 Programs
Average of 2.5 generations/program

---

*   The Boehm paper reported only on the first semester data; there was no second semester.

5. CONCLUSION

In this paper we have briefly described an integrated set of tools for the implementation and maintenance of a specific class of application. The environment is in production use, has been evaluated, and is productive for the application class. Perhaps the most important contribution of TEDIUM is that it acts as an existence proof that it is possible to:

- Design an implementation environment based upon a system analysis of the life cycle model and an automation-based method. (This is in contrast to many of the tools which automate a manual process.)

- Produce complex, operational systems using automatic programming and application directed specifications. (This is in contrast to many of the program generators which provide transformation facilities for only selected functions.)

- Maintain a design database to integrate design, testing and documentation. This design database also supports life cycle evolution. (This is in contrast to text processing tools which are independent of the implemented objects.)

Where the programming culture and operational environment permit, TEDIUM can serve as an effective environment for application development.

REFERENCES

[1] Musa, J., (ed), Stimulating Software Engineering Progress, A Report of the Software Engineering Planning Group, *ACM SIGSOFT SEN* (8,2):29-54, 1983.

[2] Osterweil, L. J., Toolpack — An Experimental Software Development Environment Research Project, *IEEE Trans. S.E.*, SE-9:673-685, 1983.

[3] Lehman, M. M., Programs, Life Cycles and Laws of Program Evolution, *Proc. IEEE*, 68:1060-1076, 1980.

[4] Freeman, P. and A. I. Wasserman, Software Development Methodologies of Ada,™ Preliminary Report, University of California, 1982.

[5] Lientz, B. and E. Swanson, *Software Maintenance Management*, Addison-Wesley, 1980.

[6] Giddings, R. V., Accommodating Uncertainty in Software Design, *COMM ACM*, 27:428-434, 1984.

[7] The General Accounting Office Report FGMSD-80-4, Contracting for Computer Software Development, 9 September 1979.

[8] Pressman, R. S., *Software Engineering, A Practitioner's Approach*, McGraw-Hill, 1982.

[9] Boehm, B. W., An Experiment in Small-Scale Applications Software Engineering, *IEEE Trans. S.E.*, SE-7:482-493, 1981.

[10] Rapid Prototyping Workshop, special issue, *ACM SIGSOFT SEN* (7,5) December 1982.

[11] Houghton, R. C., Jr., Software Development Tools: A Profile, *Computer*, May 1983, pp 63-70.

[12] Osterweil, L., Software Environment Research: Directions for the Next Five Years, *Computer*, April 1981, pp 36-37.

[13] See for example the Special Issue on Software Reusability, *IEEE Trans. S.E.*, SE-10:473-609, 1984.

[14] Blum, B. I., A Tool for Developing Information Systems, H. O. Schneider and A. I. Wasserman (eds), *Automated Tools for Information Systems Design*, North-Holland, New York, NY, pp 215-235, 1982.

[15] Blum, B. I., Three Paradigms for Developing Information Systems, *Seventh Inter. Conf. Software Engineering*, IEEE Computer Society Press, pp 534-543, 1984.

[16] Blum, B. I., An Approach to Computer Maintained Software Documentation, *NBS FIPS Software Documentation Workshop*, NBS SP 500-94, pp 110-118, 1982.

[17] Blum, B. I. and C. W. Brunn, Implementing an Appointment System with TEDIUM, *Fifth Annual Symposium on Computer Applications in Medical Care*, IEEE Computer Society Press, pp 172-181, 1981.

[18] Blum, B. I., A Methodology for Information Systems Production, *26th Meeting of the Society for General Systems Research and Systems Methodology*, 1:273-282, 1982.

[19] Lenhard, R. E., Jr., B. I. Blum, J. M. Sunderland, H. G. Braine, and R. Saral, The Johns Hopkins Oncology Clinical Information System, *J. Med. Sys.* 7:147-174, 1983.

[20] Blum, B. I., MUMPS, TEDIUM and Productivity, *First MEDCOMP*, IEEE Computer Society Press, pp 200-209, 1982.

[21] Boehm, B. W., T. E. Gray and T. Seewoldt, Prototyping vs. Specifying: A Multi-Project Experiment, *IEEE Trans. S.E.*, SE-10:290-303, 1984.

[22] Blum, B. I., Four Years' Experience with an Environment for Implementing Information Systems, draft paper.

ANALYTICAL CAD/CAE MODEL FOR EARLY-STAGE RMA ASSESSMENT

Jill V. Josselyn; Randall E. Fleming, Ph.D., OR; Ronald L. De Hoff, Ph.D., AA

Systems Control Technology, Inc.
1801 Page Mill Road, Palo Alto, CA 94304

Abstract

The ability to predict reliability, maintainability, availability (RMA) and life cycle cost for a new system during the concept and design stages has become essential in both industry and government. Cost, reliability and maintainability specifications are now routinely included in government system acquisition contracts. Both the government and contractor require effective prediction tools to monitor and compare performance at the beginning phases of a program. This ensures maximum RMA growth during later design, test and production phases. Automation of the RMA evaluation process and linkage to the design are highly desirable.

A Computer-aided Design/Computer-aided Engineering (CAD/CAE) system has been developed for the prediction of complex system reliability, maintainability, availability (RMA), safety, testability (T) and logistics support. This requires a powerful model which can produce system output from component input. Such a model must simultaneously be able to perform RMA evaluations, testability trade-offs and operation/support (O&S) cost estimations. The model discussed uses a Markov approach which as a closed-form mathematical solution provides lower operational costs and therefore permits the more extensive sensitivity analyses necessary for early-stage evaluations. This paper discusses specific CAD/CAE package application to the design, specification or allocation of RMA in complex systems. The paper also addresses unique modeling techniques currently under research which could be used to enhance large system effectiveness of Markov models.

I. Introduction

An efficient system RMA evaluation methodology must include effective techniques for predicting or calculating the failure probability of systems which include hardware/software/dissimilar replication, imperfect redundancy and maintenance. Design considerations include part quality, hardware/software redundancy, failure detection/ recovery, and communication between redundant channels to avoid system failure. In evaluating a specific configuration, trade-offs exist among reliability, maintainability, weight and support costs. Depending on the application, these factors vary in importance. Reliability and cost are significantly influenced by trade-offs between hardware/software design and maintenance strategies.

To evaluate RMA of complex designs at an early stage, a generalized analysis tool is required to identify and prioritize configurations and evaluate maintenance strategies in terms of multiple objectives including reliability, maintainability and cost. Such a tool should:

(1) give the user an estimate of reliability and availability achieved by various configurations;

(2) evaluate O&S costs and effects of preventive maintenance strategies;

(3) accommodate uncertainties in modeling data using sensitivity techniques; and

(4) be inexpensive to execute for numerous design iterations.

The integrated CAD/CAE system discussed in this paper addresses these design analysis problems. A Markov-based model [1] is used to perform trade-off design analysis of complex systems. The capabilities, advantages and current Markov method limitations of this approach are discussed. Promising results of an ongoing research program entitled "Low-cost Methods for Prediction and Evaluation of RMA in Complex Systems" are reviewed. This program is studying methods for reduction or elimination of current Markov Method limitations. Two case studies are presented which demonstrate the utility of the research results for the complex architectures common in today's highly reliable operational configurations.

II. CAD/CAE Application RMA Analysis

The use of this CAD/CAE model as an analytical tool in the early stages of design projects is shown in Figure 1. Specific input options and output from the model [2] varies with the depth and type of analysis.

RMA analysis requires that a system be viewed in terms of blocks which are constructed from engineering drawings. Modules are the building blocks upon which system design, input data and maintenance policies are based. These must be selected carefully based on engineering, judgement, knowledge of the system to be modeled, and availability of failure and/or cost data. System input can include life cycle cost parameters, costs for system failure (penalty charge), fixed charge for repair, as well as a number of variables providing user modeling options.

Subsystems are sets of modules chosen to be grouped together. Subsystems must be independent and in series. As many subsystems as possible should be created to minimize solution time. Possible reasons for including several modules in the same subsystem include dissimilar replication, analytical redundancy, or interdependent maintenance strategy. Subsystem input includes modular structure (which modules must be operational for continued subsystem performance) and an opportunistic maintenance option during preventative maintenance. Structure is input through minimum path or critical sets, which need not be disjoint.

Module input includes failure rate, cost, weight, coverage, redundancy level and maintenance decision information. Maintenance decisions involve the module level of redundancy at which system preventive maintenance will be performed. The user may also choose to perform sensitivity analysis with respect to any of the input parameters. Sensitivity is based on the percent change output per percent change of the designated input variable.

A breakdown of the system into modules and subsystems is equally valid for systems comprised of hardware, software and combinations of both [3]. Reliability analysis methods for these structural blocks are well-defined for hardware. Methods for software or combined system analysis are still under development. No industry standard currently exists.

Figure 2 is an example of a series/parallel reliability block diagram. This particular example can be broken down into 3 subsystems: A, the B-C-D group, and the E-F-G group. This type of decomposition, and definition of the operational dependencies among components, comprises the "system description" noted in Figure 1. The model then analyzes the structures, deriving RMA & cost estimates for each of the subsystems and the system as a whole. The identification of subsystems or modules which are driving system RMA or cost are then evaluated, and changes made to the component structure to minimize differences between the results and RMA system objectives.

III. Survey of Hardware System RMA Modeling Methods

System reliability, maintainability and availability (RMA) prediction necessitates powerful models which produce system output from component input. Nonredundant hardware systems are often analyzed by the piecepart count method. This involves estimating component failure rates and counting the number of components. System reliability is then a weighted sum of part failure rates. Several special properties of complex or fault-tolerant hardware/software systems render the piecepart count method inappropriate. These properties are imperfect failure coverage (probability of detection, isolation and recovery from a failure given it has occurred) between redundant components, preventive maintenance and non series-parallel system structure [4].

Most methods for predicting system reliability fall into four classifications. These are Markov, piecepart count, networks and Monte Carlo. Capabilities of each model type are shown in Table 1. Markov, piecepart count and networks are relatively low cost-to-operate compared to Monte Carlo simulation. However, Monte Carlo methods most closely model specific system details [5]. On the other hand, the extensive sensitivity analysis necessary for system design trade-offs is difficult using Monte Carlo methods.

The piecepart count method is the simplest and currently the most widely used. However, it is inadequate for use in complex hardware systems because it does not consider coverage, maintainability or system structures which are not series parallel. Network or reliability block diagram methods are suited for evaluating complex system structures but cannot account for maintenance strategy [6].

In a repairable system, maintenance is important when predicting reliability. Reliability and maintenance are highly dependent. A summary of reliability centered maintenance (RCM) methods, currently in use by the Department of Defense appears in reference 7. Markov methods are the only non Monte Carlo tools permitting consideration of maintenance policy effects [8]. Markov models are limited in the modeling of interdependent maintenance strategies for extremely large systems. This is because the number of model states increase exponentially with the number of different components.

Numerous reliability prediction software packages exist. TIGER uses Monte Carlo methods [9]. GRAMP uses Markov methods [10]. ORACLE estimates component failure rates using MILHDBK 217-D models and uses the piecepart count method to estimate system reliability [11]. Software described in reference 11 uses network or Boolean methods. A survey of Markov methods appears in reference 10.

The utility of joint application of Markov and simulation models in Fault-tolerant design-to-specs is discussed in reference 12.

IV. Markov Model Application to Complex Systems

Overview: Benefits vs. Limitations

This section provides a brief description of the Markov process on which the model is based. The process is based on defining a system in terms of all possible states. States can be thought of in terms of "conditions" of the system

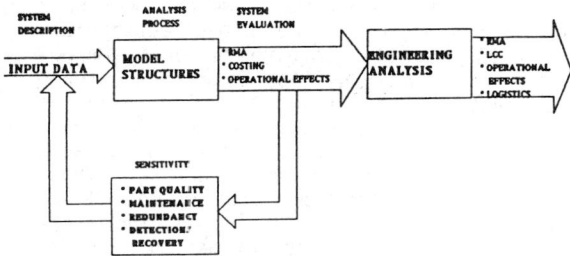

Figure 1: System Design/Analysis

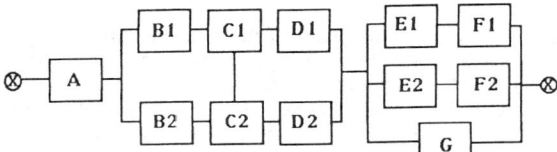

Figure 2: Reliability Block Diagram

TABLE 1: R&M PREDICTION METHODS OVERVIEW

CAPABILITY	MARKOV	PIECEPART COUNT	METHOD NETWORKS/BOOLEAN	MONTE CARLO
Low cost-to-operate	X	X	X	
Sensitivity	X	X	X	
Maintainability & related O & S cost prediction	X			X
Coverage	X		X	X
Time-dependent inputs/outputs	X			X
Generality of system structures	X		X	X
Detailed system factors modeling				X

λ A(B) - FAILURE RATE A(B)

μ A(B) = REPAIR RATE

☐ = SYSTEM OPERATING. NO MAINTENANCE.

▦ = SYSTEM UP. MAINTENANCE BEING PERFORMED ON FAILED COMPONENTS.

▨ = SYSTEM DOWN. UNDERGOING MAINTENANCE.

M = MAINTENANCE ON COMPONENT *

O = OPERATING COMPONENTS.

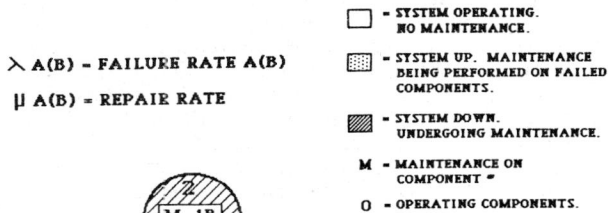

Figure 3

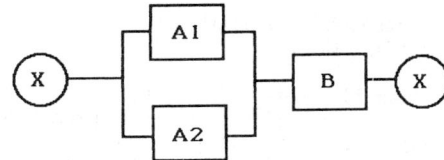

Figure 4: Reliability Block Diagram for the Hypothetical Example

TABLE 2: MARKOV MODEL BENEFITS FOR COMPLEX SYSTEM RMA AND T EVALUATION

UNIQUE CAPABILITIES AS A "STAND-ALONE" METHOD	ENHANCEMENT OF TRADITIONAL MAINTAINABILITY AND LOGISTICS SUPPORT EVALUATION METHODS	ENHANCEMENT OF TRADITIONAL SYSTEM RELIABILITY EVALUATION METHODS
o Maintenance and support policy. o Module dependencies through maintenance or system structure. o Ideally suited for "n-of-m" fault-tolerant systems with identical components. o System testability model. [3]	o Early-stage selection of optimal maintenance strategy when used in conjunction with simulation. [2] o Cross-validation of simulation results for simpler maintenance policies.	o Markov combines with fault trees or networks in hierarchical fashion. o Markov gives "in-depth" look at key portions of system. o Output from component-level failure rate or design for testability models feeds into Markov model as LRU/WRA-level input. [3]

TABLE 3: METHODS FOR COMPLEX SYSTEM RMA AND T EVALUATION USING MARKOV MODELS

CLASSIFICATION	METHODS
System* Approximation (Partitioning)	o Independent serial subsystems o Hierarchical Markov/fault tree or network o Hierarchical Markov o Hierarchical Markov/probability conditioning
Model* Approximation	o Truncation o State merging or lumping o Sequential truncation
Solution Algorithms*	o Gauss-Jordan o Eigenvalue-Eigenvector o o Differential equation (e.g., Runge-Kutte) o Monte Carlo

* Best method is a function of the structure of the system and maintenance policy.

EXAMPLE: TWO COMPONENT SERIES SYSTEM

o λ_I FAILURE RATE OF COMPONENT I. λ_1=99, λ_2=1

o ASSUME BOTH COMPONENTS DUALLY REDUNDANT

o ASSUME DON'T FIX UNTIL SYSTEM FAILS

o STATES ARE (A, B,) A = # UP FOR COMPONENT B = # UP FOR COMPONENT 2

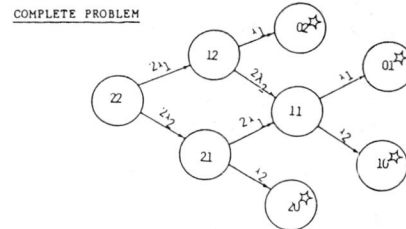

☆ SYSTEM FAILS, FIX EVERYTHING

Figure 5: Truncation Example

such as maintenance, system failure or module operating configuration.

The probability of the system being in any one of the states is defined by the specification of the transition probabilities between states and the definition of the initial state of the system. A simple Markov model is presented in Figure 3. This hypothetical example shows a five state system composed of a duplex component A's and a simplex component B. The reliability block diagram for such a system (Figure 4) shows that at least one A and one B are required to keep the system functional. Maintenance is performed whenever a component fails. The importance of this concept lies in the large number of physical and economic phenomena that can be accurately represented by the Markov process.

Today's complex systems contain hundreds of different components. Because the number of Markov states increases exponentially with the number of different dependent components modeled, these systems are usually too large to be modeled using a single Markov model. Since 5-10,000 states are the greatest number of Markov states efficiently solvable on a typical computer, 10-20 different components are the most that can be represented by a single Markov model. Because of this difficulty, Markov models have up-to-now been used only on a limited basis for complex system RMA & T evaluation.

A Markov model provides several unique benefits to the system RMA & T engineer. These can be classified into:

(1)   stand-alone benefits;

(2)   enhancement of traditional system reliability evaluation methods (fault trees, networks); and

(3)   enhancement of traditional maintainability and logistics support evaluation methods (simulations) to determine optimal maintenance procedures, integrated logistics support (ILS), and warranty/incentive contracts.

Table 2 lists specific Markov model benefits within the above categories.

Research Program: Low-Cost Methods for Complex System RMA & T

The numerous benefits available from Markov models warrant an in-depth look at methods for their application to large complex systems containing more than 10-20 different components. Current methods for large system application of Markov models fall into three categories:

(1)   system approximation or partitioning;

(2)   model approximation; and

(3)   solution algorithm efficiency improvement.

Table 3 lists specific methods which have been proposed within each of the above categories. These methods usually involve general Markov models with a given transition matrix structure. Often the best method within each classification depends heavily on the matrix structure. In a Markov model, system structure and maintenance determine the transition matrix structure. Thus, the optimal approximation or solution method depends on the specifics of the engineering problem. Methods for system approximation are defined in [1]. Methods for Markov model approximation and algorithms for solution are discussed below.

Two methods exist for Markov model approximation. These are state merging or lumping, and truncation. State merging involves the combination of several Markov states which are expected to have low probability of occurrance. Merging produces an exact solution given the reduced number of states while truncation produces an approximate solution. Conditions for mergeability or lumpability are well-known [13]. An example is the following: two states are lumpable if they have identically corresponding rows in the transition matrix. Such conditions are too restrictive for complex system RMA & T problems.

State truncation proposed in references 14 and 15 for small problems is performed through deletions of Markov states. The deleted states must have a low probability of occurrance or the truncated problem will poorly approximate the full problem. Truncation is a three-step process:

(1)   generate all Markov states;

(2)   truncate states, and

(3)   solve the truncated problem.

When truncating a state it's essential that the transition matrix for the truncated problem remain a probability matrix (rows sum to one). Figure 5 exhibits a Markov state diagram for a two component series system where both components are dually redundant. The first (second) component of the state descriptor indicates the number of working units for component 1 (2). The numbers on the arcs are state transition rates. No maintenance is performed until both units of one component fail. Repair is assumed to be instantaneous; thus the transition rates out of states denoted by "*" are identical to those out of state "22".

Figure 6 exhibits a Markov state diagram for a truncated version of Figure 5. Since component 2 rarely fails, states where the number of failures in component 2 equal or exceed those of component 1 have been truncated (22, 11, 20). State 10 was not deleted to retain the notion of a "failure due to component 2" in the model. Truncation must occur within state categories (system up, system down, preventive maintenance). A low-probability value for a "system-up" state may be a high value for a "system-down" state. Transition rates have been combined using "sum of means."

To be precise, if state j is to be truncated, P is the full transition matrix and P_T is the transition matrix with row and column j deleted, then:

$$P_T(k,m) = [P(k,j)^{-1}+P(j,m)^{-1}]^{-1} + P(k,m)$$

for j,k,m such that $p(k,j)$, $P(j,m)>0$.

A test procedure was developed to evaluate the potential effectiveness of truncation. This procedure required initial state generation using GRAMP [6] followed by user-selected truncations one state at a time. Matrix manipulations and the user-interface were accomplished using CTRL-C [8] and a routine to interface to GRAMP was developed. This procedure was used to test _potential_ effectiveness of truncation as follows:

(1) First, solve the full problem precisely using GRAMP (the problems were small enough for this).

(2) Truncate states within each state category according to increasing state occupancy probability starting with the least probable state. Run GRAMP for truncated problem.

(3) Stop when results (MTBF or reliability) deviate by more than 10% from the true answer. Maximum truncation potential is (# truncated states)/(original # of states).

The number of potential truncation states calculated will be the ideal upper limit. When problems are too large to solve exactly, the "best" states to truncate are not known. Trade-off among methods for selecting which states to truncate are being studied.

Table 4 demonstrates the results of a test for truncation potential on a two component parallel system. Component 1 consists of 7 units, 4 of which are needed to operate. Component 2 operation requires 2-of-5 units operational. Solution of the full problem, containing 45 states produces a system failure rate (per million hours) of 7.8 and an MTBF of 128,300 hours. Successful truncation of all "system up-states" having steady state probability less than 10^{-4} (45% of the states) results in a good approximation of the true result.

Table 5 exhibits truncation potential results for two component parallel systems with a variety of redundancies. The maximum truncation potential is 25% for cases of a small differential in failure rate of the components, 50% for larger differences.

Results of testing on examples similar to those in Table 4 lead to the following conclusions: The potential of truncation and sequential truncation in increasing Markov model capacity for handling large systems depends on component failure rate differentials. The more component failure rates differ, the more states can be truncated while producing a reasonable approximation to the problem. If component failure rates are "similar", approximations can be made using

identical failure rate models. The number of states in these models only increases linearly with the number of components.

Solution algorithms for Markov chains fall into two categories, the calculation of steady state probability and time-varying probability. Different algorithm types are possible within each category. Steady state probability algorithms solve the steady state occupancy probabilities of a Markov chain. This can be done by solving a linear system of equations, using a time-varying probability algorithm and letting time become large, or by simulation. Time varying probability algorithms solve for time varying state occupancy probabilities of a Markov chain given an initial state probability distribution. This is done by solving a linear system of differential equations through integration, eigenvalue or simulation methods.

The efficiency of a Markov chain solution algorithm is a function of the system and maintenance policy from which the Markov chain structure is generated. For example modeling deferred maintenance, system fault-tolerance (between non-identical components) or identical latent faults creates systems whose failed components may not be sent immediately to a repair queue. Thus, the structure of the Markov problem does not necessarily fit queing or other previously-studied specific structures. Algorithm efficiency trade-off studies are required to determine optimal algorithms as a function of system structure and maintenance policy.

Algorithm efficiency studies are currently underway. Preliminary results for two candidate steady state probability algorithms (both non-standard) exhibit vast differences in efficiency for problems assuming instantanious repair. The two algorithms compared are a conjugate gradient iterative method (CG) for solving a sparse linear system of equations and a Runge-Kutte method (RK) for solving a time-varying linear system of differential equations. In the RK cases, time is increased until convergence occurs. The "order" of a Runge-Kutte algorithm indicates the accuracy (number of terms taken) of the polynomial used in the calculation. The higher the "order", the more accurately the integration tracks the "true" value. If the "order" is too low, the algorithm does not converge. Increased accuracy is obtained at the expense of computation time. For cases considered here, an order of 30 was the lowest possible permitting covergence.

Table 6 summarizes results comparing CG and RK algorithm efficiencies on Markov chains of varying size. Runs were performed on a VAX-11/780 and were generated from standard redundant systems with instantaneous repair. Table 6 indicates that Runge-Kutte methods are much more efficient for some problems with over 200 states and can be used to solve problems with up to 8,000 states on a VAX with less than an hour of CPU time. Further tests are being made using non machine-dependent measures of efficiency to see if this is a general system result.

TRUNCATED PROBLEM

(component 2 rarely fails)

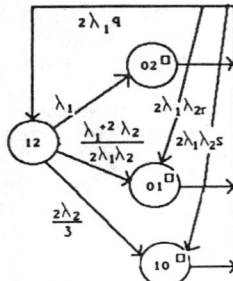

□ System Fails, Fix Everything

$$q = \frac{3\lambda_1 + 2\lambda_2}{3\lambda_1 + \lambda_2} \qquad r = \frac{5\lambda_1 + 6\lambda_2}{(\lambda_1 + 3\lambda_2)(4\lambda_1 + 3\lambda_2)}$$

$$s = \frac{9\lambda_1 + 2\lambda_2}{(3\lambda_1 + \lambda_2)(6\lambda_1 + \lambda_2)}$$

Figure 6: Truncation Example

Figure 7: Digital Telephone System

TABLE 4: SAMPLE TRUNCATION POTENTIAL TEST

o TWO COMPONENT PARALLEL SYSTEM

o COMPONENT 1: 4-of-7, FAILURE RATE 90

o COMPONENT 2: 2-of-5, FAILURE RATE 10

o RESULTS:

		# STATES	F.P.M.H.	MTBF	APPROX.
Full Problem		45	7.8	128,300	EXACT
Truncate States	10^{-6}	37	7.8	128,300	EXCELLENT
Truncate States	10^{-5}	29	7.8	128,300	EXCELLENT
Truncate States	10^{-4}	23	7.6	130,900	GOOD

TABLE 5: TRUNCATION POTENTIAL RESULTS – TWO COMPONENT PARALLEL REDUNDANT SYSTEMS

CASE	# STATES	MAXIMUM TRUNCATION POTENTIAL	COMMENTS
1	4	50%	F.R. Differential 90-10
2A	12	50%	F.R. Differential 90-10
2B	12	25%	F.R. Differential 60-40
2C	12	25%	F.R. Differential 50-50
3	16	50%	F.R. Differential 90-10 Imperfect Coverage
4	45	50%	F.R. Differential 90-10

TABLE 6: ALGORITHM STUDY – RESULTS SUMMARY

CASE	# STATES	# NONZERO MATRIX ELTS.	CG CPU*(MIN)	RK, ORDER 30 CPU*(MIN)	STATE GENERATION CPU(SEC)
1	22	117	0		.48
2	94	535	.63	.55	.56
3	198	1147	5.32	1.25	.85
4	229	2012	9.79	1.38	1.35
5	492	4461	NOT RUN	3.05	3.52
6	776	7103	NOT RUN	4.97	6.64

* ON VAX 11/780

TABLE 7

	MODULE 500	SWITCH 100
FAILURE RATES		
MTTR	8	.5
LABOR CHARGE/HR	10.	10.
FIXED CHARGE FOR REPAIRMAN	$100.	

FIXED COST FOR SYSTEM DOWN: $1000.

	SYSTEM FAILURE	MTTR, MODULE	COST/HR, MODULE
CASE I	3% SUBSCRIBERS OUT	8	10
II	6% SUBSCRIBERS OUT	8	10
III	9% SUBSCRIBERS OUT	8	10
IV	3% OUT	16	5
V	3% OUT	4	15
VI	3% OUT	2	20

TABLE 8

CASE	MTBF	MTBR	AVAIL	PARTS & LABOR	SERVICE	FAILURE	TOTAL
				$O&S/HR			
I	70.5	69.5	.898	1.14	2.84	28.42	32.4
II	576.5	62.8	.986	1.26	1.92	3.49	6.67
III	4812	62.8	.998	1.27	1.64	.43	3.34
IV	78.5	77.3	.831	1.02	2.55	25.50	29.07
V	66.5	65.6	.943	.90	3.01	30.09	34.0
VI	64.5	63.6	.970	.62	3.11	31.07	34.8

STANDARD MODULE TYPE	FAILURE RATE	QTY SPARED
	1.0	
	0.6	
A	0.4	1
B	1.2	0
C	0.1	0
D	0.3	1
E	0.4	0
O	0.3	0
R	17.0	0
S	0.3	0
-		1
Z	—	0
		3

Figure 8: High Redundancy Sonar System – Reliability & Component Failure Rates

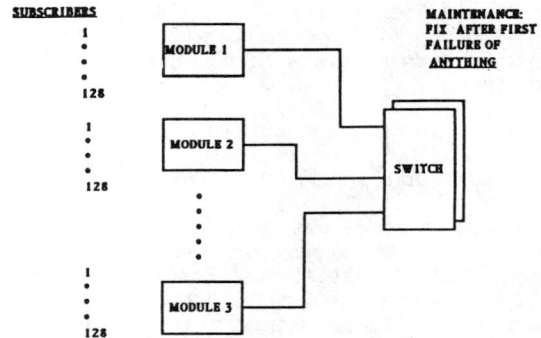

Other tests involving "standard" algorithms and systems with noninstantaneous repair are in progress. Other methods (besides CG) for solving large systems of simultaneous linear equations to be tesed include classical Jacobi and Gauss-Seidel with overrelaxation. Other methods for solving a system of first order differential equations (besides RIC) to be tesed include the Adams/Bashforth predictor/corrector and the randomization method. The Runge-Kutte methods are not expected to perform as well for noninstantaneous repair due to coexistence of very long and very short state transitions.

The right-hand column in Table 6 indicates the time required for generation of the Markov states and transition matrix elements from a system and maintenance policy description. Extrapolation of these results indicates that 200,000 states and 2 million nonzero matrix elements could be generated in one hour of VAX time. The ease of generation of large numbers of states supports the viability of a truncation algorithm.

V. Case Studies

This section addresses two case studies each with circumstances that made the problems especially difficult to solve.

The first application is a decentralized distributed telecommunications system. The functional diagram (Figure 7) depicts 32 modules, which each support 128 subscribers. The modules interface via a redundant switching unit which has previously been analyzed [16]. Failure rate data (per million hours) is shown in Table 7. Two types of sensitivity runs were performed.

This system exhibits very high component failure rates, making reliability and MTBF a poor indication of overall performance. The capability to perform frequent repair was determined to be the best way to maintain availability goals. Degraded mode analysis, revealed optimal maintenance strategies with respect to a cyclical work load profile. The paramount consideration was to minimize maintenance costs while maintaining customer support on an existing system.

Two types of sensitivity runs were performed. The first evaluated the change in system output parameters (Table 8 case I-III) with respect to the changing definition of system failure (Table 7). The second set of runs held the definition of system failures constant at 3% of subscribers without service, but varied the mean time to repair (MTTR) and labor costs per hour of repair (Table 7, cases IV-VI).

The second case study analyzes a highly redundant sonar system with limited spares. The reliability block diagram for the mission essential components, component spares and failure rates are shown in Figure 8. Availability of the on-board sonar system is highly dependent on an optimized sparing and maintenance strategy. The sparing philosophy was very constrained due to the limited room to store spares on board, and the difficulty of maintenance while at sea, (which also precluded cannibalization of modules).

Evaluation of MTBF and availability, given the specified on-board sparing constraints, was the objective of this analysis. In this case, there were too many modules to evaluate all paths and sections in a single Markov model. (Figure 8)

Due to this restriction, three conditions were selected for evaluation:

(1) Run 1 defines a lower bound, based on lack of spares for any module except for "U". Independence of sections is maintained.

(2) Run 2 defines an upper bound. One spare is available for each of A, D & U in section IV (Figure 8) and a spare string (path) available in sections I and III.

(3) Run 3 defines a logical policy, where spares for A, D & U are dedicated to the simplex units.

The modules in each path and section are all independent; critical dependencies develop due to existing spares which are allocated among different sections.

TABLE 9 CASE STUDY II RESULTS

RUN	MTBF	AVAILABILITY	TYPE
1	20450	.99994791	LOWER BOUND
2	26110	.99997282	"LOGICAL" POLICY
3	26110	.99997282	UPPER BOUND

The results in Table 9 indicate that the sparing policy in Run 3 is optimum, since MTBF and availability are identical for Runs 2 and 3. If no "logical" sparing policy had produced results close to the "upper bound," or availability goal, further required would have been required to decompose the strings in each section down to the module level.

The sonar system trade-off studies of both sparing and replacement strategies permitted a low cost approximation of operational availability. Logistical factors, including service capacity and sparing philosophy, were shown to be as important as design redundancy in optimizing availability. Policies for sparing and the logistics concerning the optimal on-board spare mix were determined.

VI. Conclusions

The analytical CAD/CAE system described has been extensively used to design, specify and allocate requirements for complex hardware and software systems. This paper focuses on the need for RMA evaluation during the early stages of program development, long before extensive failure rate data bases are available. Two case studies were presented, demonstrating the utility of the model when evaluting maintenance policy and cost implications in association with reliability analysis in large, complex systems.

This paper reviews the limitations as well as substantial advantages of using the Markov approach, which was found to be the most efficient and flexible technique. Continuing contributions to the advancements in Markov technology were discussed. Significant improvements to the process can be made through refinement of state generation logic and truncation schemes which reduce the matrix size prior to solving. Optimal solution algorithms based on the resulting matrix characteristics will also lessen some of the present Markov limitations. A basic research program is supplying promising developments to reduce or eliminate disadvantages of the Markov approach. Issues most important to modeling real systems were identifed. This paper makes the transition between theoretical modeling research to applied systems development programs.

Acknowledgements

Research in the areas of truncation methodology and complex systems was sponsored by the Office of Naval Research and the Naval Air Systems Command/Air 340R, Washington D.C. under contract #N00014-83-C-0595. This effort is titled "Low-Cost Methodologies for Prediction and Evaluation of RMA and T in Complex Systems." The CAD/CAE package, GRAMP, is a proprietary software product independently developed by Systems Control Technology.

References

1. Fleming, Randall, E., Josselyn, Jill, V., Dolny, Linda Jo, and De Hoff, Ronald, "Complex System RMA and T, Using Markov Models," Proc. RAMS, 1985.

2. Systems Control Technology, Inc., "Generalized Reliability and Maintainability Program (GRAMP) Users Manual", August 1985.

3. Shooman, M.L. "Structural Models for Software Reliability Prediction", Proceedings of the 2nd International Conference on Software Engineering, IEEE Computer Society, October 1976.

4. Arnold, Thomas F., "The Concept of Coverage and its Effect on the Reliability Model of a Repairable System," IEEE Trans Computers, v. C-22 #3, March, 1973.

5. Becker, Peter, W., "Finding the Better of Two Similar Designs by Monte Carlo Techniques," IEEE Trans. Rel., Vol. R-23 #4, October 1974.

6. Butler, David A., "Bounding the Reliability and Multistate Systems," Opns. Res., V. 30 #3, 530-44.

7. Tipton, R., et al., "Reliability Centered Maintenance Study," Final Report, Contract #DAAG 39-77-C-0169, September 1978.

8. Fleming, Randall E., "Coherent System Repair Models," T.R. #195, June 1980, ONR Contract #N00014-75-C-0561.

9. TIGER Manual, "Reliability by Design," NAVSEA TE660-AA-MMD-010.

10. Dolny, Linda Jo, Fleming, Randall, and De Hoff, R.L., "Fault Tolerant Computer System Design Using GRAMP," Proc. 1983 R&M Symposium.

11. ORACLE User's Manual (DRAFT) "Computerized MIL-HDBK 217," RADC/HONEYWELL 6180 Multics Operating System, Rome Air Development Center, 1981.

12. Fleming, Randall, Dolny, Linda Jo, and De Hoff, Ronald, "Fault-Tolerant Design-to-Specs with GRAMP and GRAMS," Proc. 1984 R&M Symposium, 403-408.

13. Papazoglou, I.A., & Gyftopoulos, E.P., "Markov Process for Reliability Analyses of Large Systems," IEEE Trans. Rel., V. R-26 #3, August 1977.

14. Singh, C., "Reliability Analysis of Large Repairable Systems," Microelectronics and Reliability, Vol. 13, 1974, 487-493.

15. Singh, C., "Reliability Calculations of Large Systems," Proc. 1975 RAMS, 188-193.

16. Piskar, R., "Hardware/Software Availability for a Phone System", Proc. 1983 RAMS, 310-315.

Biographies

Jill V. Josselyn

Ms. Josselyn received her B.A. in 1975 from the University of Massachusetts and since has done graduate work in statistics at Oregon State University. She is currently an MBA candidate in Decision and Information Sciences at the University of Santa Clara, CA. Since joining Systems Control Technology, Inc. in 1980 Ms. Josselyn has provided analysis and programming support for several reliability/maintainability/availability/testability projects. Ms. Josselyn's recent work has involved the analysis and evaluation of reliability models and failure analysis of complex, fault-tolerant computer systems. Ms. Josselyn has extensive experience with GRAMP, an RMA prediction tool, and algorithm efficiency studies associated with its development. Ms. Josselyn is a participant in a Navy-sponsored research program to develop advanced methods for RMA & T prediction. Ms. Josselyn is currently a systems engineer for the Maintenance and Logistics Systems Department at SCT.

Randall E. Fleming, Ph.D.

Dr. Fleming received a B.S. degree in Applied Mathematics magna cum laude from Brown University in 1975. He also received an M.S. degree in Statistics and a Ph.D. degree in Operations Research, from Stanford University. Since joining SCT in 1979, Dr. Fleming has provided principal support to numerous contracts in the areas of reliability, maintainability, testability, cost and statistical data collection and analysis. His primary field of expertise is in the modeling of RMA and testability for complex systems, an area he has been doing work in for seven years. This work started with his Ph.D. dissertation entitled, "Coherent System Repair Models", which developed Markov models for the maintenance of complex systems. Based on this research, Dr. Fleming developed GRAMP - a Markov model for complex system RMA prediction. Dr. Fleming is currently the principal investigator for the Navy-sponsored research program to develop advanced methods for RMA & T prediction. Dr. Fleming is a member of Sigma Xi, the Operations Research Society of America, the American Statistical Association, and the Institute of Environmental Sciences, and the IEEE Reliability Society.

Ronald L. De Hoff, Ph.D.

Dr. De Hoff graduated with high honors from Princeton University in 1971 receiving a B.S.E. degree from the Department of Aerospace and Mechanical Sciences. He received a M.S. degree from Stanford in 1972 and the Ph.D. degree in 1975 from the Department of Aeronautics and Astronautics. Dr. De Hoff received the 1977 IEEE Society on Control Systems (Bay Area Chapter) award for Outstanding Achievement in Control Engineering for the development of control strategies for the F100 turbofan jet engine using optimal control theory. Since joining Systems Control Technology, Inc. in 1975, Dr. De Hoff has worked in the areas of turbine propulsion control and diagnostic systems. He has also done work involving engine performance analysis and diagnostic system evaluation for several Air Force and Navy turbine engine monitoring systems. More recently, he has been involved in reliability, logistics, testability and database management. He is currently manager of the Maintenance and Logistics Systems Department at SCT. Dr. De Hoff is a member of Sigma Xi, Tau Beta Pi, AIAA and SAE.

Computer Printing of Syllabic Writing Systems

John S. Gourlay
James B. Unkefer

The Ohio State University Department of Computer and Information Science
2036 Neil Avenue Mall, Columbus, Ohio 43210

N. I. Balakrishnan
R. Subramanian

AT&T Bell Labs
6200 E. Broad Street, Reynoldsburg, Ohio 43213

Abstract—The application of computers to document production has naturally centered around the English language and its alphabet. The increasing importance of computers in parts of the world where English is not the native language, however, has created a demand for foreign language text processing. For languages like French, which uses essentially the same alphabet as English, and even for languages like Russian, which uses a different, but nevertheless *phonemic*, alphabet, English text processing software can be used with no conceptual changes. There are many other languages, however, that use "alphabets" with too many characters for conventional techniques. These writing systems fall into two categories, *syllabic* systems, such as the Japanese katakana and hiragana, in which each printed character corresponds to a syllable, and *ideographic* systems, such as Chinese, in which each character corresponds to an entire word. We have concentrated on the problem of adapting existing text formatting software and hardware to the printing of syllabic writing systems. We have developed a program that runs as a preprocessor to an arbitrary English based text formatting system, allowing the production of multilingual documents, incorporating both English and syllabic writing systems. An important feature of the system is that input may be prepared with ordinary English text editing facilities, the foreign language being entered in the form of an English transliteration. The preprocessor output consists of text formatter instructions to typeset the multilingual document. The preprocessor is table driven, allowing it to work for a wide variety of syllabaries and text formatters.

Introduction

The computer was invented in the United States and the technology was brought to its current state of maturity largely by the work of people in North America and Western Europe. This together with the fact that English tends to be the *lingua franca* of high technology makes it come as no surprise that the use of computers in text processing has been limited almost entirely to the processing of English text.

This English orientation can be expected to change, however, for a variety of reasons. Perhaps the most important reason is that the price of computer hardware has dropped to the point that great affluence is not a prerequisite to the use of computers. As more and more computers are installed in non-English speaking countries, more and more demand will develop for foreign language text processing. The increasing economic importance of non-Western nations outside of the computer industry will also demand foreign language processing by companies with growing foreign markets. Communication technology has also been improving, reducing the speed and cost of world-wide communication. In the shrinking world there is necessarily more contact between speakers of different native languages, creating a demand not only for foreign language processing, but also for multilingual processing. A last consideration is that the technology of printing is also changing. The advent of computer controlled laser, ink jet, and similar printers has reduced dramatically the cost of printing with large and unusual character sets, because the shapes of the printed characters can be stored and changed electronically, rather than being molded in metal.

Writing Systems

The world's writing systems can be divided into three broad categories, *phonemic*, *syllabic*, and *ideographic* [Nakanishi 80]. Phonemic writing systems are the ones with which native speakers of English are most familiar, because all the languages of the Western world are written in this way. In a phonemic writing system, each character represents a single phoneme, or sound, in the spoken language. Of course, this one-to-one correspondence is only approximate in English, but it is clearly the principle on which our writing system is constructed. German and French use essentially the same alphabet as English, although the phonemes of those languages differ somewhat. Russian, Greek, and Hebrew use different alphabets than English, but even these languages adhere to the principle of characters representing phonemes. Characteristically, all these writing systems have alphabets whose size approximates that of English.

Chinese is the only living, purely ideographic writing system. In Chinese, each character represents a different word. As a result, in principle at least, there are as many distinct characters in the Chinese writing system as there are words in the language. In fact, the number of characters is minimized in modern Chinese by the use of compound words, written as two closely spaced characters. Nevertheless, the number of characters in the Chinese writing system is on the order of ten thousand, as opposed to the 26 of English.

The syllabic systems of writing are probably the least familiar to speakers of English. Nevertheless, including Japanese, Korean, and most of the languages of the Indian subcontinent, syllabic writing systems are of great importance in terms of population and economics. These writing systems represent a kind of middle ground between the phonemic and ideographic systems in which each character represents a syllable, rather than a single phoneme or a whole word. Thus in Tamil, an important language of south India which will be used as a source of examples throughout this paper, the syllable "ṭa" is written as ⌐ while the syllable "ṭu" is written as the entirely different character ௫. It is remarkable that syllabic writing systems always seem to choose consonant-vowel pairs for representation as syllables. In Tamil phonemically there are 12 vowels and 23 consonants. Allowing for special characters to represent isolated vowels and consonants, we find that the writing system must represent 13 × 24, or 312 distinct syllables and therefore, in principle, includes 312 distinct characters. In practice some of the syllables never occur, and many others are represented as predictable compositions of more elementary symbols, so the number of symbols in mechanically printed Tamil is actually much smaller than 312, about 100. Examples of this are the syllables "ka", "ki", and "kō", which are written as க, கி, and கௌ, respectively. To a native speaker of English the character கௌ certainly can be seen as a sequence of simpler symbols. While it is not quite as obvious, the character கி also can be seen to be made up of the symbols க and ி. To the native speaker of Tamil, however, கி and கௌ are conceptually single characters, and it is a mistake to expect a Tamil speaker to treat them as composed of separable characters. Thus, we must regard Tamil as having a syllabary of about 300 characters.

Japanese is an interesting special case, because its writing alternates among three different writing systems. Two of these, katakana and hiragana, are syllabaries, while the third, kanji, is an ideographic system derived from Chinese. Katakana is used for the numerous foreign words in the language, while hiragana and kanji are used somewhat interchangeably for Japanese words. Together, the two Japanese syllabaries include several hundred characters. Another interesting feature of Japanese is that its writing may be oriented more than one way. While it is acceptable for it to be written in the left-to-right pattern used by English, it is also common for it to be written top-to-bottom in columns that are written right-to-left.

The Problem

It is evident that the three categories of writing system will require different kinds of processing when handled by computer. Among the phonemic systems, languages like French and German can be handled with English based technology with no conceptual changes. Russian and Greek, too, require little more than a change of font. Syllabic and ideographic writing systems present serious challenges to English based technology, however, because of their large character sets [Becker 84]. In both systems, keyboards for text entry would have to be unacceptably large, and text editors and video display terminals would have to be redesigned to accommodate the large number of characters. Fonts for the printing of syllabaries, while large, are still manageable with the current technology of nonimpact printers. The huge fonts for ideographic writing, however, demand novel approaches even to the storage and retrieval of character shapes.

The purpose of this paper is to report on work being done on the practical use of computers in the printing of syllabic writing systems. A number of excellent English based text formatting systems are available, such as TEX, Scribe, and Troff [Furuta 82, Knuth 84, Reid 80b], and we consider it important to take advantage of this prior work to the greatest extent possible. The same, of course, is true of existing terminals, displays, and text editors. We also see economy in taking advantage of the common features of syllabaries so that substantial work need not be repeated to add new syllabaries to the printing system's repertoire.

In order to take advantage of existing text editing hardware and software, we have made the decision to represent the foreign language input in the form of an English transliteration. This has the advantage of using the English alphabet exclusively, so that no special hardware or software is required for text entry or editing. Standard transliterations exist for many languages, and for the foreseeable future we can expect foreign language users of computer printing systems to be familiar at least with the English alphabet. The use of English alphabet transliterations has the additional advantage that the entry of multilingual documents becomes trivial, requiring no change of hardware when changing from one language to another.

In order to take advantage of existing text formatters we have designed a preprocessor that reads the transliterated multilingual document and produces text formatter commands to print the document with appropriate fonts. This requires, of course, that the printing system downstream from the preprocessor have fonts for the language to be printed. The problem of the design of such fonts is beyond the scope of this paper. It suffices to say that acceptable fonts can be produced for most modern printers using a software system such as Metafont [Knuth 79, Ghosh 83].

A last important feature of the preprocessor is that it is table driven, allowing a single piece of software to suffice for the printing of many different syllabaries simply by adding or changing table entries. The table is also designed to incorporate important information about the text formatter to be used. Thus, with a mere change of table the preprocessor can be changed from Tamil to Korean, or from TEX to Scribe, or both.

The next two sections of the paper describe the use of the prepro-

cessor, first from the point of view of an author composing a multilingual document, and then from the point of view of a designer of a table for a new syllabary. Then, following a short wrap-up discussing future work, is an appendix describing the table format.

Composing a Document

As was already briefly mentioned, the preprocessor is a program which reads an input file consisting of English text mixed with transliterated foreign languages and produces an output file which can be run through a text formatter to produce a multilingual printed document. Since the preprocessor in principle is capable of handling a variety of languages and text formatters, the first thing the user must specify in the input file is the text formatter and language or languages intended. This specification takes the very simple form of a file name, the name of the file containing the table tailoring the preprocessor to the user's purpose. So, for example, if the user wishes to compose a multilingual document containing Tamil and English to be typeset using TEX, and if a table for this purpose exists in the file `tamiltex`, then the first line of input to the preprocessor will be

```
@tamiltex
```

the `@` signifying that the word following is a command to the preprocessor rather than text to be printed.

The text input, which follows this, can be divided into two kinds—English and the transliterated form of the other language. Continuing our example using the table `tamiltex`, the foreign language is Tamil, but other tables, of course, could select Japanese, Korean, or even a group of languages.

The preprocessor has two modes of operation corresponding to these two kinds of text. When the preprocessor is in "English mode" the input text is copied to the output file without any modification. On the other hand, when the preprocessor is in "Tamil mode" it is reading the transliterated form of the Tamil text. In this case, the preprocessor reads in the transliterated text, analyses it to determine the actual vowels and consonants that build up a word, combines adjacent consonant-vowel pairs to form syllables of the Tamil language, and outputs the formatter commands which print the corresponding Tamil characters. From now on we will call the first mode of operation of the preprocessor *copy mode* and the second mode *encode mode*.

The syntax for choosing the mode of the preprocessor was chosen to be much like Scribe environments [Reid 80a] because of their proven clarity and generality. One imagines that the input file is a typescript that has been marked up by an editor with circles and marginal notes indicating special fonts or other treatments of the text that cannot be accurately reflected in a typescript. To remain within the confines of a computer text file, however, we substitute braces ({...}) for the circles and we precede the bracketed text with a command word in place of a marginal note. For example, in Scribe one might type `@chapter{...}` to indicate that the text within the braces is the title of a chapter.

When the preprocessor starts up, it is in the copy mode even before it begins reading any character from the input file. In our Tamil example, the preprocessor interrupts its copy operation for any text enclosed in a command of the form `@tamil{...}`. The preprocessor assumes that the text within the braces is the transliterated form of Tamil text and encodes it into TEX commands. For example, if the preprocessor were given the following text

```
...and the last line,
@tamil{adiyaarkku migavae}, means...
```

it will conclude that `adiyaarkku migavae` is what is to be encoded. The preprocessor output would be something like

```
...and the last line,
{\tamil abyKrPkP\a \ mVkWv}, means...
```

(recalling that TEX is the intended text processor), and the text might ultimately print like

...and the last line, அடியாரக்கு மிகவே, means...

There is also an @english{...} command that interrupts encode mode and causes its bracketed text to be processed in copy mode, and the @tamil and @english commands can be nested arbitrarily. For example, the following grouping is acceptable to the preprocessor, producing a lengthy Tamil passage in an English text, the Tamil passage itself containing a brief use of English.

```
...(English text)...
@tamil{...(Tamil text within English)...
...@english{...(English text within Tamil)...}...
....(Tamil text resumes)...
}...(English text resumes)...
```

The reason for allowing such nesting is that the document input language can mimic the author's mental organization of the text and preserve the text formatter's hierarchical structure of the document. An English word in the middle of a Tamil sentence should be notated as such, rather than as the end of a Tamil passage followed by an English word followed in turn by the beginning of another Tamil passage. This carries over into the actual formats of the various pieces of text involved. For example, if we are entering an extended Tamil passage part of which is a quotation, we might like to narrow the column to set off the quotation. If the quotation includes some English, then the English should be set in the same narrow column as the Tamil. This intention is clear if the English part of the quotation is nested within the Tamil passage in the fashion illustrated above. If, on the other hand, the Tamil were ended to accommodate the English, the implication would be that the English should be set with the wide column of the document as a whole.

This raises the question of how one can accomplish detailed control of the document format through the preprocessor. It should be possible for text formatter commands to be embedded throughout the input file and be copied unmodified to the output file. In copy mode text this generally poses no problem, but in encode mode, formatter commands must be identified so that they are not encoded. The preprocessor is intended to be formatter independent, so it contains no knowledge of the syntax of commands used by any particular text formatter. Instead, to identify something as a formatter command, we enclose it within angle brackets (<...>). For example, if we have in the input file

```
...@tamil{...<\vskip 1cm>...}...
```

then \vskip 1cm is recognized as a command (to TEX) and the preprocessor does not attempt to encode this as it did with the surrounding Tamil. The same convention is used to include commands in the English text also. Thus, within English text, the user can either specify formatter commands as they are, or they may be enclosed within < and >. In spite of this freedom in copy mode, it is preferable to use the brackets for consistency and as a way to mark clearly the formatter-dependent text of the input file.

One important use of text formatter commands is for type style changes. In English we are accustomed to using different type sizes, italics, etc., to create visual distinctions complementary to the semantics of the text. In foreign languages type style also plays an important role. The preprocessor uses a predefined, default font in printing each language. Of course, type styles in copy mode can be changed using the font selection commands of the text formatter. In encode mode, however, it is not appropriate to try to select an alternative font, even with the angle bracket notation. This is because a large syllabary might require several of the text formatter's fonts to hold all of its symbols. The preprocessor, instead, provides a mechanism similar to changing language. For example, the table tamiltex provides a bold face Tamil font which will be used if Tamil mode is invoked using @tamilb{...} instead of @tamil{...}. The output file is constructed in such a way that all font switches will apply only to the text of the current language selection command, so that the user need not worry, for example, about accidently using the Tamil character set with English text.

A last detail of the preprocessor input language is an allowance for the fact that the preprocessor attaches special meanings to certain input characters. These characters are @, {, }, <, and >. At times it is necessary to include these characters in text formatter commands or in the final printed document. Special forms exist, therefore, to instruct the preprocessor to put these characters uninterpreted into the output file. These are, respectively, @@, @{, @}, @<, and @>.

Tailoring the System to New Syllabaries

In many ways, the table input to the preprocessor depends heavily on the text formatter for which it is designed. Among other things, the table contains instructions to the preprocessor on how to change fonts and group format changes. The names chosen for fonts and the syntax of most of the later entries of the table will also depend on the formatter. Therefore, the first decision that must be made is the text formatter around which to build the table.

The second step is to decide on the set of symbols to use in constructing the characters of the language. A syllabic writing system consists of a set of *characters*, and the characters are made up of one or more *symbols*. These symbols, by themselves, may not represent any character of the language, but when they combine with others, they form the written representation of the syllables of the language. The symbols in the language may combine among themselves in many different ways. For example, they may be written one after the other as separate symbols with space between them; they may be written one above the other; or they may be written in such a way that one symbol joins with the next adjacent symbol.

By breaking the characters of the syllabary into component symbols, the number of shapes that must be printable can be reduced significantly over the total number of characters in the syllabary. Nevertheless, the number of symbols may still exceed the capacity (typically 128 characters) of a single font in the desired text formatting system. It therefore might be necessary to apportion the symbols among several fonts. Using a system such as Metafont, one must construct these fonts and install them appropriately so that the text formatter can make use of them. This step is certainly the most exacting and time-consuming one in the process of tailoring the preprocessor to a new syllabary.

The names of these fonts and the name by which the user will know the collection must be recorded in the table. The table designer may elect to provide a second type style for the language. This requires a second collection of fonts and additional entries in the table.

The next step, and probably the most important one for the users of the system, is the choice of transliteration. Some languages, for example Japanese, have standard transliterations into the English alphabet. Other languages, however, do not, and in this case one must obtain the services of a native speaker of the language to discover what English letter sequences best approximate the consonants and vowels of the foreign language. When reading text to be encoded, the preprocessor breaks the sequence into *tokens*, each representing a vowel or a consonant. The preprocessor table lists these tokens, categorizing them according to whether they are consonants or vowels. It is possible for tokens to be several characters long, because, for example, the transliteration for Japanese distinguishes between two different consonants, k and kk. It is also possible for several tokens to represent the same consonant, because, for example, Tamil speakers would read b and p as transliterations of the same consonant.

After the preprocessor has broken the text to be encoded into tokens, it attempts to match up the tokens into consonant-vowel pairs. For every possible consonant-vowel pair the table includes an output text which will use the symbols in the various fonts to construct the proper character. In some instances, such as the case of a word with an initial vowel, tokens fail to match up in the consonant-vowel pattern. Special entries in the table provide output texts for such isolated consonants and vowels. All of these output texts must be provided by the designer of the table.

With this information the table is more or less complete. The table designer may, however, include other languages in the table, repeating the above process for each language.

Further details on the format of the preprocessor table can be found in the Appendix at the end of this paper. Space limitations prohibit the inclusion here of a complete description of the table for any particular language. These will be published as separate Technical Reports by the authors' Department.

Project Status

Currently we have the preprocessor working on tables for Tamil and Japanese with the TEX text formatting program. The Japanese tables work for both katakana and hiragana, handling them as separate languages in the table structure. One Tamil font has been prepared, which has been used in the printing of this paper. We also have a font for the Japanese katakana, and we hope to extend the system to the Japanese hiragana, Korean, and other languages that use syllabaries.

Besides extending the system to other languages, we would like to use the system with other text formatters that provide the option of including specially designed fonts in the font files available to the formatter. Troff is a popular text formatter that would be a valuable addition to our group of text formatters, which now consists of TEX and soon, Scribe.

The development of fonts for different syllabaries is an area that will continue to require work. We not only need to produce new fonts for new languages that our system is asked to handle, but also need to refine the already existing fonts and develop different sizes and styles for these fonts to allow true publication quality printing of the languages.

For the longer term, several very challenging and important problems present themselves. The inclusion of the Japanese kanji presents special problems that need to be solved in order to print Japanese, and this problem carries over to the printing of languages like Chinese. In order to handle the kanji along with the hiragana and katakana, we might make use of another preprocessor and input the kanji in upper case letters. We might then still be able to make use of the syllabary preprocessor to handle the hiragana and katakana after the kanji have been taken care of. The problem of hyphenation is virtually ignored in our current implementation, as is the problem of printing direction. It is interesting to note that printing Japanese top to bottom and right to left can be accomplished by creating a new font with a 90 degree rotation relative to the font used for left to right printing. Printing text with more than one orientation in one document, however, requires additional insight.

The future of the project now has many avenues open to it as we try to improve upon and extend the scope of the original design of the system for printing syllabic languages.

Appendix: Table Format

The table begins with several lines giving the characteristics of the text formatter, and continues with tables for each of the languages it implements. The numbers prefixing the paragraphs below are line numbers in the table file.

1

The number, c, of lines to be copied from the table file to the beginning of the output file, for including macro definitions, setting parameters, etc.

2

The first line to be copied to the output file.

3

The second line to be copied to the output file.

. . .

$c + 1$

The last line to be copied to the output file.

$c + 2$

Text to be output by the preprocessor whenever it comes across the sequence @...{ in the input, where a # is replaced by the word after the @; text to be output whenever the matching } appears in the input.

$c + 3$

Text to be output to invoke a new font, where a # is replaced by the font name; text to be output to end the invocation of the font.

$c + 4$

Number, j, of languages handled by the preprocessor.

$c + 5$

The beginning of the first of j language tables.

A language table has the following format, where n is the number of the first line of the table.

n

Number, i, of fonts available in this language.

$n + 1$

User's name of a font; number of font files used for defining the characters of the language; the actual font file names. The user's font name is the name used in the input file created by the user. The font file names are used by the preprocessor to load the appropriate font before outputting the commands to print a particular character of the language.

$n + 2$

Same as above, for the second font of this language.

$n + 3$

Same as above.

. . .

$n + i$

Same as above for the last font of this language.

$n + i + 1$

The number, j, of vowels in the language.

$n + i + 2$

The number of ways in which the first vowel can be written in input; the actual input representations, separated by spaces; the actual text, enclosed in braces, that is output by the preprocessor whenever it comes across any of the combinations in the input file.

$n + i + 3$

Same as above for the second vowel.

$n + i + 4$

Same as above for the third vowel.

. . .

$n + i + j + 1$

Same as above for the last vowel.

$n + i + j + 2$

The number, k, of consonants in the language.

$n + i + j + 3$

The number of ways in which the first consonant can be written in input; the actual representations, separated by spaces; the actual text output by the preprocessor whenever it comes across any of the consonant-vowel combinations. The number of items in this third category is the number of vowels in the language plus 1 ($j+1$). The extra entry is for the consonant when it is not followed by any vowel. When vowel v combines with this consonant, the text to be output is found in entry $v + 1$ in this category. Actually, this is not the entire truth. An entry in this category has substrings of the form @f {...}, in which case the enclosed symbols are to be taken from font file f. The @f may be omitted, in which case font file 1 is used.

$n + i + j + 4$

Same information for the second consonant.

$n + i + j + 5$

Same information for the third consonant.

$n + i + j + k + 2$

Same information for the last consonant in the language.

$n + i + j + k + 3$

The number, l, of other characters in the language which can not be classified as either vowels or consonants. Punctuation marks and numerals fall under this category.

$n + i + j + k + 4$

A pair of strings separated by spaces. The second string is the text to be output whenever the first string appears in the input, and if it is enclosed in braces it may be optionally preceded by a font file specification.

$n + i + j + k + 5$

Same as above for the second character

. . .

$n + i + j + k + l + 3$

Same as above for the last character.

References

[Becker 84] Becker, Joseph D., "Multilingual Word Processing," *Scientific American* 251, July, 1984.

[Furuta 82] Furuta, Richard, *et al.*, "Document Formatting Systems: Survey, Concepts, and Issues," *Computing Surveys* 14, September, 1982.

[Ghosh 83] Ghosh, Pijush K., "An Approach to Type Design and Text Composition in Indian Scripts," Technical Report STAN-CS-83-965, Department of Computer Science, Stanford University, 1983.

[Knuth 79] Knuth, Donald E., *TEX and Metafont*, Digital Press, 1979.

[Knuth 84] Knuth, Donald E., *The TEXbook*, Addison-Wesley, 1984.

[Nakanishi 80] Nakanishi, Akira, *Writing Systems of the World*, Charles E. Tuttle Co., Inc., 1980.

[Reid 80a] Reid, Brian K., "Scribe: A Document Specification Language and its Compiler," Technical Report CMU-CS-81-100, Department of Computer Science, Carnegie-Mellon University, 1980.

[Reid 80b] Reid, Brian K. and Walker, Janet H., *Scribe Introductory User's Manual*, Unilogic, Ltd., 1980.

ES/AG:
An Environment for the Generation of Expert Problem—Solving Application Systems

R. N. Cronk, D. V. Zelinski, M. A. Parker,
P. F. McKenzie, M. Iacoviello, K. Gies

AT&T Bell Laboratories
Piscataway, New Jersey

ABSTRACT

ES/AG (Expert Systems/Application Generator) is an integrated environment of languages and tools used to create problem-solving systems from a specification of knowledge about the application domain. A major feature is the ability to tailor the knowledge base language to specific application terminology. The ES/AG environment contains tools to aid in the *specification*, *compilation*, and *use of knowledge* to solve end-user problems. In addition, facilities are available for the user to *query* the knowledge and to receive an *explanation* of how the knowledge was applied to arrive at a solution. Interfaces to user-supplied program components are also provided.

1. INTRODUCTION

Artificial Intelligence (AI) is beginning to have an effect on the marketplace in the form of *expert*, or *knowledge-based systems*. [1] [2] [3] [4] [5] [6] [7] This is creating a need for expert system building tools for use by developers (vs. AI researchers) to create systems which solve practical application problems.

Many tools for building expert systems are now being developed and marketed. [8] [9] [10] [11] [12] [13] [14] Most provide a representation for expressing task-domain knowledge and a separate problem-solving mechanism which can use the knowledge to determine or search for solutions. Knowledge is typically expressed in the form of heuristic rules or productions. The control mechanism carries out its problem-solving either in a forward-chaining (matching left hand sides of rules) or in a backward-chaining way (matching right hand sides).

As these tools begin to be used for real-world tasks, the need to provide some procedural control over the (non-procedural) rule invocation has become a major issue. Some of the tools allow specification of procedural knowledge as well as non-procedural and factual knowledge (for example, as in S.1 [15]).

However, many of the expert system tools can only be used in limited problem domains. These are typically the class of diagnosis, or selection problems where there are a finite set of solutions and the problem-solving process determines which of the solutions are the appropriate ones. [16] [17]

This paper describes the ES/AG (Expert System/Application Generator) environment - a set of tools used to create application problem-solving systems. The class of systems for which ES/AG is also applicable includes synthesis problems - creating designs or configurations of components to match end-user needs. ES/AG is implemented in a UNIX* operating system environment.

2. SPECIFYING APPLICATION KNOWLEDGE

Knowledge about a specific application task domain is represented in a *knowledge base*. This representation is tailored to the application area by describing the terminology in a simple meta-level specification - a "terminological component." [18] An ES/AG knowledge base consists of three types of task-specific knowledge: *factual*, *procedural*, and *non-procedural*.

This knowledge is represented using two types of entities: *symbols* (data

---

* UNIX is a trademark of AT&T Bell Laboratories.

elements) and *rules*.

A *symbol* specification is a frame-like declaration of the data elements used in the problem-solving model. The declaration includes the factual information associated with the symbol - name, data type, and attribute/value associations which define application-specific properties of that symbol. Figure 1 is an example of a symbol declaration which defines factual information about an equipment item. Properties may be inherited (*of type* attribute in the example) to avoid redundant declaration.

```
Symbol: Basic_Controller;

   of_type: Unit;
   drawing_number: J1365-D01;
   report_description: Peripheral Controller Unit;
   basic_configuration: Single_Port, Shelf_Mounted,
                        Bus_Access;
   optional_configurations: Dual_Port, Cabinet_Enclosed,
                            Switchable;
   material_price: 12500;
   installation_price: 575;
   controls: RQ500, RQ600;
   power_requirements: external, -48V;
```

Figure 1. Specification of factual (attribute) knowledge

The declaration may also include a *procedure block* (a sequence of calculation steps). This procedure block is invoked by the control strategy whenever it needs a value for the symbol. While the invocation sequence of procedure blocks is left to the ES/AG control strategy (see below), explicit procedural knowledge may be encoded within each block.

Procedure blocks are optional attributes of symbols and are used when the value of a symbol can be determined in an explicit way. Values may also be determined by the actions of non-procedural rules or may be supplied by the end-user of the system.

Rules represent non-procedural knowledge - heuristic "rules of thumb" about the problem-solving task. A rule specification consists of a *condition-part* (lhs) and an *action-part* (rhs). The action-part is another procedure block in which sequential control may be specified. The syntax of rules is illustrated by Figure 2.

```
Rule: Configure_Next_Node;

   subtask: distribute_equipment;

   when

      (Current_Node < Nodes_to_be_equipped)
   ->
      print_node_report (Current_Node);
      store_node_equipment (Office_File, Current_Node);
      setv (Current_Node, Current_Node+1);
```

Figure 2. Example of a rule specification.

The ordering of evaluations of conditions and invocation of actions is not explicit in the knowledge base. The ES/AG control strategy determines *when* to evaluate and invoke a rule and, if more than one rule may be applicable at a certain state, chooses *which* rule may be the best choice for invocation.

The control strategy for invoking symbol procedure blocks and rule actions is described in a following section.

Within procedure blocks, there are three basic constructs which may be used:

- *Definitions* provide a capability for defining a variable and assigning a value to that variable. The compiler establishes the data type of the variable by evaluating the type of the expression being used to assign a value to the variable.

- *Imperatives* are statements which take some action. A few imperatives (stop, setv) are ES/AG primitives. Other imperatives may be defined by the knowledge base writer and become calls to user-defined procedures and functions.

- *Local (procedural) rules* allow the knowledge base writer to include rules within a procedure block and control the selection and invocation strategy to be employed in applying the rules. These rules are considered procedural since there are analogous constructs in procedural programming languages to implement the same control. They are identified with a control prefix which indicates the common analagous construct: *if-rules* and *while-rules*.

If-rules define a set of local rules which may be invoked. A default (otherwise) condition is provided for an action to be applied if no matches are found in the rule set.

The selection and invocation strategy is simple - evaluate each rule condition in the order listed until a match is found and invoke the associated action. Only the first matched rule will be applied from the set. An example of this type of procedural rule set is shown in Figure 3.

```
if
   (Primary_Controller_Requested and
   Backup_Controller_Requested)
           ->      Controllers_Per_Node : 2;

   (Primary_Controller_Requested or
   Backup_Controller_Requested)
           ->      Controllers_Per_Node : 1;

   otherwise
           ->      Controllers_Per_Node : 0;

   end_if;
```

Figure 3. Example of procedural if-rule.

A while-rule provides a cycling mechanism for a rule condition and action. The strategy employed for a while-rule is to invoke the action if the condition is matched and to repeat the action invocation until the condition no longer holds. Figure 4 shows an example of a while-rule.

```
   sum_list : nil_list;
   node : 0;
   while
       (node < Nodes_Equipped)
     ->
           node : node+1;
           sum : ith (Type1_Qty_List, node) +
                 ith (Type2_Qty_List, node);
           sum_list : append (sum_list, sum);
           end_while;
   setv (Qty_List, sum_list);
```

Figure 4. Example of procedural while-rule

Since these rules may be nested (that is, the action-part of any rule is a procedure block which can contain local rules), user-defined strategies can be built using these two simple constructs. In the example shown in Figure 5, the system will continue to cycle through the rule set given, invoking them in the order specified until either Solved becomes true or no rules apply (i.e., the "otherwise" condition is met).

Within the knowledge base, application-specific functions may also be referenced. These functions, associated parameters, and return data types are described in the terminology component.

```
solved : false;
cannot_solve : false;
while
     (not (solved or cannot_solve))
   ->
       Inside : not Outside;
       Can_Be_Out : not Must_Be_Inside;
       if
           (Outside and DontKnow (Raining))
                   -> setv (Raining, AnswerTo ("Is it raining?"));
           (Outside and Raining)
                   -> setv (Must_Be_Inside, true);
                      print ("Go Inside.");
                      setv (Outside, false);
           ((Inside and Must_Be_Inside) or
            (Outside and Can_Be_Out))
                   -> solved : true;
           <...and more...>
           otherwise
                   -> cannot_solve : true;
       end_if;
end_while;
```

Figure 5. Combining procedural rule strategies.

3. COMPILING ES/AG KNOWLEDGE

The knowledge contained in the application knowledge base is *static knowledge* about the task domain. Thus, for run-time efficiency, it is compiled - transformed into representations which can be queried or invoked by the ES/AG application programs when needed. [19] Procedural blocks are encoded in a traditional language, and factual knowledge can be represented in several efficient ways. In addition, the compiler determines other information which is useful in solving the problem (e.g., the possible dependencies of the data).

There are two ES/AG compilers - AL and SL. AL reads the application terminology component and determines the attributes to be associated with symbols and rules, possible values to be expected for these attributes (or classes of values), application-specific functions and imperatives.

The output of the AL compiler is used to "program" the task-specific SL compiler to accept a knowledge-base using the terminology described.

The SL compiler reads the application specific knowledge base, creates code for symbol procedure blocks and rule actions and extracts information about the *structure* of the problem-solving model being described. This structure can be represented as a connectivity graph. The nodes of the graph are symbol procedure blocks and rules. The edges correspond to the symbol references used in the determination of values for those nodes.

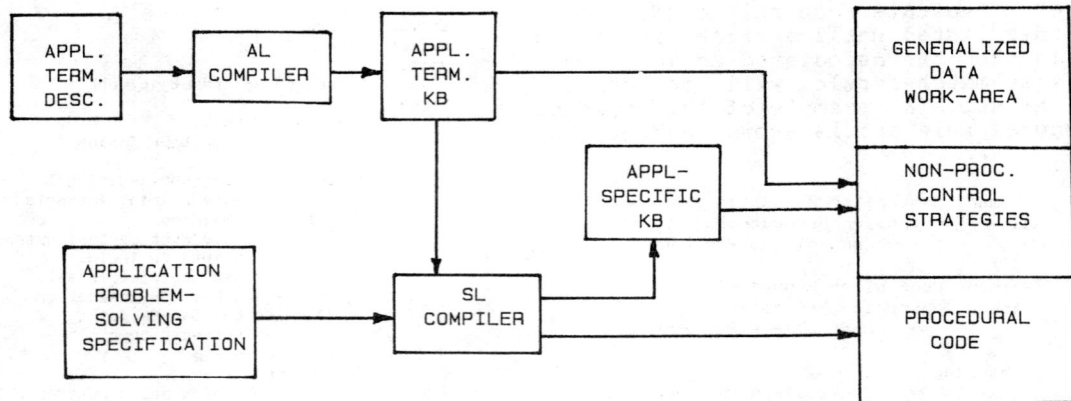

Figure 6. Overview of ES/AG Compilation

This is a static graph, and represents all possible dependencies which could occur in solving the problem. Use of this graph is helpful in focusing attention on only the rules and procedure blocks which are candidates for invocation. The dynamic data dependencies can then be represented as a subset of the full graph.

The compiler also collects the factual knowledge represented in the knowledge base and transforms it into a representation which is efficient for program retrieval and use. Figure 6 gives a simplified overview of the ES/AG compilation process.

While the SL compiler provides consistency and completeness checking for the knowledge base, another ES/AG tool provides mechanisms for *semantic validation* of attribute/value associations to symbols. To give *meaning* to attributes and values over the domain of symbols, we interpret these associations as making assertions about the defined symbols. [20] The assertions of interest involve relations among the elements of the domain. The ES/AG environment can apply *relational rules* (tests) of the attribute relations. These take the form of testing the truth value of a relationship between two expressions involving the attributes of symbols and rules.

4. USING KNOWLEDGE — THE ES/AG CONTROL STRATEGIES

In solving a problem, ES/AG uses a set of *control strategies* to effectively apply the factual, procedural, and non-procedural knowledge to the specific problem data. To do so, ES/AG must not only keep track of values for data elements, it must also keep track of the *state* of the problem-solving process. Knowing the state and changes to it leads to the ability to describe, or explain, the problem-solving steps ES/AG uses in the solution process.

To avoid the explicit statement of control flow required for sequencing calculation control blocks and rule invocations, ES/AG provides a combination of data-driven (forward-chaining) and demand-driven (backward-chaining) strategies. Backtracking within forward chaining of rule invocation cycles may also be used.

The problem-solving process proceeds in two distinct phases. The first phase involves the invocation of procedure blocks. Interaction with the user proceeds in both a forward and backward chaining way. As the user enters data, the forward dependencies are examined to determine what other values the system may determine and what rules might be candidates for evaluation. When data is requested by the user, backward chaining is employed to determine the answer and then all new determinations are propagated forward through the dependent procedure blocks and rules. Thus at any phase of interaction, the entire state of computation is current, based upon the data and values known at the time.

The second phase involves the selection and invocation of rules. When a rule is invoked, the process returns to phase I, where changes to the state are propagated forward.

The connectivity graphs (static and dynamic) are used as a simple *focus of attention* mechanism which can examine only the potentially relevant symbol procedure blocks and rule conditions which may require determination or reevaluation. The construction of the dynamic dependencies during backward chaining can be used to provide an explanation for *why* an input value is being requested. Figure 7 shows an example of this.

```
What is the serum bilirubin level (in mg/dL)? 15
What is the birthweight of the infant (in grams)? WHY

--> Low birth weight is a primary risk factor for intermediate
    serum bilirubin levels.

    This input [BirthWeight] is being requested in the
    current determination of:
      - whether or not the birthweight is low [LowBirthWeight]
      - clinical factors which could increase risk [ClinicalFactors]
      - examination of initial risk [ChangeInitialRisk]
      - a final risk based on all factors [DeterminedRisk]
      - an appropriate treatment [Treatment]

What is the birthweight of the infant (in grams)?
```

Figure 7. Example of "why" explanation.

5. ES/AG APPLICATIONS

The concepts of demand-driven and data-driven control for procedure blocks (automatic recomputation to always make the state current) and forward chaining of rules (matching lhs's of rules) are especially applicable to tasks involving configuration and design. This involves accepting user requirements and designing a configuration of components to meet those requirements.

5.1. The Design/Configuration Paradigm

A paradigm for the design (or configuration) process is the following:

- Accept the user's input of requirements (behavior, intended use, required capacities, etc.).

- From these requirements, create (using "book knowledge" or models and rules of thumb) an initial design.

- Analyze (test) the design to determine or simulate predicted behavior.

- Determine findings from the analysis by comparing predicted behavior with desired behavior.

- Use the findings to apply constraints to the types of design changes to be allowed in the next cycle.

- Apply rules to change the design parameters (within the constraints being propagated).

- Continue this *analyze-constrain-change* cycle until either the required design is completed or until it is determined that the design cannot be done.

Several design/configuration applications have been produced using the ES/AG environment. One of these, the Inductor Designer, is explained in some detail below to present some of the ES/AG capabilities.

5.2. Example — The Inductor Designer

The Inductor Designer is an application which illustrates the design process. It designs soft-iron-core inductors to meet electrical and heat requirements for low-frequency (60 Hertz) power-supply circuits. It assumes the use of standard gauges of copper wiring surrounding the soft iron core. Resulting inductance is affected by the wire size, the number of turns per unit length in the coil, the cross-sectional area of the core, the magnetic properties of the core material, and the length of the core.

The following information is requested of the user during the solution process:

- The desired inductance (in millihenries).

- The maximum allowable power dissipation (in watts/cu. in.).

- The AC current through the inductor (in amps).

- The DC current through the inductor (in amps).

- An initial guess, by the user, of the wire gauge to use in the winding of the inductor. The program will determine the final wire size required, but the better the user's initial guess, the fewer cycles required to determine the best size.

The goal of the application is to design an "acceptable" inductor having an inductance within 3% of the desired inductance, while simultaneously optimizing the power dissipation. The length of the soft iron core may be varied continuously, but must be cut from rods of discrete sizes. Wire sizes for windings are also discrete values, corresponding to standard wire gauges.

One standard for acceptance involves the aspect ratio of length to radius. Rules constrain the design such that the length must be more than twice but less than eight times the radius. This prevents the design of "pancakes" (flat, round inductors) and "pencils" (long, skinny inductors).

Rules use findings from analysis and current constraints to change the design and set additional constraints. Figures 8 and 9 show two examples from the Inductor Designer rules. The first checks for too much power dissipation and corrects it by increasing the wire size of the winding. The second is a check on the aspect ratio. Setv is an ES/AG imperative which sets the values of global symbols. Rule_Text is used for explanation of rule selection.

```
Rule: Increase_Wire_Size;

    when
        ((Power> Max_Power) and
         not Can_Decrease_Radius and
         Can_Increase_Wire_Size and
         Inductance_OK and
         Aspect_Ratio_OK)
    ->
        setv(Wire_Gauge, Wire_Gauge-1);
        setv(Min_Wire_Size, Wire_Gauge);
        setv(Min_Radius, 0.125);
        setv(Max_Radius, 100.0);
        setv(Can_Increase_Radius, (Radius<Max_Radius));
        setv(Can_Decrease_Radius, (Radius>Min_Radius));
        setv(Rule_Text,
            "wire size increased to reduce power");
```

Figure 8. Example Inductor Designer rule

```
Rule: Decrease_Aspect_Ratio;

    when
        (Aspect_Ratio_Too_Large)
    ->
        setv(Core_Volume, Core_Length*PI*(Radius**2));
        setv(Min_Radius, Radius);
        setv(Radius, Radius+0.125);
        setv(Core_Length, Core_Volume/(PI*(Radius**2)));
        setv(Rule_Text,
            "increase the radius and reduce the length");
```

Figure 9. Example Inductor Designer rule

ES/AG provides capabilities for knowledge base writers to create explanation text. In the Inductor Designer, Figure 10 shows an explanantion for the selection of the rule *Increase-Aspect-Ratio* at rule cycle 21.

For performance comparisons, the Inductor Designer was also created using a combination of OPS4 rules, FRANZ LISP, and C language routines for analysis computations. The results of the ES/AG version matched the design of the OPS4 version in all test cases. This performance comparison is shown in the first two columns of Table 1.

```
The design requirements are:
    a desired inductance (in mh) of 120.00
    a maximum power dissipation (in w/cu.in.) of 1.00
    an ac current (in amps) of 1.00
    a dc current (in amps) of 1.10

At rule cycle 21:
    The resulting design has the characteristics:
        a wire gauge of 29
        a core radius (in inches) of 0.38
        a core length (in inches) of 0.37
        the resistance (in ohms) of the core winding is 0.58
        the calculated inductance (in mh) is 120.00
        the resulting power density (in w/cu.in/) is 0.96
    Analysis indicates the following problems:
        incorrect aspect ratio (core length is too short
            relative to the core radius)
    The following constraints are active:
        the wire size cannot be decreased
        the wire size cannot be increased
    The following change is chosen:
        reduce the radius and increase the length
```

Figure 10. Inductor Designer - Explanation of Rule Selection

Since OPS4 provides only a forward-chaining strategy, another version of the ES/AG Inductor Designer was built with the backward chaining eliminated. All inputs were required to be entered before the design cycle began. This eliminated the need for ES/AG to perform the dynamic determination of whether enough data is known to invoke a procedure block or rule. The third column of Table 1 shows the performance of this version.

	OPS4	ES/AG (1)	ES/AG (2)
Size (Kbytes)	745	135	126
Time (seconds)	195	10.8	2.6

(1) forward and backward chaining
(2) forward-chaining only

Table 1. ES/AG - OPS4 Performance Comparison

5.3. Other Applications

ES/AG has been used to generate many other applications in a variety of task domains, including:

- *Local Area Network Configurator* - determines, from user needs, total equipment and cabling required to serve those needs. It also determines the number of nodes required and assigns the equipment to those nodes.

- *Software Project Cost Estimator* - implements the COCOMO model [21] for estimating large-scale software project costs (for requirements, development, and maintenance). It uses knowledge about personnel and computer resources and capabilities, size/complexity factors determined from a description of the application system, and knowledge about the software development environment.

- *CPU Capacity Model* - determines relative processing power for various CPU configurations and allows selection of upgrades to economically increase the processing throughput for various user classes.

- *Maisels Model for Hyperbilirubinemia Treatment* - uses hematofluorometric data, birth weight, age, and other clinical test findings for newborn infants to recommend a treatment to prevent kernicterus (bilirubin encephalopathy).

6. SUMMARY

ES/AG is a set of tools that generate expert system application software using a task-specific knowledge base. It uses backward and forward chaining strategies for invocation of procedure blocks to determine values of symbols and forward chaining (with backtracking) for rule evaluation and invocation.

The chief advantage of ES/AG is its ability to compile a knowledge base, performing syntax, completeness, and consistency checking as well as applying semantic rules to attribute knowledge. This compilation allows us to build reentrant, sharable code so that only one copy of the generated object code for rules and procedures is required in core. This is an important reduction in resources required for multi-user, production application systems.

But the compilation is also the primary disadvantage of ES/AG. Rules and static knowledge cannot be changed or added at execution time. Recompilation is required.

While ES/AG is not applicable for large-scale AI research efforts, it does provide an effective and efficient environment for developers wishing to create expert systems for well-defined applications in which procedural and non-procedural control strategies can be used in the problem-solving model.

7. ACKNOWLEDGEMENTS

The work on ES/AG evolved from the systems work at AT&T Bell Laboratories in the Network Administration and Engineering Laboratory. Several large-scale planning and configuration systems have been built and are now in use. The rules for the Inductor Designer were provided by Alan Parker, Supervisor of the Computer Aided Design Group in the Power Components and Military Applications Laboratory.

REFERENCES

1. Beeler, J., "Expert Systems Inching into Business," *Computerworld*, May 7, 1984.

2. McDermott, J. "R1: An Expert in the Computer Systems Domain," *Proceedings, First Annual National Conference on Artificial Intelligence*, Stanford University, 1980.

3. Hayes-Roth, F., "The Knowledge-Based Expert System: A Tutorial," *IEEE Computer*, September, 1984.

4. Hayes-Roth, F., "Knowledge-Based Expert Systems," *IEEE Computer*, October, 1984.

5. Gevaarter, W. B., "An Overview of Expert Systems," Pub. NBSIR 82-2505, National Bureau of Standards, Washington, D.C., 1982.

6. Nau, D. "Expert Computer Systems," *IEEE Computer, February, 1983*.

7. McDermott, J., "Expert Systems in Industry: A Case Study," *Tutorial Notes, The First Conference on Artificial Intelligence Applications*, Denver, CO, December, 1984.

8. Forgy, C. L., "The OPS4 Users Manual Technical Report," CMU-CS-79-132, Carnegie-Mellon University, Pittsburgh, PA, 1979.

9. Forgy, C. and McDermott, J., "OPS: A Domain-Independent Production System Language," *Proceedings of the 5th International Joint Conference on Artificial Intelligence*, 1977.

10. Michie, D., et. al., "RULEMASTER:TM A Second-Generation Knowledge-Engineering Facility," *Proceedings, The First Conference on Artificial Intelligence Applications*, Denver, CO, December, 1984.

11. Teknowledge, Inc., "M.1 Product Description," 1984.

12. Teknowledge, Inc., "S.1 Product Description," 1984.

13. Texas Instruments Inc., "Personal ConsultantTM Expert System Development Tools," Technical Report, 1984.

14. Hayes-Roth, F., Waterman, D., and Lenat, D., *Building Expert Systems*, Addison-Wesley, Reading, MA, 1983.

15. Erman, L. D., et. al., "Separating and Integrating Control in a Rule-Based Tool," *Proceedings, IEEE Workshop on Principles of Knowledge-Based Systems*, Denver, CO, December, 1984.

16. Chandrasekaran, B., "Towards a Taxonomy of Problem Solving Types," *AI Magazine*, Winter/Spring 1983.

17. Chandrasekaran, B., "Expert Systems: Matching Techniques to Tasks," Chapter 4 of *Artificial Intelligence Applications for Business*, W. Reitman (ed.), Ablex Corp., 1983.

18. Brachman, R. J., et. al., "KRYPTON: Integrating Terminology and Assertion," *Proceedings, AAAI-83*, 1983.

19. Lenat, D. B., et. al., "Cognitive Economy," Heuristic Programming Project Report HPP-79-15, Computer Science Dept., Stanford University, June, 1979.

20. Nilsson, N. J., *Problem-Solving Methods in Artificial Intelligence*, McGraw-Hill, New York, NY, 1971.

21. Boehm, B. W., *Software Engineering Economics*, Prentice-Hall, Englewood Cliffs, NJ, 1981.

A Robust Natural Language Interface to a Decision Support System

S. L. Booth, Cognitive Systems, Inc., New Haven, CT 06510
R. E. Cullingford, University of Connecticut, Storrs, CT 08268
N. H. White, Dialogue, Inc., NY, NY 10006

Decision support systems are used by financial planners, marketing analysts, securities specialists and the like, to access, manipulate, model and generate reports about information stored in large corporate databases. In this paper we describe DESI, a natural language front-end to ANALECT (tm), a decision support system providing a flexible set of tools for manipulating multidimensional data objects describing sales, stock quotes, etc., accumulated over time. DESI provides a robust interface to a database of such objects by infrequent or casual users, or users who simply do not wish to be bothered remembering the details of the database query language. Since DESI maintains models both of the database as it evolves and of its conversation with the user, it is capable of handling ungrammatical and ellipsed inputs, mispelled words, and both imperative and question forms. DESI fills in missing information needed to generate a well-formed query by looking up attributes of the object(s) being accessed. A "macro-command" facility is also provided through which the user can specify vocabulary of interest in the application domain, which DESI uses to generate sequences of queries which give the desired result.

ANALECT is a trademark of Dialogue, Inc.

1.0 Introduction: Multidimensional Decision Support Systems

The term Decision Support System (DSS) refers to a computer software system which helps managers retrieve, analyze, model or report on data which are used for tactical or strategic corporate decisions. There are many forms that a DSS can take, depending on the types of decisions being made and the amount and complexity of the data involved.

Some DSS's are primarily model-based in that there is little data and decisions are made on a mathematical model of the system in question. An example of this type of DSS might be a stock trading system which tracks one particular stock, and recommmends buy and sell timing. However, many DSS situations have voluminous amounts of data which have to be manipulated in order to provide the information necessary for an organization to act. While data base inquiry and retrieval languages often help in such situations, they usually do not have the necessary power to perform all the necessary computations. Further processing steps, either manual or computerized, have to be applied to the retrieved data in order to interpret it.

During the past decade, a number of systems have been developed which view data as *multidimensional,* and provide a set of retrieval, computational and reporting tools. Some commercial examples are EXPRESS [MDS82], ADDATA [ADS80], ANALECT [DIAL84], STRATEGEM [IP83], and System W [COM83]. A surprisingly large number of business problems can be analyzed by viewing the data involved as multidimensional.

One example that is relevant in almost any product-oriented company is sales data. Sales data can be viewed multidimensionally with dimensions of PRODUCT, MARKET, MEASURE, and TIME.

This four-dimensional data view is a fairly standard way of conceptually organizing and analyzing sales data. There are a number of variations depending on the size and complexity of the company. Often hierarchies can be represented by "splitting" a dimension into two or more sub-dimensions. For instance, markets might be grouped into regions, or products into product categories.

Another ubiquitous example is financial and accounting data which by definition has at least two dimensions, ACCOUNT and TIME and often has three or four dimensions when one goes to division-level or departmental reporting. Note that the dimensionality of data often increases as it is collected or available in more disaggregated form. There are many other applications of categorized data, having time as a basic dimension, which can be viewed multidimensionally. Associated with each of them is a set of similar operations such as averages, shares, aggregation, ratios, sorting, screening, etc.

2.0 Interfaces to Multidimensional DSS's

Users of such systems are typically not proficient computer programmers and often only do their analysis on an infrequent basis. For instance, marketing or financial plans are only developed every year. Financial reviews might only be done at the end of every month or quarter. Infrequent, non-technical users are particularly in need of user-interface support to aid their usage of a system. Typical user interfaces [VASS84] include command interpreters, menu systems, direct-manipulation systems and natural language systems.

A good natural language system can be a very efficient method of communication with a system, especially if the interface includes powerful context and referential capabilities [JAR84]. Natural language systems are also particularly attractive for infrequent, middle management personnel because of the potential for eventual voice interaction. If the system contains a model of the objects the DSS stores, the combination of DSS and natural language can be made even more powerful, since the system can "know" what kinds of operations are appropriate for different data types (dimensions).

3.0 System Overview and Sample Conversation

This section is an overview of the natural language interface (DESI) to the multidimensional analysis (MDA) component of a comprehensive DSS (ANALECT). First, we introduce some terminology which is useful for describing DSS's of the sort we are interested in. Then we give a brief overview of the major components of DESI. Finally we give an example of a conversation between a user and the DSS, mediated by the interface.

The words and phrases that appear in user inputs to DESI are normally descriptive of the user's *objects*, multidimensional associations of numeric data (marketing or financial data, for example) arranged in a time-series, and the *operations* the user wishes to carry out on them using ANALECT. The objects which are to be manipulated in an ANALECT operation are called *source* objects (of which there may be one or two), and the result of the operation is placed in a *target* object, which may be the same as one of the sources.

As stored in an ANALECT object, this data has a number of primary *dimensions,* the major descriptors of the object's organization. For example, a marketing-sales object might contain dimensions for "product," the collection of things for which sales data exists; "units," whether the data is given in terms of monetary units or simply number of products sold; "market," places where the products were sold; and "time," describing the intervals during which the products were sold. The dimensions group together *dimension values,* the constant terms which, when one is selected from each dimension, uniquely define an *item,* one of the numeric values in the database object. The dimension MARKET for example, could consist of dimension values standing for the cities in which the products are sold: ATLANTA, HOUSTON, SEATTLE, etc. The dimension values can also be organized *hierarchically.* For example, it can be declared to DESI that the term NORTHEAST is to stand for the collection of dimension values on the MARKET dimension consisting of NY, BOSTON and PHILADELPHIA.

The objects created by the user as the DSS runs can be stored in two places: the *database,* which is the long-term repository for objects the user wishes to keep across sessions; and the *workspace,* into which some of the database objects are loaded when the user wishes to work with ANALECT. New objects created in the workspace by ANALECT operations can be placed in the database for permanent storage.

As the block diagram of Figure 1 indicates, DESI, the natural language interface to ANALECT, has four major subsystems, all of which are based on existing products of artificial intelligence research:

1. A natural-language analyzer (adapted from the one described in [CULL84]), which processes typed English input into a representation of its meaning. The representation scheme used is a simple version of conceptual dependency [SCHA75], based on the database entities discussed above.

2. A recognition and diagnostic package, which is intended to examine the analyzer's output, identify the DSS command(s) being referred to, and correct or fill in any parameters needed to make a well-formed command. Ellipsis expansion, referent selection, fragmentary output and unknown words are handled here. (At this point, both the command and its parameters are still in a "conceptual" form).

3. A restricted-form natural language generator (very close to the one described in [CULL82]), which is given the output of the recognition subsystem and generates a DSS query.

4. A knowledge-base management and retrieval subsystem [CULL83], which is used to quickly find associations between conceptual forms and data/program packages (the "words" of the DSS query language in the case of the generator, and the diagnosis functions associated with each of the DSS commands in the case of the recognition subsystem).

Each of these modules will be discussed further below. To give the reader some feeling for the types of conversations a manager/analyst can have with DESI and the DSS, we present here a sample of input/output for a short session with the system, edited slightly for readability. Lowercase sentences are user input. Uppercase output is the DSS query. (The actual DSS output is not shown; it is typically a paginated printout of the contents of the target object of the DSS command, organized by its dimensional structure.)

After logging in to DESI, the user first needs to find out what the database contains. (Database objects and vocabulary defined in previous sessions are maintained by DESI on a per-user basis.)

Script started on Sun Feb 12 17:41:26 1984

DESI Version 2.13
Sun Feb 12 17:41:35 EST 1984

User:
what objects are there

DESI:
The workspace is empty

The database contains an ACCESS-type object
with dimensions:
MEASURE, MARKET, PRODUCT and TIME

You can RETRIEVE the complete object by typing

Stored objects: EX3 EX2 EX1 COMB INV1

Here the user's question has been handled directly by DESI. The user workspace currently contains nothing (the session has just started); the global database, conventionally named ACCESS, has the the dimensions shown; objects created by the user in the workspace in prior sessions and then placed back into the database are shown next.

User:
get w1 w2 and w3 in NY and Chi for 7901,
7902, and 7903, for both dollars and units,
and call that data smalldata

DESI Output:
RETRIEVE FFOBJ0 PRODUCT W1 W2 W3 MARKET
NY CHI TIME 7901 7902 7903 MEASURE D U

DESI Output:
RENAME FFOBJ0 TO SMALLDATA

Here the user has asked for a subset of the data in the ACCESS object (specified by the dimension values given) to be loaded into the workspace in the form of an object named SMALLDATA. DESI handles this by a combination of a RETRIEVE command, whose target is an object with made-up name FFOBJ0, followed by a RENAME of that object to the desired name. (DESI could have eliminated the RENAME by making SMALLDATA the target of the RETRIEVE. Such optimizations are not in the system as of this writing.)

----

get w4 and w5 as indicated above and name
it mediumdata

RETRIEVE FFOBJ1 PRODUCT W4 W5 MARKET NY
CHI TIME 7901 7902 7903 MEASURE D U

RENAME FFOBJ1 TO MEDIUMDATA

Here the "as indicated above" is analyzed as shorthand for "redo the last sequence of commands, with the new specifications overwriting the corresponding ones in the old sequence." The referent for "it" is resolved as the target of the RETRIEVE command.

combine smalldata and mediumdata into
groupdata

MERGE SMALLDATA WITH MEDIUMDATA FORMING
GROUPDATA

"Combine" is a way of referring to the DSS MERGE command. (It
can also mean EXTEND, as in "combine FOO and BAZ along
dimension BAR.")

User:
display it

DESI:
The dimensions of object GROUPDATA are:
PRODUCT MARKET TIME MEASURE
More? (y/n)

Dimension PRODUCT has values:
W1 W2 W3 W4 W5

Dimension MARKET has values:
NY CHI

Dimension TIME has values:
7901 7902 7903

Dimension MEASURE has values:
D U

Do you want to see the object's
values? (y/n)

DESI Output:
PRT GROUPDATA

DESI interprets "display" as a request for a detailed listing of the
attributes and values of the last target object. The attribute display
is handled by DESI directly. The values are shown by use of the
DSS PRT command.

---

sum smalldata over product and call it
totsmall

COLLAPSE FFOBJ3 = SMALLDATA SUM OVER
PRODUCT

RENAME FFOBJ3 TO TOTSMALL

This is an example of an arithmetic operation being applied along
one dimension of an object, yielding the reduced object TOTSMALL.

---

get from smalldata w1 dollars from 7903
and put it in w17903

SELECT FFOBJ4 FROM SMALLDATA WHERE
MEASURE EQ D AND PRODUCT EQ W1 AND
TIME EQ 7903

COMPUTE W17903 = FFOBJ4

Note that "get" is here interpreted by DESI as meaning a selection of
some data from a workspace object, rather than a RETRIEVE, as
above. The noun group "w1 dollars" has been resolved into
specifications along separate dimensions. The COMPUTE could have
been replaced by a RENAME, or eliminated altogether.

---

get same from totsmall and call it sm7903

SELECT FFOBJ5 FROM TOTSMALL WHERE MEASURE
EQ D AND PRODUCT EQ W1 AND TIME EQ
7903

RENAME FFOBJ5 TO SM7903

"Same" has been interpreted in a manner analogous to "as indicated
above" in a prior input.

---

divide w17903 by sm7903 and print
result

COMPUTE FFOBJ6 = W17903 / SM7903

PRT FFOBJ6

Here we have an example of an arithmetic operation with two objects
as arguments. The analyst is apparently interested in the ratio
between dollar sales of a given product in a given time period for all
markets versus sales for all products of a given type.

---

show all objects in workspace

Workspace objects:
FFOBJ6 SM7903 W17903 FFOBJ4 TOTSMALL
GROUPDATA MEDIUMDATA SMALLDATA

change the name of sm7903 to march79

RENAME SM7903 TO MARCH79

Here the analyst looks at the objects that currently reside in the
workspace, and gives one of them a more meaningful name.

---

average march79 over market and multiply
the result by 1.2 and put answer into
march80

COLLAPSE FFOBJ8 = MARCH79 AVG
OVER MARKET

COMPUTE FFOBJ7 = FFOBJ8 * 1.2

COMPUTE MARCH80 = FFOBJ7

This is a typical example of a "chain" of DSS commands being specified by a (not particularly grammatical) coordinate construction. DESI contains a recognition package that deals with constructions of this sort by recursively calling the recognizer on the individual component commands. The analyst seems to be making a sales growth prediction.

User:
show values for march79 and march80

DESI:
The dimensions of object MARCH79 are:
PRODUCT MARKET TIME MEASURE
More? (y/n)

The dimensions of object MARCH80 are:
PRODUCT MARKET TIME MEASURE
More? (y/n)

DESI Output:
PRT MARCH79

PRT MARCH80

User looks at his growth comparison.

----

get from mediumdata all values gt 100
and prt
SELECT FFOBJ9 FROM MEDIUMDATA WHERE
VALUE GT 100

PRT FFOBJ9

Here we see another use of "get" as a SELECTion operator, with an arithmetic comparison specified for the resultant object. The implied target object of the PRT is correctly supplied.

----

save the following objects: smalldata,
mediumdata, march79 and march80

STORE SMALLDATA MEDIUMDATA MARCH79
MARCH80

script done on Sun Feb 12 18:00:04 1984

Finally, the user stores the "interesting" objects back into the database, for possible use in future sessions.

5.0 Conceptual Analysis Subsystem

The language analyzer used by DESI is one of a class of analysis programs called *conceptual analyzers*. These are programs which attempt to map an input string directly into a meaning representation, using whatever morphological, syntactic, semantic, contextual, etc., cues are available. They are distinguished from other types of analysis programs in that they do not attempt to first analyze the input syntactically, then assign a semantic reading to the syntactic structure [e. g., WOOD70, MARC80]. Nor do they conduct a simultaneous syntactic and semantic analysis [e. g., WINO72, BROW75]. (Such analyzers are sometimes called "parsers.") Syntac-

tic features such as word order and noun-group constituency are used by a conceptual analyzer only to guide the mapping process.

The basic mechanism used by DESI's analyzer is a *predictive* one which attempts to provide *expectations* about what will be read on the basis of what has already been read. Word definitions describing the meaning structure(s) built by a word are kept "off-line" in a dictionary, and are not called into active memory until the word is actually seen in the input stream. Expectations associated with a word definition are encoded in a special type of production rule (test-action pair [NEWE72]) called a *request* [RIES75]. Requests are *activated* when the associated word definition is loaded, i. e., placed in a short-term memory of requests to be *considered*. The request consideration process repeatedly selects a request and evaluates its test part. If the test returns "non-nil," the request is said to have *fired*, its action part is evaluated, and it is removed from the request memory. Requests can check semantic, lexical, or contextual features of the run-time environment, and create or interconnect conceptual structures. Moreover, they can cause other requests to be activated or deleted. Associated with a meaning structure built by a word are a set of slots and a set of expectations embodied in requests indicating how roles are to be filled.

Consider, for example, the conceptual analysis of the sentence "John ate an apple." (We will ignore the details of how morphology and noun-grouping are managed.) The dictionary definition for "John" might look like this:

```
(def-word John
  pos noun
  topreq
  ((test t)
   (actions
    (add-word-con wsJOHN1))))

(def-wordsense wsJOHN1
  surface-form (John)
  ws-structure (person-f persname (John)))
```

Here, *def-word* is a record macro for managing the analyzer's dictionary. "John" has Part Of Speech "noun." The "top" request for "John" has a test part which always evaluates to non-nil, so the action part is always executed. The single action given here calls the function *add-word-con* to add the meaning structure for the associated wordsense (which defines a named person as shown) to the short-term memory of available concepts called the C-LIST. The word "apple" would contain a similar definition, except that the structure added to the C-LIST would be based upon the primitive *ingobj*, or ingestible object.

Neither or these words activates any further requests. The word "eat," however, does:

```
(def-word eat
  pos verb
  topreq
  ((test (:= topcon (add-word-con wsEAT1)))
   (actions
    (activate
     (actspot-req topcon (actor) couldbe-person-p)
     (objspot-req topcon (obj) couldbe-ingobj-p)))))

(def-wordsense wsEAT1
  surface-form (eat)
  ws-structure
  (ingest actor (nil)
       object (nil)))
```

Here, "eat" first adds the structure defined by the wordsense to the C-LIST, then calls the function *activate* to add two new requests to request memory. (The function := is the *run-time binding operator*, which propagates the actual name of the concept returned by *add-word-con* for this instance of "eat" into the body of the request. All instances of "topcon" will be replaced by that name. Since := always returns non-nil when used in this way, we get the effect of (test t) as in the definitions of "John" and "apple.")

The first request, named *actspot-req*, embodies a test which seeks a *person* (using *couldbe-person-p*) to fill the *actor* slot in the concept built by "eat." The place where the request looks for its actor is in the "act spot," that is, among the C-LIST items preceding the concept for "eat" in the active voice, in a prepositional phrase governed by "by" in the passive. The second request, named *objspot-req*, seeks an ingestible to fill the *obj* slot in the *ingest* structure, following that structure if the voice is active, preceding it if passive. (Both of these requests implement a fairly complicated symbolic computing activity. See [CULL84] for more details.) This simple (looking) request cluster thus embodies the syntax and semantics of "eat."

The analyzer, proceeding right-to-left through the sentence, first activates and fires the request for "John," adding the associated structure to the C-LIST. Next, the top request for "eat" adds the *ingest*, and queues up the two requests. The *actspot-req* fires immediately, since "John" is already available. The concept is inserted into the *ingest* as the *actor*, and the "John" concept disappears from the C-LIST. The *objspot-req* is a *prediction*, in this case, and does not fire when first considered. Next the topreq for "apple" fires (ignoring the determiner "an"), and the *ingobj* gets placed on the C-LIST. Now the second request for "eat" fires, and the "apple" concept becomes the *obj* filler in the *ingest*. The process terminates, leaving a well-formed conceptual structure as its result.

More complicated things happen when the words have several meanings, as for example is the case with "combine." If we restrict attention to the imperative form only, its definition is

```
(def-word combine
  pos verb
  topreq
  ((test (:= topcon (add-word-con wsCOMBINE1 wsCOMBINE2)))
   (actions
    (:= extendcon (grf '(v1) topcon))
    (:= mergecon (grf '(v2) topcon))
    (activate
     (velprepspot-req topcon extendcon (dim1)
             (along for in)
             couldbe-dimension-p)
     (velfollspot-req topcon mergecon *discard clp-p))
    (activate

     <requests to pick up the two series
       objects which are sources>

    )
   ))))
```

Here, a structure (called a *vel*) is added to the C-LIST which represents the two-ways ambiguous concept. The two calls to := propagate the names for the subcons representing the individual meanings through the rest of the request through the names "extendcon" and "mergecon." (The function *grf*, or g(et)-r(ole)-f(iller), extracts the filler associated with the slot (role) named by its first argument from the structure named by its second.)

The first call to *activate* creates requests to examine the C-LIST for features which would allow a decision about disambiguation to be made. The first, a *velprepspot-req*, searches for a dimension concept associated with a prepositional constituent governed by "along," "for" or "in." If it finds one, it *compresses* the ambiguous concept down to the EXTEND concept, and inserts the dimension concept at slot *dim1*. Usually, all the requests that were activated at the same time are suppressed at this point. The second request, using the

predicate *clp-p*, looks for a following *clausepoint*, an indicator (e. g., the end of the sentence) that the clause associated with "combine" has ended. If a clausepoint is reached without a dimension's being found, the concept is compressed to a MERGE. Since there are arrangements for staged compression steps (i. e., a 3-ways ambiguous concept may be compressed to a 2-ways ambiguous one), the computation can get quite complex.

This, in necessarily broad outline, is how DESI's basically bottom-up analysis process proceeds. The system is built on top of several dozen named requests such as *actspot-req* and *velprepspot-req*, together with about twenty specialized actions other than *activate*. Dictionary definitions are easily and flexibly created once the basic ground rules are understood. Due to the extreme simplicity of the meaning representation scheme, very few unexpected interactions have occurred between existing vocabulary and new words as they are added.

6.0 Recognition/Diagnosis Subsystem

Because of its bottom-up nature, the analysis module is prone to create fragmented output when the user's input deviates too far from grammaticality. Much of the effort in designing DESI has gone into *recognizing* an analyzer output as referring to an ANALECT command; and in *diagnosing* why it doesn't. Successful recognition of an input leads to a process of parameter validation and default-filling.

6.1 Data Structures

A series object is defined by a collection of dimensions and their corresponding dimension values. It is initially created in the workspace by: retrieving specified portions of the stored ACCESS database; issuing a command that forms a new object as a result; or creating a new object through specifications entered by the user. It may subsequently be stored in the database for future reference. When in the workspace, its structure may be modified as a result of the commands being issued. This modification is not reflected in the stored version unless overwritten by issuing a new STORE command. Thus, an object may simultaneously be defined by two different structures one as it exists on file, and one as it exists in the workspace.

If the system is to perform the functions of type checking and filling in missing parameters it must maintain models of the following information: 1) what objects are defined in the workspace; 2) what objects are defined in the database; 3) the structures of the objects as they exist in the workspace/database; and 4) the structure of the database.

The models maintained of the workspace and database are simple lists of the names of the objects defined in each. The system adds and deletes names from these lists as a result of the commands being issued. As a result of maintaining these models, the system can automatically issue commands to retrieve objects in the database when the user has not done so, since an object must be in the workspace before it can be manipulated by a command.

The object structural models consist of a collection of association lists, one for each dimension. These lists specify the structure of the object as it is stored in the database vs. the structure of the object as it exists in the workspace:

```
(dfps OBJ1
  wsstructure
  ((MEASURE U)
   (PRODUCT W1)
   (MARKET NY BOS)
   (TIME 7901 7902)
  )
```

```
dbstructure
((MEASURE U)
 (MARKET NY BOS)
 (PRODUCT W1 W2 W3)
 (TIME  7901 7902))
```

The function *dfps* is a multiple *defprop*. The "wsstructure" property gives the current structure of the object as it exists in the workspace. As shown, object OBJ1 has four dimensions: MEASURE, PRODUCT, MARKET, and TIME. The dimension values associated with each dimension are: U for the MEASURE dimension; W1 for the PRODUCT dimension; NY and BOS for the MARKET dimension; and 7901 and 7902 for the TIME dimension. The object models are used for three main purposes: 1) checking that a user parameter specification is legal for the object named; 2) filling in a specification which the user has not mentioned; and 3) answering queries regarding the current state of the database or workspace, such as "show workspace objects," or "Is NY in the Market dimension of OBJ1."

The system also makes extensive use of a global record-type data structure called an "exchange frame." Each frame carries all the information needed to define the stage of understanding of the current exchange with the user, and is passed to all the major modules of the system. An example follows:

```
(exch1
 ape-result ()       ~ holds the result produced by the parser
 fr-status ()        ~ keeps track of the current processing stage
 exchcontext ()  ~ holds contextual information
 pkg-result ()       ~ final conceptual form passed to the generater
 from-user ()        ~ holds input string given by user
 .
 .
 .
 .
)
```

Exchange frames provide a well organized method of passing large amounts of information to the major functions involved in processing, in particular, pointers to *prior exchange frames*, which are the major sources of contextual information.

6.2 Recognition

All of the semantic and syntactic knowledge needed for full "understanding" is determined by the ANALECT command being referred to. Therefore, it made sense to associate the procedures for checking parameters, filling in defaults, etc., directly with the command name. The information needed to process each command includes the following: a set of conceptual patterns designed to match the characteristic ways of referring to the command; a conceptual template to be filled in with command parameters and sent to the generator; an optional match-time function used to place restrictions on the matching process; a diagnostic function encoding the semantic information needed to process the command; and a run-time function responsible for updating the models maintained by the system.

As usual, a record macro maintains the "package" of data and functions needed to implement the recognition process:

```
(def-pkg SELECT-PKG
 targets (())

patterns                 ~ patterns used for matching
 (selectpkg1               ~ tag name for the pattern
 (FFcommand-f commtype (SELECT))
 ~ the names of the functions to be run during processing
 match-select diag-select run-select)

frame                       ~ the empty command frame
 wsSELECT
)
```

The pattern *selectpkg1* matches user inputs expressing a SELECT, with assistance from function *match-select*. Function *diag-select* checks the parameters provided and inserts them and any needed defaults into the command frame. (Note the use of the wordsense wsSELECT.) The run-time function *run-select* sends the command frame to the generator and updates the system models.

Simple pattern matching was a feasible means of recognition because of: 1) the simplified meaning representations used; 2) the small number of commands which define the system; 3) the efficiency of the method used to store and access the patterns (i. e., the knowledge-base manager described in [CULL83]); and 4) the ability to recognize partially formed concepts, or fragments (in the case of an incomplete parse). Due to the simplified meaning representations, only one pattern for the declarative form and a small number of patterns for question forms were needed for each command. (The analyzer takes care of mapping paraphrase equivalent sentences into the identical "conceptual" form.) Since the number of commands is limited to approximately 20, the total number of patterns needed for recognition small.

6.3 Diagnosis

Basically, as stated above, the purpose of the recognition phase is to determine what command the user has issued by examining the "meaning" representation produced by the parser. The method of recognition described above works perfectly well when the result of analysis is a single recognizable concept. (By "recognizable" we mean that there is a pattern stored which matches against the concept.) However, this is not always the case. There are two types of problems that can occur. The first deals with inadequecies related to the analyzer. This includes missing and/or inadequate word definitions, or inadequecies in the processing mechanics of the analyzer. The second type of problem deals with natural language phenomena such as elliptic expressions. In this case, the analyzer has performed correctly, the concept produced just needs to undergo a "pre-recognition" stage of processing.

When the parser fails, it generally produces a list of fragmented concepts that it was unable to combine into a single meaning structure. (We are assuming for purposes of discussion that only one full concept was expressed by the user.) There are two causes for this type of failure. The first is related to inadequecies in the word definitions or in the parsing mechanisms. Since these are problems which cannot be fixed at "run-time," a means of "salvaging" any information we can from the fragments was an issue we decided to take into consideration. The second is due to the presence of unknown words, i.e., words which have no meaning to the system. (Misspelled words are handled by a spelling corrector.)

Salvaging information from fragmented output must be done carefully in order to avoid erroneous results. Our approach to this problem involved using the pattern matcher in an attempt to find an indication of the command being referred to. (The pattern matcher is well suited for this purpose since the patterns are generalized forms of the command representations.) If successful, the semantic knowledge stored with the command is used in an attempt to "piece" the fragments together. Any ambiguities or uncertainties encountered would be presented to the user for clarification. In the event that the match failed the system would make its "apologies" and ask the user to continue.

If the unknown word or phrase can be associated with a word that is known to the system, then a simple substition followed by another attempt at analysis may produce a successful results (a single, recognizable concept). This method necessitates interaction with the user. A clarification dialouge is entered with the user in which the unknown word or phrase is presented. S/he was then asked if one of the words in the system's vocabulary could be used as a substitute for it. Since it was not expected that the user be familiar with the system's vocabulary, a facility for displaying it is available upon request. Once a word is chosen, the sentence is reparsed with the appropriate substitution made.

While this process may seem to be unneccessarily complicated and drawn-out, it does have an important advantage. It can be used as a means of defining new words "on the fly". The user is given the option of "adding" the unknown word to the system's vocabulary as a "synonym" for the known word. The next time the word is used (e. g., in a leter session), it will be defined and the process will not need to be repeated.

The system also needs to deal with anaphoric reference and ellipsis. Reference problems are simplified in this application domain because the user is nearly always referring to the target object(s) of a previous command when a pronoun is used. For example, the user may say "put sum of FOO and Baz into BAR," followed by "print it," or even "print." Here, the referent (implied in the second case) is resolved to BAR. The system locates prior targets by reference to the *exchcontext* field in the current exchange frame.

Ellipsed inputs are usually partial specifications of dimension or dimval parameters, missing an explicit reference to a command. Similarly, ellipsed inputs are "expanded" in the context of the previous inputs. The preceding ANALECT command frame (in its conceptual form) is retrieved from the exchange context, and subconcept(s) "congruent" to the given ones are located. Then the surrounding command is copied, with the congruent data overwritten with the new data. For example, "get foo for ny and Bos," followed by "for Chi and LA." results in a conceptual copy of the command "get <object> for Chi and LA" being sent to the generator. (The system will not overwrite the target objects in cases such as this, but will ask the user for a name.)

7.0 Conceptual Generator Subsystem

DESI's conceptual generator was adapted from a program that performs the inverse mapping to analysis: processing a well-formed "conceptual" structure into a natural language string. Since DESI's function, however, is to generate strings in the rigid ANALECT command syntax, the generator module has been greatly simplified. Mechanisms in the original program to perform tensing, aspect and modal expression, and subject-verb agreement were disabled, as were special-purpose rules (called "sketchifiers" [CULL82]) responsible for producing "advanced" English syntactic constructions such as infinitives, gerunds, imperatives, etc.

Since ANALECT commands conform to a rigid grammar, the only information needed by the generator is the syntactic specifications needed to produce well-formed command strings. These specifications are stored with the dictionary entries used to determine what word to use when expressing a concept. A typical dictionary entry, together with the corresponding wordsense entry, looks like the following:

```
(gdictdef wsEXTEND
 ()
 (((source1)
   (fo)(pr (source2)))
  ((source2)
   (fo)(fo WITH)(fo (source1))(pr (dim1 dimtag)))
  ((dim1 dimtag)
   (fo)(fo (source2))(fo USING)(pr (target)))
  ((target)
   (fo)(fo (dim1 dimtag))(fo FORMING)))
 )

(def-wordsense wsEXTEND
 surface-form (EXTEND)
 ws-structure
 (FFcommand-f commtype (EXTEND)
   source1 (series-f)
   source2 (series-f)
   dim1 (dimension-f)
   target (series-f))
 )
```

In a manner analagous to the analyzer dictionary, the record macro *gdictdef* builds a generator dictionary entry on top of a wordsense. The base meaning of the word, stored under the "ws-structure" property of the wordsense tag, is a conceptual pattern consisting of a primitive type with its case-frame, and various slots filled by sub-concepts. The "surface-form" property contains the word to be expressed corresponding to the meaning structure.

The syntactic specifications are used to order the fillers of the various slots in the generator's short-term memory, called (like the analyzer's) the C-LIST. A sentential focus, i. e., a subconcept to be "said" first, may be associated with the syntactic specifications since the specifications may be dependent on the focus. (For example, active versus passive in English). In the above dictionary entry no focus is specified (indicated by the empty list). The specifications consist of a list of syntactic predicates. These comprise an association list between the *path* to a filler and a set of predicates to order that filler with respect to other fillers. (A "path" is a list of slot-names which uniquely identifies the location of a slot-filler in a conceptual structure.) There are three types of predicates, all of which are lists. One is simply the atom 'pr' (standing for "precedes") or 'fo' ("follows"), representing the relationship between the particular filler and the word corresponding to the definition (in the above, EXTEND). Another consists of the atom 'pr' or 'fo' followed by a list. The list is a path, and the syntactic predicate states that the filler is to precede or follow the filler of that path. The last form is a list of the atom 'pr' or 'fo', followed by another atom, called a *function word* (e.g., 'USING' and 'FORMING' in the above example). This indicates that the filler to be "said" should precede or follow that word. To summarize, the syntactic predicates are used to indicate where the parts of the concept CGEN is trying to express are placed in the C-LIST relative to: the word found, remaining concepts to be expressed, and any function words.

The basic cycle used to transform the input conceptualization into the corresponding ANALECT command string is one of dictionary lookup, followed by insertion of subconcepts into the C-LIST as specified by the syntactic predicates associated with the entry found. At the beginning of each cycle, the item at the top of the C-LIST is examined. If it is a word, the generator "says" it. If it is a concept, it is sent off to the dictionary to be matched to an entry which spans as much of the concept as possible. The syntactic specifications are used to give positional information about the word found and slot-fillers which still need to be expressed. These items are placed on the C-LIST according to the specifications and the cycle is repeated. The cycle is complete when all concepts have been "expressed."

8.0 Current Status

An prototype version of DESI, programmed in Franz Lisp [FODE81], is currently running under UNIX on a DEC VAX-11/780. In addition to the vocabulary associated with the user objects, the system has a vocabulary of several hundred words, many of them several ways ambiguous. For demonstration purposes, DESI communicates with a version of the DSS, ANALECT, running on a PR1ME 750, over a dial-up telephone connection. The system has been tested with several (simulated) marketing databases and a personnel records database. Run time is dominated by the analysis phase: here, DESI reads and processes words at the rate of between on-third and one-half a second per word. Thus, a typical exchange takes on the order of 5-8 seconds (plus the time needed for the DSS to form the answer).

DESI is designed so that it can either run on the same hardware as the DSS, or on a specialized front-end processor (e. g., a single-user workstation) for increased performance. A major consumer products company (General Foods, Inc.) is currently evaluating the system for possible installation in the current fiscal year.

REFERENCES

[ADS80]

Addata Users Guide, Applied Decision Systems, Lexington MA, 1980

[BROW75]

Brown, J. S., and Burton, R. R. "Multiple Representations of Knowledge for Tutorial Reasoning," in Bobrow, D., and Collins, A. (eds.), *Representation and Understanding,* Academic Press, NY.

[CHAR80]

Charniak, E. (et. al.), *Artificial Intelligence Programming.* Erlbaum Press, Hillsdale, NJ, 1980

[COM83]

System W Reference Manual, Comshare Inc., Ann Arbor, MI, 1983

[CULL82]

Cullingford, R.E., Krueger, M.W., Selfridge, M.G., and Bienkowski, M.A. 1982. "Automated Explanations as a Component of a Computer-Aided Design System." *IEEE Trans. SM&C.* Special issue on human factors and user assistance in CAD. Vol. SMC-12, No. 2, pp. 168-182. (Mar/Apr)

[CULL83]

Cullingford, R.E. and Joseph, L.J., 1983, "A Heuristically 'Optimal' Knowledge-Base Organization Technique." IFAC *Automatica,* Vol. 19, No. 6, pp. 647-654. (November/December)

[CULL84]

Cullingford, R.E., and Pazzani, M., 1984, "Word Meaning Selection in Multi-Module Language Processing Systems." *IEEE Trans. PA&MI.* July, 1984 (in press).

[DIAL84]

ANALECT Multi Dimensional Analysis System Users Manual, Dialogue Inc, New York, NY, 1984

[FODE81]

Foderaro, J. K., and Sklower, K. L. *The Franz Lisp Manual.* Regents of the University of California, Berkeley.

[IP83]

Strategem Reference Manual, Integrated Planning, Inc., Boston, MA 1983

[JAR84]

M. Jarke, J. A. Turner, E. A. Stohr, Y. Vassiliou, N. H. White, and K. Michielsen, "A Field Evaluation of Natural Language for Data Retrieval", *Software Engineering* (in press).

[MARC80]

Marcus, M. *A Theory of Syntactic Recognition for Natural Language.* MIT Press, Cambridge, MA.

[MDS82]

Express Reference Manual, Management Decision Systems, Waltham MA, 1982

[NEWE72]

Newell, A., and Simon, H. *Human Problem Solving,* Prentice-Hall, NY, NY.

[RIES75]

Riesbeck, C. "Conceptual Analysis," in [SCHA75].

[SCHA75]

Schank, R. C. (ed.), *Conceptual Information Processing,* North-Holland, NY, 1975.

[VASS84]

Vassiliou, Y and M. Jarke, "Query Languages: A Taxonomy," in Y. Vassiliou (ed.), *Human Factors and Interactive Computer Systems,* ABLEX, Norwood, NJ.

[WINO72]

Winograd, T. *Understanding Natural Language.* Academic Press, NY, NY.

[WOOD70]

Woods, W. A. "Transition Network Grammars for Natural Language Analysis." *Comm. ACM,* Vol. 13, No. 10.

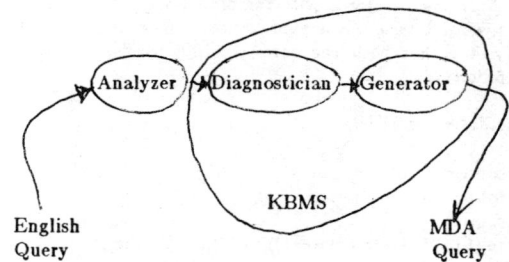

Figure 1
Structure of DESI

UNDERSTANDING ASSEMBLER BY GENERATING A HIGHER LEVEL VERSION

M. Arthur Ozeki

Science Institute, IBM Japan Ltd.
5-19 Sanbancho, Chiyoda-ku, Tokyo 102

ABSTRACT

Maintenance and modifiability are constant issues
in software development, most so when dealing with
assembly language. In order to understand assembly it must first be read. This paper presents a
prototype tool which generates a higher level version of a segment of assembly code making understanding easier. The tool is essentially an
expert system written in Prolog. The method used
is a two-pass scheme with the target code similar
to Pascal. A strong background in assembly is not
necessary, though the user should be familiar with
programming skills.

1.0 INTRODUCTION

In any type of code modification, the process of
designing control flow and deciding what new functions are to be incorporated and which functions
are to be changed is vital and often irrevocable.
Languages and specification techniques have provided convenient ways in which to make modification more flexible and readable. Before any
revision, however, comes understanding the code,
thoroughly.

When applied to the assembler language, 'understanding' becomes a menacing task not only because
it is low-level, but also since a majority of
existing code was written some time ago and maintained over a long period by various people. What
would be an optimal way to make understanding and
modifying such code easy? Documentation only
exists sparsely and probably very informally. Why
not bring the assembly code itself to a higher
level, in as complete a form as possible? We are
not speaking of creating a higher level version of
the code that can be executable as is, but at least
one that is a step towards understanding the code,
and possibly a way to give hints as to better and
more efficient ways to implement it in a structured sense [Dij72].

This paper will discuss a prototype tool consisting of an expert system coupled with a knowledge base that breaks down System/370 assembler
[IBM83] into an internal form, and uses the knowledge base to generate an equivalent higher level
abstracted version similar to Pascal [Jen74]. The
generation is done by performing a partial simulation of the actual code execution. Both the
expert system and knowledge base are written
entirely in Prolog [Clo81].

In the discussions that follow, we first elaborate on the expert system. Its structure and
examples of the knowledge base will be given. We
then will cover the actual program generation by
reviewing a segment of assembler code. In the end
further issues revolving around the techniques
used will be discussed.

2.0 THE EXPERT SYSTEM

The tool or expert system is actually an offspring
of another project which is also still under
development. The original project [Fuk85]
involves generating statement-by-statement anno-
tation for system code written in assembly.
Regardless of the final output, however, both
objectives require indepth knowledge surrounding
assembly and programming in general. For those
uncomfortable with code, high level or not, an
English-like description may be more useful. In
most cases, however, since the end result of
understanding the code will be to rewrite it, we
feel that a code-like description would be more
appropriate.

The relations between information in the knowledge base, and the inferences used to create the
equivalent higher level statements are written in
an object-oriented language based on Prolog.
Thus, variable names and hardware-related facts
(i.e., storage, registers, etc.) are defined in
the form of instances of classes.

Information related to VM/370 assembler, programming conventions, and system hardware is
included in the knowledge base. In earnest, there

237

is no end to the amount of knowledge we can collect, especially when there is no clear-cut line between what is assumed to be common knowledge and non-common knowledge. In this paper, however, we assume for the time being that all knowledge is complete and accurate.

2.1 AN EXAMPLE OF THE KNOWLEDGE BASE

Fortunately, the syntax of assembly language is simple. Using Prolog, the concept of changing assembler syntax into a more prolog-like one is not difficult. The format chosen, however, and what information should be included is the problem.

As a simple example, we will look at how a common 'load' instruction, specifically the 'LA' (load address) instruction, is handled. Figure 1 displays the inheritance relations for the 'LA' instruction which means "load the second operand address into the first operand". When the generator encounters a 'LA' instruction such as 'LA R15,LINEPATN(R14)', it first passes control to 'rx-load-immediate' (which LA is an instance of), which through parent resolution eventually passes control to 'load-instruction'. Here, the LA instruction requires that its operands be parsed and identified before knowing where to send the operands for further resolution. In this case, the operands need to be sent to the 'register' class and 'indexed-storage' class, respectively. Identification of the operands is done in the 'rx-instruction' class which is also a parent of 'rx-load-immediate'. Previous implementations lacked such structure and much overlap has been recognized since.

After the instruction and operands have been evaluated, the result should be 'R15 := LINEPATN[R14]' where LINEPATN has been recognized as an array (see section 3.2).

2.2 STRUCTURE

One of the primary objectives in designing the expert system was modifiability. The knowledge base should be mostly static but since software changes, so do even so-called 'standards' and it must be simple and efficient to modify the knowledge base components. Basically, the program generator takes as input the source code (analyzed version), and 3 types of knowledge--hardware/VM, assembly language, and programming concepts. The following is a breakdown of the 3 types, each containing a list and examples of the kinds of knowledge involved:

- Hardware/VM
  - instructions (load, compare, and/or, branch)
  - storage (indexed storage, registers, condition codes)
  - status (program status word (PSW), program interrupt codes)

- Assembly Language
  - symbols, variables
  - expressions (instruction syntax)

- Programming Concepts
  - programming conventions (counters, tables)

Figure 2 displays the overall structure of the expert system. The internal structure of each component should change with time, however, as we find more overlapping knowledge and better ways to redefine existing knowledge relationships.

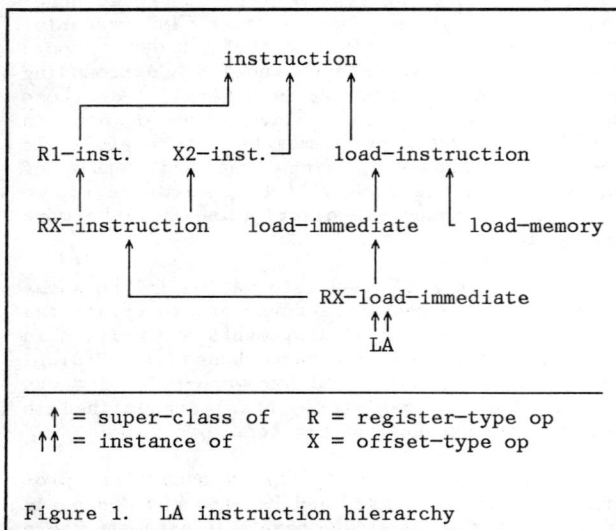

Figure 1. LA instruction hierarchy

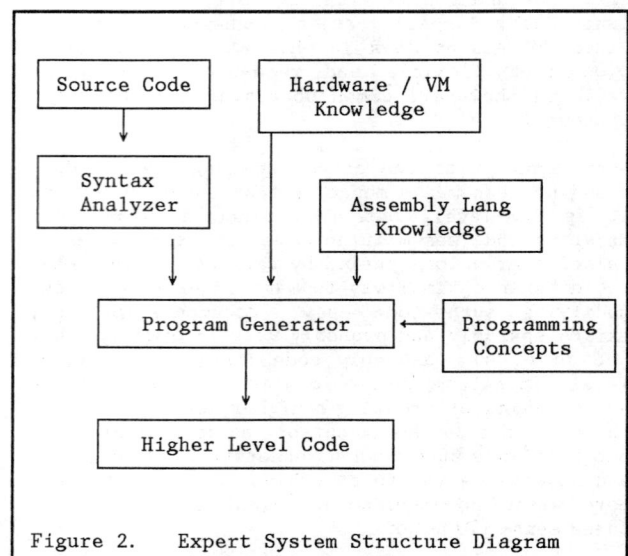

Figure 2. Expert System Structure Diagram

3.0 PROGRAM GENERATION

The method uses a two-pass scheme with the target code similar to Pascal. In the first pass, the source code is syntactically analyzed and rewritten into an internal Prolog-compatible form. Consecutively, one or more assembler statements are evaluated and for those that are directly 'translatable' (e.g., assignments), equivalent statements are generated in the pseudo-higher level target code. The second pass processes those assembler statements that require more structure, such as loops (e.g., branches).

The example we chose to use is a segment of the DMKSBL module of CP (Control Program) which handles lowercase character graphics.

3.1 DESCRIPTION OF ORIGINAL CODE

The sample segment that we have extracted from the DMKSBL module consists of a simple conditional do-loop. The loop's function is to iterate through a string of characters and create the actual fonts used on the screen. Which characters and which fonts to use are found through indirect accessing, using tables and calculating displacements. For future reference the following describes the contents of each register (or in our case parameters passed to this segment) prior to entering the loop:

1	- Relative line number
3	- Address of next letter to translate
4	- Number of letters remaining
8	- Address of next output location
12	- Base register
14/15	- Temporary work registers

In addition, there are three tables accessed from this segment: CHARTABL, CHARPATN, and LINEPATN. CHARTABL is a table of internal codes for each character. The values from CHARTABL are in turn used as displacements into CHARPATN, which again is a table of displacements into LINEPATN, which contains all the character patterns used for the screen fonts. Figure 3 is the actual segment taken from the module with the original comments placed alongside. Mnemonics are included for the reader's convenience.

```
BLOKLOOP   DS     OH
           SR     R14,R14                         clear work reg
           SR     R15,R15                         clear work reg
           IC     R15,0(,R3)                      get next character
           IC     R15,CHARTABL(R15)               get internal code for char
           MH     R15,LCHARPAT                    index to charpatn entry
           AR     R15,R1                          add current line # to index
           IC     R14,CHARPATN(R15)               get pattern # from charpatn
           MH     R14,LLINEPAT                    get index to linepatn
           LA     R15,LINEPATN(R14)               point to correct pattern
           MVC    0(LLINEPAT,R8),0(R15)           move to output area
           MVC    LLINEPAT(SKBLANKS,R8),SBLANKS   blanks too
           LA     R8,LLINEPAT+SKBLANKS(,R8)       next output area
           LA     R3,ONE(,R3)                     point to next character
           BCT    R4,BLOKLOOP                     get next code, if there's one

CHARTABL   DC     X'26'                           period
                  ...                             (other characters)
CHARPATN   DC     X'0E0f1009090000090909'         A
                  ...                             (other alphanumerics)
LINEPATN   DC     C'**            '               
                  ...                             (other patterns)
LCHARPAT   DC     AL2(L'CHARPATN)                 length of a char pattern
LLINEPAT   DC     AL2(L'LINEPATN)                 length of a line pattern
ONE        EQU    1                               number of blanks between chars
SKBLANKS   EQU    2                               number of blanks between chars
SBLANKS    DC     CL(SKBLANKS)' '                 that many blanks
```

```
Mnemonics:     SR  = subtract registers     IC  = insert character
               MH  = multiply halfword      AR  = add registers
               LA  = load address           MVC = move characters
               BCT = branch on count        DC  = define constant
```

Figure 3.   Original code segment

3.2 HIGHER LEVEL CODE GENERATION

Unlike the comments above, a statement of higher level code will not be generated for every assembler instruction. In some cases a number of assembler instructions may equal one or more higher level statements. In other cases, we have chosen to implement the assembler instruction as a function that is called. One instance of that is the MVC (move characters) instruction found within the segment. The actual definition of the MVC instruction is: "the second operand is placed in the first operand location". In our segment, the instruction "MVC 0(LLINEPAT,R8),0(R15)" would mean to move LLINEPAT bytes from the location specified by R15 to the location specified by R8, as in the following diagram:

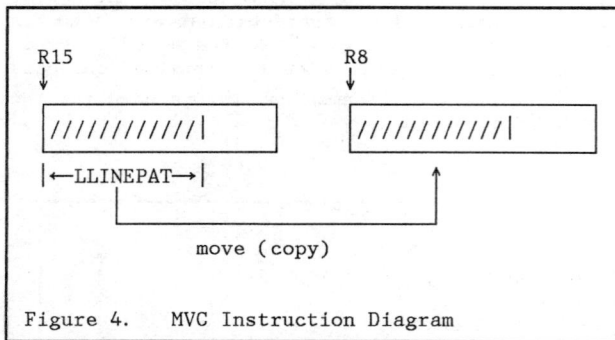

```
R15                        R8
↓                          ↓

|///////////|              |///////////|

|←—LLINEPAT—→|                      ↑
       |_____|

              move (copy)
```

Figure 4.   MVC Instruction Diagram

In this expert system we have assumed that all instructions referencing storage areas by offset will be modelled as an array of characters in the higher level version. Therefore, in any situation where a register is used as a pointer to some location, a variable with the same name as that register will be used as a displacement in an array in the higher level version. Thus, in making the MVC instruction a function, it would be a loop consisting of a character-by-character assignment from one array to another. A 'FOR' loop is used for the length of the move. Thus, the function MVC is defined as follows:

```
MVC : procedure(Source, Target, Offset, Length)
      Source : string;
      Target : array of chr;
      Offset : integer;
      Length : integer;

      for I = 0 to Length-1 do
        Target[ Offset + I ]
              := substr(Source, I, 1)
           end ;
      end ;
```

Figure 5.   MVC as a System Defined Procedure

Using the MVC function and some of these assumptions, Figure 6 shows the resulting code. The translation should be straightforward and self-explanatory. Here, the system has deduced the information that CHARTABL, CHARPATN, and LINEPATN are tables (arrays), which is why the registers are used as indices (array lengths, were also user implanted). If this information had not been placed in the knowledge base, then each of the tables would have been taken as constants. In this case, the register would have been regarded as a value and not an index. For example, in a 'IC' instruction, the results would have been:

```
original              :  IC  R14,CHARPATN(R15)
table as an array     :  R14 := CharPat[ R15 ]
table as a constant   :  R14 := CharPatn + R15
```

The difference between the second and third forms is significant. In truth the third form where CHARPATN is taken as a constant is closer to the original. Yet, for the third form to have meaning, it would have to be explicit that CHARPATN is a collection of constants beginning at the label 'CHARPATN'. But this would defeat the purpose of 'raising' the source code to a higher level. (We are not saying this is 'wrong', but only that we are trying to emphasize abstraction in the process.)

There are a number of assumptions and conditions that we have set forth so that generation is kept simple and as coherent and consistent as possible, and at the same time not degrading the resulting output. For example, the system has deduced that the 3 tables are arrays. We have assumed from the code that CHARTABL is an 'array' type by the fact that an IC instruction usually is associated with storage-offset type usage, but we have no assurance that this is true. We will, however, continue to assume datatypes depending upon their usage in instructions for the time being. In the course of covering larger segments, conflicts may arise due to this simplistic method. Since the expert system cannot extrapolate from the 4 letters 'TABL' that CHARTABL is a table, 'names' (labels) will initially be considered as 'variables' unless otherwise defined. Some of the other important assumptions are:

1) Storage areas will be modelled as arrays of characters.

2) Bytes will be modelled as characters.

3) Registers will be considered as variables.

3.3 TRADE-OFFS AND LIMITATIONS

In our scheme we have modelled the simple load instruction as an assignment statement. This probably holds true in most cases, but not always. When we transform the assembly source code into a higher level target code, a major trade-off arises when matching the two. How much conversion do we

```
/* USER DEFINED INFORMATION */

Array1¹      := array [ 1..80 ]   of chr          /* input */
Array2¹      := array [ 1..80 ]   of chr          /* output */
CharTabl     := array [ 1..256² ] of chr
CharPatn     := array [ 1..44² ]  of chr( LCharPat² )
LinePatn     := array [ 1..64² ]  of chr( LLinePat² )

/* CODE-EXTRACTABLE INFORMATION */

LCharPat     := 10
LLinePat     := 9
SKBlanks     := 2
SBlanks      := ' '
One          := 1

/* CODE */

BLOKLOOP:

do while R4 > 0
   R14 := 0
   R15 := 0
   R15 := Array1[ R3 ]
   R15 := CharTabl[ R15 ]
   R15 := R15 * LCharPat
   R15 := R15 + R1
   R14 := CharPatn[ R15 ]
   R14 := R14 * LLinePat
   R15 := LinePatn[ R14 ]
   call MVC(R15, Array2, R8, LLinePat)
   call MVC(SBlanks, Array2, R8 + LLinePat, SKBlanks)
   R8 := LLinePat + SKBlanks + R8
   R3 := One + R3
   R4 := R4 - 1
enddo;
```

¹ = generated automatically   ² = changed by user (default = 80)

Figure 6.   Translated code

want before straying away from the original implementation? For example, in our second pass, the
BCT (branch-on-count) instruction literally means
"Branch to the second operand address until the
first operand (a register) is zero, decrementing
the first operand every time". We have modelled
this as a conditional do-loop, where the control
variable (R4) is decremented every time at the
conclusion of the loop. We could have, however,
started the loop with a 'for' statement, such as
"for I = 1 to R4 do" and removed the control variable from within the loop. The second approach
may be 'cleaner' in terms of higher level code,
but it takes a clear step away from the structure
of the source code, since the BCT instruction at
the end of the loop does the actual decrementing
of the register (i.e., R4).

Secondly, it would be simple to change the variable names to something more descriptive. For
example, instead of 'CharPatn' we might put Char-
acterPatternTable. This could be done by adding a
instance variable to the instance of 'CharPatn' in
the knowledge base. This would, however, involve
more interaction with the user. We could also
replace all the occurrences of a register variable
with a more meaningful name, such as 'LettersRe-
maining' for R3 and 'NextLetterAddress' for R4.

Third, we are still experimenting with the
resulting target language. We have so far used a
Pascal-like target language, but we are also
experimenting with a more explicit form. Since
the system performs a partial simulation of the
code itself, it actually 'enacts' stores and loads
in its memory. Thus, instead of manipulating
terms, we might begin placing more concrete values
in the output. This in turn introduces more dif-
ficulties. Storing values implies a need for an
efficient means of keeping track of past evaluations. If the evaluations are concrete (e.g., 2
+ 3 = 5) then we are safe; if one value cannot be
resolved, however, a history of executions becomes
increasingly long. For example, the user might
not add some necessary knowledge such as the value

241

of a variable. We wish the target form of 'AR A,B'
(add registers A and B and store in A) to be 'A :=
A + B' where A then contains the actual value of A
+ B; but if A could not be evaluated (i.e, A was
not defined) then the system might revert to a
default target form of 'plus(A,B)'. Given B having the value 2 but A undefined, then a propagation of this type of error could lead to
something similar to 'plus(mult(minus(A,2),5),3)'
since the deeply nested A could not be evaluated.

In terms of limitations, we have yet to find a
way to supply all the necessary values for optimal
datatyping internally. Array lengths and other
constants that are not explicit in the code can
only be extracted by complicated means. For example, tables in assembly do not need an 'end' since
all accessing is done through displacements. In
addition, some other details overlooked include
the fact that a number of instructions deal primarily with only certain bits of a register, whereas
we 'assign' a value to a register in entirety.

4.0 SUMMARY AND CONCLUSION

The objective of this tool is to aid a person in
understanding assembler code. It is not meant for
the person who only wants to know what the code
does (i.e., in our case printing characters), but
for the person who wants some understanding of the
structure and implementation. After the code has
been translated, the results can be shared among
others.

The tool is not fully automated. Inputting a
piece of assembler code alone may result in a
semi-helpful but likely misleading conversion. To
get the most out of the tool, user intervention is
required, as well as time. The meaningfulness of
the results also depends on how the user interprets the code. The results, however, should be
worth the effort. If the original source code and
resulting higher level version were shown to someone with little background in programming languages, it should require much less effort to
explain the latter over the former. If the user
knew anything about the Algol-family languages, it
should take even less effort.

Programming in assembler though is often done
against conventions. The example chosen in this
paper was straightforward. The assumptions made
were correct and the results accurate. But sometimes because of the simplicity of assembler, the
unlimited number of combinations of instructions
cannot always be logically analyzed. It may be
easier and smarter to 'cheat' here and there in
assembler since it involves working at such a low
level.

At present our system can only identify simple
statements and a limited number of instructions.
The next steps include handling of larger segments
with more instructions and usage. In dealing with

larger segments, it is evident that the issues of
consistency and reliability of the results will
become increasingly important and difficult to
maintain.

5.0 REFERENCES

[Clo81] Clocksin, W.F. and C.S. Mellish (1981)
Programming in Prolog, Springer-Verlag.

[Dij72] Dijkstra, E.W. (1972) "Notes on Structured
Programming", taken from Structured
Programming, Academic Press.

[Fuk85] Fukunaga, K. (1985) "PROMPTER: A Knowledge
Based Support Tool for Code Understand-
ing", submitted to the 8th International
Conference on Software Engineering.

[IBM83] IBM System/370 Extended Architecture.
Principles of Operation, (1983) Form
SA22-7085-0, International Business
Machines Corp.

[Jen74] Jensen, K. and N. Wirth (1974) The Pascal
User Manual and Report, Springer-Ver-
lag.

Anderson, Edward
U.S. Army Electronic Proving Ground
Attn: STEEP-MT-DA
Ft. Huachuca, AZ 85613

Antczak, Tom
Jet Propulsion Laboratory
4800 Oak Grove Drive
Pasadena, CA 91109

Appleby, J.M.
General Dynamics
P.O. Box 748
Fort Worth, TX 76101

Arefi, Farah
University of Central Florida
P.O. Box 25000
Orlando, FL 32816

Balcer, Marc J.
Kulicke & Soffa Industries, Inc.
507 Prudential Road
Horsham, PA 19044

Ball, Donald J.
Sperry Systems Management
Marcus Blvd.
Great Neck, NY 11020

Balk, Herbert
U.S. Army-AMCCOM
Picatinney Arsenal
Dover, NJ 07801-5001

Banthia, Pratap
Burroughs Corporation
2888 Woodcock Blvd.
Atlanta, GA 30341

Barach, David
AT&T Bell Laboratories
6 Corporate Place, 1M142
Piscataway, NJ 08854

Barasch, Linda
Amoco Production Company
P.O. Box 3385
Tulsa, OK 74102

Barski, Peter
Haid Buckel 32
D8501 Eckental 1
West Germany

Beaucage, Andre
Ecole Polytechnique de Montreal
Edouard Montpetit
Montreal, Quebec, Canada

Becker, Mark
General Electric Company
1285 Boston Ave., Bldg. 30EE
Bridgeport, CT 06601

Belcher, R.G.
IBM Corporation
P.O. Box 390
Poughkeepsie, NY 12602

Berecz, Victor
Norden Systems/UTC
P.O. Box 5300
Norwalk, CT 06856

Biddle, Justin
The Aerospace Corporation
P.O. Box 92957
Los Angeles, CA 90009

Bitar, Imad
TRW
One Space Park
Redondo Beach, CA 90278

Block, Christopher
ISDOS, Inc.
325 E. Eisenhauer Parkway
Ann Arbor, MI 48104

Blum, Bruce
Johns Hopkins University
Johns Hopkins Road
Laurel, MD 20707

Bond, Rodney M.
10411 Storch Drive
Seabrook, MD 80706

Bowen, Jr., Freddie R.
Norfolk State University
2401 Corprew Ave.
Norfolk, VA 23504

Box, Jim
AT&T Bell Laboratories
Wheaton-Naperville Roads
Naperville, IL 60540

Bozic, Samo
Polytechnic Institute of New York
333 Jay Street
Brooklyn, NY 11201

Brautigam, John
Hazeltine Corporation
Pulaski Road
Greenlawn, NY 11740

Broner, Hans
Grumman Data Systems
1000 Woodbury Road
Woodbury, NY 11797

Bune, Marisa
AT&T Network Systems
c/o AT&T Bell Laboratories
480 Red Hill Road
Middletown, NJ 07748

Burghard, Tom
Grumman Aerospace Corporation
Stewart Ave., MS D01-31T
Bethpage, NY 11714

Byrnes, Mary Ellen
AT&T Bell Laboratories
8 Corporate Place
Piscataway, NJ 08854

Carasik, Bob
Pacific Bell
370 3rd Street, Rm. 753A
San Francisco, CA 94107

Chang, Kuang-Hua
AT&T Network Systems
6 Corporate Place
Piscataway, NJ 08854

Chang, Robert T.
Polytechnic Institute of New York
333 Jay Street
Brooklyn, NY 11201

Chou, I.-Fang
Bell Communications Research
3 Corporate Place, PYA 213303
Piscataway, NJ 08854

Christian, Kathy
General Electric Company
P.O. Box 8555
Philadelphia, PA 19101

Clark, Lori
University of Massachusetts
Amherst, MA 01003

Cline, Ralph
Quantitative Software Management
1057 Waverly Way
McLean, VA 22101

Colin, Paul
Index Technology Corporation
Five Cambridge Center
Cambridge, MA 02142

Cort, Gary
Los Alamos National Laboratory
Group P-9 MS-H805
Los Alamos, NM 87545

Cronk, Robert
AT&T Bell Laboratories
6 Corporate Place, PY1K-134
Piscataway, NJ 08854

Cullinford, R.E.
Princeton University
EE/CS Department
Engineering Quadrangle
Princeton, NJ 08544

D'Andrea, Pete
Grumman Aerospace Corporation
Stewart Ave.
Bethpage, NY 11714

Daniel, Colleen
Shell Oil Company
Bellaire Research Center
3437 Bellaire Blvd.
Houston, TX 77025

DeLoatch, Sandra J.
Norfolk State University
Norfolk, VA 23509

DeMassi, George
U.S. Army - AMCCOM
AMSMC-4AH
Dover, NJ 07801-5001

Der, Rose
IEEE Computer Society
3 Corporate Place
Piscataway, NJ 08854

Dodani, Mahesh
University of Central Florida
P.O. Box 25000
Orlando, FL 32816

Dong, Rui-Yuan
University of Illinois
Dept. of Computer Science
1304 W. Springfield Ave.
Urbana, IL 61801

Edelstein, Eugene V.
Sperry Systems Management
Marcus Blvd., MS F5
Great Neck, NY 11020

Elia, Christine
Intermetrics, Inc.
5312 Boloa Ave.
Huntington Beach, CA 92649

Erdos, Marianne E.
Hazeltine Corporation
Pulaski Road
Greenlawn, NY 11740

Estes, George E.
AT&T Network Systems
6 Corporate Place, Rm. 1E261
Piscataway, NJ 08854

Farmer, Clifford
Digital Equipment Corporation
77 Reed Road
Hudson, MA 01749

Feinberg, D.A.
Boeing Computer Services
P.O. Box 24346
Seattle, WA 98124-0346

Finnell, Charles
Teledyne Brown Engineering
788 Shrewsbury Ave.
Tinton Falls, NJ 07724

Foote, Wayland
AT&T Technologies
475 South Street
Morristown, NJ 07960

Forman, Ira R.
MCC
9430 Research Blvd.
Austin, TX 78759

Frail, R.P.
Hazeltine Corporation
Pulaski Road
Greenlawn, NY 11740

Franker, Phyllis
New York University
251 Mercer Street
New York, NY 10012

Fuhrer, James H.
Sperry Systems Management
Marcus Ave.
Great Neck, NY 11080

Gies, Kathleen
AT&T Bell Laboratories
6 Corporate Place, Rm. 1K-126
Piscataway, NJ 08854

Giterman, Hana
Advanced Technology International
135 W. 41st Street, Suite 1800
New York, NY 10036

Glickman, Stuart E.
General Electric Company
1285 Boston Ave., Bldg. 30EE
Bridgeport, CT 06601-2385

Goodman, Stuart
General Electric Company
1285 Boston Ave.
Bridgeport, CT 06601

Gourlay, John S.
Ohio State University
Dept. of Computer & Info. Sci.
2036 Neil Ave. Mall
Columbus, OH 43210

Hallenbeck, David
136 Midvale Drive
Fairport, NY 14450

Halliday, Steven A.
Environment Canada
4905 Dufferin Street
Dolonsview, Ontario, Canada M3H5T4

Henderson, Peter B.
State University of NY at Stony Brook
Department of Computer Science
Stony Brook, NY 11794

Hengstebeck, M.F.
General Dynamics
P.O. Box 748
Fort Worth, TX 76101

Hlotke, John
AT&T Network Systems
6 Corporate Place
Piscataway, NJ 08854

Huang, C.C.
AT&T Information Systems
307 Middletown-Lincroft Road
Lincroft, NJ 07738

Hurley, Anne
Xerox Corporation
Jefferson Road-Bldg. 801
Rochester, NY

Irving, Jeffrey
AT&T Bell Laboratories
Naperville-Wheaton Road
IH6M-415
Naperville, IL 60566

Janusz, Paul
U.S. Army - AMCCOM
AMSMC-QAH-A - Bldg. 62
Dover, NJ 07801-5001

Johnson, Martin
U.S. Army ISSSC
Attn: ASB-ESSD, Stop C-70
Ft. Belvoir, VA 22060-5456

Josselyn, Jill V.
Systems Control Technology, Inc.
1801 Pace Mill Road
Palo Alto, CA 94303

Juliusberger, Hans
IBM Corporation
East Fishkill B503,Z/92A,D/37A
Hopewell Juncton, NY 12533

Karohl, Jim
Perkin-Elmer
1000 Wooster Heights Road
Danbury, CT 06810

Kernighan, Brian W.
AT&T Bell Laboratories
6 Corporate Place
Piscataway, NJ 08854

Kogut, Paul
U.S. Army-CECOM
AMSEL-PA-DT
Fort Monmouth, NJ 07703

Krafcik, Richard
Avco/Lycoming Division
550 S. Main Street
Stratford, CT 06497

Lao, Check K.
Sperry Systems Management
Marcus Blvd
Great Neck, NY 11020

LaRock, Celeste
Digital Equipment Corporation
110 Spit Brook Road
Nashua, NH 03062

Levinson, Edward
Bell Communications Research
6 Corporate Place, PYA-1M-182
Piscataway, NJ 08854

Levinson, Susan
Bell Communications Research
444 Hoes Lane
Piscataway, NJ 08854

Link, Alexis
Hughes Aircraft Company
P.O. Box 3310, MS 618/L215
Fullerton, CA 92634

Luongo, John
Grumman Data Systems
175 Froehlich Farm Blvd.
Woodbury, NY 11747

Mace, Robert
Higher Order Software Inc.
2067 Massachusetts Ave.
Cambridge, MA 02140

Manning, John
Grumman Data Systems
175 Froehlich Farm Blvd.
Woodbury, NY 11797

Marciniak, John J.
Marciniak and Associates
P.O. Box 2383
Arlington, VA 22202

Mason, Christopher
Chemical Abstracts Service
2540 Olentangy River Road
Columbus, OH 43210

McKenzie, Paul
AT&T Bell Laboratories
6 Corporate Place
Piscataway, NJ 08854

Melhado, Warren K.
Sperry Systems Management
Marcus Ave.
Great Neck, NY 11020

Miller, John M.
IBM Corporation
18100 Frederick Pike
Gaithersburg, MD 20879

Modica, Leo A.
AT&T Bell Laboratories
Naperville-Wheaton Road
Room -1H 6M-442
Naperville, IL 60566

Mohanty, S.N.
MITRE Corporation
1820 Dolley Madison Ave.
McLean, VA 22102

Montanaro, George
General Electric Company
Corporate Research & Dev.
P.O. Box 8, Rm. KWC-210
Schenectady, NY 12301

Mueller, Rose
Burroughs Corporation
10850 Via Frontera
San Diego, CA 92127

Mughal, Khalid
Cornell University
Computer Science Dept.
405 Upson Hall
Ithica, NY 14850

Neftci, Sinan
3611 Ravens Crest Drive
Plainsboro, NJ 08536

Neorr, John
Boeing Computer Services
P.O. Box 24346
Seattle, WA 98124-0346

Niech, Lawrence
ITT Avionics
100 Kingsland Road, Dept. 74201
Cliffton, NJ 07014

Noyce, Michael D.
Shell Oil Company
P.O. Box 20329
Houston, TX 77025

Ozeki, M. Arthur
IBM Japan, Ltd.
5-19 Sanbancho, Chnoda-Ku
Tokyo, Japan 227

Parry, Harold
U.S. Army ISSSC
Attn: ASD-ESSD, Stop C-70
Ft. Belvoir, VA 22060-5456

Pato, Joseph N.
Brown University
P.O. Box 1910
Providence, RI 02912

Pearl, Lawrence
Digital Equipment Corporation
110 Spit Brook Road
Nashua, NH 03062

Peterson, Thomas
GTE Laboratories
40 Sylvan Road
Waltham, MA 02254

Picinich, Louis M.
Expertware
2685 Marine Way
Mountainview, CA 94043

Price, John D.
Shell Oil Company
P.O. Box 20389
Houston, TX 77025

Purdy, Steven M.
Avco/Lycoming Division
550 South Main Street
Stratford, CT 06497

Rabinowitz, Stanley
Digital Equipment Corporation
110 Spit Brook Road, ZK02-3/K06
Nashua, NH 03062

Racsok, Mark
AT&T Bell Laboratories
Whippany Road
Whippany, NJ 07981

Radding, Paul
Yourdon, Inc.
1501 Broadway
New York, NY 10036

Radtke, Steven
Bell Communications Research
3 Corporate Place
Piscataway, NJ

Reese, Randall
AT&T Information Systems
11900 N. Pecos
Denver, CO 80234

Reid, Karen
G.E.-Calma Company
501 Sycamore Drive, C5-2T
Milpitas, CA 95035-7489

Robillard, Pierre
Ecole Polytechnique de Montreal
C.P. 6079 St "A"
Montreal, Canada H3C 3Ay

Roman, Evelyn
Polytechnic Institute of New York
333 Jay Street
Brooklyn, NY 11201

Rosenbaum, Jack
Eaton/AIL Division
Deer Park, NY 11729

Rosene, A. Frederick
GTE Laboratories
77 "A" Street
Needham Heights, MA 02194

Rosenking, Jeffrey P.
Hazeltine Corporation
Pulaski Road
Greenlawn, NY 11740

Rosenthal, Sig
Computer Software Innovations Group
99 Oakland Beach Ave.
Rye, NY 10580

Royce, Wynn
Star Route Box 29
Houston, TX 78602

Russell, David Ray
Sperry Corporation
17 Ramsgate Court
Blue Bell, PA 19422

Ruston, Henry
Polytechnic Institute of New York
333 Jay Street
Brooklyn, NY 11201

Ryoich, Nakazato
Hitachi, Ltd.
515 Sycamore Lane
Davis, CA 95616

Samson-Eicher, Annette
AT&T Technologies
6 Corporate Place, Rm. 1E-250
Piscataway, NJ 08854

Sapossnek, Mark
General Electric Company
1 River Road, Bldg. 37, Rm. 523
Schenectady, NY 12345

Sayle, Karen L.
McDonnell Douglas/Astronautics Div.
5301 Bolsa Ave.
Huntington Beach, CA 92647

Schach, Stephen
Vanderbilt University
P.O. Box 70, Station B
Nashville, TN 37235

Schindler, Max
Electronic Design
3-77 Rockaway Drive
Boonton, NJ 07005

Schulz, Arno
University of Linz
Altenbergerstrasse 69
Linz, Austria A-4040

Schuman, Gail I.
Grumman Aerospace Corporation
Stewart Ave., MS A02-09
Bethpage, NY 11714

Shkolnikov, Nadia
Perkin-Elmer
11 Arlene Drive
W. Long Branch, NJ 07764

Shkolnikov, Valery
Perkin-Elmer
106 Apple Street
Tinton Falls, NJ 07724

Shooman, Martin L.
Polytechnic Institute of New York
333 Jay Street
Brooklyn, NY 11201

Siegfried, Patricia
3-M Corporation
3-M Center, 260-6A-08
St. Paul, MN 55144

Skeie, Tobby
CAE Electronics Ltd.
P.O. Box 1800
St Larent, Quebec, Canada H4L 4X4

Spear, Christian
Digital Equipment Corporation
77 Reed Road, HL02-2/H13
Hudson, MA 01749

Spota, Larry
Grumman Data Systems
1000 Woodbury Road, C11-237
Woodbury, NY 11787

Starr, John
ISDOS, Inc.
325 E. Eisenhawer Parkway
Suite 103
Ann Arbor, MI 48104

Steinberg, Amy
AT&T Network Systems
6 Corporate Place, Rm. 1E-251
Piscataway, NJ 08854

Steward, Ron
Higher Order Software Inc.
2067 Massachusetts Ave.
Cambridge, MA 02140

Stobbe, Christine
Siemens AG ZTI SOF 12
Ottohahn-Ring 6
8000 Munich 83 West Germany

Strauss, David
Bell Communications Research
3 Corporate Place
Piscataway, NJ 08854

Taormina, Kenneth
Teledyne Brown Engineering
788 Shrewsbury Ave.
Tinton Falls, NJ 07724

Tompkins, Jay W.
Amoco Production Company
P.O. Box 3385
Tulsa, OK 74102

Tsai, Wang-Choan
Bell Communications Research
3 Corporate Place, Rm. PYA 2B-308
Piscataway, NJ 08854

Turoczy, William R.
U.S. Army AMCCOM
Attn: AMCPM-CAWS-S
Building 172
Dover, NJ 07801-5001

Ural, Hasan
University of Ottawa
Computer Science Dept.
Ottawa, Ontario, Canada K1N 9B4

Valentino, Bob
Teledyne Brown Engineering
788 Shrewsbury Ave.
Tinton Falls, NJ 07724

VanBroek, G.H.M.
Nederlandse Philips Bedryven B.V.
P.O. Box 218 - Bld. BC 140
5600 MD Eindhoven
The Netherlands

Vance, Kathleen
Grumman Data Systems
1000 Woodbury Road
Woodbury, NY 11797

van Hall, Robert
Philips International B.V.
Science & Industry Division
Corporate Centre
P.O. Box 218 - Bld. TQ III-3
5600 MD Eindhoven
The Netherlands

Van Slyke, Richard
Polytechnic Institute of New York
333 Jay Street
Brooklyn, NY 11201

Versluis, John
Nederlandse Philips Bedrijven B.V.
N.P.B. S&I
P.O. Box 218 - Bld. TQ III-1
5600 MD Eindhoven
The Netherlands

Vint, John
Grumman Aerospace Corporation
Stewart Ave., MSD 01-31T
Bethpage, NY 11714

Wallace, Walt
Honeywell Corporation
13350 U.S. Highway 19 S.
MS 423-4A
Clearwater, FL 33546

Weinreb, Michael
Perkin-Elmer
1000 Wooster Heights Road
Danbury, CT 06810

Weiss, Stewart
Courant Institute
New York University
251 Mercer Street
New York, NY 10012

Wexler, Yoram
22 Kabirim Street
Haifa, 34384 Israel

Weyuker, Elaine
Courant Institute
New York University
251 Mercer Street
New York, NY 10012

White, Stephanie
Grumman Aerospace Corporation
Stewart Ave., MS B38/35
Bethpage, NY 11714

Wiechmann, James
Digital Equipment Corporation
110 Spit Brook Road
Nashua, NH 03062

Willson, Paul
U.S. Army
Picatinny Arsenal
Dover, NJ 07801-5001

Wilson, Lawrence B.
U.S. Army - ISSSC
Mail Stop C-70
Fort Belvoir, VA 22060

Wong, William
National Bureau of Standards
Bldg. 225, Rm. B266
Gaithersburg, MD 20899

Wongsawatgul, Ekawan
Eastman-Kodak
901 Elmgrove Road
FL. 2, Bldg. 5, Dept. 47
Rochester, NY 14650

Woodle, David A.
HRB Singer
P.O. Box 60
State College, PA 16840

Workman, David A.
University of Central Florida
P.O. Box 25000
Orlando, FL 32816

Wright, Sandra
Bell Northern Research
522 University Ave.
Toronto, Canada

Yoen, Chong Hok
College Militaire-Royal De Saint Jean
St Jean, Quebec, Canada

Zelinski, Dawn
AT&T Bell Laboratories
300 N. Randolphville Road
Piscataway, NJ 08854

Zellner, Rudolf
Siemans
Dept 2FT 50F42 Otto Hahn Ring #6
8000 Munich 83 West Germany

AUTHOR INDEX